The History of Human Rights

The History
of Human Rights

*From Ancient Times
to the Globalization Era*

Micheline R. Ishay

UNIVERSITY OF CALIFORNIA PRESS
Berkeley · Los Angeles · London

University of California Press
Berkeley and Los Angeles, California

University of California Press, Ltd.
London, England

Library of Congress Cataloging-in-Publication Data

Ishay, Micheline.
    The history of human rights : from ancient times
to the globalization era / Micheline R. Ishay.
        p.   cm.
    Includes bibliographical references and index.
    ISBN 0-520-23496-0 (alk. paper).
    —ISBN 0-520-23497-9 (pbk. : alk. paper)
        1. Human rights—History.   I. Title.

JC571.I73   2003
323'.09—dc21   2003012769

Manufactured in the United States of America

13   12   11   10   09   08   07   06   05   04
10   9   8   7   6   5   4   3   2   1

The paper used in this publication meets the minimum
requirements of ANSI/NISO Z39.48–1992 (R 1997)
(*Permanence of Paper*).♾

For David,
Adam, Elise, and their generation

Contents

Acknowledgments

THIS BOOK OWES A GREAT DEAL to the criticisms and suggestions of the many individuals who read earlier drafts. I want first to thank David Goldfischer, not just for his careful reading, insightful comments, and meticulous editing, but also for being a most magnificent intellectual and emotional partner. To him, and to our two wonderful children, Adam and Elise, and their generation, I dedicate this book.

I am also especially indebted to Stephen Bronner, Ginni Ishimatsu, and John Vail for their constructive criticisms and suggestions on the manuscript and for their steadfast friendship; to Sasha Breger, Lisa Burke, Eric Fattor, Bobby Pace, Chris Saeger, and Amentahru Wahlrab for their invaluable and diligent assistance with my research; to Suzanne Knott and Jan Spauschus for their judicious and thorough copyediting; and to my very able editor Reed Malcolm for his suggestions, enthusiasm, and support throughout this project.

In addition, I would like to thank many friends, colleagues, and students for their help, suggestions, and comments on parts of this book: Marc Agi, Shlomo Avineri, Benjamin Barber, Manisha Desai, Jack Donnelly, John Ehrenberg, Tom Farer, Michael Forman, Alan Gilbert, Russell Hardin, Angelique Haugeraud, Paul Kan, Max Likin, David Ost, Steve Roach, Greg Robbins, Rhoda Singer, Manfred Steger, Seth Ward, and Elizabeth Wolf. I would like also to thank Buchanan Sharp and my anonymous reviewers for their recommendations and my students, who, throughout the years, helped in the classroom in more ways than they can imagine.

I owe special thanks to my mother, Sheila Bazini, for her unwavering emotional support. Finally, I want to thank my father, Edmond Ishay, for inspiring my passion for human rights, showing me how to fight for justice, and believing in all my intellectual endeavors.

Introduction

Angelus Novus by
Paul Klee, 1920.
Courtesy of the Israel
Museum, Jerusalem.

T HERE ARE MANY HISTORIES. While some are written from the vantage point of the conquerors and oppressors, this book belongs to another tradition: that which gives voice to the oppressed. Rather than revel in the victors' parading of their slaves and the defeated, it harvests the hopes of the victims. It is not mesmerized by orators' charisma but remains attentive to the recurring dissonance between self-satisfied rhetoric and social reality. It does not leave optimism regarding humankind's noblest aspirations in the dustbin of history but follows messengers of hope through the cynicism characterizing human tyranny. It does not privilege the messianic aspirations of a single generation but recognizes the dedication of a host of human rights couriers over time.

Human rights are thus seen here as the result of a cumulative historical process that takes on a life of its own, sui generis, beyond the speeches and writings of progressive thinkers, beyond the documents and main events that compose a particular epoch. Inspired by a critical theoretical approach, this book presupposes that ideas and events are carried over from one era to another, through the media of historical texts, cultural traditions, architecture, and artistic displays. In this respect, it departs from realist perspectives on history, which privilege power over morality as the ultimate driving force of history, or postmodern interpretations of history, which question the progressive linearity of events in favor of a disconnected understanding of local discourses.[1] If the spirit of a time seems to meander whimsically and dangerously around the volcanic craters of social upheavals, it is transmitted consciously and unconsciously from one generation to another, carrying the scars of its tumultuous past. "There is no document of civilization," the critical theorist Walter Benjamin reminds us, "which is not at the same time a document of barbarism; barbarism taints also the style in which it was transmitted from one owner to another."

Barbarian and repressive policies, however, also tend to shape the direction of the social reaction. A human rights document may be marred by barbarism, yet, adding to Benjamin's observation, it is also a barometer of human rights progress. One may thus think of the history of human rights as a journey guided by lampposts across ruins left behind by ravaging and insatiable storms. In Benjamin's eloquent description of Paul Klee's painting *Angelus Novus* (The angel of history):

> [The] face [of the angel of history] is turned toward the past. Where we perceived a chain of events, he sees a single catastrophe which keeps piling wreckage and hurls it in front of his feet. The angel would like to stay, awaken the dead, and make whole what has been smashed. But a storm is blowing from Paradise; it has got caught in his wings with such violence that the angel can no longer close them. This storm irresistibly propels him into the future to which his back is turned, while the pile of debris before him grows skyward. This storm is what we call progress.[2]

THE DEFINITION, THE ARGUMENT, AND SIX HISTORICAL CONTROVERSIES

Human rights are rights held by individuals simply because they are part of the human species. They are rights shared equally by everyone regardless of sex, race, nationality, and economic background. They are universal in content. Across the centuries, conflicting political traditions have elaborated different components of human rights or differed over which elements had priority. In our day, the manifold meanings of human rights reflect the process of historical continuity and change that helped shape their present substance and helped form the Universal Declaration of Human Rights adopted by the General Assembly of the United Nations in 1948. René Cassin, one of the main drafters of the document, outlined the central tenets of human rights, comparing the declaration to the portico of a temple.

Drawing on the battle cry of the French Revolution, Cassin identified the four pillars of the declaration as "dignity, liberty, equality, and brotherhood." The twenty-seven articles of the declaration were divided among these four pillars. The pillars supported the roof of the portico: articles 28–30, which stipulated the conditions in which the rights of individuals could be realized within society and the state. Each of the pillars represents a major historical milestone. The first, covered in the first two articles of the declaration, stands for human dignity, which is shared by all individuals regardless of race, religion, creed, nationality, social origin, or sex; the second, specified in articles 3–19 of the declaration, invokes the first generation of civil liberties and other liberal rights that were fought for during the Enlightenment; the third, delineated in articles 20–26, addresses the second generation of rights, that is, those related to political, social, and economic equity and championed during the industrial revolution; the fourth, outlined in articles 27–28, focuses on the third generation of rights, those associated with communal and national solidarity as advocated during the late nineteenth century and early twentieth century and throughout the post-colonial era. In a sense, the sequence of the articles corresponds to the historical appearance of changing visions of universal rights.[3]

Yet in historical reality, each major stride forward was followed by severe setbacks. The universalism of human rights brandished during the French Revolution was slowly superseded by a nationalist reaction incubated during Napoleon's conquests, just as the internationalist hopes of socialist human rights advocates were drowned in a tidal wave of nationalism at the approach of World War I. The human rights aspirations of the Bolshevik Revolution and of two liberal sister institutions, the League of Nations and the International Labor Organization (ILO), were crushed by the rise of Stalinism and fascism during the interwar period; the establishment of the United Nations (UN) and adoption of the Universal Declaration of Human Rights were eclipsed by intensifying nationalism in the emerging Third World and global competition between two nuclear-armed superpowers. Finally, the triumphant claims made after 1989 that human rights would blossom in an unfettered global market economy were soon drowned out by rising nationalism in the former Soviet Union, Africa, the Balkans, and beyond.

This is not to say that reactionary forces have completely nullified each phase of progress in human rights. Rather, history preserves the human rights record as each generation builds on the hopes and achievements of its predecessors while struggling to free itself from authoritarianism and improve its social conditions. Yet throughout history, human rights projects—whether liberal, socialist, or "Third World" in origin—have generated contradictions concerning both how to promote human rights and who should be endowed with equal human rights. For instance, as it became clear during the nineteenth century that the masses of ordinary working people had been excluded from the liberal vision of the Enlightenment, a new socialist conception of internationalism laid claim to universal human rights promises. Furthermore, while the rise of the modern state was originally justified by claims that it would promote universal human rights, the subsequent prevalence of realpolitik and particularism inspired nineteenth- and twentieth-century efforts to embody universalism in a succession of international organizations.

If inconsistencies within each project exposed the boundaries of this or that worldview, they also moved the history of human rights forward. At the same time, the contradictory achievements of each human rights project contributed to the rise of nationalism and cultural rights. Ironically, these particularist perspectives, though directed against universalist promises, became an integral part of the Universal Declaration of Human Rights and subsequent human rights covenants, and have remained a continuing source of division within the human rights community.

Using the main points developed in the UN Declaration of Human Rights to chronicle the clashes of ideas, social movements, and armies that comprise the history of human rights, this book also engages six core controversies over human rights that have shaped human rights debate and scholarship. Thus, the historical record is offered in part to clarify several misconceptions that persist both within and outside the human rights community.

The first controversy concerns the origins of human rights. I argue that despite any temptation—especially after the events of September 11, 2001—to view religion as antithetical to a secular view of universal rights, each great religion contains important humanistic elements that anticipated our modern conceptions of rights. This does not mean that all religious contributions were equal, however, or that there is a perfect continuum from ancient to modern thinking about human rights (see chapter 1). *The second controversy* concerns the claim, which I endorse, that our modern conception of rights, wherever in the world it may be voiced, is predominantly European in origin (see chapter 2). To say that our current views of universal rights originated in the West, however, should not imply that Western rights are reducible to free-market liberalism. Despite faddish assertions that the end of the cold war represented liberalism's victory over the socialist challenge to human rights, the human rights vision currently depicted as liberal was in fact indelibly molded by the socialist ideals that grew out of nineteenth-century industrialization. The extent of modern liberalism's indebtedness to socialist thought represents the *third controversy* over human rights (see chapter 3).

The twentieth century witnessed popular assertions that cultural rights are necessary defenses against either liberal or socialist conceptions of human rights, since these conceptions presumably represent the oppressive legacy of Western domination of the rest of the world. Reminding the reader that nationalist and culturally focused arguments originated within nineteenth-century Europe, I take the position in this *fourth controversy* that demands for cultural rights must always be informed by and checked against a universalist perspective of human rights (see chapters 3, 4, and 5). At a time when proclamations of an "end of history" have been mocked by terrorists who, more dramatically than ever before, reject the very notion of universal rights, and when political realists triumphantly reassert that history is only the dismal repetition of power struggles and wars, it may be questionable, as *the fifth controversy* considers, whether there is such a thing as historical progress. Here, I will argue that human rights are not antithetical to realism, but rather complementary to sound realist policies. Further, in the post–September 11 environment, it is precisely progress in the worldwide implementation of universal rights that will most reliably advance the security goals so cherished by realists (see chapter 5). Finally, carving a middle position in a *sixth controversial* debate over whether globalization is a boon or a threat from a human rights perspective, this book draws on the legacy of history to consider broad strategies for the advancement of human rights in the twenty-first century (see chapters 5 and 6).

The Origins of Human Rights

When embarking on a history of human rights, the first question one confronts is: where does that history begin? It is a politically charged question, as difficult to answer as the one addressing the end of history. The question of the end of history has always suggested the triumph of one particular worldview over another: Friedrich Hegel's vision of history ending with the birth of the Prussian state celebrated the German liberal and cultural views of his time over others; Karl Marx's prediction that history would end with the withering of the state and the birth of a classless society emerged from a deepening struggle against the abuses of early industrialization; and Francis Fukuyama's declaration of the end of history exemplified liberal euphoria in the immediate aftermath of the Soviet collapse. Similarly, the question of the beginning of a history tends to privilege a specific status quo or value system against possible challengers or to legitimize the claims of neglected agents of history. It is in this context that one can understand the fight between religious creationists and evolutionary Darwinists in American schools, and the clash between some defenders of the Western canon and some advocates of African and Third World studies.

Tracing the origins and evolution of human rights will inescapably invite a similar debate. Those who are skeptical about the achievements of Western civilization are correct to point out that current notions of morality cannot be associated solely with European history. Modern ethics is in fact indebted to a worldwide spectrum of both secular and religious traditions. Thus, the concepts of progressive punishment and justice were professed by Hammurabi's Code of ancient Babylon; the Hindu and Buddhist religions offered the earliest defenses of the ecosystem; Confucianism promoted mass education; the ancient Greeks and Romans endorsed natural laws and the capacity of every individual to reason; Christianity and Islam each encouraged human solidarity, just as both considered the problem of moral conduct in wartime.

The first chapter of this book documents such connections between ancient values and modern human rights. Notwithstanding the different rituals and moral priorities associated with each of these traditions, all share basic views of a common good. This of course should not imply that all individuals were perceived as equal under any ancient religious or secular aegis. From Hammurabi's Code to the New Testament to the Quran, one can identify a common disdain toward indentured servants (or slaves), women, and homosexuals—all were excluded from equal social benefits. While emphasizing a universal moral embrace, all great civilizations have thus tended to rationalize unequal entitlements for the weak or the "inferior." Yet while such similarities are noteworthy, they should not overshadow one of history's most consequential realities: it has been the influence of the West, including the influence of the Western concept of universal rights, that has prevailed.

The Enlightenment Legacy of Human Rights

If the civilizations and ethical contributions of China, India, and the Muslim world towered over those of medieval Europe, it is equally true that the legacy of the European Enlightenment, for our current understanding of human rights, supersedes other influences. The necessary conditions for the Enlightenment, which combined to bring an end to the Middle Ages in Europe, included the scientific revolution, the rise of mercantilism, the launching of maritime explorations of the globe, the consolidation of the nation-state, and the emergence of a middle class. These developments stimulated the expansion of Western power even as they created propitious prospects for the development of modern conceptions of human rights. They ultimately shattered feudalism and challenged the previously uncontested divine rights of kings.

As Europe was plagued by religious wars pitting Catholics and Protestants in a struggle to redefine religious and political structures, human rights visionaries like Hugo Grotius, Samuel Pufendorf, Emmerich de Vattel, and René Descartes constructed a new secular language, affirming a common humanity that transcended religious sectarianism. Over the next two centuries, revolutionaries in England, America, and France would use a similar discourse to fight aristocratic privileges or colonial authority and to reorganize their societies based on human rights principles. Armed with the scientific confidence of their era, they struggled for the right to life, for freedom of religion and opinion, and for property rights.

Notwithstanding the incontestable debt of modern conceptions of human rights to the European Enlightenment, the positive legacy of that era remains widely contested. Many rightly argue that the Enlightenment did not fulfill its universal human rights promises. In the early nineteenth century, slavery continued in the European colonies and in America. Throughout the European dominated world (with the exception of revolutionary France), women had failed to achieve equal rights with men, propertyless men were denied the right to vote and other political rights, children's rights continued to be usurped, and the right to sexual preference was not even considered. Given those shortcomings, critics argue that the Enlightenment human rights legacy represents little more than an imperialist masquerade aimed at subduing the rest of the world under the pretense of promoting universality.

While the development of capitalism in Europe contributed to the circumstances necessary for the development of a secular and universal language of human rights, the early European liberal agenda inadvertently taught that very language to its challengers. Thus, the international language of power and the language of resistance were simultaneously born in the cradle of the European Enlightenment. The Enlightenment thinkers not only invented the language of human rights discourse, they discussed issues that continue to preoccupy current human rights debates. Now as then, we find ourselves pondering the role of the state as both the guardian of basic rights and as the behemoth against which one's rights need to be defended. Both during the Enlightenment and today, this dual allegiance to one's state and to universal human rights has contributed to the perpetuation of a double standard of moral behavior in which various appeals to human rights obligations remain subordinated to "the national interest." Further, we are still embroiled in Enlightenment debates over whether a laissez-faire approach to markets is the best way to promote democratic institutions and global peace, as Immanuel Kant and Thomas Paine contended, and we remain engaged in the Enlightenment argument over when and how one may justly wage war. The current forms of these debates, one should add, are not merely a contemporary variant of the liberal tradition but have been modified and enriched by the socialist contribution.

The Socialist Contribution to Human Rights

The nineteenth-century industrial revolution and the growth of the labor movement opened the gates of freedom to previously marginalized individuals who challenged the classical liberal economic conception of social justice. Despite the important socialist contribution to human rights discourse, the human rights legacy of the socialist—and especially the Marxist—tradition is today widely dismissed. Bearing in mind the atrocities that have been committed by communist regimes in the name of human rights, this book nevertheless attempts to correct the historical record by showing that the struggles for universal suffrage, social justice, and workers' rights—principles endorsed in the Universal Declaration of Human Rights (articles 18–21) and in the two International Covenants adopted by the United Nations in 1966—were socialist in origin.

Indeed, the Chartists in England and the European labor parties played a large role in the campaign for voting and social rights. Disenfranchised from the political process, propertyless workers realized that without a political voice, they would not be able to address the widening economic gap between themselves and the rising industrial capitalists. In other words, the historical struggle for universal suffrage was launched by the Chartist and socialist movements. As Marx put it in the *New York Daily Tribune* in 1850, "The carrying of universal suffrage in England . . . [is] a far more socialistic measure than anything which has been honored with that name on the Continent."[4]

While liberals retained their preoccupation with liberty, Chartists and socialists focused on the troubling possibility that economic inequity could make liberty a hollow concept—a belief that resonated powerfully with the bourgeoning class of urban workingmen and workingwomen. In this sense, socialists became legitimate heirs of the Enlightenment, applying the universal promises of "liberté, égalité, fraternité" to the political realities of the nineteenth century.

From the nineteenth century onward, radical and reformist socialists alike called for redefining the liberal agenda to include increased economic equity, the right to organize trade unions, child welfare, universal suffrage, restriction of the workday, the right to education, and other social welfare rights. Most of these principles were encapsulated in the 1966 International Covenant on Economic, Social and Cultural Rights. By then, these key elements of the original socialist platform had long been embraced as mainstream tenets of liberalism.

Cultural Relativism versus Universalism

One of the most intense debates within the human rights community is the one pitting universalists of liberal or socialist persuasions against cultural relativists. Three historical misconceptions, each of which requires explanation, have confused this debate. The first is the tendency to lump together second- and third-generation rights. The second is the effort to collapse first- and second-generation rights into a single Western perspective. The third is rooted in ignorance of the Western roots of third-generation rights.

Fusing socialist and cultural rights views (or second- and third-generation rights) into one philosophical tradition, as implied by the language of the International Covenant on Economic, Social and Cultural Rights, overlooks important differences that exist between these two traditions. For instance, "second-generation" socialists have long criticized the "third-generation" conception of group rights or rights to self-determination. Indeed, the notion of the right to self-determination, as defined by various international bills of rights, fails to specify which nationality or group should end up being favored over another when their claims conflict. Given the abuses that have occurred in the name of national and cultural rights since the end of the cold war, contemporary human rights advocates would profit from a familiarity with the criteria offered by late-nineteenth- and early-twentieth-century socialists for distinguishing between legitimate and illegitimate claims on behalf of groups.

Efforts to fuse liberal and socialist perspectives on rights (first- and second-generation rights) into one Western philosophical tradition echo the current Third World litany against Western cultural values, or what Samuel Huntington described in terms of "the West versus the Rest."[5] After centuries of colonialism and an accelerating globalization process dominated by Western media, Western technology, Western values, and Western products, arguments employed to defend the alleged uniqueness of non-Western cultural traditions against Western values (or vice versa) may seem almost farcical. Weren't the great leaders of the anti-colonial national liberation movements, like Jawaharlal Nehru, Léopold Senghor, and Ho Chi Minh, educated in the West, and weren't their agendas clearly indebted to different strands of the Western human rights tradition? Don't many clauses of the International Covenant on Economic, Social and Cultural Rights incorporate first- and second-generation rights traditions of obviously Western origin? What should we make of appeals to national or ethnic solidarity that completely ignore the Western human rights tradition? There may be, one should note, a questionable motive for selectively insisting on group or cultural rights, since failing to qualify those rights can ultimately provide dominant elites in particular societies opportunities to oppress individuals and religious and cultural minorities for not fitting with their self-serving conceptions of traditional values. At the same time, it is worth noting that a universal human rights agenda insensitive to existing power relations may serve as a tool with which to mask the particular national interests of powerful countries.[6]

More specifically, antagonism between liberal (first-generation) and developing world (third-generation) rights discourses currently plagues the human rights community. That division is based on the assumption that Western values are associated largely with individual civil and political rights, whereas people in developing countries emphasize rights related to the welfare of groups consistent with their cultural and religious traditions.[7] Many defenders of such cultural rights are forgetful or unaware of nineteenth-century European adherence (particularly among Italians and Germans) to the notion of cultural rights, a principle that was employed in the struggle against unqualified individualism and the Enlightenment's conception of universalism. The nationalist writings of Johann Gottlieb Fichte, Giuseppe Mazzini, John Stuart Mill, and Theodor Herzl, among other social thinkers of the nineteenth century, foreshadowed the twentieth century's quest for the codification of the right to self-determination.[8]

This book sheds light on these misunderstandings. A key point is that cultural relativism is a recurrent product of a historical failure to promote universal rights discourses in practice, rather than a legitimate alternative to the comprehensive vision offered by a universal stand on justice.[9] The invocation of cultural rights tends to occur when a specific group feels deprived of political, social, and economic rights. Inspired by a radical perspective on Kantian ethics—as discussed by critical theorists like Ernst Bloch, Lucien Goldman, Jürgen Habermas, and many others—this book upholds, however, a flexible conception of international justice. It emphasizes the importance of conducting dialogues across cultures in a spirit of tolerance, it respects the indivisible and inalienable notions of universal political, social, and economic rights, yet it is sensitive to the various socioeconomic and cultural circumstances that have historically privileged the emergence of certain conceptions of rights in particular parts of the world.

The Tension between Security and Human Rights

Once again, at the beginning of a new millennium, we find particularism and nationalism undermining universal human rights aspirations, confirming the views of relativists and realists that human rights do not progress, but rather wax and wane along with a cyclical pattern of history. Against that view, this book argues that those human rights themes that survive the tests and contradictions of history provide in the long run a corpus of shared perceptions of universal human rights that transcends class, ethnic, and gender distinctions. Indeed, despite various setbacks, the history of human rights shows a clear dimension of progress: slavery has been abolished (even if vestiges, intolerable though they may be, remain), women in most of the world have been granted the right to vote, and workers are endowed with more social and economic protection than ever before. While the victims of one era have sometimes emerged as avenging aggressors in the next, they have been, however, more likely to reappear as powerful human rights crusaders. The propertyless Fourth Estate of the eighteenth century would become the revolutionaries of 1848 and 1871, just as eighteenth-century Jacobin women and rebellious slaves would energize the suffragettes and abolitionists of the nineteenth century. Moreover, the marginalization of colonized peoples gave way to successful anti-colonial struggle following World War II, and so on.

Of course, some realists were eager to point out in the aftermath of September 11, 2001, that the seemingly enhanced post–cold war role for human rights in foreign policy has now been reversed, revealing the true face of a history condemned, like Sisyphus confronting his eternal curse, to the struggle of power against power. Human rights must be seen, according to this view, at best as subordinate to security objectives, at worst as antithetical to security. Indeed, the emergency Patriot Act signed by President George W. Bush six weeks after the World Trade Center and Pentagon attacks shows the fragility of such freedoms in times of war, as does increased support for some repressive regimes in the name of the war on terror. Challenging this perspective, this book argues that the vulnerability of national borders in our era of globalization calls now more than ever for the development of a broader strategy of security founded on human rights and global economic welfare.

Does Globalization Advance Human Rights?

Calling for a human rights–oriented security strategy begs, however, a broader question: Is globalization promoting or undermining human rights prospects? While there is clear evidence that globalization coincides with a widening gap between the rich and the poor within societies and between rich and poor countries, the information age has redefined and created new spatial opportunities for human rights. With the globalization of the economy and communications and the emergence of developing post-colonial states, new rights have been added to the human rights corpus. These include rights to a healthy environment, to sustainable development, to culture, to immigration, and to political asylum.

Yet even as rights are redefined and widened, how can we effectively protect the rights of workers and the less privileged when the state is ever more vulnerable to market pressures and more constrained in its role as a buffer against the ill effects of global economic forces? At a time when there is widening agreement that sovereignty should not protect regimes that stifle human rights, should international human rights monitoring agencies be further empowered? If so, can these agencies maintain their effectiveness when democratic forces at the national level may be weakening, nationalism is rampant, and the private realm is under tighter control?

Examining the roles of the state, civil society, and the private realm as agents of change throughout history provides important insights into ways to optimize human rights prospects for the future. This book concludes with a review of the changing spatial and institutional dynamics of human rights interaction at critical historical junctures: the Middle Ages, the Enlightenment, the industrial revolution, the anti-colonial struggle, and the age of globalization. For example, railroads and the industrial revolution helped create new forums for social protest (trade unions, labor movements, etc.). Today, one may wonder whether information technology and globalization have created superior human rights opportunities (e.g., proliferating nongovernmental organizations and human rights websites), or whether the decline of older forms of social resistance (public rallies, strikes, etc.) outweighs the alleged advantages of the information age. In other words, one may ask whether we have too hastily deserted the old public spaces of human rights politics in exchange for the magical realism of the Internet, and whether the private realm is growing progressively more vulnerable to surveillance and control.

STRUCTURE

Each of the chapters that follow is divided into four corresponding parts: a historical background focusing on select critical events that helped launched the most important human rights campaigns; the main human rights themes of each period, broken down into several subsections; a review of the debate, within each period, over acceptable ways to promote human rights; and a discussion of the inclusiveness of prevailing views of human rights during each period, that is, a chapter-by-chapter response to the question, human rights for whom?

This book attempts to provide a useful path for navigating through the main historical events, speeches, and legal documents that led up to the ratification of the 1948 Universal Declaration of Human Rights. While highlighting the pre-Enlightenment period, chapter 1, unlike subsequent chapters, does not emphasize any specific historical period. It shows how Cassin's major human rights themes were indebted to ancient views of tolerance, social and economic justice, just war, and universality. These themes, as laid out in chapter 1, guide the chapters that follow. Consistent with that structure, the analysis of the relatively shorter period since 1948, and in particular the treatment of our current globalized era, relies more on an imagination stretching to grasp the direction toward which the forces of history are blowing the winds of social change. In an effort to reach an intelligent lay audience that may have limited patience with technical language and abstract theoretical speculation, this book addresses questions of academic and political importance in ordinary prose. For the scholar, the student, the activist, and the wider community concerned with human rights, this history can help illuminate the controversies and commonly held misconceptions that continue to beset the human rights debate.

Chapter One

Early Ethical Contributions to Human Rights

The Creation of Adam
by Michelangelo, 1508–
1512. Detail: hands of
God and Adam. Courtesy
of the Vatican Museum,
Vatican City.

T HERE ARE NO UNIVERSAL ETHICS. This was at least what the Greek historian Herodotus argued more than two thousand years ago, illustrating his point with a story about the Persian king Darius. The king, wrote Herodotus, summoned several Greeks and asked them how much money it would take for them to eat the dead bodies of their fathers. Outraged, they proclaimed their refusal to perform such a gruesome act at any price, adding that cremation of the dead was a sacred obligation. Darius then called upon some Indians, who by custom ate their deceased parents, and asked them if they would consider burning the bodies of their fathers. Insulted, they replied that such an act would be a horrible crime. The lesson, concluded Herodotus, was simply that each nation regards its own customs as superior.[1]

Through the ages, Herodotus's observation seemed an apt characterization of humankind's immersion in war after war, its dark implications nowhere more apparent than in the twentieth century's near triumph of Nazism and fascism, in which doctrines of national supremacy were used to justify the annihilation of presumably inferior cultures and races. When those forces were finally turned back after six years of brutal world war, the survivors were determined as never before to resurrect a lasting universal ethics from the ashes of unprecedented destruction. At Dumbarton Oaks in 1945, the victorious Allied powers set the stage for a new international order; at San Francisco that same year, they unveiled their plan for an international organization that would secure peace and human rights; and in New York three years later, the General Assembly of the United Nations ratified the Universal Declaration of Human Rights.

Overcoming obstacles posed by divergent cultures and deeply rooted ideological divisions, the source of so much bloodshed across the centuries, would hardly be an easy task. None were more aware of that challenge than the members of the Human Rights Commission, which had been charged in 1945 with the drafting of the declaration. After all, the commission members themselves, under the leadership of Eleanor Roosevelt (1884–1962), represented starkly contrasting cultural backgrounds and philosophies. One may wonder how the Chinese Confucian philosopher, diplomat, and commission vice-chairman Pen-Chung Chang (1892–1957), the Lebanese existentialist philosopher and rapporteur Charles Malik (1906–1987), and the French legal scholar and later Nobel Prize laureate René Cassin (1887–1976) were able to arrive at a common understanding of human rights. Yet despite constant philosophical rivalries between Malik and Chang, coupled with the political tension between Cassin, a Jew who had lost twenty-nine relatives in the Holocaust and who was a supporter of the creation of a Jewish state, and Malik, a spokesperson for the Arab League (formed in 1945), these strong personalities managed to work together toward the drafting of the declaration. One might also wonder how the eight delegates representing states embroiled in armed conflict with each other found a way to put their differences aside. Remarkably, all of the human rights commissioners, deeply committed to their mission, responded to their historical mandate by transcending the myriad differences that set them apart.[2]

Struggling to find a common language, they commissioned the United Nations Educational, Scientific and Cultural Organization (UNESCO) to conduct an inquiry into the diversity of human rights viewpoints across the globe. UNESCO in turn circulated a questionnaire to various thinkers and writers from member states, seeking their particular understandings of human rights, as drawn from their religious, cultural and intellectual backgrounds. "How," asked one of UNESCO's participants, the French Thomist philosopher Jacques Maritain (1882–1973), "can we imagine an agreement of minds between men who come from the four corners of the globe and who not only belong to different cultures and civilizations, but are of antagonistic spiritual associations and schools of thought?"[3] Yet finding such an agreement was the mandate of the Human Rights Commission as it began to derive a common language of human rights from a host of cultural, religious, and political traditions.

In their search for a new universal ethics, the commission members affirmed that the history of the philosophic tradition of human rights extended beyond the "narrow limits of the Western tradition and [that] its beginning in the West as well as in the East coincides with the beginning of philosophy."[4] In that sense, from the onset of their work, they challenged the premise that universal human rights were purely a Western invention traceable to the eighteenth-century European Enlightenment. Instead, they would look to all the world's great religions and cultures for the universal notions of the common good that had inspired the Enlightenment's human rights visionaries.

The outcome of their discussions culminated in the development and ratification, on December 10, 1948, of the Universal Declaration of Human Rights, the preeminent document of international rights summarizing secular and religious notions of rights that had evolved throughout the centuries. The first nineteen articles of the declaration captured rights related to various personal liberties (life, security of one's person, diverse protections against cruel treatment, equality before the law, etc.), rights that had been fought for during the Enlightenment; articles 20–26 addressed rights related to social and economic equity (social security, the right to work, the right to just remuneration, the freedom to join trade unions, limitation of working hours, periodic holidays with pay, the right to education, etc.) championed during the industrial revolutionary era; and articles 27–28 focused on rights associated with communal and national solidarity, advocated during the late nineteenth century and early twentieth century and throughout the post-colonial era.

According to René Cassin, these clusters of rights embodied generations of rights, each summed up, in chronological order, by one of the three words of the famous French revolutionary motto "Liberté, égalité, fraternité." This legendary tripartite slogan helps provide the main themes of this book; it also contributes to the structure of this chapter. Elaborating on UNESCO participants' views, this chapter stresses early ethical contributions to the spirit that informed the Universal Declaration. It highlights ancient texts that informed the drafting of this document, rather than the historical events (or the contradictions between theory and historical reality) on which subsequent chapters are based. It begins with a general discussion of religious and secular universalism, followed by a look at ancient understandings of liberty, then by an assessment of old texts on equality and an overview of ancient thought on the promotion of justice, and ends with a discussion of the pre-Enlightenment question: fraternity for whom?

RELIGIOUS AND SECULAR NOTIONS OF UNIVERSALISM

Despite the many controversies regarding the origins of human rights, one should note that few of the drafters of the Universal Declaration and few of UNESCO's respondents disputed that religious humanism and ancient traditions influence our secular and modern understanding of rights. Putting aside the issue of divine revelation, which has at various times led to arbitrary interpretations and applications, most religious texts incorporate a notion of universalism containing altruistic guidelines that could apply if not to all individuals, as a contemporary definition would require, then to a substantial portion of humanity. While human rights force us to think about universality in political and economic terms, they benefit from such portrayals of universal brotherly love as one finds in Micah (the Hebrew Bible), Paul (the New Testament), the Buddha, and others, and also, in a different way, from the detached universal love professed by the Stoics, like Epictetus, and advocates like Plato, Aristotle, and Cicero. While the Greek and Roman notions of laws and rights, eclipsed during the Middle Ages, would be reinvoked during the Enlightenment, other non-Western notions of the common good would be reclaimed during the anti-colonial struggles and in our globalized era.

Maintaining that human rights transcend religious and ideological differences, René Cassin nonetheless recognized their religious and natural law foundations. By proclaiming that all human beings "should act toward one another in a spirit of brotherhood," the first article of the declaration corresponded to the biblical injunction "love thy neighbour as thyself" and "love the stranger as you love yourself" (Leviticus 19:18–33 Jerusalem Bible [hereafter JB]).[5] We must not lose sight of fundamentals, Cassin claimed, in noting that "the concept of human rights comes from the Bible, from the Old Testament, from the Ten Commandments. Whether these principles were centered on the church, the mosque, or the *polis,* they were often phrased in terms of duties, which now presume rights. For instance, Thou shall not murder is the right to life. Thou shall not steal is the right to own property, and so on and so forth. We must not forget that Judaism gave the world the concept of human rights."[6]

Some may argue that the Jewish precepts invoked by Cassin were, however, themselves traceable in part to Hammurabi's Code, the oldest surviving collection of laws.[7] The Babylonian code narrates the moral principles of a people, sanctioning punishments for those who transgress the law; discussing how one should marry, divorce, and work the land; proposing ways to regulate the wages of agricultural laborers and craftsmen; and establishing duties and fees for doctors, veterinary surgeons, builders and sailors. The laws of ancient Israel, after all, had been influenced by the Jewish experience in both Egypt and Mesopotamia. Indeed, the book of Exodus describes the period of Jewish emancipation from slavery in Egypt, but also invokes the Babylonian talion principle of progressive punishment: "eye for eye, tooth for tooth, hand for hand, foot for foot, burning for burning, wound for wound, bruise for bruise" (Exodus 21:24–25 JB).

Yet unlike Hammurabi's Code, ancient Jewish laws did not differentiate between the rights of patricians (or free individuals) and those of commoners. Jewish laws even went a step further, explicitly placing the rights of Jews and Gentiles on an equal footing. The Bible claimed that God's statutes and laws were for everyone (Leviticus 18:5 JB), and God's call for Jewish emancipation was voiced in terms of the uplifting of other peoples as well: "Are you not as much mine as the children of the Ethiopians, O children of Israel? Says the Lord. Have I not brought up Israel out of the Land of Egypt, and the Philistines from Kaftor, and the Syrians from Kir?" (Amos 9:7 JB). That aspect of ancient Jewish tradition has long been invoked to counter criticism about Jewish particularism associated with the notion of a "chosen people," providing a basis for some rabbis to respond that "Israel was not elected for honor, or for particular privilege, but for service."[8]

Cassin, along with the political scientist S. V. Puntambekar, one of the respondents to UNESCO's questionnaire, was also aware of the contribution to universalism of some aspects of Hinduism and Buddhism.[9] For Puntambekar, Hinduism offered important "spiritual aims and values for mankind," beyond the "demands of economic technocracy, political bureaucracy and religious idiosyncrasy." "Both Manu and Buddha," he claimed, "propounded a code as it were of ten essential human freedoms and controls or virtues of good life." The first five tenets of social assurances included: "freedom from violence (Ahimsa), freedom from want (Asteya), freedom from exploitation (Aparigraha), freedom from early death and disease (Armritatva and Arogya)." To these five freedoms corresponded five virtues or controls: "absence of intolerance (Akrodha), compassion (Bhutadaya, Adroha), knowledge (Jnana, Vidya), freedom of conscience and freedom from fear, frustration and despair (Pravrtti, Abhaya, Dhrti)."[10]

One may add to Puntambekar's account that the *dharma,* the religious and moral law governing individual conduct, understood in the Vedas, also offers universally encompassing prescriptive and descriptive guidelines of morality. Yet Hinduism's cosmological focus, in which organic and inorganic matters interrelate in a symbiotic whole, should not imply that individuals are passive cogs in a preordained universe, exempt from moral actions and judgments. Their rights need first to be earned as they ideally accomplish a life journey of moral duties.[11] They should first strive for *kama,* or pleasures derived from the human senses under the control of the mind: for example, pleasures derived from art, music, literature, and sexual activity. Gaining material control, in economic and political *(artha)* terms, without being subject to greed and desire, is as central as learning to perform just actions *(dharma)*.

Specific to Buddhism is the concept of selflessness *(anatma)*, a notion that along with the idea of the individual's innate suffering *(duhkha)* involves feelings of universal compassion. After leading an ascetic life of renunciation for six years, the Buddha understood that detachment from the world could not be an ultimate solution. Drawing lessons from his years of solitude, he realized that in the process of self-negation, the sufferings of other creatures became more evident and compassion for other creatures immanent. Proposing a "middle path" between self-indulgence and self-renunciation, the Buddha's ultimate aim was to reach Nirvana, a realm in which all living things are free from pain and suffering.[12] His devotion to compassion and solidarity later became the cornerstone of the Mahayana school of Buddhism, which urges individuals to work toward the salvation of others—a message that has been disseminated throughout the world by the fourteenth Dalai Lama of Tibet.

Chung-Shu Lo, a Chinese philosopher and special consultant to UNESCO, drew on the classic *Book of History* to illustrate comparable sentiments in the Chinese cultural tradition. "Heaven," he quoted, "sees as other people see; Heaven hears as our people hear. Heaven is compassionate towards the people. What the people desire, Heaven will be found to bring about. A ruler has a duty to heaven to take care of the interest of his people. In loving his people, the ruler follows the will of Heaven." Like Buddhism, "Chinese ethical teaching emphasized the sympathetic attitude of regarding all one's fellow men as having the same desires, and therefore the same rights, as one would like to enjoy oneself."[13]

More specific and central to the Chinese tradition was *The Analects,* the teachings of Confucius (ca. 551–479 B.C.E.). Offered in the form of

---

THE DALAI LAMA, "HUMAN RIGHTS AND UNIVERSAL RESPONSIBILITIES," 1988

When we demand the rights and freedoms we so cherish we should also be aware of our human responsibilities. If we accept that others have an equal right to peace and happiness as ourselves, have we not a responsibility to do what we can to help those in need and at least avoid harming them? Closing our eyes to our neighbor's suffering in order to better enjoy our own freedom and good fortune is a rejection of such responsibilities. We need to develop a concern for the problems of others, whether they be individuals or entire peoples.

From *The Dalai Lama: A Policy of Kindness,* 112 (www.snowlionpub.com).

---

aphorisms, sayings, and anecdotes, Confucius's reply to questions posed by his disciples served as a guide to human conduct. As in Buddhism, heavenly inspiration should not lead to a life of detachment from the world. "One cannot herd with birds and beasts," stated Confucius; "Am I not a member of this human race? Who then is there for me to associate with? While the way is to be found in the Empire, I will not change places with him [i.e., the way]."[14] One way to promote change was by promoting good actions inspired by the Way, by which Confucius meant individuals' efforts to actualize themselves and to pursue an altruistic and dutiful path. That conception of human purpose would resonate throughout the ages, appearing, for example, in the opening quotation in a 1950 UNESCO Statement on Race.[15]

Confucius elaborated, over two millennia ago, an ethical position that encompassed aspects of current views on human rights. Indeed, he believed that all individuals, even commoners, possessed rational, aesthetic, political, social, historical, and transcendental qualities that could be cultivated through education.[16] This led him to become a staunch advocate of education and personal self-actualization. "Gentlemen should devote their minds to learning, attaining the Way rather than securing food."[17] At the same time, Confucius elaborated a position closely related to that of modern defenders of group rights. The more individuals broaden themselves, the more they are capable of deepening their self-awareness. Their persistence in deepening their self-awareness is the basis for their fruitful interaction with an ever-expanding network of human relations that includes the family, the community, the state, and the world.[18] At each of these levels of social interaction, individuals need to express their commitment *(li)* to a social unit, which in turn has entitlements of its own.

As long as government took an interest in the economic and moral welfare of its people, Confucius maintained, peace, stability, and security—contemporary human rights postulates—would be assured. The notion of peace and social order, he also argued, was not merely an external condition, but also a reflection of an individual's internal order, since "if a man manages to make himself correct, what difficulty will there be for him to take part in government?"[19] Personal order can be developed through self-cultivation, and social order and universal peace can be generated by inner clairvoyance, kindness, and rituals. When a "gentleman is reverent and does nothing amiss, is respectful towards others and observant of the rites, [then] all within the Four Seas are his brothers."[20]

For another UNESCO respondent, Richard McKeon, professor of philosophy and Greek, the major Western influence on human rights as developed during the eighteenth century was traceable to the Greeks and the Romans.[21] While various ethical traditions in different regions of the world were preoccupied with similar concerns, the Greeks and Romans seemed to have crossed a particular threshold in the development of human rights thought. We should recognize, as McKeon enjoined, that the Stoics introduced the term *cosmopolite,* which meant "citizen of the world," and that Zeno of Citium (335–263 B.C.E.) wrote that "a well-admired republic is founded on the principle that human beings should not be separated within cities and nations under laws particular to themselves, because all humans are compatriots . . . , and because there is only one life and one order of things (cosmos)."[22]

Stoicism had its origin in the views of Socrates (469–399 B.C.E.) and Plato (ca. 428–347 B.C.E.). Socrates had already imagined, according to Plato's *Republic,* the possibility that a person could be rendered invisible by wearing the mythical ring of Gyges. Would that person behave unjustly, knowing she or he could get away with it? In a long argument, Socrates maintained first that people have a general comprehension of what constitutes the good, and second, that coupled with that understanding, the need to seek internal and external harmony led most to pursue an altruistic path. Because goodness is not a particular characteristic but can be found in every topic of inquiry, he concluded that goodness is universal. It was in the process of deepening their understanding of the common element of goodness that Plato and Socrates showed their allegiance to a universal view of human goodness and, in a sense, human rights, and refuted the Sophists' claim that goodness and justice are relative to the customs of each society—a view that they believed was often offered to disguise the interests of the stronger. In the presentation of this argument more than two thousand years ago, Socrates and Plato highlighted key controversies of the human rights debate that continue even today to divide advocates of cultural relativism, on the one hand, and defenders of a universalist agenda, on the other.

Proving the existence of universal goodness did not automatically imply that one was driven to perform righteous actions. Socrates and Plato (somewhat similarly to the Buddha and Confucius) understood that such motivation was conditioned by the harmonious balancing of three elements of the soul: intellect, emotion, and desire. The unjust person, like the unjust government, lives in an unsatisfactory state of internal discord, trying to overcome the constant malaise prompted by insatiable desire.[23] A just individual, like a just government, keeps in harmony the constitutive elements of her or his soul. According to Socrates and Plato,

individuals fell into three classes (rulers, guardians, and commoners), depending upon which part of the soul was dominant, and it was the task
of a good government to keep this social division in balance. Socrates
further suggested that justice was a state in which all people knew their
place and in which the passion of the multitude was controlled by the
wisdom of the superior few. In this respect, right and justice did not belong to this or that class, but to the functioning of society as a whole.

With Plato, Aristotle (384–322 B.C.E.) held that virtue needed to be
a central characteristic of human life, which should aim at the common
good. At the same time, he rejected Plato's theory of an essential universal goodness. Adding a tangible character to Plato's teachings, he explained that the form of goodness had to match its empirical content. In
other words, virtue was not innate, but a capacity that needed to be developed. For instance, we become just by performing good actions, and
courageous by performing acts of courage. Continuing to act in a certain way inculcates habits. The virtuous individual thus deserved respect
for good habit formation and his or her search for a balanced life. In the
same vein as the Buddha's middle path between self-indulgence and self-
renunciation, Aristotle called for a Golden Mean between extreme forms
of emotion. By urging people to consult their inner motivations while
promoting the common good, Aristotle, with Plato and the Buddha, provided important insight into the psychological prerequisites for effective
ethical action. However, Aristotle's notion of prudence called for a more
"engaged" attitude toward the world than did those of his predecessors.
Prudence, the keystone of all virtues, Aristotle maintained, was manifested in acting so that the idea of right could take its concrete form.

Plato's and Aristotle's views gradually gained influence, resonating,
for example, in the writings of Epictetus (ca. 55–135) and the Roman
statesman and legal scholar Marcus Tullius Cicero (106–43 B.C.E.).
Epictetus advanced the idea of Stoicism, which stressed the importance
of regulating passions and physical desires through reason. Challenging
the common assumption of freedom, Epictetus maintained that neither
kings, nor their friends, nor slaves were truly free. Only those who were
not enslaved by their bodily desires, passions, and emotions and who
could overcome the fear of death could be truly free. Diogenes and
Socrates were Epictetus's heroes, for they (like the Buddha and Confucius) called for a detached love of the common good, of the gods, and
of their real country: the universe.[24]

Cicero's general indebtedness to Greek sources in his account of Roman history also reflected the particular influence of Plato and Aristotle.

Like them, Cicero sanctified individuals' capacity to reason critically for themselves: "Since there is nothing better than reason, and since it exists both in man and God, the first common possession of man and God is reason."[25] Cicero went beyond the Greeks in an effort to translate these ideals into natural laws *(ius naturales)*: "There is in fact a true law—namely right reason—which in accordance with nature, applies to all men, and is unchangeable and eternal."[26] These universal laws of justice were distinguishable from customary laws, or the laws of the nations *(ius gentium)*. The notion that everything is just by virtue of custom or the laws, claimed Cicero, was a foolish idea. "Would that be true," asked Cicero, "even if these laws had been enacted by tyrants?" He appealed to universal natural laws that transcended customary and civil laws, and he endorsed with the Stoics of his time the idea of "a citizen of the whole universe, as it were of a single city."[27]

What distinguished the earlier Greek Stoics from Cicero, however, was their explicit assertion that reason and the capacity for good judgment were not limited to free citizens but were possessed by everyone, no matter their race, rank, or wealth, including those living beyond the Greek city-states. With the legacy of Stoicism and early Greek ethical perspectives, Cicero's thought embodied ideals to fit a greater region of human interactions in which the division between citizens and foreigners was blurred, and in which individuals from different social backgrounds—as diverse as those of the emperor Marcus Aurelius and the slave scholar Epictetus—could claim to be honorary members.

Another of UNESCO's respondents, the French philosopher Pierre Teilhard de Chardin (1881–1955), from the Society of Jesus, blended Christianity and science to conclude, in a Stoic universalist vein, that whether "we like it or not, humanity," after World War II, "was collectivizing, 'totalising' itself, under the influence of physical and spiritual forces of a worldwide nature."[28] These unifying forces, seeking a harmony beyond liberalism and socialism, could be traced to Christianity, echoed another respondent, the Polish historian Sergius Hessen (1887–1950). "It would be easy to show that this modern idea of democracy is deeply rooted in the new attitude, which Christianity has brought into the world," Hessen explained, for "[t]rue charity includes equality, liberty and fraternity. They are inseparable components of Christian love."[29]

Like Stoicism and the viewpoints of Roman legal moralists such as Cicero, Christianity, based on the birth and teachings of Jesus (ca. 6 B.C.E.–30 C.E.), promoted a notion of equal moral status for all human beings. But whereas the Stoics grounded moral equality on the human capacity to reason, Christians saw individuals as equal by virtue of their capacity to love their neighbors as themselves. They were also equal because they were all potentially immortal and precious in the eyes of God and his son Jesus. "There is no such thing as Jew and Greek," advocated the apostle Paul, "slave and freeman, male and female: for you are all one person in Jesus Christ" (Galatians 3:28–29 New English Bible [hereafter NEB]). The Christian notion of universalism and its missionary attitude were also stressed by allowing members an easier admission to the Jewish covenant with God, as a result of Paul's repudiation of the Jewish requirements of male circumcision and observance of dietary law.[30] Paul asserted against Peter that "if we are in union with Jesus Christ, . . . the only thing that counts is faith active in love" (Galatians 5:6 NEB).

Did it follow that Christian universalist attitudes as revealed in the New Testament would extend to slavery in a more charitable fashion than was done in the Hebrew Bible or in the Roman world? The answer is unclear. In Judaism, slaves (or indentured servants) possessed rights and were automatically enfranchised after a certain specified time, as long as they were not foreign slaves acquired in war. In the Roman world of early Christianity, in contrast to biblical times, slaves were denied any form of rights and were placed under the absolute control of their masters. For Christians, however, as long as slaves received the words of Jesus, they were perceived as free individuals under the canopy of God. Paul is even reported to have urged slaves to seize liberty if the chance arose (1 Corinthians 7:21–22 NEB). Yet Paul and other early Christian leaders hardly called unequivocally for the emancipation of slaves. A certain acceptance of the condition of slavery was also apparent. For instance, knowing the severe punishment dictated by the law for runaway slaves, Paul sent back a fugitive, Onesimus, to his master Philemon, and asked him to redeem the converted slave (the letter of Paul to Philemon 1–25 NEB). In Colossians, Paul even advised slaves' subordination to their masters: "[S]laves, give entire obedience to your earthly masters, not merely with an outward show of service, to curry favour with men, but with single-mindedness, out of reverence for the Lord" (Colossians 3:22–23 NEB).

It was the Islamic tradition that inspired the Indian poet and philosopher Hamayun Kabir in his reply to UNESCO's questionnaire. If anything, Kabir felt that "the Western conception has to a large extent receded from the theory and practice of democracy set up by Islam, which did succeed in overcoming the distinction of race and colour to an extent experienced neither before nor since."[31] Whether Kabir's statement is true or not, it is clear that principles of solidarity and justice are discussed in the Quran, the fundamental source of Islamic teaching.

The Quran consists of 114 chapters (surahs) that according to the Muslim tradition were revealed to Mohammed prior to his death in 632. As in Christianity and Judaism, Abrahamic monotheism governs the Muslim religion, which spread rapidly in the Middle East and eventually extended to Persia, Turkey, parts of the Slavic world, Indonesia, and China. Though every creature is part of an autonomous universe, which has its own law, the Islamic, Judaic, and Christian universe is—in contrast to Hinduism's and Buddhism's cosmological deities—endowed by God, who reigns unchallenged in the heavens and on earth. But along with Judaism, Islam repudiated the Christian belief in intermediaries between God and his creation.

Notwithstanding these points of difference with other religious perspectives, Quranic verses offer a universal message reminiscent of the ethical perspectives of the older religions: "O mankind! We created you from a single pair of a male and a female and made you into Nations and tribes, that ye may know each other, not that you may despise each other" (surah 49:13).[32] Having identified a common point of origin for all creatures, Mohammed, like some of his Hellenic predecessors, further recognized the universality and objective nature of moral goodness shared by different religious communities. Islam therefore invited all people to the truth; and should disputes arise between different religious groups over its meaning, it is Allah "that will show you the truth of the matters in which ye dispute" (surah 5:48).

LIBERTY: THE ORIGINS OF TOLERANCE

Even if one can easily show that the "right to life and security" (article 3 of the Universal Declaration) has deep roots in ancient religions and cultures, it would be excessive to claim that what we understand today as liberty is equally traceable to the pre-Enlightenment period. Nonetheless, it is worth drawing attention to some of the inklings of these notions within various traditions, if only to show that the idea of liberty was not born *ex nihilo* during the Enlightenment. Often defined as a variety of injunctions, many religious invocations of duties, as Cassin observed, correspond closely to secular conceptions of rights. Thus "thou shall not kill" implies the right to secure one's life, just as "thou shall not steal" implies a right to property. Generally, standardized legislation,

progressive punishments, fair ruling, freedom of conscience, religious toleration, the right to life and the security of one's person, among other
conceptions one may associate with liberty or freedom, were not un-
known in ancient religious and secular texts.

The rules contained in Hammurabi's Code had a far-reaching influence
in this respect. Aiming at ensuring the integrity of the judiciary, they called
for the removal of corrupt judges.[33] There were also laws against
calumny: if a person were wrongly accused, the accuser would suffer the
punishment that would have been inflicted on the accused.[34] Yet the most
important contribution of Hammurabi's laws resides in the notion of progressive justice, illustrated by the talion principle of "eye for eye, tooth
for tooth." A strict "eye for eye" rule was dictated, however, only if the
victim was a freeman (a patrician) or from the same rank; if the victim
was a commoner, the punishment was a payment of a fine in silver. In
other words, talion was exacted only when the victim was of the same
rank as the aggressor, otherwise the penalty was in the form of monetary compensation.

The incorporation of the talion law in the Hebrew Bible does not retain this Babylonian social differentiation. Yet, like Hammurabi's Code,
the Hebrew Bible condemns bribery and the corruption of judges, "for
a bribe blinds the eyes of the wise, and perverts the words of the righteous" (Deuteronomy 16:19–20 JB). Without punishing with Babylonian severity the levelers of wrongful accusations, the Bible nonetheless
denounces "false witness against [one's] neighbor" (Exodus 23:2–3 JB).
God's laws as reported in the Bible are more universal than Hammurabi's
Code. Not only must one "love thy neighbour as thyself," but rules apply equally to alien and native: "judge righteously between every man
and his brother, and the stranger that is with him" (Leviticus 19:18 JB;
Deuteronomy 1:16–17 JB). Vexing or oppressing strangers and the poor
was unacceptable ("He that oppresses the poor blasphemes his maker,"
Proverbs 14:31–35 JB), for the Jews themselves had been "strangers in
the land of Egypt" (Exodus 22:20 JB). Even discrimination against the
disabled was castigated: "[T]hou shalt not curse the deaf, nor put a stum-
bling block before the blind" (Leviticus 19:14–15 JB). In the Hebrew
Bible, the same rules of justice apply to the stranger, the poor, and the
disabled.

For 450 years, according to the Bible and the Roman historian Jose-
phus's record, these rules of justice were implemented by a theocratic nation and administered by judges who rose amidst the people to free them
from their oppressors. By the time of the prophet Samuel (ca. 1100 B.C.E),

the Jewish people had selected a king. In contrast to other centers of monarchy, such as Egypt and Mesopotamia, in the kingdom of Judah the king was never deified or perceived as an ambassador of God on earth. A leader of the people in war and peace, the king was never allowed, in the 500 years of the kingdom, to make laws. Laws were revealed and interpreted by the prophets and not by the king, who reigned only in the profane sphere.[35] "He that rules over men must be just, ruling in the fear of God," professed Samuel (2 Samuel 23:3–4 JB).

Like Hammurabi's Code and the Hebrew Bible, ancient Indian texts also contained precursors of modern conceptions of rights. Kautilya's *Arthashastra* (ca. 300 B.C.E.), in particular, provided an almanac of just rulings for kings. For instance, judges were admonished to show integrity and impartiality. "Judges and magistrates shall not impose a fine when it is not prescribed, impose a fine higher or lower than the prescribed one, award physical punishment when it is not prescribed."[36] As in the Hebrew Bible, kings were not regarded as high priests, but in religious matters were subordinate to the Brahmins, who, like the Hebrew prophets, retained for thousands of years their position as an intellectual aristocracy.[37]

Though there were different punishments for civil offenses and criminal charges, the *Arthashastra* includes no application of the talion law. With the exception of the Brahmins, people might be sentenced to death (with or without torture) not only if they committed murder or treason, but also if they robbed (more than ten cattle), stole the king's property or a soldier's weapon, or damaged waterworks (as a result of a scuffle or a dispute).[38] For lesser crimes, mutilation or monetary penalty were in order, but there was no "eye for eye, bruise for bruise" punishment corresponding to one's offense. Monetary fines, for instance, could substitute for the mutilation of a body part (finger, nose, eye, hand, etc.).[39] To elicit confessions of crimes, torture was an accepted form of judicial investigation. Once again, Brahmins and holy men were spared that ordeal, along with others such as minors, the aged, the sick, the debilitated, the insane, the starving, and pregnant women.[40]

Buddhism, in a sense, went further than Hinduism in advancing a conception of freedom, as its expression of non-attachment provides all individuals with the strength to reach new introspective insights and freedom of conscience by questioning the truthfulness of apparent reality, all imposed dogma, and hence, all totalitarian ideas. This attitude was evidenced in May 1999, when, in the biggest demonstration in China since the 1989 Tiananmen Square massacre, twenty thousand members of the "Buddhist Law" sat silently in the lotus position for fifteen hours to protest against the Chinese government. More than two thousand years before Immanuel Kant's pamphlet against obscurantism, "Enlightenment," the Buddha told his followers to think for themselves and to take responsibility for their own future: "Just as the experts test gold by burning it, cutting and applying it on a touchstone, my statements should be accepted only after critical examination and not out of respect for me."[41]

In contrast to Theravada, which celebrates the subjective world of detachment, Mahayana Buddhism, in particular, challenges the path of the eternal skeptic who finds consolation in a cynical and quixotic world of ephemeral truth.[42] Instead, the active reassertion of oneself in the community of humankind is seen as a renewed commitment to the positive values of life itself. For Mahayana monks and nuns, the vow of compassion precedes Nirvana.[43] As they integrate into the community of humankind, Mahayana Buddhists follow basic universal Buddhist moral tenets of conduct: abstain from killing, abstain from stealing, abstain from unlawful sexual intercourse, abstain from lying, abstain from the use of intoxicants.[44] With the exception of the last, these creeds are similar to the commandments invoked in the Decalogue: thou shall not kill, thou shall not steal, and thou shall not covet thy neighbor's wife. With the exception of adultery, the gist of these injunctions is reflected in the very first clauses of the Universal Declaration of Human Rights, which praise the spirit of brotherhood and the right to life, liberty, and the security of one's person. Further, to alleviate suffering, the Buddha recommended that everyone follow the Eightfold Noble Path, by which one would avoid harming oneself and others through the cultivation of "right views, right intention, right effort, right action, right livelihood, right speech, right mindfulness, right meditation."[45]

In the mid–third century B.C.E., some two hundred years after the death of the Buddha, his teaching was adopted by King Asoka, who ruled over the greater part of India, in an area spreading from Afghanistan to Madras. In Buddhism, he found useful guidelines for implementing justice throughout his kingdom. Believing that there was no "greater task than to strive for universal welfare," he promoted toleration of religious ideas: "All sects receive honour from me, and I deem the essential point is fidelity to their doctrines and their practices."[46] His twenty-eight-year rule, after initial wars, was mainly dedicated to instituting peace. Missionary yet tolerant in its scope, Buddhism became, under his control, a vehicle for conversion by persuasion rather than force.

About the same time that Asoka was ruling in India, the Ch'in emperor Shih Huang Ti reigned over China. After building the Great Wall of China to keep invaders from infiltrating from the north, he turned, it is said, "his weapons into bells and statues."[47] Just as the Buddha had inspired Asoka, Confucius's early teachings inspired the universal emperor.

An exemplary ruler, Confucius believed, was a prerequisite for implementing the principles of justice. Confucius distinguished five attributes of a good leader: "to be generous without its costing him anything, works others hard without their complaining, has desires without being greedy, is casual without being arrogant, and is awe-inspiring without appearing fierce." He deplored four "wicked" forms of statesmanship: "to impose the death penalty without first attempting to reform is to be cruel; to expect results without first giving warning is to be tyrannical; to insist on a time limit when tardy in issuing orders is to cause injury. When something has to be given to others anyway, to be miserly in the actual giving is to be officious."[48] A state, Confucius maintained, could possibly exist without tax revenue and an army, but it could never be legitimate without good faith. Only laws based upon morality could command the respect of its people. Along with the unity of the human race, these principles were, according to Confucius, the universal end of any just government.[49]

A just government would be durable if order was based on the teaching of virtue and justice. Confucius's teaching commitment was such that he promised never to refuse to teach someone something in exchange for a small present.[50] "In instruction," Confucius stated, "there is no separation into categories."[51] Learning is a paramount quality:

> To love benevolence without loving learning is liable to lead to foolishness. To love cleverness without loving learning is liable to lead to deviation from the right path. To love forthrightness in word without loving learning is liable to lead to harmful behaviour. To love forthrightness without loving learning is liable to lead to intolerance. To love courage without loving learning is liable to lead to insubordination. To love unbending strength without loving learning is liable to lead to indiscipline.[52]

Where some scholars have argued that Confucius remained skeptical about the intellectual capacity of the common people, others maintain that he was a staunch advocate of public education with no distinction based on class, sex, or race.[53] In any event, Confucius insisted that only through study could a ruler become sufficiently wise to be entrusted with national leadership.

The early Greeks and Romans embraced similar principles of education and just government. Socrates' teaching, like Confucius's, was based on a questioning style. It offered a critical method of inquiry for understanding justice and ethics, based on exposing errors and confusion in the arguments of Socrates' opponents. Such a skeptical perspective, combined with a commitment to the public debate of contentious issues, is central to the notion of freedom of speech advocated centuries later. This should not suggest that Socrates was a moral relativist. At the heart of Socrates' ethics, as reported by his greatest disciple, Plato, was the challenge to conceptions of rights that promote the interests of the stronger. "Might was not right," argued Socrates, rejecting uncritical obedience to the laws of society or self-interest, in opposition to Thrasymachus and other Sophists of his time. Individuals' education was not driven merely by skepticism and self-interest, but also by virtue and morality.

That morality was much subordinated to the ideal of the philosopher king or the statesman. Like the Confucian ruler, Plato's state ruler needed to be knowledgeable and wise, one who, unlike a tyrant, did not need to rule unwilling subjects by force, one who strove to maintain peace and the welfare of his subjects.[54] The chief virtue of a just republic for Plato, as for Confucius, was division of labor and the specialization of functions, which put everyone in their proper place and provided what was due to them. Later, Plato crystallized the wisdom of temperance in the state of the *Laws,* hailing a law-abiding disposition and respect for the institutions of the state.

Beyond that ethical purpose, Aristotle maintained, the statesman would need to seize opportunities and show the ability to conduct state affairs both pragmatically and for a worthy end. With the understanding that "good laws make good men," the lawgiver needed to create a just political and ethical order in which freemen could enjoy equality with each other in the *polis:* a place that, in contrast to the authoritarian realm of the household, was composed of equal citizens "who shared in ruling and ruled by turn."[55] It was a forum where reason, rather than hierarchy, was the governing principle. With this distinction between the private and the public realm, only heads of households were entrusted with the capacity to be citizens, to exercise their freedom of expression and their political rights. By *right* Aristotle meant a "right in benefit to the whole state and the common interest of the citizen."[56]

Neither the Greek nor the Roman Empire mirrored Plato and Aristotle's ideal *polis* or Stoic teaching. Both Greek and Roman civilization were built on a fundamental distinction between the citizen and the non-citizen, between the free and the unfree. Yet Greek philosophy, with its love of wisdom and its respect for the rule of law, was bequeathed to the Roman world and later to European civilization. Inspired by Greek philosophy, Cicero, among others, would become a revered champion of the rule of law and republican government, influencing the development of Roman law, often described as Rome's "most enduring contribution to world history." Under Roman law, *ius civile* (state law) regulated the relations between citizens, and *ius gentium* (international law) harmonized relations between nations. The Greek and the Roman worlds, despite their limitations, would inspire Christianity and its canonical laws, and offered a concept of secular citizenship that would be broadened throughout the Enlightenment and subsequent centuries.

Early Christianity attempted to expand the Greek and Roman view of the commonwealth by including slaves as equal sons and daughters of God. Yet the early Christian view on ethics and law did not really differ from that of Judaism. Matthew reported Jesus as having said, in the Sermon on the Mount, that he came not to destroy the law and the Jewish prophets but to complete them (Matthew 5:17–18 NEB). Not only did Jesus venerate the Jewish commandments and laws as sacrosanct, he also regarded his work as the advancement of righteous human intentions; this was, in his opinion, as important as literal compliance with the Hebrew laws. In his view, it was not sufficient to abstain from committing a crime; indulging in such an idea was equally reprehensible. That "you shall love the Lord your God with all your heart, with all your soul . . . is the first and greatest commandment. And the second is like it: Love your neighbour as yourself" (Matthew 22:37–39 NEB).

A good Samaritan was thus not merely a law-abiding citizen but an individual whose actions were internally motivated by love for God and neighbor. Such a person would deserve honor in the afterlife. In Jesus' reported words: "I tell you, unless you show yourselves far better than Pharisees and the doctors of law, you can never enter the kingdom of Heaven" (Matthew 5:20 NEB). From the perspective of ethical contributions, one can argue, Christianity never fully broke with the Jewish conception of law. In that sense, Jesus should be seen more as a reformer of Judaism than as a revolutionary innovator.

While Christ had himself rejected involvement in politics, and his followers did not seek political power to advance their cause, the conversion of the Roman emperor Flavius Valerius Constantine (306–337) made Christianity an official state religion, inaugurating an age in which Christianity and politics were deemed compatible pursuits. Constantine ended persecution of Christians, and after uniting the two halves of his empire called for religious tolerance in the Edict of Milan in 313. That early commitment to tolerance would prove short-lived as the gradual dismemberment of the Roman Empire heralded the arrival of the Dark Ages, which lasted from the fifth to the eleventh century. Christianity, under the rule of the Church Councils, would become a source of violence, intolerance, and persecution.

If Islam's rapid spread was based largely on the sword, it soon began to emphasize tolerance. It is worth noting that the Quran shares with the Hebrew Bible, Christianity, and other sources of religious and secular ethics the notion of impartial justice: "God commanded justice and good."[57] The real test of impartiality is the ability to treat a person justly even if one harbored some aversion toward that person. In this test of character, distorting the truth is futile, for "God is well informed" (surah 5:8). Like the Decalogue, the Quran upholds the sanctity of life: "take no life, which Allah hath made sacred, except by way of justice and law" (surah 6:151). Slaying an innocent individual, says the Quran, is like slaying the whole people (surah 5:32).

According to the Quran, to receive individual protection under God's law requires not only evidence of individuals' righteous conduct but also of their religious faith.[58] This leads to the question of religious freedom. "Let there be no compulsion in religion," commanded Mohammed. While "Allah is the protector of those who have faith,"[59] Jews and Christians would also remain safe as long as they paid a tribute to the king. Later this protection was extended to Zoroastrians and Hindus. Yet perfect equality with Muslims was awarded only to those who accepted Islamic teaching. Throughout the Middle Ages, a doctrine of tolerance was nonetheless extended outside the Muslim kingdoms. Indeed, when Damascus was captured, the conqueror Khalid (?–642) secured the lives, property, and churches of the inhabitants. Even more remarkable was the extent of tolerance in the Moorish kingdom of Spain, where Muslims, Jews, and Christians lived under the rule of the caliphs of Cordova from 800 to 1000 C.E., enjoying equality, full freedom of conscience, and equal protection for person and property.[60]

Mohammed cautioned, however, that only the righteous who believe in the Quran, and not merely in the Jewish or Christian scriptures, will be rewarded on the last Day of Judgment (surah 2:62). Does that then imply that nonbelievers are ineligible for God's protection and justice on earth as well as in heaven? The Quran provides those without faith the possibility of redeeming themselves through voluntary conversion (surahs 6:108, 9:6). In the premodern Shari'a (Islamic law), however, the repercussion for remaining a non-Muslim or a nonbeliever was that one was not granted the same legal rights as Muslims.[61] Even worse, under the same laws, Muslims who repudiated their religion faced a sentence of death. As in Christianity, the religious freedom described at the outset by Mohammed was later eroded by the practices of his adherents. As recently as February 1989, the persistence of that dark strand within the Islamic tradition was dramatized by the death sentence imposed in absentia on the novelist Salman Rushdie, whose novel *The Satanic Verses* had been denounced as apostasy by the Iranian leader and Shiite cleric Ayatollah Khomeini.[62] Viewing Islam solely in terms of Khomeinism and other extremist interpretations would, however, overlook the richness of a religion whose tradition of tolerance is matched by a commitment to economic and social justice.

EQUALITY: EARLY NOTIONS OF ECONOMIC AND SOCIAL JUSTICE

Article 22 of the Universal Declaration stipulates that each human possesses "economic, social, and cultural rights . . . indispensable for his dignity and the free development of his personality." While the modern struggle over economic rights grew out of the industrial revolution and the subsequent working class movement, it is also true that calls for economic justice originated in ancient times. Traditions from Hammurabi's Code to early Islamic thought incorporated aspects comparable both to Plato's communist vision of economic redistribution and to Aristotle's defense of property, setting the stage for the tempestuous debates and struggles of the past three centuries.

In the laws promulgated by Hammurabi's Code, one can already find provisions that took into consideration differences in social status. A surgeon's fees, for instance, would vary, since a freeman had to pay more than a commoner or a slave.[63] At the same time, there were also laws protecting the right of commoners to own land. Members of various trades such as archers, cobblers, scribes, and singers were often granted land by the crown in exchange for service (not to be read as feudal service).[64] The Babylonian laws also guaranteed restitution of stolen property, ensuring a person's right to claim his or her own goods before a judge.[65] There were also laws securing employees' rights, so that a master, for instance, owed a shepherd his full wage before the master made any claims against him (e.g., for a reduction in the flock). The object of this clause, it might be inferred, "was to protect a shepherd, a poor man, against extortion by a rich owner of cattle."[66] Hammurabi's letters to governors and princes confirm that the king took pains to preserve the interests of the weak and the helpless.

The Hebrews also believed in the importance of protecting contracts and the right to property, and expressed it with the injunctions "thou shall not steal" or "covet . . . anything that is thy neighbor's" (Exodus 20:13–14 JB).[67] An important modification to the right to property was that it should not be exercised at the expense of the poor, since "the rich man's wealth is his strong city and the ruination of the lowly is their poverty" (Proverbs 10:15 JB). This view coincided with an organic belief in a social covenant with God, in which the interest of each was intertwined with the interests of others, as illustrated by the injunction "[W]hen you knock down the fruit of your olive tree, you shalt not go over the branches a second time: it shall be for the stranger, for the fatherless and for the widow" (Deuteronomy 24:20–21 JB).

In the same spirit, the poor man should not be refused a loan, and interest should not be extracted from him (Exodus 22:20–27 JB), nor should one delay paying the wages of the needy. Modern social concerns such as the right to rest from work were also invoked for everyone, including servants: "[R]emember to keep holy the Sabbath day, six days you may labor, but the seventh is the Sabbath of your lord" (Exodus 20:8–9 JB). An additional preoccupation, reminiscent of modern views on environmental rights, is also mentioned in the Bible: for "six years thou shalt sow the land, and shalt gather in its fruit; but the seventh year thou shalt let it rest and lie fallow; that the poor of thy people may eat: and what they leave, the beasts of the field shall eat" (Exodus 23:10–11 JB).[68]

In Hinduism, the importance of animals and the environment is far more pronounced. Indeed, one can find extensive references in the Vedas and other authoritative texts, such as the *Arthashastra,* to regulations against cruelty to animals and for the general protection of wildlife.[69] Because of the belief in the distribution of souls among different sentient beings and because any individual might well have been an animal in a previous life, Hinduism calls for respect for all animals and the environment.[70] Although the Hebrew Bible refers to environmental preoccupations by invoking individuals' duty to respect God's creations and the need to leave the earth unlabored every seventh year, it nonetheless asserts human domination "over the fish of the sea, and over the fowl of the air, and over the cattle, and over all the earth, and over every creeping thing that creepeth upon the earth" (Genesis 1:26 JB). One should not be surprised that Hinduism, more biocentric in character than Judaism, has such influence over the deep ecology movement and over principles that might well have inspired UN legal provisions calling for improvement of all aspects of the environment.[71]

A harmony between humans and nature is consistent with the Hindu idea of cosmological balance. Hence, as in the Mesopotamian and Jewish examples, a just Indian king needed to enforce the right to property in a spirit of harmony and common good. Indeed, the *Arthashastra* asserts that no one will occupy the property of another except with good reason, and that if property has been wrongfully appropriated during war, the kings shall restitute it to its owners.[72] In these and other instances, the universal spirit of the common good, animated by the *dharma,* might be superseded by "greed and desire for each other's property," warned the *Mahabharata* scriptures—a trend that "generally brings moral decay."[73] Stealing was considered a grave sin, further strengthening the notion of entitlement over property. Yet different forms of punishment in traditional Hinduism showed these laws securing property were often written to benefit the higher caste.[74]

Nevertheless, contractual work arrangements, described in the *Arthashastra* with the same concern as in Hammurabi's Code and the Hebrew Bible, were honored in clauses setting forth both employers' and employees' rights. Although an employer had the right to require an employee to work for pay, an employee was not obliged to work against his will if he was sick. "An employee shall have the right, if he is ill, in distress, incapable of doing his work or if the work is vile: to have his contract annulled or to have it done by someone else." Further, "[A]n employee shall not be obliged to work against his will, to continue working for his previous employer if he had completed the task allotted to him." With the employee's consent any additional work beyond the contractual agreement would receive adequate compensation.[75]

In the same spirit, the texts in the Buddhist Pali Canon command followers not to steal; hence the right to property.[76] At the same time, the Buddhist tradition recommended some forms of economic redistribution. In later Buddhist literature, the sage Nagarjuna's advice to royalty depicted the functioning of a welfare state that limited the incomes of the well off: "To dispel the suffering of children, the elderly, and the sick, please fix farm revenues for doctors and barbers throughout the land." In certain circumstances, as the Buddhist scholar Robert Thurman has noted, Nagarjuna also urged the state "to intervene in the realm of private affairs to forestall bankruptcy," to guarantee universal health care, to set up "hostels, parks, canals, irrigation, ponds, rest houses, wells, beds, food, grass, and firewood," to care for travelers, and to provide shelters for beggars, cripples, and wandering ascetics.[77] Property, especially that owned by the Sangha (the Buddhist community of monks and nuns), can also be seen as communitarian and, in the characterization of the Buddhist scholar Masao Abe, even communistic. For instance, despite the Chinese Communists' hostilities toward Tibetan Buddhists, which began in the 1960s, Mao's commune and a Zen monastery may not be as different as one might think. The difference, Abe maintains, is one of attitude and scale.[78]

Although not as egalitarian as Mao, Confucius did not accept the prevailing political views of his time, which held that wealth and power should be the predominant values. A benevolent leader, he maintained, needed to enhance the economic well-being of his people. Confucius's condemnation of a high taxation of the public would later be reiterated by one of his followers, Chen Te-hsiu, who called for the end of abusive tax collection.[79] In the same vein, Confucius also believed that "where there is even distribution there is no such thing as poverty, where there is harmony there is no such thing as underpopulation and where there is stability there is no such thing as overturning."[80] A benevolent government should provide people with what is really beneficial for them and discourage the rich from taking complete control of society's wealth: "A gentleman gives to help the needy and not to maintain the rich in style."[81]

Plato, too, realized that struggles over wealth would have a pernicious effect on the good order and functioning of his ideal government. Anticipating the socialist or communist view of human rights, Plato asserted that to turn rulers away from greed, there was no alternative but to abolish wealth, the source of cupidity and hostility. Since private property would virtually disappear, "[T]here won't in fact be any quarrels which are caused by having money."[82] He abhorred industrialism and commercialism because they were sources of conflict and believed that a self-sufficient agricultural community fostered the most temperate and pacifist type of population.

"[W]e find, however, more dispute between those who share property in common," Aristotle later countered, "than we do among separate holders of possession."[83] According to Aristotle, ownership in common could generate tension between the lazy and the industrious worker; it would defy a natural human enjoyment, which individuals should benefit from without excess; it did not entrust individuals with the capacity to exercise the virtues of "temperance" and "liberality," "for it is in the use of articles of property that liberality is practiced."[84] Property rights were paramount for the Greeks' and Aristotle's notion of citizenship: property ownership provided the entitlement to participate in public affairs and qualified a man to be a citizen.[85] Aristotle believed that if they owned sufficient property, individuals would free themselves from daily preoccupations and find the leisure necessary to participate in the activities of the *polis,* an idea that would influence the liberal tradition of the Enlightenment.[86]

Capturing the tension of these two antithetical Greek positions, Christianity, through the Ten Commandments, upholds the sanctity of individual life and the importance of not stealing.[87] Though there is no call for the abolition of property, as in Plato's *Republic,* the pernicious effect of greed is nonetheless evoked in the New Testament by Jesus' condemnation of the merchants of the temple, and later by James's warning to wealthy men that misery will come upon them (James 5:1–6 NEB). The general Christian attitude toward excesses of wealth is best characterized by Jesus' famous statement that "it is easier for a camel to pass through the eye of a needle, than for a rich man to enter the kingdom of God" (Mark 10:25–26 NEB). Echoed today by Peruvian liberation theologist Gustavo Gutiérrez, universal compassion toward the poor, the sick, and the disabled remains a persistent theme in Christian thought.

The Quran also recognizes basic economic and related rights for in-

---

GUSTAVO GUTIÉRREZ, "ON LIBERATION AND DEVELOPMENT,"
***THE DENSITY OF THE PRESENT,* 1992**

Thus we affirm life as the primary human right and, from a Christian viewpoint, as a gift of God which must be defended. . . . It has helped us to recover an evangelical perspective (so important to people like Las Casas in the sixteenth century) on the idolatrous nature of human profit as promoted by "savage capitalism," which tramples the dignity of human beings and turns them into the victims of a cruel and sacrilegious cult. At the same time it is important to observe that poverty is not only a matter of not having. The poor are brimming with abilities and possibilities. The poor often possess a culture with its own values, from their race, their history, and their language; with energies like those shown in the struggle for life by women's organizations throughout the continent; with inventive and creative power that resists, against all odds, what today is being called the crisis of paradigms.

From *The Density of the Present: Selected Writings* by Gustavo Gutiérrez, 132–133.

dividuals.[88] These include protection against defamation (surah 24:16) and against poverty (surah 22:7–8), as well as rights to a place of residence (surah 2:85), to dignity, to sustenance (surah 17:70), to asylum from oppression, and so forth (surah 4:97–99).[89] The doctrine of social service, defined in terms of alleviating suffering and helping the needy, constitutes an integral part of Islamic teaching. Praying to God and other religious acts should always be complemented by active service to the disadvantaged (surahs 2:188, 3:14, 4:29, 4:30, 4:33). The Quran promises prosperity in exchange for such social services. Accumulating wealth without recognizing the rights of the poor, however, is threatened with the harshest punishment in the hereafter and perceived as one of the main causes of the decay of societies.

HOW TO PROMOTE JUSTICE?

If an excess of wealth was a cause of misery, would coercive measures promoting social or economic justice be justified? Some traditions stress preaching or educating, others invoke the sword, and others insist on passive resistance. When war was seen as inevitable, the Hebrews considered guidelines to ensure that it would be waged justly. Further developed by Christians, Muslims, and others, these principles would culminate in the celebrated theories of Augustine of Hippo (354–430), Thomas Aquinas (1225–1274), Hugo Grotius (1583–1645), and other natural law theorists. In modern times, these early visions were encapsulated by the 1864 Geneva Convention (amended in 1949), an international convention that required, for the first time, the protection of prisoners of war, recognition of their rights, and assistance for the wounded regardless of the side for which they had fought.

It is well known that the Hebrew Bible demands adherence to the critical commandment "thou shall not kill." Weren't Adam and his heirs, made in the image of God, therefore deserving of having their lives venerated? The preservation of human life and the search for peace were paramount duties for Jews, maintained the Jewish philosopher Maimonides (1135–1204), holding out hope that there would be no war and no hunger and no oppression. One should also recall that modern insistence on the right to peace, celebrated by the UN Declaration on the Right of Peoples to Peace (1984), harks as far back as Micah in the Old Testament, who demanded that a "nation shall not lift a sword against nation, nor shall they learn war anymore" (Micah 3:14–16 JB).

Of course, wars remained unavoidable, and for that eventuality, moral prescriptions promoting humane conduct were drafted. The book of Exodus stipulates that war can be initiated only when peace has been offered to the enemy and has been rejected. It also discusses the different types of treatment to be accorded prisoners of war, and the requirement to offer safety to the inhabitants of a besieged city should they surrender. Elsewhere, the Bible urges the Israelites to conduct themselves compassionately in war: "If thy enemy be hungry, give him bread to eat, if he be thirsty, give him water to drink" (Proverbs 25:21 JB), it enjoins, while warning against the wanton robbery of an enemy's property. In all instances, stolen goods needed to be restituted: "[R]eturn a stray ox and ass to the enemy" (Exodus 23:4–5 JB).

The Hindu tradition offers more pervasive constraints on recourse to violence than one finds in the Old Testament. The ideal of *ahimsa*, "non-injury" or the absence of the desire to harm, is regarded as one of the keystones of Hindu ethics and has influenced many thinkers and political figures, including Mahatma Gandhi (1869–1948), whose political technique of passive resistance, *satyagraha*, was inspired by many Hindu sources. Originally, *ahimsa* was unrelated to vegetarianism, but the two practices reinforce one another through the protection offered both humans and animals. The spirit of nonviolence was further recommended to kings.[90] Although a right to rebel is not spelled out, kings are warned of the possibility of rebellions if they are tyrannical or cause the impoverishment of the population. A just king observes the *Arthashastra*, will

---

MICAH 3:14–16 JERUSALEM BIBLE

But in the last days it shall come to pass, that the mountain of the house of the Lord shall be established on the top of the mountains, and it shall be exalted above the hills; and peoples shall stream towards it. And many nations shall come, and say, Come and let us go up to the mountain of the house of the Lord and to the house of the God and Y'aaqov; and he will teach us of his ways, and we will walk in his paths: For Tora shall go forth from Ziyyon, and the word of the Lord from Yerushalayim. And he shall judge between many peoples, and decide concerning strong nations afar off; and they shall beat their swords into ploughshares, and their spears into pruninghooks: nation shall not lift up a sword against a nation, nor shall they learn war anymore. But they shall sit every man under his vine and under his fig tree; and none shall make them afraid: for the mouth of the Lord of hosts has spoken it. For let all people walk everyone in the name of his god and we will walk in the name of the Lord our God for ever and ever.

be safe from attack by his subjects and will preserve their loyalty during wartime.[91]

The Buddhist understanding of war shows clear similarities with Hinduism. The injunction not to kill or injure any human, animal, or insect reflects the pacifist Buddhist attitude. Warfare is depicted as self-defeating, since, according to the Buddha, "[V]ictory breeds more hatred, the defeated live in pain; the peaceful person lives happily, giving up victory and defeat. . . . The slayer gets a slayer in return. The conqueror gets one who conquers him."[92] War might still be fought, though only in self-defense. All alternatives, including diplomatic efforts, compromise, compensation, threats, or demonstrations, needed first to be considered. If those proved futile, then one should weigh the possible outcome of a war and refrain from fighting if the prospects for success were poor. It is imperative, from a Buddhist standpoint, to minimize casualties, whenever possible, and maintain moral conduct during and after a war.[93]

Confucianism also aimed to promote peace. During the time of Confucius, China consisted of many small squabbling states. The feudal system had deteriorated, and political crises had been accompanied by a profound sense of moral decline. To avoid chaos and the eruption of vi-

---

MAHATMA GANDHI, "PASSIVE RESISTANCE," 1907

Passive resistance is an all-sided sword, it can be used anyhow; it blesses him who uses it and him against whom it is used. Without drawing a drop of blood it produces far-reaching results. It never rusts and cannot be stolen. Competition between passive resisters does not exhaust. The sword of passive resistance does not require a scabbard. It is strange indeed that you should consider such a weapon to be a weapon merely of the weak. . . . Kings will always use their kingly weapons. To use force is bred in them. They want to command, but those who have to obey commands do not want guns: and these are in a majority throughout the world. They have to learn either body-force or soul-force. Where they learn the former, both the rulers and the ruled become like so many madmen; but where they learn soul-force, the commands of the rulers do not go beyond the point of their swords, for true men disregard unjust commands. Peasants have never been subdued by the sword, and never will be. They do not know the use of the sword, and they are not frightened by the use of it by others. The nation is great which rests its head upon death as its pillow. Those who defy death are free from all fear. For those who are labouring under the delusive charms of brute-force, this picture is not overdrawn. The fact is that, in India, the nation at large has generally used passive resistance in all departments of life. We cease to cooperate with our rulers when they displease us. This is passive resistance.

From *The Selected Works of Mahatma Gandhi*, vol. 4, 176–177.

---

olence, Confucius continued to profess the cultivation of the self, which he saw as the root of social order, just as social order was the basis for political stability and universal peace. Even the expansion of one's state should be conducted peacefully: "If . . . the people of far-off lands still do not submit," argued Confucius, "then the ruler must attract them by enhancing the prestige *(te)* of his culture, and when they have been duly attracted, he contents them."[94]

In the early Warring States period (475–221 B.C.E.), Mencius (372–259 B.C.E.), a renowned follower of Confucius, defended the right to fight a war of self-defense against foreign aggression. At the same time, Mencius considered as just causes for war the overthrow of tyrannical regimes, and, with Confucius, the expansion of the territory of a benevolent government not to gain possession of a state but to enlighten a subjugated people.[95] Against an unfit ruler, Mencius recommended criticism and rehabilitation, but called for revolution as a last resort. Whether Mencius called for a people's rights to revolution and to depose a king is unclear; he encouraged, however, the responsible members of a ruling house to overthrow an abusive ruler.[96]

Chinese unity, and peace in general, were dear to Confucius and his followers, just as unity and peace among the Greek city-states were to Plato and the Stoics. Greeks should "love their fellow Greeks, and think of Greece as their own land, in whose common religion they share." "Should hostility arise between two states," Plato argued with Socrates, "one should not reduce another Greek people to slavery"; and when fighting barbarians, "one should treat them as the Greeks now treat each other."[97] Neither stripping corpses on battlegrounds, nor desecrating the enemy's temples, nor burning the enemy's houses and lands were justifiable acts of war, they insisted, as the Jews had before them. An enemy should also be permitted to recover bodies and bury his dead after a battle, as Greek custom obliged.[98]

MENCIUS, "AGAINST TYRANNY," FOURTH CENTURY B.C.E.

The people are of supreme importance; the altars to the gods of earth and grain come next; last comes the ruler. . . . When a feudal lord endangers the altars to the gods of earth and grain he should be replaced. When the sacrificial animals are sleek, the offerings are clean and the sacrifices are observed at due times, and yet floods and droughts come, then the altars should be replaced.

From *Mencius,* bk. 7, pt. B, sec. 14.

While exalting with Plato the importance of courage among warriors, the Roman Cicero joined him in his criticism of war, describing his disgust over the spoliation caused by Philip, Alexander, and many others who had brought fame upon themselves at the expense of their own people.[99] With the Stoics, Cicero believed that the world was one great city, and that everyone had an obligation to all things pertaining to world affairs and peace. "Wars are unjust" when undeclared or "undertaken without provocation." Only a war waged for revenge or defense, he claimed, "can actually be just."[100]

Central to the foundation of early Christianity was the repudiation of violence and the proclamation of solidarity with other human beings. Jesus, following Old Testament teachings, called for loving one's enemy as one loves one's neighbor (Matthew 5:43–44 NEB), and famously commanded his followers to respond to a slap in the face by turning the other cheek (Matthew 5:39 NEB). Until the Christian church became the creed of the Roman Empire, Christians were to maintain an unbending position toward fighting and military service. Christians, unlike Jews, wrote Origen (ca. 185–254), head of the Patristic school in Palestine, were not allowed to fight their enemies: "We draw not the sword against any people and we do not learn the art of war. . . . We do not march with the emperor into the field even when he commands us to do so. We fight for him in that we form an army of our own, an army of piety and prayer."[101] When Christianity was adopted by the emperor Constantine as the religion of the state, this belief was modified, and it was indelibly altered during the conquest and conversion of the northern barbarians.

The great bishops of the church, such as Augustine of Hippo, now rejected the prior commitment to pacifism. After the sack of Rome by the Goths in 410, Augustine declared, in *De civitate Dei,* that some form of revenge or killing in a "just war" was permissible, but should only be considered *ad extremis.* Yet how could the idea of a just war be reconciled with the injunction "thou shall not kill"? Augustine made in this respect a critical distinction between two societies. Drawing on Plato, he characterized the earthly city as one founded on material appetites and possessive impulses. The city of God, on the other hand, was founded in the hope of universal heavenly peace and spiritual salvation. This implied a dual organization of human society, in which spiritual concerns came under the province of the church and secular interests under the aegis of a secular authority. Because the earthly city was intrinsically sinful in character, one needed to develop some form of remedy to prevent abuses. The consideration of a just war was one such effort.[102] If, in the earthly city, war needed to be waged as a last recourse, it was unjustified if undertaken for the purpose of profit and brigandage and justified if undertaken in order to crush oppression. The Christian soldier, like the Israelite, needed to show compassion toward an enemy, since, Augustine reminded, he was, after all, fighting for peace.

More influenced by Aristotle than Plato, and thus, relatively speaking, by the earthly quality of human morality and activities, Thomas Aquinas would later elaborate a theory of just war. Wars were just, he claimed, when waged with self-restraint by sovereign authorities for self-defense, for the sake of the common good, and with peaceful ends. Provided that the ends were just, wars could be waged either openly or by means of ambushes. On the other hand, Aquinas perceived that wars were unjust if they were motivated by self-aggrandizement or the lust for power, or were conducted with cruelty. In an Augustinian mode, he also viewed as unlawful the taking up of arms by clerics or spiritual leaders.[103] Revised later by Hugo Grotius and other international legal scholars, Aquinas's *jus bellum* view set the stage for a new way of thinking about morality in such inevitably "sinful" human situations as wars.

The notion of specified limits on the use of violence is also embedded in Islamic teaching, as the Quran echoes the biblical standard of "life for life, eye for eye, nose for nose, ear for ear, tooth for tooth and wound for wound equal for equal." Yet following the teaching of Jesus and Mohammed, one can still "remit retaliation by way of charity" (surah 5:45). While retaliation against an evil must be proportionate to that evil (surah 42:40), there are instances in which retaliation by means of war, or jihad (literally meaning "exertion") is, as in the Christian notions of just war, legitimated. The Quran justifies wars for self-defense to protect Islamic communities against internal or external aggression by non-Islamic populations, and wars waged against those who "violate their oaths" by breaking a treaty (surahs 9:12, 9:13, 42:40–43).[104]

If God commands us to go to war, a better afterlife, exhorts the Quran, is promised to the true soldiers of faith: "And if ye are slain or die, in the way of Allah, forgiveness and mercy from Allah are far better than all they could amass [in wealth]" (surah 3:157). If some modern Islamic religious zealots, such as Osama bin Laden, have found in the concept of the holy war a justification for terrorist activities, they have overlooked the fact that the same Quran, drawing from the Hebrew Bible, urges a soldier of faith "to protect the life of non-combatants, aged ones, children and women, as well as the life of imprisoned soldiers."[105] Temperance, the Quran states, is also mandated: "Fight in the name of God those who fight you; but exceed not the limit. For God loves not those who exceed the limit. . . . Fight till there is no persecution, and the judgment be God's. But if they desist, let there be no hostilities save against the unjust."[106] One should not forget, after all, that Islamic juridical writings urging tolerance and moderation in war, such as the Abbou Hassan of Baghdad (1036), the Hedaya (1196), and the Vikayat printed in Spain

---

ON JIHAD

Quran, Surah 111:97

Remember . . . the kindness of God to you who were formerly enemies. He has now bound your hearts together, so that through His goodness you may become brothers.

Sobhi Mahmassani, "The Principle of International Law in Light of Islamic Doctrine," 1966

Islamic law . . . is essentially a law of peace, built on human equality, religious tolerance and universal brotherhood. . . .

War, in theory, is just and permissible only as a defensive measure, on grounds of extreme necessity, namely to protect the freedom of religion, to repel aggression, to prevent injustice and to protect social order. . . .

This defensive war, when permissible, is moreover subjected by Islamic jurisprudence to strict regulations and rules. In their human character they were unparalleled in their time and are comparable in content only to modern regulations recognized to-day by international conferences and treaties.

Thus, a declaration of war has to be preceded by notification sent to the enemy. Detailed provisions are laid down for the use of human methods of warfare and fair treatment of enemy persons and property. Acts of cruelty and unnecessary destruction and suffering are expressly proscribed. Provision is also made for the termination of war and the settlement of its consequences.

From Hague Academy for International Law, *Recueil des cours.*

Osama bin Laden, "Jihad," from "Fatwah," 1998

In compliance with God's order, we issue the following fatwa to all Muslims: the ruling to kill the Americans and their allies—civilians and military—is an individual duty for every Muslim who can do it in any country in which it is possible to do it, in order to liberate the Al-Aqsa Mosque [Jerusalem] and the holy mosque [Mecca] from their grip, and in order for their armies to move out of the lands of Islam. . . . This is in accordance with the words of almighty God, "and fight the pagans all together as they fight you all together," and "fight them until there is no more tumult or oppression, and there prevail justice and faith in God."

From *Al-Quds al-'Arabi*, February 23, 1998, http://www.ict.org.il/articles/fatwah.htm.

(1280) were composed five hundred years before Grotius and the Christian humanists. Those views live on in the contemporary Islamic writings of the Lebanese jurist Sobhi Mahmassani.

FRATERNITY, OR HUMAN RIGHTS FOR WHOM?

If brotherly compassion or universal humanity in war and elsewhere were unconditionally mandated by Muslims and others in many ancient texts, the notion of universality evolved throughout history, carrying narrower meanings in Hammurabi's and Mohammed's times than in Jefferson's or Lenin's. Slaves, women, foreigners, and homosexuals, among others, were rarely considered full-fledged members of early universal projects. Yet the ancients sketched out the fundamentals of a universal ethics that the moderns would further elaborate, by gradually including new actors within their conception of humanity.

Hammurabi's Code included protection for widows, sick wives, raped virgins, daughters-in-law, and daughters.[107] For example, the code stipulated, "If a man (carnally) knows his daughter, they shall banish that man from the city."[108] Yet women were not granted the same rights as men, and their rights varied depending upon their social class. An adulterous wife (and her lover) was subject to death at her husband's discretion, but women did not have the same prerogative against adulterous husbands.[109] Adultery was perceived as an offense against the husband, not the wife. A woman who killed her husband or her unborn child was subject to the most severe punishment: "If a women has procured the death of her husband on the account of another man, they shall impale that woman."[110] It is unclear whether a husband committing the same crime would have suffered the same punishment.[111]

The laws of Hammurabi were not universal in the modern sense of the word, because slaves were endowed with fewer rights than patricians or freemen. The majority of slaves in Babylon, the major center of Mesopotamia, belonged to the palace, the temples, or the rich. Slaves were either acquired in war or purchased in markets at home and abroad. A large number were born Babylonians, and because of poverty either sold themselves, were sold by their fathers, or had been seized by creditors. Unlike Roman slaves, Babylonian slaves were able to marry, and their masters were not granted the power of life and death over them.[112] A slave concubine could be redeemed, and generally after a certain number of years a Babylonian slave, who often was a debtor, could also be released: "If a man has become liable to arrest under a bond and has sold his wife, his son or his daughter or gives (them) into servitude, for three years they shall do work in the house of him who has bought them in servitude; in the fourth year their release shall be granted."[113]

There were also restrictions in the Hebrews' vision of universality. Perpetual slavery was abolished for Hebrew slaves but not for foreign slaves.[114] As in Babylonia, debtors in Israel worked as slaves. But for enslaved Hebrews (or indentured servants), a seven-year limit was set on bondage. During one's years of servitude, both Hebrew and non-Hebrew slaves retained some rights and were not subject to the absolute power of the master. For instance, if a master beat his slave to death, he would himself face death, and if he maimed a slave, he had to set the slave free (Exodus 21:20 JB). In these instances, a particular interpretation of the talion law was ordained. Further, like Hebrew slaves, foreign slaves, once circumcised, could partake in religious worship, and, like other members of the community, were forbidden to work on the Sabbath (Exodus 20:9–10 JB).

The Bible depicts the worthy deeds of many women of unquestionable stature, including Sarah, Miriam, Deborah, Hannah, Esther, Ruth, Naomi, and others, but, like indentured servants or slaves, these women— whether judges, prophetesses, heroines, or commoners helping the cause of their people—did not enjoy equal rights with freemen. It is also accurate that various biblical clauses, like Hammurabi's, called for the protection of women. For example, if a man strikes and hurts "a women with child, so that her fruit depart from her; and yet no further harm ensue: he shall be surely punished, according as the woman's husband will lay upon him; and he shall pay as the judge determines. But if any harm ensue, then thou shalt give life for life" (Exodus 21:22–24 JB).

Despite admonitions not to inflict pain on widows and pregnant wives (Exodus 22:21 JB) and the centrality of women in household religious rituals, women were always subordinate to men and at times were regarded as the property of their husbands. There are references in the Bible to marriage by purchase. Hosea, for instance, noted that he bought his wife for fifteen pieces of silver (Hosea 2 JB), and Boaz spoke of Ruth as one "whom I have purchased" (Ruth 4:10 JB).[115] The notion of women as property is also evoked by the Ten Commandments' prohibition against coveting one's neighbor's wife. A woman could not divorce her husband for adultery or at will unless her husband agreed; and Hebrew daughters, like Babylonian ones, could inherit only if there were no sons living at the time of their father's death. A woman who committed adultery, like a man who had sex with another man, was perceived to have committed an "abomination" punishable by death (Leviticus 20:13 JB). In other instances, however, adulterous women and homosexuals were punished by being cut off from the people of Israel, or stoned (Leviticus 20:19 JB).[116] Although it is unclear whether these punishments were enforced, the Bible shows no signs of tolerance for male homosexual behavior. By contrast, lesbianism was apparently indulged in early Judaism because it did not involve genital penetration.[117]

Encompassing inorganic as well as organic entities, the structure of the universe depicted in ancient Hindu texts was even more hierarchical than that of Judaism. The natural and social stratification was articulated in alimentary and figurative terms: you are more than the one you eat, and less than the one by whom you are eaten. More concretely, society was divided into four major castes: Brahmins (priests), rulers and warriors *(kshatriyas),* commoners *(vaishyas),* and servants *(shudras).* The principle of karma, premised on the idea of reincarnation, suggested that members of a lower caste could aspire to social mobility in another life cycle if they had lived righteously and performed their duties on earth. In the physical realm, however, upward mobility was a vain enterprise, and intermarriage was discouraged in order to uphold the purity of the higher castes.[118]

This should not suggest that the higher echelons were permitted to trample on the lower ones; after all, individuals could be reborn as members of an inferior caste. Whereas moral guidelines were true for all, tasks and punishments varied according to an individual's caste: "Taking into consideration the laws of the castes, districts, guilds, and families, a king who knows justice should establish the particular law of each."[119] Unlike those in the other castes, male Brahmins were exempt from the death penalty and corporal punishments. *The Laws of Manu* proclaimed "ten places in which the three lower classes may be punished, but a priest should depart uninjured."[120] In extreme cases such as murder, a Brahmin could be sent into exile or sent to work in the mines. The caste system and especially the suffering of members of the lowest caste, the Untouchables, would finally confront significant opposition in the mid-twentieth century, when Indian lawyer Bhimrao Ambedkar (1891–1956) campaigned for the political and social rights of the Untouchables.[121]

There existed safeguards for women in the *Arthashastra,* such as the protection of pregnant women against torture and unhealthy incarceration, but their rights were very restricted. Women from lower castes or in bonded labor were provided with some protections from unjust beating or other forms of mistreatment. For instance, the punishment a husband could inflict on a woman was limited to three slaps, and a woman could run away if she was mistreated by her husband.[122] According to *The Laws of Manu,* however, a husband could inflict more severe punishment on his wife.[123] All in all, a woman was always dependent on and subservient to a man. Manu stated that "in childhood, a woman should be under her father's control, in youth under her husband's, and when her husband is dead, under her sons'. She should not have independence."[124] Women were also included in lists of property, along with deposits and pledges.[125] A wife could not, without the consent of her spouse, drink, indulge in sports, travel for leisure, or attend performances. She was prohibited from leaving the household when her husband was either asleep or drunk.[126]

There is no corresponding evidence of strict physical and sexual control over homosexuals in the orthodox Vedic tradition. In the *Mahabharata,* homosexuality, along with sodomy and pederasty, was perceived as at most perverse, and less offensive than miscegenation. In more secular post-Vedic texts, such as the *Arthashastra,* a higher fine was prescribed for male than for female homosexuality. A relaxation in control over sexual behavior, however, can be found later on in the *Kamasutra,* whose author defines *kama* as "a state where all our senses and our mind get satisfaction." Modern disapproval of homosexuality may well be attributable to a cultural and nationalist reaction against mores of foreign domination in India.[127]

BHIMRAO RAMJI AMBEDKAR, *ANNIHILATION OF CASTE,* 1945

It is a pity that Caste even to-day has its defenders. The defenses are many. It is defended on the ground that the Caste System is but another name for division of labour and if division of labour is a necessary feature of every civilized society then it is argued that there is nothing wrong in the Caste System. . . . Civilized society undoubtedly needs division of labour. But in no civilized society is division of labour accompanied by this unnatural division of labourers into water-tight compartments. Caste System is not merely a division of labourers which is quite different from division of labour—it is an hierarchy in which the division of labourers are graded one above the other. . . .

. . . What is your ideal society if you do not want Caste is a question that is bound to be asked of you. If you ask me, my ideal would be a society based on *Liberty, Equality,* and *Fraternity.*

From *Annihilation of Caste: With a Reply to Mahatma Gandhi,* 19–20, 38.

Some restricted rights also applied to servants or bonded slaves. Like Babylonian and Hebrew slavery, "the supposed slavery in India was of . . . mild character and limited extent, as compared with the slavery known to the Hellenic world."[128] The word *dasa,* translated as slave, represented the condition of unfree labor, which had fewer rights than other categories of workers (male or female). There were two other categories of unfree laborer: the *underadsatva* and the *ahitaka.* The former alluded to a person in distress who exchanged work for protection, and the latter to a person who was pledged or mortgaged against a debt, or against ransom demanded after being captured in war. In all these cases, individuals' labor was limited to a particular time, depending upon their particular condition and the amount owed.[129] A slave was entitled to keep property and to pass it on to his kin. There were fines for not redeeming a slave or for remortgaging a slave without his or her consent.[130]

If the Vedas inspired some of the thinking of the Buddha, he nonetheless refuted some important aspects of Hinduism (Brahmanism), in particular the notions of a caste system and privileges based on birth. If any hierarchy existed, the Buddha asserted, it was one solely based on the character and quality of a righteous person: "I do not call a man a brahmana because of his origin or of his mother. He is indeed arrogant, and he is wealthy; but the poor man who is free from all attachments, him I call indeed a brahmana. Him I call a brahmana whose knowledge is deep, who possesses wisdom, who knows the right way and the wrong, and has attained the highest end."[131]

Buddhist universalist notions of justice were not without flaws: they did not fully extend to women. It is true that Buddhist monasteries became the first schools open to students of all castes and both sexes. In addition, the position of women in ancient Tibetan society, it is argued, was better than that in India, Southeast Asia, or China. Vajrayana, or Tantric Buddhism, for example, glorified a considerable number of female teachers and saints, and upheld their writings as authoritative. At the same time, women were not granted the same privileges as men. With great hesitance the Buddha permitted the ordination of nuns; but once ordained they still maintained a status inferior to that of monks.[132] To be born or reborn as a woman was seen at times in Buddhism as a form of punishment. "Any woman," stated the celestial Buddha Bhaishajyaguru, "who is afflicted by various disadvantages of womanhood and who wishes to be liberated from being born as a loathsome female should bear my name in mind, and she will not be reborn in the female state."[133]

"[If she] abhors her femaleness and constantly aspires to masculinity, [she] will be reborn as a man."[134]

The ancient Buddhist disposition toward homosexuality (not to be confused with the cultural attitude of many contemporary Buddhists) was more charitable than its view on the position of women. There were very few instances in which male homosexual relations were condemned (there are no specific references to lesbianism). This was partly due to the fact that most of the record pertaining to that issue was related to monastic life, and in that sphere of avowed celibacy, all forms of sexual activity—whether heterosexual or homosexual—were denounced. Early Buddhist texts reject same-sex preference for men; later, in the case of India, China, and Tibet, Buddhism remained relatively neutral about homosexual practices. In Japan, however, "[I]t was extolled and praised as a mysterious practice."[135]

Discrimination also existed in Confucius's thought. One clearly negative aspect of the Confucian notion of social stability, from the perspective of our modern concept of universality, is the insistence on an orderly hierarchy premised on five relationships: those between father and son, ruler and minister, husband and wife, older and younger sibling, and older and younger friend. The problematic legacy lies in that of the "three bonds," namely in the authority of the ruler over the minister, the father over the son, and the husband over the wife. In the words of the classical legal scholar Han Fei Tzu, during the Han dynasty (206 B.C.E.—220 C.E.), "[T]he minister serves the king, the son serves the father, and the wife serves the husband. If the three are followed, the world will be in peace; if the three are violated the world is in chaos."[136] Despite the Confucian disciple Mencius's call for ethical responsibility at each level of power, hierarchy, justified in the name of social stability—the linchpin of Confucian thought—is elevated above the concept of universal rights.

The tension between personal awareness through universal education and a fixed view of hierarchical stratification is replicated in Confucius's discussion on justice and the law. Confucius condemned leaders who put individuals to death without first attempting to reform them, including teaching them about right and wrong.[137] At the same time, he did not believe that individuals were born with similar faculties or that they were equal in intelligence. Men of low intelligence, he explained, cannot acquire the capacity for self-control. Laws thus should be enforced when education failed to check the passions of the commoner. With this in mind, he recommended that the ordinary code of criminal law be applied to the uneducated lower class, whereas higher officials, assumed to be role models by virtue of their position and education, should be governed by different laws.[138]

Despite these tendencies toward authoritarianism, Confucianism, like Buddhism, did not advocate slavery, nor were slaves listed among any of six classes of people in the state—namely, kings and princes, scholars and great officials, artisans, farmers, merchants, and women.[139] However, the role of women, as in all of the other great religions, was subordinate to that of men. "In one household," said Confucius, "it is the women and the small men that are difficult to deal with. If you let them get too close, they become insolent. If you keep them at a distance, they complain."[140] Depiction of the mother as caretaker and descriptions of her family duties are so prevalent throughout the classic texts that one should not be surprised that many Confucians characterized women as submissive to men and deplored instances of their dominance or political control as an abnormal social phenomenon.[141] At times, women did become government officials or were appointed as commissioners. Yet, all in all, dutiful subservience to men was the general condition of women, and adultery was severely punished by law. Interestingly, lesbianism was more acceptable than adultery. One may wonder, given the conservative aspect of the Confucian family and the importance of filial lineage, why homosexuality (male or female) was not severely condemned. As long as one fulfilled familial and social obligations, however, Confucians did not single out homosexual behavior for special rebuke.[142]

Plato, through his narrative on Socrates, was unique among his contemporaries in his position on women. Not only did he encourage the fair treatment of women, a group that had few rights in ancient Greece, Plato was among the first Western thinkers to assert that women had similar abilities to men, and that depending upon their individual capacities, they should be able to fulfill the same tasks as their male counterparts: "There is therefore no function in society which is peculiar to woman as woman or man as man; natural abilities are similarly distributed in each sex, and it is natural for women to share all occupations with men, though in all women will be the weaker partners."[143] A revolutionary for his time, Plato maintained that women should receive the same kind of education as men and should be eligible for the same kinds of offices. Although Plato disparaged homosexuality somewhat in the *Laws,* Socrates, along with Xenophon and other Athenians of his day, discussed homosexual friendship in a more sympathetic way.[144] Last, there was no discussion of the tasks of slaves in Plato's *Republic,* which led some to argue that Plato was implicitly calling for the abolition of slavery.

Aristotle joined Plato's academy and adhered to many of its principles, yet the Thracian native also significantly modified Plato's ethical thought. This was particularly striking in Aristotle's problematic justification of slavery. Like Plato and Confucius, Aristotle argued that the highest form of human existence resided in the life of the rational being, who should strive to extend the full capacity of his or her reasoning. Unlike his predecessor, he inferred from this that the function of lower beings, that is, slaves, was to serve the higher forms of life. Because barbarians were less rational than Greeks, they were by nature suited to be enslaved as a "living tool": "A slave is a sort of living piece of property; and like any other servant is a tool in charge of other tools."[145] He also departed from Plato's view of women by asserting, "[B]etween male and female the former is by nature superior and ruler, the latter inferior and subject. And this may hold good for mankind in general."[146] Aristotle's position was undoubtedly influenced by the condition of women in Hellenic society and the prevailing norm of support for slavery.

Though inconsistent, Aristotle's views toward homosexuals were more generous than his positions on women. He viewed the homosexual disposition sometimes as bad habit formation, but at other times as "natural."[147] "When nature is responsible, no one would call such persons immoral, any more than they would women because they are passive in intercourse rather than active."[148]

In Hellenic times, as in early Christianity, women were often admired and appointed as deaconesses. As mentioned earlier, the New Testament, like the Hebrew Bible, narrates the positive deeds of some virtuous women. The purity of Mary, the mother of Jesus, served as an example of virtue for women, as did the models provided by the nurturing character of many others, such as the nameless woman who anointed Jesus for his burial (Mark 14:3–9 NEB). In Romans, Paul welcomes the help of several Christian women co-workers and friends like Phoebe, Prisca, Aquila, Thyphaena, and Tryphosa (Romans 16:1–15 NEB). Further, the New Testament records compassionate attitudes toward women's transgressions. John, for instance, reports that when Jesus heard that an adulteress was about to be put to death for her violations of Mosaic laws, he warned her accusers with the famous statement, "[T]hat one of you who is faultless shall throw the first stone" (John 8:7–8 NEB).

At the same time, the New Testament contains many examples of support for the subjugation of women. Not only were women required to keep silent in church, they were also condemned to learn in silence under the authority of their husbands. Christianity rationalized women's inferior status by blaming Eve for the original sin, characterizing her as the deceiver of Adam and God's trust (1 Timothy 2:11–15 NEB). Because of Eve's transgression, women were to pledge their submission to their husbands, the New Testament stated, as part of their Christian duty: "for the man is the head of the wife, just as Christ also is the head of the church" (Ephesians 5:22–24 NEB; see also Colossians 3:18–23 NEB). Moreover, indulging in carnal pleasure was condemned as sinful, whether the act was heterosexual or homosexual.

Drawing mainly from Leviticus (18:22 and 20:13) and the lessons of the promiscuous cities of Sodom and Gomorrah, Paul warned that "no fornicators or idolaters, none who are guilty of adultery or homosexual perversion, no thieves or grabbers or drunkards or slanderers or swindlers, will possess the kingdom of God" (1 Corinthians 6:9–10 NEB).[149] Homosexuality was generally seen as a perversion of the natural act of procreation—a view that has persisted to this day within the Catholic Church and some other Christian sects.[150]

Like the two monotheistic religions that preceded it, the Islamic claim to universality was undermined by its attitude toward women, homosexuals, and slaves—an attitude that, however, varied depending upon the source of Islamic teaching. The Quran, for instance, unlike the later juristic tradition of Islam, provides relatively favorable comments regarding the status of women, pointing to God as the source of both male and female creation and making Adam's mate, Eve, "of equal nature" (surahs 4:1, 4:7, 16:72, 30:21, 49:13). Unlike Christianity, the Quran does not hold Eve solely responsible for the original sin, instead regarding Eve

---

**POPE PAUL VI, SACRED CONGREGATION
FOR THE DOCTRINE OF THE FAITH, 1975**

[N]o pastoral method can be employed which would give moral justification to these acts on the grounds that they would be consonant with the condition of [homosexuals]. For according to the objective moral order, homosexual relations are acts which lack an essential and indispensable finality. In Sacred Scripture they are condemned as a serious depravity and even presented as the sad consequence of rejecting God. This judgment of Scripture does not of course permit us to conclude that all those who suffer from this anomaly are personally responsible for it, but it does attest to the fact that homosexual acts are intrinsically disordered and can in no case be approved of.

---

and Adam as equally guilty of challenging God's will in the Garden of Eden. Further, Quranic injunctions apply to both women and men, who remain equally accountable for their actions in purgatory—actions that determine whether they will ultimately reach hell or heaven.[151] The Quran also encourages the protection of married women (surahs 2:187, 4:19, 7:189), demands husbands' fair treatment of women they divorce (surah 2:231–232), gives women ownership of the dower (or dowry) previously paid by the bride's father, and prohibits female infanticide.

Compared with the relatively reformist attitude of the Quran regarding women's status, the juristic elaboration of the Shari'a deals with women in a more discriminatory fashion. In the Shari'a, women are clearly viewed as inferior individuals in need of male tutelage, compelled to strict obedience, confined to a secluded domestic role in the patriarchal family, limited to monogamy (compared to the male option of polygamy), forced to accept their husband's prerogative in terminating a marriage, subject to the loss of child custody rights once divorced, entitled to only half the inheritance of a comparable male heir, assigned inferior juridical status, and prescribed chastity, sexual "decency," and other restrictions on behavior.[152]

Any forms of sexual indulgence outside of marital vows are prohibited. Thus, along with adultery, Islam (following Judaism and Christianity) severely condemns same-sex intimate behavior (although women's homosexuality is considered less harmful), and the Sharia'a law even considers it a crime (surahs 15:73–74, 26:165–166).[153] Islamic universal notions of justice are constrained with respect not only to their position on women, but to their position on slavery as well. Although owners are urged to treat their slaves in a just and humane way and "enable them to earn their freedom for a certain sum" (surahs 4:92, 5:89, 8:80, 9:177, 24:33, 58:33), the Quran does not call for the prohibition of slavery (or indentured servitude).

One may question, given the severity of some punishments and the lesser rights enjoyed by women, slaves, and homosexuals, the extent to which the ancient traditions contributed to the development of human rights. Yet so long as one recognizes the very different historical context in which they evolved, one can claim that even the Babylonian laws were universalist in a narrow and formal sense of the term, for they were a priori and imposed consistent standards, thereby removing judgments from the whims of kings. They not only celebrated the idea of just and impartial rulings, establishing the integrity of the court, they also announced for the first time the ideas of property rights and progressive punishment. These ideas later reappeared in the ancient Hebrew laws and in the modern liberal view of human rights.

The Hebrews' great respect for the sanctity of individual life and reciprocal entitlements would later echo throughout the human rights revolutions of the Enlightenment. Thomas Hobbes's view of the supremacy of the right to life, to be upheld, if necessary, against the state, was indebted to "thou shall not kill." John Locke's justification of property rights and his consideration of the need to leave enough for other people, and Jean-Jacques Rousseau's organic view of the social contract were influenced, among other things, by the biblical injunction that "thou shall not steal," as well as by the Bible's organic view of the common good.[154] Hugo Grotius restated the biblical moral obligation toward one's enemy in terms of natural law, and Immanuel Kant transformed it into a categorical imperative. In many respects, the moral injunctions contained in the Bible paved the way for liberal and socialist conceptions of human rights.

Were we to focus solely on such features of Hinduism as the institution of slavery, bonded labor, women's subordination to men, uncharitable behavior toward homosexuals (although relatively less harsh than in other religions), and particularly on the justification for the caste system, we could assert that Hindu moral values failed to contribute to the advance of any universal ethics.[155] Hindu moral values, however, also forbade harming any living creatures and insisted on truthfulness, freedom from malice, compassion, and tolerance. Nor should we overlook the importance accorded to just actions in times of both peace and war and to duties to one's community, as well as to provisions for property rights and a fair relationship between employers and employees. All these provisions later found their way into modern notions of human rights. Yet what constituted the most original contribution of both Hinduism and Buddhism to the recent development of rights was the room they provided for environmental and animal rights. In this respect, Hinduism and Buddhism offered a foundation for the ecological movements of the late twentieth century.

Despite the sexist language of some early scriptures, the Buddhist attitude toward women was relatively liberal compared to others during the same period and was very advanced on the issue of homosexuality. Buddhism prided itself on its emancipating spirit: "[A]s the great ocean has one flavor, the taste of salt, so does the doctrine and the discipline of the Buddha have but one flavor—the flavor of emancipation."[156] Indeed, one should not forget the Buddhist repudiation of the caste system, its anti-dogmatic stand on truth, its vow of universal compassion, its adherence to a progressive economic and welfare rights system, its commitment to the well-being of animals and the environment, and its pacifist orientation. For all these reasons, the contribution of Buddhist scriptures, as a forerunner of modern notions of human rights, is undeniable.

Confucian ethics incorporated views of varying compatibility with contemporary perspectives on human rights. On the one hand, the government was seen as obligated to provide people with education, as well as economic and social welfare—attitudes that are consistent with the notion of individual rights. Confucianism was also, apparently, tolerant of homosexuality. On the other hand, individuals could not exist in isolation from their family, community, nation, and the world. They therefore needed to act dutifully based upon their expected roles in these various settings and within a rigidly stratified social hierarchy. From a human rights perspective, Confucianism highlights the danger that stability, a cornerstone of Confucian thought, can supplant the notion of individual rights, particularly women's rights.

Despite the Platonic vision of social hierarchy and Aristotle's support for and Cicero's de facto acceptance of slavery and women's subordination, their legacies remain central to Western ethics. By entrusting people with the capacity to reason critically and a capacity for inner goodness, an ability to search for just courses of action and develop good governments, they provided a philosophical basis for challenging oppressive regimes, thereby laying the foundation for human rights activism. Aristotle's confidence in the middle class and in the benefits of a limited accumulation of wealth and Plato's challenge to private property planted the seeds for later debates between liberal and socialist advocates of human rights. Their disagreements over women's abilities and rights (and perhaps on slavery as well) initiated the as yet unfinished journey of human rights debate on those issues. With the Stoics and the application of their ideas by Cicero, the notion of natural rights had clearly enlarged its scope beyond the Greek city-states to gradually embrace the community of humankind.

One may conclude that Catholic universalism, though advanced for its time, was, like its Judaic predecessor, initially marred by an ungenerous attitude toward women, slaves, and homosexuals. Further, while the notion of good motivation, as advocated by Jesus, was morally relevant, it remains problematic to hold someone responsible before the law merely for wrong motivations. Christianity had stressed Heaven as an ultimate tribunal that would hold individuals accountable for their "sinful" motivations and actions on earth. Later, however, by stressing the importance of providing relevant moral guidelines to rulers, Christian leaders such as Augustine and, more particularly, Aquinas, focused on earthly preoccupations by elaborating provisional ethical considerations for particular circumstances like war. Both paved the way for later efforts to distinguish permissible from impermissible acts during wartime, a tradition of thought that culminated in the ratification of wartime moral standards in the Geneva Convention.

The Islamic conception of jihad, built on the ideas advanced in early Hebrew and Christian just-war theory, contributed to a body of thought that continues to shape contemporary debate. In the spirit of the talion law, Islam called for proportional retribution against those who transgressed the law. The legalistic Islamic attitude recognized many of the rights invoked in other religions as well as in secular ethics, such as the rights to life, dignity, sustenance, asylum, and so forth. The rights of children in particular were celebrated, many centuries before the worldwide agreement represented by the UN Convention on the Rights of the Child (1989). One should not disregard, however, the harsh Islamic restrictions on women and homosexuals despite the relatively more magnanimous Quranic attitude toward women. In addition, although the Quran urged the good treatment of slaves, it fell far short of calling for the abolition of slavery. Finally, although religious minorities' rights were advocated, their legal rights were often even more restricted than those of nonbelievers. Least protected were defectors from Islam, who forfeited their rights.

Islamic beliefs in the superiority of the faithful over the unfaithful are not unique. As noted earlier, the Greek historian Herodotus maintained thousands of years ago not only that all national customs were different, but that each group believed itself to be morally superior. Today, from the Gush Emunim in Israel, to Christian militias in the United States, to Hamas in the West Bank, to the BJP in India, to the Komeito in Japan, claims of religious and national superiority are voiced without inhibition, in apparent confirmation of Herodotus's early perception.[157] Even should we put such extreme voices aside, clear differences exist among the reviewed ethical works. Some are religious and others are secular in their orientation; some are more tolerant than others; some, like Judaism, Christianity, and Islam, are monotheistic, and others, like Hinduism, Buddhism, and Confucianism, are not. Some, like Hammurabi's Code, Judaism, and Islam, have an anthropocentric focus, and others, like Hinduism and Buddhism, are cosmological in their orientation.

Notwithstanding the different moral priorities contained in each of these ethical stances, it is clear that that all of the aforementioned traditions—although not always exposed directly to each other—share basic views of a common good, thereby reinforcing the Socratic argument for a universal goodness. They all urge protection for the poor, the disabled, the sick, and the powerless, praise good and impartial rulings, encourage some forms of social and economic justice, condemn arbitrary killing, offer moral prescriptions for wartime, and so forth. This should not imply that all individuals were perceived as equal under a specific religious or secular aegis. Bearing in mind the nuances of each of the ancient views of ethics presented in this chapter, one can identify a common disdain toward indentured servants or slaves, women, and homosexuals, as all were excluded from equal social benefits. As the forces of history, however, unveiled conflicting power relations and created conjectural opportunities for the inclusion of new social participants, these previously invisible historical agents would eventually become more visible, forcefully asserting their political rights as members of the greater community of humankind.

As we now proceed toward the Enlightenment, the question that needs to be answered is how, despite the worldwide ethical heritage discussed in this chapter, Western ethics became the major contributor to the development of human rights. Wasn't Buddhism, for instance, better qualified for such a mission, given its greater tolerance for women and homosexuals and its criticism of any form of rigid social hierarchy? Of course, one could argue against that view, suggesting, for example, that Buddhism might have been either too soft in its recommendations or too monastic in its orientation, and that it lacked the anthropocentric and legalistic character of religious ethics associated with Judaism, Christianity, Islam, or the ancient Greek and Roman contributions.

The centrality of individuals' entitlements and the importance of the prescriptive character of laws are undoubtedly decisive perspectives for the later development of international human rights law. In this case, one may still wonder why Islam, which incorporated a strong legalistic tradition and prevailed as the most tolerant of medieval civilizations, did not become the leading force in the advancement of human rights against the exclusionary moral crusade of the Christian church during the Dark Ages.

The answer to this question does not reside solely in the character of this or that religious or secular moral injunction, but can also be found in the way in which Judeo-Christian morality was secularized, separated from politics, and strengthened in influence by the advent of capitalism and colonialism, at the expense of other notions of ethics. The next chapter discusses the emergence of the modern view of human rights, focusing on the way in which Judeo-Christian ethics was privileged thanks to the development of capitalism in Europe, secularized with the progress of the Reformation and the democratic revolutions of the eighteenth century, and, finally, transformed into a liberal discourse that dominates our current conception of human rights.

Chapter Two

Human Rights
and the Enlightenment

THE DEVELOPMENT OF A LIBERAL
AND SECULAR PERSPECTIVE ON HUMAN RIGHTS

*The Oath of the
Tennis Court* by
Jacques-Louis David,
1791. Courtesy of the
Musée National du
Chateau de Versailles
at Versailles.

I F A CIVILIZED NATION "lacks in its eyes and in the eyes of others, a universal and universally valid embodiment in laws," observed the German philosopher Friedrich Hegel (1770–1831), "it fails to secure recognition from others."[1] India, China, Roman Christendom, and the Arab Islamic world met these standards and were recognized as the great civilizations of the fifteenth and sixteenth centuries. In addition to its economic achievements, each showed the capacity for transcending the horizon of local and parochial thinking, and each exhibited a set of encompassing moral criteria that commanded the respect of others. The next three centuries, however, were to witness a revolutionary change in human thought as for the first time a secular and relatively more egalitarian approach to universal morality emerged in Europe and spread throughout the world under the revolutionary banner of the Enlightenment.

The birth of secular universalism took the form of an assault on the intellectual and political edifice of Roman Catholicism. That structure, seemingly impregnable during the Middle Ages, now collapsed under the blows struck by the Renaissance and the Protestant Reformation, opening up room for the emergence of humanist thought. Christian ethics thus shifted from a docile dependence on revealed knowledge toward an embrace of religious freedom and freedom of opinion in general. Simultaneously, feudal authoritarianism grounded on divine inspiration yielded to the modern concept of the nation-state, justified by its protection of natural and individual rights. The monopolistic feudal economy gave way to mercantilism and later to free markets based on the individual's right to private property. Finally, a religious tradition that had often sanctioned merciless and arbitrary killings was now confronted with laws premised on the individual's right to life, and with an insistence that even warfare must conform to universal standards of justice.

With these transformations, a secularized version of Judeo-Christian ethics lent itself to the development of a broad liberal discourse on human rights, a discourse that has shaped contemporary thinking. This chapter will illustrate why current human rights debates can be best understood as an extension of Enlightenment arguments that date back to the seventeenth and eighteenth centuries. Now as then, we find ourselves wondering whether the state is the best mechanism with which to defend basic rights, or a formidable Leviathan against which one's rights need to be defended. As in the eighteenth century, we are still questioning whether free markets are the best way to promote democratic institutions and global peace, and under which conditions one may justly wage war. This chapter also alerts the reader to the sufferings of those who remained excluded from initial Enlightenment conceptions of (purportedly) universal rights. As subsequent chapters will show, the victims of one era can become either the avenging aggressors or the human rights crusaders of the next age.

Because our modern conceptions of human rights originated in Europe and America, the story of their inception is embedded in the political, economic, and technological changes associated with the rise of the West and the relative decline of rival civilizations. Thus, before turning to the Western origins of particular rights, this chapter begins with a brief overview of the changes that contributed to the rise of the West over other civilizations. Chief among those changes were the development of modern science, the rise of mercantilism (which led to the consolidation of the nation-state), the great voyages of discovery that would bring the world's wealth within Europe's grasp, and the emergence of a middle class as a powerful source of revolutionary change. These developments laid the foundations for four great historical events in the Western world: the Reformation and the English, American, and French Revolutions. Much of this chapter will look at how each of these events animated key dimensions of the emerging liberal vision of human rights. That vision today reigns triumphant, though not uncontested, throughout the West, and has passionate, often embattled adherents throughout the rest of the world.

The liberal worldview first emerged out of the struggle for freedom of religion and opinion that began with the Reformation, laying the groundwork for subsequent claims for a universal right to life (including calls for the abolition of torture and the death penalty) and the right to property—along with counterclaims on behalf of an equitable distribution of wealth. As each of these components of the liberal tradition emerged, adherents began the political struggle—still under way—to develop effective means to promote the rights they championed. The final section of this chapter addresses the inconsistencies and limitations that beset early liberal thought (including the exclusion of women, the propertyless, blacks, colonized peoples, homosexuals, Jews, and other nationalities), inconsistencies that helped provoke the development of the nineteenth-century challenge to the liberal human rights agenda. Let us first consider how the West emerged as the leading power, outpacing other civilizations, notably in India, China, and the Islamic world, and attaining the capacity to dominate the world and, consequently, to shape an increasingly global debate over human rights.

FROM ANCIENT CIVILIZATIONS TO THE RISE OF THE WEST

India, China, and Islamic Civilizations

At the close of the fifteenth century, as Vasco da Gama's expedition found its way around the Cape of Good Hope to Indian waters, it was far from apparent that the West was on the verge of ascendancy to global predominance. Indeed, three rivals, India, China, and the Islamic world, could not only claim to match or exceed Western accomplishments, but could not then be ruled out as formidable contenders for global power. India, under Muslim Moghul rule, had reached a level of civilization marked by respect for learning and growing religious tolerance whose achievements in architecture and painting surpassed those of medieval Europe. Under the leadership of Akabar (1542–1605), religious minorities were granted legal status. The "Great Moghul" not only condemned Indian practices such as the immolation of widows and enslavement, his tolerance for all religions was exemplary. For half a century, his successors continued his efforts to wed Hindu and Muslim cultures. The mingling of these traditions found sublime expressions in naturalist painting, refined ceramics, textiles, and monumental architecture.[2] An empire built on a regularized tax system supported all these cultural endeavors and also provided the central treasury with funds for rulers to secure the loyalty of military and bureaucratic officers.

Chinese civilization was at least equally impressive, not least in inventiveness, as its production of paper, printing (around 700), gunpowder, the mariner's compass, the sternpost rudder, and the wheelbarrow all predated their appearance in Europe. China's silks, ceramics, jades, and bronze castings (accomplished fifteen hundred years before Europeans mastered that metal) found a market in far-flung parts of Asia and Europe. Moreover, the Chinese, under the influence of Confucianism, possessed an advanced ethical and political system presided over by a scholarly bureaucracy, which not only maintained great administrative continuity but made possible the centralized management of a vast state. If rebellions took place, provinces broke away, or rulers changed, the politico-religious system persisted. It was later emulated in Korea and Vietnam. Experimentation with newly available crops made possible the rapid growth of the Chinese population, which had reached perhaps 160 million by 1600.[3] Despite many famines, the food situation in China was typically better than that in Europe in the previous millennium.[4]

The Arab-Islamic Mediterranean and the Middle East region also enjoyed a brilliant civilization that predated the emergence of Italian commercial cities.[5] As Islam spread, Arabia, Persia, and the Ottoman Empire surfaced as major centers of religious, intellectual, cultural, artistic, and architectural influence whose reach extended to North Africa, China, and northern and Southeast Asia, threatening Europe as a result of its penetration of southern Spain. The Abbasid civilization (750–1258), second of the two great dynasties of the Muslim empire, had already marked its greatness by undertaking the translation of the Greek classics into Arabic, and the works of Plato, Aristotle, Euclid, and Galen were integrated into a flourishing Arab culture.[6] Subsequent translations of Arabic works in the late European Middle Ages testify to the great reputation that Arab thinkers such as Al-Kindi enjoyed in Europe. Persian contributions to medical studies penetrated the Arab world and became the standard texts for Western training. In contrast to China, trade and maritime expeditions were more central to the Islamic world. The prominence of Muslim trade in the early Middle Ages was prompted by flexible commercial instruments and practices adopted as early as the eighth century and picked up only centuries later in Europe.[7] Cultural and commercial traffic with the European world was almost one-way, attesting to the superior quality of Arab civilization.[8]

Given the strength of Indian, Chinese, and Islamic civilizations relative to the West, one may wonder why none of them successfully propagated a universal ethics of rights. Inevitably, the unexpected speed of the West's ascendance drew the interest and speculation of many historians. Writings on this question have been controversial, as various scholars emphasize different economic, cultural, and institutional variables. Some stress the uniqueness of Western capitalism and scientific development, while others counter that a similar form of capitalism existed in Islam, or that science flourished in China before the modern West.[9] At times, such disagreements have fueled heated academic debates between "Eurocentric" defenders and "anti-Eurocentric" critics. While the fundamental sources of strength and weaknesses of civilizations will remain contentious, we can nevertheless point to particular reasons for the relative decline of India, China, and the Islamic cultures, and corresponding factors that help account for the rise of Europe, as well as for the influence of its human rights legacy.

Indian agriculture, based on the caste system, was less productive than that of other areas of Asia, and small manufacturing (mainly handicraft production) in towns was organized around hereditary guilds.[10] Not only did heavy taxation leave the peasantry destitute, but the cost of trading also hindered the prospects for artisans who might have wished to become merchants. These obstacles, coupled with Hindu reliance on the caste system, may have frozen occupational mobility to a larger extent than it did in feudal Europe. Moreover, despite the partial unity achieved during the Moghul Empire, limited communications and inadequate military technology made it difficult for rulers to retain loyalty in various critical areas.[11] This fragmentation of loyalty, reminiscent of that in late medieval Europe, was exacerbated by the religious intolerance and relentless wars of the last Moghul leader, Aurungzebe, whose regime was countered by many popular revolts that ultimately led to the decline of the Moghul Empire.[12] That decline coincided with the emergence of European predominance. European traders had acquired only a few coastal stations in India since the Portuguese appropriation of Goa in 1510, but opportunities for trade increased after the decline of the Moghul Empire. Despite rivalries and unlike earlier conquerors, Europeans would stay in India for centuries and would extract substantial economic gains.

Despite the strength of Chinese civilization, the Ming dynasty gradually shifted its energy inward, focusing on agrarianism and away from technology, industry, and its earlier naval exploration of Asia and the Indian Ocean, leaving Europeans freer to secure their dominance over the seas and expand their colonial control over the globe.[13] China's power, its centralized unity, and its isolationism might have ultimately worked against the expansion of its civilization and possibly against the spread of a Confucian sense of universal justice. It was precisely the European states' fragmentation and competition, Jared Diamond argues, that enabled the Genovese Christopher Columbus to bargain with several monarchs and finally earn the financial support of the Spanish king for his naval expedition. By contrast, in unified China, there was no alternative site with which to challenge the shortsighted decision to forgo maritime exploration. European scientific discoveries, Diamond speculates, might also have benefited from that disunity.[14]

In comparison, Maxime Rodinson has maintained that there seemed to be nothing inherent in Islamic civilizations that would have precluded further economic development,[15] unless we consider the fact that the lands the Muslim Mediterranean world acquired were not as rich as the regions colonized by the Europeans in the Americas. Islamic overseas trade emphasized luxury goods and did not compensate for the general shortage in important sectors such as agriculture.[16] Another potential source of economic weakness was that the population of the Islamic Near East comprised only 28 million people, which was relatively low compared to that of China, India, and Europe in the 1600s.[17] Behind the Ottoman frontiers, a multiracial policy was organized to integrate different religions into the growing empire. Yet the expansion of the empire engendered heavy military expenses, which created great stresses for the state. Further back in Islamic history, in Cordoba, private property had been protected against the caliph, and in general, medieval Islamic governments were not known for seizing commercial property. Later, "[T]he Ottoman empire as heir to all this came to operate an economic system that rested on confiscation, despoilment, and a total, calculated, insecurity of life and property."[18] Whereas Europeans took advantage of feudal fragmentation to develop a mercantile society, the Ottoman Empire's structural fragility gradually weakened its economy, contributing to its diminishing cultural, legal, and ethical influence and its final disintegration.

The Rise of the West and the Legacy of the Enlightenment

In contrast to these sources of weakness within India, China, and the Islamic world, an amalgamation of simultaneously favorable circumstances stimulated the rise of the West and its capacity to develop and diffuse a modern discourse of human rights. They included the Reformation, the inception of science, the rise of mercantilism, the consolidation of the nation-state, maritime expeditions, and the emergence of a revolutionary middle class, developments that served to hone human rights demands throughout such major social upheavals as the English, American, and French Revolutions.[19] A new universal discourse of rights took hold, committed to reason and individual free choice, to scientific planning and the rules of law, to contractual agreement and economic interdependence. The emerging commercial nation-state was then entrusted to diffuse these ideals worldwide in the spirit of peace and cooperation.

With the advance of the Reformation, from 1546 to the Treaty of Westphalia in 1648, the universalist message of the church had been severely compromised. While the separation of the Greek Orthodox churches from

Rome had provoked the first rupture in Christian unity, the Protestant Reformation of the sixteenth and seventeenth centuries contributed decisively to its decline. Erupting in Germany, religious conflict soon spread through Europe to France, Holland, and Spain, and to England. Yet if a series of long-lasting religious wars eroded the initial aspirations of Christendom, the international nature of the wars incited the development of a new vision of world unity based on rational thinking rather than on revealed truth—principles that had shown their divisive nature during the wars of religion. By asserting individual responsibility in matters of salvation and in seeking happiness on earth, the Protestant influence helped advance a new credo relying on individual choice and rights. The belief in the value of individuals and their capacity to reason was further strengthened by a burst of scientific breakthroughs.

Despite the long phase of religious crisis, scientific discoveries abounded. Striving to free themselves from the universities, which remained a stronghold of Catholicism, British, French, Italian, and German scientists joined a growing number of independent societies, such as the Royal Society in London, the Academy of Science in Paris, the Academia della Scienza in Naples, and the Collegium Carolinum in Brunswick, Germany. Their collaboration over distances was facilitated by the invention of the printing press, and common standards of measurement were promoted by the development of such precision instruments as the telescope, the microscope, the barometer, and the pendulum clock. The drive behind the scientific revolution might have been of divine inspiration, but it was Galileo, Descartes, and Newton, rather than God, who were stirring the imaginations of their contemporaries. By painting a picture of the enrichment of human life through new discoveries, each presented an accessible world open to human consciousness and built upon universal and secular laws—laws that would later help shape secular visions of human rights.

As both scientific progress and the wars of the Reformation were undermining the Catholic Church, changes in economic life were also reshaping the social landscape of Europe. While feudalism decayed, mercantilism emerged as an economic system that unified, strengthened, and financially enriched the nation. It did so by means of strict governmental regulation of the entire national economy, usually through policies designed to secure an accumulation of bullion, the expansion of a favorable trade balance, and the development of agriculture and manufacturing. Proponents of mercantilist theories maintained that global wealth was relatively fixed. The best way to acquire new resources and to preserve as large a share as possible of this limited wealth, they believed, was through a rationally and scientifically planned state, aspiring to sufficient size and strength to sustain national development. By relying upon the mercantilist and later the commercial state as a way to promote economic interdependence and possibly peaceful conditions, mercantilists would also inspire the vision of many human rights champions of the Enlightenment.

Circumstances, of course, would not equally favor all who aspired to apply the mercantilist approach. In the sixteenth and seventeenth centuries, German and Italian cities—notwithstanding the call of Niccolò Machiavelli (1469–1527), in *Il principe,* for the unification of his country—lacked the necessary political strength to appropriate resources on a large national scale. In eastern Europe, states such as Austria, Poland, and Russia, although large in size, were overwhelmingly dominated by agrarian production and could not achieve the benefits of a mercantile economy. However, the conditions necessary for the progress of mercantilism were present in the Low Countries (especially in the period from the Treaty of Westphalia until the early 1700s), as well as in England and France.[20]

Critical to the rise of the West over other civilizations was the discovery, colonization, and mercantilist exploitation of the new world. The developing global economy, initiated by the Portuguese and Spanish in the sixteenth and seventeenth centuries, moved during the eighteenth century into the hands of the British, the French, and the Dutch. While India and China still commanded admiration, these Western powers were ascending as the new leaders of the international economy. The conquest of America was particularly valuable for the Europeans because of its vast natural resources, whose exploitation required masses of human labor that were supplied by Africa. Many Europeans regarded the indigenous populations of their colonies as barbarians, justifying the enslavement of Africans, the killing or subjugation of American Indians, and similar abuses of other native peoples.

As overseas empires spread, the expansion of money markets dissolved old social bonds, transformed the guild character of the Middle Ages, and strengthened the town economy, leaving the surrounding countryside subservient to the interests of the town. The shift from the village to the town changed the landscape of social relationships that had been prevalent in feudal societies.[21] With the emergence of towns as the heart of human society, autonomous spheres of social activity proliferated amid the ruins of the Catholic commonwealth. In addition, labor was in-

creasingly divided according to specialization. With the subsequent at-
omization of society, mercantilism reached new levels of speed and efficiency. This fragmentation into various spheres of specialization undermined the self-sufficient character of feudal society, exacerbating the need
for a new form of social interdependence surrounding the exchange of
commodities and the necessity of a contractual discourse premised on
rights.

This parceling of sixteenth- and seventeenth-century political and economic life created space for the development of a relatively autonomous
class, the bourgeoisie, which was concentrated in urban sites. Economically speaking, the bourgeoisie stood between the nobility and the clergy
on the one hand and the peasantry on the other hand. Its members earned
their living by manufacturing, shopkeeping, banking, trading—in general, by the various activities that had been stimulated by the expansion
of commerce. In countries like England and France or regions like
Flanders—where governments helped create a national market and an
industrious nationwide labor supply for their great merchants—the bourgeoisie became even more prominent, and succeeded in gaining a degree
of economic strength independent of the political and religious control
of their provinces. Needless to say, a merchant backed by a national
monarchy was in a much stronger position than one supported by a city,
such as Augsburg or Venice. National governments could endorse local
merchants, subsidize exports, and pay bounties for goods whose production they wished to encourage, or erect tariff barriers against imports
to protect their own producers from competition. A national tariff system was thus gradually superimposed on the old network of provincial
and municipal tariffs.[22]

From the mid–seventeenth century to the eighteenth century, the European bourgeoisie, however, felt trapped within a tale of two economies,
that is, between a prosperous international economy and the still backward, traditionalist, and autarkic national market. The nobility still
dominated the government, public administration, the church, and most
social institutions. It resisted any change in the status quo that might undermine its political privileges. These conflicts of interests were exemplified in Molière's play *Le bourgeois gentilhomme,* which portrayed a
ruined nobleman begging for more loans from an enriched bourgeois.
Art was imitating life, reproducing the economic wealth and political
frustration of the burgeoning middle class. The needs of the bourgeoisie,
in the end, collided with monarchical interests, fueling the English, American, and French Revolutions. Facing resistance, the political demands

of this new class in formation grew more revolutionary and universalist in orientation; as it gained power, it also revealed its particularist tendency.[23]

During the English Puritan revolution (1642–1648), universal claims of rights were first advanced against Charles I's effort to restore his centralized power at the expense of Parliament. Seeking funds to crush a Scottish rebellion in 1637, the king convoked the English Parliament for the first time in eleven years. Neither that Short Parliament (1640) nor the subsequent Long Parliament (1640–1660) supported that goal. Instead, new members of the Long Parliament, led by Oliver Cromwell (1599–1658), John Hampden (1594–1643), and John Pym (ca. 1583–1643), challenged royal authority, culminating in the execution of Charles I and the establishment of the republic. After using the support of radicals like the Levellers (whose influence had spread among the rank and file of the army fighting the king) to press popular demands, such as the rights to life, property, and religious freedom, Cromwell turned against those democratic supporters and purged them from the army.

Despite these dramatic turns of events, the revolution ultimately empowered the propertied class by granting sovereignty to Parliament and dissolving prerogative courts. It overlooked the demands of starving peasants, led by the communist Diggers, who tried but failed to radicalize the revolution by calling for broader political representation and a more egalitarian redistribution of wealth. With the monarchical restoration, human rights hopes that had been unleashed by the English Revolution were thwarted. Yet the revolutionary spirit remained alive amidst peasants' grief and despair. It was to reemerge in a brief explosion during the 1688 Glorious Revolution, as the bourgeois fought for parliamentary and civil rights—later embraced by the English Bill of Rights.

In the late eighteenth century, England became overburdened by the cost of its colonial possessions and resorted to imposing inequitable taxes on the American colonies. The colonists rebelled. The English revolution of the 1640s provided a worthwhile example of resistance for them to emulate. Fighting for independence from England, they recalled the British Levellers' struggle for the rights to life, to property, to manhood suffrage, and the rights to rebel against tyrannical authorities and to establish republican institutions. With the ratification of the Declaration of Independence in 1776, they were soon able to celebrate their new human rights achievements.

As in the English Revolution, the new American republic was initially divided. Competing economic interests separated merchants, farmers, and plantation owners. There were also differences between the new and old states of the confederation, and already some tensions between Southern slave-owning states and Northern states. While these tensions would ultimately result in a civil war (1860–1865), in the 1770s, supporters of independence in both North and South were drawn together in opposition to the British crown and its American loyalists. After their fight for independence from England, Americans inscribed in the 1788 constitution rights that favored wealthy property owners. However restricted the human rights claimed by the American republic, the success of the revolution drew international admiration.

French soldiers who had fought on the side of the American revolutionaries returned to France to extol the accomplishments of the American revolutionaries. With the country on the verge of national bankruptcy and confronting a nobility unwilling to share its power, many of these returning soldiers would follow the horde of hungry peasants and angry bourgeois from the streets of Paris to the Tennis Court, where the Third Estate General rallied and affirmed that it now constituted the National Assembly. The mixture of solemnity and optimism of that first revolutionary moment was admirably captured by the neoclassical painter Jacques-Louis David (1748–1825) in his *Oath of the Tennis Court* (1791). A month later, on July 14, 1789, the movement took the streets as a crowd stormed the Bastille. Soon after, the revolutionary leaders drafted the Declaration of the Rights of Man and of the Citizen, one of the most important human rights documents of the eighteenth century, affirming the principles of the new state based on the rule of universal law, equal individual citizenship, and collective sovereignty of the people. With it, Jacobins and defenders of the French *patrie* proclaimed a new world in which "liberty, equality, and fraternity" would become, they hoped, universal norms.

Yet social divisions in France, initially eclipsed by the Third Estate in its fight against the *ancien régime,* now reemerged as voting rights were restricted to owners of property, along the lines of the British and American example. Struggling to repel invading armies, the Third Estate was further divided by domestic social tensions. If the influence of property owners during the early phase of the revolutionary wars soon yielded to the ascent of a popular force, the sansculottes (1792–1794), the execution of their leader, Maximilien de Robespierre (1758–1794), marked the end of the revolutionary process and the empowerment of a new regime of notables whose ranks were drawn from monarchists and moderate republicans. As in England and America, the revolutionary universalism of the French middle class gave way to an era of conservatism. Those seventeenth- and eighteenth-century struggles represented, however, the first important affirmations of liberal ideas, and they were crucial for establishing the secular foundation of human rights. These important events also serve as a guide to the first part of our journey, which begins with the historical struggle for freedom of religion and opinion and leads to assertions of rights to life and to property.

FREEDOM OF RELIGION AND OPINION

The fight for freedom of religion and opinion repeatedly jolted medieval Christendom. Religious intolerance had long since superseded the charitable and universalist promise of the Gospels. The pervasive Christian fear of the Turks, a result of the Crusades (1096–1099, 1147–1149, 1189–1192, and 1202–1204), contributed to sharpening Catholic intolerance toward other religious groups. In addition to Muslims, European Jews were considered foreigners and often personae non gratae in Western Christendom, and as such were subjected to various levels of discrimination. The Fourth Lateran Council (1215), for instance, banned Jews from government employment. In 1290, Jews were expelled from England, in 1306, from France. In Spain, initial tolerance gave way to persecution during the Inquisition (1492), and Jews were forced to choose between conversion and eviction. In addition, Jews were often accused of performing acts of sacrilege and murdering children, charges that intensified during the Crusades and the Black Plague (1347–1351), and as a result were often targeted as scapegoats and massacred.

Challengers from within the Catholic faith endured similar persecutions in the medieval age. The church, jealously guarding its wealth, was unwilling to accommodate sprouting heretic groups whose demands for a new spirituality called for a genuine solidarity with and renewed interest in the plight of the poor. The Cathari, the Humiliati, and the Waldenses were among the early heretic groups whose members defied the monopoly of the Catholic Church only to be subjected to many forms of discrimination and even public immolation. For those dissenters and sinners who evaded earthly punishment, Dante's *Inferno* (1306–1308 and 1321) and Michelangelo's *Last Judgment* (1534–1541) served as reminders of their fate in hell. Similar Catholic intransigence existed in the Spanish colonies, where, despite protests by the Dominican priest Bartolomé de las Casas, Indians were persecuted without mercy in the name of Catholicism.[24] Catholic efforts to crush all opposition finally encountered a force that could not be suppressed, as the rise of Protestantism reshaped prospects for religious freedom and helped ultimately to launch the broader Enlightenment struggle for human rights.

Against the indisputable authority of a highly hierarchical Catholic Church, its spectacular and mundane authority, its claim to each person's body and soul, its control of the individual's destiny and the promise of eternal felicity in heaven—all demanding unconditional obedience to the feudal church—Protestantism proposed radical reforms. Martin Luther (1483–1546), the first to formulate Protestant principles, called for the centrality of the Bible as primary authority on issues of faith; the return to simple liturgies; separation between church and state; and individual responsibility in matters of salvation and in finding happiness on earth. Luther's notion that "a Christian man is the most entirely free lord of all, subject to none," while at the same time he was the "dutiful servant

---

BARTOLOMÉ DE LAS CASAS, *IN DEFENSE OF THE INDIANS*, 1548

[Y]ou seek Indians so that gently, mildly, quietly, humanely and in a Christian manner you may instruct them in the word of God and by your labor bring them to Christ's flock, imprinting the gentle Christ on their minds, you perform the work of an apostle and will receive an imperishable crown of glory from our sacrificed lamb. But if it be in order that by sword, fire, massacre, trickery, violence, tyranny, cruelty, and in inhumanity that is worse than barbaric you may destroy and plunder utterly harmless peoples who are ready to renounce evil and receive the word of God, you are children of the devil and the most horrible plunderers of all. . . . Now if we shall have shown that among our Indians of the western and southern shores (granting that we call them barbarians and that they are barbarians) there are important kingdoms, large numbers of people who live settled lives in a society, great cities, kings, contracts of the law of nations, will it not stand proved that the Reverend Doctor Sepúlveda has spoken wrongly and viciously against peoples like these, either out of malice or ignorance of Aristotle's teaching, and therefore, has falsely and perhaps irreparably slandered them before the entire world. From the fact that the Indians are barbarians it does not necessarily follow that they are incapable of government and have to be ruled by others, except to be taught about the Catholic faith and to be admitted to the holy sacraments. They are not ignorant, inhuman, or bestial. Rather, long before they heard the word Spaniard they had properly organized states, wisely ordered by excellent laws, religion, and custom. They cultivated friendship and, bound together in common fellowship, lived in populous cities in which they wisely administered the affairs of both peace and war justly and equitably, truly governed by laws that at very many points surpass ours.

From *In Defense of the Indians*, 40, 42.

---

of all, subject to everybody," restated Paul's injunction: "[O]we no man anything, but to love one another."[25] This became a rallying cry against the abuses of the Catholic Church.

Luther's views, as espoused, or revised, by supporters like Jean Calvin (1509–1564), had far-reaching political repercussions: they not only undercut the power structure cemented by the feudal church, but also the system of privileges granted by divine grace. The progress of the Protestant reformation alarmed the Catholic custodians of the status quo, and eventually also Luther himself, who feared social chaos and ended up condemning in 1524 the German peasant rebellion against manorial lords. Even as Luther reverted to a more conservative view of Protestantism, hostility between Protestants and Catholics escalated, culminating in a religious conflict that plagued late-sixteenth- and seventeenth-century Europe.

The 1555 Augsburg Peace seemed to resolve the conflict by officially recognizing Lutheranism in the Holy Roman Empire. According to the principle of *cujus regio, ejus religio,* each prince was to decide for himself whether he or his state should be Catholic or Lutheran. Yet the continuous spread of Protestantism was now becoming more threatening for Catholics, who ended up mobilizing armed forces against Lutheran advances. This religious clash led to a series of wars that spread throughout Europe: the French civil wars of 1562–1598; the Dutch revolution against Philip II of Spain in 1567–1579; the Spanish Armada Católica against England in 1588; the Scottish rebellion against Mary Stuart in 1565–1568; the Thirty Years' War of 1618–1648; and the Puritan revolution of 1642–1648 in England.

Revolted by the appalling atrocities committed in the name of God during these religious conflicts, the Dutch legal scholar Hugo Grotius (1583–1645) urged warring parties to maintain a spirit of religious tolerance. "It seems unjust," he said, "to persecute with punishments those who receive the laws of Christ as true, but entertain doubts or errors on some external points."[26] During the English civil war, the spokesman of the Levellers, John Lilburne (1614–1657), proclaimed that "all men by nature are the children of Adam, and regardless of religious differences, they are all equal and alike in power, dignity, authority and majesty."[27]

In the end, the struggle for religious freedom during the wars of the Reformation won some enduring success. The Treaty of Westphalia, ratified in October 1648, put an end to the wars of religion. It granted, for instance, "the privilege of emigration to the subjects of such states if they dissented from the religion of their territorial lord; and whereas later, for the better preserving of greater concord among the states, it was agreed that no one should seduce another's subjects to his religion."[28] It stopped short of providing individuals with freedom of religion, but the treaty nevertheless asserted the right to religious asylum and states' prerogative to select their own religion. The treaty also divided Europe according to religious spheres of influence. A balance of power between Catholics and Protestants was achieved in Germany; England asserted its Anglican colors; Calvinism maintained a strong foothold in the Netherlands; France and the Italian states (despite intermittent occupations by the Austrian Empire) remained loyal to the papacy.

With his famous *Letter concerning Toleration* (1690), the English philosopher John Locke (1632–1704) moved beyond the conservative concessions of Westphalia, demanding the individual's, rather than the state's, right to select a religion. Such a right, he argued, comes from "an inward persuasion of the mind, without which nothing can be acceptable to God."[29] Yet the battle for religious freedom was far from over. In France, an important advance in that struggle had been the Edict of Nantes (1598), in which Henry IV had sought to end the French wars of religion by guaranteeing religious freedom to French Protestants (or Huguenots). In 1658, however, Louis XIV revoked the edict, depriving the Huguenots of all civil and religious liberties. In England, the Parliament passed the Tolerant Act in 1689, which, though allowing some dissenters to practice their religion, continued to exclude Jewish and Catholic worship. Alarmed by these violations, Locke called for a clearer separation between the church and the state. "Political society," he maintained, "is instituted for no other end, but only to secure every man's possession of the things of this life. The care of each man's soul, and of the things of heaven, which neither does belong to the commonwealth nor can be subjected to it, is left entirely to man's self."[30] With these statements, Locke opened a new chapter in the struggle for religious freedom and freedom of opinion.

The context for reviving that struggle was propitious. Throughout Europe, the most dramatic effort to silence opinions (of religious or secular nature) was the *Index librorum prohibitorum*—a list of proscribed books developed by the Roman Catholic Church that included the work of the well-known scientist Galileo. Licensing (or control over publication) came to be regarded by many in England as an excess of Roman Catholic influence. So, when the Puritans disestablished the Anglican successor to the Roman church and the English Parliament reinstated licensing in 1643, the political pamphleteer John Milton (1608–1674) rose in protest: "He who kills a good book kills reason itself, kills the image of God . . . in the eye," he exclaimed in *Areopagetica,* a book that remains a classic plea for the freedom of the press.[31] While conceding the need for criminal prosecutions in response to some types of publications, Milton proclaimed the importance of freedom of opinion: "[G]ive me the liberty to know, to utter, and to argue freely, above all liberties. . . . If truth is let free, it will overcome and win over all possible errors."[32] Milton's beliefs ultimately prevailed, leading in 1695 to the abandonment of prepublication censorship in England. This victory became an important milestone in the fight for freedom of opinion and the press, and was repeatedly invoked throughout the American and French Revolutions.

Given the strong communal theocratic beliefs held by the early English Pilgrims in America, one may have wondered whether American soil would prove fertile for the development of Milton's and Locke's perspectives. The Pilgrims, after all, represented the radical fringe of the English Reformation. For them, the Reformation had not gone far enough, having ended by merely supplanting one ruler (the pope) with another (the British crown). They believed that nowhere in England could they find a true church, and concluded that their ultimate salvation required their migration to the New World. In the first Puritan colonies of Plymouth and Boston, as in Calvin's Geneva, the church was an integral part of the state. The fundamental laws were drawn from the Bible, and only where the Bible was silent could men create laws.[33] By the second half of the seventeenth century, Calvinism in America had grown to such an extent that the French and the Dutch were unable to limit its expansion.[34] Its growing influence in America, however, would ultimately clash with that of the established English church.

The major cleavage among the churches in colonial America divided Anglicans from Puritan dissenters. With growing political tensions between England and the American colonists, this split might well have been a necessary condition for ensuring pluralism and religious tolerance. The rapid spread of religious sects during the prerevolutionary period, called the "Great Awakening," further secured this prospect.[35] The Methodist movement seized upon the elements of feelings and conscience that Protestant orthodoxy had tended to neglect and gave a renewed and devotional impetus to the doctrine of grace and to the tradition of moral earnestness. In the middle years of the eighteenth century, waves of revivals and conversions led by Congregationalists and Presbyterians spread through the colonies. Many small, independent, Bible-centered groups, which often professed allegiance to Baptist teachings, also came into being during this period.

Undoubtedly, the spread of divergent churches, combined with the increasing influence of the press, helped to influence the prerevolutionary spirit. There were initial efforts to hinder the freedom of the press, which paralleled similar attempts in England. The 1735 trial of the German immigrant printer John Peter Zenger, indicted for his attacks on Governor Cosby of New York, and the 1765 British Stamp Act, which placed a severe tax on newspapers, were among the many efforts to control the press.[36] The Stamp Act, in particular, intensified colonial resentment of the British, which was already growing in response to other taxes, and unleashed a radical form of journalism against the crown. Anti-British printers and activists such as Isaiah Thomas (1749–1831) and Samuel Adams (1722–1803) were among the inciters of the rebellious spirit of the 1770s. Nothing, however, could surpass the agitational journalism of Thomas Paine (1737–1809), whose work was actually read out loud to the revolutionary troops before battle. The "last Cord between England and America" was now broken, Paine announced in 1776, while urging his American compatriots to stand against England. "O ye that love mankind! Ye that dare oppose not only the tyranny but the tyrant, stand forth! . . . Let none other be heard among us than those of *a good citizen, an open and resolute friend, and a virtuous supporter of the rights of mankind and of the free and independent states of America.*"[37]

Such combative pleas on behalf of freedom influenced the founding fathers. Thomas Jefferson (1743–1826) championed the right of the individual to religious opinion and freedom of conscience based on the reasoning of Locke, Paine, and the French *philosophes*. "Religion," Jefferson asserted, "is a matter which lies solely between man and his God," and therefore it was necessary that "a wall of separation [be] erected between the Church and the State."[38] This position was restated in the Virginia Act for Establishing Religious Freedom (1786), a statute that entrusted people with the right to follow the dictates of their conscience and called on the state to tolerate all religions without favoring one in particular.[39] Three years later, the concept of the separation of church and state took its place as the first article of the Bill of Rights, part of the new Constitution of the United States of America. The struggle to separate church and state was not completed on the day the Bill of Rights (1791) was adopted, however. Instead, "The wall was slowly erected stone by stone, in some states earlier than in others, in some states more completely than in others."[40] Even today, this partition is fragile and under challenge, as some Christian groups seek to institute religious curricula (e.g., prayers, the teaching of Creationism, etc.) in American public schools.

After American independence, limits on state control over the press needed to be secured. In anticipation of a war with France, a law restricting criticism by the press was passed in 1798. The Sedition Act, defined in national security terms, made criminal the publication of "any false, scandalous and malicious writing . . . against the government of the United States, or either House of Congress . . . or the President . . . with the intent to defame [them], to bring them into contempt or disrepute."[41] Thomas Jefferson's first inaugural address, however, provided the moral grounding for jurists to repudiate that act: "If there be among us those who wish to dissolve the Union or to change its republican form," he claimed, "let them stand undisturbed as monuments of safety with which error of opinion may be tolerated where reason is left free to combat it."[42] When the threat of war passed, the Sedition Act was repealed and freedom of the press restored.

On the other side of the Atlantic, French intellectuals welcomed the winds of freedom coming from revolutionary America. Baron de Montesquieu (1689–1755), Jean-Jacques Rousseau (1712–1778), Voltaire (1694–1778), Baron Paul-Henri d'Holbach (1723–1789), and Denis Diderot (1713–1784), among many other French thinkers, had proclaimed the importance of freedom of expression and other civil rights long before the American Revolution.[43] They saw in revolutionary America the realization of such ideals. Voltaire, more than any other deist philosopher of his time, has been identified as the archenemy of revealed knowledge and intolerance.[44] "What is toleration?" he asked in 1764. "It is the natural attribute of humanity. We are all formed of weakness and error: let us pardon reciprocally each other's folly. That is the first law of nature."[45]

Such a law of nature, advancing "freedom of communication of ideas and opinion," was later singled out as "one of the most precious of the rights of man" in the French Declaration of the Rights of Man and of the Citizen (1789).[46] In its fight against religious intolerance, the French revolutionary *patrie* became the first country in the world ever to grant Jews civic emancipation and to allow them to hold public office—and this well before the hard-won legislative passage of the 1826 Maryland "Jewish Bill of Emancipation" in America. If the American Revolution left the church free from state supervision, with complete freedom in moral and educational tasks, the French revolutionary government im-

THE FRENCH DECLARATION OF THE RIGHTS
OF MAN AND OF THE CITIZEN, 1789

... The National Assembly recognizes and proclaims, in the presence and under the auspices of the Supreme Being, the following rights of man and citizen.

1. Men are born and remain free and equal in rights; social distinctions may be based only upon general usefulness.

2. The aim of every political association is the preservation of the natural and inalienable rights of man; these rights are liberty, property, security, and resistance to oppression.

3. The source of all sovereignty resides essentially in the nation; no group, no individual may exercise authority not emanating expressly therefrom.

4. Liberty consists of the power to do whatever is not injurious to others; thus the enjoyment of the natural rights of every man has for its limits only those that assure other members of society the enjoyment of those same rights; such limits may be determined only by law.

5. The law has the right to forbid only actions which are injurious to society. Whatever is not forbidden by law may not be prevented, and no one may be constrained to do what it does not prescribe.

6. Law is the expression of the general will; all citizens have the right to concur personally, or through their representatives, in its formation; it must be the same for all, whether it protects or punishes. All citizens, being equal before it, are equally admissible to all public offices, positions, and employments, according to their capacity, and without other distinction than that of virtues and talents.

7. No man may be accused, arrested, or detained except in the cases determined by law, and according to the forms prescribed thereby. All who solicit, expedite, or execute arbitrary orders, or have them executed, must be punished; but every citizen summoned or apprehended in pursuance of the law must obey immediately; he renders himself culpable by resistance.

8. The law is to establish only penalties that are absolutely and obviously necessary; and no one may be punished except by virtue of a law established and promulgated prior to the offence and legally applied.

9. Since every man is presumed innocent until declared guilty, if arrest be deemed indispensable, all unnecessary severity for securing the person of the accused must be severely repressed by law.

10. No one is to be disquieted because of his opinions, even religious, provided their manifestation does not disturb the public order established by law.

11. Free communication of ideas and opinions is one of the most precious of the rights of man. Consequently, every citizen may speak, write, and print freely, subject to responsibility for the abuse of such liberty in the cases determined by law.

12. The guarantee of the rights of man and citizen necessitates a public force; such a force, therefore, is instituted for the advantage of all and not for the particular benefit of those to whom it is entrusted.

13. For the maintenance of the public force and for the expenses of adminis-

tration a common tax is indispensable; it must be assessed equally on all citizens in proportion to their means.

14. Citizens have the right to ascertain, by themselves or through their representatives, the necessity of the public tax, to consent to it freely, to supervise its use, and to determine its quota, assessment, payment, and duration.

15. Society has the right to require of every public agent an accounting of his administration.

16. Every society in which the guarantee of rights is not assured or separation of powers not determined has no constitution at all . . .

17. Since property is a sacred and inviolable right, no one may be deprived thereof unless a legally established public necessity obviously requires it, and upon condition of a just and previous indemnity.

---

plemented a more restricted and regulated policy toward the church. Its lands were placed at the disposal of the *patrie,* the clergy was provided with an honorable stipend, and bishops and clergymen were elected like any other public officials.[47] Such a policy was designed to control the power of the clergy, which was closely allied with the feudal nobility. Not surprisingly, as the conflict between the supporters of the ancient regime and the defenders of the French Revolution deepened, anticlerical measures assumed proportions not known in the New World. Indeed, after refractory French priests rose in revolt on the side of the aristocracy and allied with the royalists in the Vendéean counterrevolution, the young Jacobin government was marked by attacks on priests, including the wholesale closure of churches and the enthronement of the Goddess of Reason in Notre-Dame Cathedral. The de-Christianization process, further inflamed by an ultra-atheist group called the Enragés, might have alienated believers among the French peasantry and could have led to domestic chaos at a time when France was fighting a war with external enemies. At least this was what Robespierre believed. He thus called for a patriotic compromise, based on Rousseau's view of civic religion, that he identified as the cult of the Supreme Being (or the cult of reason). Religious feasts were celebrated under the banner of universal reason and were organized in order to raise popular feelings of solidarity against the old regime.

The triumph of reason associated with the Enlightenment reached its pinnacle during the French Revolution. Despite many setbacks over the succeeding centuries, the fight for freedom of religion and opinion was not in vain. Those rights would be recognized in the twentieth century as fundamental human rights proclaimed in the first clause of the UN

Universal Declaration of Human Rights (1948), in article 9 of the European Convention for the Protection of Human Rights and Fundamental Freedoms (1950), article 13 of the American Convention on Human Rights (1969), article 18 of the International Covenant on Civil and Political Rights (1966), and in article 8 of the African Charter on Human and Peoples' Rights (1986).

THE RIGHT TO LIFE

Appeals to trust the human capacity to reason and think freely long preceded the Enlightenment, as chapter 1 showed. Such efforts were rooted in the writings of ancient Greek and Roman political thinkers, who ultimately provided European Enlightenment thinkers and leaders with new moral tools in their struggle against tyranny. Because of these struggles surrounding the human capacity for rational thought, the Enlightenment was aptly described by the German philosopher Immanuel Kant (1724–1804) as the "Age of Reason." Reflecting on the wisdom of nature and its laws, which some characterized as God's imprint on earth, European visionaries of the new age employed reason not merely as a new way to combat religious oppression and arbitrary ruling, but also as a starting point to further individual rights, starting with the right to life. With the injunction "thou shall not kill," Judaism had already instructed people to honor individuals' right to life, an entitlement not only respected by other monotheistic religions, such as Christianity and Islam, but also by Buddhism, Hinduism, and Confucianism. The difference was that reason rather than revelation or mystical devotion was now advanced as the basis for such a belief.

Unfolding historical events had already shown that many who acted in God's name could easily dismiss religious formulations of the sanctity of life. The record of human carnage created by waves of religious fanaticism during the Reformation evidenced the futility of bartering human lives for religious power. If life could be so casually disposed of by rulers, whose "revealed" wisdom could not be questioned, then new criteria other than revelation needed to be developed to constrain their arbitrary actions. Where else could humanists of the Reformation appeal, but to human reason, to its universalist attributes, to its deist and peaceful intent? If religion could not unite everyone, then reason would provide more concrete guidelines for transcending religious and parochial differences.

Brandishing a torch of optimism amidst the graveyards of the English civil war, the English philosopher Thomas Hobbes (1588–1679) argued for a fundamental right of nature, namely that "each man has to use his own power, as he will himself for the preservation of his own nature—that is to say of his own life."[48] From this natural right derived "a precept or general rule of reason *that every man ought to endeavor peace, as far as he has hope of obtaining it.*"[49] To secure that inalienable right to life, an individual could consider entering a social contract to join the commonwealth. For no reason other than the security of one's life and peace, maintained Hobbes, should one surrender other forms of liberty enjoyed in the precivilized state of nature.

With other Enlightenment social contract theorists, Hobbes understood the state of nature as a hypothetical place in which no government existed. By speculating on how humans would fare under those conditions, one could identify why one would consider entering into a social contract that would secure minimal rights. For Hobbes, the right to life was essential, and a social contract would be void if it did not defend this right. The human rights discourse was emerging as a worldview wedded to realpolitik concerns. Ironically, one of the first realists in international politics was also a human rights advocate. His assertion of a right to life would ultimately be echoed in many international bills of rights (article 3 of the UN Universal Declaration, article 6 of the International Covenant on Civil and Political Rights, article 2 of the European Convention, article 4 of the American Convention, and article 4 of the African Charter).

If indicted by the state, Hobbes further argued, one should not be forced to incriminate oneself. In short, for Hobbes, self-defense in all circumstances was a paramount human right.[50] No matter how much the protection of one's body and life was trumpeted as inalienable during the Enlightenment and thereafter, what such protection meant in practice would become the subject of many controversies. When applied to those accused of crimes, for example, it was unclear where to place limits concerning imprisonment, torture, and the death penalty. In the same year as Hobbes's death, the Habeas Corpus Act of 1679 was promulgated in England as an ancient common law writ intended to correct violations of personal liberty by the state. In the spirit of the Magna Carta, granted in 1215 by King John to his barons, the Habeas Corpus established appropriate processes for checking the illegal imprisonment of people by inferior courts.[51] Ten years later, the English Bill of Rights restated similar rights and liberties of subjects by condemning abuses of those accused or convicted of crimes: "[E]xcessive bail ought not to be required, nor excessive fines imposed, nor cruel or unusual punishments inflicted."[52] Although there had been no explicit legalization of "cruel punishments" or torture in England, torture was hardly forbidden. The threat of "pressing to death" under weights, for instance, was used to compel the accused to testify in court, while the rack and other instruments of torture were employed to elicit legally admissible confessions.[53]

THE ENGLISH BILL OF RIGHTS, 1689

. . . Thereupon the said lords spiritual and temporal, and commons, pursuant to their respective letters and elections, being now assembled in a full and free representative of this nation, taking into their most serious consideration the best means for attaining the ends aforesaid; do in the first place (as their ancestors in like case have usually done) the vindicating and asserting their ancient rights and liberties, declare:

1. That the pretended power of suspending of laws, or the execution of laws, by regal authority, without consent of parliament, is illegal.

2. That the pretended power of dispensing with laws, or the execution of laws, by regal authority, as it hath been assumed and exercised of later, without consent of parliament, is illegal.

3. That the commission for erecting the later court of commissioner for ecclesiastical causes, and all other commissions and courts of like nature are illegal and pernicious.

4. That levying money for or to the use of the crown, by pretence of prerogative, without grant of parliament, for longer time, or in other manner than the same is or shall be granted, is illegal.

5. That it is the right of the subjects to petition the King, and all commitments and prosecutions for such petitioning, are illegal.

6. That the raising or keeping a standing army within the kingdom in time of peace, unless it be with consent of parliament, is against the law.

7. That the subjects which are protestants, may have arms for their defence suitable to their condition, and as allowed by law.

8. That the election of members of parliament ought to be free.

9. That the freedom of speech, and debates or proceedings in parliament, ought not to be impeached or questioned in any court or place out of parliament.

10. That excessive bail ought not to be required, nor excessive fines imposed; nor cruel and unusual punishments inflicted.

11. That jurors ought to be duly impanelled and returned, and jurors which pass upon men in trials for high treason ought to be freeholders.

12. That all grants and promises of fines and forfeitures of particular persons before conviction, are illegal and void.

13. And that for redress of all grievances, and for the amending, strengthening, and preserving of the laws, parliament ought to be held frequently. . . .

Whether in Europe, China, Japan, India, the Middle East, or elsewhere, the most intricate and horrible tortures were used as common forms of interrogation and punishment.[54] Some, like Sir Francis Bacon (1561–1626), defended the efficiency of torture; others, like Hobbes, qualified its usage. If torture was used, Hobbes suggested, it should be under very specific circumstances and only to promote the search for truth, and this with the understanding that "accusations upon torture are not to be reputed as testimonies."[55] Yet the eighteenth century also witnessed vociferous condemnations of torture. Indebted to Montesquieu, the Italian criminologist and economist Cesare Beccaria (1738–1794) claimed that punishments should be relative to the severity of the offense, and imposed only when a defendant's guilt was proven. With compelling logic, he argued that

> [t]he dilemma is not a novelty: either the crime is certain or it is not; if it is certain, then no punishment is called for other than what is established by law and other torments are superfluous because the criminal's confession is superfluous; . . . if it is not certain, then an innocent man should not be made to suffer, because in law, such a man's crimes have not been yet proven. . . . [Further, a] sensitive but guiltless man will tend to admit guilt if he believes that, in that way, he can make the pain stop.[56]

In France, where the use of *supplice* (referring specifically to the public torture and execution of criminals) was one of the great evils of judicial procedure up to the time of the French Revolution, Beccaria found in Voltaire a kindred spirit who would condemn torture repeatedly in his writings: "It is as absurd to inflict torture to seek out truth as it is to order a duel to assess who is the culprit," Voltaire wrote. "[O]ften the robust and guilty one resists the ordeal, whereas the debilitated innocent succumbs to it."[57] If Voltaire and Beccaria's outcries against torture often fell on deaf ears in the eighteenth century, they were very much in the minds of the drafters of the major twentieth-century international legal documents on human rights.[58]

The right to life and to the integrity of one's body, including the condemnation of illegal imprisonment, was invoked with each unfolding war and period of political turmoil during the eighteenth century. During the Seven Years' War (1756–1763), Rousseau defended life "as an essential gift of nature";[59] during the American revolutionary war, Jefferson echoed that view in the 1776 Virginia Declaration of Rights; and in pre-revolutionary France, Kant admonished rulers, in *The Metaphysics of Morals* (1785), for treating individuals as a means rather than an end.

This stipulation of an essential law of nature, along with related personal guarantees mentioned in the Habeas Corpus and the English Bill of Rights, would have lasting effects on the promulgation of the American Bill of Rights and the 1789 French Declaration of the Rights of Man and of the Citizen—the two documents most responsible for modern legal formulations of human rights.[60] By the end of the eighteenth century, torture was widely denounced as a relic of the barbarism of another age, as the mark of a savagery decried as "Gothic."[61]

The question of the death penalty for criminals (or the limitations of the "inalienable" right to life), however, created a deeper divide among intellectuals.[62] The death penalty was taken for granted throughout the history of medieval criminal law. John Locke, among others, reiterated in modern terms the argument that life could be forfeited if anyone attempted to violate another's natural rights.[63] Should a criminal be punished with death, he asked? "Each transgression," he answered, "may be punished to that degree and with so much severity, as will suffice to make it an ill bargain to the offender, give him cause to repent, and terrify others from doing the like. Every offense that can be committed in the state of nature may be also punished equally, and as far forth as it may in commonwealth."[64] More than half a century later, Rousseau echoed Locke's view, observing that "it is in order that we may not fall victims to an assassin that we consent to die if we ourselves turn assassins."[65]

Rousseau's influence on the German philosopher Kant was considerable. Like Rousseau, Kant did not see any contradiction between his support for the right to life (defined as a categorical imperative) and his defense of capital punishment. Referring to the idea of retributive punishment (the talion law), he maintained that "if [an individual] has committed a murder, he must die. In this case, no possible substitute can satisfy justice."[66] Aside from murder cases, Kant identified other crimes punishable by death, including crimes against the state. Invoking the Scottish rebellion of 1745, he believed that conspirators against the state deserved the death penalty, yet he warned that if a great part of the population was accomplice to such a plot, a sovereign should not get rid of all his subjects and reduce the country to chaos.[67] He thus urged sovereigns, perhaps with a favorable eye toward the early achievements of the French revolutionaries, to consider other punishments, including granting mercy, so that the community of people might be preserved. Clearly, he suggested, "[T]he state will not wish to blunt the people's feelings by a spectacle of mass slaughter."[68]

Yet the spectacle of death as a form of punishment was not about to end with Kant's warnings. How many deaths by torture would be deemed necessary to revive the collapsing *ancien régime?* How many times would the guillotine dull its blade on the necks of enemies of the French Revolution? Executions were then public events and belonged to a series of rituals in which power was either "eclipsed" or "restored." "The public execution of the seventeenth and early eighteenth century," Michel Foucault has insightfully stated, "was not . . . with all its theater of horror, a lingering hang-over from an earlier age. Its ruthlessness, its spectacle, its physical violence, its unbalanced play of forces, its meticulous ceremonial, its entire apparatus were inscribed in the political functioning of the penal system."[69]

The horrible displays of public execution, often preceded by torture, stirred the minds of many Enlightenment humanists, who decried the savagery of their contemporaries. "For most people," Beccaria complained, "the death penalty becomes a spectacle and for a few an object of compassion mixed with scorn."[70] Beccaria's thesis was that the severity of the death penalty was inferior to the prospect of life imprisonment as a deterrent to murder. "With the death penalty," he explained, "every lesson which is given to the nation requires a new crime; with permanent penal servitude, a single crime gives many lasting lessons." He argued further, *"Murder which we have preached to us as a terrible crime, we see instituted without disgust and without anger."*[71] Only in extreme circumstances was Beccaria willing to consider the death of a citizen: if the life of that citizen truly jeopardized the survival of the social contract, and when "the nation stands to gain or lose its freedom, or in periods of anarchy, when disorder replaces the law."[72]

Beccaria's powerful arguments against the death penalty had wide influence. First published in 1767, his work was soon well known in British colonial circles and was reflected in calls from American political leaders such as Benjamin Franklin (1706–1790) and Benjamin Rush (1746–1813) to abolish the death penalty. For Rush, death penalty laws were "as unchristian as those which tolerate or justify revenge."[73] In France, Voltaire drew on Beccaria to criticize the French penal system: "[A] Roman citizen could be condemned to death only for crimes that threatened the security of the state. Our masters, our first legislators, respected the blood of their compatriots, while we lavishly waste that of ours."[74]

Influenced by Beccaria, whose ideas were popularized in France by Voltaire, Robespierre called in 1791 for the repeal of the death penalty, on the grounds that it was an unjust and ineffective way to deter crime.

When the state becomes an executioner, he maintained, it does not act like an individual who has been attacked and is using force in self-defense, but like a cold-blooded barbarian: "In the eyes of truth and justice, the scenes of death that society commands with so much ceremony are nothing but cowardly murders, solemn crimes committed according to legal procedures, but by the nation at large."[75] Just a year later, when Beccaria made his exception allowing the death penalty in cases where national security was at risk, Robespierre called for the death of Louis XVI after the king's intercepted flight to the foreign enemies of France:

> Yes the death penalty in general is a crime and for that one reason: that according to the indestructible laws of nature, it can be justified only in cases where it is necessary for the security of the person or the state. . . . Society can prevent [common-law offenses] by other means and render the culprit harmless to injure her further. But when a king is dethroned in the midst of a revolution whose laws are still in the making, a king whose very name draws the scourge of war onto a nation in tumult, neither prison nor exile can destroy the influence that his existence continues to exert on the public welfare. . . . Louis must die in order that our country must live.[76]

Robespierre's seemingly dichotomous view on capital punishment reflected the Enlightenment's divide over this issue. Today's controversy on this matter dramatizes the Enlightenment's legacy as supporters and opponents of the death penalty echo and expand upon positions defined two centuries ago. Thus modern abolitionists argue about the futility of capital punishment as a deterrent against crimes; that judicial errors have condemned the innocent to death; that perpetrators are often social victims who should be provided with the possibility to redeem themselves; and that society's deliberate violence can only generate more violence.[77] These views are opposed by defenders of the death penalty who, in reply, assert that killing murderers indeed provides a deterrent, that only death ensures that a convicted murderer will not kill again, and that the families of murder victims deserve nothing less than the killer's death and may require it as the psychological closure necessary for resuming their lives.

The liberal camp remains split over the idea of capital punishment (particularly in the United States), and tensions over this issue are evidenced by the careful wording of some current human rights documents. For example, the 1966 United Nations International Covenant on Civil and Political Rights states in article 2 that "in countries which have not abolished the death penalty, sentence of death may be imposed only for the most serious crimes in accordance with law in force at the time of the commission of the crime." Article 4 states that "anyone sentenced to death shall have the right to seek pardon or commutation of the sentence." This prudent language may well underline the divisiveness generated by a more general question, namely, under what conditions may the state deprive an individual of inalienable rights? Liberals' answers to this question diverge, not just with regard to the question of the death penalty, but also with regard to another central tenet of liberal rights: the right to private property.

THE RIGHT TO PRIVATE PROPERTY

New forms of mercantilist activities that emerged during the Renaissance rekindled efforts to define the individual's right to private property. Strengthened by trade overseas, the call for such a right by merchants and the rising bourgeoisie could no longer be dismissed. With the advance of Lutheranism and the Reformation, the fight for property rights was initially couched in the terminology of revelation. The English Levellers, for instance, identified property earned as the fruits of one's labor as sacred under the biblical injunction "thou shall not steal."[78] The work ethic of the emerging capitalist age was consistent with the Protestant vision of man's providential destiny on earth, Max Weber later explained in his *Protestant Ethics and the Spirit of Capitalism*. Indeed, Protestants maintained that only through relentless work on the land, God's imprint on earth, could individuals reach an intimate communion with the Almighty. Regarded as a radical human rights affirmation in the seventeenth century, the right to property would become a major source of contention in nineteenth- and twentieth-century human rights discourse.

If Hobbes could apply the importance of an inalienable natural right to the property of one's own body and life, the Levellers would extrapolate from that the equally sacrosanct right to acquire property from one's work. Yet not everyone among the English rebels agreed with this formulation. Parliamentary Independents like Cromwell and Henry Ireton (1611–1651) argued at the 1647 General Council of the Army in Putney that equating the right to life with the right to property was tantamount to claiming a right to take anything that one may want, irrespective of the rights of others. If the right to property is a natural right, proposed Ireton, "then show me what step or difference there is why I may not by the same right take your property."[79] A Leveller spokesman, Thomas Rainborough (?–1648), replied that this was merely a mischaracterization of the Levellers' position, which was consistent with respect for others' natural rights.[80] This view had been developed a year earlier by the English pamphleteer and Leveller Richard Overton (1631–1664). In his tract entitled "An Arrow against all Tyrants," he stated:

> To every individual in nature is given an individual property by nature not to be invaded or usurped by any. For everyone, as he is himself, so he has a self propriety, else he could not be himself; and of this no second may presume to deprive of without manifest violation and affront to the very principles of nature and of the rules of equity and justice between man and man. Mine and thine cannot be, except this. No man has power over my rights and liberties, and I over no man.[81]

Debating the legitimacy of property rights as a natural right was not a mere semantic exercise but had additional civil rights implications, including implications for the question of universal manhood suffrage. For Independents like Cromwell and Ireton, only property in freehold land or chartered trading rights entitled men to voting rights. Levellers, on the other hand, argued for a less restrictive property franchise than the one stipulated by the Independents. They believed that all men except servants, alms recipients, and beggars should be granted voting rights. This was consistent with their belief that political freedom was best ensured when individuals (e.g., soldiers and craftsmen) were engaged in independent activity.[82]

Despite these differences over what constituted reasonable qualifications for political freedom and manhood suffrage, Independents and Levellers alike equated political freedom with some sort of individual property ownership and independence. Thus they introduced the liberal notion that freedom is first earned through independent economic activity. Although the right to vote remained limited, the right to property was eventually won, albeit at a high human cost, and feudal land tenures and arbitrary taxation were abolished in England. Whereas the first phase of the revolution (1642–1648) empowered the propertied by granting sovereignty to Parliament,[83] the second phase galvanized more radical concerns, voiced by peasants like the Diggers, who were animated by the vision of an agricultural communist society.

The Diggers' beliefs were more radical than those of the Levellers, who had the support of independent men of small property. Under the leadership of Gerrard Winstanley (1609–1669) and William Everard (1575–1650), the Diggers, who conceived of the English civil wars as a struggle against the king and the great landowners, asked for the establishment of communal property. Now that Charles had been executed, they argued, land should be available for the very poor to cultivate. They also called for further legal and political democracy and the rejection of the state church. Their increasing activities, however, alarmed the commonwealth government and triggered the hostility of local landowners. Harassed by legal actions and mob violence, they had dispersed by the end of March 1650.

With the restoration of Charles II in 1660, the disbanding of the New Model Army, which had won the English civil war for Parliament, and the return of confiscated estates to the crown and to bishops, the liberal as well as the radical hopes of the civil wars seemed vanquished. Yet the debates that unfolded throughout the two periods of the English civil war were to inform subsequent debates over property and political rights. Not only did these early English civil war debates on property and voting rights anticipate future liberal tensions, they also heralded some of the radical dimensions of the nineteenth-century socialist critique of liberalism. Starting with Locke, forty years after the English civil wars, the Levellers' position was once again echoed during the relatively more conservative settlement of the 1688 Glorious Revolution.

Like the Levellers, Locke argued in 1689 that "everyman has a property in his person; this nobody has a right to but himself. The labor of his body and the work of his hand, we may say, are properly his."[84] In

---

**GERRARD WINSTANLEY, "A DECLARATION
FROM THE POOR OPPRESSED PEOPLE OF ENGLAND," 1649**

We whose names are subscribed, do in the name of all the poor oppressed people in England declare unto you, that call yourselves lords of manors, and lords of the land, that in regard the King of Righteousness, our Maker, hath enlightened our hearts so far as to see that the earth was so made purposely for you to be lords of it, and we to be your slaves, servants, and beggars; but it was made to be a common livelihood to all, without respect of persons; and that your buying and selling of land, and the fruits of it, one to another is the cursed thing, and was brought in by war; which hath and still does establish murder and theft in the hands of some branches of mankind over others, which is the greatest outward burden and unrighteous power that the Creation groans under. . . .

And while we are made to labour the earth together, with one consent willing mind; and while we are made free, that every one, friend and foe, shall enjoy the benefit of their creation, that is, to have food and raiment from the earth, their mother; and every one subject to give account of their thought, words and actions to none but to the one only Righteous Judge and Prince of Peace, the Spirit of Righteousness that dwells and that is now rising up to the rule in every creature, and in the whole globe.

From *Selections from His Works,* 44–45.

---

urging individuals not to spoil or waste God's creation and to leave enough for everyone's subsistence, Locke also voiced some of the more collectivist concerns expressed in the English civil wars. Further, he maintained that the rights to life and property were inalienable rights of nature that the state, to gain moral legitimacy, had to secure. Without spelling out how people's political voice would be heard in civil society— other than suggesting people's right to rebel if a government failed to respect its mandate—Locke offered innovative proposals to curb political abuses. By proposing a separation of powers (legislative, executive, and federative) based on a system of checks and balances, he developed a unique institutional model for safeguarding natural rights principles, principles that would inspire eighteenth-century European revolutionaries.

American revolutionaries enthusiastically modeled their new government according to ideas advanced by Locke, the Levellers, and Montesquieu, who owed his popularity to his lucid philosophizing about English institutions. What the American founding fathers took from the British, following Locke's *Second Treatise* (1690) and Montesquieu's *Spirit of Laws* (1748), was the idea of the division and the balancing of power. Indeed, the constitution clearly reflected the view that unless the three classes of governmental power—the legislative, the executive and the judicial—were separated, political freedom and the certainty of basic human rights would not secured. In an atmosphere of protests against a centralized sovereign power, American revolutionaries developed a unique federal system by allocating power between central and local governments and drafting all constitutions so as to limit each level of government by means of a separation of powers.

Following Paine's impassioned condemnation of the British monarchy in *Common Sense,* they also rejected the English system of constitutional monarchy, which was identified with George III. Along with Paine, many expressed their dislike for special hereditary privileges, a position exemplified by the constitution of Massachusetts (and many other state constitutions), which affirmed that no government should be instituted "for the profit, honor or private interest of any one man, family or class of men."[85] Not only did the Declaration of Independence reject monarchy, it also called for the protection of inalienable rights, famously referring to the rights to life, liberty, and the pursuit of happiness. The same year it was signed, George Mason placed property rights in the first clause of the Virginia Declaration of Rights. In the spirit of Locke, the Virginia Declaration granted people the right "to institute a new government" should the state fail in its mandate to secure individual rights.

THE UNITED STATES DECLARATION OF INDEPENDENCE, 1776

When in the course of human events it becomes necessary for one people to dissolve the political bands which have connected them with another and to assume, among the powers of the earth, the separate and equal station to which the laws of nature and of nature's God entitle them, a decent respect to the opinions of mankind requires that they should declare the causes which impel them to the separation.

We hold these truths to be self-evident, that all men are created equal; that they are endowed by their Creator with uncertain unalienable rights; that among these are life, liberty, and the pursuit of happiness. That to secure these rights, governments are instituted among men, deriving their just powers from the consent of the governed; that, whenever any form of government becomes destructive of these ends, it is the right of the people to alter or to abolish it, and to institute a new government, laying its foundation on such principles, and organizing its powers in such form, as to them shall seem most likely to effect their safety and happiness. Prudence, indeed, will dictate that governments long established should not be changed for light and transient causes; and, accordingly, all experience hath shown that mankind are more disposed to suffer, while evils are sufferable, than to right themselves by abolishing the forms to which they are accustomed. But when a long train of abuses and usurpations, pursuing invariably the same object, evinces a design to reduce them under absolute despotism, it is their right, it is their duty, to throw off such government and to provide new guards for their future security. Such has been the patient sufferance of these colonies, and such is now the necessity which constrains them to alter their former systems of government. The history of the present King of Great Britain is a history of repeated injuries and usurpations, all having, in direct object, the establishment of an absolute tyranny over these States. . . .

We, therefore, the representatives of the United States of America, in general Congress assembled, appealing to the Supreme Judge of the world for the rectitude of our intentions, do, in the name and by the authority of the good people of these colonies, solemnly publish and declare, that these united colonies are, and of right ought to be, free and independent states: that they are absolved from all allegiance to the British crown, and that all political connection between them and the state of Great Britain is, and ought to be, totally dissolved; and that, as free and independent states, they have full power to levy war, conclude peace, contract alliances, establish commerce, and to do all other acts and things which independent states may of right do. And, for the support of this declaration, with a firm reliance on the protection of Divine Providence, we mutually pledge to each other our lives, our fortunes, and our sacred honor.

This should not suggest that all state constitutions were fully egalitarian, as even the most liberal ended up providing advantages to the
owners of property. That principle was expressed in some of the state
constitutions that supported manhood suffrage for those who showed
"sufficient evidence of attachment to the community."[86] Even the most
radical proponents of the revolution accepted that premise. Benjamin
Franklin, presumably a staunch believer in the equality of all men, insisted that to allow those who had no land to vote in legislative elections
was "an impropriety."[87] Thomas Jefferson contended that suffrage
should be extended to "everyman who fights or pays."[88] James Madison voiced concern about the following dilemma: "[A]llow the right to
vote exclusively to those with property, and the rights of persons may be
oppressed. . . . Extend it equally to all, and the rights of property or the
claims of justice may be overruled by a majority without property."[89]

The Constitutional Convention initially called for universal male suffrage but soon adopted, following Samuel Adams's draft, a restriction
on the franchise. Under the restriction, a white man was allowed to vote
if he owned real estate worth £3 a year or real and personal property
with a value of £60.[90] As a result, the voting constituency was far less
than half of the adult male population.[91] The property franchise was
justified along the same lines as those advanced by advocates of the Parliamentary cause during the English civil war, namely that political freedom and public office holding would be best served by white independent men who were either free of material concerns or had property at
stake. In some instances, the property franchise was fixed at a very considerable figure; in Massachusetts, for example, it was established at
£1,000, in Maryland at £5,000, and in South Carolina at £10,000.[92]
These requirements were consistent with the political ascendancy of a
propertied ruling elite that included rich governors and senators—all
elected by the wealthy sector of the electorate.

Despite these conservative features of its outcome, the American Revolution inspired people to fight tyrannical regimes and to spread the human rights credo of an emerging liberal age. Constitutionalism, federalism, limited government, property and civic rights were not new ideas
in Europe. John Adams (1735–1826), a great figure of the Continental
Congress (1774–1777) and the second president of the United States
(1797–1801), would later report that the American Revolution was
"Locke, Sidney, Rousseau, and de Mably," that is, the ideas of European
philosophers put into practice. The American struggle for independence
turned the human rights aspirations of the French into a tangible possi-

bility. As the news of the revolution spread in French salons, clubs, and the press, it began to stir members of the Third Estate, who felt increasingly frustrated by the political corruption and economic abuses of the *ancien régime*.

The fall of the Bastille opened the gates for the arrival of new civic rights, and the Declaration of the Rights of Man and of the Citizen hailed universal rights previously acclaimed by the Americans. Its article 7, for instance, stated that no one "may be deprived of property rights unless a legally established public necessity requires it and upon condition of a just and previous indemnity." In reference to political freedom, it declared that "sovereignty resides essentially in the nation. . . . The law is the expression of the general will; all citizens have the right to contribute personally or through their representatives. . . . All citizens being equal before it, are equally admissible to all public offices, positions and employment according to their capacity, and without other distinction than that of virtues and talents" (articles 3 and 6).[93]

These words initially suggested that in contrast to the American system, no property qualification would be required for political participation and manhood suffrage. Yet after having fought strenuously for the elimination of privileges granted to the nobility, Abbé de Sieyès (1748–1836) and other like-minded deputies found no inconsistency in favoring male taxpayers or property owners as the only eligible "active" voting citizens capable of holding public office. "All the inhabitants of a country should enjoy the right of a passive citizen . . . but those alone who contribute to the public establishment are like the true shareholders in the great social enterprise. They alone are the true active citizens, the true members of the association."[94] With revolutionaries like Jacques Guillaume Thouret and Rabaut Saint Etienne, Sieyès presented a report that formed the basis for subsequent legislation on suffrage qualifications and office holding. Only three months after the French declaration of rights was issued, voting rights and public office holding were denied to passive citizens—including domestic servants, women, and all those who did not pay taxes equivalent to three days of labor. Invoking the principles of the declaration, Robespierre was among the few who protested the decree:

> What sort of system is it in which an honest man, despoiled by an unjust oppressor, sinks into the class of the *helots* while his despoiler is raised by this very crime to the ranks of the citizens . . . in short, what is the worth of my much vaunted right to belong to the sovereign body if the assessor of taxes has the power to deprive me of it by reducing my contribution by

a cent if it is subject at once to the caprice of man and the inconsistency of
fortune?[95]

Although the property-based franchise was set at a lower threshold
than the one adopted in the United States, it reflected the liberal and bourgeois character of the initial phase of the French Revolution. Revolutionaries such as Abbé de Sieyès, Marquis de Lafayette (1757–1834),
Georges Danton (1759–1794), Pierre-Joseph Cambon (1756–1820), and
François-Antoine Boissy d'Anglas (1756–1826) were all proponents of
a rapid expansion of commerce and the unrestricted accumulation of
property. They opposed supporters of the popular class, like Robespierre
and Louis de Saint-Just (1767–1794), who were associated with the more
radical phase of the French Revolution. Robespierre had warned the Jacobins to limit the free accumulation of wealth. The right to property,
he insisted, should not be permitted to infringe upon the rights of others, in particular those of the poorer citizens: the sansculottes (the urban
popular class) and the peasantry. He also proposed a progressive tax on
incomes and the drawing of a clear distinction between property rights
justly and unjustly exercised; only the former type, he believed, should
be protected by the state. His views, however, were defeated and omitted from the constitution of 1793, and the property qualification was
maintained.[96]

This decision reflected the eighteenth century's endorsement of property as a right and voting as a male privilege to be earned. It also illustrated the tension of a bourgeois consciousness torn between self-interest
and a humanistic opposition to feudalism and self-interest. J. A. Pocock
aptly remarks that the social thought of the eighteenth century can be
envisaged as a single momentous quarrel oscillating between the worldwide compassion of Roman patriotism and the particularism of private
investors. The Enlightenment's inability to reconcile economic and political rights sharpened domestic social divisions that would later be further intensified by the rise of the nineteenth-century labor movement.

The notion of property, recognized as an inalienable right by the UN
Universal Declaration of Human Rights, the American Convention on
Human Rights (article 2), and the African Charter on Human and
Peoples' Rights (article 14), would remain a point of contention among
the participating members of the UN. For instance, soon after the establishment of the UN, the Soviet Union rejected article 17 of the Universal Declaration, insisting that large units of property should be in the
hands of the state (see chapters 3 and 4). Meanwhile, the question of

how to implement liberal rights internationally added another source of division to the human rights debate as conflicting views on that question further shaped the developing liberal character of human rights.

THE STATE AND JUST-WAR THEORY

The Enlightenment's vision of human rights stipulated that rights to property, religious freedom, and life needed to be protected by the state not only against aggressive individuals, but also against predatory states. Today, as during the Enlightenment, the state is both admired as an efficient vehicle for promoting human rights and feared for its potential to abuse those rights, especially during wartime. Italian interstate conflicts in the fourteenth century had already prompted lawyers like Bartolo de Sassoferrato (1314–1357) and Baldo degli Ubaldi (1327–1400) to address the proper wartime conduct of states. Their doctrines became influential in Spain, Portugal, and Germany. Machiavelli, in the fifteenth century, further elaborated guidelines aimed at tempering conflicts over the unification of Italy. The Dominican friar Francisco de Vitorio (1485–1546) joined the critical chorus, condemning in the sixteenth century the conquests and colonial policies of the Spanish empire and defending the rights of non-Christians and American natives, thereby becoming the founder of the Spanish school of international law.[97]

Throughout Europe, the wars of the Reformation intensified debates over the international application of natural law and highlighted the role and responsibility of states as central actors in the world community. Mercantilists looked to the state as the best vehicle to promote their interests and pursue their economic ventures. At the same time, the state, rather than the supranational authority of the Catholic Commonwealth, was also envisioned as the most efficient vehicle for the advancement of human rights norms—norms consistent with religious tolerance and mercantilist pursuits. "Just wars" were thus rationalized accordingly.

The German publicist and jurist Samuel Pufendorf (1632–1694), the English scholar and jurist Richard Zouche (1590–1661), the Swiss jurist Emmerich de Vattel (1714–1767), and the Dutch legal scholar Hugo Grotius were major participants in the debates over just war.[98] Each offered advice to state leaders, finding in Islam and medieval Catholic scholasticism important contributions to this question.[99] Because of the growing importance of the nation-state, they also pledged loyalty to the mercantilist state, which they viewed as an important mechanism for waging just wars and promoting peace and human rights. Their views, above all, captured a period in transition between the medieval system of international law and the birth of the modern international system, between a system established under the control of the Roman papacy and the emperor and one based on state sovereignties as sanctioned by the Treaty of Westphalia.

No one was better able than Hugo Grotius, one of the most influential legal thinkers of his time, to imagine the changes of the time and new possibilities for international cooperation. To mitigate the occurrence and the effects of the wars that plagued his epoch, he called on heads of states to restrain violence for reasons of humanity and freedom of religion. State leaders, he argued, along with others, needed first to avail themselves of negotiations and diplomacy. If military action was inevitable, he insisted that it needed to be both tempered and used only for the right reasons. Natural law instructed leaders on whether and how to initiate a just war and provided guidelines consistent with the prevailing spirit of mercantilism and free enterprise. With Pufendorf and other legal theorists, Grotius defined just wars as wars waged for defense, recovery of property, and punishment of the unjust.[100] Preventive war undertaken because of fear of an imminent attack, he added, was also legitimate. Which types of war were then forbidden according to natural law? Those infringing upon natural law principles, namely, wars for the appropriation of others' property, wars that subjugated "any people by force on the grounds that they deserved to be slaves," wars aimed at repressing religious differences, and wars driven by expediency rather than necessity.[101]

Retaining many of Grotius's teachings, Pufendorf partly disagreed with his Dutch counterpart, asserting, "[F]ear alone does not suffice as a just reason for war, unless we determine with a morally evident certitude that there is an intention to hurt us."[102] Customary laws, Pufendorf further elaborated, needed to be adopted by states intervening on behalf of a third party:

> It is obvious that people wage war not only on their own behalf, but often on the behalf of others. But for this to be done rightly, a just cause for warring is required, at least in the one who is being assisted. In the one who is going to render aid to the other, however, there should be some special bond by which he is connected to the chief belligerent, one that makes it appropriate for him, in order to meet his obligation to one man, to treat another who is equally a man in a hostile fashion.[103]

At first glance, Pufendorf's notion of a "special bond" is evasive and seems to contrast with his initial insistence on the need for clear criteria before waging preventive war. Indeed, an unqualified notion of a "special bond" could indulge a third party's whimsical preferences by encouraging that party to act only when its perceived national self-interest was at stake and exempting it from acting on humanitarian grounds. Reflecting his epoch's preoccupation with curtailing the strong authority of the Catholic commonwealth, Pufendorf's views also illustrate growing sentiments favoring the sovereignty of nation-states in intervention and other matters.

That concern was deemed so important that neither Grotius, Vattel, Pufendorf, Christian von Wolff (1679–1754), nor any other Enlightenment humanist thinker advanced the idea of a supranational state reminiscent of papal or imperial dominion. If anything, the natural law among nations was characterized by its advisory nature: it informed nations of their mutual advantages and the range of actions that were "permissible" if they were to abide by the rule of nature and reason. "The law of nations," Grotius commented, "derive[s] its authority from the consent of all, or at least of many nations. It was proper to add MANY, because scarce any right can be found common to all nations, except the law of nature, which itself too is generally called the law of nations. Nay, frequently in one part of the world, that is held for the law of the nations, which is not so in another."[104] The law of nature encouraged cooperative behavior among nations but rejected the idea that the state ought to be subjugated to a supranational power. Referring to the example of the Roman province, Grotius asserted, "For those nations are not sovereign states of themselves, in the present acceptation of the word; but are subordinate members of a great state, as slaves are members of a household."[105]

Such a statement resulted in the commonly held belief that natural law could be secured by strong states without any need for authoritative supranational political structures. This view also grew out of the concomitant historical development of human rights norms and mercantilism. Mercantilism required a strong state to launch trade expeditions overseas, yet it also needed new international norms of cooperation to prevent wars and other possible obstructions to the free flow of goods. If the seventeenth century united the interest of the mercantile nobility and that of merchants, by the eighteenth century such an alliance was questioned. For members of the rising middle class, state mercantilism would prove to be too restrictive both domestically, where they were excluded from the political process, and internationally, where the weak political leverage of property owners undercut opportunities for trade.

The towering Scottish economist Adam Smith (1723–1790) formulated best the principles of this new economic challenge. Against the monopolistic nature of both feudalism and mercantilism, Smith saw in the pursuit of individual self-interest the possibility of an unimpeded development of the common good. In a concept he introduced in *The Theory of Moral Sentiments* (1759) and developed in the *Wealth of Nations* (1776), Smith depicted self-seeking individuals as being led by "an invisible hand . . . [that] without knowing it, without intending it, [serves to] advance the interest of the society."[106] The system of perfect liberty, he asserted in his 1776 masterpiece, must operate according to the drives and constraints of human nature as channeled by intelligently tailored institutions.[107] Should such institutions ensure free economic competition, the individual's constant drive for self-improvement, pitted against others driven by the same competitive urge, would maximize the prosperity of the entire society.

Reviewing four main historical stages of political organization—the age of huntsmen, nomadic agriculture, feudal or manorial farming, and commercial interdependence—Smith concluded that the final stage represented the highest form of individual liberty. Insightfully, he observed that a civil government established for the purpose of protecting property rights "is in reality instituted for the defense of the rich against the poor, or of those who have property against those who have none at all."[108] Yet the forces of the market, he explained, constituted a mechanism that would drive the prices of commodities down to their "natural" and most affordable level, despite short-term aberrations and inequality. Praising a guild-free wage and private ownership rather than government-constrained enterprises, he introduced the case for what would become known as laissez-faire capitalism.[109]

Left largely unexplored by Smith, however, was the question of which form of government was best suited to ensuring free markets. In the second half of the seventeenth century and throughout the eighteenth century, many visionaries viewed a republican regime as the best way to promote laissez-faire policies and peace between nations and to ensure liberal rights domestically. Cromwell and Lilburne had justified the pursuit of an English revolutionary war on behalf of a British republic, but it was with Jean-Jacques Rousseau that the concept of the nation-state, justified by his theory of the social contract, was substantially broadened. Rousseau went beyond Hobbes's notion that the state should be protective yet authoritarian, and further than Locke's view of a minimal liberal state ratified by a social contract of atomistic individuals. The state had a different task, insisted Rousseau. It needed to be identified with people's will, or the *volonté générale* (the general will), an organic entity that transcended the sum total of the individuals who comprised it. In the state, individuals were not merely securing the rights they acquired in the state of nature but were creating a new entity, one committed to the common welfare. Later joined by revolutionaries and illuminati like Jefferson, Paine, Robespierre, and Kant, Rousseau advanced the idea that inequitable and unrepresentative states were by nature the basis of global disorder. It was only by means of just political institutions that the rights of a citizen could blossom and war would disappear.

What would promote the development of such political institutions? The spread of commerce would encourage republicanism, argued Paine. By rendering individuals as well as nations useful to one another, the necessity for war would be eclipsed. "If commerce were permitted to act to the universal extent it is capable," Paine explained, "it would extirpate the system of war, and produce a revolution in the uncivilized state of Governments. The invention of commerce has arisen since those Governments began, and it is the greatest approach towards universal civilization that has been made by any means not immediately flowing from moral principles."[110] The principle of republicanism, now linked with the spirit of laissez-faire, was widely viewed as a panacea against the outbreak of wars. Echoing Paine, Kant remarked that "civil freedom could no longer be infringed without disadvantage to all trades and industries, and especially to commerce," and vice versa.[111] That view, essentially unchanged since its eighteenth-century origins, would find expression in the post–cold war foreign policy doctrine of the world's only superpower, which linked world peace to the synergetic expansion of markets and democracy.

Yet not everyone was so optimistic about the widely accepted affinity between commerce and human rights. Rousseau had warned the Polish and Corsican governments that commerce bred inequity and war. In the tradition of the French Physiocrats, Rousseau, like François Quesnay (1694–1774), instead favored representative states based on self-sufficient agrarian economies.[112] "Leave all the money to others," . . . [f]arm well your fields without worrying about the rest . . . financial systems produce venal souls," wrote Rousseau, pointing to the possible flaws of a human rights vision predicated solely on commercial transactions, a view later shared by Jefferson and Robespierre.[113] Whether capitalism should be applied solely to agriculture, as the Physiocrats suggested, or to commerce, as Smith argued in repudiating the Physiocrats' belief system, all of the sympathizers of the revolutions agreed on a central point: republican institutions were the only way to promote peace and human rights.

Should a republican supranational entity be instituted to force aggressive states to enter the civilized world community? With the exception of Kant, no supporters of the French Revolution were willing to endorse such an option. In *Abridgement of the Project for Perpetual Peace* (1713), the French publicist and reformist Abbé Charles de Saint-Pierre (1658–1743), following Henry IV's idea of a "grand design plan," proposed the establishment of a European confederation that would name a permanent, indissoluble arbitration council to solve disputes between states and even stipulated that the council's arbitration would be binding.[114] Yet as Rousseau argued in his *Judgement on Perpetual Peace* (1756), the development of international harmony and rights could never be achieved by self-serving princes and monarchical regimes. Sympathetic to the objectives of the world federation proposed by Saint-Pierre, he nevertheless remained skeptical about its viability and deplored the repressive tendencies of big governmental institutions that were sure to be manifest in such a supranational behemoth.[115]

Addressing part of Rousseau's concerns, and loyal to the spirit of the categorical imperative that invited individuals "to act according to principles which can be adopted at the same time as universal law," Kant further explored the idea of a cosmopolitan confederation premised on republican states.[116] He suggested that since individuals had relinquished their "lawless freedom" for their own good upon entering the republican state, the state now needed to surrender some of its "lawless freedom" for the sake of global welfare. The "general will," he insisted, could only exist peacefully as long as each state recognized an authority above itself. In an effort to develop accountable domestic and international institutions for securing human rights, he envisioned that

> [t]here shall be no war, either between individual human beings in the state of nature, or between separate states, which, although internally law-governed, still live in a lawless condition in their external relationships with one another. . . . [W]e must simply act as if it could really come about (which is perhaps impossible), and turn our efforts towards realising it and towards establishing that constitution which seems most suitable for this purpose (perhaps that of republicanism in all states, individually and collectively).[117]

Whereas most intellectuals and politicians remained unconvinced, at the end of the eighteenth century, that such a confederation of states was feasible, many agreed with Kant and Paine that republicanism and some version of laissez-faire would favor peace. If, while constructing this republican and laissez-faire order, war had become a necessity to eradicate the vestige of the old regimes, then the eighteenth century needed to redefine the seventeenth century's contribution to just-war theory. Indeed, though condemned in principle, revolutionary wars were now deemed just so long as they promoted property rights for all, laissez-faire economic policies, and republicanism.

In the 1770s, there was seldom disagreement among supporters of republicanism over the justice of a revolutionary war to redress American rights usurped by the British. At one end of the spectrum, revolutionaries like John Dickenson (1732–1808) continued to praise the king while calling for some form of resistance. At the other end of the spectrum were defenses of the people's right to change the government at any time. As one speaker at the annual orations in colonial Boston expressed it, civil liberty is "a power existing in the people at large, at any time, for any cause, . . . to alter or annihilate both the mode and essence of any government and adopt a new one in its stead."[118] The Declaration of Independence ultimately advanced a relatively more moderate position on the justifications of revolutionary change: "Whenever any form of government becomes destructive of these ends [life, liberty, and property], it is the right of the people to alter or to abolish it, and to institute new government, laying its foundations on such principles and organizing its power in such form, as shall seem most likely to affect their safety and happiness."[119] Although America did not use the sword to spread its revolutionary message beyond its natural frontiers, its example inspired others to take up arms against tyranny.

Soon after the fall of the Bastille, French revolutionaries found themselves facing troops sent by foreign dynasties that feared the diffusion of human rights ideas beyond the newly established French *patrie*. Drafted in a *levée en masse,* French soldiers of the new patriotic army saw themselves as the liberators of Europe. "O! Ye Austrians, ye Prussians!" wrote Paine in his address to the people of France, "ye who turn your bayonets against us, it is for you, it is for all Europe, it is for all mankind, and not for France alone that she raises the standard of liberty and equality."[120] Robespierre defined the objectives of the French revolutionary wars in similar terms:

> We wish an order of things . . . where distinctions arise only from equality itself; . . . where industry is an adornment to the liberty that ennobles it, and commerce the source of public wealth, not simply of monstrous riches for a few families. . . . May France stand for the glory of all people, fight

the terror of oppressors, console the oppressed, become the ornament of the universe; and in sealing our work with our blood may we see at last the dawn of universal felicity gleam before us. This is our ambition, this is our aim.[121]

The credo of the Declaration of the Rights of Man and of the Citizen, invoking the vision of universal felicity, justified the wars against the enemies of the French revolutionaries. With counterrevolutionary forces on the rise at home and abroad, Robespierre even called for the institution of a strong centralized government: "The object of constitutional government," he explained, "is to preserve the Republic; the object of the revolutionary government is to establish it."[122] If centralism could be depicted as essential for warding off the enemies of the revolution, it would be less easy to rationalize the creation of an expedient judiciary machine during the last phase (1793–1794) of the French Revolution, a vehicle for killing many less radical revolutionaries like Danton or the feminist Olympe de Gouge (1748–1793).

Was Saturn now eating his own children? asked Danton before his execution. It might have been the similar use of violence on behalf of a revolutionary cause in the early nineteenth century that prompted the Spanish painter Goya to paint with disturbing sensationalism a fear-crazed old man, Saturn, driven by the blind instinct of self-preservation, eating one of his children (1821). The revolutionary excesses carried out during the Red Terror and its aftermath begged crucial questions: Which means are justified to promote human rights? Do all means justify their human rights goals? These questions would be widely debated within the socialist movement in the nineteenth and twentieth centuries. In the late eighteenth century, however, violence and war were generally accepted as means of last resort for implementing republican ideals—with the assumption that once republics were established worldwide, wars would vanish. Would revolutionary wars, however, in fact lead to a world federation that would secure the rights upheld domestically by new republican regimes? Even Kant, the only defender of a confederation of republican states, remained conflicted on that question. On the one hand, he saluted the French Revolution "as a moral predisposition within the human race."[123] On the other hand, consistent with his central belief in the supremacy of individual life, he denounced "any uprising that bursts into rebellion . . . [as] the worst punishable crime in a community."[124] It is left unclear from Kant's statements how France could have fought against despotism except through resistance to authority, rebellion, the breach of agreements, killings, or interference with the internal affairs of the enemy's country—recourses that were all condemned by Kant.[125]

Nevertheless, if Kant was unique in trying to grapple with the problem of ends and means, his inconsistency on how to promote human rights was in fact symptomatic of his era. Many revolutionaries were unclear about how to proceed with a just-war strategy. For instance, no one asked at what point in the revolutionary war process republicanism and commerce would triumph, or what the acceptable extent was to which violence could be used to save the revolution. These incongruities and omissions were born in the tumult of an uncertain age that lacked historical precedents for a democratic revolutionary struggle. Yet the eighteenth century's standards nevertheless offered an important contribution to the human rights debates over means of implementation. The eighteenth century revisited the seventeenth century's criteria for just wars—that is, those waged for self-defense, the recovery of property, and freedom of religion—by considering legitimate the right to wage wars to establish a more inclusive republican sovereignty and to promote republican ideals.

The late Enlightenment's preference for laissez-faire economics over a supranational authority as central to the spread of republican ideals and peace is still shared by many Western politicians. Despite increased international recognition of human rights today, nothing contained in the UN charter authorizes "the United Nations to intervene in matters which are essentially within the domestic jurisdiction of any state" (article 2). Nevertheless, recent inconsistent humanitarian justifications for military interventions reflect continued liberal ambivalence about loyalty to the national interest versus solidarity with an international authority predicated on human rights. Both during the Enlightenment and today, this dual allegiance has contributed to the perpetuation of a double standard of moral behavior in which various appeals to human rights obligations remain subordinated to "the national interest."

HUMAN RIGHTS FOR WHOM?

In addition to being characterized by such conflicts over means and ends, the eighteenth century universal liberal agenda was undermined by another set of concerns over who would be the primary beneficiaries of human rights. Unquestionably, the social conditions of many improved during the Enlightenment. The struggle for the right to life, freedom of religion and opinion, and property rights broke the back of feudal regimes and transformed humankind's prospects for realizing human rights. Despite the Enlightenment's critical contribution to the development of the modern human rights agenda, the revolutions of the mid–seventeenth and eighteenth centuries remained incomplete. Many individuals were still considered ineligible to be entrusted with all the freedoms invoked by the English, American, and French declarations of rights. Propertyless male citizens and all women were considered secondary or passive citizens and denied voting rights and political participation; women's legal status continued to be subjugated to the authority of their husbands; with rare exceptions, slavery persisted; the rights of indigenous populations within European colonies were violated; in many places, homosexuality was still regarded as a criminal act; the civil rights of Jews continued to be denied even in revolutionary countries; and finally, despite the pledge of the French revolutionary army to liberate all European nationalities, their lack of political freedom remained unchanged under Napoleon's continental system.

As the drama of revolutionary upheavals unfolded, the Enlightenment era gradually revealed the limits of its universal promise of rights. The English civil war might have coincided with the development of fundamental rights (i.e., the right to life, freedom of opinion, and property), but those rights were not extended to everyone. The emergence of radical groups like the British agrarian communists the Diggers, who strove to be recognized as full-fledged citizens under the British sky, attested to the exclusive character of the revolution; their hopes for civil equality were soon thwarted by the political ascendancy of men of property. The Diggers' disillusionment with the revolutionary process was well described by Gerrard Winstanley: "[S]ome of your great offices, . . . told me that we Diggers took away other men's property from them by digging upon the common; yet they have taken mine and other men's property of money (got by honest labour) in taxes and free quarter to advance themselves, and not allowed us what they promised us; for it [is] this beam in their own eyes they cannot see."[126]

Similar sentiments against the inequitable resolution of the American Revolution were expressed by Thomas Jefferson, who complained in 1785 that "the property of this country is absolutely concentrated in a very few hands."[127] More consequential outrage was expressed by the 1786–1787 Shay's Rebellion in western Massachusetts. Rebuffed after an appeal to the state legislature for relief, debt-ridden farmers organized a rebellion under the leadership of Daniel Shay (1747–1825). The rebels argued that the state legislature was in the hands of the wealthy and was being used for their benefit. Growing support for the rebellion worried many in the upper classes in other states. Their concerns were ultimately allayed when the federal arsenal crushed the rebellion. As a result of the rebellion, however, the Massachusetts legislature enacted laws easing the economic condition of debtors.[128]

Similar popular disillusionment over the consolidation of power by French propertied men could be observed in revolutionary France. Robespierre's proposal to limit the accumulation of wealth and grant every man the right to vote was rejected by the French National Assembly. Economically disadvantaged and politically disempowered, members of the Fourth Estate—the peasantry and the sansculottes—were not able to bridge the growing economic gap between themselves and the wealthier sector of the population. Though they were briefly in power, their radical agenda did not outlast Robespierre's revolutionary government and was superseded (in 1794) by the Thermidorian reaction. The Thermidorians wanted to guarantee the social preeminence and political authority of the bourgeoisie within the liberal regime. With Thermidor, the progressive forces of the Enlightenment era were in retreat, challenged by the interests of a greedy commercial class.

By casting aside dated customs and old economic structures, the emerging commercial age had initially infused women with new emancipatory hopes. "With every great revolutionary movement," observed Friedrich Engels, "the question of free love came into the foreground."[129] Coinciding with the advent of Protestantism, sexual revolutionaries argued that a monogamous partnership based on mutual love should replace arranged marriage. Theoretically, a single moral standard would now have to be applied to both sexes.[130] This prospect unleashed radical speculations by Milton, who, with the clergyman Hugh Peters (1598–1660) and Ms. Attaway, defended the freedom to divorce. The essayist and playwright Francis Osborne (1593–1659) entertained even more daring propositions by celebrating polygamy and annually renewable marriage contracts, and the novelist Henry Neville (1620–1694) depicted a cheerful polygamous utopia in the *Island of the Pines* (1668).[131]

In reality, these assaults on conventional thinking were ephemeral, soon supplanted by a conservative backlash that defended the inequality of the sexes and a strict division of labor between men and women. Although the social condition of Englishwomen was better than that of most women in other parts of Europe, their legal position remained inferior to that of men. They were, for instance, subjected to different forms of punishment than were men, for the same offense. They were not allowed to sit on the same bench as their husbands when in church and were often subjected to beatings.[132] Some contract theorists, such as Pufendorf, Hobbes, and Locke, had recognized some form of women's equality in the hypothetical state of nature, but none entertained such ideas when considering women's status in civil society. Women, they assumed, would consent to their husbands or male political authorities in exchange for protection once they entered a conjugal or a social contract.[133] At the turn of the seventeenth century, a British feminist writer, Mary Astell (1666–1731), highlighted her era's double standard, comparing the limits placed on the power of sovereigns with the almost limitless power of husbands over wives. Sarcastically, she asked, "If the authority of the husband, so far as it extends, is sacred and inalienable, why not that of the Prince?"[134]

Her concerns were echoed throughout the eighteenth century. In 1775, Thomas Paine deplored the plight of women in the *Pennsylvania Magazine:* "Society, instead of alleviating [women's] condition, is to them the source of new miseries."[135] Abigail Adams (1744–1818) suggested in a famous letter to her husband John, "Remember the Ladies" (1776), that he be more generous than his ancestors as he helped orchestrate America's independence from Great Britain. She warned him not to grant husbands unlimited power over their wives: "Remember all men would be tyrants if they could." Despite her warning that women were determined to foment a rebellion if they had no political voice, John Adams scornfully rebuffed her request, asserting that "we know better than to repeal our Masculine systems."[136] Confirming this position, the constitution avoided mentioning women, that is, one-half of the population under its jurisdiction.

The French Declaration of the Rights of Man and of the Citizen, like the American constitution, excluded women from political participation. With the hope of converting Queen Marie-Antoinette to the women's cause, the French pamphleteer and playwright Olympe de Gouge, echoing the views of the French philosopher the Marquis de Condorcet (1743–1794) and Etta Palm d'Aelders (1743–?), wrote a Declaration of the Rights of Women in 1791. In it, she called for respect for women's natural rights as equal to the rights of male citizens outlined in the 1789 declaration. Writing in a time which still viewed women as passive citizens, dependent socially and economically on the male sex, she added a special proviso to protect women from plights specific to their gender. Her declaration included the right to have one's children recognized by their fathers and various other protections for unmarried women to be provided by the state.[137] Invigorated by the militancy of the French-women, the English writer Mary Wollstonecraft (1759–1797), in her *Vindication of the Rights of Woman* (1792), made a similarly passionate and insightful plea for women's education combined with social and political equality.[138]

French law was not changed in response to the important role women had assumed in the revolutionary process. While they were active in popular assemblies, galleries, and clubs, and even risked their lives in the battle to save the revolution, women were nonetheless denied the full rights of citizens. Their dual role was justified by Louis-Marie Prudhomme (1752–1832) who, without scruple, urged Frenchwomen of all ages and all stations to arm themselves with burning torches for the sake of the revolution, but who continued, "[o]nce the country is purged of all these hired brigands, we will see you return to your dwellings to take up once again the accustomed yoke of domestic duties."[139] In the final stage of the French Revolution, women's opportunities were further curtailed. French deputies like Philippe Fabre d'Eglantine (1750–1794), Jean-Baptiste Amar (1755–1816), and Pierre Gaspard Chaumette (1763–1794) decided that organized women's activities, including women's involvement in political associations, were threatening, and forbade their existence.[140] With the Thermidor, and later with the establishment of the Napoleonic Code, women's hopes of emancipation were crushed.

While women and propertyless individuals remained at the margin of English, American, and French societies, France advanced considerably the status of homosexuals, slaves, and Jews.[141] At the beginning of the revolution, the death penalty was removed for all sexual crimes. With the revision of the criminal codes under Napoleon, homosexuals were granted the same rights as other citizens. To be more specific, the codes now left unpunished any sexual activity occurring in private between consenting adults (whether between women, men, or men and women), as long as their actions were not the subject of public indecency. The French legislated for the first time in favor of sexual privacy, while sexual freedom remained severely restricted in the English and American penal books (although prosecutions of sodomy or "acts against nature" were rare).[142]

On the issue of slavery, Montesquieu's work *L'esprit des lois* was a pivotal contribution to the abolitionist cause. It influenced many other French revolutionaries, like the constitutional monarchist the Comte de Mirabeau (1749–1791) and Lafayette, as well as members of the 1788 Black Friends Association, which supported the emancipation of slaves.

OLYMPE DE GOUGE, THE DECLARATION OF THE RIGHTS OF WOMAN, 1790

. . . Mothers, daughters, sisters [and] representatives of the nation demand to be constituted into a national assembly. Believing that ignorance, omission, or scorn for the rights of woman are the only cause of public misfortunes and of the corruption of governments, [the women] have resolved to set forth in a solemn declaration the natural inalienable and sacred rights of woman in order that this declaration constantly exposed before all the members of the society, will cease-lessly remind them of their rights and duties; in order that the authoritative acts of women and the authoritative acts of men may be at any moment compared with and respectful of the purpose of all political institutions and in order that cit-izens' demands, henceforth based on simple and incontestable principles, will al-ways support the constitution, good morals, and the happiness of all. Conse-quently, the sex that is as superior in beauty as it is in courage during the sufferings of maternity recognizes and declares in the presence and under the auspices of the Supreme Being, the following Rights of Woman and of Female Citizens. . . .

Article I. Woman is born free and lives equal to man in her rights. Social distinc-tions can be based only on the common utility.

Article II. The purpose of any political association is the conservation of the nat-ural and imprescriptible rights of woman and man; these rights are liberty, prop-erty, security, and especially resistance to oppression. . . .

Article VI. The law must be the expression of the general will; all female and male citizens must contribute either personally or through their representatives to its formation; it must be the same for all: male and female citizens, being equal in the eyes of the law, must be equally admitted to all honors, positions, and pub-lic employment according to their capacity and without other distinctions besides those of their virtues and talents. . . .

Article XI. The free communication of thoughts and opinions is one of the most precious rights of woman, since that liberty assures the recognition of children by their fathers. Any female citizen thus may say freely, I am the mother of a child which belongs to you, without being forced by a barbarous prejudice to hide the truth; [an exception may be made] to respond to the abuse of this liberty in cases determined by the law. . . .

Article XIII. For the support of the public force and the expenses of administra-tion, the contributions of woman and man are equal; she shares all the duties *[corvées]* and all the painful tasks; therefore, she must have the same share in the distribution of positions, employment, offices, honors, and jobs *[industrie]*. . . .

Article XVII. Property belongs to both sexes whether united or separate; for each it is an inviolable and sacred right; no one can be deprived of it, since it is the true patrimony of nature, unless the legally determined public need obviously dic-tates it, and then only with a just and prior indemnity. . . .

Nevertheless, the fear that the eradication of the slave system would contribute to the decline of French national wealth silenced many initial sympathizers. Slavery and the slave trade, essential to the maintenance of colonial plantations, thus remained in place for the next five years.[143] Vincent Ogé, a young representative of the Assembly of the Colonists, went to Paris in 1789 to press mulatto claims for equal civil and political status on the grounds that mulattoes were men of property and slave owners. His plea was rejected.[144] Yet Robespierre, along with the parish priests and revolutionary sympathizers Abbé Grégoire (1750–1831) and Abbé Raynal (1713–1796) went further, decrying the lot of slaves in the colonies. Their efforts were countered by individuals like Antoine Barnave (1761–1793), a lawyer for the city of Grenoble and a central figure in the French National Assembly, who unscrupulously warned his audience against abolition. "Abandon the colonies," he said on behalf of the Colonial Committee, "and the sources of prosperity will disappear."[145] With the spread of slave rebellions in the 1790s in Saint Domingue (now the Dominican Republic), Haiti, Guadeloupe, and Martinique, the Committee of Public Safety[146] finally adopted, at the National Convention on February 4, 1794, a decree abolishing slavery. Yet the taste of emancipation enjoyed by former slaves soured eight years later, in 1802, when Napoleon restored colonial slavery.

The British, who abolished the slave trade in their colonies in 1807,

---

ENTRY FOR *NEGRO* IN *ENCYCLOPAEDIA BRITANNICA*, 1798

Negro, *Homo pelli nigra*, a name given to a variety of the human species, who are entirely black, are found in the Torrid Zone, especially in that part of Africa which lies within the tropics. In the complexion of negroes we meet with various shades; but they likewise differ far from other men in all the features of their face. Round cheeks, high cheek-bones, a forehead somewhat elevated, a short, broad, flat nose, thick lips, small ears, ugliness, and irregularity of shape, characterize their external appearance. The negro women have their loins greatly depressed, and very large buttocks, which give the back the shape of a saddle. Vices the most notorious seem to be the portion of this unhappy race: idleness, treachery, revenge, cruelty, impudence, stealing, lying, profanity, debauchery, nastiness and intemperance, are said to have extinguished the principles of natural law, and to have silenced the reproofs of conscience. They are strangers to every sentiment of compassion, and are an awful example of the corruption of man when left to himself.

From *Encyclopaedia Britannica, or a Dictionary of Arts, Sciences and Miscellaneous Literature*, 3d ed. (Edinburgh: A. Bell and C. Macfarquhar, 1798). (Modeled on *La grande encyclopédie*.)

---

were nonetheless influenced by the early French revolutionary example. In North America, however, abolitionist efforts were less successful as Thomas Paine's passionate denunciation of the African slave trade in 1775 was rejected.[147] Although he kept slaves on his estate, Jefferson shared some of Paine's discomfort, and in 1782 called for the abolition of slavery and for respect for Indians.[148] Nonetheless, the interests of slave owners on the Southern plantations prevailed in the constitution. Indeed, articles 1 and 4 perpetuated slavery and, with a perverse mathematical logic, called for counting each black and mulatto as three-fifths of a person; Article 1 also excluded Native Americans from apportionment for representation.[149]

Despite the limitations described above, France carried the torch of freedom further than any other country. It was the first country to free slaves, decriminalize homosexual activity, and emancipate Jews. The Declaration of the Rights of Man and of the Citizen had proclaimed freedom of religion and opinion, yet it was initially unclear whether Jews would qualify as citizens. The Prince de Broglie (1756–1794), an officer from Colmar, spoke against the idea, arguing that the Jews' "present existence can be regarded as a great misfortune for [the Alsace] province." Blaming Jews for lending enormous sums of money, he called for denying them the title and rights of citizen.[150] The Bishop of Nancy, La Fare (1752–1829), joined the anti-Semitic chorus by stating that Jews were foreigners and should not be allowed to enjoy rights held by the French people.[151] Yet after tumultuous discussions of the rights of the Jewish communities, a deputy of the National Assembly, Adrien Jean Francois Duport, proposed a daring motion that would finally admit Jews as equal citizens of the republic. The motion passed on September 27, 1791.[152] The French decision was soon emulated in Holland, Germany, Austria, Hungary, and England.[153]

Granting minority rights and freeing all repressed nationalities throughout Europe was part of the French revolutionary agenda.[154] With the decree of November 19, 1792, the Constituent Assembly declared "in the name of the French nation [the decree] will bring fraternity to all people wishing to recover their liberty."[155] Revolutionary principles as celebrated by the French began to spread through all of Europe, not only through "wars of liberation," but also through well-organized local minority groups who had been influenced by French republican ideals. In the most despotically governed countries of eastern Europe, such as Hungary, political unrest took the form of conspiracies. In England and Prussia, Jacobin clubs, such as the London Corresponding Society and the Wednesday Society, proliferated.

By 1807, French armies under Napoleon Bonaparte had swept across Europe. Napoleon now organized a continental system to unite Europe and cripple Britain by cutting off its trade.[156] The system attempted to organize the economy of continental Europe with France as its center. It promulgated an internationalist human rights ideology that presupposed the consent of the European peoples to a new era of republican governance. European Jacobins initially regarded Napoleon as their liberator. He spoke repeatedly of the Enlightenment and urged all people to work with him against the medievalism, feudalism, ignorance, and obscurantism still prevailing in Europe. Hopes were high that France would continue to champion the principles of liberty and equality, and that Napoleon, whose victories spread these principles abroad, was the "man of destiny," what Hegel called "the world spirit on a white horse." For the continental bourgeoisie, The Declaration of the Rights of Man and of the Citizen became the charter of a new world, the constitution of a universal society that Europe should exemplify.

The rhetoric of a French crusade to liberate enslaved people, however, was soon swept aside in Napoleon's policies, as the deeds of the liberator began to resemble the play of old-fashioned power politics. The united European flag, which Napoleon brandished during the "wars of liberation" against absolutist regimes, served mainly to increase France's economic power and national prestige at the expense of its allies. Indeed, national emancipation was not really granted to Jacobins outside of France. The unification of Italy, for instance, may have been implied by the creation of the Italian kingdom, but the new state was promptly truncated by the French annexation of one-third of the peninsula, including all the territory north of Rome to France. Sections of Croatia, Carnolia, and the Dalmatian coast, annexed as the Illyrian provinces, were given a strictly administrative unity: the name was borrowed from a Roman prefecture, and the language favored there was not Croat, nor Italian, but French. The unfulfilled promises of national emancipation began to be ever more deeply resented by the subjects of the Napoleonic Empire.

It was nevertheless the case that the rational reforms Napoleon introduced in Italy and in the German states helped shatter feudal particularism and clear the way for the development of national institutions. As a champion of liberal reforms in spite of himself, Napoleon taught the Italians and the Germans how to reorganize their national institutions—a lesson that would later help them build their respective national states. However, he failed to perceive that nationalist sentiment, which he hoped to arouse against absolutist regimes, would instead turn on him and his empire. The first signs of his decline coincided with what was ostensibly his period of greatest power. As the expansion of French reach became increasingly identified with blatant imperialism, the seeds of nationalist revolt began to bear fruit—first in Spain and then in Austria—and finally broke Napoleon's power at the Battle of Waterloo in 1815.

The reestablishment of the old dynasties during the 1815 Congress of Vienna suppressed even the limited liberties instituted by the French emperor. The resulting Concert of Europe was specifically designed to prevent revolutions based on either individual rights or national self-determination. The new European balance of power, however, did not succeed in extinguishing the hope of emancipation brandished by revolutionary France, and rebellious sentiments would now be directed against aristocratic regimes. If advocates of human rights ideals were now, at least temporarily, on the defensive in Europe, the Enlightenment had nevertheless transformed the Western world. Slavery had been temporarily abolished in the French colonies. The United States entered a new century as the first constitutional republic founded on human rights principles. The idea of national liberation, temporarily suppressed, was ready to reemerge with a vengeance in the nineteenth century. Many women had recognized their inferior legal status and were resolved to change it. Finally, the first stirrings of popular demand for economic justice had challenged the classic liberal assumption that free markets and human rights were always compatible.

Chapter Three

Human Rights and the Industrial Age

THE DEVELOPMENT OF A SOCIALIST PERSPECTIVE ON HUMAN RIGHTS

Liberty Leading the People by Eugène Delacroix, 1830. Detail: Liberty and Gavroche. Louvre, Paris. Photo by Hervé Lewandowski. Courtesy of Réunion des Musées Nationaux/ Art Resource, New York, N.Y.

W AS IT NAPOLEON'S FALL AT WATERLOO, the repressive climate of the Congress of Vienna, the industrial revolution, or slavery in the American South and elsewhere that triggered the tempestuous social upheavals of the nineteenth century? It was no single event, but rather a succession of political jolts that fed a chain reaction of popular unrest as workers rose to demand economic and political power, liberal nationalists strove for independence from tyrannical dynasties, serfs and slaves struggled to free themselves from bondage, and suffragettes demanded rights for women. Their outrage in the face of social inequity shaped the nineteenth-century human rights debate — a debate that intensified as conservative forces succumbed to the advance of capitalism and as rapid industrialization spawned social conflict.

The progress of capitalism brought socialism to the forefront of the nineteenth-century struggle for human rights. Seeking to demythologize the abstract rationalism of the Enlightenment while embracing its internationalist spirit, Karl Marx, Friedrich Engels, and others proposed a materialist understanding of rights sensitive to economic forces, historical change, and conflicting class interests. Armed with a new approach, they confronted early Enlightenment assumptions, asking why only those with property should be allowed to vote, and still more boldly, whether a capitalist state could ever truly represent the people's interests. In answering the latter question, socialists were divided between the appeal of Louis Blanc (1811–1882) for reform and the revolutionary call of Louis Auguste Blanqui (1805–1881) to overthrow the capitalist system. The establishment of an international working-class organization in 1864 raised hopes that these revolutionary and reformist factions of socialism (a worldview interchangeable with Marxism during the nineteenth century) could unite against the ever more defiant advance of imperialism. In the end, however, just as nationalism had poisoned the internationalist hopes of the French Revolution, nationalism on the eve of World War I would ultimately overwhelm the internationalist aspirations of the socialist movement.

Many social democrats, in building their critique against the revolutionary strand of Marxist thought, have questioned whether a Marxist could really believe in human rights. Post-structuralists have also denounced the institutionalization of Marxist ideals as disciplinary and repressive.[1] Notwithstanding important insights offered by these critics, it would be wrong to overlook Marxism's (or socialism's) nineteenth-century historical contributions because of the human rights abuses later inflicted by communist regimes. If liberalism—rightly celebrated for its contribution to civil rights—is more than its colonial legacy, socialism—which championed the rights of the hardworking and powerless poor—is more than Stalinism and Maoism.

Bearing in mind atrocities committed by communist regimes in the name of human rights, this chapter aims to correct the early historical record by showing that the struggle for universal suffrage, social justice, and workers' rights—principles endorsed by the two International Covenants adopted by the United Nations in 1966—were socialist in origin. This should not imply that all nineteenth-century human rights emissaries were socialist; there were certainly non-socialist advocates of self-determination, the rights of women, and the emancipation of slaves. Yet while liberals retained their preoccupation with liberty, socialists focused on the troubling possibility that economic inequity could make liberty a hollow concept—a belief that resonated powerfully with the bourgeoning class of urban workingmen and workingwomen. In this sense, socialists became legitimate heirs of the Enlightenment, applying the universal promises of "liberté, égalité, fraternité" to the political realities of the nineteenth century. The following discussion thus highlights the socialist contribution to central human rights themes—such as universal suffrage, economic welfare, labor rights, education, slavery, and women's rights—in contraposition to other relevant discourses on similar issues. These positions were developed in the epicenters of major political cataclysms, such as the defeat of Napoleon and the Congress of Vienna, the revolutions of the 1830s and 1848, the Paris Commune of 1871, and the American Civil War of 1861–1865: all critical turning points in the struggle to advance a progressive political and social human rights agenda.

Against the religious revival orchestrated by Europe's monarchs after the Congress of Vienna (1815), socialists proposed a secular "historical materialist" approach to human rights. Inspired by a new ethos, they rejected aristocratic and liberal restrictions on voting rights and more broadly questioned the inequality engendered by the notion of property rights. Rejecting the liberal belief that free markets and trade would advance human rights, socialists remained divided over the best means of implementing their egalitarian vision. Socialists embraced a more inclusive agenda than the one professed by liberals in the previous century, and the broadened struggle of the nineteenth century would achieve partial recognition of the human rights of slaves, women, homosexuals, children, national minorities, and the people of the colonies. With the arrival of the twentieth century, internal tensions within the socialist project were overtaken by the nationalist tide that preceded World War I, a tide that crushed socialism's internationalist aspirations. Beginning with the industrial revolution, the next section provides a historical context for understanding subsequent revolutionary developments in human rights.

THE INDUSTRIAL AGE

England led the way toward industrialization as the agricultural innovations of the mid–eighteenth century helped ignite British economic dynamism. Many landowners, seeking to increase their income, began experimenting with improved methods of cultivation, introducing fertilizers, new methods of crop rotation, and new tools (i.e., the drill seeder and horse-hoe) into the rural economy.[2] To overcome barriers associated with the old communal village system, they proposed an enclosure system as a new method of agricultural production.[3] With a market extending from the Americas to Europe, and with unchallenged maritime superiority, British merchants were able to sell more, move capital with ease, and finance technological innovations. The steam engine, applied to cotton mills during the late eighteenth century, enabled England to outstrip the more labor-intensive Asian production of cotton.[4] The appearance of the first successful locomotive in 1829 also provided England with an enormous economic advantage. Some wealthy landowners contributed to the new economic expansion by channeling part of their profits into newly established industries, particularly textile production and the extraction of coal and iron. Other countries, such as the United States, France, Belgium, Holland, and, at a later stage, Germany, Italy, and Japan followed a similar trajectory. Nonetheless until the late nineteenth century, England's economic leadership of the world remained unchallenged.

The route toward industrialization, however, created growing social hardships, as rural poor in search of work migrated en masse to industrial sites, worsening urban poverty. The widening gap between rich and poor ultimately sparked popular rebellions and prompted the revival of human rights discourses. Depending upon the period, the country, and the nature of its government, these revolts were liberal, socialist, or nationalist in character. The conservative climate created by the Congress of Vienna unleashed a predominantly liberal and nationalist reaction that peaked in the 1830s. The spread of industrialization, combined with liberal intransigence in sharing power with more progressive forces during the 1848 revolutions, fueled socialist militancy. The 1848 revolutions, in that sense, were a watershed. In the most industrialized countries, they broke the liberal-radical republican alliance against legitimist regimes and catalyzed the formation of the most radical human rights perspectives of the century.[5] From that point on, the socialist movement shifted to the forefront of the struggle for civil, political, and economic rights.

In autarkic and industrially backward societies, such as those in eastern Europe (e.g., Poland), or in nationally fragmented countries, like Italy and Germany, liberal nationalists, calling for self-determination or national unity, continued to be the dominant forces of the opposition. The American Civil War reflected a hybrid of these trends: Northern industrialization stimulated radical movements, while the agricultural South experienced a nationalist bid for independence. More importantly, the North-South conflict galvanized the anti-slavery cause. In Europe, socialist militancy on behalf of human rights was rekindled by the Paris Commune of 1871. By the end of the nineteenth century, however, nationalism was on the rise everywhere, challenging the socialist human rights project, stimulating the colonial appetites of newly consolidated states (such as Italy, Germany, and Japan), and contributing to the imperial rivalries that precipitated World War I.

From the Congress of Vienna, to the 1830s Revolutions, to the 1848 Revolutions

In the first decades of the nineteenth century, Italian, German, and other liberal (as well as more radical) forces were momentarily repressed by the establishment of the Congress of Vienna. Indeed, the major powers that defeated Napoleon in 1815 were determined to produce an aristocratic balance of power that would suppress popular appetites for Jacobin liberties while preventing the domination of any single power. The German states, thirty-nine in number, were joined in a loose confederation in which each state remained virtually sovereign—a situation that precluded resolution of the rivalry between Austria and Prussia. The congress ignored the yearning of German, Hungarian, Italian, Polish, and other nationalists for unified homelands. To counter the influence of the French Revolution and to reestablish conservative legitimacy, European aristocrats reintroduced religion, which found new forms of expression, both in a rich corpus of theological writings and in the strengthening of the church.

The restoration of monarchical rule and the spread of religious fervor fomented, however, violent popular reactions throughout Europe during the 1830s, uprisings that the French romantic painter Eugène Delacroix (1793–1863) vividly rendered in his much celebrated *Liberty Leading the People* (1831).[6] Against monarchical and religious order, more and more revolutionaries were invoking a secular and republican discourse of human rights. Throughout that decade, liberals, united with radical republicans, fought for political reforms or against repressive foreign regimes. In Spain, *liberales* were pitted against religious and monarchical forces in recurrent outbreaks of violence. Between 1812 and 1876, liberal constitutions were annulled as frequently as they were introduced.[7] For eighty years, Portugal underwent a similar struggle that finally ended with a constitutional monarchy. In South America, the leaders of the Latin American Independence movement, Simón Bolívar (1783–1830) and José de San Martín (1778–1850), unleashed civil wars and revolutions against Spanish colonial possessions between 1810 and 1824, and independent South American nations were to emerge from wars against Spain in the early nineteenth century.[8] Following Alexander Ypsilanti's call to free "the fatherland from its chains," Greek nationalists won their independence from Turkey in 1830. In France, the rebellion of liberals and radicals led by General Lafayette during the 1830 "July days" resulted in the abdication of Charles X and the crowning of a seemingly liberal monarch, Louis-Philippe.

The French July days sparked similar rebellions elsewhere in Europe. In Brussels, liberal rebels' seizure of the Hôtel de Ville led, despite Dutch opposition, to Belgian independence and the inauguration of a constitutional monarchy.[9] Polish liberal nationalists also saw in the fall of the French Bourbon dynasty a timely moment to rebel against the Polish king Nicholas. Yet the Poles were not as fortunate as the Belgians, as the newly proclaimed Polish republic was soon dismantled by Russian troops and superseded by a more repressive regime.[10] In Italy and Germany, authorities put down similar uprisings. Even as national liberation movements were crushed in Poland, Italy, and Hungary, popular culture embraced the lyrical music of Frédéric Chopin (1810–1849), Giuseppe Verdi

(1813–1901), and Franz Liszt (1811–1886) as symbols of national identity and liberation. The success of Latin American and Greek nationalists, followed by the 1848 revolutions, would later help revive the struggle, stirring these and other repressed nationalities to insist on the right to self-determination and other political reforms.

In Great Britain, social change initially advanced the liberal human rights agenda. The 1830 Paris insurrection had provided the British middle class with a new sense of confidence in confronting two remaining obstacles to their triumph over the landowning aristocracy: unequal political representation and the tax on imported grain imposed by the Corn Law (1815). Fearing that the spread of violence would cross the English Channel, the House of Lords allowed passage of the 1832 Reform Bill, which implemented a flat property qualification tax for eligible male voters. Still conservative in scope, the bill nonetheless widened the electoral base and provided the business class, already strengthened by industrialization, with a political position rivaling that of the old aristocratic elite. By 1846, following the repeal of the Corn Law (thanks to a liberal-radical alliance), industrialists' interests were finally privileged over those of landowners.

Yet these liberal victories were accompanied by a new development in the history of human rights, for it was in Britain during this period that the material and political aspirations of the working class first became politically salient. The workdays of children and women (and soon after, men) were reduced to ten hours in 1847. The Chartist Movement—a social movement for parliamentary reform named after the People's Charter (1837)—played a large role in the campaign for voting and social rights.[11] If one can argue that the Chartist movement was not, strictly speaking, socialist, it was nevertheless a working-class movement radicalized by its political experience, and hence can be seen as a precursor to what would later become the modern socialist labor movement.[12] Not all of the demands of the Chartists were initially met; male suffrage remained limited, and property qualifications for membership in the House of Commons continued to limit public participation. Indeed, despite significant strides for labor rights, the principal result of the revolutionary agitation of 1830–1832 in England, France, and Belgium was a decisive victory for the ascending class of wealthy capitalists over the aristocracy. As the bourgeoisie accumulated capital, built up industrial plants, and augmented the national wealth, only a relatively small share of that wealth went to an increasingly alienated working class.

From the 1848 Revolutions to the Paris Commune

Frustrated by harsh working conditions, insecure jobs, and exclusion from political participation, after 1830 the working class turned increasingly to socialism. In France, political radicalization found powerful artistic expression: the painter Gustave Courbet (1819–1877) depicted the plight of the poor with striking realism, while the writer Honoré de Balzac (1799–1850) brilliantly described the lives of unscrupulous financiers in *The Human Comedy*. On the political scene, many advocates of the working class, like the socialist Louis Blanc, were now ready to revive the radical republicanism of the French Revolution. In the face of Louis-Philippe's unshakable opposition to electoral reforms that would benefit either the middle or working classes, riots erupted, barricades were formed, and the February revolutionaries of 1848, like those of the July revolution of 1830, removed the king.[13]

Guided by Louis Blanc's socialist vision, the city of Paris established national workshops to relieve the distress of the unemployed. Favoring an uncompromising liberal agenda, however, the newly formed Constituent Assembly soon dissolved these social projects and proclaimed martial law against any form of social resistance. Over twenty thousand men from the workshops, joined by unnumbered thousands from working-class districts of the city, took up arms against the government in a terrifying class war. Ten thousand were killed or wounded in the three "Bloody June Days," and eleven thousand insurgents were taken prisoner and deported to the colonies.[14] With Louis Napoleon's institution of the Second Empire (1852–1870), a conservative regime was restored.

Despite the defeat of the 1848 French insurgency, the specter of revolution continued to threaten the European middle and upper classes. With the French uprising, revolts spread almost simultaneously from city to city, from country to country. "There has never been anything closer to the world-revolution of which the insurrectionaries of the period dreamt than this [1848] spontaneous and general conflagration," noted one historian.[15] In less industrialized and regionally decentralized countries, the 1848 revolutions took a nationalist form. The Italian uprising against the Austrian monarchy revealed, throughout the peninsula, an enthusiasm for independence animated by liberal nationalist forces. Weakened by internal divisions, the rebellion was, however, ultimately crushed by Austrian troops.

In the multicultural empire of the Habsburgs, the spread of liberal nationalist fervor was also difficult to contain. Lajos Kossuth (1802–1894) sparked the flame of independence by demanding home rule for the Hungarian people, but as in the Italian case, the Hungarian rebels were defeated. In Germany, a similar experiment in national unification was also thwarted, in part due to a division between advocates of a "little Germany" (excluding Austria-Hungary) and a "greater Germany"(excluding only Hungary). In a less acute way, the rebellions also affected Spain, Denmark, and Rumania, and, intermittently, Ireland, Greece, and Britain.

The ill-fated revolutions of 1848, however, were not waged in vain; hopes for political and welfare reforms and human rights were now brewing with more intensity as Chartists and socialists assumed leading positions in the human rights struggle of the nineteenth century. The socialists and the British Chartist Movement inspired others to renew their quest for universal suffrage. Across Europe, socialists joined the anti-slavery movement, supported women's political and social rights, denounced the plight of child factory workers, called for the right of all children to public education, advanced the right to a safe work environment, and pressed for the reduction of daily working hours. In 1864, socialists and anarchists helped found an international socialist organization, the First International, that gathered together for the first time representatives of socialist movements worldwide, working together to develop policies and strategies for promoting political, social, and economic rights. Their endeavors were further inflamed by another influential, albeit short-lived, social explosion in France.

Between March and May 1871, French socialists and anarchists set up a revolutionary municipal council, the Paris Commune. Refusing the harsh terms of the German peace settlement that followed the Franco-Prussian war, French Communards took over the streets of Paris, challenging wealthy bourgeoisie, aristocrats, and the clergy while demanding government control over prices and wages, as well as better working conditions. Moreover, the Communards demanded rights for the working class, the development of workers' cooperatives, a reduction of working hours, free public education for all children, professional education for young workers, and housing rights (including a suspension of rent increases that had gone into effect during the German siege of Paris). Many defended women's right to equal pay for equal work. Legislation subsidizing single mothers and day nurseries for their children was passed.[16] In May 1871, fearing defeat, conservatives in the French National Assembly sent the National Guard to crush the Paris Commune in a bloodbath that claimed some fifteen thousand lives in one week. Those who survived were prosecuted and exiled by a military court. The repression failed, however, to uproot hopes for social welfare and human rights: the experience of the Paris Commune reignited labor activism throughout Europe.

Social democratic parties, generally indebted to Marxist doctrine, sprang up in most of the countries of continental Europe. In Germany, the social democratic movement grew rapidly, despite the initial attempt of Otto von Bismarck (1815–1898) to suppress it through anti-socialist legislation and to undercut its appeal by enacting social reforms. The Danish and Norwegian Social Democratic Parties were established during the 1870s; the Belgian Labor Party was formed in 1885; and the Swedish socialist movement began in 1889. In central Europe, social democratic parties gradually assumed a more important political role, as did the Austrian Social Democratic Party (founded in 1888). In England, the Labour Party emerged as a strong independent force able to gain important welfare concessions from liberal and conservative governments.

The American Civil War and the Anti-Slavery Cause

Just as in Europe, America's early industrialization sparked a wave of human rights debate. European immigrants, arriving in the New World, carried with them new human rights ideas from their homelands. By the mid–nineteenth century, American progressives shared the same views of social rights as their European counterparts. Inciting civil disobedience against unjust laws, the political thinker Henry David Thoreau (1817–1862) inspired many Americans in the fight for trade unions and women's suffrage and the struggle against slavery.[17] When the question of national unity became increasingly critical as American expanded westward, the American statesman and writer Carl Schurz (1829–1906) influenced many contemporaries by invoking liberal nationalist principles and identifying America as the "Great Empire of Liberty." The cohesiveness of the "Great Empire of Liberty" was challenged, however, as Northern states asked for tariff barriers to protect their young industries from competition from British goods. Wishing to purchase manufactured goods as cheaply as possible, Southern states rejected this type of protectionism.[18]

A more fundamental conflict was over their different approaches to slavery. As long as Northern wage earners regarded the gap between themselves and capitalists as tolerable, workers supported the Republican Party and its twin goals: the destruction of slavery and the enhancement of free wage labor in Northern industries.[19] These positions contrasted starkly with that of a South whose economy depended on slavery. In an effort to mitigate tensions, the 1820 Missouri Compromise was reached, requiring that for each slave-owning state admitted to the Union, a non-slaving-owning state would be admitted. To offset the inequality resulting from the addition of California (1850) as a non-slave-owning state, the Northern states agreed to Southern demands that they enforce harsher laws against fugitive slaves.

The plight of a growing number of fugitive slaves who escaped from Southern to Northern states, and its poignant evocation in the best-selling novel by Harriet Beecher Stowe (1811–1896), *Uncle Tom's Cabin* (1852), helped fuel Northern support for the abolitionist cause. Correspondingly, secessionist and pro-slavery ideas, promoted in fiction like *Cannibals All!* (1857), by George Fitzhugh (1806–1881), spread widely in the South. Many Southerners, feeling that their interests were being subordinated to those of Northern states, began to identify "Yankees" as foreigners. The 1860 election of abolitionist Abraham Lincoln (1809–1865) as president further fomented secessionist sentiments and precipitated a long Civil War (1861–1865) pitting North against South. During the Civil War, nationalism revealed its Janus face. While Northerners appealed to nationalism to save the Union, Southerners called on the right of the Confederate states to self-determination. With the North's victory, the United States was reunified, setting the stage for its emergence as a major economic power committed to liberal political principles and the spirit of private enterprise. More significantly, as the United States rejected slavery within its borders, the international abolitionist movement scored a decisive triumph on behalf of human rights.

In short, the Congress of Vienna, the 1830s and 1848 revolutions, the Paris Commune, and the American Civil War were events that both catalyzed and sharpened the most progressive universal vision of human rights of the nineteenth century, a vision later challenged by intensifying nationalism and World War I. These historical episodes provide us with important signposts to guide us through the important human rights developments covered in the remainder of this chapter, namely, the demands for a secular and historical materialist approach to human rights, the struggle for universal suffrage, economic equity, and other social rights, the challenge to the state and capitalism as vehicles for promoting human rights, and the broadening of the human rights agenda.

CHALLENGING THE LIBERAL VISION OF RIGHTS

The establishment of the Congress of Vienna showed that the great powers could unite against a common internal threat to their ruling elites, as the monarchs of Prussia, Austria-Hungary, and Russia pledged each other mutual assistance in their efforts to quell democratic challenges by their subjects. Yet the Jacobin taste for freedom, previously aroused throughout Europe by revolutionary France, was not about to be so easily denied. If anything, the aristocratic hold on power sanctioned by the congress helped intensify a liberal nationalist riposte animated by romantic ideals. As European industrialization intensified, it also fomented a socialist response. While liberal romantics had initially inflamed socialists' hope for justice, they ultimately failed to share power with them. For many socialists, the "bourgeois betrayal" of 1848 urged them to a new course of action drawn from historical lessons and a materialistic interpretation of rights.

By the time Napoleon was sent to exile in Saint Helena (1815), a romantic and religious intellectual climate was spreading in revulsion against the French rationalist and secular influence. Edmund Burke (1729–1797) and Joseph de Maistre (1753–1821) had already anticipated, as the end of the eighteenth century approached, a yearning for a return to monarchy and for a collective stability centered on faith, emotionalism, tradition, and discipline.[20] Many conservatives, like the French poet and diplomat Chateaubriand (1768–1848) and the British poet William Wordsworth (1770–1859), echoed their views. In an effort to erect royal bulwarks against the raging liberal tides that had outlasted the defeat of Napoleon, monarchies restored organized religion.

The Roman Catholic Church, for example, regained its privileged position in France and, without recovering the lands lost during the French Revolution, resumed its control over education. In Prussia, a new national church was created in 1817 by merging Lutheran and Calvinist elements. With the spirit of tolerance still in place in most European countries (with the exception of Russia), religious fervor and theological debate was encouraged. Leading Protestant and Catholic scholars like the Prussian Friedrich Schleiermacher (1768–1834), the French abbé Félicité Robert de Lamennais (1782–1854), the Bavarian Catholic J. J. Ignaz von Döllinger (1799–1890), and the Danish religious existentialist Søren Kierkegaard (1813–1855) participated in interfaith exchanges. These religious conversations created a hospitable climate for the exploration of non-monotheistic religions such as Hinduism and Buddhism.[21]

The new religious attitude of the age also flavored the nature of the liberal and nationalist reactions of the 1830s. If monarchies and aristocracies saw in religion a means toward social stability, others used religious worship as a way to rouse the masses against the new conservatism inaugurated in Vienna or against the false promises of freedom of the Napoleonic era. Liberal thinkers like Johann Gottlieb Fichte (1762–1814) who initially saw in Napoleon a great hero were now turning against the basic postulates of the Enlightenment and against all notions of universality based on an abstract notion of reason. Fichte and others opted for a different message of self-determination, blending some liberal views on rights with mystical (or religious) conceptions of solidarity centered on love of the nation.[22] With other romantics, Fichte upheld an organic view of the nation while idealizing the subjective will; he looked back to tradition while contemplating new venues for cultural development.[23] If some romantics saw history as a process to be orchestrated by a ruling elite faithful to its traditions, others identified it as a cyclical mechanism in which wars and violence were romanticized as weapons against oppression.

While predominantly liberal in character, romanticism recruited individuals from across the political spectrum. Precursors of socialism such as Claude Henri Saint-Simon (1760–1825), Charles Fourier (1772–1837), and Robert Owen (1771–1858) were not insensitive to the liberal passion for justice that animated their romantic contemporaries. Each had developed a utopian vision in which individuals from different social milieus would work in harmony to promote the common good. The unique technological capacity of the industrial age, Saint-Simon argued, could provide all people with the opportunity to ascend to a social position commensurate with their talent while working toward the improvement of the collective good, as in a gigantic workshop. In a similar vein, Fourier imagined model communities, called the *phalanstères* (phalanxes), which would encourage individuals in a self-sufficient, small agricultural society to perform tasks congenial with their temperaments and inclinations.[24] In England, Robert Owen, often viewed as the Welsh Fourier, placed less importance on human passion than his French contemporary, but he also envisioned cooperative villages where settlers, in addition to raising crops, could strengthen their bodies and cultivate their minds.[25] Saint-Simon's, Fourier's, and Owen's visions of social harmony between classes coincided with the bourgeois liberal-radical association against the nobility during the 1830s revolutions.

Yet this association was fragile. In 1848, the strengthened French middle class proved unwilling to share its newly acquired power with Louis Blanc and other leaders of the working class. Outraged by the liberal "treason" of the Bloody June Days, many, like the German political philosopher Karl Marx (1818–1883), denounced the conservative restoration of "property, family, religion, and order."[26] It soon became clear to the defeated socialist forces that a new perspective on human rights was needed, one stripped of all elements of liberal ideology that undermined the goal of social justice. Saint-Simon, Fourier, and Owen might have paved the road to socialism, but they were utopian in their belief that peaceful cooperation between classes was possible under capitalism.

This was at least what Marx, Friedrich Engels (1820–1895), Auguste Blanqui, and others asserted as they watched the crushing of the popular protests of 1848. The ideals of human rights developed hitherto, they claimed, were associated with the pretense of a universal liberal and religious morality that camouflaged the particular interests of the bourgeoisie. Since the influences of liberalism and romanticism were part of the problem, they took upon themselves the task of disabusing their contemporaries of their idealism. In *The German Ideology* (1845), Marx had already initiated this endeavor by condemning German philosophers from David Friedrich Strauss (1808–1874) to Max Stirner (1806–1856), who confined their philosophical works to religious criticism. In their approaches, Marx maintained, every "dominant relationship was pronounced a religious relationship and transformed into a cult, a cult of law, a cult of the State, etc."[27] The time had come, he believed, to create a secular and international labor movement.

While Marx was one of the most influential socialist voices of his time, his anti-religious position was rejected by the Christian socialist groups that sprouted in nearly every European country and in the United States. These groups developed the view that Christians should feel obligated to ameliorate the economic and political conditions of the working class. Champions of such tenets came from diverse backgrounds and included the abbé Félicité Robert de Lamennais in France, the religious "communist" Wilhelm Weitling (1808–1871) in Germany, the British theologian Frederick Denison Maurice (1805–1872), and the American manufacturer Stephen Colwell (1800–1872).[28] For Marx, however, in the final analysis, the use of religion always benefited the preservation of the ruling elite. By consoling the masses, who are urged to resign themselves to their plight on earth with the promise of heavenly reward, religion becomes nothing more than "the opium of the people." With his collaborator Friedrich Engels, Marx provided the emerging labor movement with a more tangible universal creed.

Marx's "On the Jewish Question" exemplified the radical critique of all forms of religious or particularist emancipation. The Jews of Germany were not entitled to special privileges when the rest of the country was still under the yoke of authoritarianism. "As Germans," he admonished advocates of Jewish emancipation, "you ought to work for the political emancipation of Germany, and as human beings, for the emancipation of mankind."[29] The emancipation of one religious group over the rest of society perpetuated social divisiveness and undercut the possibility of collective action against authoritarian rule. Singling out Jews, for instance, in opposition to the Christian state, would allow people to harbor resentment against a particular group. How could the opposition between Christians and Jews be resolved, Marx asked? "By making it impossible. By *abolishing religion.*"[30]

Real freedom called for terrestrial opportunities, for economic and political emancipation. The universal principles of human rights advocated during the American and French Revolutions, Marx pointed out, were therefore inconsistent. By celebrating the free exercise of religion, the Declaration of the Rights of Man and of the Citizen and the constitutions of Pennsylvania and New Hampshire, he wrote, praised "the right of separation" and fragmentation, thereby denying citizens the opportunity to develop a common human rights agenda.[31]

Like religious rights, the notion of cultural rights, so strongly advocated by liberal nationalists in nineteenth-century Europe (and later championed during the twentieth-century post-colonial struggle), faced criticism. Although the idea of group loyalty contemplated by romantics influenced socialist concepts of solidarity, most socialists rejected the disjunction between group solidarity and universal human rights. Challenging liberal ambiguities, many socialists asked, who were the primary beneficiaries of a particular culture or religion? What was the political and economic program advocated by champions of any particular culture or religion? Was culture (or religion) a right sui generis that did not need further qualification? How should these rights be prioritized in relation to other universal rights? The critical nature of these questions was intended to unveil potentially exclusionary aspects of any given political agenda. In this respect, the contemporary conflation of social, economic, and cultural rights in one international human rights covenant, the International Covenant on Economic, Social and Cultural Rights, overlooks the socialists' rejection of unqualified notions of religious and cultural forms of emancipation.

Equally important for the development of a socialist perspective of human rights was the argument that changing social forces throughout history could account for why some rights were privileged at various times over others (e.g., group rights, or class privileges, over universal rights).

By 1848, many had witnessed human rights history coming full circle as French revolutionary ideas had risen, were overturned by conservatism, and were reembraced by progressive forces during the industrial revolution. In this respect one cannot overlook Hegel's influence on socialist thought. Hegel's contribution to the understanding of historical development was enormous. Described in terms of thesis-antithesis-synthesis, his system sought to explain how contradictory dialectic forces pushed the wheel of history toward freedom. In this motion, morality and rights were contingent upon different historical stages of the Spirit (or Zeitgeist). The Spirit was essentially a providential embodiment of history shaped by the actions and values of individuals and states. Yet the Spirit was not following a predetermined cyclical narrative, which romantics like Joseph de Maistre and, later, Friedrich Nietzsche (1844–1900) depicted in terms of the recurrent rise and decay of societies and mores, but was progressing, despite some regressive phases, toward freedom.

Because historical progress had come to a halt with Napoleon's defeat and the Congress of Vienna, Hegel's *Philosophy of Right* (1821) proposed to unify the Enlightenment's desire for human rights progress with the liberal romantics' yearning for self-determination. In light of the French failure, Hegel now conferred upon the German people the task of advancing the progress of history by building an exemplary liberal Prussian state. Not all classes, he believed, however, were able to ensure the evolution of history. The three classes he identified, namely, the agricultural, the business, and the bureaucratic (or civil servant), reflected three modes of morality—conservatism, individualism, and universalism. Freedom, expressed by the exchange of free property, was associated only with the world and consciousness of the middle class (businessmen and civil servants), "the pillars of the state, so far as honesty and intelligence are concerned."[32]

While praising Hegel's system, Marx and Engels rejected his political conclusion. History was more than the contorted movement of the Spirit through time; instead, it needed to be accounted for by the actual transformation of social reality. A materialist interpretation of Hegel's historical dialectic, they maintained, would provide practical judgments based on historical lessons, and would offer new human rights directions for the emerging labor movement. The material conditions of life, as related to the social forces of production, first needed to be prioritized. In *The German Ideology,* Marx articulated what most socialists embraced, that "the first premise of all human history is . . . the existence of living individuals. Thus the first act to be established is the physical organization of these individuals and their consequent relation to the rest of nature."[33] The production of life not only created social relations shaped by the forces of production, it also generated moral rationalizations relative to time, space, and class.

Such was the argument Engels further developed against the German philosopher Eugen Dühring's ahistorical characterization of morality, truth, and rights. Consistent with Marx's position, Engels asserted that the conception of right and wrong has "varied so much from nation to nation and from age to age that they have been in direct contradiction to each other."[34] He also maintained that moral theories of rights are the product of economic stages of societies, and in particular of the dominant class. Hence, the notions of freedom and rights are futile if not discussed in terms of historical circumstances, or in terms of material contingencies and possibilities. Such an interpretation of rights would lead one to question the validity of our current ahistorical and classless international human rights covenants. Moreover, if rights are contingent on changing historical and material circumstances, would it be unreasonable to wonder whether a socialist understanding of rights is as relativistic (and thus arbitrary) as the liberal notion of cultural rights, which Marx dismissed? The argument that conceptions of rights depend upon class and social historical conditions indeed reveals prima facie a certain level of relativism by implying that no human rights are universally and permanently valid.

Aware of that potential accusation of historical relativism, early-twentieth-century Austro-Marxists and socialist scholars belonging to the Frankfurt School have all invoked Immanuel Kant's axiomatic and a priori principles of ethics, enabling them to ground more firmly their unequivocal adherence to universal principles of human rights. In the words

---

FRIEDRICH ENGELS, ON RIGHT AND HISTORY, *THE ANTI-DÜHRING*, 1878

We maintain . . . that all former moral theories are the product, in the last analysis, of the economic stage which society has reached at that particular epoch. And as society has hitherto moved into class antagonisms, morality was always a class morality; it has either justified the domination and the interests of the ruling class, or, as soon as the oppressed class has become powerful enough, it has represented the revolt against this domination and the future interests of the oppressed. That in this process there has on the whole been progress in morality, as in all other branches of human knowledge, cannot be doubted.

From *The Anti-Dühring*, in Karl Marx and Friedrich Engels, *The Marx-Engels Reader*, 726.

of the German socialist philosopher Karl Vorländer (1860–1928), Kantian ethics represent "the final bastion to which we can retreat whenever
ethical skepticism obstructs the naïve moral judgement of class maxims
discovered by science." More recently, others, like Alan Gilbert, have
stressed the relevance for socialist thought of a timeless yet limited moral
objectivity drawn from an Aristotelian reading of Marx.[35]

Socialists provided another reason for rejecting the view that all class
visions of morality, at whatever historical stage—feudal, bourgeois, or
proletarian—should be evaluated on an equal footing. Whereas Hegel,
like many of his contemporaries, relied on the middle class to carry the
universal message of rights, after 1848, Marx, Blanc, Blanqui, and many
other socialists entrusted proletarians with this mission. Because they had
"nothing to lose but their chains," Marx wrote, proletarians were in a
uniquely critical position to imagine a more egalitarian society in which
universal human rights ideals would be sustained (rather than contra-
dicted) by the economic and institutional infrastructure of society.[36] The
emancipation of slaves in America and throughout the rest of the world,
and the establishment of the Paris Commune of 1871 were seen as important evidence of such historical progress.

There were also, however, critical human rights setbacks. In May of
1871, the First International workers' association decried the merciless
shooting of thousands of defenders of the Paris Commune. Over half of
the ten thousand sentenced by court-martial were sent to exile in Caledonia. The subsequent rise of nationalism, fanned by the emergence of
competition among the great imperial powers in the late nineteenth century, further hindered human rights progress. From a historical dialectic
understanding of human rights, however, history is never really amnesic.
It retains the forces of progressive change against repression, which are
invoked and revised by new generations. Each generation builds on the
hopes of the past as it strives to improve its social conditions or to free
itself from authoritarianism. From such a perspective, the human rights
themes that survive the tests and contradictions of history may provide
in the long run a corpus of shared perceptions of universal human rights
that transcend class distinctions and economic inequity. In Engels's
words, "That in this process there has been on the whole progress in
morality, as in all other branches of human knowledge, cannot be
doubted. A real human morality, which transcends class antagonisms and
their legacies in thought, becomes possible only at a stage of society which
has not only overcome class contradictions but has even forgotten them

in practical life."[37] Despite regressions and repressions, an internationalist socialist agenda based on universal suffrage and social and economic rights was developed throughout the nineteenth century. Many of its principles continue, by and large, to stand the test of time, as shown by the UN International Covenant on Economic, Social and Cultural Rights. It is to these contributions that we now turn.

UNIVERSAL SUFFRAGE, ECONOMIC AND SOCIAL RIGHTS

In principle, the Enlightenment offered all white men the option to become voting members of society should they acquire enough property, earn a sufficient income, and pay adequate tax. In the industrial reality of the nineteenth century, however, the gap between the rich and the working class had grown so wide that this opportunity had become a mere chimera. Efforts to address voting rights inequities thus went hand in hand with hopes to redress economic and social disparities. Today, it is commonly held that civil and political rights are linked with the liberal tradition, whereas social and economic rights are usually associated with a socialist ideology. This perception is further evidenced by the United Nations' ratification of two separate covenants: the International Covenant on Civil and Political Rights and the International Covenant on Economic, Social and Cultural Rights. A careful review of the nineteenth century, however, shows that for most socialists, the struggles for political and economic rights were closely linked. Their demands, however, were strongly opposed by aristocratic forces in the first decades after the Congress of Vienna and were later resisted by the bourgeoisie wherever it had ascended to power.

Despite a brief revival of Jacobinism at the end of the eighteenth century, spearheaded by the French agitator Gracchus Babeuf (1760–1797), the radical forces of the French Revolution had been effectively suppressed. Babeuf perished on the scaffold, after conspiring in 1795 to lead a nascent urban proletariat against the establishment of a bourgeois regime.[38] His spirit, however, survived underground during the Napoleonic regime, the Congress of Vienna, and the Restoration (1815–1830), taking the shape of conspiratorial sects. Babeuf's successor, Michel Buonarroti (1761–1837), escaped abroad after the French government retaliated against Babeuf's "Conspiracy of the Equals," and spent the remainder of his life transmitting Babouvist thought to secret societies such as the Carbonari, which flourished in western Europe.[39] Babeuf and his followers had concluded that as long as the propertyless were restricted from political participation, they would have to fight an uphill battle to gain equal economic and social rights.

The republican uprisings following the July revolution of 1830 and liberal victories against conservative strongholds throughout Europe in the 1830s inflamed the spirit of many progressive thinkers. In France, liberals quickly discovered that the democratic tone assumed by the new monarchy in 1830 was a posture that concealed Louis-Philippe's love for power. While the doctrine of divine right was expunged from the 1830 constitution, and the power of the king slightly restricted by the establishment of two legislative chambers, alteration to the electoral system was minimal. A proposal to grant all taxpayers the right to vote was hastily eliminated from discussion. The French bourgeoisie was, nonetheless, endowed with electoral power.[40] The European middle class gained similar electoral successes in Spain, Belgium, and Greece, though its efforts were aborted in Poland, Germany, and Italy.

If the tocsin of freedom had sounded once again for many European liberals, nothing happened to advance the case of the working class in France or elsewhere. Frustrated and deprived of voting rights, many progressive thinkers began to work tenaciously for the eradication of unequal property, which was now seen as the key obstacle in the fight for political equality. Having turned to socialism while a member of the Charbonnerie (the French branch of the Carbonari) during the Restoration, the French thinker Etienne Cabet (1788–1856) imagined in his *Voyage en Icarie* (1839) a system of utopian communism in which private property would be excluded and every social inequality, down to differences in clothing, would be eradicated. All citizens would give the benefits of their labor to the community on an equal basis and take from a collective storehouse whatever they needed.[41]

Such early socialist visions aiming toward equality and social welfare were fostered by the rapid industrialization of England and France. Germany and Italy during this period, by contrast, were undergoing only the first faint stirrings of the industrial revolution. The working class was still a feeble minority, upstaged by liberals' demands for more civil and political rights. Admiring the progress of social ideals in England and France, the German philosopher Moses Hess (1812–1875) argued in *The Philosophy of the Act* (1842) that it was first necessary to develop a material philosophy to enact freedom and equality. "The time has come," he wrote, "for the philosophy of spirit to make a philosophy of action."[42]

Progressive thinkers in Italy were undergoing a similar evolution in their thinking. Yet for most Italians, the goal of social justice required a prior accomplishment: winning the fight against the Habsburg yoke. Giuseppe Mazzini (1805–1872), the head of the liberal Giovane Italia (the Italian youth movement), led the national struggle. He asked his compatriots, "What is a Country . . . but the place in which our individual rights are most secure? What is a Society, but a collection of men who have agreed to bring the strength of the many in support of the rights of each?"[43]

That industrialism was most advanced in England may account for the early development of a self-conscious British working class, able to coordinate its efforts and petition for social rights. Distressed masses of factory and craft workers gathered in English cities. Those who managed to keep their jobs were often forced to work in unsanitary and dangerous conditions. For most of the people working in the blazing, satanic mills of industrial civilizations, these were truly "the worst of times," with seasons of never-ending darkness and winters of eternal despair.[44] Because they lacked the political access necessary to promote peaceful change, insurrection was in the air. Fearing the spread of the 1830s revolutions on the continent, British conservatives reluctantly yielded. In 1832, they passed the First Reform Bill, which widened male suffrage. Though conservative in nature, the bill opened the door for other concessions.

A new Poor Law (also called the Speenhamland Law) was enacted in 1834, resulting in an increase in spending for public relief, but it was accompanied by a policy that viewed pauperism among workers as a moral failing. Under the new law, all relief to the able-bodied in their own homes was forbidden, so that all who wished to be granted help had to live in workhouses, where, to discourage relief seekers, conditions were intentionally made callous and humiliating. Ultimately, all claimants were forced to forfeit their civil and political rights.[45] The Reform Bill of 1832 and the Poor Law amendment of 1834 could be regarded, as Karl Polanyi later argued, "as the starting point of modern capitalism . . . because they put an end to the rule of the benevolent landlord and his allowance system."[46]

Additional reform acts followed. In 1835, the Municipal Corporations Act standardized and modernized the local governments in English cities, dismantled the old local oligarchies, and paved the way for a uniform electoral and administrative machinery. More important was the passing of the 1833 Factory Act, which forbade employing children less than nine years old in the textile mills. In 1842, the employment of women as well as girls and boys under ten in coal mines was prohibited. The greatest success for the working class arrived in 1847 with the Ten Hours Act, which limited the daily work hours of women, children, and men.

Efforts to promote these social rights were led by the Chartist Movement. When the Reform Bill continued to exclude workers from political power, the Chartists, under the guidance of London radical William Lovett (1800–1877), drafted a People's Charter (1837) calling for equal representation, universal suffrage, the abolition of property qualifications, annual reelection of parliaments, and vote by secret ballot. Those who remained excluded from political participation, Chartists claimed, could only see the laws as "despotic enactments." "The universal political right of every human being," they held, "is superior and stands apart from all customs, forms, or ancient usage; a fundamental right not in the power of man to confer, or justly to deprive him of."[47] Their petition, however, was rebuffed in 1838. It would be several more decades before the enactment of universal male suffrage, and women's voting rights would not be granted until the following century (see the last section of this chapter).

Meanwhile, in France, the socialist anarchist Pierre-Joseph Proudhon (1809–1865) launched a radical attack against the problem of poverty intensified by industrialization. "Property is theft!" he proclaimed in his famous inflammatory essay *What Is Property? or an Inquiry into the Principle of Right and of Government* (1840). While he acclaimed most of the basic rights celebrated by the French Declaration of the Rights of Man and of the Citizen—namely, the rights to liberty, equality, and security—he rejected the idea that property was an inalienable right. Property, Proudhon maintained, is an asocial right: it ossifies inequalities without offering corrective measures. "The rich man's desire for property has to be continually defended against the poor man's desire for property. What a contradiction!"[48]

A few years later, in Germany, Karl Marx reached similar conclusions. The French declaration, he remarked, announced that inalienable rights are those in defense of equality, liberty, security, and property. Yet if the right to property is the right to enjoy and dispose of property regardless of its impact on society as a whole, then it is nothing but the right to self-interest. As long as property rights are the concrete application of liberty and equality, then liberty and equality are nothing more than an abstraction, or rather the rights of egoistic and "selfish monads." As for the concept of the right to security, he claimed, the declaration and the French constitution of 1793 did not raise civil society above egoism. "On the contrary," Marx wrote, "security is the insurance of its egoism." The

Declaration of the Rights of Man and of the Citizen, he added, did not celebrate the rights of man as a citizen, but secured the rights of "the bourgeois, who is considered to be the essential and true man."[49]

General Cavaignac's merciless use of force to defend liberal political gains against the 1848 Bloody June Days rebels seemed to prove Marx correct. If socialist forces were defeated in 1848, their hope for manhood suffrage was not, and it was initially adopted in the new liberal republican constitution of that year. At first, the French National Assembly of November 4 provided all male citizens of twenty years of age and in possession of civil rights with the right to vote. Electors were allowed to select

---

THE CHARTIST PETITION ADOPTED AT
THE CROWN AND ANCHOR MEETING, LONDON, 1837

A LAW FOR EQUALLY REPRESENTING THE PEOPLE OF GREAT BRITAIN AND IRELAND

That the United Kingdom be divided into 200 electoral districts; dividing, as nearly as possible, an equal number of inhabitants; and that each district do send a representative to Parliament.

UNIVERSAL SUFFRAGE

That every person producing proof of his being 21 years of age, to the clerk of the parish in which he has resided six months, shall be entitled to have his name registered as a voter. . . .

ANNUAL PARLIAMENTS

That a general election do take place on the 24th of June in each year . . .

NO PROPERTY QUALIFICATIONS

That there shall be no property qualifications for members; but on a requisition, signed by 200 voters, in favour of any candidate being presented to the clerk of the parish in which they reside, such candidate shall be put in the nomination. And the list of all candidates nominated throughout the districts shall be stuck on the church door in every parish, to enable voters to judge of their qualifications.

VOTE BY BALLOT

That each voter must vote in the parish in which he resides. That each parish provide as many balloting boxes as there are candidates proposed in the district; and that a temporary place be fitted up in each parish church for the purpose of secret voting. . . .

SITTINGS AND PAYMENTS TO MEMBERS

. . . That all electoral officers shall be elected by universal suffrage. . . .

From Dorothy Thompson, The Early Chartists, 64–66.

---

a president for a term of four years and a single-chamber legislature for a term of three years.[50] France thus became the first country in the world to adopt universal manhood suffrage. Yet within two months of the election, on May 31, 1850, the National Assembly reimposed property qualifications on the right to vote.[51]

Watching the French events from England, where he had fled out of fear for his life, Louis Blanc decried the betrayal by liberal forces, forces that he, along with other socialists, had helped to overthrow Louis-Philippe's monarchy. Highlighting the inconsistency of his liberal and conservative compatriots, he exclaimed:

> But the poor man, you say, has the *right* to better his position? So! And what difference does it make, if he has not the power to do so. What does the right to be cured matter to a sick man whom no one is curing? Right considered abstractly is the mirage that has kept the people in abused condition since 1789. . . . Let us say it then for once and for all: freedom consists, not only in the RIGHTS that have been accorded, but also in the power given men to develop and exercise their faculties, under the reign of justice and the safeguard of law.[52]

Blanc had hoped, as he explained in 1848, that a newly constituted government would gradually transform privately owned workplaces into social workshops designed to alleviate the lot of the needy.

The right to work, he further claimed, was an essential right that needed to be secured by the state. "That which the proletarians lack to free themselves," he explained, "are the tools of labor; these the government must furnish them."[53] In this respect, he echoed Charles Fourier, who had earlier maintained the futility of wrangling over the rights of man "without thinking of the most essential, that of labor, without which the others are nothing."[54] Observing the dismantling of the social workshop in Paris and the perpetuation of oppressive workhouses, Marx, in "The Class Struggles in France, 1848–1850," cast doubt on such a right being secured by a capitalist state built on an inequitable economic system of forced wage labor. "The right to work," he deplored, "is in the bourgeois sense an absurdity, a miserable pious wish."[55]

Despite the Bloody June Days massacre, the events of 1848 spurred renewed political efforts by the Chartist Movement in England. Bearing in mind the events that led to the restriction of manhood suffrage in France, Marx turned his attention to England, and wrote in the *New York Daily Tribune* (1850) that "the carrying of universal suffrage in England would be a far more socialistic measure than anything which has been honoured with that name on the Continent."[56] Lord John Russell (1792–

1878), who had been instrumental in the passing of the first electoral Reform Bill, ended up backing the Chartist electoral reform proposals in 1852.[57] Yet the Second Reform Act was passed only in 1867, after years of parliamentary resistance.

Whereas the First Reform Bill added some two hundred thousand voters to the rolls, the Second Reform Act added nearly a million. In some towns the electorate was tripled or quadrupled. Despite significant changes, the Second Reform Act was challenged. When workers protested property and residency requirements, the illiteracy of the working class was invoked to limit their right to vote. Even the liberal progressive thinker John Stuart Mill (1806–1879), who favored representative democracy, continued to argue in 1861 for the literacy requirement: "[U]niversal teaching must precede universal enfranchisement."[58]

Additional legislation improved the Second Reform Act and managed to erode the political advantage of the middle and upper classes. To counter political corruption, the 1872 Ballot Act was introduced, and in 1883 the New Corruption Practices Act outlined penalties for bribery; in 1884 an extension of the franchise was offered for borough and county voters; and in 1885 new legislation ensured a better distribution of parliamentary seats in order to guarantee equitable political representation for industrial centers.[59] The control of the upper class in voting matters would finally be broken by the Act of 1918, which adopted universal suffrage without further qualification, assuring a final Chartist and socialist victory in the fight for voting rights.[60]

The United States underwent a similar battle to secure manhood suffrage. The constitution of New Hampshire (1784) might have stipulated that "all government of right originates from the people, is founded on the consent and instituted for the general good," but in practice, the United States had not abandoned its oligarchic political system. By 1822, however, rapid industrialization had gathered in the towns a landless and voteless class that demanded political leverage to lessen its economic hardship. The journalist and founder of the New York Working Man's Party George Henry Evans (1805–1856) voiced the discontent of that class, pointing out that "the history of the political parties in this state is a history of political inequities, all tending to enacting and enforcing oppressive and unequal laws."[61] His and the similar pleas of others fell on deaf ears. Many, like chief justice of the supreme court of New York James Kent (1763–1847), opposed liberalizing elections, suggesting that "universal suffrage jeopardizes property and puts it into the power of the poor and the profligate to control the affluent."[62]

A literacy test requiring an ability to read the constitution further limited manhood suffrage. In the South, white illiterates had the alternative of a poll tax for which few blacks could qualify. Soon after the Civil War, William Wells Brown (1842–1884), considered the first black American novelist, decried such discrimination: "It is said that the slaves are too ignorant to exercise the elective franchise judiciously. To this we reply, they are as intelligent as the average 'poor white' and were intelligent enough to the Unionist during the Great struggle, when the Federal Government needed friends. . . . Impartial suffrage is what we demand for the colored people of the Southern States."[63]

When electoral restrictions did not suffice to prevent blacks from exercising their right to vote, extralegal measures were used to keep them from going to the polls. Under what were known as Jim Crow laws, which characterized Southern practice starting in the 1870s, racial segregation of whites and blacks was enforced on public transportation and in schools, parks, cemeteries, theaters, restaurants, and other public spheres. In addition to the literacy test restriction, these and other discriminatory laws, backed by orchestrated policies of intimidation (including lynching), prevented blacks from implementing their right to vote. Representative of the techniques employed to bar blacks from the voting pool were the ones used in North Carolina, where a "Call to Arms" urged "Anglo-Saxons" on the eve of an election to "go to the polls tomorrow and if you find the Negro voting tell him to leave the polls and if he refuses, kill him, shoot him down in his tracks."[64] Not until 1954 did the United States Supreme Court rule Jim Crow legislation unconstitutional.

Such legal remedies, however, can leave open wounds. Few blacks are surprised today when disproportionate numbers of votes in black neighborhoods are disqualified, as famously occurred in Florida during the 2000 presidential election. In that case, the use of obsolete voting machines was compounded by the state's use of a highly inaccurate list of purported felons—a list used to prevent thousands of innocent blacks from exercising their legal right to vote. That election only confirmed lingering feelings among blacks of alienation from the political system. Furthermore, the openly disproportionate influence of the wealthy in political financing has stimulated a struggle for campaign reform reminiscent of the nineteenth-century socialists' fight against property qualification as a prerequisite for voting rights.

However imperfect today's American electoral system, one should not forget the distance traveled since socialists launched the first campaigns for universal voting rights. As workers first entered the electorate, labor parties were created to harness their votes.[65] Yet whether in the United States or in Europe, male workers' representation started out disproportionately low and remained so even after the introduction of extensive male suffrage. This was generally due to the required voting age (generally twenty-five years and older) and residency requirements (typically one year). In some countries, such as Germany and Sweden, socialists sought temporary alliances with liberal parties in their pursuit of additional electoral reforms. In that quest for electoral allies, however, socialists ended up obscuring the class character of their demand for social rights. The designation *working class* or *proletariat* gave way to terms like *all the oppressed, the exploited, the poor, the masses, the people,* and finally even *the nation.*[66] The diminishing role of strictly economic arguments in advancing the cause of voting rights may have helped shore up the myth that the struggle for universal voting rights was liberal—rather than socialist—in its origin.

As long as property qualification continued to limit American and European workers' ability to vote, socialists headed the fight for equal political and economic rights. To counter claims that only educated citizens should vote, many called for public education and educational reforms. In the spirit of Robert Owen's 1816 plea for children's education, Marx and Engels called in 1840 for recognizing the right of children to a free public education.[67] "The *rights* of children and juveniles must be vindicated," Marx reiterated in 1868. Provision for education and other legislation protecting the rights of children, he further argued, needed to be "enforced by the power of the state."[68]

Some could argue that the right to education would not affect the right to citizenship, since children by definition could not vote.[69] Yet as Marx aptly suggested, "[T]he more enlightened part of the working class understands that the future of its class, and therefore of mankind, altogether depends upon the formation of the working class."[70] It follows that "the right of education is a genuine social right of citizenship, because the aim of education during childhood is to shape the future of adulthood."[71] These positions were not fought for in vain. By the end of the nineteenth century, it was generally understood that political democracy needed an educated electorate and that technologically advanced manufacturing needed educated workers and technicians. Hence, opposition waned and elementary education became free and compulsory. Later, in the twentieth century, advocates of children's rights were once again vindicated when article 26 of the Universal Declaration of Human Rights and article 13 of the Covenant on Economic, Social and Cultural Rights proclaimed that childhood education was a fundamental human right.

The right to a free education, to work, to safe working conditions, to public health care, to form free associations and trade unions—all core clauses of the Covenant on Economic, Social and Cultural Rights—originated in the filthy and hazardous conditions of European and American mines and factories. While such social rights were first invoked in the nineteenth century, social legislative protections would receive greater attention in the twentieth century, which saw the rise of the welfare state. Outside of western Europe, the United States, Australia, and New Zealand, labor legislation progressed at an even slower pace. The hardwon legislation promoting voting rights and the right to form trade unions (such as the 1824 and 1871 British acts and the 1884 French act), however, laid the groundwork for later progress in collective bargaining efforts and for a new activism in the struggle to advance social rights.

If nineteenth-century political and social gains seem small from today's perspective, they were nonetheless critical and were attained at the price of relentless struggle. Political obstacles to workers' demands led many to dream of revolution: when the forces of power relented, reformist visions gained in appeal. Just as eighteenth-century liberal activists debated the best means for promoting civil rights, the nineteenth-century

---

KARL MARX, ON EDUCATION AND CHILD LABOR, 1866

Proceeding from this standpoint, we say that no parent and no employer ought to be allowed to use juvenile labour, except when combined with education.

By education we understand three things.

Firstly: *mental education.*

Secondly: *bodily education,* such as is given in schools of gymnastics, and by military exercise.

Thirdly: *technological training,* which imparts the general principles of all processes of production, and simultaneously initiates the child and young person in the practical use and handling of the elementary instruments of all trades. . . .

The combination of paid productive labour, mental education, bodily exercise and polytechnic training, will raise the working class far above the level of the higher middle classes.

It is self-understood that the employment of all persons from [nine] and to seventeen years (inclusively) in nightwork and all health-injuring trades must be strictly prohibited by law.

From "Instruction to the Delegates to the Geneva Congress," in Marx, *The First International and After,* vol. 3 of *Political Writings,* 88–91.

---

socialist agenda considered which measures needed to be implemented in the face of political adversity. Like their eighteenth-century human rights precursors, socialists debated the use of political strategies ranging from reform to revolution.

CHALLENGING CAPITALISM AND THE STATE

The State or International Organization?
Political Reform or Revolution?

Most Enlightenment human rights visionaries imagined that a peaceful world, predicated upon liberal rights, would be realized during the coming era of free economic exchange. "Civil freedom," Kant declared early on, "can no longer be easily infringed without disadvantage to commerce."[72] During the same period, Adam Smith painted an image of the common good shaped by an "invisible hand," able to orchestrate individuals' pursuit of self-interest. "If commerce were permitted to act to the universal extent it is capable," wrote Thomas Paine, echoing Kant and Smith, "it would extirpate the system of war, and produce a revolution in the uncivilized state of Governments."[73] Free commerce, most liberals believed, would encourage peace and the spread of republican states by rendering individuals and as well as nations useful to one another.

With an industrial bourgeoisie on the rise, aristocrats on the defensive, and workers living in urban poverty, the Enlightenment's association of commerce among liberal states with peace and justice was nonetheless vividly challenged. Whereas anarchists rejected the mechanism of the state as a viable instrument for promoting human rights, socialists were split between proponents of the revolutionary overthrow of the capitalist state and advocates of state reforms. Despite differences over tactics, all endorsed the development of an international socialist organization able to harmonize global human rights activism. Yet that organization, the First International, ultimately failed to develop a coordinated international policy prior to World War I, a failure that reflected national as well as strategic divisions and culminated in the collapse of the International.

In the 1830s, and more specifically after 1848, many radicals distrusted the capacity of the state to become more inclusive and to promote political and social rights for all citizens. Anarchists rejected the idea of bestowing upon the state the task of implementing human rights principles, an idea that was influential among the early socialists; the state was seen as inherently a tool of elite interests and domination. "Politics," claimed Proudhon, "is the science of liberty. The government of man by man (under whatever name it be disguised) is oppression."[74] In the same spirit, the Russian anarchist Mikhail Bakunin (1814–1876) later proclaimed, "[T]he state is authority, domination and force, organized by the property owning and so-called enlightened classes against the masses."[75] Any political ideals, once institutionalized by regimes of any type, he argued, ended up serving the interests of the elite in power. Recurrent general strikes, claimed Bakunin and other anarchists, were the only way to assure the essential rights of the working class in its struggle against the inexorable tendency toward state corruption.[76]

Marx launched a scathing critique of anarchist positions regarding the state. Deploring with the anarchists the exclusionary nature of the emerging capitalist state, he nevertheless viewed the state apparatus as a necessary mechanism for regulating conflicts in civil society. Bonapartism was inevitable in France after 1850, he contended, for none of the warring classes was sufficiently well organized to run the country. In circumstances pitting one group against the other, the state ends up serving a consolidating role, Marx wrote, anticipating the insightful reflections of Antonio Gramsci (1891–1937) on the role of the state and civil society.[77] Yet when the state arose to settle class antagonisms, Engels observed, "[I]t is normally the state of the most powerful, economically ruling class, which by its means becomes also the politically ruling class, and so acquires new means of holding down and exploiting the oppressed class."[78]

While strikes were seen as an important way for the working class to dramatize its plight, Marx and Engels rejected the anarchist view of strikes as ends in themselves and maintained that strikes alone were inadequate to eradicate existing social inequities. What workers actually needed to do, Marx stated, was to follow the example of the bourgeoisie by seizing the reins of state power. The bourgeoisie had so far been involved in a constant battle against aristocrats and domestic and foreign competitors; and "[i]n all these battles [the bourgeoisie] sees itself compelled to appeal to the proletariat, to ask for its help, and thus to drag it into the political arena." Yet ironically, in these conflicts, "[T]he bourgeoisie itself . . . supplies the proletariat with its own elements of political and general education; in other words, it furnishes the proletariat with weapons for fighting the bourgeoisie."[79] Henceforth, like the French bourgeoisie who stole the political stage in 1848, marginalizing and ex-

ecuting the radicals who helped them, proletarians needed to capture the
state, Marx urged, and to establish a dictatorship "as a transit point to
the abolition of class distinctions generally, to the abolition of all the
relations of production on which they rest."[80]

At the Hague Congress of 1872, Marx modified his revolutionary
position, asserting that the means for achieving socialist goals were not
identical everywhere. "We know," Marx proclaimed, "that the institutions, customs and traditions in the different countries must be taken into
account; and we do not deny the existence of countries like America, England, and . . . I might add Holland, where the workers may achieve their
aims by peaceful means. But this is not true of all countries."[81] As for the
idea of the meaning of the dictatorship of the proletariat, the German social democrat Karl Kautsky (1854–1938) noted, Marx had referred to it
as *a state of affairs* and not *as a form of government,* a state of affairs
that must necessarily arise when the proletariat achieves political power
and finds itself fighting against reactionary forces. For Marx, the state of
affairs that existed during the Paris Commune, added Kautsky, was not
predicated on the abolition of all forms of democracy. Indeed, as Marx
explained, "The Commune was formed of the municipal councilors, chosen by *universal suffrage* in the various wards of the town . . . *universal
suffrage* was to serve the people constituted in communes, as individual
suffrage serves every other employer in the search for the workmen and
managers in his business."[82] No matter the intensity of his initial dis-

---

FRIEDRICH ENGELS, ON VIOLENCE, "PRINCIPLES OF COMMUNISM," 1847

Question 16: Will it be possible to bring about the abolition of private property by
peaceful methods?

Answer: It is to be desired that this could happen, and Communists certainly would
be the last to resist it. The Communists know only too well that all conspiracies
are not only futile but even harmful. They know only too well that revolutions are
not made deliberately and arbitrarily, but that everywhere and at all times they
have been the necessary outcome of circumstances entirely independent of the
will and the leadership of particular parties and entire classes. But they also see
that the development of the proletariat is in nearly every civilised country forcibly
suppressed, and that thus the opponents of the Communists are working with all
their might towards a revolution. Should the oppressed proletariat in the end be
goaded into a revolution, we Communists will then defend the cause of the proletarians by deed just as well as we do now by word.

From "Principles of Communism," in Karl Marx and Friedrich Engels, *Collected Works,* vol. 6,
349–350.

---

agreement with reformist and utopian socialist views, Marx's revolutionary perspective was softened in light of the social gains he saw occurring in several of the advanced industrial countries.

With the spread of labor movements and the passing of social welfare laws, reformist positions gained more influence. In Germany, the socialist Ferdinand Lassalle (1825–1864) argued in 1862 that the state, despite conservative gains in the French elections of 1848 and 1849, was the sole possible promoter of freedom and human rights. It was ultimately the "state," Lassalle suggested, "whose function is to carry on this development of freedom, this development of the human race until its freedom is reached."[83] If his position had initially been marginalized as the German Social Democratic Party rose to prominence in the 1880s, it now became linked to Marx's reformist strand of thought, which gained legitimacy and influenced socialist leaders like Eduard Bernstein (1850–1932) and Karl Kautsky.[84]

In England, Fabian (or evolutionary) socialists espoused a similar perspective. The British Fabian Sydney Webb (1859–1947) assumed that the inherent flaws of capitalism would necessarily lead to the incremental development of socialism. If economic conditions were ripe, the Fabians believed, local and cooperative communities would gradually take control of the means of production and distribution.[85] Fabians observed that many inroads had already been made, and they expressed confidence that "the inevitable convergence of all the economic tendencies towards Socialism" was imminent.[86] The eloquent French socialist Jean Jaurès (1849–1914) echoed their views, suggesting that the moral and socialist development of humankind was slow but ineluctable. Like Marx, Jaurès identified the evolution of history as interweaving between ideals and material conditions; and like other evolutionists, he explained the development of humanity in biological terms, as the "product of a long physiological evolution" from animality to the state.[87]

Whether the capitalist state's willingness to promote human rights was an absurd proposition, as anarchists and revolutionary socialists argued, or a possibility, as socialist revisionists maintained, all deplored what they regarded as the nefarious international impacts of capitalism on social rights. As Marx and Engels prophetically argued in 1848, capitalism did not stop at national borders: "It compels all nations, on pain of extinction, to adopt the bourgeois mode of production."[88]

Since the state was permeable to the imperatives of the market and too weak to counter social ills resulting from the emerging international economy, the institutionalization of working-class solidarity was becoming a necessity. "Workers of the world, unite!" became the socialist rallying cry after 1848. Inspired by the spontaneous efforts of workers in London and Paris, and in support of the 1863 Polish national rising, Marx reiterated his famous motto in the 1864 Inaugural Address of the Workingmen's Association, a federative human rights organization. With the establishment of the First International (1864–1876), well before the League of Nations, the International Labor Organization, and the United Nations, workers' political and economic rights were for the first time endorsed and actively promoted by an institution with representatives from around the world.

Though the members of the First International agreed on what constituted socialist rights, debates over strategies of implementation quickly led to deep cleavages.[89] Bakunin and other anarchists favored a federal order without a state, along with general strikes and other forms of direct action by the working class. They regarded not only the state but

---

**KARL MARX, INAUGURAL ADDRESS
OF THE WORKINGMEN'S INTERNATIONAL ASSOCIATION, 1864**

Past experience has shown how disregard of that bond of brotherhood which ought to exist between the workmen of different countries, and incite them to stand firmly by each other in all their struggles for emancipation, will be chastised by the common discomfiture of their incoherent efforts. This thought prompted the working men of different countries assembled on September 28, 1864, in public meeting at St. Martin's Hall, to found the International Association.

Another conviction swayed that meeting.

If the emancipation of the working classes requires their fraternal concurrence of different nations, how are they to fulfill that great mission with a foreign policy in pursuit of criminal designs, playing upon national prejudices, and squandering in piratical wars the people's blood and treasure. . . . The shameless approval, mock sympathy, or idiotic indifference, with which the upper classes of Europe have witnessed [European power politics], have taught the working classes the duty to master themselves the mysteries of international politics; to watch the diplomatic acts of their respective Governments; to counteract them, if necessary, by all means in their power; when unable to prevent, to combine in simultaneous denunciations, and to vindicate the simple laws of morals and justice, which ought to govern the relations of private individuals, as the rules paramount of the intercourse of nations.

The fight for such a foreign policy forms part of the general struggle for the emancipation of the working classes.

Proletarians of all countries, Unite!

From Karl Marx and Friedrich Engels, *Collected Works,* vol. 20, 12–13.

---

later the International itself—the two possible political means by which human rights could be enforced—as centralist and authoritarian by nature. British trade unionists, on the other hand, whose activities had been legalized by the Trade Union Act of 1871, believed that working conditions could be enhanced through parliamentary reforms. While the influence of anarchists was dramatically weakened with the dissolution of the First International, additional controversies between anarchists, reformists, and revolutionaries would continue beyond the establishment of the Second International (1889–1914).

Unlike the First International, the Second International was based mainly on organized parties from various nations. It had no mandatory power but was recognized by its member parties as their highest moral authority. The International held congresses every two to four years to debate policy and orchestrate international working-class action. In 1890, it called for demonstrations every May Day in support of an eight-hour workday. Domestic political issues often became part of the agenda of the Second International. Marxism was the dominant ideology, though other trends and influences were also present. In 1896, anarchists were ultimately excluded from the International, leaving socialists to examine the validity of emerging revisionist thought.[90] At the 1900 Paris Congress, for instance, they accepted the possibility of joining a bourgeois government, as the French socialist Alexandre Millerand (1859–1943) had done a year earlier, as "a temporary expedient and . . . in exceptional cases."[91] At its next meeting, however, the International condemned the revisionist ideas of Eduard Bernstein, who had justified socialist support for colonialism. These debates over strategy and disputes over colonial matters and war would prove pivotal for the survival of the Second International.

Beyond State Boundaries: Colonialism, International War, or Pacifism?

One could argue that long before the socialists, such seventeenth-century thinkers as Grotius and Pufendorf, along with other international legal scholars, had already developed guidelines, drawn from natural law, for the purpose of preventing wars. Just wars were seen as a last resort, to be waged only for self-defense, the recovery of property, the pursuit of religious tolerance, or against tyrannical subjugation, and were legitimate only as long as they were conducted with restraint. A century later, in *Perpetual Peace*, Kant laid out a proposal for a confederation of nations to resolve conflicts, a project that would later inspire the First and Second Internationals. He also offered preventive and restraining measures to be adopted prior to or during wartime, such as the abolition of standing armies, the prohibition of foreign debts, the endorsement of less predatory regimes (such as those with republican constitutions), and the proscription of wars of extermination that would make perpetual peace possible only "on the vast graveyard of the human race."[92]

The Swiss J. Henri Dunant (1828–1910) continued that tradition in the nineteenth century, calling for the care of wounded soldiers at the battlefield. Soon after he witnessed the horror of the Battle of Solferino (1859), which pitted French and Italian troops against Austrian armies, he proposed to establish a permanent system of humanitarian assistance in wartime.[93] His efforts led to the ratification of the Geneva Convention (1864), a treaty that required all signatory states to secure the rights of the wounded and to respect the immunity of those providing assistance, regardless of their nationalities. The Hague Peace Conference

---

J. HENRI DUNANT, *MEMORY OF SOLFERINO*, 1862

At the entrance to the church was a Hungarian who never ceased to call out, begging for a doctor in heartbreaking Italian. A burst of grapeshot had ploughed into his back, which looked as if it had been furrowed with steel claws, laying bare a great area of red quivering flesh. The rest of his swollen body was all black and green, and he could find no comfortable position to sit or lie in. I moistened great masses of lint in cold water and tried to place this under him, but it was not long before gangrene carried him off. . . . The feeling one has of one's own utter inadequacy in such extraordinary and solemn circumstances is unspeakable. It is indeed, excessively distressing to realize that you can never do more than help those who are just before you—that you must keep waiting men who are calling out and begging you to come. When you start to go somewhere, it is hours before you get there, for you are stopped by one begging for help, then by another, held up at every step by the crowd of poor wretches who press before and about you. Then you find yourself asking: "why go to the right, when there are all these men on the left who will die without a word of kindness or comfort, without so much as a glass of water to quench their burning thirst?" The moral sense of all the importance of human life; the humane desire to lighten a little the torments of all these poor wretches, or restore their shattered courage; the furious and relentless activity which a man summons up at such moments: all these combine to create a kind of energy which gives one a positive craving to relieve as many as one can. . . . If an international relief society had existed at the time of Solferino . . . what endless good they could have done! . . . It is . . . important to reach an agreement and concert measures in advance, because when hostilities once begin, the belligerents are already ill-disposed to each other, and thenceforth regard all questions from the one limited standpoint of their own subjects.

(1899), which secured, along with the rights of victims, the rights of prisoners of war, was a catalyst for the establishment of the International Committee of the Red Cross and parallel institutions (such as the Ottoman Red Crescent Society and the Japanese Red Cross Society, or Nippon Seikijuji Sha).[94] The mushrooming numbers of trained medical personnel in combat zones as early as the 1864 Prussian-Danish war, the 1866 Austro-Prussian war, and the 1870–1871 Franco-Prussian war vindicated Dunant's quest for human compassion in wartime.[95]

Like Dunant, nineteenth-century socialists regarded themselves as heirs of eighteenth-century ideals of human rights and world peace. Yet they opposed the Enlightenment belief that peace could be secured in the competitive jungle of a free market society. If anything, wars were perceived as the end game of the economically advantaged class, which sought to promote its political and economic power worldwide. Inequities of property generated by laissez-faire economic policies, the socialist Rosa Luxemburg (1870–1919) and others charged, were not only at the root of social injustice but, as Rousseau had remarked early on, the source of wars between nations.[96] Wars would vanish once social and economic injustice disappeared, many hoped. Meanwhile, nearly every congress of the two Internationals opened with questions about how the workers of the world could prevent war.[97]

The 1868 Brussels Congress of the First International concluded that the Austro-Prussian War was "one between governments," in which workers were advised to be "neutral."[98] Similar statements were issued after the outbreak of the Franco-Prussian war, calling on "workers in every country not only to speak loudly and clearly against all such wars between peoples," but also to refuse all "work which might contribute to the killing of men." The International also launched a propaganda campaign "so as to make every worker who is obliged to join a standing army clear as to his human rights, and to prescribe to him, in the event of war breaking out, certain principles of conduct."[99] The 1886 London Congress of the Second International and the 1889 Congress of Paris reiterated the importance of workers' active resistance to war. They urged working-class representatives to vote against military credits, to denounce militarism, to advocate disarmament, to replace standing armies with popular militias, and to set up an international court of arbitration for the peaceful settlement of interstate disputes.[100]

By 1886, colonial disputes were threatening to spark wars between the great powers. Yet as early as 1865, the International had voiced its position on a "colonial" matter: the American Civil War. Most members

saw that conflict as a colonial war, since the South's institution of slavery was reminiscent of the colonialists' treatment of populations in the
areas they colonized. Soon after the establishment of the First International, Marx drafted a letter, signed by each member of the International
General Council, congratulating President Lincoln on his reelection. "If
resistance to the Slave Power was the reserved watchword of your first
election," Marx wrote to Lincoln, "the triumphant warcry of your reelection is, Death to slavery." The letter also pledged Lincoln the support of the European working class: "[T]he working men of Europe feel
sure that, as the American independence initiated a new era of ascendancy for the middle class, so the anti-American anti-slavery war will do
for the working classes."[101]

Beyond the American Civil War, colonial concerns divided many socialists. For instance, most socialists generally attributed Britain's war
against the Boer Republic in South Africa to the interest of British ruling elites in acquiring the profitable gold mines of South Africa. Yet some
Fabians, such as the famous British socialist George Bernard Shaw (1856–
1950), justified the war, suggesting that the natives of the Transvaal
needed to be protected from slavery and from extermination at the hands
of the Boer oligarchy. Colonialism was morally legitimate, Shaw wrote,
as long as it civilized the indigenous population.[102] While many Fabians
endorsed Shaw's views, the publication of his manifesto stirred the indignation of the British Labour movement.

Eduard Bernstein developed a similar position to the one advocated
by Shaw, in his defense of German efforts to gain a voice in the partition
of China. Colonialism, explained Bernstein, was justifiable as long as natural resources needed to be exploited. "Since we enjoy the tropics, . . .
there can be no real objection to our cultivating the crops ourselves."
"The right of savages to the soil they occupy," he further maintained,
could only be recognized as a conditional right. The cultivation of the
lands, rather than conquest, was what provided historical and legal title
to an occupier. Following Mill and other liberal "enlightened" imperialists, Bernstein argued that capitalism would help educate stagnant civilizations and lead them toward eventual independence.[103]

With few supporters, Bernstein's views, like Shaw's, were rebuffed by
his own party. In the Mainz Congress of 1900, the German Social Democratic Party reiterated its rejection of annexation of foreign land and
the exploitation of indigenous people.[104] Other labor parties, like those
in Belgium, France, and Italy, were beset by similar controversies over
colonial policies. Fifty years before Western liberal democracies followed

suit, the Amsterdam Congress adopted a resolution rejecting "the so-called civilizing mission, in terms of which capitalism seeks to justify its colonial policy," a policy that forced native peoples into servitude.[105]

At the turn of the century, the fear of a war among major powers, instigated by colonial disputes, still haunted socialists. The international socialist Congress of Stuttgart (1907) decided to adopt a clearer resolution against militarism and the ongoing arms race between the major powers:

> Wars between capitalist states are, as a rule, the outcome of the competition on the world market, for each state seeks not only to secure its existing markets, but also to conquer new ones. . . . If a war threatens to break out, it is the duty of the working classes and their parliamentary representatives . . . to exert every effort in order to prevent the outbreak of war by means they consider most effective. . . . In case war should break out anyway, it is their duty to intervene in favor of its speedy termination, and with all their powers to utilize the economic and political crisis created by the war to rouse the masses and thereby to hasten the downfall of capitalist rule.[106]

As relations among the European powers worsened, the next congress of the Second International restated its demand for an international arbitration court to settle disputes between nations, and it pledged its commitment to transnational actions among workers in the event of a war.

JOHN STUART MILL, ON COLONIALISM,
***CONSIDERATIONS ON REPRESENTATIVE GOVERNMENT*, 1861**

Free States, like all others, may possess dependencies, acquired either by conquest or by colonization; and our own is the greatest instance of the kind in modern history. It is a most important question, how such dependencies ought to be governed.

. . . [There are some] dependencies whose population is in a sufficiently advanced state to be fitted for representative government. But there are others which have not attained that state, and which, if held at all, must be governed by the dominant country, or by persons delegated for that purpose by it. This mode of government is as legitimate as any other, if it is the one which in the existing state of civilization of the subject people, most facilitates their transition to a higher stage of improvement. There are, as we have already seen, conditions of society in which vigorous despotism is in itself the best mode of government for training the people in what is specifically wanting to render them capable of a higher civilization.

From *Considerations on Representative Government*, in *Three Essays*, 401, 408.

The war clouds hovering over Europe did not disperse, however. A major conflict involving all the major powers was now imminent. The Kantian ideal of a federation of republics, peacefully bound by commercial ties, as had been advocated during the Enlightenment, seemed more illusory than ever, as the competition over markets continued to yield imperialist and nationalist policies. Surrendering to nationalist forces as soon as World War I began, the socialist parties abruptly dropped their positions and declared support for their respective governments. This "betrayal," decried by Rosa Luxemburg, Vladimir Lenin (1870–1924), and other socialist leaders, led to the final collapse of the Second International as Europe plunged into a long and bloody world war.

In short, just as the aftermath of the French Revolution had betrayed an earlier vision of human rights, nationalism, war, and divergences over strategy would now contribute to the unraveling of a powerful human rights movement. While hopes for the spread of social rights were suddenly curtailed by the outbreak of the twentieth century's first world war, the industrial revolution and the rise of socialism had nevertheless modified the early human rights discourse. If socialists were responsible for the first emulation of a supranational authority to resist either the aggressive politics of states or their colonial enterprises, their position also represented the first historical assertion that all humans, regardless of wealth, gender, race, or age, were entitled to both political and social rights. In this respect, they broadened the narrow definition of universalism they inherited from the Enlightenment, articulating a broad commitment to enhance simultaneously, rather than selectively, the rights of slaves, children, women, homosexuals, and Jews.

HUMAN RIGHTS FOR WHOM?

Notwithstanding enormous opposition, human rights progress was evident in the nineteenth century. Slavery was abolished nearly everywhere and manhood suffrage adopted in many industrialized countries by the end of the century. Still, although women's calls for voting rights could be heard loud and clear, most remained disenfranchised until the twentieth century. If child labor was now restricted and public education mandated in many countries, the road to child welfare was far from being completed. If homosexuality was now better tolerated as gender roles were redefined by industrialization, homophobia continued to prevail. If Jewish emancipation was on the rise in most European countries, so was the tide of anti-Semitism. Finally, whereas independence was recognized for many European nationalities, national liberation for the people of the colonies was still a distant dream.

The near-end of slavery and the enfranchisement of propertyless male citizens can be recorded as the main nineteenth century achievements on behalf of human rights. While the struggle for political and social rights was more predominant in countries with a high concentration of industrial workers, the call for the right to national self-determination was more prevalent in industrially backward and ethnically divided countries, such as the Austro-Hungarian and Ottoman Empires. Having begun with the story of efforts to promote social rights universally, this chapter ends by considering individuals' calls for self-determination and more particular rights, appeals that would further guide the direction of the twentieth-century human rights agenda.

Revolutionary France had prided itself on the emancipation of its slaves. In 1802, however, the wheel of progress came to a halt. Despite the resistance of black leaders such as Toussaint-Louverture (1743–1803) and Jacques Dessaline (1758–1806), Napoleon restored slavery in the French colonies.[107] Joseph-Arthur de Gobineau (1816–1882), among other intellectuals, reflected the mood of nineteenth-century racism, arguing that blacks and other "inferior" races belonged to a degenerate species: they "have not the same blood in [their veins], continual adulterations having affected the quality of [their] blood."[108] Great humanists did not escape racist beliefs. Hegel saw blacks as "children who remain immersed in their state of uninterested *naïveté*," resigned to their fate as slaves.[109] While philosophers succumbed to racism, eminent scientists proved willing to distort evidence in order to corroborate the perceived inequality of the races. The liberal biologist Charles Darwin (1809–1882) and the eugenicist Francis Galton (1822–1911), among many others, tendentiously interpreted and even altered their findings in support of their racist bias.[110]

It indeed required deep prejudice to ignore the horrors of the slave trade. Crammed into ships like cattle, many Africans died during their journey from disease, starvation, or the whip of their captors.[111] Those who survived could look forward to a life of despair, deprived of dignity and all human rights. Outraged, a French officer in Saint Domingue reported how planters mercilessly overworked their slaves and treated them "when old and infirm, worse than their dogs and horses."[112] If they even faintly resisted their calamitous life, they were cruelly punished or put to death. While visiting Guiana, a Dutch army officer witnessed "a girl of eighteen, suspended naked by her wrists from the trees, who had received a hundred lashes." When the Dutch officer interceded, the overseer doubled her punishment. Throughout the day, that officer also listened to a slave being flogged to death. "My ears were stunned," he wrote, "with the clang of the whip and the dismal yells of the wretched Negroes on whom it was exercised from morning to night."[113]

Objects of their owners' whims, many intrepid slaves nevertheless organized rebellions. Uprisings occurred in every slave-holding society. Throughout the eighteenth century, slave rebellions in China became sufficiently widespread that women were ultimately favored over men for slave labor. In the European colonies, slave rebellions broke out from the late eighteenth century onward, in Saint Domingue (1791), Jamaica (1760, 1798, and 1831–1832), Barbados (1816), and British Guiana (1823). With the 1802 French decision to resume slavery, the baton of the anti-slavery cause passed to Britain. While many abolitionists held racist attitudes, the cruel circumstances of slavery rallied the voices of the outraged. Popular pressure was such that in 1807 Britain abolished its slave trade. The anti-slavery movement was further invigorated when the British Parliament passed the Abolition Act of 1833, freeing slaves on its Caribbean plantations the following year.

The change in British policy had an immediate impact in Latin America, where Venezuela (1810), Argentina (1812), Chile (1823), Mexico (1829), and Peru (1854) all abolished slavery. Spain signed a treaty with Britain agreeing to abolish the slave trade by 1820, but the trade in fact continued in the remaining Spanish colonies until 1880. The British then turned their attention to Southeast Asia. If the Act 5 of 1843 enabled British courts not to enforce claims to a slave, the Penal Code of 1861 made holding a slave a crime. Moving onto the African continent, British forces took control of places such as Nigeria, Malawi, and Zanzibar that thrived on slavery, and abolished the institution in each country.[114]

In the United States, the problem was more complex than in Great Britain, since slavery was a domestic rather than a colonial problem. Though the United States had abolished slavery between 1777 and 1804 in all states north of Maryland, pro-slavery sentiment remained strong among owners of the great plantations of the Southern states. By the 1830s, facing continuous resistance from the Southern states, whose economy was heavily dependent on the labor-intensive production of cotton, some abolitionists resorted to militant activism. Exasperated by the cruelty of the status quo, William Lloyd Garrison (1805–1879), the founder of the American Anti-Slavery Society (1830–1870), threatened, "Let Southern oppressors tremble—let their secret abettors tremble—let their

Northern apologists tremble—let all the enemies of the persecuted blacks tremble."[115] He drew support from clergymen like Theodore Dwight Weld (1803–1895) and Theodore Parker (1810–1860); from intellectuals and literati like John Greenleaf Whittier (1807–1892), James Russell Lowell (1819–1891), and Lydia Maria Child (1802–1880); and not least from the free black community, notably Frederick Douglass (1817–1895) and William Wells Brown.[116]

Obstacles, however, hindered the progress of the abolitionist movement. The U.S. Constitution had left the question of slavery to individual states, and many believed that the anti-slavery crusade was jeopardizing the harmony of the Union. Yet the power of abolitionism would only increase as Northerners rose in indignation against the brutality of fugitive slave hunters, who had been encouraged by the Fugitive Law of 1850. Tension over slavery exacerbated the economic conflict between the industrial North and the agrarian South, and the South finally seceded in 1861, precipitating the Civil War. Starting with the goal of simply restoring the Union, President Abraham Lincoln decided in 1863 to proclaim the emancipation of all slaves throughout the Confederacy. At the end of the war, that edict paved the way for the Thirteenth Amendment (1865) to the United States Constitution, enfranchising former slaves in all states of the Union.

In the Caucasus and Central Asia, slavery had been converted into serfdom during the sixteenth and seventeenth centuries, thereby providing peasant serfs with slightly better rights than their previous status had afforded. By the nineteenth century, it became clear to Tsar Alexander II (1818–1881, r. 1855–1881) that that was not enough; hence, the first step he took toward modernizing Russia was to abolish serfdom. Convinced that it was better to abolish serfdom from above than to wait until the serfs begin to liberate themselves from below, Alexander II proclaimed a settlement on February 19, 1861, in which peasants were freed from serfdom and entitled to become owners of land.[117] (In reality, the terms were inauspicious for peasants. In his attempt to compensate landowners for their loss, the tsar demanded high prices for the purchase of land.) Other important reforms followed the emancipation act. By the end of the century, slavery was almost completely abolished worldwide, as Cuba (1880–1886), Brazil (1883–1888), and China (1910) followed the global anti-slavery trend. In Korea, where slavery had been officially abolished in 1898, the institution persisted until 1930.

One noteworthy aspect of these fights against slavery was the role of emerging international organizations and transnational activism. As early as 1815, responding to public outrage regarding slavery, delegates to the Congress of Vienna announced, in the Eight Power Declaration, that "the public voice in all civilized countries calls aloud for its prompt suppression."[118] If this statement paid only lip service to the anti-slavery cause, it nonetheless helped galvanize international activism against the slave trade. International campaigns brought together journalists and intellectuals from all over the world, and anti-slavery societies, such as the French Société des amis des noirs and the British and Foreign Society of the Abolition of the Slave Trade, all pressured governments to halt the slave trade.[119]

To foment international support, the British and Foreign Society of the Abolition of the Slave Trade sponsored its first World Anti-Slavery Conference in 1840.[120] Later, with the establishment of the First International in 1864, socialists also joined the transnational movement against slavery. All these anti-slavery efforts led to the General Act of the Berlin Conference (1884), which stipulated that "trading in slaves is forbidden in compatibility with principles of international law," and to other similar international documents enacted in the late nineteenth century.[121] In 1926, the League of Nations' adoption of the Convention to Suppress the Slave Trade and Slavery in the former German and Turkish colonies ultimately became (with some later amendments) the primary international document prohibiting the practice of slavery.

With the progress of the abolitionist cause and the emergence of socialism, the early social pleas of the Levellers, Diggers, and sansculottes had become central to the nineteenth-century human rights agenda. The end of slavery, albeit an important goal, was only one milestone toward political and social emancipation for workers regardless of color and sex. Many bourgeois who had joined the abolitionist movement were also driven by utilitarian motives. Adam Smith had provided landowners with such an instrumental rationale for abolition when he suggested, in 1776, that "[a] slave . . . who can acquire nothing but his maintenance, consults his own ease by making the land produce as little as possible over and above that maintenance."[122] On the other hand, he further explained, free workers cost their employers less because they are more parsimonious and efficient in maintaining themselves. By holding property, they "have a plain interest that the whole produce should be as great as possible, in order that their own proportion may be so."[123] During the first decades of the nineteenth century, labor-saving agricultural machinery and other changes affecting agrarian economies had strengthened the case against the cost-effectiveness of slave labor.[124]

Liberal defenders of property rights, like Smith, of course were unlikely to detect any irony in the observation that "free" workers might
be cheaper then slaves. The darker side of that calculation, however, was
not lost on Karl Marx, who observed in *Capital:*

> If the slave is a property of a particular *master;* the worker must indeed sell
> himself to capital; but not to a particular capitalist, and so within certain
> limitations, he may choose to sell himself to whomever he wishes. The
> effect of all these differences is to make the free worker's work more inten-
> sive, more continuous, more flexible and skilled than that of the slave, quite
> apart from the fact that they fit him for quite a different historical role.[125]

The role that Marx had in mind for workers was that of advancing the
new human rights agenda of the industrial age by demanding the actu-
alization of the universal promises of political and economic equality proclaimed during the French Revolution.

If socialists generally supported universal suffrage without distinction
as to race or sex, some, like the German socialist August Bebel (1840–
1913), feared that bourgeois "feminism" could undermine the agenda
of the party, while others argued that the struggle for women's suffrage
would best await the achievement of manhood suffrage.[126] In principle,
nevertheless, the right to vote was considered universal and inalienable,
an important means to alleviate the plight of the needy and to promote
social and economic rights. Thus, mobilization in pursuit of political
rights was directly linked to activism on behalf of economic and social
rights. Social welfare for the poor would no longer be left to whimsical,
charitable impulses at the margins of a market-driven distribution of
wealth, but would now be demanded as a right by a working-class electorate. As the main producers of the economic life of their societies, propertyless males now insisted on assuming a role that the Enlightenment
and industrial age had initially denied them: that of active citizen.

Though most women visibly contributed to the economic life of their
countries, they continued to be perceived as passive citizens. The transition to industrialization and to urban sites provided women, irrespective of economic background, with opportune venues in which to com-
municate their plight and champion their rights. Clara Zetkin (1857–
1933), a socialist feminist and a leading figure of the German Social Democratic Party, provided an insightful class analysis of the condition of
women in general since the inception of capitalism. "There is a woman
question," she stated, "for the women of the proletariat, of the middle

bourgeoisie and the intelligentsia, and of the Upper Ten Thousand; it takes various forms depending upon the class situation of these strata."[127]

Women of the Upper Ten Thousand, Zetkin observed, had the luxury of employing servants to perform household and childcare tasks. Should they "desire to give their lives a serious content," however, "they must first raise the demand for free and independent control over their property," a right they lost after marriage. Their struggle, she pointed out, was similar to that of the early liberals' struggle against the aristocratic elite for property rights. As women's working clubs and groups proliferated in the late nineteenth century, wealthy women became sponsors of such organizations. "[Club sponsors] must see life from our standpoint to know what we most need, and to do that they must be friends, not patrons, and in helping us they help themselves," proclaimed one club member.[128]

As market competition enabled large firms to drive small-scale producers to ruin, the economic condition of women from the petty-bourgeoisie and the middle class became more precarious. Fearing economic uncertainty, men of these circles began to "think twice or thrice before they decided to marry . . . and . . . are pushed into marriage to a lesser degree as social arrangements make a comfortable bachelor life possible even without a legal wife."[129] Industrialization also ended up creating a growing pool of unmarried, educated women who, postponing or dreading the prospect of economically unstable marriages, joined the workforce for the first time. In such milieus, women demanded equal pay for equal work, as well as the right to equal access to education that would enable them to enter white-collar professions. Without questioning the economic system, explained Zetkin, they competed with men at every level of professional activity. When male resistance persisted, they organized and intensified their political struggle. Women's militancy had found a new impetus, as suffragette organizations mushroomed in Europe and America throughout the late nineteenth century.

Working-class women were without doubt those most afflicted by industrialization. They did not have to fight for the right to enter the workplace, like their middle-class counterparts, argued Zetkin. They were already there, used and exploited as the cheapest segment of the labor force of the emerging capitalist system. Working long hours in textile factories or in horrendous conditions in the mines and metal industries, they also assumed childcare responsibilities; at the same time, they were deprived of the extended family support system that had prevailed in peasant societies.[130] "Neither as a person nor as a woman or wife does [the working class woman] have the possibility to live a full life as an individual," deplored Zetkin.[131] Hence, her struggle would not be directed against the men of her own class, but would be linked to the proletarian campaign against all forms of exploitation, Zetkin suggested, echoing Engels and Bebel.

The suffragette struggle was indeed incomplete for Bebel, who argued that "if the bourgeois suffragists would achieve their aims and would bring about equal rights for men and women, they would still fail to abolish that sex slavery which marriage, in its present form, is to countless women; they would fail to abolish prostitution; they would fail to abolish the economic dependence of wives."[132] Marriage based on love and yearned for by the heroic female characters of Jane Austen's and Emily Brontë's novels, and by many suffragettes of that time, did not guarantee economic independence for women. For Engels, echoing Bebel, it perpetuated women's economic dependence and provided extramarital opportunities for unfaithful men. A true "love marriage," suggested Engels, "was proclaimed as a human right and indeed not only as a *droit de l'homme,* one of the rights of man, but also, for once in a way, as a *droit de la femme,* one of the rights of woman."[133] Despite the reaffirmation of Bebel, Engels, Zetkin, and others of socialist solidarity with women's rights, the suffragette movement throughout Europe and in the United States was primarily liberal in character.

Early victories of the suffragette movement were achieved in New Zealand (1893), Australia (1902), Finland (1906), and Norway (1913), which became the first countries to grant women the right to vote in national elections, an achievement realized after only a decade of women's activism.[134] The struggle for women's voting rights became particularly intense in the United States and Great Britain in the mid- to late nineteenth century. In the United States, at the Seneca Falls Convention in 1848, middle- and upper-class women called for general principles of equality between the sexes: the rights to own property, to custody of their children in case of divorce, to keep their own earnings, to sign contracts, to serve on juries, and to equal education. Their aspirations were closely associated with those of the abolitionist movement, for which they had worked assiduously. For all the ongoing discussion about the rights of black men, the convention, however, initially ignored those of poor women, let alone black women. At the second women's rights convention, in 1851, Sojourner Truth (1797–1883), a black woman born in slavery, reminded her audience in an impassioned speech of just that omission.

Unfortunately, Truth's call for more freedom, along with the appeals of white middle-class women, was ignored at the end of the Civil War. Though slavery was abolished by the Thirteenth Amendment (1865) and equal protection of the law guaranteed by federal law as a result of the Fourteenth Amendment (1868), women's rights continued to be denigrated. Angered by this exclusion, a second wave of feminism was propelled forward, leading in 1868 to the creation of two rival organizations: the National Women's Suffrage Association (NWSA), a liberal organization presided over by Susan B. Anthony (1820–1906) and Elizabeth Cady Stanton (1815–1902), and the more conservative American Women's Suffrage Association (AWSA), led by Lucy Stone (1818–1893). Despite their differences, the feminist leadership in these two associations increasingly reflected the agenda of wealthy and middle-class women. Twenty years after their establishment, the two organizations were finally united in the suffrage movement to fight more effectively for women's right to vote. In 1920, their efforts finally bore fruit as the Nineteenth Amendment to the United States constitution established women's suffrage.

In Britain, as in the United States, early industrialization contributed to the founding of small suffrage organizations. Like the corresponding American organizations, early British feminist associations recruited middle- and upper-class women, who shaped the organizational agenda by calling for the expansion of educational and occupational opportunities, as well as for property law reforms for married women. Initially, they were, like their American counterparts, involved in the anti-slavery movement. After the Second Reform Act of 1867 broadened manhood suffrage, activism on behalf of women's enfranchisement gained momentum. Frustrations generated by electoral setbacks from the 1860s to 1880s further incited women's militancy. The Women's Franchise League,

---

SOJOURNER TRUTH, "AIN'T I A WOMAN?" 1851

That man over there says women need to be helped into carriages, and lifted over ditches, and to have the best place everywhere. Nobody helps me into carriages or over puddles, or gives me the best place—and ain't I a woman? Look at my arms! I have plowed and planted and gathered into barns, and no man could head me—and ain't I a woman? I could work as much and eat as much as a man— when I could get it—and bear the lashes as well! And ain't I a woman? I have borne thirteen children and seen most of 'em sold into slavery, and when I cried out with my mother's grief, none but Jesus heard me—and ain't I a woman?

From Lyman Tower Sargent, *Political Thought in the United States: A Documentary History*, 235.

---

an association advocating voting rights, equality with males in matters of divorce, child custody, and inheritance, was established in 1889. Less than a decade later, in 1897, the more conservative National Union of Women's Suffrage Societies was founded, promoting suffrage for middle-class women under the presidency of Millicent Fawcett (1847–1929).[135] At the turn of the nineteenth century, the Women's Social and Political Union (WSPU), led by Emmeline Pankhurst (1858–1929) and her daughters Christabel (1880–1958) and Sylvia (1882–1960), added new strength to the suffrage cause. Yet soon Sylvia, exasperated with the WSPU's insufficient commitment to promoting voting rights for propertyless women, broke away from her mother and sister to form, along with other socialist

---

SUSAN B. ANTHONY AND ELIZABETH CADY STANTON, "THE DECLARATION OF SENTIMENTS," DELIVERED AT THE SENECA FALLS CONVENTION, 1848

The history of mankind is a history of repeated injuries and usurpations on the part of man toward woman, having in direct object the establishment of an absolute tyranny over her. To prove this, let facts be submitted to a candid world.

He has never permitted her to exercise her inalienable right to the elective franchise.

He has compelled her to submit to laws, in the formation of which she had no voice.

He has withheld from her rights which are given to the most ignorant and degraded men—both natives and foreigners.

. . . After depriving her all rights as a married woman, if single, and the owner of property, he has taxed her to support a government which recognizes her only when her property can be made profitable to it.

He has monopolized nearly all the profitable employments, and from those she is permitted to follow, she receives but a scanty remuneration. He closes against her all the avenues of wealth and distinction which he considers most honorable to himself. As a teacher of theology, medicine, or law, she is not known.

He has denied her the facilities for obtaining a thorough education, all colleges being closed against her.

He allows her in Church, as well as State, but in a subordinate position, claiming Apostolic authority for her exclusion from the ministry, and, with some exceptions, from any public participation in the affairs of the Church.

He has usurped the prerogative of Jehovah himself, claiming it as his right to assign for her a sphere of action, when that belongs to her conscience and to her God.

He has endeavored, in every way that he could, to destroy her confidence in her own powers, to lessen her self-respect, and to make her willing to lead a dependent and abject life.

---

women, the Women's Freedom League—a new movement that gradually gained publicity by emphasizing illegal tactics.[136]

As, by the early twentieth century, the movement began to attract women from all social backgrounds, ideological differences dissolved and a unity of purpose emerged, leading to the 1918 achievement of universal suffrage. The example of the British suffragettes spread beyond the Western world. Following the WSPU's militant tactics, the Women's Suffrage Alliance, for instance, a Chinese socialist feminist group in Nanking, China, stormed the parliament building armed with weapons, proclaiming the equality of the sexes and demanding the right to vote. Suffragettes around the world applauded their commitment, which energized women's activism.[137] Even if women were generally not endowed with the right to vote in the nineteenth century, women's militancy helped lay the foundation for twentieth-century progress in human rights.

If industrialization coincided with the emergence of public sympathy for women's cause, it also prompted greater compassion toward working children. Children's employment, of course, had been the norm in pre-industrial societies. Whereas formal education was reserved for the privileged classes, at age six most children were already working in the family household, in the field (e.g., plowing and herding cattle), or in handicraft manufacturing. The seventeenth century's attitude toward childhood was severe. The French general controller of finance under Louis XIV, Jean-Baptist Colbert (1619–1683), would have raised many modern psychologists' eyebrows when he declared, "[E]xperience had always shown that idleness in the first years of a child's life is the real source of all disorders in later life."[138]

Children's contribution to the economy continued with the emergence of industrialization. The early employment of young children not only added directly to the workforce; it freed their mothers to work in the factories. In general, entrepreneurs were eager to employ children and women: both earned less for the same task than did adult males. Anyone who caught a glimpse of nineteenth-century textile mills, coal mines, or glassmaking and chemical factories, however, would have seen children suffering from unhealthy and hazardous working environments, chronic exhaustion, and malnourishment. The experiences of two great fictional characters, the title character in Charles Dickens's *David Copperfield* and Cosette in Victor Hugo's *Les misérables,* vividly illustrate the plight of nineteenth-century working-class children.

Indignation over children's distress ultimately rallied progressive forces throughout Europe. As early as 1802, the British Parliament passed the Factory Health and Morals Act, which applied principally to both male and female apprentices in cotton and woolen mills.[139] Yet lack of enforcement perpetuated the cruel labor environment for children. When Robert Owen arrived at the New Lanark textile mill in 1816, he discovered children as young as five working thirteen hours a day. He stopped employing children under ten and reduced their labor to ten hours a day. The younger children were sent to nurseries and primary schools that Owen had built. Older children continued to work in the factory but also attended secondary school for part of the day.[140] The Factory Act of 1833 addressed some flaws of earlier acts: it forbade the hiring of children younger than nine years old to work in factories and also stipulated the need for paid inspectors to enforce child-protection laws. In 1842, additional legislation restricted the work of children in coal mines and prohibited underground work for girls. Despite the resistance of champions of free market policies, the working class scored a victory with an 1847 act that limited the work of both children and adults to ten hours a day.[141]

In 1832, the New England Association of Farmers, Mechanics and Other Workingmen in the United States called for similar reforms. "Children should not be allowed to labor in the factories from morning till night, without any time for healthy recreation and mental culture." This "endangers their . . . well-being and health," making regulation necessary.[142] Responding to trade union pressure, Massachusetts (1842), followed by Connecticut (1855), limited the workday for children under twelve years old to ten hours. In 1881, the American Federation of Labor,

---

ROBERT OWEN, ON EDUCATION, *A NEW VIEW OF SOCIETY*, 1817

Far better would it be for the children, their parents, and for society, that the first should not commence employment until they attain the age of twelve, when their education might be finished, and their bodies would be more competent to undergo the fatigue and exertions required of them. . . .

The National Plan for the formation of characters should *include* all the modern improvements of education, without regard to the system of any one individual; and should not exclude the child of any one subject in the empire. Anything short of this would be an act of intolerance and injustice to the excluded, and of injury to society. . . .

From *A New View of Society: A Facsimile Reproduction of the Third Edition Printed in London in 1817*, 66.

---

at its first annual convention, called upon states to bar children under fourteen from all employment.[143]

Like the British and Americans, many French were outraged by the plight of children. The wife of a French glass manufacturer described in 1835 the status of these youngsters: "In times of pressure, when the workers keep laboring through the night, the children must also stay awake and work, and . . . when these poor creatures, succumbing to sleep, stop working, they are aroused by any means necessary, including the lash."[144] Popular pressure resulted in the passage of the French Child Labor Law of 1841. It limited children of eight to eleven years to an eight-hour workday and children of twelve to sixteen to twelve hours a day.[145]

Similar legislation for the protection of the young was adopted in other European countries. Yet widespread lack of enforcement continued to corrupt the integrity of early child labor legislation. To address that problem and to broaden the campaign on behalf of children, organized international efforts began with the first International Labor Conference in Berlin in 1890. Although agreement on standards was not reached at that time, similar conferences and other international efforts followed. In 1900, the International Association of Labor Legislation was established in Basel, with branches in sixteen countries, each organized to promote child labor provisions as part of broader international labor legislation. Thanks to these advances, children were progressively less pressured to perform like adults in the labor force and were gradually provided with more legal protection, schooling, and freedom from the harsh demands of the working world of adults.

Rapid changes in the family structure resulting from industrialization not only had an impact on women's and children's social welfare, but also contributed to the redefinition of gender roles, a process that gradually challenged traditional sexual identification.[146] Homosexuality flourished in the late nineteenth century. This should not imply that it was nonexistent in pre-industrial societies, but rather that the economic fragility of the nuclear middle-class family, coupled with the growth of cities—with their theaters and other entertainments—and the impersonal character of an individualized market economy all created propitious conditions for the development of a homosexual subculture.[147] At the same time, as an increasing number of working women demonstrated abilities conventionally limited to men, "effeminate" men were increasingly regarded as a threat to patriarchy. As the sociologist David Greenberg has observed, "[T]he preservation of male domination in the face of women's aspirations to equality depended on men possessing qualities that clearly differentiated them from women. It consequently became necessary to police men who lacked those qualities just as women who exhibited them."[148] The short imprisonment of the great British writer Oscar Wilde (1854–1900) on a charge of sodomy attested to such policing measures. Yet no one described more eloquently than the French novelist Marcel Proust (1871–1922) the suffering and ostracism of homosexuals. Unsurprisingly, many homosexuals, like Wilde, the American poet Walt Whitman (1819–1992), the British political activist Edward Carpenter (1844–1929), and the French novelist André Gide (1869–1951), found solace in socialism, an ideology that claimed to represent the cause of the persecuted.[149]

If homosexuality was socially condemned in the nineteenth century, it was nevertheless legally permitted in most European countries that had fallen within the sphere of Napoleon's power. These included Belgium, Italy, Portugal, Rumania, Russia, and Spain and its former colonies. Those countries that had remained outside the French orbit of influence, such as Prussia and the Austro-Hungarian Empire, retained harsh punishments, including the death penalty, for "sexual offenses." In 1866, Denmark, followed by Germany and the English-speaking common-law countries, modified the harsh character of these laws, ensuring an initial yet incomplete victory for the rights of homosexuals.[150]

More than homosexuals, Jews and other national minorities were the subjects of great political attention. With the exception of France and Holland, where Jews were granted civil and political rights after the French Revolution, the emancipation of northeastern European (or

---

MARCEL PROUST, *SODOM AND GOMORRAH*, 1921

Their [homosexuals'] honour precarious, their liberty provisional, lasting only until the discovery of their crime; their position unstable, like that of the poet one day fêted in every drawing room and applauded in every theater of London, and the next driven from every lodging, unable to find a pillow upon which to lay his head. . . . What they have been calling their love . . . springs not from an ideal of beauty which they have chosen but from an incurable disease; like the Jews . . . shunning one another, seeking out those who are most directly their opposite, who do not want their company brought into company of their own kind by the ostracism to which they are subjected, the opprobrium into which they have finally been invested, by a persecution similar to that of Israel, with the physical and moral characteristics of a race, sometimes beautiful, often hideous, finding . . . a relief in frequenting the society of their kind, and even some support of their existence.

Ashkenazi) Jews throughout Europe was more advanced in countries that had moved rapidly toward industrialization and had adopted civil reforms. In England, following the Catholic emancipation, Jews were for the first time allowed to hold public office both in Parliament and the House of Lords. In Germany, working under discriminatory circumstances, Jews were finally recognized as citizens by the North German Federation in 1869.[151] The reorganization of the Austrian Empire, resulting from its conflict with Prussia, led in 1867 to political equality for Jews throughout the empire, including in Hungary.

In less industrialized eastern European countries, particularly in Russia, Jews, confined to the territories of the Pale and restricted from traveling, faced severe discrimination. In 1856, Alexander II provided limited rights to Jews; that liberal phase, however, ended with the Polish rebellion of 1863. Thereafter, the fate of Jews deteriorated drastically. Russia was the only country in Europe where anti-Semitism was the official policy of the government. The Slavophile state organized and condoned numerous pogroms. That climate fostered the circulation of the *Protocols of the Elders of Zion*—a tract that falsely alleged that Jews were conspiring to conquer the world.[152] From 1881 to 1911, Russia added new restrictions against the Jewish population, leading in 1882 to one of the greatest expulsions of Jews (55,000 in one year) since the Spanish Inquisition.[153] Repudiation of these anti-Semitic laws would begin only with the quasi-constitutional Russian monarchy of 1905, and only after the Bolshevik Revolution would legislative decrees announce the emancipation of all citizens regardless of religious creed. Such legislation, of course, did not prevent the ordeal that Jews would later face within the Soviet Union.[154]

The Sephardic Jews (or Sephardim) of southern Europe, the Ottoman Empire, and the Arab world were relatively better off.[155] In Italy, Jews had briefly enjoyed freedom during the Napoleonic era, before they were forced to return to the ghettos. With the advance of Italian nationalism, they would soon be emancipated a second time, as early as 1848 in Piedmont and later throughout Italy.[156] In the Ottoman Empire, Sephardim were tolerated and protected by the state, while still perceived as juridically inferior to Muslims. In 1839, non-Muslim nationals, however, benefited from enactment of a law guaranteeing "life, honor, and property of all subjects." Soon after these reforms, Christians and Jews alike were allowed to participate in local and regional councils, and in 1867 a new citizenship law provided all minorities with full citizen rights regardless of religious differences.[157]

Despite the spirit of emancipation that was sweeping throughout western and southern Europe, anti-Semitism was simultaneously on the rise. Most striking was its appearance in countries that had assimilated a great part of their Jewish population, such as France, a nation that had prided itself on entrusting Jews with civil rights during the early phase of the French Revolution. In 1895, the public trial and conviction of the innocent Captain Alfred Dreyfus—the only Jew serving on the general staff of the French army, who was charged with high treason against the state—unleashed an anti-Semitic mob. "Death to Dreyfus, death to the Jews," they shouted, to the indignation of many French intellectuals.[158] "J'accuse" replied the French writer Emile Zola (1840–1902), in what would become a famous journal headline denouncing the blatant anti-Semitism and false allegations of high-ranking French officials.[159] The racism and anti-Semitism prevailing in various political, clerical, and popular milieus did not stop at the borders of the French Third Republic, but was spreading throughout Europe. Witnessing the rise of anti-Semitism after the Dreyfus Affair, and disillusioned with what he had once perceived as the Parisian citadel of tolerance, the assimilated German Jewish journalist

---

EMILE ZOLA, "J'ACCUSE," 1898

I accuse Lt-Col du Paty de Clam of having been the diabolical agent of a miscarriage of justice (though unwittingly, I am willing to believe) and then having defended his evil deed for the past three years through the most preposterous and most blameworthy machinations.

I accuse General Mercier of having been an accomplice, at least by weak-mindedness, to one of the most iniquitous acts of this century.

I accuse General Billot of having had in his hands undeniable proof that Dreyfus was innocent and of having suppressed it, of having committed this crime against justice and against humanity for political purposes, so that the General Staff, which had been compromised, would not lose face. . . .

I accuse the War Office of having conducted an abominable campaign in the press (especially in L'éclair and L'echo de Paris) in order to cover up its misdeeds and lead public opinion astray.

As for the persons I have accused, I do not know them; I have never seen them; I feel no rancour or hatred towards them. To me, they are mere entities, mere embodiments of social malfeasance. And the action I am taking here is merely a revolutionary means to hasten the revelation of truth and justice.

I have but one goal: that light be shed, in the name of mankind which has suffered so much and has the right to happiness. My ardent protest is merely a cry from my very soul. Let them dare to summon me before a court of law! Let the inquiry be held in broad daylight!

From *Aurore*, January 13, 1898.

Theodore Herzl (1860–1904) began to imagine a safe haven for Jews, in Uganda, Argentina, or Palestine.[160] In 1897, he called for the first Zionist Congress, an assembly that would launch the Zionist Movement.

Zionism was just one expression of the liberal nationalism that was rampant throughout late-nineteenth-century Europe.[161] Nationalism drew support primarily from the bourgeoisie, who regarded nationhood as an important form of political emancipation from multinational empires. Following the German national unification and the Italian Risorgimento, liberal nationalism became an explosive force in the Austro-Hungarian Empire and the surrounding regions of central and southeastern Europe. Nationalist aspirations progressively undermined the political cohesion of the multiethnic Ottoman Empire. That enormous empire, which stretched from the Balkans to Asia Minor, to Palestine and North Africa, was gradually destabilized by the emerging separatism of the Christian Balkan peoples and later by that of the Muslims.

Such calls for self-determination, however defensible, bore decreasing resemblance to the benign vision originally offered by liberal proponents such as Giuseppe Mazzini, who had advocated a united Europe of free peoples, in which national singularities would be transcended by pan-European harmony. In 1914, that vision of peace and universal human rights was dashed as conflicting nationalist and imperialist positions unleashed the Great War, in which nearly every nation found itself battling with some of its neighbors. The socialist human rights ideal that workers would have no nation was buried in the trenches of World War I. In her poignant "Junius Pamphlet," Rosa Luxemburg decried the horror of the war and despaired over the death of her internationalist comrades:

> Never has a war killed off whole nations; never, within the past century, has it swept over all of the great and established lands of civilized Europe. Millions of human lives were destroyed in the Vosges, in the Ardennes, in Belgium, in Poland, in the Carpathians and on the Save; millions have been hopelessly crippled. But nine-tenths of these millions come from the ranks of the working class of the cities and the farms. It is our strength, our hope that was mowed down, day after day, before the scythe of death. They were the best, the most intelligent, the most thoroughly schooled forces of international socialism, the bearers of the holiest traditions, of the highest heroism, the modern labor movement, the vanguard of the whole proletariat, the workers of England, France, Belgium, Germany and Russia who are being gagged and butchered in masses.[162]

At the beginning of the nineteenth century, nationalism had crushed the liberal internationalist aspirations of the Enlightenment, as it now destroyed the socialist human rights vision. Unsurprisingly, revulsion against this new cycle of nationalism and the violence generated by the unfolding events of two world wars would influence subsequent human rights efforts to try to prevent war. And numerous voices for human rights—those of women, oppressed nationalities, colonized peoples, blacks, homosexuals, and child welfare advocates—all temporarily silenced by the drums of war—would assume in the second part of the twentieth century a more active contribution to the drafting of the human rights agenda.

Chapter Four

The World Wars

THE INSTITUTIONALIZATION OF INTERNATIONAL RIGHTS AND THE RIGHT TO SELF-DETERMINATION

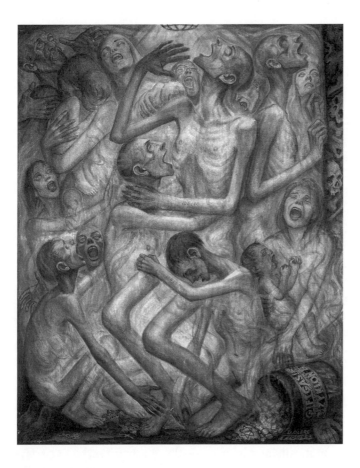

Gassing, oil on burlap,
65 × 52½ inches. Gift of
the Olere Family, Museum of
Jewish Heritage—A Living
Memorial to the Holocaust,
New York, N.Y. David
Olère was deported from
Drancy to Auschwitz, March
2, 1943, no. 106144.

A S THE NEW TWENTIETH CENTURY RAPIDLY DESCENDED into a period of wars and great disillusionment, nationalist and cultural relativist positions rose to occupy a central place in the human rights agenda. Hardly new, these relativist claims of rights endorsed in ancient times by Herodotus had reemerged intermittently, growing stronger and more strident with each successive collapse of universalist visions of human rights. In the twentieth century, struggles carried out on the basis of claims to a right to self-determination would precipitate the breakup of empires and end colonialism. Yet as the plight of excluded nations entered the discourse of rights, it soon unearthed deep-seated schisms, pitting relativists against universalist human rights advocates. No matter how justified the struggles of various oppressed groups, the right to self-determination should be regarded as a formal and abstract right, devoid of content—unless one considers the fairness of the political, social, and economic arrangements awaiting the individuals comprising these subjugated groups once they achieve independence. Toward the goal of informing the relativist versus universalist debate, which has now entered a third century, this chapter considers the merits of early socialist and anti-colonial conceptions of the meaning of self-determination.

If no new broad perspective on universal rights was advanced during the twentieth century, were there any noteworthy innovations during the first part of the twentieth century with respect to human rights? What was distinctive was the scale of the worldwide effort to advance human rights both domestically and internationally. As wars reached new levels of destructive power and became global in scope, proponents of different ideologies could agree on the need to create international institutions (e.g., the League of Nations and the UN) that could help preserve peace. On the domestic front, they could also shore up the legitimacy of states buffeted by warfare and economic depression. Indeed, the early Bolsheviks hoped that a socialist state would ensure the social and economic welfare of all citizens, and Franklin Roosevelt (1882–1945), following the example set by Otto von Bismarck in nineteenth-century Germany, presided over the construction of a welfare state committed to establishing a social safety net that would protect all Americans—an example that was soon emulated by European states.

These national and international endeavors emerged from the series of social cataclysms that distinguished the first half of the twentieth century: the dismantlement of great empires following World War I, the Bolshevik Revolution, the establishment of the League of Nations and the International Labor Organization during the interwar period, the creation of the United Nations, and the anti-colonial struggle following World War II. An examination of these events can help us understand how early discourses linked self-determination to human rights; and how, after each of the world wars, the institutionalization of human rights efforts was shaped by conflicting ideological and geopolitical interests that ultimately privileged some human rights actors while overlooking others.

THE END OF EMPIRES

On the eve of the twentieth century, liberals, realists, and socialists alike focused on ways to develop viable structures for implementing competing visions of peace inherited from the nineteenth century. The importance of such structures was intensified as nationalism and the right to national self-determination (a component of what would later be called "third-generation," or solidarity, rights), originally articulated in reaction to Napoleon's conquests, moved to the center stage of world politics.[1] First came the nationalism of consolidating states like Italy (1867), Germany (1871), and Japan (1868–1912). Subsequently, international politics was increasingly shaped by the appeal of calls for self-determination that spread throughout the weakening Ottoman and Austro-Hungarian empires. Those calls were cultural no less than political, evoked as strongly, for example, in Hungarian composer Béla Bartók's *String Quartet No. 2* (1917) as in any political tract of that period. Yet ethnic quests for self-determination, coupled with growing jingoism as European powers competed for influence in southeastern Europe and the colonial world, were leading not to the realization of new rights, but to a descent into world war. Otto Bauer (1881–1938), Vladimir Lenin (1870–1924), and Rosa Luxemburg, addressing the Balkan and Polish problems, would offer later generations useful tools for assessing the question of self-determination in general.

While the Ottoman and Austrian Empires were confronting the dis-
integrating pressures of national independence movements, newly consolidated nations, such as the United States, Germany, Italy, and Japan,
were seeking to expand their territories. Unification enabled these countries both to extend their economic reach and to expand territorially.[2]
The Monroe Doctrine (1823) had paved the way for U.S. dominance over
Central and South America, a war against Mexico (1848) and a series
of devastating blows against the native population had subdued the continent, and by the end of the century, American power was expanding
further westward into the Pacific. With the establishment of a modern
state apparatus, Japan was also developing imperialist interests, which
were manifested in its war with China (1894–1895) and in the 1910 edict
proclaiming its annexation of Korea.[3] Soon after their respective unifi-
cations, Germany and Italy also began to experiment with colonialism.
Germany moved into Cameroon, East and South-West Africa (now
Namibia), while Italy occupied Somalia and Libya; yet their expansion
was soon limited by the fact that Britain and France (and to a lesser extent Holland, Portugal, and Spain) already occupied the greater part of
the colonial world.

The Crisis of Agadir (1911), in which German aspirations collided with
France's established colonial interests in North Africa, marked the esca-
lation of colonial disputes into the extreme form of power politics that
characterized the period leading up to World War I. That war was more
than an outgrowth of continental conflicts between two military alliances;
it was also driven by the major powers' interest in conquering or preserving markets and colonies. It was a frightening period, which the Austrian composer Gustav Mahler (1860–1911) echoed with tragic accu-
racy in his dissonant and chromatic *Sixth Symphony*, which seemed to
threaten the extinction of tonality.

Nationalism and Efforts to Institutionalize
Human Rights after World War I

As World War I approached, power politics, commercial rivalry, and nationalism were fused into a Darwinist conception of foreign policy that
culminated in unprecedented carnage.[4] The Great War, however, also led
to radical reappraisals of human rights perspectives on the legitimacy of
states. Two decades earlier, the German philosopher Friedrich Nietzsche
(1844–1900) had presaged the trend toward European self-destruction
and self-awakening. "This is the great spectacle," he wrote in *The Ge-*

nealogy of Morals, "of a hundred acts that will occupy Europe for the next two centuries, the most terrible and problematic, but also the most hopeful spectacles."[5] Indeed, during the devastating war and its aftermath, two opposed efforts to institutionalize human rights emerged: the triumph of Bolshevism in Russia, initially premised on international socialism, and the nearly simultaneous establishment of the League of Nations and the International Labor Organization, predicated upon progressive liberal notions of human rights. Failure to implement such visions later corresponded to the rise of particularist perspectives, to fascism, and a renewed descent into total war.

With the Second International socialist organization in disarray and with a devastating world war in progress, many progressives hoped that the Bolshevik Revolution and its 1918 human rights declaration would not only implement for the first time a workers' rights agenda in one state, but would spread socialist principles of human rights throughout the world. At first, Soviet foreign minister Leon Trotsky (1879–1940) saw himself not as a representative of the Russian state, but as a spokesperson for the workers of the world. He would not conduct state diplomacy, he claimed, but would "issue some revolutionary proclamations to the peoples and then close up the joint."[6] Despite early near-successes in Hungary, Germany, and elsewhere, efforts to expand the socialist revolution westward failed, and as Joseph Stalin (1879–1953) consolidated his rule, the dream of international socialist rights yielded in the Soviet Union to a repressive bureaucratic state.

Stalin's "socialism in one country" meant that preservation of socialist aspirations to world revolution would be linked to the strengthening of the Soviet state against capitalist "aggression." That view dictated a policy of rapid industrialization, which was used to justify mass terror against the peasantry and to suppress all internal opposition. In foreign policy, the proclamation of the unity between socialism and Soviet power in the Comintern (the Third International) forced socialists outside the USSR either to remain loyal to Soviet interests and security concerns, or to pursue their own conception of socialism as determined by the individual socialist parties within each state. The resulting divisions in the socialist camp were never reconciled.

Like the socialists, the liberal U.S. president Woodrow Wilson (1856–1924) developed an alternative to the power politics associated with World War I; an alternative, however, based on a liberal and free market understanding of human rights. He rejected the balance of power "determined by the sword."[7] Instead, he argued, in the same liberal perspective as Giuseppe Mazzini, that the inherent inequality of power among states would be countered by the "common strength" of nations to enforce peace based on an "equality of rights."[8] While Wilson hoped that peace would be reinforced by the spread of liberal democracy based on the U.S. model, his specific proposal was for a redrawing of European boundaries predicated upon the principle of national self-determination. In 1919, at the Treaty of Versailles, the League of Nations was created in the spirit of Wilson's vision. At the same conference, the International Labor Organization (ILO) was formed as an affiliated agency of the League of Nations.

The various means Wilson offered for enforcing peace and social justice were, however, foreclosed. The United States failed to join the League of Nations, in large part because the Senate opposed yielding to an international organization its constitutional mandate to decide on U.S. involvement in war. By the early 1930s, the League's inaction in the face of open aggression by Italy and Japan revealed the difficulty of enforcing "collective security" by means of an international organization based on sovereign states. The war ultimately paralyzed the actions of the League, brought international labor legislation to a standstill, and slowed the ratification of ILO standards.

The inability to construct a viable human rights mechanism to secure either liberal or socialist rights in domestic and global politics during the interwar period provided fertile soil for the spread of particularist trends. Nationalist and realpolitik leaders soon exploited popular frustrations on the eve of World War II. That reassertion of state power in an intense period of nationalism culminated in fascism: a conception even more conducive to unlimited aggression against democratic values than the virulent nationalism associated with World War I. The impending horror was powerfully evoked in Pablo Picasso's acclaimed *Guernica* (1937), which depicted a town's destruction during the Spanish Civil War.

**WOODROW WILSON, ADDRESS AT INDEPENDENCE HALL,
PHILADELPHIA, JULY 4, 1914**

My dream is that as the years go by and the world knows more and more of America, it . . . will turn to America for the moral aspirations which lie at the basis of all freedom, . . . and that America will come into the full light of day when all shall know that she puts human rights above all other rights, and that her flag is the flag not only of America but of humanity.

From *The Papers of Woodrow Wilson*, vol. 30, 254.

New Efforts to Institutionalize Human Rights after World War II

The triumph over fascist power politics at the price of tens of millions of lives launched a renewed effort to implement universal rights worldwide. The end of World War II, like the end of World War I, kindled new human rights projects, liberal in nature, like the Bretton Woods system and the Marshall Plan for Europe, exemplifying the conviction that international commerce was a key to peace. The establishment of the United Nations (1945) also illustrated a potentially more practical approach to collective security than the one underlying the failed League of Nations, emphasizing this time enforcement by the great powers. The founders had realized that a basic agreement among the major powers on important international issues was essential for effective cooperation in the maintenance of peace or the application of sanctions against an aggressor. Their fear of international instability was confirmed as people in the colonies demanded sovereign control over their countries and as the East-West rivalry intensified.

In the immediate aftermath of World War II, however, it seemed plausible that the stage had finally been set for the global implementation of a liberal vision of human rights. The United States, founded explicitly on the basis of that vision, now produced half of the world's goods and possessed an atomic monopoly that provided an unchallengeable military advantage. Moreover, the nightmarish costs of world war had created strong elite support for a policy of liberal internationalism—that is, support for a global structure to provide free markets, political liberty, and collective security.

Economic liberalism and liberal political rights appeared to go hand in hand with the institutionalization of the welfare state. The 1929 Great Depression, followed by World War II, created human misery on a scale that challenged the non-interventionist or limited role of the state. Following Franklin Roosevelt's New Deal policy in the 1930s, Britain and France also adopted welfare strategies to address economic crisis and large-scale unemployment. After the war, emerging welfare states were seen as robust enough to counterbalance the destructive domestic repercussions of concentrated wealth and internationally mobile capital.

If the welfare state were combined with economic interdependence and political freedom, world peace and security might then be achieved by means of the United Nations: a forum for sovereign states to coordinate global progress, with the great powers working together to avoid regression toward the balance-of-power politics and extreme nationalism of the interwar period. The United Nations, proclaimed President Roosevelt in 1945, would "spell the end of the system of unilateral action, . . . the balances of power, and all the expedients that have been tried for centuries—and have always failed."[9]

Standing in the way of that liberal human rights vision—that is, of economic interdependence, free-market democracy, collective security, and expansion of the system to embrace the emerging post-colonial world—was the challenge offered by proponents of world socialism. In France and Italy, communists had proven themselves as leaders of the anti-fascist resistance, and emerged as a prospective governing party in early postwar elections.[10] The Communist Party in Czechoslovakia polled more than twice as many votes as any other party in free elections in 1946, and communists achieved power in Albania and Yugoslavia.[11] The communist model also had appeal for aspiring national leaders in what was to become known as the "Third World." The lure of socialism as a facet of self-determination could be linked both to widespread poverty and the fear that liberal development schemes were a new guise for continued domination by their former Western masters. A major inspiration was the 1949 victory in China by a mass peasant movement under the communist leadership of Mao Tse-tung (1893–1976).

With no real colonies, the United States seemed well positioned to expedite liberation from colonial rule and to integrate newly emerging states into the world market system while promoting the establishment of democratic political structures. At the wartime meeting with British Prime Minister Winston Churchill that produced the Atlantic Charter, President Franklin Roosevelt argued for extending the charter globally: "[I]f we are to achieve a stable peace it must involve the development of backward countries. . . . I can't believe that we can fight a war against fascist slavery, and at the same time not work to free people all over the world from a backward colonial policy."[12]

Soon after World War II, as a nationalist tide rose across the Asian and African continents, European colonial powers initially resisted Roosevelt's calls for independence in the colonies. Yet the war had so weakened Western imperial powers that maintaining offshore dominions in the face of anti-colonial struggle was becoming unbearable. Britain had already understood that eventual independence in India and elsewhere in Asia was inevitable. The war and Japanese imperialist inroads in Asia had intensified the anti-colonial struggle and abruptly accelerated the British timetable for departure. As colonial resistance intensified, the French and Dutch followed Britain and abandoned their Asian possessions. In Africa, the Western powers (Britain, France, Belgium, Portugal, and Spain) clung more firmly to their possessions, delaying the decolonization process.

Throughout the developing world, aspiring and post-colonial nationalist leaders soon had to face additional difficulties, this time in the form of United States or Soviet "assistance," either of which was a certain harbinger of superpower efforts to harness their states as instruments for waging the cold war. One way out of this Hobson's choice seemed to be the abandonment of either liberal or socialist human rights—whose proponents might welcome one of the superpowers—in favor of cultivating nationalist and particularist doctrines rationalized in terms of indigenous culture. From ethnic movements in Africa to Islamist movements in the Middle East, "cults of authenticity" arose that resembled Western realism and at times mimicked the models of fascist power drawn from pre–World War II Europe.[13]

Increasingly dropping any pretense of promoting the universal human rights on which they based their legitimacy, both superpowers opportunistically sought support among whichever self-determination movements seemed susceptible to their influence.[14] The United States found itself backing autocrats like Jonas Savimbi in Angola and arming Islamic fundamentalists in Afghanistan. The Soviets did not hesitate to seek support from regimes that imprisoned or killed domestic communists or socialists, as in the case of Nigeria, Ethiopia, Iraq, Syria, Egypt, and the Islamic regime of the Ayatollah Khomeini in Iran. For both superpowers, there were some cases where their proclaimed human rights values and power politics could be harmonized; where that was impossible, crude cold war power politics generally prevailed.[15] Of course, such struggles over the ideological content underlying proclamations of self-determination long predated the cold war. The nineteenth-century history of the right to self-determination, as it continued to unfold into the twentieth century, would, however, gain greater international attention during the world wars and their aftermath.

THE RIGHT TO SELF-DETERMINATION

Indeed, during the twentieth century, the right to a homeland recurrently emerged as a pivotal human rights issue in international affairs, surfacing with a vengeance whenever a universal rights project collapsed in failure. At the time of the ratification of the Covenant of the League of Nations, however, few foresaw that the notion of national rights would be invoked by imperialist and fascist leaders, contributing to the horrors of another world war, just as few would have predicted, following World War II, that such rights would be elaborated, albeit vaguely, in international legal documents. Indeed, article 1 of the two main human rights covenants adopted by the UN in 1966 stipulated, "[A]ll peoples have the right of self-determination. By virtue of [that] right they freely determine their political status and freely pursue their economic and cultural development." Nevertheless, that legal codification of self-determination neither specified which type of political regime a newly independent state would establish, nor entertained the possibility that legitimizing one group's national aspirations would come at the expense of others'.

The criteria for justifying anyone's right to self-determination are, from a legal perspective, far from obvious, and they needed further elaboration. The search for appropriate standards for implementing self-determination rights started before World War I, as a nationalist tide swept Central and Eastern Europe, fragmenting the Ottoman and Austro-Hungarian Empires. After the Great War, in the wake of the collapse of those empires and with the establishment of the League of Nations, the national question moved to the center of international political debate. The League's endorsement of self-determination did not extend to the colonized peoples, who, as their European masters were further weakened by a second world war, intensified their insistence on a right to self-rule in their homelands.

Before World War I

Far more than anywhere else, Central and Eastern Europe experienced an explosion of nationalist sentiment. In Russia, the Polish Party carried the torch of patriotic insurrection, alerting authorities to the possibility of copycat insurrections in Byelorussia, Ukraine, and throughout most of its vast territory, which stretched from Poland to Siberia and encompassed peoples who spoke more than a hundred different languages. In Austria-Hungary, the problem was particularly recondite. After all, "Austria was a Slav house with a German façade":[16] a country in which Czechs, Slovaks, Romanians, and Ruthenians (Ukrainians), among twelve other ethnic groups, were calling for secession.

With the ever more defiant ascendance of nationalism at the eve of World War I puncturing the universalist hopes of the Second International, many socialists reflected on Marx's and Engels's early view of the national question, namely that "proletarians have no country" and that "national differences and antagonism between peoples are daily more and more vanishing, owing to the development of the bourgeoisie . . . and the uniformity in the mode of production."[17] Their views were further predicated upon the idea that the modern nation-state would initially promote capitalism throughout the world, and later create the revolutionary conditions for internationalist solidarity among proletarians. In other words, self-determination was not an absolute right, but rather a stepping stone toward the promotion of universal rights.

Indeed, until socioeconomic conditions favored such a transformation, Marx considered the struggle for self-determination for oppressed people as one of many possible tactics in the pursuit of international justice. Regarding the question of Irish independence, for instance, Marx changed his position over time, depending upon his assessment of the opportunities offered to the working class. Initially, he favored autonomy for the small island, while preserving union with England, hoping that a Chartist victory in England would benefit both the Irish and British working classes. Later, in the 1860s, he modified his opinion, supporting Irish nationhood, with the expectation that the secession of oppressed Irish nationals would weaken the economic, political, military, and ideological strength of the British dominant class.[18]

With recurrent outbreaks of nationalist calls for self-determination in the Ottoman and Austro-Hungarian Empires and throughout Eastern Europe, leading socialists such as Bauer, Luxemburg, Lenin, and Stalin considered different points developed by Marx and Engels on the national question. In his *Question of Nationalities and Social Democracy* (1907), Bauer distinguished himself by envisioning, in the divided multiethnic Habsburg context, some form of socialist internationalist accommodation to the increasing pressure of nationalism. Rather than acknowledging a right to secede, which could prove economically and political disruptive to neighboring nationalities, Bauer proposed the establishment of cultural autonomy within a greater federal state. While considering with Marx the importance of capitalism and state formation for the consolidation of the proletariat, he also believed that workers from different ethnic backgrounds might initially resist integration within a socialist state. "The socialist community," Bauer wrote, "will never be able to include whole nations within its own make-up by the use of force. Imagine the masses of the people enjoying the blessing of national culture and an active part in legislation and government, and finally supplied with armies, would it be possible to subordinate such a nation to the rule of war?"[19]

There are ways, Bauer maintained, to enlist workers to shape the cultural and national discourse without the use of force. "In a society, based upon ownership of the means of production, the ruling classes, once the knights and now the educated classes, constitute the nation by shaping, through language and education, a national 'affinity of character.'"[20] As national unity was imposed from above, the masses, Bauer continued, remained excluded from that enterprise. Local regions, molded by the division of labor imposed by capitalism, ended up clinging to fragmented parochial loyalties, thereby missing out on opportunities to influence the course of an emerging national culture.

How should this problem be addressed? Bauer proposed for consideration "the implementation of the nationality principle," a rule by which an external federal power would serve local communities.[21] While representative national entities would be responsible for matters related to their cultural and national life, the federal state would be concerned with foreign policy and domestic economic policy between different nationalities. To counter economic disputes that could emerge from inequities between wealthy and impoverished areas, a nationality could join conationals in more productive areas without having to claim a small homeland or evict other nationals to create a greater one.[22] Finally, "the unregulated migration of individuals, dominated by the blind laws of capitalist competition, will then cease and will be replaced by a conscious regulation of migration by the socialist communities."[23] While such an intricate, socially engineered solution might be unrealistic, Bauer's proposal of a multicultural coexistence within states, consistent with human rights principles, prefigured the search for innovative ways to resolve ethnic conflicts, short of the unqualified endorsement of a right to self-determination.

Warning of the potential costs of secession for economically weak nationalities and the elitist trends of the nationalist movements, the status of group rights was further qualified by the socialist Rosa Luxemburg as she grappled with the complexities of the Polish question. Poles, like Austrians, were also dealing with the national question. After being repeatedly crushed by Russia throughout the nineteenth century, Polish hopes for self-determination had been rekindled after the 1905 Russian revolution. On the right, the Polish League, led by the integral nationalist or fascist Roman Dmowski (1864–1939), advocated struggle not only against Russia but also against Ukrainians and Jews. On the left, the Polish Socialist Party, dominated by the figure of Josef Pilsudski (1867–1937), saw in an independent socialist Poland the possibility of destroying the reactionary Russian tsardom. Luxemburg distinguished herself by opposing both Dmowoski and Pilsudski, along with the Russian Social Democratic Labor Party's rush to endorse a right to self-determination in Poland.[24]

Any alliance between the working class and Polish nationalists, or with the nationalist bourgeois elite, in any oppressed country, Luxemburg warned, would subvert the future establishment of democratic socialist regimes. Anticipating the fate of mid-twentieth-century anti-colonial struggles, she argued that " 'national movements' and struggles for 'national interests,' are usually class movements of the ruling strata of the bourgeoisie, which can in any given case represent the interest of the other strata of the population only insofar as under the form of 'national interests' it defends progressive forms of historical development, and insofar as the working class has not yet distinguished itself from the mass of the 'nation' (led by the bourgeoisie) into an independent, enlightened political class."[25]

Further, in the spirit of Marx and Engels, she held that such a right to self-determination was an abstract and futile notion, since it did not take into account "the material social conditions of the environment in a given historical epoch." Therefore, she continued, this right was as ridiculous and pointless as the "right of each man to eat off gold plates, which, as Nicolas Chernyshevski wrote, he would be ready to sell at any moment for a ruble."[26] Luxemburg lauded Marx and Engels for speaking out early against the nationalism of Balkan Slavs and supporting the integrity of the Ottoman Empire. They always judged their support for nationalist movements from an economic materialist standpoint, she pointed out, rather than "from the 'eternal' sentimental formulae of liberalism."[27]

This should not suggest that Luxemburg was unwilling to consider socialist concessions to the quest for self-determination. In general, "[t]he position of socialists with respect to the nationality problem depends primarily on the concrete circumstances of each case, which differ significantly among countries."[28] Political independence, she claimed, could be considered only if people could achieve economic self-sufficiency, including sovereign control over their economic resources. For industrially backward countries like Poland or Czechoslovakia, such a right was utopian. Attacking the Polish nationalists of her day, Luxemburg further argued that secession from Russia would ultimately undermine the interests of the Polish proletariat by perpetuating their economic dependence on Russia as a junior trading partner and diminishing their ability to coordinate struggle with Russian workers against Russian authoritarianism.

All socialists did not share her views. Less circumspect on secessionist appeals than Luxemburg, Lenin considered that the intensity of repression experienced by oppressed or colonized nationalities warranted a "tactical alliance" with bourgeois elites in the struggle for self-determination. Rebuffing Luxemburg's anti-secessionist position for Poland, Lenin drew on Marx's legacy, maintaining that independent states were more likely to modernize and hence more likely to foster the emergence of national and then international working-class solidarity. Nevertheless, he reproached Luxemburg, economic maturity was not the only standard needed to justify national liberation claims. "We cannot say whether Asia will have time before the downfall of capitalism to become crystallized into a system of independent national states, like Europe," Lenin wrote, "but it remains an undisputed fact that capitalism, having awakened Asia, has called forth national movements everywhere in the continent, too; that the tendency of these movements is toward the creation of national states there; that the best conditions for the development of capitalism are ensured precisely by these states."[29]

This, of course, did not imply that Lenin favored all forms of nationalism. Nationalism from "above" was different than nationalism from "below," he argued, distinguishing the oppressive nationalism of tsarist Russia from the justifiable nationalism of oppressed Poland. In the case of an oppressed nationality, he encouraged workers to consider tactical alliances with elements of the bourgeoisie. A repudiation of the right to self-determination, he further replied to Luxemburg, "is tantamount to defending the privileges of the dominating nation and police methods of administration as against democratic methods."[30] Hence, he urged socialist countries and proletarians in imperialist countries to help the lib-

---

V. I. LENIN, *ON THE NATIONAL LIBERATION MOVEMENT*, 1920

. . . The cornerstone of the whole policy of the Communist International in the national and colonial question must be to bring together the proletarians and the masses of the toilers of all nations and countries for the joint revolutionary struggle for the overthrow of the landlords and the bourgeoisie; for this alone guarantees victory over capitalism, without which the abolition of national oppression and inequality is impossible.

From "Preliminary Draft Theses on the National and Colonial Questions: For the 2nd Congress of the Communist International (1920)," in Lenin, *Collected Works*, vol. 31, 146.

eration movements of oppressed nations. Revising Marx's famous motto, he called on "workers of all countries and of all oppressed nations to unite!"[31] Many leaders of Third World national liberation movements would later echo that rallying cry.

To address the national question in Russia, the Balkans, and throughout Eastern Europe, Lenin sent Joseph Stalin to Vienna in 1913 to write an article on Marxism and the national question. If Stalin, as the French scholar Michael Löwy has correctly reminded us, developed a more rigid—and hence a less interesting—conception of nationalism than one can find in Lenin, his position would nevertheless have an important impact on nationalities within the Soviet Union.[32] Initially, Bauer might have inspired aspects of Stalin's view that "a nation is a historical, evolved stable community of language, territory, economic life, and psychological make-up manifested in a community of culture."[33] Yet Stalin did not believe that national autonomy would help the development of nations. "[W]herein," he asked, "does such national autonomy, as advocated by Bauer, differ from the utopia of the old nationalist, who endeavored to turn back the wheel of history?" Bauer's federalism, he argued, was mistakenly based on the national demarcation of workers, rather than on regional autonomy. Therefore, Stalin argued, Bauer "spreads noxious ideas of mutual mistrust and aloofness among the workers of the different nationalities."[34]

Rejecting Bauer's proposal, Stalin asserted that history was now bearing out Marx's prediction that national differences would disappear under capitalism. By 1920, with the failure to internationalize the Bolshevik Revolution, the tendency was toward Soviet unity rather than respect for national diversity. Stating that a nation exists only when all four characteristics of nationality are present at the same time (common language, territory, economic life, and psychic formation), Stalin, unlike Lenin, did not make any particular distinction between tsarist oppressive nationalism and the nationalism of the oppressed nations.

However, in a later article, "The Policy of the Soviet Government on the National Question in Russia" (1920), Stalin clarified his position, supporting the secessionism of anti-colonial movements in India, Egypt, Morocco, and elsewhere, while rejecting demands for secession within the regions bordering Russia. Precisely because Western powers were rejecting the secessionism of the former while supporting that of the latter, the Soviet government, Stalin argued, needed to formulate positions in conformity with what he perceived to be the interests of the revolution.[35]

The Aftermath of the Great War

Like Stalin, Europeans applied a double standard, favoring the independence of the nationalities in the Balkans and ignoring appeals for self-
determination in their colonies. If Bauer, Luxemburg, and Lenin had made
distinctive contributions to the national question, their insights were not
taken into account by the victorious World War I powers. Aspects of
Lenin's position were echoed in Woodrow Wilson's "Fourteen Points
Address" (1918), which called for the independence of nationalities in
the Balkan states, the proclamation of a Polish homeland, and sovereignty
for the Turkish portion of the Ottoman Empire. Wilson's famous address
concluded with a sweeping invocation of the right to self-determination.
"An evident principle runs through the whole programme I have outlined," he stated. "It is the principle of justice to all peoples and nationalities, and their right to live on equal terms of liberty and safety with
one another, whether they be strong or weak. Unless this principle be
made its foundation, no part of the structure of international justice can
stand."[36] These rights, he hoped, could be realized by a League of Nations, which would establish borders for homogenous ethnic groups,
thereby presumably removing a major cause of war.

   This idea was further debated in the 1919 Paris Conference, convened
by the victors of World War I to settle the fate of the defeated. Residing
in France during the Paris Conference, Ho Chi Minh (1890–1969), the
future founder of the Vietnamese state, submitted a petition to the U.S.
delegation in hopes that Wilson would intervene on behalf of the Vietnamese against their French occupiers. The European victors, however,
were concerned with ways to punish the Germans and maintain their
colonies, and were not eager to discuss with the American president the
destiny of subjugated peoples. Ho's plea to the delegates fell on deaf ears.[37]

   The League of Nations, instituted shortly after the conference, did not
promote the rights of the colonized, as Ho and Wilson had hoped. As
soon as the League was established, it revealed its exclusionary character. Indeed, the Covenant of the League placed the fate of some nationalities (e.g., in the Middle East) under a system of mandates administered by the victorious colonial powers, which agreed to bring the
mandate territories toward self-government (article 22).[38] It also stipulated that each European power was responsible for ensuring racial and
religious impartiality in the territories under its supervision. In 1919, fearing that discrimination against minorities would result from Polish national independence, the League ratified the Polish Minority Treaty, which

endorsed Polish self-determination, encouraged efforts to protect its minorities, and offered specific protection for its Jewish minority.[39]

Despite these protective clauses, the concept of self-determination proved destructive for those who needed protection in Europe. Invoking Wilson's notion of national unity and territorial sovereignty for homogenous ethnic groups, Germany used the presence of three million Germans within Czechoslovakia's borders as justification for its occupation of the Sudetenland. With Nazism on the rise, an oppressive form of nationalism began to terrorize Europe. Nazism, like fascism an aggressive and integral nationalist ideology cloaked in populist rhetoric, had mushroomed in popularity once postwar German grievances were inflamed by hyperinflation and economic depression in the Weimar Republic.

The social and economic troubles within Europe during the years following 1918 had been greatly intensified by the carnage of World War I, especially in societies that were not fully modernized. This was true of Germany and Italy, which had entered the war expecting great territorial gains, along with achievement of equal social and economic status with the older societies of the West. While Italy was among the victors and Germany was defeated, the relative backwardness of their political, social, and economic structures placed a particularly immense strain on both their societies. The Treaty of Versailles, which ordered enormous German reparations to the victors, was the final coup de grace for the German economy.

Soon, emerging fascist parties began to exploit national feelings of disappointment, a sense of unjust victimization, and the desire to overcome their perceived social and economic disadvantage, galvanizing the masses with visions of past grandeur and future glory. Whereas Adolf Hitler (1889–1945) prophesied a Third Reich that would reign for ten thousand years, Benito Mussolini (1885–1945) strove to revive the magnificence of ancient Rome. In Italy and Germany, under the respective leadership of Mussolini and Hitler, fascism became the dominant political force. Repudiating republican and liberal institutions, both leaders were now calling for individual sacrifice to the fascist state.

Yet for the Italian duce, national redemption did not entail a struggle between workers and capitalists, as Marx believed, but relentless warfare between proletarian nations (such as Italy) and European plutocracies. Such a war, explained Mussolini, "keys up all human energies to their maximum tension and sets the seal of nobility on those people who have the courage to face it."[40] With other Nazi theorists, Hitler added a racial component to Mussolini's conception of the national struggle. In

THE POLISH MINORITY TREATY, 1919

Article 7

All Polish nationals shall be equal before the law and shall enjoy the same civil and political rights without distinction as to race, language, or religion.

Differences of religion, creed, or confession shall not prejudice any Polish national in matters relating to the enjoyment of civil or political rights, as for instance admission to public employments, functions, and honours, or the exercise of professions and industries.

No restriction shall be imposed on the free use by any Polish national of any language in private intercourse, in commerce, in religion, in the press, or in publications of any kind, or at public meetings.

Notwithstanding any establishment by the Polish Government of an official language, adequate facilities shall be given to Polish nationals of non-Polish speech for the use of their language, either orally or in writing, before the courts.

Article 8

Polish nationals who belong to racial, religious, or linguistic minorities shall enjoy the same treatment and security in law and in fact as the other Polish nationals. In particular they shall have an equal right to establish, manage, and control at their own expense charitable, religious, and social institutions, schools and other educational establishments, with the right to use their own language and to exercise their religion freely therein.

Article 9

Poland will provide in the public educational system in towns and districts in which a considerable proportion of Polish nationals of other than Polish speech are resident adequate facilities for ensuring that in the primary schools the instruction shall be given to the children of such Polish nationals through the medium of their own language. This provision shall not prevent the Polish Government from making the teaching of the Polish language obligatory in the said schools.

In towns and districts where there is a considerable proportion of Polish nationals belonging to racial, religious, or linguistic minorities, these minorities shall be assured an equitable share in the enjoyment and application of the sums which may be provided out of public funds under the State, municipal, or other budget, for educational, religious, or charitable purposes.

Article 10

Educational Committees appointed locally by the Jewish communities of Poland will, subject to the general control of the State, provide for the domination of the proportional share of public funds allocated to Jewish schools in accordance with Article 9, and for the organization and management of these schools.

Mein Kampf (1925–1927), he saw in the future German triumph purification of German blood from contamination by inferior races and the purge and genocide of "enemies from within": the Jews and Gypsies. No mere fantasy, this dark vision was realized in the gas chambers of Auschwitz and other concentration camps, as depicted in David Olère's *Gassing* and countless other artistic remembrances. "Oppressed" and "victimized" nations were now becoming merciless tyrants, revealing the potentially cruel face of national consolidation and the dark side of the right to self-determination.

By founding the principle of self-determination primarily on ethnic and cultural—rather than democratic—rights within given borders, Wilson inadvertently offered equal moral weight to irreconcilable conceptions of national autonomy. Thus, a Sudeten German senator in 1929 had no difficulty making the case that German inhabitants of Czechoslovakia were "not an ethnological minority in the territory occupied by the Czechs but a part of the totality of the German people, thrust beyond the present state and frontiers."[41] Such justifications can degenerate into a Hobbesian "state of nature" fueling international conflict. Wilson's conception offered no response to the arbitrary rationalization for state power represented by the Nazi advance into Austria and the Sudetenland.

As Nazism engulfed Europe in war, several imperial powers of Europe were defeated by Germany, as were France, Belgium, and the Netherlands, or were fighting desperately for survival, as was Great Britain. Weakened at home by a ruthless occupation, they became more vulnerable to overseas challenges. Hence, maintaining European control in Asian colonies soon turned out to be an arduous task. The Japanese, who had assumed the dubious role of liberator in Asia, speedily defeated European forces there, signaling to Vietnam, Indonesia, and India that their previous masters were not as powerful as they might have imagined. If the Japanese initially supplanted colonial control with their own, they nonetheless ultimately helped galvanize nationalist movements throughout many areas of Asia.

The Anti-Colonial Struggle after World War II

Just as the League of Nations had quickly proven unable to fulfill its early hopes, the United Nations, erected on human rights promises, soon betrayed its founding principles as the Western victors in World War II sought to preserve their colonial possessions. Lenin's early call for oppressed nationalities to rise against their colonial masters would finally be loud and clear after World War II. Nationalist resistance against England, led by two Western-educated Indian leaders, Mahatma Gandhi (1869–1948) and Jawaharlal Nehru (1889–1964), yielded an early anti-colonial victory in Asia in 1948. As early as 1924, Gandhi had argued for India's right to independence: "The whole world is shivering from the pains of labour, the indications of a new life are manifest everywhere, and a regenerated India must find a place among the new-born nations of the world. This rejuvenated India cannot accept any over-lord, she must be free and independent."[42] The British embroilment in World War II created opportunities that Indian nationalists were not about to miss.

As the prospect of self-determination loomed, Nehru began to imagine a newly independent India. Inclined toward socialism, Nehru's views were not cast in a definite mold. While warning against the excesses of the West, his major objective was to carry India into the modern age of scientific discovery and socioeconomic progress. He claimed that this "modern idea of nationhood," effectively realized in Britain and France, could be achieved in India. If "the inexorable logic of the age presents the country with radically different alternatives: union plus independence or disunion plus dependence," national unity was the clear way to set India on the path toward freedom.[43] Nehru, however, fell short of preserving the overall unity of India in its struggle for independence, as the growing Muslim separatist movement soon led to the creation of Pakistan (1947).

Further decolonization in Asia was now imminent. With the exception of India, whose partition resulted in approximately 800,000 deaths, this process was generally more orderly in the British colonies than it was in those of the French and Dutch.[44] In 1947, Britain granted independence to Ceylon (now Sri Lanka), in 1948 to Burma, in 1957 to the Federation of Malaya, and in 1959 to Singapore, which was later joined by Sarawak and North Borneo to form in 1963 the state of Malaysia. In contrast, the French and the Dutch were holding on more tightly to their colonial possessions. After a protracted Indonesian war for independence, which left thousands dead and wounded on both sides, the Dutch finally recognized the fully independent Federation of Indonesia in 1949.

In Indochina, the Vietnamese revolt against the French would take nine years to succeed. In his 1945 Declaration of Independence, Ho Chi Minh described how the French colonialists "have built more prisons than schools. . . . They have robbed us of our rice fields, our mines, our forests, and our raw materials. . . . They have mercilessly slain our patriots." The

HO CHI MINH, DECLARATION OF INDEPENDENCE
OF THE DEMOCRATIC REPUBLIC OF VIETNAM, 1945

All men are created equal: they are endowed by their Creator with certain unalienable Rights; among these are Life, Liberty, and the pursuit of Happiness.

This immortal statement was made in the Declaration of Independence of the United States of America in 1776. In a broader sense, this means: All peoples on the earth are equal from birth, all the peoples have a right to live, to be happy and free.

The Declaration of the French Revolution made in 1791 on the Rights of Man and the Citizen also states: "All men are born free and with equal rights, and must always remain free and have equal rights."

Those are undeniable truths.

Nevertheless, for more than eighty years, the French imperialists, abusing the standard of Liberty, Equality, and Fraternity, have violated our Fatherland and oppressed our fellow citizens. They have acted contrary to the ideals of humanity and justice. . . .

. . . In the autumn of 1940, when the Japanese fascists violated Indochina's territory to establish new bases in their fight against the Allies, the French imperialists went down on their bended knees and handed over our country to them.

Thus, from that date, our people were subjected to the double yoke of the French and the Japanese. Their sufferings and miseries increased. The result was that, from the end of last year to the beginning of this year, from Quang Tri Province to the North of Viet-Nam, more than two million of our fellow citizens died from starvation. On March 9 [1945], the French troops were disarmed by the Japanese. The French colonists either fled or surrendered, showing that not only were they incapable of "protecting" us, but that, in the span of five years, they twice sold our country to the Japanese.

On several occasions before March 9, the Viet Minh League urged the French to ally themselves with it against the Japanese. Instead of agreeing to this proposal, the French colonists so intensified their terrorist activities against the Viet Minh members that before fleeing they massacred a great number of our political prisoners detained at Yen Bay and Cao Bang.

Notwithstanding all this, our fellow citizens have always manifested toward the French a tolerant and humane attitude. Even after the Japanese *Putsch* of March 1945, the Viet Minh League helped many Frenchmen to cross the frontier, rescued some of them from Japanese jails, and protected French lives and property.

From the autumn of 1940, our country had in fact ceased to be a French colony and had become a Japanese possession.

After the Japanese had surrendered to the Allies, our whole people rose to regain our national sovereignty and to found the Democratic Republic of Viet-Nam.

The truth is that we have wrested our independence from the Japanese and not from the French.

The French have fled, the Japanese have capitulated, Emperor Bao Dai has abdicated. Our people have broken the chains which for nearly a century have fettered them and have won independence for the Fatherland. Our people at the same time have overthrown the monarchic regime that has reigned supreme for dozens of centuries. In its place has been established the present Democratic Republic.

From *On Revolution: Selected Writings, 1920–1966*, 143–144.

long Vietnamese guerilla war against the French occupiers culminated in the siege and defeat of French forces at Dien Bien Phu (1954), a battle in which two thousand French soldiers died, forcing the French government to renounce its colonial claim on Vietnam.[45]

In 1954, two Vietnamese delegations—one composed of supporters of the Marxist Ho Chi Minh, the other of followers of Bao Dai (1913–1997)—met with representatives of eight countries in Geneva to seek an acceptable plan for the design of post-colonial Indochina. They concluded with an agreement according to which Vietnam was to be divided into North and South at the seventeenth parallel until national elections, scheduled for 1956, would reunite the country. Certain that free elections would result in a victory for Ho Chi Minh, the United States initiated two decades of effort to forge an independent South Vietnam, first approving the seizure of power by the despotic Ngo Dinh Diem, and then, when Diem's inept and repressive policies helped stimulate armed rebellion, supporting the coup that led to his death in 1963. The North had for several years been increasing its support for the leftist uprising by the Vietcong (South Vietnamese communists), with the aim of driving the Americans out and reunifying the country. Having fought the Japanese and then the French, North Vietnam and its Vietcong allies were now waging what would prove to be the longest conflict against the perpetuation of the colonial system of the great powers. "Nothing is as dear to the heart of the Vietnamese as independence and liberation," said Ho Chi Minh in response to American air strikes—a message that became the motto of the North Vietnamese cause. In 1975, six years after the death of Ho, the communists finally succeeded in reunifying Vietnam under the leadership of the North. In doing so, they had withstood more bombs than had been dropped on all of Europe and Asia combined during World War II, the devastation of villages by the incendiary chemical agent napalm, the defoliation of their land by massive air drops of herbicides, and more than one million deaths.[46]

In Africa, the decolonization process started later. Although some signs of African agitation appeared in the interwar period, the end of World War II unleashed sustained demands for independence. In Africa, the shift from allegiance to one's ethnic group to aspirations to nationhood occurred more slowly than in Asia, since the areas occupied by African ethnic groups had little correspondence with the national borders drawn by the colonial powers. As that difficult process of unification proceeded, African nationalists like Ghana's leader Kwame Nkrumah (1909–1972) made demands for self-determination to an increasingly sympathetic

United Nations audience. The British had already decided that their economically underdeveloped African colonies were an economic and political liability, and they finally accepted nationalist leaders' demands for self-governance. In the late 1950s, bloodied by anti-colonial uprisings, the French and Belgians reached the same conclusion.

In Algeria, however, the French refused any concessions to the nationalist movement. French brutality only intensified National Liberal Front terrorist activities and was decried by many French intellectuals, among them Albert Camus, who called for the indictment of French torturers while condemning Algerian terrorism.[47] After eight years of bloody war, French forces under General Charles de Gaulle withdrew in 1962, allowing Algeria to declare its independence. Another violent struggle for national independence in Africa took place against Portugal, under the dictatorship of Oliveira Salazar (1889–1970), which stubbornly held onto its colonies in Angola and Mozambique. Worn out by the conflict in Angola, the Portuguese finally granted independence to their two colonies in 1975.[48]

If many African nationalist leaders, like the Senegalese poet and first president Léopold Sédar Senghor (1906–2001), championed the cause of national liberation and human rights, many other elected African governments, such as those in Zimbabwe, the Ivory Coast, Zambia, and Botswana, gave way over time to one-party rule. No one was better able

---

KWAME NKRUMAH, SPEECH AT THE UNITED NATIONS, 1960

The great tide of history flows and as it flows it carries to the shores of reality the stubborn facts of life and man's relations, one with another. One cardinal fact of our time is the momentous impact of Africa's awakening upon the modern world. The flowing tide of African nationalism sweeps everything before it and constitutes a challenge to the colonial powers to make a just restitution for the years of injustice and crime committed against our continent.

But Africa does not seek vengeance. It is against her very nature to harbour malice. Over two hundred million of our people cry out with one voice of tremendous power—and what do we say? We do not ask for death for our oppressors, we do not pronounce wishes of ill-fate for our slave masters, we make an assertion of a just and positive demand. Our voice booms across the oceans and mountains, over the hills and valleys, in the desert places and through the vast expanse of mankind's habitation, and it calls out for the freedom of Africa. Africa wants her freedom, Africa must be free. It is a simple call, but it is also a signal lighting a red warning to those who would tend to ignore it.

From *I Speak of Freedom: A Statement of African Ideology*, 262.

than the West Indian psychoanalyst and social philosopher Frantz Fanon (1925–1961) to articulate the dynamic linking anti-colonial struggle to the emergence of post-independence dictatorship. Vile colonial subjugation justified the violence of the oppressed and the necessity of self-determination, argued Fanon, in the spirit of Lenin. Yet true self-determination, Fanon argued, could not be achieved when an indigenous elite who had already internalized the forces of domination, ended up under international pressure, perpetuating the unequal social and economic structure inherited from colonialism. In this respect, Fanon shared Luxemburg's earlier disbelief that the nationalist indigenous bourgeois elite could promote equal rights after independence.

To destroy the vestiges of Western domination that persisted after independence, many Africans, like the liberal nationalists of the early nineteenth century, proposed to develop a genuine national culture freed from Western universal rationalist pretense, while retaining the human rights promises of Western civilization. "In our return to our cultural roots," Senghor suggested, "and particularly to the Negro-African method of knowledge and comprehension of the world, we can reject European methods, but we also cannot forget Europe's lessons in building a nation, the socialist state."[49] Echoing Senghor, Fanon emphasized the importance of culture for the building of a nation: "It is the fight for national existence which sets culture moving and opens to it the doors of creation."[50]

As former colonies began to join the community of nations in the 1960s, the notion of cultural rights, as understood by Fanon and others, was intrinsically linked to the right to self-determination. This association was expressed in article 27 of the Universal Declaration of Human Rights, which specified that "[e]veryone has the right freely to participate in the cultural life of the community, to enjoy the arts and to share in scientific advancement and its benefits." Later, article 1 of the 1966 International Covenant on Economic, Social and Cultural Rights con-

---

ALBERT CAMUS, ON ALGERIAN MISERY, 1939

I don't believe that one can suppress poverty in one day. But I have to say that I never saw a European population as miserable as this Arab population. . . . It is against this disproportion and excess of poverty that we need to fight. . . .

From *Alger républicain*, January 1, 1939 (my translation).

firmed a universal right to self-determination. In 1986, the African Charter on Human and Peoples' Rights reiterated these clauses.

If self-determination and cultural development may be necessary collective rights responses to colonialism, ethnic oppression, or genocide, such rights, however, do not specify how new independent governments will treat their citizens (including their minorities). Unqualified group rights can be used to inflict the very harms they purport to protect against. Elites of newly independent states can easily appeal to or reinvent ancestral traditions in order to justify women's or minorities' unequal rights or other forms of social and economic discrimination. Such a justification of the right to define one's own culture as the prerogative of sovereign states was the outcome of nearly all Third World anti-colonial struggles.

The early socialist critique of the unconditional right to self-determination and culture, while overlooked in current human rights discourse and legal documents, stands the test of time. If Lenin, and later Wilson, helped provide the necessary optimism for brutalized and oppressed nationalities to pursue their right to independence from intractable imperialist controls, Luxemburg warned that most newly formed countries were too weak economically to maintain genuine sovereignty, and she cautioned against popular alliances with a self-interested nationalist elite or bourgeoisie. Such alliances, Fanon believed, with Luxemburg, would

---

FRANTZ FANON, *THE WRETCHED OF THE EARTH*, 1963

We believe that the conscious and organized undertaking by a colonized people to re-establish the sovereignty of that nation constitutes the most complete and obvious cultural manifestation that exists. It is not alone the success of the struggle which afterward gives validity and vigor to culture; culture is not put into cold storage during the conflict. The struggle itself in its development and in its internal progression sends culture along different paths and traces out entirely new ones for it. The struggle for freedom does not give back to the national culture its former value and shapes; this struggle which aims at a fundamentally different set of relations between men cannot leave intact either the form or the content of the people's culture. After the conflict there is not only the disappearance of colonialism but also the disappearance of the colonized man. . . .

. . . The consciousness of self is not the closing of the door to communication. Philosophic thought teaches us, on the contrary, that it is its guarantee. National consciousness, which is not nationalism, is the only thing that will give us an international dimension.

From *The Wretched of the Earth,* 245–246.

---

mainly benefit the elite and perpetuate oppression. Since resources are almost certain to be distributed inequitably within any given territory, the breakup of existing states is bound to favor one regionally concentrated ethnic group over another, as exemplified today in the former Yugoslavia. Bauer's vision of a federation of multiethnic groups, activated at the grassroots level and committed to economic and social equity, may provide a better solution than calls for unlimited self-determination in the post–cold war era. Self-determination may have been a necessity, as Lenin mentioned, for colonized states. Yet in an ever more enmeshed globalized world, which has eroded the sovereignty of the state, cultural autonomy within a federative multiethnic state offers an alternative solution to possible human rights abuses associated with conflicts over self-determination.[51]

In short, universal human rights are always potentially endangered by particularist and vague conceptions of rights framed in terms of the "national interest," "national security," the right to "national self-determination," or "cultural rights." If, in principle, a flexible interpretation of rights points to tolerance, evasive notions of rights tend to favor the interests of the strongest. Bauer, Lenin, Luxemburg, Wilson, and later, Fanon shaped the terms of a debate in which we must continue to engage, offering critical questions and insights to assess under which conditions and for whose benefits one should justify self-determination. Should all forms of self-determination be endorsed? Should one first consider cultural autonomy, in hopes of avoiding struggles over vital economic resources and to avoid tempting ever smaller ethnic or religious factions to seek secession? Should the case for self-determination be judged in terms of the level of oppression suffered by a given nationality? To what extent should one consider who the primary beneficiaries (and the likely losers) are, both within and outside the group struggling for independence? Is the political agenda of the national movement framed in terms of universal human rights? To what extent is the prospective independent state economically viable? Seeking answers to these questions is an inescapable part of any effort to evaluate demands for independence in terms of the likely consequences for human rights.

Further, finding the answers to how and when to promote either cultural autonomy or self-determination requires an assessment of the capacity of governmental and international institutions to peacefully balance conflicting demands. The bloodshed of World War I made the design and construction of such institutions a central concern of human rights architects, as discussed in the following section.

INSTITUTIONALIZING HUMAN RIGHTS

Nineteenth-century socialists had already pointed out the inability of government institutions to protect social rights or to counter the pernicious social effects of commercial rivalries, imperialism, and war. World War I proved them right. Just as Jacobins during the French Revolution had entrusted the republican *patrie* with the task of spreading liberal and secular rights throughout Europe, now communists from all over the world turned their hopes for the internationalization of human rights to the unfolding Bolshevik Revolution. By now, however, socialists had long been torn over the appropriate means with which to realize social and economic principles of rights. While some believed that violence and a vanguard party were necessary to lead the revolution and eradicate the vestiges of tsarist tyranny, others were committed to promoting reforms in the parliamentary arena or within newly established organizations like the International Labor Organization (ILO) and the League of Nations.

On the other side of the Atlantic, economic depression during the interwar period had taught President Roosevelt that the state's legitimacy required extending government spending in the public sector and addressing the needs of the poor. The same lessons would apply to Europe after World War II as the Marshall Plan and Bretton Woods helped restore the social capacity of the devastated countries of Western Europe. Yet if welfare states were to emerge, their ability to flourish would require peace, a need that now would inspire interest in constructing a stronger international organization than the defunct League of Nations. The UN, its champions hoped, would unite states with different social and political agendas in support of one critical end: preventing interstate violence on the scale attained by the two world wars. From the perspective of the socialists, support for the United Nations was a stage in the debate over means and ends that dated back to the era of the Bolshevik Revolution.

Promoting Socialist Rights: Means and Ends during the Bolshevik Revolution

The road to a socialist revolution in Russia had been marked by Russian defeat in the 1905 war with Japan, spreading starvation, and a continuously intransigent autocratic regime. Discontent in Russia had been mounting at the end of the nineteenth century as peasants rebelled against landlords and workers organized strikes in factories. In 1905, the tsarist regime was further destabilized by what became known as "Bloody Sunday," when a crowd of two hundred thousand men, women, and children singing "God save the Tsar" gathered peacefully at the Winter Palace to ask for reforms. Fearful officials, who were left in charge of defending the palace when the tsar fled, ordered troops to fire into the crowd. Several hundred were killed. The event horrified workers and peasants throughout Russia and beyond. To prevent the spread of rebellion, the tsar grudgingly offered some concessions, granting more rights to property owners, a small fraction of the population. That proved insufficient. The fragile tsarist regime would soon require far broader popular support, as his 1914 decision to mobilize his army in defense of Serbia ended all hope of averting World War I.

As casualties mounted, the tsarist regime confronted growing resistance. The death or injury of two million Russians and the spread of famine throughout the country inflamed the revolutionary climate, and workers' demonstrations proliferated. When his troops refused to fire on insurgent workers in Petrograd, middle-class opponents of his regime demanded the appointment of a new ministry and the formation of a new Duma.[52] The time seemed propitious for promoting justice. By March of 1917, social democrats and social revolutionaries called for the removal of the tsar, a tsar who had resisted democratic reforms and had sent masses of peasants into battle, in some cases without rifles. The tsar finally abdicated without resistance and was replaced by a provisional government under the leadership of liberal and socialist forces.[53] Popular support for the new government, however, soon dissipated. As the war continued, army desertions mounted while strikes, riots, and food lines filled the streets with starving and angry crowds.

On October 25 of the Gregorian calendar (or November 2), with the slogan "Peace, land, and bread," the Bolsheviks and the socialist revo-

---

RUSSIAN CORRESPONDENT OF THE JOURNAL *LE MATIN*, JANUARY 22, 1905

The soldiers of the Preobrazhensky regiment, without any summons to disperse, shot down the unfortunate people as if they were playing at bloodshed. Several hundred fell; more than a hundred and fifty are killed. They are almost all children, women, and young people. It is terrible. Blood flows on all sides. At 5 o'clock the crowd is driven back, cut down and repelled on all sides. The people, terror-stricken, fly in every direction. Scared women and children slip, fall, rise to their feet, only to fall again farther on. At this moment a sharp word of command is heard and the victims fall en masse. There had been no disturbances to speak of. The whole crowd is unarmed and has not uttered a single threat.

lutionaries of the left took over the provisional government in a blood-less transfer of power. As Lenin assumed power, he issued a decree calling for an immediate armistice and a peace "without annexation or indem-nities," and a decree ordering the abolition of property and the distri-bution of land to the peasants who worked on it. The Declaration of the Rights of the Toiling and Exploited Peoples of 1918 stated the revolu-tion's goal: "the suppression of all forms of exploitation of man by man . . . [and] to reorganize society on a socialistic basis."[54] Next came a series of measures proclaiming workers' control of factories, national-izing the banks, abolishing the old courts in favor of revolutionary tri-bunals, establishing a workers' militia, removing legal class privileges and titles, abolishing inheritance, separating church and state, establishing the legal equality of the sexes, and Westernizing the Gregorian calendar. As in the French revolutionary experience, however, disagreements soon arose over what means were acceptable for suppressing a counterrevolution, and over how to internationalize the revolution during the war—disagreements that divided the Leninist regime from many of the revolu-tion's initial supporters.

Prior to the revolution, Lenin had stated that in a society dominated by an impoverished peasantry, revolution could not await the full-fledged development of capitalism to ensure the maturity of working-class consciousness. In "What Is to Be Done?" (1902), he proposed the creation of a vanguard working-class elite to generate political con-sciousness *among all classes of the population.*"[55] As riots and military mutiny spread in 1917, challenging the liberal influence of the provisional government, he called for a transition by force from capitalism to com-munism. "Democracy for the vast majority of the people," Lenin pro-claimed, "and suppression by force, i.e., exclusion from democracy, of the exploiters and oppressors of the people—this is the change democ-racy undergoes during the *transition* from capitalism to communism." He continued, "It might be suppression, but it should nonetheless be a momentary state of affairs, in which the exploited majority suppresses the exploiting minority." Only when capitalist exploitation had been crushed, Lenin stated, reiterating Marx, "then the state . . . ceases to exist, and it becomes possible to speak of freedom."[56]

Yet at what cost were Lenin and his followers willing to build a so-cialist society? The dictatorial management of politics that Lenin referred to as "momentary" was initially justified by the war waged at home against the tsarist White Army forces and their foreign supporters. The civil war was now used to rationalize the spread of a Red Terror, which

DECLARATION OF THE RIGHTS OF THE TOILING AND EXPLOITED PEOPLES, 1918

Chapter One

1. Russia is proclaimed a Republic of Soviets or Workers', Soldiers', and Peasants' Deputies. All central and local authority is vested in these Soviets.

2. The Russian Soviet Republic is established on the basis of a free union of free nations, a federation of National Soviet Republics.

Chapter Two

The Constituent Assembly sets for itself as a fundamental task the suppression of all forms of exploitation of man by man and the complete abolition of class distinctions in society. It aims to crush unmercifully the exploiter, to reorganize society on a socialistic basis, and to bring about the triumph of Socialism throughout the world. It further resolves:

1. In order to bring about the socialization of land, private ownership of land is abolished. The entire land fund is declared the property of the nation and turned over free of cost to the toilers on the basis of equal right to its use. All forests, subsoil resources, and waters of national importance as well as all livestock and machinery, model farms, and agricultural enterprises are declared to be national property.

2. As a first step to the complete transfer of the factories, shops, mines, railways, and other means of production and transportation to the Soviet Republic or Workers and Peasants, and in order to ensure the supremacy of the toiling masses over the exploiters, the Constituent Assembly ratifies the Soviet law on workers' control and that on the Supreme Council of National Economy.

3. The Constituent Assembly ratifies the transfer of all banks to the ownership of the workers' and peasants' government as one of the conditions for the emancipation of the toiling masses from the yoke of capitalism. . . .

Chapter Three

1. The Constituent Assembly expresses its firm determination to snatch mankind from the claws of capitalism and imperialism which have brought on this most criminal of all wars and have drenched the world with blood. It approves whole-heartedly the policy of the Soviet Government in breaking with the secret treaties, in organizing extensive fraternization between the workers and peasants in the ranks of the opposing armies and in its efforts to bring about, at all costs, by revolutionary means, a democratic peace between nations on the principle of no annexation, no indemnity, and free self-determination of nations. . . .

Chapter Four

4. At the same time, desiring to bring about a really free and voluntary, and consequently more complete and lasting, union of the toiling classes of all nations in Russia, the Constituent Assembly confines itself to the formulation of the fundamental principles of a federation of the Soviet Republics of Russia, leaving to the workers and peasants of each nation to decide independently at their own plenipotentiary Soviet Congress whether or not they desire, and if so on what conditions, to take part in the federated government and other federal Soviet institutions.

erupted in an atmosphere similar to that of 1793–1794 in France. In Russia, thousands upon thousands of dissidents were taken prisoner and killed.[57] The political police, the Cheka, indiscriminately targeted individuals from the bourgeoisie and the aristocracy, as if "a dividing line between bourgeois and worker can [ever] be drawn accurately," argued Karl Kautsky, castigating the actions of the Bolsheviks. "In the Soviet Union not only were the means of production and consumption taken from the 'bourgeoisie' without any compensation, not only were they deprived of all political rights; they were at the same time victims of oppression and they alone were liable to do compulsory work!" The harsh treatment of the bourgeoisie reflected only "the proletariat's thirst for revenge in its crudest form."[58]

From her German prison cell, where she was incarcerated for her opposition to the world war, Rosa Luxemburg celebrated the unfolding Bolshevik Revolution with greater enthusiasm than the reformist Kautsky. Nevertheless in the letters she sent to the editor of the Spartacus League (1914–1918), she joined Kautsky's condemnation of Trotsky and Lenin's radical elimination of democracy. Such an act, she wrote, "is worse than the disease it is supposed to cure, for it stops up the very living source from which alone can come the correction of all the innate shortcomings of social institutions. That source is the active, untrammeled, energetic political life of the broadest masses of the people." While during the initial phase of the revolution, some form of democratic centralism might be justified, it was an "undisputable fact" that without universal suffrage, without "a free and untrammeled press, without the unlimited right of association and assemblage, the rule of the broad mass of the people is entirely unthinkable."[59]

The Bolshevik suppression of democracy and the ensuing period of terror, explained Kautsky, reflected the poor preparation of the working class in its efforts to assume power. Central to these reflections was Kautsky's and other reformers' rejection of the idea that the replacement of the capitalist system of production by a socialist one required a violent revolution. More constructive, he maintained, would be the development of a labor party that would win broad support within society. Instead, under the Bolsheviks, "[B]usiness concerns were expropriated without any attempt being made to discover where it would be possible to organize them on socialist lines." Such measures not only precipitated a cycle of violence, they also left industries in the hands of incompetent workers and managers.[60] After all, even socialist ends do not justify any means, he reiterated in *Terrorism and Communism* (1919): "Just as one does not champion the right to live by sacrificing those things which give life content and purpose, one ought not to defend one's principles by abandoning them."[61]

Conceding sarcastically that under "normal" conditions a "normal" person may obey the commandment "thou shalt not kill," Trotsky, in his role as leader of the Red Army, pointed out that in a situation of self-defense and war, the moral injunctions invoked by Kautsky and other "social moralists" were untenable.[62] One needs to adopt a different moral yardstick, Trotsky argued, when a victim is fighting an oppressor. Invoking the Civil War in the United States, he distinguished between "[a] slaveholder who through cunning and violence shackles a slave in chains, and a slave who through cunning and violence breaks the chains—let not the contemptible eunuchs tell us that they are equals before a court of morality."[63] At the same time, Trotsky wanted to distinguish himself from the brutality of fellow Bolshevik Joseph Stalin. Thus, he argued that not all means are acceptable, only those that increase the power of humanity over nature and those seeking the abolition of the power of one person over another. Hence, what are permissible are only those methods that "*really* lead to the liberation of humanity," he insisted in an effort to distinguish himself from Stalin's brutality.[64]

On the international front, Trotsky, with Lenin, condemned imperialism and its barbarous effects as objectionable means toward reprehensible ends. Because the second International Socialist Organization, the only mechanism for fighting imperialism, was dissolved under the "chauvinist" concessions of European labor parties to "bourgeois" parties during the war, Bolshevik Russia, they argued, needed to rekindle a spirit of international solidarity among proletarians. Prior to the collapse of Germany, subsequent popular rebellions around Europe appeared to herald the world revolution anticipated by communists like Trotsky and galvanized Russian efforts to expand the revolution across its borders.

Luxemburg, with her comrade Karl Liebknecht and other Bolshevik leaders, had already concurred that the success of the Russian revolution depended upon simultaneous working-class revolts on "the part of the French, English, Italian and especially, the German proletariat." At this historical crossroads, Luxemburg wrote, the choice was between an imperialist war and a proletarian revolution. With great optimism, she held that "the great historical law" was "making headway [toward socialism]—like a mountain stream which had been diverted from its course and has plunged into the depths, it now reappears, sparkling and gurgling, in an unexpected place."[65]

The revolution was, however, in peril, as Bolsheviks were fighting within and outside their national boundaries. In 1918, to gain a respite from war, Lenin had been forced to sign the Brest Litovsk peace treaty, which ceded parts of western Russia to Germany. Assuming that a proletarian revolution in Germany was imminent, he resisted the internationalist drive of the left wing of the Bolshevik party against the ratification of such a treaty. He subsequently explained his difficult decision:

> The revolution will not come as quickly as expected. History has proved this, and we must be able to take this as a fact, reckon with the fact that the world socialist revolution cannot begin so easily in the advanced countries as the revolution began in Russia. . . . But to start a revolution in a country in which capitalism is developed, in which it has produced a democratic culture and organization, provided it to everybody—to do so without preparation would be wrong, absurd. We are only just approaching the painful period of the beginning of socialist revolution.[66]

For Luxemburg, along with Liebknecht, the treaty was a big blow to hopes for an international proletarian uprising against imperialism and capitalist greed. It was not a real peace, they argued, but a Bolshevik capitulation to German militarism; it represented nothing more than Lenin's disillusionment with revolutionary opportunities in Germany and would result in nothing less than the economic strangulation and isolation of the Bolshevik revolution from all sides. Any socialist party, Luxemburg continued, would fail in its task and perish, by carrying out "the dictatorship of the proletariat and the socialist revolution in a single country surrounded by reactionary imperialist rule and in the fury of the bloodiest world war in human history."[67] Stalin's proclamation of "Socialism in one country" and his merciless purge of his fellow Bolsheviks following Lenin's death (1924) would later confirm her darkest fears.

The 1919 socialist conference held in Bern at the end of the war proved an ephemeral effort to resurrect the idea of a Second International. The conference had been called principally to influence the discussions held at the Paris Conference that was convened by the victors of the war. Drawing on the spirit of the International Socialist Organization and the reports by British Fabian Leonard Woolf (1880–1969) on international governance, detailing as early as 1915 a peace program orchestrated by a supranational organization, socialist delegates in Bern called for the establishment of a league of people rather than a league of representative governments.[68] In time of conflict, they argued, member states of the League needed to surrender their sovereign powers to a supranational entity, which should be able to back its decisions by exercising economic pressure.[69]

The League of Nations, the ILO, and the Emergence of the Welfare State

The League of Nations was not to become a supranational entity transcending the interests of the more powerful states, as socialist envoys to Paris hoped. Rather, it embodied the victorious Allied powers' principle of collective security, in which all world states would join against any future aggressor. Mainly, it was envisioned as a forum for arbitration of international disputes and a mechanism for overseeing the reduction of armaments. While the Assembly of the League included representatives from all member states, endowed with executive authority, the council would combine permanent representation of the leading Allied powers, with rotating membership for all other states, and non-permanent states included on a rotation basis. The Secretariat, the third office, represented the permanent and more specialized civil service of the League.[70] The League was also designed to work in close association with an independent Permanent Court of Justice located at the Hague.

LEONARD WOOLF, *INTERNATIONAL GOVERNMENT*, 1915

On the conclusion of the war the working classes of all industrial countries must unite to . . . establish some international authority to settle points of difference among nations by compulsory conciliation and arbitration. It would clearly be desirable, if possible, that they (the terms of peace) should include provisions obliging Germany, along with the rest of Europe, to submit to some form of international organization designed to prevent future war. . . .

. . . The problem is not a new one. It has for many centuries exercised the minds of those people who, because they were civilized, have at all times been contemptuously called theorists and Utopians by plain men, their contemporaries; but periodically, when the world is swept by the cataclysm called war, plain men, amazed to find that they are not civilized, have themselves raised a cry for the instant solution to the problem. One cannot, however, avoid some doubt whether the most opportune moment for solving it is the hurried and temporary reaction which comes to men when they see what a very barbarous and inefficient method of arranging international affairs they have adopted in the arbitrament of arms. . . .

. . . It is true that human society is so simple that if a majority of men want to fight, no International Law, no treaties or tribunals will prevent them; on the other hand, society is so complex that though the majority of men and women do not want to fight, if there are no laws and rules of conduct, and no pacific methods of settling disputes, they will find themselves at one another's throats before they are aware of or desire it.

From Leonard Woolf and the Fabian Society, *International Government: Two Reports*, 3–4, 6–7.

The preamble of the Covenant of the League laid down its principal missions, namely, to "promote international cooperation and to achieve international peace and security" and to compel member states "not to resort to war" and to abide by international law and treaty obligations.[71] The covenant also advocated humanitarian and human rights principles to be overseen by the Allied powers, including humane working conditions, the prohibition of trafficking in women and children, the prevention and control of disease, and self-determination. Yet as we have seen earlier, not all nationalities were granted the right to a homeland after the war. Under the pressure of major colonial powers, the League established a system for allocating Asian and African colonies among the Allied powers in the form of mandates. To reassure critics, the covenant included clauses urging colonial powers to guarantee, under the mandatory system, the political advancement of indigenous people, freedom of conscience and religion, just laws, and the prohibition of abuses (such as trafficking in slaves, arms, or alcohol).

At least equally pertinent, however, for the advancement of international social justice was the establishment of the International Labor Organization (ILO), an affiliated agency of the League, during the Paris Conference. As the preamble of the ILO's charter indicated, the main thrust of this new organization, in relation to the League of Nations, was to enforce labor standards, in part as a way to reduce the motives for war. The new Labor Charter, ratified by the members of the League, called for establishment of a maximum working day and week, the provision of an adequate living wage, protection against sickness, disease, and injury arising out of a worker's employment, the protection of children, women, and immigrant workers, freedom of association, and so forth.

THE PREAMBLE OF THE ILO CHARTER, 1919

Whereas the League of Nations has for its object the establishment of universal peace, and such a peace can be established only if it is based upon social justice. . . . Whereas conditions of labor exist involving injustice, hardship and privation to large numbers of people as to produce unrest so great that the peace and harmony of the world are imperilled. . . . Whereas also the failure of nations to adopt humane conditions of labor is an obstacle in the way of other nations which desire to improve the conditions in their own countries. . . . The High Contracting Parties, moved by sentiments of justice and humanity as well as by desire to secure the permanent peace of the world, agree to the following [standards].

The composition of the ILO bore considerable similarity to the structure of the League of Nations. It was divided into three arms—the General Conference, corresponding to the League Assembly, the Governing Body, similar to the League Council, and the International Labor Office, analogous to the League's Secretariat in Geneva. Despite the socialist impulse behind the text issued by the ILO, collaboration between employers and employees was to be secured by the ILO's tripartite composition, which included state representatives, employers, and employees.

The co-optation of socialist principles by the League and ILO was facilitated by the widening gap between European socialist reformers and Bolshevik revolutionary communists. The Allies' fear of the spread of Bolshevik ideas had been allayed with Lenin's ratification of the Peace Treaty of Brest Litovsk, and further calmed when socialists declared at the Bern conference that they "stood resolutely for democracy." Later, most European labor representatives, like Emile Vandervelde (1866–1938) and Philipp Scheidmann (1865–1939), further distanced themselves from the Bolshevik revolution and all use of violence to attain socialism. Under Sidney Webb's influence, the "socialist commonwealth" redefined its mission at the 1920 Geneva Congress by condemning the "dictatorship of the proletariat": "socialism will not base its political organization upon dictatorship. It cannot seek to suppress Democracy; its historic mission, on the contrary, is to carry Democracy to completion."[72] This was the coup de grace for a united socialist strategy.

The League's and ILO's efforts to counter economic inequity and conflicts between nations, feeble from the outset, would quickly collapse under the pressure of nationalism and war. From the outset, the opposition of the U.S. Congress to U.S. membership in the League, despite Wilson's desperate efforts, weakened the organization's credibility. Ultimately, neither the League nor the initial internationalist human rights promise of the Bolshevik regime, soon completely crushed by Stalin, would stand in the way of continuing imperialism, fascism, and the advent of World War II. Nevertheless, the combination of the Great War together with the Great Depression had impelled European and American statesmen to seek popular legitimacy by introducing many of the economic and social safety-net policies that socialists had long promoted. Thanks to a corporate alliance of government, business, and workers, the welfare state was born.

The connection between imperialist wars and welfare policies can be traced to the nineteenth century, when Bismarck was leading his country toward modernization and expansion while advocating social welfare as a way of foiling the appeal of German socialism. The fear of a communist rebellion similar to the one experienced during the short period of the Paris Commune, which led to 30,000 deaths, must have haunted the Iron Chancellor and explained why, starting in 1883, at the peak of German expansionist policies in Togo, the Cameroon, portions of southwest Africa, New Guinea, and Samoa, he secured the passage of social legislation that included compulsory sickness insurance for workers, an accident insurance plan, and a comprehensive pension for the aged and disabled.[73]

As the laissez-faire liberal dream of "a commercial peace" yielded to the nightmare of trench warfare at the battles of the Marne and Verdun, European states extended Bismarck's strategy, implementing regulatory control over their national economies. In England, France, and Germany, the railroad, shipping, and armament industries fell under the control of the government. Subsequently, each of these governments took extraordinary steps to control natural resources and other commodities, to introduce general price controls on basic foods, to ration and regulate consumption, and to oversee financial markets.[74] Both the imperatives of the war and continuing socialist pressure for more labor rights prompted states to make suffrage and welfare concessions. Foreseeing that trend, the French minister of commerce Etienne Clémentel (1864–1936) declared, "I have become convinced that a new era is emerging, one in which our old and excessive love must bow before the necessity of organization and union."[75]

The Great Depression (1929–1939) made that collectivist impulse a greater necessity. In England, the depression saw growth in the percentage of gross national product devoted to social welfare spending. France timidly followed the British example, despite Leon Blum's Popular Front (1936–1938) effort to institute, against great resistance, paid vacations and the forty-hour week.[76] Elected two years after the onset of the Great Depression, American president Franklin Roosevelt proposed a set of social protection policies under the label of the New Deal. Reflecting the views of the British economist John Maynard Keynes (1883–1946), this policy would involve increased government spending to create jobs, increase purchasing power, and stimulate the economy. With the massive expansion of the American state during World War II, that model would guide America for several subsequent decades.

Meanwhile, in much of Europe, Japan, and South America, the Great

THE SOVIET CONSTITUTION OF 1936

5. Socialist ownership in the U.S.S.R. has either the form of state ownership (public property) or the form of co-operative and collective farm ownership (property of individual collective farms, property of co-operative associations). . . .

9. Alongside the socialist system of economy, which is the dominant form of economy in the U.S.S.R., the law allows small private economy of individual peasants and handicraftsmen based on individual labour and excluding the exploitation of the labour of others. . . .

13. The Union of Soviet Socialist Republics is a federal state, formed on the basis of the voluntary association of the Soviet Socialist Republics with equal rights: Russian Soviet Federated Socialist Republic, Ukrainian Soviet Socialist Republic, Belorussian, Azerbaijan, Georgian, Armenian, Turkmenian, Uzbek, Tajik, Kazakh, Kirghiz. . . .

16. Every Union republic has its own constitution, which takes into account the specific features of the republic and is drawn up in full conformity with the Constitution of the U.S.S.R.

17. Each Union republic retains its right freely to secede from the U.S.S.R. . . .

64. The supreme executive and administrative organ of state power in the U.S.S.R. is the Council of People's Commissars of the U.S.S.R. . . .

79. The supreme executive and administrative organ of state power of a Union republic is the Council of People's Commissars of the Union republic. . . .

112. Judges are independent and subject only to the law. . . .

118. Citizens of the U.S.S.R. have the right to work—the right to receive guaranteed work with payment for their work in accordance with its quantity and quality. . . .

122. Women in the U.S.S.R. are accorded equal rights with men in all fields of economic, state, cultural, social and political life. The possibility of exercising these rights of women is ensured by affording women equally with men the right to work, payment for work, rest and leisure, social insurance and education, and by state protection of the interests of mother and child, maternity leave with pay, and the provision of a wide network of maternity homes, nurseries and kindergartens. . . .

124. To ensure to citizens freedom of conscience the church of the U.S.S.R. is separated from the state and the school from the church. Freedom to perform religious rites and freedom for anti-religious propaganda is recognized for all citizens.

125. In accordance with the interests of the toilers, for the purpose of strengthening the socialist system, the citizens of the U.S.S.R. are guaranteed:

a) Freedom of speech

b) Freedom of press

c) Freedom of assembly and meetings

d) Freedom of street processions and demonstrations. . . .

126. In accordance with the interests of the toilers and for the purpose of developing the organizational self-expression and political activity of the masses of the people, citizens of the U.S.S.R. are ensured the right of combining in public

organizations: trade unions, co-operative associations, youth organizations, sport and defense organizations, cultural, technical, and scientific societies, and for the most active and conscientious citizens from the ranks of the working class and other strata of the toilers, of uniting in the Communist Party of the U.S.S.R., which is the vanguard of the toilers in their struggle for strengthening and developing the socialist system and which represents the leading nucleus of all organizations of the toilers, both public and state. . . .

134. Deputies to all soviets of toilers' deputies, the Supreme Council of the U.S.S.R., Supreme Councils of the Union republics, territorial and province soviets of toilers' deputies, Supreme Councils of autonomous republics, soviets of toilers' deputies of autonomous provinces, regional, district, city, and village soviets of toilers' deputies . . . are elected by the electors on the basis of universal, equal and direct suffrage by secret ballot.

Depression was to foster extremist ideologies calling for a fusion between nationalism and a distorted variant of socialism, which Hitler designated as national socialism. In an effort to transcend the right and the left, Mussolini, Hitler, Francisco Franco of Spain (1892–1975), the Brazilian leader Getulio Varga (1883–1945), the Argentinean Juan Perón (1895–1974), and others urged workers to cooperate with employers toward the advancement of a new modern corporate and fascist state. Even as Stalin was consolidating his totalitarian regime, in the midst of murdering and purging, he was still seeking popular legitimacy by issuing, in 1936, a model of a socialist constitution predicated on social and welfare rights. It would take another world war to repudiate the fascist combination of political dictatorship and economic nationalism, on the one hand, and the illusion that a totalitarian state could penetrate every sphere of social activity to promote a mythical notion of the common good, on the other hand.

After World War II: The Universal Declaration of Human Rights

Indeed, the effort to create a global economic system after the war, premised on the unimpeded flow of capital, had been prompted in large measure by lessons drawn from the interwar period, when protectionist trade policies had contributed to intensifying nationalism and global depression. Those conditions in turn had helped ignite the mass appeal of fascism, whose resurgence, argued liberals, would now be prevented by policies fostering economic recovery and interdependence. The Bretton Woods system and the Marshall Plan for Europe (originally envisioned to include the Soviet-occupied territories and the Soviet Union itself) exemplified this approach, as did the 1950 Schuman plan for common Franco-German production of coal and steel as "the first step in the federation of Europe."[77] Jean Monnet, architect of European integration, maintained that economic interdependence offered a way "to unite men, to solve the problems which divided them, and to seek their common interest."[78]

The new world order, it seemed, would be a world of peaceful national societies enjoying liberal and even certain socialist rights, to be determined within each state by democratic institutions and pluralistic debate. It would be a world founded on "four essential human freedoms," declared Roosevelt in his 1941 message to Congress, a world predicated on freedom of expression and belief and freedom from want and fear.[79] In this universalist vision, as long as the state maintained a basic commitment to property rights, economic growth, and a degree of social justice—that is, the goals of the modern welfare state—its role appeared to be fundamentally compatible with laissez-faire capitalism. Appropriating aspects of early socialist principles of human rights, the welfare state after World War II proved a formidable force when pitted against the alternative Soviet model. Although communists would continue to denounce that "laissez-faire plus welfare" worldview, all the victorious leaders, following the atrocities generated by the war, agreed that an international organization stronger than the League of Nations was needed to counter interstate conflicts and promote social justice.

At Dumbarton Oaks in 1944, as victory approached, China, the Soviet Union, the United States, and the United Kingdom began to formulate proposals for a world organization that would succeed the League of Nations. "This time," said Roosevelt, "we won't make the mistake of waiting to set up the machinery of peace."[80] They agreed that all peace-loving states would in principle be eligible for membership and began the process of establishing the specific structure and functions of the United Nations. A subsequent conference, reuniting the big three— Winston Churchill (1874–1965), Roosevelt, and Stalin—convened a year later at Yalta, on the Crimean Sea, to resolve lingering disagreements from Dumbarton Oaks over the voting system of the proposed Security Council and the membership provisions concerning the constituent republics of the Soviet Union.

The main functions of the various UN organs were further detailed at the San Francisco conference of April 12, 1945, a conference that convened the main powers, prospective members of the UN, and nongovernmental organizations (NGOs). There, the Security Council, which included all the great powers as permanent members, with each having veto power over all decisions, was entrusted with the mission of maintaining peace (articles 22–32). A General Assembly comprising all members would be the plenary organ or "global town meeting" of the UN, and unlike the Security Council, would operate under majority rule and vote on non-binding resolutions (articles 9–22). The Economic and Social Council, working under the authority of the General Assembly, would

---

FRANKLIN D. ROOSEVELT, "THE FOUR FREEDOMS," ADDRESS TO THE UNITED STATES CONGRESS, 1941

For there is nothing mysterious about the foundations of a healthy and strong democracy. The basic things expected by our people of their political and economic systems are simple. They are:

Equality of opportunity for youth and for others.

Jobs for those who can work.

Security for those who need it.

The ending of special privilege for the few.

The preservation of civil liberties for all.

The enjoyment of the fruits of scientific progress in a wider and constantly rising standard of living.

These are the simple, basic things that must never be lost sight of in the turmoil and unbelievable complexity of our modern world. The inner and abiding strength of our economic and political systems is dependent upon the degree to which they fulfill these expectations. . . .

. . . In the future days, which we seek to make secure, we look forward to a world founded upon four essential human freedoms.

The first is freedom of speech and expression—everywhere in the world.

The second is freedom of every person to worship God in his own way—everywhere in the world.

The third is freedom from want—which, translated into world terms, means economic understandings which will secure to every nation a healthy peacetime life for its inhabitants—everywhere in the world.

The fourth is freedom from fear—which, translated into world terms, means a worldwide reduction of armaments to such a point and in such a thorough fashion that no nation will be in a position to commit an act of physical aggression against any neighbor—anywhere in the world.

That is no vision of a distant millennium. It is a definite basis for a kind of world attainable in our own time and generation. That kind of world is the very antithesis of the so-called new order of tyranny which dictators seek to create with the crash of a bomb.

---

carry out many committee functions (such as those of the Commission on Human Rights, the Sub-Commission on the Prevention of Discrimination and Protection of Minorities, and the Commission on the Status of Women) in pursuit of economic and social goals (articles 55–72).

In addition, there would be a Secretariat, which consisted of officials and civil servants who performed administrative, linguistic, secretarial, staff, and housekeeping functions for the other organs. These activities would be headed by a secretary-general, who was designed to be "the chief administrative officer of the Organization" (articles 97–101). An International Court of Justice, succeeding the Permanent Court of International Justice, would function outside of UN auspices as a semi-independent entity headquartered at the Hague. With fifteen judges elected by the Security Council and the General Assembly, only states consenting that the Court adjudicate their controversies would be parties to international arbitration. When states failed to comply with a decision of the court, the injured party would have recourse to the Security Council. In short, whatever the court's interpretation of treaties and international customs, its decision remained advisory (articles 92–97).

The proposal for a United Nations organization was not accepted without vociferous protests from small and medium states. Two months before the meeting in San Francisco, Latin American states held a conference assembling twenty nations at Chapultepec, Mexico, to exert pressure against the prominence of great power influence in the new international organization, and they submitted recommendations to be discussed at the San Francisco conference.[81] At the San Francisco meeting, Australia, New Zealand, India, and the Philippines joined the chorus of disenchanted countries. With Chile, Cuba, and Panama initially in the forefront, the protesting countries called for a stronger human rights commitment. Joining Gandhi's effort, Carlos Romulo of the Philippines (1899–1985), Ho Chi Minh, Kwame Nkrumah, and the American black leader W. E. B. Du Bois (1868–1963) all condemned the proposal for ignoring human rights in general, and specifically for overlooking the rights of minority and indigenous people living under colonial control.

Amendments to the UN calling for an increase in the General Assembly's authority, the weakening of the Security Council, and human rights provisions were now advanced. Amidst heated deliberations, NGOs such as the American Jewish Committee, the World Trade Union Congress, the Provisional World Council of Dominated Nations, the West Indies National Council, the Sino-Korean People's League, and the

Council of Christians rushed to the side of small and medium states to keep the pressure on the great powers.[82]

These pressures proved sufficiently intense to force the major powers to amend the charter and its preamble, and to make human rights a central part of UN activities. In the memorandum NGO activists issued on May 2, 1945, to American Secretary of State Edward Stettinius (1900–1949), they urged the American delegation to take a leadership position in demanding that human rights become a central purpose of the UN, asked all member states of the UN to assume the obligation of guaranteeing human rights, and called for the establishment of a human rights commission. Without the forceful presentation of Frederick Nolde (1899–1972) of the Council of Churches, followed by the persuasive plea of Judge Joseph Proskauer (1877–1971), president of the American Jewish Committee, Stettinius acknowledged he would not have "realized the [emotional] intensity on this subject." Three days later, the United States, along with Britain, France, and the USSR, conceded and backed the NGOs' human rights proposals.[83] The charter would now include the statement that "[w]e the people of the United Nations [are] determined . . . to reaffirm faith in fundamental human rights," followed by several passages with clear human rights references, and ending with a recommendation for the formation of a Trusteeship Council system as a sixth main organ (articles 75–91) designed to oversee the rights of the people of the colonies and work toward their self-determination.[84] The revised charter thus marked an important success for human rights activists. Yet while the charter stressed the importance of the "dignity and worth of the human person and the equality of rights," it also reaffirmed the principle of non-intervention by the organization in matters essentially within the domestic jurisdiction of the member states, thereby appearing to preclude international intervention to protect human rights. The centrality of the sovereign state as the final authority in human rights affairs was reiterated in the founding document of the United Nations. The Westphalian system was not altered, as the new order recognized the sovereignty of all states while conceding the reality that the great powers had disproportionate influence. The exception was that the two defeated major powers, Germany and Japan, would not be named among the permanent five in the Security Council.

Yet justice beyond state jurisdiction was still needed for the six million Jewish men, women, and children who had been forced down the corridors of death in the concentration camps of Dachau, Auschwitz, Belzec, Majdanek, and Treblinka. In their nightmarish journey, they had

THE UNITED NATIONS CHARTER, 1945

Article 1

The purposes of the United Nations are:

1. To maintain international peace and security, and to that end: to take effective collective measures for the prevention and removal of threats to the peace, and for the suppression of acts of aggression and other breaches of the peace, and to bring about by peaceful means, and in conformity with the principles of justice and international law, adjustment or settlement of international disputes or situations which might lead to a breach of the peace;

2. To develop friendly relations among nations based on respect for the principle of equal rights and self-determination of peoples, and to take other appropriate measures to strengthen universal peace;

3. To achieve international cooperation in solving international problems of an economic, social, cultural, or humanitarian character, and in promoting and encouraging respect for human rights and for fundamental freedoms for all without distinction as to race, sex, language, or religion; and

4. To be a center for harmonizing the actions of nations in the attainment of these common ends. . . .

Article 55

With a view to the creation of conditions of stability and well-being which are necessary for peaceful and friendly relations among nations based on respect for the principle of equal rights and self-determination of peoples, the United Nations shall promote:

a. higher standards of living, full employment, and conditions of economic and social progress and development;

b. solutions of international economic, social, health, and related problems; and international cultural and educational cooperation; and

c. universal respect for, and observance of, human rights and fundamental freedoms for all without distinction as to race, sex, language, or religion. . . .

Article 62

1. The Economic and Social Council may make or initiate studies and reports with respect to international economic, social, cultural, educational, health, and related matters and may make recommendations with respect to any such matters to the General Assembly, to the members of the United Nations, and to the specialized agencies concerned.

2. It may make recommendations for the purpose of promoting respect for, and observance of, human rights and fundamental freedoms for all.

3. It may prepare draft conventions for submission to the General Assembly, with respect to matters falling within its competence.

4. It may call, in accordance with the rules prescribed by the United Nations, international conferences on matters falling within its competence.

been enslaved, exhausted by agonizing labor, tortured, starved, and ultimately consumed in crematoria or open fires, while world governments averted their eyes. There were heroic individuals, one should note, like the Swedish diplomat Raoul Wallenberg (1912–1947), who was able to stop the deportation of some of the last remaining Jews from Hungary in 1944; the now famous Nazi businessman Oskar Schindler (1908–1974), who, while using Jewish slaves as workers, ultimately prevented their deportation to extermination camps; or the German pastor Martin Niemöller (1892–1984), founder of a "Pastor Emergency League" (Pfarnobund) that fought against Nazi racial policy. His brave acts took him to the concentration camps of Sachsenhausen and Dachau. Freed by the Allied forces at the end of the war, he was persuaded of the Germans' collective guilt and urged his compatriots to assume responsibility for the human tragedy associated with the Holocaust. However important and heroic such individuals were, they could not bring a halt to the extermination of the Jews.

While Jews were the primary victims of Nazism, many others were also persecuted by the Nazi regime merely for who they were or for what they believed in, including Gypsies, the handicapped, homosexuals, Jehovah's Witnesses, social democrats, and anyone else who was seen as an obstacle to Hitler's dreams of racial superiority and lebensraum. While the Polish-Jewish legal scholar Raphael Lemkin (1901–1959) might have coined the word *genocide* for the first time in 1944, atrocities that could be described by that new word preceded the Holocaust. While smaller in scale, the horrors surrounding the World War I deportation of 1,750,000 Armenians (1915–1916) by Turkish troops to Syria and Mesopotamia remains a neglected subject, and one still omitted in Turkish history books.[85] In the course of their forced exodus, more than half a million died of starvation or were killed by Turkish troops. Many Chinese still remember with bitterness "the rape of Nanking," in which, dur-

---

MARTIN NIEMÖLLER, "THEY CAME," 1968

First they came for the communists and I did not speak out because I was not a communist.

Then they came for the trade unionists and I did not speak out because I was not a trade unionist.

Then they came for the Jews and I did not speak out because I was not a Jew.

Finally, they came for me and there was no one left to speak out.

From the *Congressional Record*, October 14, 1968.

---

ing the interminable month of December 1937, Japanese soldiers carrying out Premier Matsui Iwane's (1878–1948) orders perpetrated mass
executions, tens of thousands of rapes, and the looting and burning of
towns and cities as they moved deeper into China.[86] Japan, like Turkey
and unlike Germany, has until now failed to assume responsibility for
these massacres.

"Never again!" was the rallying cry of Jews and human rights activists
after World War II. The Nuremberg trials (1945–1946) and the Tokyo
trial (1946), in which former Nazi and Japanese leaders were indicted and
tried as war criminals by an international military tribunal, vindicated the
persecuted. They also set a new precedent in international law, namely
that no one, whether a ruler, a public official, or a private individual, was
immune from punishment for war crimes. These crimes included crimes
against peace—namely, the planning, initiating, and waging of wars of
aggression in violation of international treaties and agreements; crimes
against humanity—that is, exterminations, deportations, and genocide;
war crimes—namely, violations of the laws of war; and "a common plan
or conspiracy to commit" criminal acts listed in the first three categories.[87]
These principles—later informed the UN Convention on the Prevention
and Punishment of the Crime of Genocide—were adopted unanimously
as the first human rights treaty by the General Assembly, on December
9, 1948, one day before the ratification of the Universal Declaration of
Human Rights.[88]

December 10 was also an important milestone for the members of the
human rights commission, headed by the remarkable Eleanor Roosevelt
(1884–1962). The widow of the late President had worked relentlessly
on the drafting of the Universal Declaration. Until this vote, the UN, noted
the Filipino diplomat Carlos Romulo (1899–1985), had been "on trial
for its life." The recent drama of the Holocaust and, more generally, the
killing of over fifty million people in World War II had highlighted the
significance of the work of the human rights commission members. Addressing the General Assembly on December 10, Eleanor Roosevelt proclaimed, "This Declaration may well become the international Magna
Carta of all men everywhere. We hope its proclamation by the General
Assembly will be an event comparable to the proclamation of the Declaration of the Rights of Man by the French people of 1789, the adoption of the Bill of Rights by the people of the United States, and the adoption of comparable declarations at different times in other countries."[89]

One prominent member of the human rights commission, Charles Malik, had preceded Eleanor Roosevelt and assured the Assembly the day

before the vote that the declaration reflected and synthesized many rights traditions.[90] (See chapter 1.) In addition to Roosevelt, who was both chairperson and member, the commission included eighteen members representing a diversity of nations: Australia, Belgium, Byelorussia, Chile, China, Egypt, France, India, Iran, Lebanon, Panama, the Philippines, Ukraine, the United Kingdom, the United States, Uruguay, the USSR, and Yugoslavia.[91]

To help the work of the human rights drafting committee, a questionnaire had been commissioned from a UNESCO philosophers' committee to study various rights traditions, including Chinese, Islamic, Hindu, American, and European worldviews on human rights as well as their customary legal perspectives. Seventy responses came back from noted scholars and leaders. They included, to list just a few, the views of the pacifist leader of the Indian independence movement, Mahatma

---

UNITED NATIONS CONVENTION ON THE PREVENTION AND PUNISHMENT OF THE CRIME OF GENOCIDE, ADOPTED 1948, RATIFIED 1951

Article I—The Contracting Parties confirm that genocide, whether committed in time of peace or in time of war, is a crime under international law which they undertake to prevent and to punish.

Article II—In the present Convention, genocide means any of the following acts committed with intent to destroy, in whole or in part, a national, ethnical, racial, or religious group as such:

    a. Killing members of the group;

    b. Causing serious bodily or mental harm to members of the group;

    c. Deliberately inflicting on the group conditions of life calculated to bring about its physical destruction in whole or in part;

    d. Imposing measures intended to prevent births within groups;

    e. Forcibly transferring children of the group to another group.

Article III—The following acts shall be punishable:

    a. Genocide;

    b. Conspiring to commit genocide;

    c. Direct and public incitement to commit genocide;

    d. Attempt to commit genocide;

    e. Complicity in genocide.

Article IV—Persons committing genocide or any of the other acts enumerated in article III shall be punished, whether they are constitutionally responsible rulers, public officials, or private individuals.

Gandhi, the Italian philosopher and historian Benedetto Croce (1866–1952), the Indian and Muslim poet and philosopher Hamayun Kabir, the Indian social scientist S. V. Puntambekar, the Chinese philosophy professor Chung-Shu Lo, the English novelist and essayist Aldous Huxley (1894–1963), the French Jesuit and paleontologist Teilhard de Chardin (1866–1952), the British professor and diplomat E. H. Carr (1892–1982), the Polish historian Sergius Hessen, the American professor of international law and international relations Quincy Wright (1890–1970), the Russian professor of law Boris A. Tchechko, and the Spanish author and diplomat Don Salvador de Maderiaga (1886–1978).[92]

The UNESCO committee was convinced that the members of the UN shared common convictions on which human rights depended. Affirming that the history of the philosophical tradition of human rights extended beyond Western tradition, they further argued that while human rights varied across cultures and were built upon different institutions and different political and economic backgrounds, the United Nations members nonetheless believed in similar principles:

> [T]hat men and women, all over the world, have the right to live a life
> that is free from the haunting fear of poverty and insecurity. They believe
> that they should have a more complete access to the heritage, in all its
> aspects and dimensions, of the civilization, so painfully built by human
> rights effort. They believe that science and the arts should combine to
> serve alike peace and the well-being, spiritual as well as material, of all
> men and women without discrimination of any kind. They believe that,
> given goodwill between nations, the power is in their hands to advance
> the achievement of this well-being more swiftly than in any previous age.[93]

Eleanor Roosevelt and the gifted framers who surrounded her shared the spirit of the UNESCO committee. For a year and a half, Roosevelt worked toward the drafting of the final document in close collaboration with three eminent scholars: the Chinese philosopher, diplomat, and commission vice-chairman Pen-Chung Chang, the Lebanese existentialist philosopher and rapporteur Charles Malik, and the French legal scholar and later Nobel Prize laureate René Cassin. Despite philosophical and political rivalries between these great minds, each human rights commissioner understood what was at stake, and all responded to their historical call by transcending personal and philosophical differences. Ideological gaps within the wider human rights commission, and more particularly the chilly relations between the East and the West, however, often tarnished the optimism of the commission members.

Illustrative of such intrinsic ideological and philosophical differences was the first major argument during the first session of the human rights commission, in which the definition of human nature was discussed. Malik's provocative questions—"Is man merely a social being? Is he merely an animal? Is he merely an economic being?"—generated a heated debate between advocates of individual and collective rights. Warning against the danger of collectivism that ultimately absorbed "the human person in his individuality and ultimately inviolability," Malik asserted the centrality of a person's mind and consciousness, the sanctity of individual property rights, and individual protection against religious, state, and other forms of external coercion. His position prompted reactions from communist representatives like Yugoslav Vladislav Ribnikar (1900–1955) and the Russian representative Valentin Tepliakov. In the words of Ribnikar, "[T]he psychology of individualism has been used by the ruling class in most countries to preserve its own privileges; a modern declaration of rights should not only consider the rights favored by the ruling class."[94] How can one understand individual rights and obligations apart from those of one's own community, asked Tepliakov.[95]

The Soviet representatives, unsurprisingly, gave priority to social and economic rights and equivalent civic duties, while American representatives favored political and civil rights. Central to this controversy was a face-off between proponents of central planning and advocates of programs that provided some room for the "invisible hand" to operate.[96] This unleashed tempestuous accusations on each side; for instance, in response to American accusations of civil and political human rights abuses in the Soviet republic, Soviet delegates would point out that aside from making "slanderous allegations," the United States was "hypocritically" maintaining segregation in its own country, depriving Southern blacks of their fundamental civil, political, and economic rights.[97]

Fearing additional incursions into domestic politics, and given their minority status in the overall composition of the United Nations in 1948, the Russians insisted that the state should be left as the primary authority for securing human rights. While representatives of states like India and Egypt were sympathetic to the inclusion of social and economic rights, they preferred broad principles concerning implementation, reminding other members of the commission that poor nations could only hope to actualize these rights gradually.[98] With the increasing number of post-colonial states after the adoption of the Universal Declaration, the issue of group and self-determination rights, predicated upon social, eco-

Eleanor Roosevelt and the Universal Declaration of Human Rights, 1949. Courtesy
of the Franklin D. Roosevelt Presidential Library and Museum, Hyde Park, N.Y.

nomic, and cultural rights, would begin to shift the emphasis of human
rights discourse. Meanwhile, growing hostilities between the two superpowers intensified the ideological controversy.

In 1948, Roosevelt, with great dexterity, succeeded in forging a compromise, convincing President Harry Truman's reluctant administration
(1945–1952) of the importance of incorporating socioeconomic clauses
in the Universal Declaration and insisting that these clauses were consistent with her late husband's New Deal and "four freedoms" vision.[99]
With the Soviet bloc abstaining, the declaration was adopted. The information in it, initially compiled by John Humphrey (1905–1995) and
drafted into a document by Cassin, could be compared, to use Cassin's
words, to "the portico of a temple."[100] Influenced by the spirit of the
French Revolution motto, Cassin identified the four foundation blocks
of the declaration as "dignity, liberty, equality, and brotherhood." Under "dignity" were values shared by all individuals regardless of religion,
creed, ethnicity, or sex (articles 1–2); under liberty were rights related to
individual life, liberty, and personal security (articles 3–19); under equal-

ity were rights related to public and political participation (articles 20–26); under brotherhood were economic, social, and cultural rights (articles 27–28). Finally, the roof of the portico (articles 28–30) highlighted the conditions in which the rights of individuals in society and the state could be realized.[101]

When this important, albeit non-binding, document was put to a vote, the UN had only fifty-eight member states. Fifty ratified the declaration, while Byelorussia, Czechoslovakia, Poland, Saudi Arabia, South Africa, Ukraine, the Soviet Union, and Yugoslavia abstained. Those countries worried that this document, predominantly "individualist" in its selected category of rights, would challenge the sanctity of domestic jurisdiction guaranteed by the legally binding UN charter.[102] These fears proved warranted, as state practice, and regular invocations of the declaration over time, turned the document into respected customary international law. More importantly, human rights commissioners knew that the declaration was but a first step toward the development of a more specific legally binding covenant of human rights.

Despite Cassin's continuous call for the indivisibility of human rights, ongoing dispute between members of the commission over the relationship between civil and political rights, on the one hand, and economic and social rights, on the other hand, as well as over the appropriate means with which to implement, supervise, and protect human rights, led to a decision to develop two covenants.[103] The looming cold war rivalry and the admission of newly independent states in the United Nations eager to integrate socioeconomic clauses into the covenant explained that resolution. When challenged about this division, Roosevelt backed an Indian resolution in the General Assembly, which pointed out that "though equally fundamental and therefore important, economic, social, and cultural rights formed a separate category of rights from the civil and political rights in that they were justiciable rights and their method of implementation was different."[104]

Two covenants were therefore presented and adopted by the General Assembly in 1966, entering into force in 1976. Upon ratification of these human rights covenants, states were no longer able to claim that human rights remained simply within their domestic jurisdictions. The two covenants also shared two provisions in common: one affirming the right to self-determination (article 1), and a second prohibiting any form of discrimination on grounds of race, color, sex, language, religion, or political or other opinions (article 2). These two clauses were perceived as fundamental prerequisites for the realization of other human rights.

The International Covenant on Civil and Political Rights focused more specifically on the civil and political dimensions of the Universal Declaration (see articles 2–21). Pressed by the Soviet Union, it excluded, for instance, the right to property. The International Covenant on Economic, Social and Cultural Rights, on the other hand, expanded upon the few social and economic clauses stipulated in the Universal Declaration (see its articles 21–27). Yet beyond the ideological differences, exacerbated by cold war hostilities, the salient difference between these two covenants was stated in article 2 of the Covenant on Civil and Political Rights, which stipulated that the listed rights would be protected immediately, while article 2 of the Covenant on Economic, Social and Cultural Rights stipulated that states should recognize the rights contained therein and should implement them progressively, consistent with other specific programs.

In the story of the UN approach to human rights, one should not depreciate the work of NGOs as human rights promoters, standard setters, and, later, fact finders in the early days of the UN.[105] While far less numerous than today, NGOs were responsible for the incorporation of human rights clauses into the UN charter, for a significant part of the language used in the Universal Declaration, and for the adoption and domestic ratification of major human rights treaties, such as the Declaration of the Rights of the Child (1959), the Covenant on Civil and Political Rights (1966), the Covenant on Economic, Social and Cultural Rights (1966), the Convention on the Elimination of All Forms of Racial Discrimination (1966), and the Convention on the Elimination of Discrimination against Women (1967). In 1948, their influence was reflected in article 71 of the UN charter, which encouraged the UN Economic and Social Council to "make suitable arrangements for consultation with nongovernmental organizations." UNESCO also became an important center for NGO activities. There were only forty-one NGOs holding consultative positions in 1948, predating the explosive increase in human rights NGOs over the coming decades.

If NGOs were able to generate pressure, provide expert opinion, and channel demands that the General Assembly might then deliberate in a broad international forum, the Security Council was the entity entrusted with the executive power of securing peace and resolving conflict. The UN charter had set the tone: it prescribed that all members "refrain in their international relations from the threat or use of force against the territorial integrity or political independence of any state, or in any other manner inconsistent with the purposes of the United Nations" (article 2). Yet to harness the powers of UN members to intervene against aggression, the charter allowed exceptions, such as the use of force in cases of individual or collective self-defense (article 51), actions against the "enemy states" of World War II (article 107), joint actions by the five permanent members, consistent with the availability of troops (article 43), and any other use of force authorized by the Security Council.[106] In short, the council could make binding decisions to impose both military and non-military sanctions against peace-violating states.

Furthermore, articles 51–54 of the UN charter encouraged regional organizations such as the Arab League, the Pact of Rio de Janeiro (1947), the North Atlantic Treaty Organization (NATO, 1949), the security treaty between Australia, New Zealand, and the United States (ANZUS, 1951), the South-East Asia Treaty Organization (SEATO, 1954), the Central Treaty Organization (CENTO, 1954), the Warsaw Pact (1955), and the Organization of African Unity (1963) to settle local disputes and prevent or repel acts of aggression. All such actions, however, needed to be reported to the Security Council, "[F]or no enforcement action shall be taken under regional arrangements or by regional agencies without the authorization of the Security Council" (article 53).

The Cold War: Social and Economic Rights versus Civil Rights

The effectiveness of these systems proved to be very limited. In the climate of the cold war, agreements on guidelines within the Security Council for the formation of a UN military force, under article 43, never succeeded as formulated. The first test for the UN was over Korea. Seizing the opportunity provided by a Soviet boycott of the Security Council in protest against the seating of Taiwan (as opposed to the People's Republic of China) as a permanent member of the Security Council, UN forces, led by the United States, intervened on the side of South Korea against North Korea's invasion. While that UN action preserved the independence of South Korea, the subsequent return of Soviet representatives to the Security Council ensured its paralysis in addressing subsequent cold war conflicts.

When collective military or non-military sanctions (e.g., economic and military boycotts or moral condemnation) failed, the UN was authorized to send a new Emergency Force, UNEF, a non-fighting military peacekeeping presence, to report on border violations and any forms of aggression, and to serve as a buffer between hostile forces once a cease-fire or a truce had been achieved. Throughout the cold war, from Indonesia to the Middle East, Africa, Kashmir, Cyprus, and the Sinai, and, more precisely, in areas in which the interests of the Americans and the Soviets converged, the UNEF was able to intervene successfully either as a local police force or to restrain hostilities.

The cold war, however, undercut the constructive tone of the San Francisco conference. For a brief time, the two superpowers had seemed united in trying to develop the UN as an efficient international institution predicated upon human rights principles and capable of mediating international conflicts. Soon ideological differences surfaced, shaping the UN structure, the content of fundamental human rights documents, and the actions (and inactions) of the organization. Engulfed in cold war politics, the UN became a battleground between superpowers' economic and geopolitical interests. In such a competition, invocations of human rights principles became a subterfuge for advancing the realpolitik interests of East and West. Both sides, in the end, used the UN principally as one means of courting world opinion.

Looming over varied European and Third World conceptions of socialist principles of human rights was Stalin's Soviet Union, a military superpower that combined massive internal repression with espousal of a world socialist revolution. For Stalin, Soviet security and power was the precondition for the global defeat of capitalism, and communists everywhere were obligated to subordinate their struggle to Soviet geostrategic concerns.[107] Thus, the Soviets prevented the communist regimes of Eastern Europe from accepting Marshall Plan assistance, maintaining that it represented an effort by "the imperialist circles of the United States" to create "a situation where the world [capitalist] economic system would recover hegemony, and the socialist area would first be pushed back to its frontiers of 1939 and then fully liquidated."[108] In response, the Soviet Union established the Council on Mutual Economic Assistance (Comecon) to prevent the encroachment of capitalism into its bloc.

After largely ignoring the Third World during the Stalin era, the Soviets began to support nationalist leaders on the basis—at least prospectively—of common opposition to the West, despite the fact that many of the regimes (e.g., of Nasser in Egypt and Nehru in India) were openly anticommunist. Later, the Soviets began to support socialist or communist "vanguard" movements and regimes in countries such as Vietnam, Laos, Algeria, Cuba, Nicaragua, Democratic Yemen, Ghana, Guinea, Mali, Mozambique, Angola, Rhodesia, and South Africa.

Responding to Soviet efforts to harness socialist movements in Europe and the Third World, liberal notions of human rights soon collapsed into a foreign policy based on realpolitik. While the rhetorical commitment to universal liberal rights continued, in practice, the United States soon dropped whichever elements of liberal human rights seemed incompatible with state power and the interests of private capital. George Kennan, widely celebrated for his formulation of U.S. containment doctrine, provided a (somewhat overstated) version of the new "realism" in a classified document he wrote as head of the State Department's Policy Planning Staff in 1948. "We have about 50 percent of the world's wealth, but only 6.3 percent of the world's population," Kennan noted. "Our real task in the coming period is . . . to maintain this position of disparity. . . . We need not deceive ourselves that we can afford today the luxury of altruism and world-benefaction. . . . We should cease to talk about vague and . . . unreal objectives such as human rights . . . [W]e are going to have to deal in straight power concepts."[109]

Where faced with choices between universal liberal political rights and protecting the interests of private capital, Kennan's strand of power politics was likely to prevail. In 1948, the Central Intelligence Agency (CIA) inaugurated its cold war campaign of worldwide covert action by interfering in Italian national elections, which had threatened to place a communist government in power.[110] In Japan, the overt establishment of democratic institutions was coupled to the covert creation of a one-party state, as the CIA funded the pro-American Liberal Democratic Party while infiltrating and sabotaging the Japanese socialist movement. From Iran to Guatemala to Chile, U.S. "security" policy now seemingly required overthrowing democratically elected regimes. From Southeast Asia to Central America, the same security considerations dictated suppressing mass social movements while supporting pro-Western despotic elites.

In the United States, the administration most explicitly wedded to realpolitik, that of President Richard Nixon (1913–1994), extended the concept of national security to include security against domestic opponents. The result was the use of the machinery of the state to undermine civil liberties and to prevent the election of George McGovern, a presidential candidate who rejected the basic tenets of cold war foreign policy. The resulting Watergate scandal would ultimately force Nixon from office.[111] If socioeconomic rights were strengthened by the welfare state at the height of the cold war, civil liberties were simultaneously threatened. More broadly, it may be the case that war and economic depression tend to drive countries in the direction of social and economic justice at the expense of civil and political rights.

In general, throughout the Third World, the cynical use of universal principles such as self-determination, socialism, or liberal democracy ended up following the power-politics, or realpolitik, standard set by Bismarck a century earlier. United States leaders during the 1950s could thus simultaneously call for the liberation of Eastern Europe from communism, demand Soviet respect for the sovereignty of Yugoslavia's anti-Soviet communist state (and later for Communist China), fund a French colonial war to prevent national self-determination in Indochina, and support tyrants like the Angolan Jonas Savimbi. Similarly, the Soviets supported "national liberation movements" within Western spheres of control, endorsed new independent regimes, such as those in Nigeria and India, which repressed their communist opposition, used force to crush hopes for freedom in Hungary and Czechoslovakia, and broke with communist regimes in Yugoslavia, China, Cambodia, and Albania over challenges to Soviet foreign policy.

Superpower leaders turned toward reshaping their state machinery for the conduct of a new global power struggle as the cold war underlined the impotence of the UN. The realist conception of a world cloaked in human rights rhetoric and dominated by autonomous "security-seeking" states was progressively reified in the form of huge nuclear arsenals and by an unfolding Third World carnage financed by the superpowers. By the 1960s, the "national security" policies of the two states had put directly at risk the lives of the entire human species, creating a danger of mutual nuclear annihilation that was superbly captured by Stanley Kubrick's satirical movie *Dr. Strangelove*. Whatever the origins of the conflict, the security managers of each government could now plausibly identify their counterparts on the other side of the Iron Curtain as the single greatest threat to the security and human rights of their state's inhabitants.

The Iron Curtain had indeed signified the paralysis of twentieth-century efforts to institutionalize human rights on a global scale. The inability to construct a viable mechanism, whether in the form of a model socialist state, after the Russian revolution, or in the form of the League of Nations, had revealed the weaknesses of both Wilsonian liberalism and Bolshevik communism. The rise of fascism, leading to the bloodletting of World War II, had momentarily revived the effort to design a just and peaceful world, leading to the establishment of the United Nations. Then it had seemed apparent, in light of the legacy of belligerent nationalism, that it was no longer safe for humankind once again to invest states alone with the task of securing even a narrow conception of basic rights.

The aftermath of World War II had introduced into global politics the notion that the state now existed to secure the political and welfare rights of all of its inhabitants, and by extension, that a Kantian supranational mechanism needed to be put in place. Unfortunately, the structure of the UN would not only reveal the continuing influence of the Enlightenment but also underline its inability to overcome continuing ideological and interstate rivalry. Despite these setbacks, the 1948 Universal Declaration of Human Rights had provided unmistakable evidence of progress in the global effort to extend new rights to oppressed minorities and to enlarge prevailing conceptions of who deserved inclusion in a universal human rights regime.

HUMAN RIGHTS FOR WHOM?

If the spread of industrialization and colonialism in the nineteenth century helped spur new conceptions of political and socioeconomic rights, the twentieth century, despite the setbacks of the world wars, was to be the era in which many of these political and social demands were institutionalized in the West. Throughout the first half of the twentieth century, slavery, in whatever forms, was once and for all legally banned worldwide, women across the globe were gradually entrusted with the right to vote, and the rights of children were codified in international treaties. While oppressed throughout that century, homosexuals, along with women, gained recognition, if not legally, at least socially, as important human rights partners in the new Western social movements. Following World War II, in response to the Jewish Holocaust and colonial oppression, minority rights and the right to a homeland became central components of the human rights agenda.

Workers in industrialized countries had already become seasoned human rights activists during the nineteenth century; if the onset of World War I had converted some of them to nationalism, years of carnage in the trenches had reintensified their demands for social and economic reforms. The Bolshevik victory in Russia and its pledge to ignite worldwide revolution fanned the optimism of socialist workers, yet they were soon disheartened by Lenin's acceptance of the 1918 Peace Treaty of Brest Litovsk, signaling his retreat from that vision of an international uprising. After the war, many turned their hopes toward the welfare rights promises of the League of Nations, and more specifically to the agenda of the ILO. Among the League's early successes was the Slavery Convention of 1926, which pledged to suppress the remaining slave trade and to abolish all forms of slavery in colonial territories and elsewhere.

Competing with the Bolshevik model for popular approval, and recognizing the social flaws generated by a laissez-faire economy, the victorious countries of World War I also began incorporating many of the principles developed by nineteenth-century socialists into their international treaties. When Roosevelt assumed the presidency three years after the onset of the Great Depression, he proposed a New Deal that represented a middle way between laissez-faire capitalism and socialism—an example industrialized countries would follow with conviction after World War II.

Meanwhile, during the interwar period, demagogues of industrially backward economies preached a populist, nationalist, and even a fascist alternative, channeling workers' frustration toward imagined enemies from within and from without. If the industrialized West was suffering, the depression had far harsher consequences for the entire underdeveloped world. As the advanced economies sharply reduced their imports of food and raw materials, the result in the colonial world was catastrophic for the "poor men and women who had dug and carried loads since the beginning of time."[112] From Peru to Ghana to Malaysia, peasants were migrating en masse to overcrowded cities, and students were rioting, contributing to the deepening crisis of colonialism. To control spreading unrest, European governments prodded their colonial administrators to improve workers' conditions, which, in places like the central African copper belt, were horrendous.[113]

After World War II, the problem of the colonies was at least initially subordinated to concern over the economic devastation of Europe, whose workers were, in several countries, on the verge of electing communist governments to power. European leaders turned their attention inward, focusing on workers' rights and welfare protections at home. At the same time, the need for sustained economic growth prompted construction of a new international regime—represented by the Bretton Woods system and the Marshall Plan—designed to speed European recovery and to encourage growing trade. World War II had given way to the cold war, and these domestic and international responses confirmed on a broader scale the success of Bismarck's policy in the nineteenth century—namely that warfare strengthened the interventionist capacity of the state.

Such partial concessions to socialist demands, as Bismarck had shown, were a necessary quid pro quo for power building and domestic legitimacy, especially necessary while conducting war. As liberal governments confronted domestic and international challenges in the name of workers' rights, principles protecting both social and state rights were incorporated into major international legal documents. The inalienable rights of state sovereignty were stipulated in the UN charter, and social and economic rights were spelled out in the UN Universal Declaration of Human Rights (articles 22–26). These included assertions that everyone has the right to social security, to work, to the free choice of employment, to equal pay for equal work, to join trade unions, to rest and leisure, to periodic paid holidays, and to an adequate standard of living (including medical care, food, clothing, housing, free education, etc.).

These principles were reiterated in subsequent human rights documents (e.g., the International Covenant on Economic, Social and Cultural Rights), as the co-optation of socialist principles of rights helped prevent outright communist victories in places like France and Italy and helped galvanize Western mobilization to wage the cold war against the Soviet Union. Left out of that human rights agenda, workers of the colonized world intensified their demands for rights, by now concentrated into a single core demand: the right to national independence. In the first years after 1945, the growing power of anti-colonial movements coincided with a moment of great weakness for Britain, France, and the lesser colonial powers. In some cases peacefully, in others only after exhausting wars, the Europeans would finally relinquish colonial control.

If World War I had helped trigger the development of welfare policies, the major roles played by women during that war also broke down the remaining opposition to women's suffrage in the United States and hastened the enfranchisement of women in Europe and elsewhere. In the period from 1914 to 1939, women in twenty-eight additional countries gained voting rights equal to those of men. These countries included Soviet Russia (1917); Canada (1918); Germany, Austria, Poland, and Czechoslovakia (1919); the United States and Hungary (1920); Great Britain (1918 and 1928); Burma (now Myanmar; 1922); Ecuador (1929); South Africa (1930); Brazil, Uruguay, and Thailand (1932); Turkey and Cuba (1934); and the Philippines (1937). In a number of these countries, women were initially granted the right to vote in municipal or other local elections, and only later the right to vote in national elections.

With the progress of the Bolshevik Revolution, social protections were added to the women's human rights agenda. As early as 1917, the new Soviet government began to enact new legislation granting women equal civil rights, voluntary marriage and divorce, legal contraception and abortion, state-supported childcare, employment rights, and maternity leave provisions. Lenin understood, despite all these new laws, that women's oppression would continue as long as they remained unpaid workers in the household: "[E]ven when women have full rights, they still remain downtrodden because all housework is left to them." Recognizing that developing the material conditions necessary for emancipating women from household bondage was a far more arduous mission, he proposed to socialize housekeeping by creating community kitchens, public dining rooms, laundries, repair shops, nurseries, kindergartens, and so forth.[114] In short, Lenin recognized that granting women equal rights under the law would in itself be insufficient to overcome prevailing male chauvinism within the Soviet Union. In any event, the civil war against tsarist and foreign troops, and particularly the ascent of Stalin to power, would result in reversals of many of women's initial gains. In 1936, abortion of first pregnancies was outlawed, and all abortions were outlawed in 1944. Divorcées were subjected to a fine and common-law marriage lost legal recognition.[115]

Outside of the world's first socialist state, women's political, social, and economic rights began to receive attention in international treaties after World War I. The League of Nations opened official positions equally to men and women (article 7 of the covenant) and prohibited trafficking in women and children (article 23). A 1918 recommendation stipulated that women should receive equal wages for equal work. It added that women should not be employed in any industry during a period of ten weeks before or after childbirth, and employers were forbidden to

---

V. I. LENIN, "A GREAT BEGINNING," 1919

. . . Take the position of women. Not a single democratic party in the world, not even in any of the most advanced bourgeois republics, has done in this sphere in tens of years a hundredth part of what we did in the very first year we were in power. In the literal sense, we did not leave a single brick standing of the despicable laws which placed women in a state of inferiority compared with men, of the laws restricting divorce, of the disgusting formalities attending divorce proceedings, of the laws on illegitimate children and on searching for their fathers, etc. . . .

. . . Do we in practice devote sufficient attention to this question, which, theoretically, is indisputable for every Communist? Of course not. Do we devote sufficient care to the *young shoots* of Communism which have already sprung up in this sphere? Again we must say emphatically, No! Public dining rooms, *crèches,* kindergartens—these are examples of the shoots, the simple everyday means, which assume nothing pompous, grandiloquent or solemn, but which can *in fact emancipate women,* which can in fact lessen and abolish their inferiority to men in regard to their role in social production and in social life.

From *Women and Society,* 13–14.

---

give female employees work to take home with them after working hours.[116] A 1926 recommendation declared that whenever a small group of female immigrants traveled unaccompanied, they should receive assistance to secure their rights and to give them moral support.[117]

The rise of Nazism and fascism proved major setbacks for the progress of women's rights. With the Nazi motto "Kinder, Kirche, Küche" women were prescribed a life spent raising their children, going to church, and busying themselves in the kitchen. Fascist leaders also believed in glorifying the role of motherhood as a female's greatest contribution to the state: "For the highest calling of the National Socialist, a woman is not just to bear children, but consciously and out of total devotion to her role and duty as mother to raise children for her people."[118] If women in fascist Italy were encouraged more than their German counterparts to enter professions hitherto closed to women, they were still supposed to produce children and preserve the family. The feminist movements in these countries, under the influence of the regimented mores of their time, were now reduced to timidly calling for women's suffrage as a way to open public life "to maternal influences" and not to female politicians.[119]

This suffocating moral veil was lifted at the end of the war, rekindling a new era of women's struggle. In 1945, the UN charter reaffirmed "faith in fundamental human rights . . . in the equal rights of men and women" (preamble)—principles reiterated in the Universal Declaration of Human Rights (article 2). Immediately after World War II, France, Italy, Romania, Yugoslavia, and China passed universal suffrage laws. Eleanor Roosevelt's strong belief "in active citizenship, for men and women equally, as a simple matter of right and justice" would soon be recognized by the 1953 Convention on the Political Rights of Women.[120] Sixty ratifying states concluded that women should be entitled to vote in all elections on equal terms with men. Aware that women continued to be "subject to ancient laws, customs and practices" inconsistent with the Universal Declaration, the UN General Assembly called on all governments to "abolish them," and adopted, a few years later, in 1967, the Convention on the Elimination of Discrimination against Women, which included, among other rights, the right to equal education and equal remuneration.

By the late 1960s, more than one hundred countries had given women the right to vote. Nearly all countries that had gained independence after World War II guaranteed equal voting rights to women and men in their constitutions. Last among Western countries, Switzerland granted women full voting rights only in 1971. In many of the conservative Arab states adjacent to the Persian Gulf, women continue to be denied voting and other fundamental rights. With that important exception, the recognition of universal suffrage and women's civil rights was a triumph for women. Social and economic protection for women and mothers has remained a central issue for the feminist agenda.

The fight for women's rights would have direct implications for the plight of children. In the nineteenth century, as the industrial revolution progressed, many European countries began to regulate child labor, making education universal and compulsory. Examples of legislation designed to protect children include the English Elementary Act of 1870 and the 1882 promulgation of a similar French law. With the implementation of compulsory education for children, women were gradually released from some of their daily caretaking tasks. The advance in children's rights cannot be attributed solely to the moral progress of employers; instead, there had been a realization that an increasingly complex industrial environment required workers with at least a basic education. That capitalist motive, socialists hoped, would ultimately contribute to the development of the working-class consciousness necessary for building a just society.

Unsurprisingly, among the first acts called for by the Bolshevik state, as it envisioned the arrival of a new generation of socialist men and women, was "the carrying out of universal free of charge compulsory general and polytechnical education for all children of both sexes up to the age of 17." The Soviet government also became a leader in the development and subsidizing of factory nurseries to improve health and sanitation for children. "Our state institutions of guardianships," maintained A. Goikhbarg, "show parents that social care of children gives far better results than the private individual, inexpert and irrational care by individual parents who are 'loving,' but in the matter of bringing up children ignorant."[121]

The World Wars and the Russian civil war, followed by economic disintegration, left a great number of orphans and homeless children, propelling the Soviet government to secure boarding institutions and infant homes. As the reconstruction of a society devastated by war began, children were among the first to benefit from state intervention in delivering social services and in securing basic rights. This social policy soon changed. Under Stalin's collectivization policy, the children of the Kulaks were left to fend for themselves or were deported to their death. It was one of the "most degrading periods in the history of Soviet child welfare," where "the goals became so corrupt that children were held responsible for their parents' behavior"—a period in which children were taught to place loyalty to the state above that due to their own parents.[122]

Fascist and Nazi leaders attempted to extract loyalty from children with methods similar to those designed under Stalin's terror. In Germany, the study of Hitler's *Mein Kampf* was used to instill Nazi racist doctrine in children, and for the Hitler Youth in particular, education emphasized sports and paramilitary training. If the goal of female education was invariably to prepare girls for motherhood (girls would become citizens only upon marriage), for boys the motto was "Live faithfully, fight bravely, and die laughing."[123] Italian and Spanish fascists, among others, realized along with the Nazis the necessity of free compulsory education for propagating their regimes, and made national and religious traditions the heart of school curricula.[124]

While more children were going to school, many would be killed at the front, their bodies draped with the patriotic flags of their countries. In the aftermath of the war in Europe, waves of orphans and homeless children, wandering the streets in despair, drew the attention of the international community, just as had occurred after World War I. A special committee appointed by the League of Nations had already been established to draft various conventions related to the protection of children, including the 1921 International Convention for the Suppression of the Traffic in Women and Children, the 1924 Declaration of the Rights of Children (also called the Declaration of Geneva), and the 1926 Slavery Convention. Equally concerned about the suffering of children during World War II, the General Assembly launched efforts to revise the 1924 Declaration of the Rights of Children. Article 25(2) of the Universal Declaration of Human Rights had stipulated in 1948 that "motherhood and childhood are entitled to special care and assistance," and the UN Declaration of the Rights of the Child was finally ratified in 1959.

Formulated in terms of the rights of a child, rather than, as in the Geneva Declaration, in terms of humankind's duty to a child, the 1959 declaration provided, aside from material needs, attention to children's emotional needs. The declaration may have been instrumental in the promotion of children's rights throughout the world, yet many felt—despite article 24 of the Covenant on Civil and Political Rights stating that every child regardless of race, sex, and background was entitled to protective measures—that it would also later be important to create a binding international instrument, as finally occurred in 1989. Children were still suffering from many forms of abuse in the developed world, while also victimized under colonialism and apartheid.[125]

After all, the colonial powers had shared similar goals with respect to children's education: to train a limited number of mid-level bureaucrats, and particularly, as in the case of France, to impose its culture and language. Predictably, the anti-colonial movement would attempt to expand education by restoring national dignity and a new consciousness stripped of foreign influence. Even with a better state-run pub-

---

UNITED NATIONS DECLARATION OF THE RIGHTS OF THE CHILD, 1959

Principle 2—The child shall enjoy special protection, and shall be given opportunities and facilities, by law and by other means, to enable him to develop physically, mentally, morally, spiritually and socially in a healthy and normal manner and in conditions of freedom and dignity. In the enactment of laws for this purpose, the best interests of the child shall be the paramount considerations. . . .

Principle 4—The child shall enjoy the benefits of social security. He shall be entitled to grow and develop in health; to this end, special care and protection shall be provided both to him and to his mother, including adequate pre-natal and post-natal care. The child shall have the right to adequate nutrition, housing, recreation and medical services.

Principle 5—The child who is physically, mentally or socially handicapped shall be given the special treatment, education and care required by his particular condition.

Principle 6—The child, for the full and harmonious development of his personality, needs love and understanding. He shall, wherever possible, grow up in the care and under the responsibility of his parents, and, in any case, in an atmosphere of affection and of moral and material security; a child of tender years shall not, save in exceptional circumstances, be separated from his mother. Society and the public authorities shall have the duty to extend particular care to children without a family and to those without adequate means of support. Payment of State and other assistance towards maintenance of children of large families is desirable. . . .

Principle 9—The child shall be protected against all forms of neglect, cruelty and exploitation. He shall not be the subject of traffic, in any form. The child shall not be admitted to employment before an appropriate minimum age; he shall in no case be caused or permitted to engage in any occupation or employment which would prejudice his health or education, or interfere with his physical, mental or moral development.

Principle 10—The child shall be protected from practices which may foster racial, religious and any other form of discrimination. He shall be brought up in a spirit of understanding, tolerance, friendship among peoples, peace and universal brotherhood, and in full consciousness that his energy and talents should be devoted to the service of his fellow men.

---

lic education system, the suffering, labor, and sexual exploitation of children would remain a great challenge in the developing world and would continue to preoccupy the children's and women's rights advocates of the new millennium.

As women entered the labor force, gender relations were gradually redefined, opening, from the nineteenth century on, social spaces for a freer expression of homosexual and lesbian preferences. These spaces were noticeable in European countries that, under the influence of the Napoleonic Code and the continental system, had already decriminalized homosexuality. In the nineteenth century, countries outside that sphere, such as England and Germany, lagged behind. In the early years of the twentieth century in England, the trial of Oscar Wilde had sent a chilling message regarding Victorian morality to the homosexual community. In 1905, by contrast, the German Reichstag—under pressure from the German physician Magnus Hirschfeld (1868–1935) and socialists like Bebel and Adolfe Thiele—modified an 1871 German legal code (Paragraph 175) stipulating that "a male who indulged with another male or who allowed himself to participate in such activities will be punished with jail."[126] With the repeal of Paragraph 175, Germany became one of the first countries to witness the development of a public gay and lesbian movement before 1918.

During the Bolshevik Revolution, along with new legislation mandating equality for women, criminal penalties for adultery and homosexuality were also abandoned; all private consensual sexual activity was now perceived as beyond the concern of the state.[127] As a result the Soviet Union raised hopes in the 1920s for many gay writers seeking a new haven to escape homophobic societies. The Soviet Union even sent representatives to meetings of Magnus Hirschfeld's League for Sexual Reform, and Hirschfeld himself was well received when he toured the Soviet Union in 1926. This climate of tolerance, however, changed completely under Stalin. In 1934, homosexuality was recriminalized and made punishable by a five-year prison term. During the mid-to-late 1930s, 3,000 Muscovite homosexuals were imprisoned in labor camps on the Baltic, and mass arrests of homosexuals were also carried out in Leningrad, Kharkov, and Odessa.[128] What accounted for such a rapid political change? One explanation, offered by Herbert Marcuse (1898–1979), was that rapid industrialization, as was occurring in the Soviet Union, tended to re-create a reactionary morality similar to that adopted by Victorian capitalists as social mores were geared toward the efficient control of both production and reproduction.[129]

After a period of progress achieved by the German gay movement in the early decades of the twentieth century, along with the emergence of a gay subculture in European cities such as Paris and Amsterdam, the trend was reversed in the early 1930s. With the rise of Nazism, homosexuality, now deemed a "vice" and a "disease" that would erode the vigor of a conquering people, was outlawed in Germany. Forced to wear an identifying pink triangle, homosexuals in German-occupied territory during World War II were relentlessly subjected to beatings and other humiliations and were often executed along with Jews and political dissidents in concentration camps. In fascist Italy, homosexuals were occasionally harassed but were not persecuted as in Germany, nor were homosexual acts outlawed.

If the glorification of a desexualized masculinity reached its apogee during the height of Nazism and fascism, the idealization of order and a conservative division of labor between the sexes, despite the significant roles played by women during the war, remained appealing to a postwar generation devastated by violence and chaos. Cold war fears at the onset of the nuclear age inspired political conservatism, which, by the end of the 1940s, had degenerated in the United States into the period of McCarthyism. In that climate, not only alleged communists, but all perceived political and social "deviants," including homosexuals, were seen as subversive. It is ironic that Roy Cohn, the most zealous prosecutor working for McCarthy, as well as J. Edgar Hoover, who as head of the Federal Bureau of Investigation (FBI) was leading the national search for communists and homosexuals, were most likely closeted gays.[130]

HEINZ HEGER, *THE MEN WITH THE PINK TRIANGLE*, 1972

Thousands upon thousands of homosexuals must have lost their tormented lives there, victims of a deliberate operation of destruction by the Hitler regime. And yet till this very day no one has come forward to describe this and honour its victims. It seems that "good taste" nowadays prevents people from speaking of the destruction of concentration camp victims, particularly when they were homosexuals. . . .

. . . My request for compensation for the years [spent in a] concentration camp was rejected by our democratic authorities, for as a pink triangle prisoner, a homosexual, I had been condemned for a criminal offense, even if I'd not harmed anyone. No restitution is granted to "criminal" concentration-camp victims. I therefore found employment in a commercial office, which hardly fulfilled my ambitions of a career, but none the less provided me with an income.

From *The Men with the Pink Triangle*, 38.

Even in northern Europe, these were difficult times for homosexuals. In Norway, the state church warned against a "world conspiracy of homosexuals,"[131] and in England, 2,109 homosexuals, including the mathematical genius Alan Turing, were arrested for "gross indecency," punishable by two years in prison. The fact that Turing, whose decoding device had cracked the "Enigma" code used by the German military, was arguably the individual most responsible for British survival during World War II, did not spare him from persecution.[132] In general, in the conservative climate of the 1950s, homosexuality was widely castigated either as a crime or as a form of mental illness.[133]

The 1950s, however, incubated a sexual revolution that would dramatically change gender relations and attitudes toward sexuality. As mounting opposition to the Vietnam War during the late 1960s galvanized the New Left movement, women and gays found a new partner in their fight against sexism and homophobia. The alliance with the emerging student movement was intensified after a New York City police raid on June 27, 1969, on a Greenwich Village gay bar called the Stonewall Inn. Within a few days, large numbers of gays in New York, San Francisco, and Minneapolis took to the streets to demand an end to police harassment. Breaking with a long history of suffering in silence, the gay liberation movement, with the assistance of radical student groups, began spreading across the college and university campuses of the United States and Western Europe.[134] By the early 1970s, the movement had successfully campaigned, in England and elsewhere, to decriminalize homosexual conduct. These victories were, however, limited to Western states;

LUCIAN TRUSCOTT IV, "GAY POWER COMES TO SHERIDAN SQUARE," 1969

Sheridan Square this weekend looked like something from a William Burroughs novel as the sudden specter of "gay power" erected its brazen head and spat out a fairy tale the likes of which the area has never seen.

The forces of faggotry, spurred by a Friday night raid on one of the city's largest, most popular, and longest lived gay bars, the Stonewall Inn, rallied Saturday night in an unprecedented protest against the raid and continued Sunday night to assert presence, possibility, and pride until the early hours of Monday morning. "I'm a faggot, and I'm proud of it!" "Gay Power!" "I like boys"—these and many other slogans were heard all three nights as the show of force by the city's finery met the force of the city's finest. The result was a kind of liberation, as the gay brigade emerged from the bars, back rooms, and bedrooms of the Village and became street people.

From *The Village Voice*, July 3, 1969.

---

gay repression, as discussed in the next chapter, continued in less developed countries, such as those in Latin America, and in post-colonial countries around the world. And even in the West, homophobia remained well entrenched, an ancient prejudice that could not be uprooted overnight.

The same could be said of anti-Semitism, another historical reaction to what some would always regard as disturbing challenges to social conformity. If the American and French Revolutions, and later, the 1848 revolution, had promised, in their embrace of universal human rights, to carry Jews to a better future, the late nineteenth century and early twentieth century had yielded sober recognition of the limits of the Enlightenment. In a sense, the trial of Oscar Wilde was for homosexuals what the Dreyfus Affair had represented for the Jews of the early twentieth century: both were vivid illustrations of xenophobia and the limits of human rights. Pogroms in Kishnev (1903) and Odessa (1905) were echoed in England by the anti-Semitic prose of political philosopher Houston Steward Chamberlain (1855–1927), whose prejudice toward Jews mirrored that of Austria's Christian Social Party and the Czech Social Party of that time.[135]

The nationalism of the Great War deepened European anti-Semitism as Jews were increasingly identified, particularly in Germany, as outsiders. Other groups suffered as well. Because of worries about the treatment of Eastern and Central European minorities, prospective members of the League of Nations after World War I, including Bulgaria, Montenegro, Romania, Serbia, and Turkey, were required, as a condition of their admission to the League, to ratify minority rights treaties.[136] The Polish Minority Treaty, in particular, contained special protective provisions with respect to Jews. This and other minority treaties were regarded as essential for averting secessionist demands by minorities in Central Europe and in the colonial world. While many European Jews were comforted, however naively, by these new protective measures, others were convinced that a more reliable path toward safety would be the establishment of a national Jewish homeland in Palestine. Under a plan produced by British Prime Minister Arthur Balfour (1848–1930), it became British policy to support their cause.

Meanwhile, Eastern European Jews found brief respite from the long history of Russian pogroms when one of the first acts of the Bolshevik Provisional Government decreed that "all restriction on the Russian citizens which had been enacted by existing laws on account of their belonging to any creed, confession, or nationality shall be abolished."[137] Under Lenin's leadership, Jews were identified as a nationality under Soviet law, and in the 1920s, the far eastern territory known as Birobidzhan was selected as the Jewish Autonomous Region. These projects came to an abrupt end under Stalin.[138]

In general, after initial advances, minority rights were gradually eroded during the interwar period. Soviet Jews were progressively excluded from all positions of power, influence, and prestige. Despite the faint protests of France, Italy, and the United Kingdom, Poland withdrew unilaterally from the Polish Minority Treaty in 1934. The Germans, who had never really recognized the legitimacy of the Treaty of Versailles, were soon challenging it, trying to recover Upper Silesia and the Polish Corridor from Poland—areas inhabited by a million Germans. With the ascent of nationalism, fascism, and Nazism, the well-elaborated minority treaties of the League became worthless for the mistreated minorities of Central and Eastern Europe. The ultimate reflection of the obliteration of minority rights was, of course, the murder of six million Jews during World War II.

The horror of the Holocaust would shape new international humanitarian law for decades to come. One of the first conventions drafted after the war to protect minority rights was the Convention on the Prevention and Punishment of the Crime of Genocide, adopted in 1948. Of particular significance was article 2 of the convention, which extended protection to either a minority or a majority "national, ethnic, racial and religious group."[139] Article 14 of the European Convention for the Protection of Human Rights and Fundamental Freedoms (1950) stipulated that "the enjoyment of rights and freedoms set forth in this Convention shall be secured without discrimination on any ground such as sex, race, colour, religion, political or other opinion, national or social origin, association with a national minority, property, birth or other status."[140] Similar language can be found in the International Covenant on Civil and Political Rights (article 27) and the Helsinki Accords (1975; paragraph 4 of principle 7).[141]

Following World War II, in cases of severe oppression or genocide, the international community found itself more inclined to favor self-determination. The Jewish survivors of concentration camps, and later the indigenous inhabitants of colonial states, would garner considerable sympathy in world public opinion as they struggled for self-determination. Yet the subsequent creation of a Jewish state in 1948 continues to epitomize the dilemma of self-determination in areas under previous colonial mandates. Even if an oppressed nationality deserves a right to a safe homeland, its existence within new borders is often realized at the expense of other groups, imposing on them economic hardship and the loss of self-governance. Without careful planning to avert those dangers, the victims of yesterday may well become the aggressors of tomorrow.

Nationalism and the quest for self-determination have continued to challenge the notion of universal rights ever since the French revolutionary wars. These divisive movements arose out of the failures of a succession of efforts to implement universalistic conceptions, beginning with the American and French Revolutions and culminating in the United Nations' Universal Declaration of Human Rights. What are the lessons that one can then draw from these cycles of internationalism and nationalism? While nationalism, and particularly the creation of an independent homeland, as Lenin and Wilson argued, might be a much needed means of escaping chronic abuse of minority rights, new states based on ethnicity or religion, as Luxemburg and Fanon foresaw, can simply re-create the same forms of oppression. Hence the question remains, following Bauer and others: what are the best social and economic arrangements for securing social justice and stability, and what are the most appropriate means with which to implement these ideals, thereby removing the incentive for oppressed minorities to secede?

Such questions regarding the relationship between means and ends have not been limited to questions of majority versus minority rights. The issue of which means can be employed for a just end was a central preoccupation of the socialist movements that flourished in the early twentieth century. A temporary dictatorship of the proletariat, argued Lenin, was essential for eradicating the authoritarian institutions that had prevailed under the tsar. A labor party, retorted Karl Kautsky, was a better venue for educating the public and implementing reforms while averting inevitable revolutionary abuses. Grassroots participation in any revolutionary process, Luxemburg cautioned, remained a vital check against the abuses of whatever political elite held power. Despite their differences, Lenin's socialist critics were animated by a common interest, the development of a political platform in which all share the benefits, and by a mindfulness of how excessive means can jeopardize valuable ends.

From that perspective, many socialists repudiated the presumed necessity of Stalin's repression of gays, women, the pauperized bourgeois, and Kulak peasants as acceptable means toward achieving a socialist model of human rights, just as one could question the repressive politics of erstwhile colonized countries of various ideological stripes who have sought to modernize at the expense of human rights. While the architects of the United Nations certainly intended to create a venue that would peacefully resolve existing conflicts between nations and groups, its very structure, including its human rights mechanisms, excludes attention to the human rights violations of the major powers, which remain in critical instances protected by the veto privilege of the Security Council. The UN's guiding principle of national sovereignty would also limit its capacity to protect human rights; those who framed that structure may have erroneously hoped that marginalized and oppressed individuals in authoritarian and poor states (e.g., women in theocratic Islamic societies) would be allowed to express their human rights grievances through legal channels similar to those that existed in the West.

Cynical positions regarding power politics or attentiveness to the horrors of colonialism, Nazism, and Stalinism should not, however, blind us to genuine human rights progress. After all, the twentieth century witnessed the final abolition of the slave trade, the vast improvement of workers' rights in industrialized states, the recognition of universal suffrage in most countries of the world, substantial advances in homosexual rights, and greater recognition of children's and minority rights in the West. At the same time, recent decades have witnessed a growing chasm between the fundamental rights enjoyed in the developed and the developing world, alerting us to the urgent need to guarantee the basic rights of billions of continuously neglected humans. Would globalization impede or advance the hopes and rights of the wretched of the earth? This important question is addressed in the next chapter.

Chapter Five

Globalization and Its Impact on Human Rights

ILWU rank and file make
their voices heard, 1999.
Photo by David Bacon.

A S THE SUPERPOWER RIVALRIES fanned old ideological controversies, the world was changing. An ever-expanding market economy, new forms of production, and dramatic innovations in information technology fed a process of globalization that contributed to the West's victory in the cold war. Two linked strands of "triumphalism" followed the fall of the Berlin Wall. Some proclaimed, with Charles Krauthammer, the arrival of "the unipolar moment," in which United States power reigned supreme over the globe.[1] For others, it was, as Francis Fukuyama put it, "the end of history," as liberalism and a globalized free market achieved final victory in the historical world struggle over contending conceptions of rights.[2]

There certainly seemed to be good reasons for post–cold war optimism over prospects for promoting human rights. With the development of global information technology, Human Rights Peacenet, Amnesty International, and a multitude of other websites now offered human rights advocates unprecedented possibilities for fighting with their fingertips. One cannot overlook the success of the human rights community's "infopressure" on the Mexican government during the Chiapas rebellion or the human rights "infoactivity" during the turbulent events in Tiananmen Square or against Indonesia's repression in East Timor. The proliferation of human rights–oriented NGOs and the post–cold war mushrooming of human rights activities—such as the International Women's Conference in Beijing and the launching of humanitarian interventions—have also kindled new hopes for the advancement of human rights.

Yet even if a new global communications revolution may be enhancing human rights opportunities, globalization is also associated with two more disturbing trends. First, it has been accompanied by a growing gap between rich and poor countries. Second, it has inspired backlashes in the name of various purportedly threatened beliefs and ways of life—at least one of which, we learned on September 11, 2001, can lash out with a global reach. These two trends are plausibly linked, since widespread despair over economic prospects could presumably feed rage against the countries and elites that benefit most from an integrated world economy.

A revealing exchange between the *New York Times* journalist Thomas Friedman, and the editor of *Le monde diplomatique,* Ignacio Ramonet, highlights conflicting perceptions over these two trends of globalization. For Friedman, globalization provides opportunities for more than just the wealthy. To his French interlocutor, he says, "Ask the high-tech workers in Bangalore, India, or Taiwan or the Bordeaux region of France, or Finland, or coastal China, or Idaho what they think of the opportunities created by globalization. . . . What about all the human rights and environmental organizations that have been empowered by the Internet and globalization, don't they count?"[3] Exasperated, Ramonet replies, "My dear Friedman, do reread the 1999 Human Development Report from the United Nations Development Programme. It confirms that 1.3 billion people (or one quarter of humanity) live on less than a dollar a day." "The political consequences [of globalization]," Ramonet adds, "have been ghastly. . . . Borders are increasingly contested, and pockets of minorities give rise to dreams of annexation, secession, and ethnic cleansing."[4] Some, as we came to realize on September 11, were even dreaming of the annihilation of the United States, the powerhouse of globalization.

Contention over the benefits of globalization continues to divide the human rights community. If the advance of a more integrated world has enabled many to contemplate the idea of a global citizenry sharing ascendant values of human rights and dignity, these very advances have also exacerbated the fear that national, cultural, and economic difference will overwhelm such universalist aspirations. That anxiety has intensified as the Trojan horse of globalization has successfully infiltrated the fortress of the nation-state, diluting forces of democratic opposition in civil society and even besieging the realm of privacy, the once sacrosanct bastion of the liberal edifice. Yet as human rights activists grasped for ways to resist these globalization effects, Osama bin Laden and Al Qaeda launched a violent campaign that imperiled globalization, though hardly in the name of democracy or individual liberties.

The tight international security controls that have emerged in response to September 11 have cast a shadow over efforts to promote human rights either domestically or globally, apparently vindicating once again the realist perspective that national interests ultimately override such internationalist concerns. In rejecting that conclusion, this chapter argues that global justice and human rights belong now more than ever at the center of any strategy that hopes to achieve long-term security. Moreover, growing recognition of that linkage between human rights and security may well pave the way for the development of new human rights realism in foreign policy. Even if the first impulse for Americans after September 11 was to protect their borders and kill the terrorists in the caves of Tora Bora, those reactions have been followed by the growing realization that military measures are hopeless if they ignore some universal aspirations for social justice and rights.

Toward the goal of evaluating the role of human rights in the emerging post–September 11 era, this chapter proposes first to review the various ways globalization has redefined the main concerns of human rights for the new millennium and shaped changing opportunities and security challenges for human rights. It also evaluates the status and actions of deprived citizens and human rights actors in our globalization era. To set the stage for addressing the debate over globalization and human rights, this chapter begins with a look at the wave of cold war–era human rights militancy that began in the late 1960s and then turns to the second wave of activism unleashed by the shocks of 1989.

GLOBALIZATION AND PROTEST MOVEMENTS

From 1968 to 1989: New Social Movements and the Waning of the Cold War

In May 1968, Paris became the epicenter of a student uprising that reverberated in the United States, Mexico, Germany, Czechoslovakia, Italy, and elsewhere. In Paris, street combat between protesters and police soon unleashed waves of working-class strikes throughout Europe that briefly paralyzed the economy of such countries as France and Italy. This was the time of the Algerian crisis that led to that nation's independence from France, the Tet offensive that turned the tide against the United States in Vietnam, the assassination of civil rights leader Martin Luther King, Jr. (1929–1968) and U.S. presidential hopeful Robert Kennedy (1925–1968), and the Soviet repression of the Prague Spring. These events coincided with the explosive growth of a new global student society, which in turn fueled a vast student political movement. Sensing the strength of their numbers as the post–World War II baby boom generation began arriving in annual waves at universities in Europe and America, students became convinced that they could change the world.

Despite those hopes, 1968 proved not to be a revolution as had occurred in 1789, 1848, or 1917, since those in power were quite prepared to prevent a real social revolution in the Western world. It was, however, the most widespread resistance since World War II, fanned by the new technological instruments of globalization: students everywhere read the same books, now often published internationally at the same time, took the same cheap air flights from Paris to Havana and São Paulo, dressed in the same hippie style, sang the same anti-war and Beatles songs, lived the same free lifestyle, and, whether in the Sorbonne or at Berkeley, challenged the emerging postwar consumer society. With them, pop, conceptualist, and neo-dada artists like Andy Warhol (1928–1987), Cesar Baldaccini (1921–1998), and Yves Klein (1928–1962) were unearthing the ironical mass appeal of materialism and the modern urban condition. Artists and students became, however, despite the warnings of their anti-consumerist gurus, the beneficiaries of an emerging globalized counterculture. Similar political ideas were broadcast and televised on each

---

MARTIN LUTHER KING JR., "I HAVE A DREAM,"
KEYNOTE ADDRESS OF THE CIVIL RIGHTS MARCH ON WASHINGTON, D.C., 1963

So I say to you, my friends, that even though we must face the difficulties of today and tomorrow, I still have a dream. It is a dream deeply rooted in the American dream that one day this nation will rise up and live out the true meaning of its creed—we hold these truths to be self-evident, that all men are created equal.

I have a dream that one day on the red hills of Georgia, sons of former slaves and sons of former slave-owners will be able to sit down together at the table of brotherhood.

I have a dream that one day, even the state of Mississippi, a state sweltering with the heat of injustice, sweltering with the heat of oppression, will be transformed into an oasis of freedom and justice.

I have a dream that one day, that one day my four little children will one day live in a nation where they will not be judged by the color of their skin but by the content of their character. I have a dream today!

I have a dream that one day, down in Alabama, with its vicious racists, with its governor having his lips dripping with the words of interposition and nullification, that one day, right there in Alabama, little black boys and black girls will be able to join hands with little white boys and white girls as sisters and brothers. I have a dream today!

I have a dream that one day every valley shall be exalted, every hill and mountain shall be made low, the rough places shall be made plain and the crooked places shall be made straight and the glory of the Lord will be revealed and all flesh shall see it together.

From *A Testament of Hope,* 217.

---

side of the Atlantic, and thus comparable ideological concerns were entertained, with efforts to develop a movement dissociated from both American capitalism and Soviet oppression in communist regimes. The struggle by Czech students to realize their president Alexander Dubcek's call for "socialism with a human face" evoked yearnings similar to those of American and Western European students seeking to transcend cold war conformity by joining the New Left. As a young playwright, future Czech President Vaclav Havel (1936–) would find himself alternately imprisoned as a dissident and fraternizing with the Western counterculture when allowed to travel abroad. Notwithstanding a violent fringe, stu-

---

VACLAV HAVEL, *THE POWER OF THE POWERLESS*, 1978

A specter is haunting Eastern Europe: the specter of what in the West is called "dissent." This specter has not appeared out of thin air. It is a natural and inevitable consequence of the present historical phase of the system it is haunting. It was born at a time when this system, for a thousand reasons, can no longer base itself on the unadulterated, brutal, and arbitrary application of power, eliminating all expressions of non-conformity. What is more, the system has become so ossified politically that there is practically no way for such nonconformity to be implemented within its official structures. . . . Is it within the power of the "dissidents"—as a category of subcitizen outside the power establishment—to have any influence at all on society and the social system? Can they actually change anything? . . .

The essential aims of life are present naturally in every person. In everyone there is some longing for humanity's rightful dignity, for moral integrity, for free expression of being and a sense of transcendence over the world of existence. Yet, at the same time, each person is capable, to a greater or lesser degree, of coming to terms with living within the lie. Each person somehow succumbs to a profane trivialization of his inherent humanity, and to utilitarianism. In everyone there is some willingness to merge with the anonymous crowd and to flow comfortably along with it down the river of pseudo-life. This is much more than a simple conflict between two identities. It is something far worse; it is a challenge to the very notion of identity itself. . . .

A person who has been seduced by the consumer value system, whose identity is dissolved in an amalgam of the accouterments of mass civilization, and who has no roots in the order of being, no sense of responsibility for anything higher than his own personal survival, is a demoralized person. . . .

Living within the truth, as humanity's revolt against an enforced position, is, on the contrary, an attempt to regain control over one's sense of responsibility.

---

dents generally opted for green rather than red politics, anti-nuclear and pacifist positions rather than bellicose ones.

Various guerilla movements for anti-colonial liberation and ultra-left Latin Americans were making more serious attempts at revolutionary transformation of their societies. Yet with the exception of the internationalism of the revolutionary Che Guevara (1928–1967), Senghor, and a few other like-minded leaders, Vietnamese, Palestinian, Basque, and Irish Republican Army leaders reflected the nationalist preoccupations of most movements of liberation.[5] With the Sino-Soviet split deepened by the Soviet invasion of Czechoslovakia, few were left who believed in Moscow's continuing claim to support proletarian internationalism.

If the anti-imperialist revolutions in the Third World reinvigorated human rights activism in the West, its particularistic and nationalist dimension influenced the course of the new social movement. During its initial phase, mass activism in the West seemed animated by a common sense of purpose (e.g., in the anti–Algerian war movement in France and the civil rights and anti–Vietnam War movements in the United States).[6] As mass movements faded, a new era of identity politics began in which blacks, feminists, Latinos, and gays focused on promoting their particular agendas.[7]

The 1970s oil crisis, inflation and stagnating growth, hobbled liberal governments in England and the United States, and set the stage for a conservative backlash. With the victory of Margaret Thatcher (1925–) in England, followed by that of Ronald Reagan (1911–) in the United States, attacks were launched against trade unions and the welfare state.

CHE GUEVARA, SPEECH DELIVERED BEFORE THE GENERAL ASSEMBLY OF THE UNITED NATIONS, 1964, AND THE AFRO-ASIAN SOLIDARITY CONFERENCE, 1965

Immense problems are presented to our two worlds, the world of the socialist countries and this one which is known as the third world. They are problems that are directly related to man and his well-being and to the struggle against the main culprits guilty of our backwardness. All we countries and peoples who are aware of our duties and of the dangers that the situation entails must take definite steps to solve these problems so that our friendship can be cemented on two planes, the economic and the political, which can never be separate. We must form a large compact bloc that will in turn help other countries liberate themselves not only from imperialist political power but from imperialist economic power as well. The question of armed liberation from an oppressive political power must be handled in accordance with the rules of proletarian internationalism.

From *Che: Selected Works of Ernesto Guevara*, 356–357.

In this upsurge of neo-conservatism, announced by Reaganomics and Thatcherism, some traditional left and right views were blurred. One could even imagine conservatives joining their liberal foes to boycott the beleaguered segregationist South African apartheid regime. In reality, political dissent was tolerated under the aegis of multiculturalism as long it as it did not threaten the pace of economic integration and globalization.

The forces of globalization proved sufficiently powerful to infiltrate the communist fortress and erode the Soviet empire. Outspent in its competitive war with the United States in every possible realm, and facing an inflexible, sclerotic, and steadily shrinking centralized economy, the USSR's only hope of remaining a significant power was to undertake radical political and economic change. Under the bywords *uskorieniie* (acceleration), *glasnost* (openness), and *perestroika* (restructuring), Mikhail Gorbachev (1931–) launched new reforms that soon unraveled into seething popular discontent. Decentralization and political autonomy were no longer sufficient for the Baltic states, nor for the other nationalities of the Soviet Union, which were now pressing vociferously for independence. Fights for national independence and growing worker dissatisfaction, coupled with a fierce power struggle within the politburo over the nature and pace of reform, would ultimately culminate in the downfall of Gorbachev.

Meanwhile, throughout the communist bloc, human rights activists sensed the vulnerability of Soviet power and seized the opportunity to push more aggressively for political reforms. Solidarity, a Polish alliance between socialists, democrats, nationalists, and Catholics led by Gdansk shipyard union leader Lech Walesa (1943–) showed the way, demanding throughout the 1980s free trade unionism and political freedom in the face of military opposition and fear of a Soviet invasion. The Soviets, however, did not roll their tanks onto the streets of Warsaw, signaling to human rights activists within the rest of the communist countries that there would be no repeat of the suppression of similar movements in Hungary (1956) and Czechoslovakia (1968).

Yet on June 4, 1989, the very day that elections in Poland sealed the defeat of the communist regime there, China was sending troops to crush the thousands of students and workers gathered in protest at Tiananmen Square in Beijing. The news of the death of Hu Yaobang, the Chinese secretary-general who had been ousted for his sympathetic views toward the student democracy movement, had sparked a series of student demonstrations. Workers angered by rampant official corruption joined students as they defiantly erected a "goddess of democracy" on the legendary square. The world was watching and thousands conveyed supporting messages via the Internet.

Deng Xiaoping (1904–1997), China's aged leader, recognized a Chinese Solidarity movement in the making and resolved to stop at all costs the spread of the "Polish disease."[8] On the night of June 3, after days of peaceful protests, shots were heard as tanks and armed troops entered Beijing. As they reached the square, they began to fire indiscriminately, killing men, women, and children sitting on balconies. Those who sat in front of the tanks were brutally run over, those who kneeled down were machine-gunned. There were scenes of mayhem and slaughter throughout the city, which soon lapsed into stunned silence.[9]

While Communist officials in Eastern Europe were tempted similarly to crush their respective oppositions with an iron fist, they realized they could not count on Soviet help, and their intransigence succumbed to mounting popular dissatisfaction that spread rapidly through Hungary, East Germany, and the rest of the Eastern bloc with varied levels of intensity. As Czechoslovakia underwent a "velvet revolution," Romania approached the brink of civil war.[10] The collapse of the Berlin Wall in November 1989 signified the end of these struggles and the collapse of the world's division into two ideological camps—in short, the end of the cold war.

By overthrowing communism in Europe, the protests of 1989 succeeded where the Prague Spring of 1968 had failed. What many of the 1989 protesters did not expect, however, was that their victory over communism would open the floodgates of a raging laissez-faire tide that would bring dire social and economic malaise, political corruption, and great uncertainty over their future. In this respect 1989 failed to avert what the Parisian and American protesters of 1968 had sought to resist: the uncontested triumph of capitalism. With all boundaries removed, globalization no longer faced meaningful opposition anywhere in the world.

The Aftermath of 1989 and Its Impact

Soon after the fall of the Berlin Wall, Europeans signed the 1991 Maastricht Treaty, a free trade agreement designed to deepen European economic cohesion. Because of British opposition to the welfare rights invoked earlier by the Council of Europe in the Social Charter (1961), European Union social policy was gradually weakened, triggering uncoordinated strikes throughout Europe.[11] In 1992, the United States, Canada, and Mexico ratified the North American Free Trade Agreement (NAFTA), which would gradually eliminate most tariffs and other trade barriers. One act of resistance against this neo-liberal pact was almost immediate as peasants of the impoverished Chiapas region of Mexico, led by the mysterious Subcomandante Marcos, launched a rebellion. For them, NAFTA did not mean the return of their land or their autonomy, but the prospect of even less power to shape their lives as they faced transnational economic forces. Their rebellion ignited instantaneous domestic and international support. The speed with which the news of an indigenous struggle circulated and the rapidity of the resulting mobilization of support were unprecedented.[12] Global communication had penetrated the countryside of Mexico and become a recognized tool for human struggle, forestalling any temptation on the part of the Mexican government to crush the uprising and fueling the demands of indigenous movements in Brazil, Chile, and elsewhere.

The human rights movement against globalization would later take

---

SUBCOMANDANTE MARCOS,
"A LETTER ADDRESSED TO THE PEOPLE OF THE UNITED STATES," 1995

The U.S. government has been wrong, not just a few times, in its foreign policy. When this has occurred, it's because it made a mistake in the man it backed up. History gives us ample examples of this.

In the first half of this decade, the U.S. government made a mistake backing Carlos Salinas de Gortari. It made a mistake signing NAFTA, which lacked the support of the majority of the North American people, and which spelled a summary execution of Mexico's indigenous people.

On the dawn of 1994 we rose up not seeking power, not in response to a foreign mandate. We rose to say: "We are here."

The Mexican government, our government, had forgotten us and was ready to perpetrate a genocide without bullets or bombs; it was ready to annihilate us with the quiet death of sickness, of misery, of oblivion. The U.S. government became the accomplice of the Mexican government in this genocide. With the signing of NAFTA, the U.S. government acted as guarantor of—and gave its blessing to— the murder of millions of Mexicans. . . .

What are the North American people afraid of? Should they fear our wooden rifles, our bare feet, our exhausted bodies, our language, our culture? Should they fear our shout that demands democracy, liberty, and justice? Aren't these three truths the foundation that inspired the birth of the United States of America? Aren't democracy, liberty, and justice rights that belong to all human beings?

From *Our Word Is Our Weapon: Selected Writings,* 169.

on a new shape as thousands upon thousands of people turned out to protest a succession of International Monetary Fund (IMF), World Bank, World Trade Organization (WTO), and major world power (Group of Eight, or G8) meetings.[13] This new anti-globalization movement, which first demonstrated its strength in the streets of Seattle and Washington, D.C., would soon spread throughout the world. In May 2000, 80,000 protesters gathered in Argentina to confront the IMF as over seven million workers joined a twenty-four-hour strike to protest IMF anti-labor measures.[14] In the same year, 15,000 Colombian workers struck against the IMF's loan conditions, which called for cuts in social services; 10,000 protested in Costa Rica over IMF-prescribed policies of privatization; between 20,000 and 50,000 protestors assembled in Prague to demonstrate against the "evils" of globalization; over 40,000 Ecuadorians demonstrated against the United States and the IMF's neo-liberal economic rules; and large protests erupted in Honduras against IMF austerity measures.[15]

The year 2001 witnessed a similar wave of human rights militancy against the IMF and the WTO, particularly in India, Indonesia, Kenya, Malawi, Nigeria, Paraguay, Peru, South Africa, South Korea, and Turkey, culminating in the gathering of 150,000 protesters in Genoa, Italy, to protest the August 2001 G8 summit. Most of these protesters do not oppose international trade, as is commonly held, but instead seek international regulations to secure the rights of women, children, and labor to promote development and protect the environment. Despite the political fragmentation of these various groups, a transnational human rights movement is in the making, resurrecting the spirit of 1968 as it consolidates its agenda after each cycle of demonstrations.

Not all anti-globalization movements since the end of the cold war, however, have struggled on behalf of human rights. "I don't believe in democracy because I don't believe any group at any time can change the course and goals of their ancestors by their free will," claimed Dragoslav Boka, the Serb film director, as the Balkans were crumbling under nationalist strife.[16] His position is far from unique. North of Serbia, in the Eastern and Central European republics, or far to the south, in Somalia, Rwanda, and Sierra Leone, or to the southeast, in Pakistan and India, few regimes have proved impervious to the impact of nationalism since the shocks of 1989, or remained untarnished by war or its ripple effects.

Worse, the fight against modernity and globalization has also energized extreme fundamentalist groups. Growing economic gaps and social inequities in the Palestinian territories, Afghanistan, and India, among other places, has fed the appeal of groups like Hamas, the Taliban, and the Indian BJP. In climates of social and economic turbulence, fundamentalist organizations have provided badly needed social services while striving to reorder society along traditional lines under the claim of providential protection. If defined as a reaction to globalization, fundamentalism nonetheless necessarily remains contaminated by the very culture it opposes.[17] The horrors committed by fundamentalist terrorists during the attack on the World Trade Center and the Pentagon could not have reached such a large scale without the technology generated by the world they so much abhorred. They were fighting, for a radically different purpose and with wholly different means, the same icons of global capitalism and American power previously challenged by leftist human rights advocates. The anti-globalization trend has indeed produced strange bedfellows.

In an effort to discredit the progressive anti-globalization movement, Britain's Secretary for International Development, Clare Short, went as far as stating that "their demands turned out to be very similar to those of bin Laden's network."[18] Fearful of giving apparent credence to such assessments, a sense of paralysis has gripped the anti-globalization movement in the wake of September 11. An understanding of these two conflicting strands of anti-globalization activism, as they have evolved since 1989, will be critical to formulating a new human rights agenda for this millennium. This requires first an understanding of how various trends of globalization have shaped our evolving human rights perspectives since the end of the cold war, a topic we now turn to discuss.

DEFINING RIGHTS IN THE ERA OF GLOBALIZATION

While some still see globalization as nothing more than an extension of capitalism on an unprecedented scale, most agree that globalization presents new features that have an impact on various aspects of human rights—features that cannot be reduced to a single phenomenon.[19] Indeed, globalization is now widely viewed as an amalgamation of a host of international processes characterized by a growing market economy, new forms of production, and impressive developments in information technology. Each of these dimensions of globalization has undergone substantial change since the beginning of the cold war, change that has had different impacts across countries, groups, and classes. The human rights agenda of this era is being shaped in the context of these global developments.

Weakened by the expansion of a globalized free market economy, trade unions and labor rights activists, for instance, have been reenergized in recent years as they seek to make labor rights central to the human rights debate. Poor countries, less attractive to investment, continue to challenge IMF austerity policies and to press for a right to sustainable development. The unprecedented ravaging of the global environment has prompted the emergence of an active international ecology movement. The abuses of a growing illegal immigrant labor force and the hardships suffered by refugees fleeing from poverty, repression, or war have led to calls for fairer immigration and refugee laws. Diffused by a global telecommunications network, Western culture seems more omnipresent and is now more forcefully resisted by many nationalists and advocates of different cultural rights.

Cultural differences have continued to divide the human rights community, as evidenced by specific labor, environmental, and immigration rights debates and treaties. There are signs, however, that human rights activism is overcoming its cultural and economic differences while broadening and internationalizing its agenda. Conversely, some protectionists, alarmed over what they regard as the transfer of power from the nation to pernicious international forces, are joining militant right-wing movements in the industrialized countries, and many of the most destitute within the southern hemisphere also attack globalization, driven by the religious conviction that their struggle will be rewarded in heaven.

Economic Globalization and the Question of Labor and Development Rights

Clearly the reaction against globalization is not uniform. If the goal of the free trade regime developed after World War II was to extend labor rights and reduce the national economic disparities intensified by that war, the institutional legacy of Bretton Woods is today challenged by both its right-wing and left-wing critics as the source of social and labor inequities.

Created in 1944 to restore a stable world economy following the impending defeat of Japan and Germany, Bretton Woods developed new international financial mechanisms, establishing the Bank for Reconstruction and Development to make long-term capital available to states in urgent need of foreign aid and an International Monetary Fund aimed at financing short-term imbalances in international payments in order to stabilize exchange rates. Under the direction of one of its chief architects, John Maynard Keynes, Bretton Woods further guaranteed that domestic economic objectives would not be subordinated to global financial imperatives, but rather that countries could adjust their balance of payment deficits or surpluses incrementally, remaining responsive to social and domestic concerns. Bretton Woods thus embodied a "compromise between free traders, who desire open global markets, and the social democrats, who desire national prosperity and full employment," thereby establishing an auspicious climate for the promotion of labor and welfare rights.[20]

Within a few decades, the global economic environment had substantially changed. If the rise of private international finance and the emergence of the European currency market placed growing pressure on the Bretton Woods regime by the late 1960s, the 1973 oil crisis represented its coup de grace, precipitating financial deregulation and increased privatization. To fill the vacuum, the General Agreement on Tariffs and Trade (GATT), established in 1948 to abolish quotas and reduce tariff duties among the contracting nations, found new impetus. In a series of negotiating rounds, it moved beyond tariffs and sought to grapple with non-tariff barriers as well. Amplified and enlarged at several subsequent rounds of negotiations, GATT significantly increased the level of foreign investment, creating levels of capital mobility that would begin to erode the bargaining power of organized labor.

Economic integration on the scale that occurred would not have been possible without the development of new technologies. The invention of the transistor and, later, semiconductors, the spread of television, the development of the computer, the onset of satellite communications, microprocessors, the Internet, and in general the ever more effective packaging of data for mass consumption all marked the road to the information age. Making an international transaction could now be faster and more economical than doing business locally. New technologies also facilitated shifts in distribution, consumption, and management. Mass production, which had characterized the Fordist economy, began to yield to flexible production.[21]

While exploiting opportunities created by new information technologies, the post-Fordist economy also represented an effort to respond rapidly to unexpected changes in labor and diverse market conditions, including demographic changes, by emphasizing labor flexibility (e.g., the growing use of part-time workers), infrastructure flexibility (e.g., leased office space rather than company-owned buildings), production flexibility (e.g., extensive use of machines rather than human labor), institutional flexibility (e.g., organizations that managed contracts rather than products), and political flexibility (e.g., state encouragement of privatization).[22]

If businesses and ever growing multinational corporations hailed flexibility in production and labor force recruitment, that flexibility dramatically undermined the bargaining leverage of trade unions. On the collapse of communism in 1989, increasingly flexible and globalized world production further shrank the power of labor, as private capital and states now rushed to broaden and deepen the free trade regime, establishing or fortifying new regional economic agreements such as Maastricht (1991), NAFTA (1992), and the Association of South East Asian Nations (ASEAN) Free Trade Area (1992). Already reeling, organized labor was now confronted with a new threat as calls for a stronger global organization to extend free trade and to resolve disputes led to the establishment of the World Trade Organization as the successor to GATT. With 104 countries as founding members, the WTO has brought greater transparency and predictability to the global business environment, integrating more tightly national economies, as Karl Marx and Friedrich Engels predicted—if prematurely—more than one hundred and fifty years ago:

> [T]he bourgeoisie, by the rapid improvement of all instruments of production, by the immensely facilitated means of communications, draws all, even the most barbarian nations, into civilization. The cheap prices of its commodities are the heavy artillery with which it batters down all Chinese walls, with which it forces the barbarians' intensely obstinate hatred of foreigners to capitulate. It compels all nations, on pain of extinction, to adopt the bourgeois mode of production. . . . In one word, it creates a world after its own image.[23]

Financiers and advocates of globalization began to engage in self-congratulatory exercises as they perceived the arrival of a world created after their own image. "The integration of marginalized societies is the best thing that has happened in the lifetime of the post-war generation," recently claimed Peter Martin.[24] Pointing to the success of globalization in Asia, Martin Wolf noted that real per capita incomes had risen sevenfold from 1965 to 1995.[25] Rebuffing human rights outcries against the exploitation of child labor, Ted Fisherman forecast that "the economic output of the developing world will soon outstrip that of developed countries and by the turn of the century will account for over 60 per cent of everything the world produces." Just when his own children would be in the midst of their working years, Fisherman complained, Taiwan, Thailand, and Indonesia would rank higher in gross national product than Great Britain, reversing the economic divide between developed and developing countries.[26]

A less selective look at the facts, however, tells a different story. Recent reports from the United Nations Development Programme show that the poorest countries are getting poorer, not just in relative terms, but also in absolute terms. Around 1.2 billion people live on less than $1 a day, and 2.8 billion on less than $2 a day. In Africa, reality shows its cruelest face: 46 percent of the population earns less than $1 a day, and foreign direct investment has fallen sharply since the mid-1990s, the $9.1 billion invested in 2000 amounting to less than 1 percent of total world investment.[27] In Latin America and the Caribbean, the percentage of people living in poverty has increased, peaking at 40 percent during the 1990s.[28]

While it is true that transitional economies, such as a few of the former communist countries and the so-called Asian Tigers (Hong Kong, Singapore, South Korea, and Taiwan) have been more effectively incorporated into the global financial system, the poorest developing countries have often been excluded from direct investment and IMF loans.[29] It is also worth mentioning that none of the much-vaunted Asian Tiger economies have built their commercial power on the precepts of Adam Smith or David Ricardo; their power reflects, rather, a long history of protectionism, managed trade policies, massive U.S. government aid during the cold war, and records of using political repression to discipline the labor force.[30]

Unsurprisingly, numerous Asian states have preferred to invoke their inalienable right to economic development, as opposed to civil and political rights. The nineteenth century's socialist belief that the fight for economic rights is intrinsically linked to political freedom continues to be overlooked in elite circles in China and by the authoritarian regimes that prevail in much of the developing world. Since the drafting of the International Covenant on Economic, Social and Cultural Rights, leaders of the less developed states have urged the West to be patient, holding that development initially requires sacrificing civil and political rights. Ironically, some human rights advocates on both right and left have concurred that the short-term cost of development is deepening poverty and political repression. Whereas free-traders saw the ineluctability of economic austerity policies as the price of modernization, to be followed by the establishment of legitimate institutions that would promote civil liberties, many Marxists agreed that the suffering of the masses was an inevitable feature of rapid industrialization and economic development: it was the very pervasiveness of suffering that would kindle working-class consciousness and the ultimate struggle for human emancipation.[31]

To those who believed, with student protesters in the 1970s, that development was not diametrically opposed to human dignity and political freedom, IMF structural adjustment policies, backed by repressive and punitive regimes (such as those in Chile, Argentina, and Mexico), seemed to mock their beliefs. In Argentina and Chile, political opponents of military regimes pursuing neo-liberal economic policies were tortured or simply "disappeared." Even Mexico's elected civilian government ordered troops to open fire on a peaceful demonstration of several thousand students. Economic policies in the developing world would continue to fuel protest movements, as evidenced in a succession of large rallies in Costa Rica, Ecuador, Honduras, Peru, Mexico, and elsewhere. Now more than ever, those protestors would insist that sustainable, more inclusive and independent economic development policies must be consistent with political and social rights. Economic development programs, argued Nobel Prize–winning Indian economist Amartya Sen (1933–), should not require "blood, sweat and tears" sacrifice by a population, but adopt a more congenial approach with respect for human freedom as their central tenet.[32] Article 1 of the UN Declaration on Environment and Development, drafted at Rio de Janeiro (1992), encapsulates some of his concerns: "Human beings are at the center of concerns for sustainable development. They are entitled to a healthy and productive life in harmony with nature."

AMARTYA SEN, *DEVELOPMENT AS FREEDOM*, 1999

Within the narrower views of development (in terms of, say, GNP growth or industrialization), it is often asked whether the freedom of political participation and dissent is or is not "conducive to development." In the light of the foundational view of development as freedom, this question would seem to be defectively formulated, since it misses the crucial understanding that political participation and development are *constitutive* parts of development itself. . . .

The relevance of the deprivation of basic political freedoms or civil rights, for an adequate understanding of development, does not have to be established through their indirect contribution to *other* features of development (such as the growth of GNP or the promotion of industrialization). These freedoms are part and parcel of enriching the process of development.

From *Development as Freedom*, 36–37.

With foreign aid receding in the 1990s, that goal seemed a mere chimera, leading the World Bank to recommend an increase in foreign aid by the developed countries of ten billion dollars annually to lift about twenty-five million people out of poverty. The United Nations' development goals for 2015 recommended a more ambitious plan, namely to raise about five hundred million people above the poverty line.[33] These recommendations fell, however, on deaf ears, at least until after the events of September 11. As the war against terror unfolded, even a conservative United States leadership concluded that it could not cut back on foreign aid to poor countries, as it had in the 1990s, and effectively fight terrorism. "Besides being a moral question, poverty reduction is now recognized as a necessity for peace and security," stated the deputy managing director of the IMF, Eduardo Aninat, as he attempted with others to formulate a more balanced approach to financial globalization.[34]

Most developing countries aspire today not to avoid globalization, but to harness it in a way that reduces poverty while increasing national revenue. Indeed, most developing countries compete to attract foreign investment, offering tax incentives and reassurances that labor costs will be controlled. Human rights activists in these countries have so far welcomed foreign investments that create jobs, while repeatedly condemning the job-cutting consequences of IMF stimulus packages. Western labor activists, on the other hand, object to the threats of capital flight to regions with cheap labor, a threat used to undermine their fight for higher wages and better working conditions. These conflicting interests have widened the gulf between the human rights priorities within privileged and poor states.

Organized labor continues to be divided on two fronts: internationally, between workers from rich countries and workers from poor countries, and domestically, between the interests of union members—who comprise a shrinking portion of the workforce—and unrepresented workers. Since the 1970s, trade unions and labor in general have been on the defensive as industrial and manufacturing centers have spread outside the industrialized western hemisphere and post-Fordism has fragmented the workforce. Making matters even worse for trade unions in countries such as England and the United States, corporate flexibility in hiring and firing places downward pressure on wages (while tending to increase employment). By contrast, in European countries like France, Germany, and Italy, limitations on laying off workers protect wages at the expense of economic growth, with consequently higher rates of unemployment.[35]

The erosion of European labor rights policies became more apparent when, during the Maastricht talks, the British government opposed the Social Charter advocated by an economically integrated European Union, on the grounds that that it provided too much prominence to trade unions.[36] While free-traders often contest the charge that economic integration yields poverty, pointing to the rise in wages and living conditions for workers in general, they tend to overlook the growing gap between wages for high-skilled and low-skilled workers, or the latter group's worsening prospects since the 1980s.[37] The difficulty in maintaining labor rights across the board was further evidenced during the implementation of NAFTA. Of the "nineteen labor rights cases brought against the three governments under NAFTA," reported *Public Citizen,* "not one has resulted in fines or penalties against the offending country."[38]

More alarming was the WTO Multilateral Agreement on Investment, in which the twenty wealthy nations comprising the Organization for Economic Cooperation and Development (OECD) negotiated new rules extending benefits to foreign corporations as if they were national firms, thus removing all restrictions on transnational investment. Had the agreement been adopted, it would have had nefarious effects on worker, health, and environmental rights legislation. The negotiations were ambushed by 600 organizations in nearly 70 countries, in addition to a "tidal wave of electronically amplified opposition," characterized by Guy Jonquière of the *Financial Times* as an assault by "network guerillas."[39]

If the world has changed enormously since World War II, and, in particular, over the last three decades, the sclerotic organized labor movement has been slow to adjust. Creative in its intentions, the ILO was never able to translate its findings and analyses into action. As a new protest movement mobilized with increasing strength at each G8, IMF, and WTO summit, many progressive labor activists and scholars like Robert Cox, Jay Manzur, and Kathleen Newland, along with the president of the American Federation of Labor and Congress of Industrial Organizations (AFL-CIO), Lane Kirkland, began calling for broader international solidarity between labor unions, international governmental organizations, activist lawyers, nongovernmental organizations, progressive governments, human rights, and consumer groups.[40] "The broad human rights movements and the unions have a lot to learn from each other," affirmed Amnesty International, "and both could benefit from working more closely together" as they fight to overcome cultural, economic, and other obstacles dividing labor within and between nations.[41]

The Global Environment and Environmental Rights

The intensification of human-inflicted damage on the environment, exacerbated by globalization, has also helped redefine and energize human rights militancy. While the West, as the original site of the industrial revolution, had long been the major source of pollution, by the mid–twentieth century emerging southern hemisphere and socialist industrializing states were contributing substantially to the problem.[42] The combined and ever growing effect of world pollution and diminishing resources since World War II has no historic parallel, making the question of the right to a healthy environment, identified in the International Covenant on Economic, Social and Cultural Rights (article 11), a critical human rights issue.

Environmental spoilage extends beyond territorial boundaries; it is heedless of national, cultural, or religious identities. Ozone depletion, marine pollution, deforestation, desertification, soil exhaustion, acid rain, carbon dioxide emissions, hazardous wastes, and nuclear risks affect each of us.[43] This may be the reasonable price for the triumph of modernity over barbarism, proselytize some globalizers. "Let us not [however] flatter ourselves overmuch on account of our human conquests over nature," warned Engels, prophetically, over a century ago:

> For each such conquest takes its revenge on us. Each of them, it is true, has in the first place the consequences on which we counted, but in the second and third places it has quite different unforeseen effects which only too often cancel out the first. The people of Mesopotamia, Greece, Asia Minor, and elsewhere destroyed the forests to obtain cultivable lands, never dreamed that that they were laying the basis for the present devastated condition of those countries, by removing along with the forest the collecting centers and reservoirs of moisture. . . . Thus at every step we are reminded that we by no means rule over nature like a conqueror over a foreign people, like someone standing outside nature—but that we have, with flesh, blood, and brain belonged to nature, and exist in its midst, and that all our mastery of it consists in the fact that we have the advantage over all other creatures of being able to know the law and correctly apply its laws.[44]

That our fate, should we continue toward environmental catastrophe, will increasingly be common to all humankind has stimulated the imagination of popular writers from Michael Crichton (*Andromeda Strain,* 1969, and *Jurassic Park,* 1990), to Elizabeth Hand (*Glimmering,* 1999), to Jane Jensen (*Millennium Rising,* 1999). Popular fears of environmental disasters, however exaggerated, should not imply that all countries and people share a similar level of guilt, are equally impacted, or enjoy a comparable ability to reverse the unregulated drive to conquer nature. There exists a great and growing disparity between rich and poor societies. Even if rich countries have passed stricter environmental regulations, as John Micklethwait and Adrian Woldridge would argue against environmentalist critics of globalization,[45] the United States (more than other developed countries) and the OECD member states contribute the lion's share of global pollution, averaging four times the level per capita produced by the rest of the world.[46] In short, economic development has meant that the worst polluters have also been the most powerful states, with disproportionate influence over future environmental policy.

While localized pollution in cities and manufacturing regions across the globe may be similar, there are still enormous differences among societies. Poorer, more agrarian societies continue to experience rapid population growth, complicating prospects for development and placing stress on basic local resources like water and food supplies. On a global scale, however, the primary threat to ecosystems has stemmed from developed countries. Because environmental threats ultimately affect the whole earth, concern over further degradation has spurred the activism of a global ecological movement.

Its agenda reflects the divergent interests of developed and developing countries, as well as differing cultural backgrounds and ideologies. Preserving the unspoiled wilderness and restoring despoiled areas to their pristine condition while elevating a mystical and cosmological consciousness underlines the vision of the deep ecology movement, which encompasses individuals from the right to the left of the political spectrum. While inspired by Eastern mysticism, the biocentric focus of this group overlooks the way in which indigenous groups, expelled from natural preservation parks (as they were, e.g., by Project Tiger in India and Southeast Asia), are deprived of the environment that had provided their daily subsistence over the centuries. Deep ecology thus remains a Western ecological outlook.[47]

For many, like the Indian scholar Ramachandra Guha, deep ecology and development projects throughout the Third World are antithetical to environmental positions associated with egalitarian justice. "Commodities have grown, but nature has shrunk," echoes his compatriot Vandana Shiva, whose concern is to halt the commodification of the natural world, which has particularly severe consequences for women, "the poorest among the poor, . . . because with nature, they are the primary sustainers of society."[48] Other ecological feminists (or ecofeminists—

namely, feminists associated with deep ecological tenets), like Mary Daly and Susan Griffin, elevate the very nurturing relationship between women and nature, as one that should guide peaceful political arrangements outside the confines of patriarchal hierarchy—arrangements that would be immune from predatory conquest over women and nature.[49]

Nevertheless, the feminist stand on ecology is far from unified: it remains divided along ideological persuasions and regions of the world. Many socialist feminists have rejected the belief that women are closer to nature as an essentialist attribution of women's capacity, further contesting the idea that patriarchy is the basis of all forms of domination irrespective of social and economic circumstances.[50] The premise of that critique is also shared by red-green political advocates, who argue that the current ecological crisis cannot be resolved without an improvement of social conditions and better distribution of wealth. From this perspective, argued German critical theorist Herbert Marcuse, "[T]he structure of capitalist productivity is inherently expansionist: more and more, it reduces the last remaining natural space outside the world of labor and of organized and manipulated leisure." In that sense, "[T]he ecological movement is attacking the 'living space' of capitalism, the expansion of the realm of profit, of waste and production."[51]

Despite the hopes of leftist advocates, the fight against environmental degradation has often been easily co-opted, as we witness in the incorporation of "green rhetoric" in WTO debates, and as corporate advertising exhorts each of us to protect the environment.[52] Businesses from the cosmetic industry to paper companies and even to petroleum companies are reassuring their ecologically conscious consumers of their commitment to the environment. These same companies, of course, routinely oppose any environmental regulations that interfere with their pursuit of profits. Some free market enthusiasts, like Alan Binder, believe it will be sufficient to develop a system in which permits to pollute consistent with some acceptable ceiling on total emissions are auctioned to the highest bidders.[53]

Having entered mainstream policy debate more than other human rights issues, environmental rights have found recognition in many international meetings, such as the Stockholm Conference (1982) sponsored by the UN environmental program and the meetings of multilateral NGOs and national governments convened to discuss the broader environmental crisis. Many specific treaties were subsequently ratified, such as those aiming to control maritime pollution: the London Dumping Convention (1972), the MARPOL International Convention for the Prevention of Pollution from Ships (1973), and the United Nations Law of the Sea (1982), among others. Other international agreements have focused on not spreading hazardous waste, as evidenced by the UN ratification of the Basel Convention (1989), or on limiting air pollution, as exemplified by the UN Vienna and Montreal Protocols (1985 and 1987).[54]

In 1992, the UN environmental conference held in Rio de Janeiro established more comprehensive agreements targeting the preservation of biodiversity and addressing the environmental and development concerns of poor states, greenhouse gas emission regulations, and so forth. As greenhouse emissions remained a major issue, a conference in Kyoto (1997) convened 160 signatory nations to the UN Framework Convention to sign an agreement to reduce global emissions by about 5.2 percent by 2012—by 8 percent for the European Union, 7 percent for the United States, 6 percent for Japan, and varying other amounts for 21 other industrial countries. The Bush administration, questioning the veracity of the scientific community whose consensus on the danger of inaction had led to the treaty, opted not to enforce the Kyoto agreement, reflecting the continuing hurdles confronting efforts to construct a global environmental regime. If the election of a conservative American president has caused a setback for environmentalists, the rise of extreme rightwing movements in Western Europe and the events of September 11 have raised concerns over reversals in another area of great concern for human rights activism: that of immigration.

Global Migration and the Question of Citizens' Rights

Migration, whether by those in search of greater safety and sustenance or by those bound in the chains of captors, has characterized human life from prehistory to the present. Its various manifestations have included ancient nomadic societies, the Jewish Diaspora, the slave trade from Africa to the Americas, the waves traveling from Europe to the colonies, and then, the reverse flow as those once colonized sought new lives in the countries of their former European masters. Wars, scarcity, and the lure of greater opportunity have remained throughout the centuries the main factors driving migration, exacerbating what the German-American philosopher Hannah Arendt (1906–1975) characterized as the calamity of stateless people. What has changed is the visibility of refugees as the global reach of modern mass media has combined with growing recognition that migrants have rights, rights that call into question established conceptions of citizenship and national and cultural identity.

As have other major wars, World War II brought new waves of migration, including, at its conclusion, two mass expulsions of German populations. Thus, in 1945, the Soviet Union expelled millions of Germans from densely populated German territory that had been awarded to Poland, and the restored Czech government expelled a similar number from the Sudetenland. When, two years later, a Britain greatly weakened by war relinquished India, the resulting partition unleashed the flight of millions of Muslims northward to the new state of Pakistan, even as millions of Hindus fled south to India. A year later, in 1948, the British abandoned Palestine, to which Jewish survivors of the European Holocaust had fled in search of a safer homeland. When the establishment of Israel sparked the first Israeli-Arab war, yet another refugee problem was created as hundreds of thousands of Palestinians fled or were driven outside the borders established by the victorious Jewish state, then herded into what became permanent refugee camps within the surrounding Arab countries. The tragedy of those displaced by wars gave impetus to the creation of a new international agency to assist refugees, the Office of the United Nations High Commissioner for Refugees, and to the United Nations' 1951 Convention Relating to the Status of Refugees.

Initially, refugees were understood as individuals who left their homelands out of well-founded fear of persecution from authoritarian states.

HANNAH ARENDT, ON THE RIGHTS OF STATELESS PEOPLE,
THE ORIGINS OF TOTALITARIANISM, **1951**

The calamity of the rightless is not that they are deprived of life, liberty, and the pursuit of happiness, or of equality before the law and freedom of opinion—formulas which were designed to solve problems *within* given communities—but that they no longer belong to any community whatsoever. Their plight is not that they are not equal before the law, but that no law exists for them; not that they are oppressed but that nobody wants even to oppress them. Only in the last stage of a rather lengthy process is their right to live threatened; only if they remain perfectly "superfluous," if nobody can be found to "claim" them, may their lives be in danger. Even the Nazis started their extermination of Jews by first depriving them of all legal status (the status of second-class citizenship) and cutting them off from the world of the living by herding them into ghettos and concentration camps; and before they set the gas chambers into motion they had carefully tested the ground and found out to their satisfaction that no country would claim these people. The point is that a condition of complete rightlessness was created before the right to live was challenged.

From *The Origins of Totalitarianism,* 295–296. Reprinted by permission of Harcourt, Inc.

As anti-colonial and civil wars, leading to newly independent states in the 1960s and 1970s, spawned more waves of refugees, the definition of persecution, hence of refugee rights, was broadened, first with the 1968 UN Protocol Relating to the Status of Refugees and then with the 1969 UN Convention Governing the Specific Aspects of Refugee Problems in Africa, promulgated by the Organization of African Unity. "The term refugee," stipulated the 1969 document, "also applies to every person who owing to external aggression, occupation, foreign domination or events seriously disturbing public order in either part or the whole of his country of origin or nationality, is compelled to leave his place or habitual residence in order to seek refuge in another place outside his country of origin or nationality."[55]

Throughout the same period, European countries became the recipients of a growing flow of immigrants from their former colonies, transforming their erstwhile ethnically homogenous societies into increasingly pluralistic ones. Highly skilled immigrants were favored over low-skilled ones, who formed the bulk of those who arrived in flight from oppression or starvation. Yet low-skilled immigration has proven of great value to the aging and gentrified industrialized societies of Western Europe, which can explain why Europe has allowed an exponential increase of immigrants from less developed countries to OECD countries. Between 1955 and 1988, a total of 24.5 million people immigrated to West Germany; 21.9 million to France; and 25 million to the United Kingdom, the Low Countries, Switzerland, and Scandinavia. Altogether more than 100 million postwar migrants reached the countries of the OECD between 1945 and 1995. The number of immigrants to the United States is harder to determine given the magnitude of illegal immigration across the Mexican border; one credible estimate is between 1 and 1.5 million per year in the 1980s and 1990s.[56]

Whatever the precise count, the trend has been sufficiently significant to stir up controversial attitudes, including cultural prejudices against immigrants, as host countries attempt to redefine the boundary of citizenship and the notion of citizens' rights. Four main approaches to citizenship translate into different perspectives on immigrant rights. At one end of the spectrum, the conception of citizenship offered by the anthropologist Clifford Geertz stresses the importance of national ethnicity, as "the congruities of blood, speech, custom and so on" form "the primordial bonds" that define and distinguish one society from another.[57] While some proponents of states as cultural enforcers are tolerant of immigrants as long as the cultural spirit (or ethnic composition) of the state remains unchallenged, many sympathizers of such a view tend to see immigrants as intruders, prompting them to favor exclusionary immigration policies. Founded on the principle of *jus sanguinis,* or citizenry as a community of blood descent, Germany, for instance, until important 1999 reforms in its immigration laws, had no legal mechanism for enabling second- or even third-generation immigrants to become citizens.[58]

At the other end of the spectrum, promoters of republicanism favor a civic and political approach to nationhood traditionally associated with French revolutionary ideals of universality. From this perspective, citizenship "owes the character of its existence to what its constituent members have in common," like universal legal procedures, common work, and a shared sense of collective values. This requires, claims political theorist Benjamin Barber, the transcendence of cultural and other particular interests and the development of a notion of the common good in the public realm.[59] For immigrants to states adhering to such republican ideals, such as France and the Netherlands, it is sufficient to be born in those territories or to reside there for a certain time, *jus soli,* to be granted citizenship.[60]

Between these two approaches resides the multiculturalist approach to citizenship. This position holds that there is no necessary contradiction between non-territorial communities of interest and national unity. The fear that "polyethnic rights impede the integration of immigrants by creating a confusing halfway house between their old nation and citizenship in the new one" is simply unfounded, argues the philosopher Will Kymlicka.[61] Yet where critics of a republicanist approach rightly point to the danger that cultural or other forms of particularity will end up being subsumed by the assimilationist will of the majority, they often fail to propose which guidelines (other than civic rights) should be applied in order to tighten the social fabric of the state.[62] The United States and Sweden, by preserving one official lingua franca and by cultivating respect for their liberal institutions, come close to exemplifying this approach, granting citizenship to all individuals born in their territories, and ensuring automatic immigration according to a set of rules that take into account marriage, the reuniting of families, and so on.

The United States has been relatively lenient in its immigration policy, turning a blind eye to illegal immigration in order to secure a cheap labor force while withholding from illegal immigrants the social services provided to citizens, as well as any obligation to keep them should their labor become unnecessary. The events of September 11 resulted in significant changes, producing a climate of fear in which President George W.

Bush (1946–) rescinded his initial offer to grant American citizenship to two million illegal Mexican workers and issued tougher immigration policies, restricting tourism and foreign student visas.[63] The Europeans have undertaken a similar reversal of liberal immigration policies in the context of rising anti-immigration fervor. In March 2002, Dutch voters in Rotterdam stunned Europe by granting Pim Fortuyn's right-wing Leefbaar (livable) Nederland Party 35 percent of the vote in local elections, based largely on his call for a halt to Muslim immigration. Only Fortuyn's assassination on May 8, 2002, prevented his party's ascension as a major force in Dutch politics. Others, like Jean-Marie Le Pen of the Front Nationale Populaire, have echoed such sentiments in France, which has, with Italy, Germany, the Netherlands, Belgium, Denmark, and other countries, tightened immigration laws since September 11.[64]

In the aftermath of the September tragedy, one may wonder whether internationalists' arguments in favor of applying the same principles of citizenship within and beyond national boundaries are still relevant. "Only democratic citizenship," the German theorist Jürgen Habermas once advocated, "can prepare the way for a condition of world citizenship which does not close itself off with particular biases, and accepts a worldwide form of political communication."[65] What should unite various groups, according to the British historian Eric Hobsbawm, is a common thirst for equality and justice and a program aimed at advancing the needs of all.[66] From this it follows that even if open-door policies for immigrants might be impractical, those who were allowed in would be treated as citizens, subject to the obligations (such as payment of taxes) as well as the benefits of citizenship.[67] Yet no country has ever adopted such open immigration policies, and none would begin to consider that position now in light of new fears of terrorist attacks. One could argue against the skeptics that greater efforts at integrating the immigrant population from the Muslim world would have greatly undermined the appeal of Islamic fundamentalism in the West. Inhospitable immigration policies and the rise of xenophobia in the streets of Hamburg, Marseilles, and Brussels have only served to fuel support for violent extremist groups like Al Qaeda.

To overcome divisions and disenchantments within the labor force, it is not surprising that progressives like the Italian and American scholars Antonio Negri and Michael Hardt have placed their hopes in the possible development of a global citizenship, in large measure created by the expanded need for labor mobility. "Capital itself," they remark, has demanded increased mobility of labor power and continuous migrations across national boundaries. Developed economies are "utterly dependent on the influx of workers from the subordinate regions of the world." Hence, one needs to recognize the changing cartography of capitalist production as human rights activists struggle to promote full rights of citizenship for all workers, regardless of their ethnic background. Such an agenda would provide the divided workforce with the capacity to make broader social and economic demands in an ever more fragmented post-Fordist world. The opportunity for freedom of movement as well as "the right to stay still and enjoy one place rather than being forced to move constantly" under conditions of fear and great uncertainty is an important human rights issue. In a globalized world economy, the "general right to control its own movement," insist Negri and Hardt, "is the multitude's ultimate demand for global citizenship."[68] One can only hope that such a vision will ultimately alter the climate of intolerance in which the economic need for immigrants is too often coupled to unfair treatment and outright hostility once they arrive.

One cannot overlook the fact that prior to September 11, international legislation against inhumane deportation laws and practices, unscrupulous trafficking in children and women for sexual and labor exploitation, and the calamitous conditions experienced by refugees was already well-established. Ill treatment of foreigners had galvanized governmental and nongovernmental organizations to fight, if not for global citizenship, then at least for international laws more amicable toward displaced individuals. Tempering their competitive interests, immigration associations in host countries had joined together to forge a transnational coalition. Following adoption of the 1986 Single European Act, "more than 2,500 immigrants' associations in fourteen host countries established the Council of Immigrant Associations in Europe."[69] A long list of alliances, including religious organizations and NGOs devoted to labor, women's, migrant, and other human rights, such as the International Confederation of Free Trade Unions, the Women's International League for Peace and Freedom, the World Council of Churches, and the Migrants Forum in Asia, have paved the way for concerted campaigns such as the designation of an official International Migrants' Day, which was finally proclaimed by the United Nations on December 4, 2000.

Since the 1949 ILO convention, contracting states have agreed to treat immigrants "without discrimination in respect to nationality, race, religion, or sex."[70] Each subsequent convention of the ILO, the European Council, and the UN—such as the 1955 Convention of the European Council, the 1978 UNESCO Declaration on Race and Racial Prejudice, the 1990 UN Convention on the Protection of the Rights of All Migrant Workers and Their Families, and so forth—has further promoted the social and cultural rights of migrant workers and their families.[71] Yet while these various instruments have produced important guidelines and pressures for recipient states, the sovereign authority of the state to control entry across its borders has enjoyed stronger international legal protection than is provided by immigration and refugee rights treaties and laws, underlining the tension between liberal immigration rights policies and the right of states to grant citizenship.[72] After the attack against America, this conflict was further dramatized, heightening the risk of a "clash of civilizations" over the rights to protect one's culture.

Cultural Globalization and Cultural Rights

Since the early nineteenth century, the concept of cultural rights has been invoked by subject peoples against their rulers, starting with the uprisings against Napoleon, then against the Austro-Hungarian and Ottoman Empires, and ultimately was wielded as a weapon against colonial control throughout Africa and Asia. As globalization erodes national distinctions, cultural rights revive them, intensifying efforts to protect national patrimonies against waves of immigrants, foreign imports, or the overall homogenization of the world into universal consumerism. Over the last third of the twentieth century, the notion of group, or cultural, rights became recognized as an important category of human rights aimed at protecting diverse conceptions of human needs and values.

Defensive in orientation, assertions of cultural rights reflect resistance against what is seen as the overwhelming influence of Western—and particularly American—cultural influence throughout the non-Western world, an influence that, since the end of colonialism, has been strengthened by the development of a global telecommunications infrastructure, which has led to the ever growing transmission of cultural artifacts from the developed to the developing world. There are no territorial boundaries for CNN, McDonald's, and Nike, as well as "no foreign countries" for Gillette's chairman Alfred M. Zein.[73] With English as the dominant language of international communication, and with cheaper transportation fueling mushrooming Western commerce and tourism, these global structures have also forged common values shared by a worldwide elite increasingly eager to benefit from globalized enterprises.

Immigration and telecommunications have also provided venues for a reverse flow of cultural influence, from south to north, as the latter ex-

UNITED NATIONS CONVENTION ON THE PROTECTION OF THE RIGHTS OF ALL MIGRANT WORKERS AND THEIR FAMILIES, 1990

Part III: Human Rights of All Migrant Workers and of Their Families

ARTICLE 13

2. Migrant workers and members of their families shall have the right to freedom of expression; this right shall include freedom to seek, receive and impart information and ideas of all kinds, regardless of frontiers, either orally, in writing or in print, in the form of art or through any other media of their choice. . . .

ARTICLE 16

7. When a migrant worker or a member of his or her family is arrested or committed to prison or custody pending trial or is detained in any other manner:

   a. The consular or diplomatic authorities of his or her State of origin or of a State representing the interests of that State shall, if he or she so requests, be informed without delay of his or her arrest or detention and of the reasons therefor;

   c. The person concerned shall be informed without delay of this right and of rights deriving from relevant treaties, if any, applicable between the States concerned, to correspond and to meet with representatives of the said authorities and to make arrangements with them for his or her legal representation. . . .

ARTICLE 17

6. Whenever a migrant worker is deprived of his or her liberty, the competent authorities of the State concerned shall pay attention to the problems that may be posed for members of his or her family, in particular for spouses and minor children. . . .

ARTICLE 18

1. Migrant workers and members of their families shall have the right to equality with nationals of the State concerned before the courts and tribunals. In determination of any criminal charge against or of their rights and obligations in a suit of law, they shall be entitled to a fair and public hearing by a competent, independent and impartial tribunal established by law. . . .

ARTICLE 25

1. Migrant workers shall enjoy treatment not less favorable than that which applies to nationals of the State of employment in respect of remuneration and:

   a. Other conditions of work, that is to say, overtime, hours of work, weekly rest, holidays with pay, safety, health, termination of the employment relationship and any other conditions of work which, according to national law and practice, are covered by these terms;

   b. Other terms of employment, that is to say, minimum age of employment, restriction on home work and any other matters which, according to national law and practice, are considered a term of employment.

periences a growing taste for "exotic" music, food, ideas, and literature, enriching the multicultural tendencies of many Westerners. Yet this cultural influence is far from equal, as Western consumerism only takes on the colors of those aspects of culture it can commodify and ultimately swallow. In the end, as Benjamin Barber points out, "MTV and McDonald's and Disneyland are American cultural icons," combined in the form of a seemingly innocent Trojan-American horse that stealthily penetrates other nations' cultures.[74] While some cannot help but admire the shining steed and wind up reinterpreting their lives in relation to television dramas like *Dynasty* and *Dallas* (or more recent shows like *Seinfeld* and *Friends*),[75] many others root for heroic resistance figures like José Bové (1953–), the French farmer who in August 1999 defied the great beast by trashing a McDonald's restaurant in the south of France. The strongest reaction, however, comes from some of the most impoverished countries, whose masses, excluded from the benefits of globalization, seek refuge under the veil of religious fundamentalism, where despair is exchanged for rage and hopes of a better afterlife.[76] Thus understood, fundamentalism, a politicized religious movement shaped in reaction to modernity, is an intrinsic yet contradictory condition of globalization.

JOSÉ BOVÉ

"McDonald's as a Symbol" Interview, 1999

The objective was to have a non-violent but symbolically forceful action, in broad daylight and with the largest possible participation. We wanted the authorities to be fully aware of what was going to happen, so we explained to the police in advance that the purpose of the rally was to dismantle the McDonald's. . . .

"Seattle-on-Tarn" Interview, 2000

I was chatting about the day's events with the designers of the magazine *Charlie Hebdo* and others, when one of them drew a picture of a *sans-culotte,* the name for the poor in the French Revolution. That's what made me think of the slogan "Liberty, Equality, Fraternity." The struggle of the *sans-culottes* was no different from ours today.

The victory of the *sans-culottes* was appropriated by the stooges of the state, so that the slogan "Liberty, Equality, Fraternity," painted on the façade of every town hall, has lost its meaning. It's up to us, in the streets, to rehabilitate democracy from the grass roots, to take over the slogan and give it back its original meaning.

From José Bové and François Dufour, *The World Is Not for Sale: Farmers against Junk Food,* 5–6, 190–191.

Many defenders of cultural rights have cautioned against Eurocentric criticism of other societies, arguing that Western cultural hegemony has developed at the expense of the needs and values of subjugated people. A relativistic approach, many have long professed, offers at the very least a more generous attitude toward otherwise misrepresented or muffled cultural influences. "[R]elativism," claims cultural rights advocate Alison Dundes Renteln, seeks "to alleviate but not obliterate prejudice, even if tolerance is not an integral part of the theory."[77] The post-structuralist feminist Jane Flax has argued that women's suffering, as an important form of group affliction, would have remained an inaudible and invisible right under any universal discourse, which often masks power interests; hence a more fragmented (or genealogic) and relativistic interpretation of rights sheds new light on different varieties of human experience.[78] A "sentimental" or compassionate education, argues the American pragmatic philosopher Richard Rorty in a similar vein, should "sufficiently acquaint people of different kinds with one another so that they are less tempted to think of those different from themselves as only quasi-human."[79]

Yet from a liberal or socialist internationalist human rights perspective, adopting a cultural relativist stance on rights can lead one to overlook cases where culture is used to justify oppression of one group by another. Were all indigenous cultures that preceded colonialism tolerant toward the rights of women, the needy, or foreigners? Are these cultural traditions consistent with the Universal Declaration? How are we to identify the genuine cultural ambassadors of a nation when the voice of the multitude is suppressed? What if national or local elites can easily manipulate sentiments toward others in ways that may serve their own interest in wielding power? In short, cultural rights have little merit for internationalist defenders of human rights when women and the untouchables of this world are silenced and abused in the name of an imagined tradition. Identity politics, as John Rawls and Eric Hobsbawm have claimed, must always be assessed in terms of an internationalist position, whether this position emphasizes liberal or socialist principles.[80]

Many have carved a middle road, identifying, and at times exaggerating, these two poles (the universalist versus the relativist) as stylized "ideal types," preferring, like the British philosopher Bikhu Parekh, a minimalist universal pluralist vision of human worth and achievement in the arts and in social and intellectual life, while promoting a cross-cultural dialogue.[81] The irony, however, is that despite different points of emphasis, cultural, multicultural, universalist, and religious proponents of rights advertise their positions as the only ones truly consistent with compromise, tolerance, cultural diversity, and justice.[82]

Why then so much controversy within the human rights community on this issue? Undoubtedly, important epistemological differences separate one interpretation of rights from another. Nevertheless, liberal internationalists prefer an interpretation of rights endowing all people with the capacity to reason and shape their destinies; socialists favor a socioeconomic definition of universal rights to redress social inequity between individuals; post-structuralists, and oddly enough pragmatists, understand the importance of elevating particular cultural interests as a weapon against the manifold sources of domination, regardless of their basis of moral legitimacy; and communitarians celebrate the importance of an organic communal spirit in the face of an ever more impersonal and alienating world.

Notwithstanding important differences between these and other grammars of knowledge and existence, it is also useful to observe how each human rights tradition is initially animated by a different problem. Whereas staunch internationalists fear a world of competing cultures, which would ensure the triumph of either the mightiest or the most belligerent fundamentalists at the expense of justice, cultural rights proponents worry that tendentious "universal" moral perspectives of the most powerful players will prevail over the cultural values of subordinated nations. Whereas the former focus on new political, social, and economic arrangements or on law and institutions as means to strengthen a global human rights regime, the latter fear that such an emphasis on an all-inclusive social alternative will overshadow the demand for specific rights.

If both universalists and relativists identify important concerns, one must understand these approaches not merely in terms of what they oppose or fear, but also in the context of existing power relations, relations principally shaped by the socioeconomic conditions of our time. The globalization of the economy, despite the view of its cultural rights critics, is not adverse to cultural diversity, as long as globalization offers exotic products for consumption by a gentrified world thirsty for novelties, and insofar as it produces cultural spaces in which one can escape the vicissitudes imposed by modernity. Let us not forget that despite competing cultural values within and between the south and the north, cultural assaults against globalization are easily co-opted by the very forces they challenge. The music of social protest, like reggae and African-American rap, has lost its political significance by the time it reaches a mainstream audience on MTV, just as 1960s counterculture artists found their message radically transformed in the consumer-oriented hands of 1994 Woodstock promoters or in the ads of Coca-Cola and Nike.

One can even argue that the promotion of cultural rights and values was advanced, if not institutionally ossified, with the march of globalization. With the waning of colonialism, the codification of cultural rights clauses, such as those contained in the International Covenant on Economic, Social and Cultural Rights, was followed by subsequent rights treaties pertaining to labor, environmental, developmental, and immigration rights. Revised international labor standards, such as those promulgated by the 1989 Convention concerning Indigenous and Tribal Peoples in Independent Countries, have, for instance, focused their attention on the situation of indigenous workers and their specific social, cultural, and economic conditions, which "distinguish them from other sections of the national community and peoples."[83] The Rio Declaration on Environment and Development also recognized the importance of indigenous "identity, culture and interests" in stimulating indigenous groups' "effective participation in the achievement of sustainable development" and the management of their environment (article 22). Acceptance of different cultural traditions for immigrants has also found recognition in various UN immigration treaties and regional Western legal documents, which, in the cases of Sweden, the Netherlands, and Belgium, guarantee immigrants the right to use their mother tongue or to perform religious practices that would otherwise be illegal (such as rituals involving animal sacrifice).[84]

While cultural rights clauses in diverse international human rights treaties remain impressive, one must note that their implementation may now be challenged by the post–September 11 reaction to fundamentalism and fears of security threats—fears that can spill beyond the focus on Al Qaeda to include everyone of Arab origin or Muslim faith. If in times of peace, invocations of cultural and group rights had already led to the fragmentation of the human rights community, the context of the war on terror will only increase the magnitude of the challenge. The human rights agenda of the beginning of this millennium needs to fight emerging fascist forces, whether in their Islamic or Western manifestations, while simultaneously confronting the selfishness of an ever more privatized corporate world. An alliance of purpose and action, premised upon civil, political, social, and economic rights, becomes a growing necessity, even when the question of which universality should be adopted has not yet been fully settled.

One can only hope that a new dialogue is evolving not merely in the corridors of international institutions and in cosmopolitan elite salons, but among those who live in the shadow of corporate power, as grass-roots human rights groups coordinate their actions in and beyond the streets of Seattle, Washington, Prague, and Genoa. Despite recurrent set-backs, that universal in the making is one that would fuel and inject positivist international laws with a new internationalist human rights spirit. It is one that would challenge co-optation and the cosmetic formalism of human rights treaties in the face of the daily human rights demands of ordinary people throughout the world. It is one that should not fear to take creative positions that defy the Manichean "with us or against us" characterization of the post–September 11 world. In doing so, it must continue to offer a democratic alternative to the mystical irrationalism of leaders from the impoverished south, while holding accountable the power centers of the north.

AFTER SEPTEMBER 11: SECURITY VERSUS HUMAN RIGHTS

The cultural and internationalist tension within the human rights community, which intensified with the advance of globalization, reached a crippling impasse after September 11. Imagining the future direction of the human rights movement at the dawn of the new millennium is a formidable endeavor. If, as discussed earlier, the first critical test for the human rights community is to renew its universalist aspirations, bridging developed and developing world concerns and reasserting the inalienability and indivisibility of civil-political and socioeconomic rights, it is also confronted with another test. As the major powers continue to shape, mediate, and resolve conflicts consistent with their geopolitical and other interests, the second challenge for the human rights community lies in its ability to confront a narrow national security agenda. More concretely, how can the human rights movement cope with the suppression of civil and human rights in the name of wartime requirements? How can one make the case that security and human rights are not always antithetical?

Civil and Other Human Rights in Wartime

Indisputably, the war against terrorism has affected civil liberties and other human rights in the West, offering new license for governments around the world to crush dissidents in the name of a global war against terrorism. The Patriot Act, passed in the shattering aftermath of the September 11 attacks, has provided U.S. authorities with greater invasive power in the private realm. It has expanded the federal government's ability to conduct electronic surveillance and issue nationwide search warrants, permits the detaining of immigrants for a week without their being charged with a crime or immigration violation, and broadens FBI access to private records (including library, bank, motel, and grocery store records). While it includes a sunset provision and expires in 2004, civil rights watchdog groups fear that such laws will have a chilling effect on free speech as the government is tempted to apply the Patriot Act to political dissidents. The act, warned John Sellers, a leading organizer of the Seattle 1999 protest, "will be wielded as a very blunt weapon against a lot of very important movements for justice in this country that happen to disagree with the status quo."[85]

While the Europeans have long enshrined privacy rights, both in their comprehensive 1950 European Convention for the Protection of Human Rights and Fundamental Freedoms and in the 2000 Charter of Fundamental Rights of the European Union, the September calamity has ignited European debate over whether such privacy guarantees are compatible with security objectives. "The [p]rinciple of protecting the people's personal data must not stand in the way of fighting against crimes and terrorism," recently stated Otto Schiller, the German interior minister.[86] His concern has been echoed in fifteen European countries where new rules would subject everyone who uses the Internet or a telephone to greater surveillance. These laws, human rights custodians worry, would have the effect of creating a massive electronic data bank containing information about everyone's private activities.

Other countries have jumped on the anti-terrorism bandwagon as an opportunity to justify greater internal repression. A month after September 11, Chinese Foreign Ministry spokesman Sun Yuxi conveyed his government's new anti-terrorist stand, blurring the distinction between Al Qaeda terrorism and Muslim separatist claims: "We hope that efforts to fight against East Turkistan terrorist forces will become a part of the international efforts and should also win support and understanding,"[87] he stated, in hopes of heading off an international outcry as China detained, tortured, and executed Muslim (Uighur) separatists. Russia also used America's war on terror, invoking the danger of Islamic extremism to legitimize its own brutal military occupation of Chechnya.[88] Finally, the Israeli government similarly used the opportunity to label its conflict

EUROPEAN CONVENTION FOR THE PROTECTION OF HUMAN RIGHTS AND FUNDAMENTAL FREEDOMS, AND ITS EIGHT PROTOCOLS, 1950

Article 4

2. No one shall be held in slavery or servitude.

3. No one shall be required to perform forced or compulsory labor

4. For the purpose of this Article the term "forced or compulsory labor" shall not include:

(a) any work required to be done in the ordinary course of detention imposed according to the provisions of Article 5 of this Convention or during conditional release from such detention;

(b) any service of a military character or, in case of conscientious objectors in countries where they are recognized, service exacted instead of compulsory military service;

(c) any service exacted in case of emergency or calamity threatening the life or well-being of the community;

(d) any work or service which forms part of normal civic obligations. . . .

Article 5

3. Everyone arrested or detained in accordance with the provisions of paragraph 1 (c) of this Article shall be brought promptly before a judge or other officer authorized by law to exercise judicial power and shall be entitled to trial within a reasonable time or to release pending trial. Release may be conditioned by guarantees to appear for trial.

4. Everyone who is deprived of his liberty by arrest or detention shall be entitled to take proceedings by which the lawfulness of his detention shall be decided speedily by a court and his release ordered if the detention is not lawful.

5. Everyone who has been the victim of arrest or detention in contravention of the provisions of this Article shall have an enforceable right to compensation. . . .

Article 9

1. Everyone has the right to freedom of thought, conscience and religion; this right includes freedom to change his religion or belief and freedom, either alone or in community with others and in public or private, to manifest his religion or belief, in worship, teaching, practice and observance.

2. Freedom to manifest one's religion or beliefs shall be subject only to such limitations as are prescribed by law and are necessary in a democratic society in the interests of public safety, for the protection of public order, health or morals, or for the protection of the rights and freedoms of others.

with the Palestinians as part of the war on terror, as it applied increasingly harsh measures against the population of the occupied territories. It comes as little surprise that countries such as Russia and China, with weak civil liberties traditions, have used September 11 as a pretext for human rights abuses. The aftermath of September 11 has also shown that liberal democracies, where protection of civil rights is a foundation of governance, are also prone to impinging on well-established rights in times of economic crisis and war.

Are all human rights, by implication, under jeopardy in times of scarcity and conflict? Historically, while it is true that freedom of expression and other civil rights were undermined in the West during the world wars, the Great Depression, and the cold war, conversely, during these same periods, liberal governments increased their attention to welfare rights programs. War and serious economic crises tend to create xenophobia, increase repression of all forms of domestic dissent, and encourage a political climate in which the rights to free speech and to privacy are muted by patriotic fervor; these circumstances, however, also favor stronger governmental intervention in the economy. Nevertheless, efforts at such times to increase military expenditures, limit inflation and unemployment, and stimulate consumer confidence and purchasing power are a daunting task for any state. Since governments must give priority to retaining popular legitimacy during times of crisis, there is a strong incentive to focus in particular on the social and economic welfare of their citizens.

Unsurprisingly, during the Great Depression, full employment became the cornerstone of European and U.S. economic policy as John Maynard Keynes became the new prophet of democratic capitalism. If assistance to the poor and the unemployed had hitherto depended on the discretion of whichever leadership happened to be in power at the time, welfare programs would, under the Roosevelt administration, be more systematically instituted as legal, social, and economic rights, and would be strengthened by the development of the welfare state during World War II and the cold war, while spreading throughout the Western world. Yet if wars and depressions have stimulated welfare rights institutions as prophylactic mechanisms necessary to temper the whims of the market, they have also eroded the edifice of fundamental liberties liberal states enjoy in peacetime.[89]

During wars, the liberal doves of yesterday, cloaked in a banner of nationalism, have shown how easily they can metamorphose into un-

apologetic hawks, targeting and stripping the liberties of individuals perceived as a possible threat to either social stability or the national interest. Once President Woodrow Wilson led the United States into World
War I for the avowed purpose of making the world safe for democracy,
domestic liberals, progressives, and radicals found their civil liberties increasingly suppressed. During the Great Depression, President Franklin
Roosevelt restricted the rights of communists to freely express their views.
Following the December 1941 Japanese attack on Pearl Harbor, it was
again the Roosevelt administration that presided over the wartime internment of 110,000 innocent Americans who were detained solely because they were of Japanese descent. The cold war revival of anticommunist fervor produced the notorious demagoguery of Senator Joe
McCarthy and the House Un-American Activities Committee, as the
blacklisting of those accused of having communist sympathies left dissidents fearful of expressing their views. Finally, mounting opposition to
the Vietnam War inspired the Nixon administration to infiltrate and dis-
rupt anti-war organizations, authorize the auditing of tax returns of
prominent opponents of the war, and hire a secret group (the Plumbers)
to conduct illegal actions against troublesome politicians, journalists, and
anti-war activists.[90]

If each of these episodic civil rights setbacks coincided with a new drive
toward the fortification of welfare rights, should we then concur, as hundreds of innocent sons of Allah were unjustly detained after September
11 without appropriate legal representation in the United States and elsewhere, that the state is about to resume a more interventionist role? If
wars also tend to stimulate welfare programs, should we anticipate that
Western states would now intensify efforts to address economic inequity?
In his recent history of upper-class American politics, the Republican historian Kevin Phillips has predicted a domestic reawakening of mass militancy as the social gap between rich and poor has widened and as corporate corruption has reached the level last encountered during the early
decades of the twentieth century. If Phillips is right, then today's junc-
tion between growing popular resentment and the government's need for
wartime social cohesion should result in a revival of New Deal–style programs designed to curtail the power of the rich and provide greater economic security for ordinary Americans.[91] If this is the case, the onset of
that trend will apparently have to await the end of the conservative administration of President Bush.

As of 2003, powerful conservative voices are still claiming that these domestic social concerns are at best of marginal concern, as the United States faces a more formidable enemy from without that now threatens the lives of millions of Americans with weapons of mass destruction.[92] Security concerns, they claim, as George Kennan did at the outset of the cold war, will always ultimately prevail over any form of human rights considerations. With security concerns now central to the foreign policy agenda, should we agree with Kenneth Waltz, Paul Kennedy, and other like-minded scholars that realism is the only sound worldview and that the history of world politics is characterized by a never-ending Vichean cycle of national growth and decline? Accepting this position, which implies that the entire struggle for universal human rights is quixotic, in fact overlooks the historical progress in human rights recounted in the preceding chapters of this book.

Of course, the advance of human rights is slow and suggestive of unfinished labor. Indeed, after September 11, it may have appeared that the march of human rights progress had come to a full stop, proving once again the realist perspective that state security must prevail over other ethical and human rights considerations. Yet one can argue instead that global justice and human rights belong now more than ever at the center of any strategy that hopes to achieve long-term security. Those drawn to that argument may find it useful to consider how security and human rights have been connected since the origins of the modern system of states, and how a current human rights agenda might continue to build on that tradition.

KEVIN PHILLIPS, *WEALTH AND DEMOCRACY*, 2002

If economic trauma has stimulated radicalism, so has war, both directly and indirectly. The immediate effects have usually been to divert reform, to submerge divisions in patriotism and temporary unity. But as we have seen, some major war proves too burdensome, economic prospects and divisions worsen, and the politics of frustration takes a critical leap forward. As the twenty-first century gets under way, the imbalance of wealth and democracy in the United States is unsustainable, at least by traditional yardsticks. Market theology and unelected leadership have been displacing politics and elections. Either democracy must be renewed, with politics brought back to life, or wealth is likely to cement a new and less democratic regime—plutocracy by some other name. Over the coming decades, American exceptionalism may face its greatest test simply in convincing the American people to continue to believe in its comfort and reassurance.

From *Wealth and Democracy: The Politics of the American Rich*, 422.

The Legacy of Human Rights and Security

Traditionally, while human rights is understood as a worldview encompassing the rights and well-being of all individuals across boundaries, security, as conceptualized within the realist perspective, comprises assertions of rights that belong to states or nations. This commonly perceived tension does not reflect a historical tradition in which national security and universal human rights can be understood in terms of an unfolding debate within the discourse on human rights. The history of the interdependence of human rights and security worldviews, as associated with the nation-state, began with the spread of the Reformation wars and mercantilism. It was in this historical context that the realist political thinker Thomas Hobbes argued, in *Leviathan,* that the state would become the framework wherein individuals could seek protection from war. One should not forget that Hobbes's linkage between the right to security and allegiance to the state, rather than to papal authority, was revolutionary in its implications. By basing sovereignty on natural rights, Hobbes also opened the door to liberalism—to what was later called the first generation of civil and political rights—and to three centuries of debate over the human rights basis for state legitimacy. Current realists who describe their own view as "statist" and "Hobbesian" seem to have forgotten that the central concern of Hobbes was how best to realize the universal individual human right to security, as opposed to some notion of national security as an end in itself.

John Locke further developed the liberal conception of human rights, inquiring more deeply than Hobbes into what constituted natural rights and hence what was required to justify the state. Coeval with the emergence of the English bourgeoisie, he proposed to add to Hobbes's concern for security (or life) the rights to political liberty and private property—rights that greatly influenced the founders of the American republic in 1776. It was Rousseau's social contract, however, that identified and legitimized for the first time the nation-state as the embodiment of the "general will" of the people, a collectivist view that influenced the French Declaration of the Rights of Man and of the Citizen (1789). Subsequently, Robespierre, Paine, and Kant justified the raison d'être of the state only insofar as it would secure these vital universal rights domestically and internationally. Many other great visionaries maintained with them that with the development of republican institutions and commerce, human rights would prevail around the world.

But could the state secure the rights of all people, or even the rights

of its own citizens? The culmination of the French revolution in the conquests of Napoleon suggested otherwise. The hope for a state predicated
upon human rights was further challenged as the industrial revolution
and global capitalism sharply divided humankind into an elite class enjoying security, liberty, and property and disenfranchised masses that did
not enjoy any of those human rights.

The industrial revolution had created new conditions in which it became increasingly clear that rights to life, liberty, and property were insufficient to legitimize the state. As capital could increasingly escape the
boundaries of states, some began to insist that the liberal state and the
free market economy were preventing the realization of the universal
rights advocated during the French Revolution. The unlimited pursuit of
property rights, socialists now argued, would mainly benefit a minority
who were initially advantaged. Put another way, the instruments of state
power were being used to preserve the security of the capitalist class while
depriving ordinary working people of security and other human rights.
The familiar prescription offered by Marx and Engels maintained, particularly after the civil war or Bloody June Days of 1848, that ultimately
the betrayed working proletariat should seize the reins of state power in
order to promote socialist rights worldwide.

Over time, that call for global revolution faced increasing competition from those who sought to reform the state, a possibility enhanced
by the spread of labor movements and the passing of social welfare laws.
In Germany, the socialist Ferdinand Lassalle argued in 1862 that the state
was the sole possible promoter of freedom and human rights. In England
and elsewhere, the Fabians and other evolutionary socialists espoused a
similar perspective. The eloquent French socialist Jean Jaurès echoed their
views, suggesting that the state would carry the moral and socialist development of humankind slowly but ineluctably forward.

Fear of communist rebellion now spurred reform. In 1883, at the zenith
of German expansionist policies, German Chancellor Bismarck secured
the passage of social legislation, including compulsory sickness insurance
for workers, an accident insurance plan, and a comprehensive pension
for the aged and disabled. In a sense, Bismarck set the stage for what
would become the standard response of realist statecraft to the problem
of reconciling human rights and security in the world's industrialized
states. Domestic workers would be appeased with redistributed wealth
and, ultimately, universal suffrage, making it safe to largely ignore the
economic and political aspirations of the remainder of the world's poor.

An enormous problem interfered with this solution in which universal rights could be achieved domestically while power politics would prevail in international affairs. That problem was the twentieth-century emergence of the phenomenon of world war. The scale of wartime destruction was now so immense that security seemed to demand some sort of effective international organization. The first to reach this conclusion were the socialists, who not only proclaimed that universal human rights were the only way to prevent world war, but established the First International (1864–1876) to gather representatives from around the world for the purpose of creating a global regime based on human rights and peace.

After World War I, liberals also arrived at the idea that human rights and security required an international organization. One of the two organizations set up after World War I, the ILO, grafted socialist convictions onto liberal thought, insisting that world peace could only be preserved if workers' rights were respected in all countries. The other attempt to construct a liberal peace, the League of Nations, like its successor, the UN, placed the goal of non-aggression at the center of its search for international peace. The UN, building on the failure of the League of Nations, sought to combine respect for the division of the world into large and small powers with a more developed vision of universal human rights, as witnessed by the 1948 Universal Declaration of Human Rights.

Yet the old Bismarckian vision of combining global geopolitics with domestic harmony was resurrected by the cold war, during which the prevailing narrow view of security called once again for sacrificing international human rights in pursuit of what was considered the more pressing national interest in managing the U.S.-Soviet relationship. Whether the preferred agenda was an arms buildup and anti-Soviet interventionism or arms control and restraint in the use of force, the issue of human rights was generally regarded as a marginal one. This marginalization, and the view of national security that justified it, have since been seriously challenged. As the state becomes more vulnerable to the global reach of both private economic interests and weapons of mass destruction, which may soon originate from the poorest regions of the world, it has become increasingly clear that national security can no longer be achieved at the expense of human rights. If anything, the advances of human rights and global economic justice have become the only reliable paths to security, thereby extending the Bismarckian equation to the international realm.

Indeed, this progression is recognizable throughout modern history. Each historical cycle of world violence created the need to develop stronger mechanisms to protect individual rights within and between nations. If the Enlightenment had introduced into world politics the notion that the state existed to secure the universal rights of all its inhabitants, and by extension to exemplify those rights for all humankind, the industrial revolution had planted the seeds for a more interventionist state and a stronger international organization to promote human rights and counter conflicts between states. Last, the twentieth century was an era in which the establishment of the welfare state represented an improvement over the purely greed-driven capitalist state, and the UN an advance over the impotent League of Nations. In other words, if the wars and social revolutions of the eighteenth and nineteenth centuries strengthened the capacity of the state, and the two world wars and the cold war institutionalized the domestic welfare state, the mounting potential for violence incubated by globalization might well bring the task of securing global welfare into the realm of practical politics.

The result is that today's realists, seeking only security, find themselves drawn toward policies designed to advance human rights, a lesson that even the sole superpower can no longer afford to overlook. Thus, U.S. National Security Advisor Condoleezza Rice had argued before September 11 that realism required U.S. foreign policy to avoid humanitarian and human rights efforts. Reversing that view, she later stressed the complementarity of realism and idealism, so that "to continue to build . . . a balance of power that favors freedom, we must extend as broadly as possible the benefits of liberty and prosperity that we in the developed world enjoy. We have a responsibility to build a world that is not only safer but better."[93] As a result, the Bush administration, rejecting much of the foreign policy platform of candidate Bush, found itself committed to nation building in Afghanistan, to celebrating the right of Afghan girls to go to school, and to increasing the foreign aid budget, all because, as the president expressed it, "Hope is the answer to terror," as the United States vowed to become the new Jacobin soldiers of universal rights and democracy.

One may disparage these discourses as merely another step toward a more enlightened imperialism. Noam Chomsky, Antonio Negri, Michael Hardt, and Michael Ignatieff have all argued recently (though from different perspectives) that we have entered a new stage of globalization orchestrated by American imperialism.[94] For Ignatieff, it is not the imperialism of the past, "built on colonies, conquest and the white man's burden," but one reveling in a "global hegemony whose grace notes are free markets, human rights and democracy, enforced by the most awesome military power the world has ever known."[95] While imperial greed should always be denounced, the moral evaluations of empires, Ignatieff reminds us, get complicated when the policies of empire might benefit the Kosovars, Afghanis, Iraqis, and others. One can argue that if the American empire is well on its way to shaping the new international order, human rights may well benefit from exploiting the search for moral legitimacy associated with empire building. Of course, from the Roman Empire to that of the British Commonwealth, history warns us that the extension of empires inevitably breeds local contempt and violent backlashes that grow increasingly unmanageable. Yet even should the United States ultimately follow that familiar path, its current emphasis on legitimizing its global reach still provides important opportunities for a progressive agenda. In short, as foreign policymakers, preoccupied after September 11 with security, begin to acknowledge the relevance of human rights, the human rights community should be prepared to offer a substantive agenda linking human rights and international security. The following offers five preliminary guidelines for shaping what one might call a new realist human rights agenda for the twenty-first century: recognizing the legitimacy of core national security concerns, seizing human rights opportunities amid great power politics, reevaluating the appropriate means toward human rights ends, reassessing the limit to imposing human rights from outside, and confronting the overall need for a new human rights realism in our globalized economy.

Just as foreign policy analysts can no longer develop grand strategies which overlook basic human rights in poor societies capable of lashing out with a global reach, human rights activists cannot dismiss Western fears of mass destruction attacks as merely ideological manipulations to further geopolitical ends. Human rights activists should propose alternatives to narrow security concerns, rather then rejecting them outright. For instance, given how the new U.S. Department of Homeland Security is amassing broad powers in the name of national security, it is especially important to subject it to strong civil rights oversight and accountability, as advocated by Human Rights Watch and other human rights NGOs, which supported an amendment to the Homeland Security Bill that included the establishment of an effective assistant inspector general for civil rights and civil liberties, as well as a civil rights officer with policy and oversight functions.[96] Campaigning for such initiatives offers a practical path toward reconciling homeland security requirements with civil and privacy rights, and pressures along those lines have already served notice on policymakers that they need to explain convincingly how their homeland security policies can be reconciled with the protection of rights.

When security concerns bring major powers into conflict with brutal regimes, human rights activists should work to ensure that intervention serves to advance human rights. In this respect, the war against the Taliban, if not undertaken to liberate women from feudal slavery, had considerable beneficial consequences for women's rights, just as NATO's intervention in Kosovo might well have averted a repetition of Serbia's genocidal war, dramatized by the events in Srebrenica, against Muslims in Bosnia. While human rights rhetoric often masks other motives, and while the United States routinely maintains a double standard, favoring regimes that commit gross human rights violations (e.g., Saudi Arabia and China) when it serves its interests, a new realism of human rights should nevertheless seize opportunities to advance its cause whenever Western powers confront repressive governments. Certainly, human rights activists should condemn repressive regimes with equal fervor regardless of whether they are seen as friend or foe by the United States or the European Union. While it remains critically important to draw attention to grave human rights abuses that are ignored by the media and on no one's political agenda, human rights advocates should not shrink from actively opposing a cruel regime, such as that of Iraqi leader Saddam Hussein (1937–), simply because it has become the bête noire of the United States or other major powers. One can deplore the long record of human rights abuses in the foreign or domestic policies of the five permanent members of the UN Security Council and still support those instances in which their common cause advances human rights.

Human rights activists have traditionally condemned shortsighted great powers' foreign policies that have ultimately bred human rights abuses. For instance, many rightly criticized U.S. support of the mujahideen during the Afghan war against the Soviet Union and the subsequent U.S. indifference to the plight of the Afghanis after Soviet withdrawal. Such critical stands are hardly sufficient. The human rights community should feel obligated to offer viable policies, whether for liberating women from the Taliban regime or for freeing individuals within current repressive and authoritarian regimes. Thus, when power politics or the "CNN effect" draws the world's attention toward the brutality of particular regimes, a new human rights realism will assess in critical instances whether war is a legitimate last resort or whether the cost in likely casualties outweighs the prospective ends.

Just as the question of means and ends divided early-twentieth-century socialists, pitting Karl Kautsky and Rosa Luxemburg against Trotsky and Lenin on the question of what means were justified for achieving a socialist vision of rights, the question of the appropriate means for moving human rights principles forward is today equally divisive. For instance, while there might be broad agreement that toppling Saddam Hussein's dictatorial regime and restoring democracy and human rights for Iraqis was an honorable goal, the difficult question remained whether an intervention in Iraq might override the envisioned ends, namely that a prolonged U.S. military intervention and occupation might undermine the long-term prospects for human rights in the region. Obviously, there would have been fewer critics of military intervention if one could have foreseen that resistance would be short-lived and the cost in human lives low. While no one knows with certainty the outcome of any impending war, reflexive judgments are no substitute for sober assessments of whether ongoing political and military operations are consistent with human rights objectives and whether the considered means justify the envisioned ends.

Even if one could predict with certainty that human rights abuses could be greatly reduced at the cost of very few casualties, the question remains whether external forces are sufficient for sustaining improvements in human rights. Although, for instance, one can applaud U.S. policies in Afghanistan that quickly freed women from their burkas, the intervention against the Taliban regime would not have been possible without the cooperation of the Northern Alliance. While one can rightly claim that the groups composing the alliance were hardly democratic, they nevertheless represented a vital source of support for a new post-Taliban government. Generally, finding viable local or exiled sources of resistance remains imperative whenever outside military intervention is being considered to redress human rights violations. Not only is domestic support for intervention important in the short term, in its absence the long-term task of creating the infrastructure to maintain democracy in societies devastated by civil war is prone to being seen as another form of imperialism, resulting in growing resistance.

Thus, one should acknowledge the reasonableness of Michael Walzer's warning that outsiders' attempts at improvements are unlikely to take hold absent strong local support.[97] Taken to its extreme conclusion, however, this position may imply that short of an unfolding genocide, the world should refrain from interfering in cases of severe human rights violations. This line of thinking can inadvertently provide an unacceptable reward for effective totalitarianism, ensuring that once the iron fist of tyranny has silenced internal resistance, all hopes for outside help disappear as well. In practice, this view marks an unacceptable retreat from the conviction that an inalienable, indivisible perspective on human rights as endorsed by the Universal Declaration of Human Rights, is not a Western privilege but should be enjoyed by everyone everywhere. Hence, the task confronting a human rights realist is to carve a space between the charge of indifference linked to a non-interventionist position and the possible accusation of imperialism associated with humanitarian intervention.

If security strategies need always to be understood in the framework of our globalizing economy, a new human rights realism should actively support initiatives, wherever voiced, that integrate security, economic development, and human rights, such as the one discussed in July 2000 in Okinawa, Japan. There, under the Miyazaki Initiatives, the G8 foreign ministers called for "a culture of prevention" in addressing security threats. That culture would be based on "the UN charter, democracy, respect for human rights, the rule of law, good governance, sustainable development and other fundamental values, which constitute the foundation of international peace and security."[98] Whereas one may characterize these statements as purely cosmetic rhetoric, a new human rights realism would hold accountable the merchants of human rights ideals and press for the implementation of their decisions.

A campaign to apply that public pressure implies a clear rejection of the conviction shared by many human rights scholars and activists that globalization is simply antithetical to the advancement of human rights. One should recognize that there are aspects of capitalism that represent dramatic improvement when compared to the feudal arrangements that prevail in much of the southern hemisphere: its progressive capacity and its formidable power to develop the forces of production, to generate new needs, and to kindle humans' unlimited possibilities.[99] That hardly entails an endorsement of neo-liberal ideology, which can be held accountable for rules imposed on developing countries by the institutions controlling globalization (e.g., the IMF) that have perpetuated—or even worsened—poverty.

How then could a new human rights realism free globalization from its destructive trends? While a new human rights realism should always condemn the harsh conditions of workers in sweatshops, it should also acknowledge that the often romanticized alternative of self-sufficient feudalism may be even worse. In reality, millions of young women beyond the reach of globalization are left with no choice but to be subjugated under patriarchal domination or under the arbitrary tyranny of local mullahs in one or another remote corner of countries like Pakistan or Nigeria. For women and other destitute people within the most impoverished regions of the world, opportunities for change offered by market-driven economic growth (e.g., through microlending) should be welcomed when synchronized with redistributive policies that ensure real opportunities to escape poverty as well as with democratic aspirations.

While economic growth is vital to rescuing the poor, so are the institutions of the state. In other words, realizing the advantage of a market economy, a human rights realist perspective would call for more state intervention, not less—to develop economic infrastructure, public health and education, and civil institutions.[100] In the same vein, one should call for the implementation of supportive regulatory mechanisms within international financial institutions. Extending the campaign to forgive the debts of third world countries, for instance, could help enable many developing countries to combine economic development with a measure of social justice. Needless to say, keeping people alive, controlling the spread of epidemics, and providing clean water cannot be left solely to the work of the "invisible hand." In this respect, from the perspective of a new human rights realism, globalization is not an end, as its proselytes would like to have it, but should be seen as a means of advancing political, civil, social, and economic rights not just for the privileged but also for the "wretched of the earth."

One cannot relegate the task of building such a global welfare mechanism to policymakers or the providential caprices of history. That task belongs to the active intervention of the human rights community, which in the current climate of fear must vigilantly resist narrow and short-sighted security, cultural, and economic pressures. These forces always result in the fragmentation of what should remain the inalienable and indivisible mission of the human rights community, namely the relentless fight for civil, political, social, and economic rights for the visible, less visible, and conveniently invisible among us, within and beyond every national border.

HUMAN RIGHTS FOR WHOM?

This fight remains even more important as the jubilation at the end of the cold war has yielded to a more sobering environment for the pursuit of human rights. Indeed, the pressures of globalization (environmental degradation, the weakening of trade unions, harsh immigration policies, etc.) have further complicated the daunting search for a unified human rights agenda. At the same time, each of these negative aspects of globalization has redirected the specific agenda of various social groups: trade unions, women's groups, children's rights activists, gay rights groups, and advocates for minorities and the disabled. Over time, one may hope that a common understanding of the new challenges presented by globalization will enable each group to unify and to build a more encompassing program.

For over a century and a half, trade unions have fought for workers' rights to decent pay and better working conditions, and for improved social welfare, including health care, education, and social security. Generations of struggle for basic democratic rights, such as the right to organize in the workplace, have culminated in the International Confederation of Free Trade Unions, an organization that now embraces 127 million men and women in 136 countries on five continents. Yet with the decline of trade unions in recent decades, this movement is now under attack on a global scale.

Partly because of the spread of privatization, and partly because of the emergence of post-Fordist globalized production, trade unions in the West have suffered progressive losses in membership and have consequently lost some of the leverage they applied in earlier battles with employers. Despite the optimistic predictions of globalizers, average wages in the United States have been stagnant and have even dropped for the lowest-skilled workers. With growing numbers dependent on social security and welfare benefits, many governments have raised eligibility requirements while cutting payments. In many countries, government spending on education and health has also declined.

In the developing world, for much of the time since independence, trade unions have faced significant interference from governments and even, in some cases, outright control by them. While trade unions in many countries have played a key role in the move toward democratization, they are now facing a new crisis as their former strongholds, sectors like teaching, transport, and civil service, are undermined by privatization and public sector cuts. Worse, as competition becomes global and intensifies, bringing a new level of insecurity to developed nations and increased poverty to much of the developing world, one-fifth of the world's population has been left in conditions of utter poverty as more than 700 million workingmen and workingwomen are not productively employed, let alone properly represented.[101]

While it is true that the Universal Declaration of Human Rights (articles 21–27) and many clauses of the Covenant on Economic, Social and

Cultural Rights have codified workers' rights, enforcing a standard international social clause remains, in trade and business summits, a divisive issue. Western labor activists believe that a common social standard would prevent division between workers and dampen capital flight to poorer regions of the world, while rights activists in the developing world, recognizing that lower labor costs are a key incentive for attracting foreign investment, have denounced such measures as dismissive of the needs of poorer societies.

Domestically, trade unions in the southern hemisphere face other difficulties in their fight to secure the rights of their members, to represent workers in the informal sector, and to prevent forced labor. The last problem, little noticed by Western media, in fact represents an alarming reversal for human rights. Despite the banning of slavery in 1926 and in the 1957 Supplementary Convention on the Abolition of Slavery, the practice has not disappeared but has taken on a new form, with the current world total of slaves reaching approximately 27 million. Fifteen to twenty million of those bonded laborers are concentrated in India, Pakistan, Bangladesh, and Nepal. "There are more slaves alive today," argues the British scholar Kevin Bales, "than all the people stolen from Africa in the time of the transatlantic slave trade."[102] That one should never be forced to barter one's freedom for fear of one's life had already been affirmed by Rousseau in the eighteenth century.[103] Slavery remains, despite the Enlightenment's outcry, the nineteenth-century anti-slavery fight, and subsequent abolitionist treaties, a plague for many of the world's poorest people.

Chattel slavery, in which a captured person is born or sold into permanent servitude, still exists in places like Mauritania, yet represents only a very small part of modern slavery.[104] Debt bondage, common in Pakistan and India, is the most prevalent form of slavery today. It occurs when people who are desperately in debt are forced to submit to an agreement in which they (or their children) work without compensation until their employer decides they have paid off their obligations. Another form of modern slavery results when vulnerable people accept (or, as children, are forced by their parents to accept) a contract for guaranteed work and are transported far from home, only to find themselves, in effect, imprisoned and forced to work (child prostitution is a notorious example). That type of slavery is prevalent in Southeast Asia, Brazil, and some Arab states. While these forms of slavery are more widespread in developing countries, immigrants in Western countries, fearing deportation or illegal status, are often exposed to similar forms of bondage. Removed from the public eye, domestic workers, especially women, have remained more vulnerable to exploitative conditions.

Such persistent areas of female exploitation should not obscure the successes of the women's liberation movement in condemning the treatment of women as second-class citizens. In her international best-seller *The Second Sex* (1949), Simone de Beauvoir raised postwar feminist consciousness to a new height. With the emergence of the service sector in the West, women poured into the workforce after World War II, only to remain stigmatized because of their sex. Betty Friedan's *The Feminine Mystique* (1963) captured their tedious domestic lives and degrading daily experiences and, along with Kate Millett's *Sexual Politics* (1969), galvanized the women's movement in the late 1960s. Feminists had concluded that polite requests for change were insufficient and that they needed to develop a new organization to press their demands. The National Organization for Women was established in the United States and, despite a membership that ranged from moderate to radical, found consensus on six measures essential to ensuring women's equality: en-

---

SIMONE DE BEAUVOIR, *THE SECOND SEX*, 1949

It is through gainful employment that woman has traversed most of the distance that separated her from the male; and nothing else can guarantee her liberty in practice. Once she ceases to be a parasite, the system based on her dependence crumbles; between her and the universe there is no longer any need for a masculine mediator.

The curse that is upon woman as vassal consists, as we have seen, in the fact that she is not permitted to do anything; so she persists in the vain pursuit of her true being through narcissism, love, or religion. When she is productive, active, she regains her transcendence; in her projects she concretely affirms her status as subject; in connection with the aims she pursues, with the money and the rights she takes possession of, she makes trial of and senses her responsibility. Many women are aware of these advantages, even among those in very modest positions. . . .

When at last it will be possible for every human being thus to set his pride beyond the sexual differentiation, in the laborious glory of free existence, then only will woman be able to identify her personal history, her problems, her doubts, her hopes, with those of humanity; then only will she be able to seek her life and her works to reveal the whole of reality and not merely her personal self. As long as she still has to struggle to become a human being, she cannot become a creator. . . .

What is certain is that hitherto woman's possibilities have been suppressed and lost to humanity, and that it is high time she be permitted to take her chances in her own interest and in the interest of all.

---

forcement of laws banning employment discrimination; maternity leave rights; child-care centers that could enable mothers to work; tax deductions for child-care expenses; equal and unsegregated education; and job-training opportunities for poor women.

As globalization facilitated the erection of transnational social networks, the women's liberation movement spread throughout the world. The goals of feminism, however, varied from country to country, depending upon the level of repression. Western feminists were fighting to change sexist stigma and to achieve social and economic equality, African women were demanding the removal of the bride price, and feminists of the Muslim world were seeking the relaxation of the dress code and regulations enforcing separation of the sexes. Growing awareness of these issues prompted the 1979 adoption of the UN Convention on the Elimination of All Forms of Discrimination against Women (CEDAW), later ratified by 131 countries with the glaring exception of the United States, which stood out as the only industrialized country not to sign it.

Despite CEDAW's demand for equal remuneration (article 2d), women continue to be paid less than men for the same work. In less developed countries, women receive about one-half to two-thirds less pay than men, while in more developed countries, they earn about one-third to one-fifth less than men.[105] More broadly, as the total number of people living below the poverty line has increased substantially, there has been a significantly higher proportion of women among the poor than men. The feminization of poverty has worsened due to a substantial increase in female-headed households and the feminization of low-wage work, as well as lower educational levels in some regions of the world. Employed in badly ventilated Central American textile factories, maquiladores women work in harsh conditions for just $1 to $2 for each nine- to ten-hour workday. While the "Asian miracle" has generated unprecedented employment opportunities for women seeking to escape rural poverty in that part of the world, many are soon physically exhausted or injured by the fast pace of industrial production, exposed to hazardous substances, or fired as soon as they get married or pregnant (in contraposition to CEDAW's article 11.2a).

In response to the increased migration associated with globalization, CEDAW also affirms the right of women to immigrate to more prosperous regions with greater employment opportunities and better welfare systems (article 15.4). In reality, conforming to the norms of their traditional cultures, the less skilled are often less likely to initiate migration themselves, but instead follow their husbands or other relatives. Once they

UNITED NATIONS CONVENTION ON THE ELIMINATION
OF ALL FORMS OF DISCRIMINATION AGAINST WOMEN, 1979

Part I: Article 1

For the purposes of the present Convention, the term "discrimination against women" shall mean any distinction, exclusion or restriction made on the basis of sex which has the effect or purpose of impairing or nullifying the recognition, enjoyment or exercise by women, irrespective of their marital status, on a basis of equality of men and women, of human rights and fundamental freedoms in the political, economic, social, cultural, civil or any other field. . . .

Part II: Article 7

States Parties shall take all appropriate measures to eliminate discrimination against women in the political and public life of the country and, in particular, shall ensure, on equal terms with men, the right:

a. To vote in all elections and public referenda and to be eligible for election to all publicly elected bodies;

b. To participate in the formulation of government policy and the implementation thereof and to hold public office and perform all public functions at all levels of government;

c. To participate in non-governmental organizations and associations concerned with public and political life of the country. . . .

Part III: Article 11

1. States Parties shall take all appropriate measures to eliminate discrimination against women in the field of employment in order to ensure, on a basis of equality of men and women, the same rights, in particular;

a. The right to work as an inalienable right of all human beings;

b. The right to the same employment opportunities, including the application of the same criteria for selection in matters of employment;

c. The right to free choice of profession and employment, the right to promotion, job security and all benefits and conditions of service and the right to receive vocational training and retraining, including apprenticeships, advanced vocational training and recurrent training;

d. The right to equal remuneration, including benefits, and to equal treatment in respect of work of equal value, as well as equality of treatment in the evaluation of the quality of work;

e. The right to social security, particularly in cases of retirement, unemployment, sickness, invalidity and old age and other incapacity to work, as well as the right to paid leave;

f. The right to protection of health and to safety in working conditions, including the safeguarding of the function of reproduction.

2. In order to prevent discrimination against women on the grounds of marriage or maternity and to ensure their effective right to work, States Parties shall take appropriate measures:

a. To prohibit, subject to the imposition of sanctions, dismissal on the grounds of pregnancy or of maternity leave and discrimination in dismissals on the basis of marital status;

b. To introduce maternity leave with pay or with comparable social benefits without loss of former employment, seniority or social allowances;

c. To encourage the provision of the necessary supporting social services to enable parents to combine family obligations with work responsibilities and participation in public life, in particular through promoting the establishment and development of a network of child-care facilities;

d. To provide special protection to women during pregnancy in types of work proved to be harmful to them.

3. Protective legislation relating to matters covered in this article shall be reviewed periodically in the light of scientific and technological knowledge and shall be revised, repealed or extended as necessary.

---

migrate, they tend to join the domestic service or other activities in the informal sector—a sphere in which they experience long working hours, no benefits, a high dependence on their employers for food and housing, and limited freedom of movement.[106] Some southern and Southeast Asian countries that receive immigrants have also placed specific restrictions on women, allowing them to emigrate only if they have completed most of their child-bearing life.[107]

As immigrants or refugees of war, women have fewer opportunities and recognized rights than men. Along with the West's increased attentiveness to ethnic conflict after the cold war, women's refugee rights have received greater attention in human rights circles. While women can claim refugee status based on five criteria stipulated under the 1951 Convention Relating to the Status of Refugees—legitimate fear of persecution due to race, religion, nationality, membership in particular social groups, or political opinion—for many women refuge seekers, these grounds do not reflect the type of gender-specific persecution they endure. In 1991, the guidelines of the UN High Commissioner for Refugees recommended that evaluators respond with greater sensitivity to gender as they assess refugee status eligibility. Subsequent Canadian laws are more comprehensive, broadening the application of the term *refugee* and allowing, for instance, a Turkish woman and her three children, repeatedly assaulted and threatened, to seek refuge from a Muslim country where single women are expected to live under the protection of a male relative. Without changing the five criteria, some countries have begun recognizing the special circumstances of women seeking refugee status, as in the case of a young Mali woman, Amina Diop, who, forced to undergo genital mutilation and fearing an impending arranged marriage, fled to France, where she received asylum.[108] While a few countries are expanding their legal interpretation of the term *refugee*, the United States, along with most others, has generally continued to deny gender-based persecution claims beyond the five standard refugee criteria.[109]

With rampant nationalist wars characterizing our globalized era, one important advance for women's protection in wartime has been the recognition of war rape as a crime against humanity. It is true that the crime of rape has long existed under customary international law. The Lieber Code made rape a capital offense, and the Hague and Geneva Conventions barred rape and other sexual brutality. The international military tribunal in Tokyo following World War II condemned rape and other sexual violations.[110] Regrettably, the atrocious offenses committed against women in Nanking, Borneo, the Philippines, and French Indochina were mentioned only in passing, viewed as part of the barbarous collection of crimes and tales of horror traditionally associated with the normal "collateral damage" of war. Finally, with the 1993 inception of the International Criminal Tribunals for the Former Yugoslavia and for Rwanda,

---

CATHERINE A. MACKINNON, "CRIMES OF WAR, CRIMES OF PEACE," 1993

When the women survive, the rapes tend to be regarded as an inevitability of armed conflict, part of the war of all against all, or as a continuation of the hostilities of civil life of all men against all women. Rape does occur in war among and between all sides; rape is a daily act by men against women and is always an act of domination by men over women. But the fact that these rapes are part of an ethnic war of extermination, being misrepresented as a civil war among equal aggressors, means that Muslim and Croatian women are facing twice as many rapists with twice as many excuses, two layers of impunity serving to justify the rapes: just war and just life. . . . It is rape unto death, rape as massacre, rape to kill or make the victims wish they were dead. It is rape as an instrument of forced exile, to make you leave your home and never come back. It is rape to be seen and heard by others, rape as spectacle. It is rape to shatter a people, to drive a wedge through a community. It is the rape of misogyny liberated by xenophobia and unleashed by official command. . . . Do not say it is not sex for the men. When the men are told to take the women away and not to bring them back, they rape them, *then* kill them, then sometimes rape them again, cut off their breasts, and rip out their wombs.

From Stephen Shute and Susan Hurley, eds., *On Human Rights*, 88–89.

the adjudication of rape and sexual violence as crimes against humanity has now transformed jurisprudence, enabling criminal prosecutors, since 2001, to indict war rapists, and warning future perpetrators of the heavy cost of their crimes.[111]

As long as women are forced to take a back seat in traditional societies, to accept their inferior status in public and professional arenas, or to hide behind the veil of religious obscurantism, they will be easily discriminated against, treated as male property, seized as war trophies, and subjected to various abuses in their households. In the world's cruelest theocratic regime, the Taliban of Afghanistan displayed an extreme version of how poor countries may attempt to restore the appearance of stability amidst economic chaos by attempting to take absolute control over women and minorities. With less excess, this trend is not unique, reminding women of the Janus face of globalization as one face welcomes women to the entrepreneurial world of the next millennium while the other traps them in the terrible grip of poverty and oppression. Women need to consider the dark side of globalization as they attempt to develop a women's rights platform that bridges the cultural and socioeconomic divide between rich and poor. The 1995 Beijing Declaration of the Fourth World Conference on Women strengthened such efforts and provided a new platform for the promotion of women's rights as human rights.

On a related issue, the rights of the girl were included in the Beijing Declaration, in CEDAW, and more broadly under the 1989 Convention on the Rights of the Child (CRC). Yet many came to believe that the CRC needed to be revised to reflect the changing conditions of the international order by shedding light on the particular afflictions of children in developing countries. A working group was established in 1979, leading to the adoption of a revised CRC in 1989. The drafting committee reaffirmed the indivisibility between the civil, economic, social, and cultural rights of children, addressing issues heightened by contemporary concerns, such as exploitative labor conditions, sexual exploitation, refugee status, involvement in armed conflicts, and the juvenile justice system.

Article 32 of the revised 1989 Convention on the Rights of the Child recognized "the right of the child to be protected from economic exploitation and from performing any work that is likely to be hazardous."[112] In reality, many signatory countries, such as India, Pakistan, and Thailand, fail to enforce restrictions on child labor. While the boundary between acceptable and unacceptable child labor is not always clear, the reports of the UN on such abuses worldwide leave no doubt as to the intolerable exploitative conditions of countless children: "Thousands of girls between the ages of 12 and 15 work in the small industrial enterprises at Kao-hsiung in southern Taiwan. . . . Some children [in Colombia] are employed 280 meters underground in mines at the bottom of shafts and in tunnels excavated in the rock. . . . [O]ne million Mexican children are employed as seasonal workers in the United States."[113]

To prevent sexual exploitation, the 1989 convention also stated, as had the 1926 Slavery Convention and the 1949 Convention on the Suppression of the Traffic in Persons and of the Exploitation of the Prostitution of Others, that state parties shall prevent "(a) the inducement or coercion of a child to engage in any unlawful sexual activity; (b) the exploitative use of children in prostitution or other unlawful sexual practices; (c) the exploitative use of children in pornographic performances and materials."[114] The cruel reality of child prostitution and the ever growing trafficking in children, however, challenge these and other human rights legal instruments.

There are well over one million child prostitutes worldwide, assert scholars Kenneth J. Hermann and Michael Jupp.[115] Many girls as young as eight in Thailand and the Philippines are sold by their parents and smuggled across borders with the promise that they will be working in factories or as entertainers, waitresses, or servants. In reality, they are beaten and raped on the road, then forced, as indentured servants, to provide sex for their masters and to become indebted prostitutes, supplying brothels catering to a growing sex tourism industry. There may be 20,000 underage prostitutes in Thailand, 575,000 in India, and 500,000 in Brazil.[116]

KEVIN BALES, ON PROSTITUTION, *DISPOSABLE PEOPLE,* 1999

Though she is only fifteen, Siri is now resigned to being a prostitute. After she was sold and taken to the brothel, she discovered that the work was not what she thought it would be. Like many rural Thais, Siri had a sheltered childhood and she was ignorant of what it meant to work in a brothel. Her first client hurt her and at the first opportunity she ran away. On the street with no money she was quickly caught, dragged back, beaten, and raped. That night she was forced to take on a chain of clients until the early morning. The beatings and the work continued night after night until her will was broken. Now she is sure that she is a bad person, very bad to have deserved what has happened to her. . . .

In Thailand prostitution is illegal, yet girls like Siri are sold into sex slavery by the thousands.

From *Disposable People: New Slavery in the Global Economy,* 36–37.

If poverty has devastating consequences for children, war, which so often grips the poorest countries, claims children as its first innocent victims or recruits them as its agents. This common pattern led to the adoption of article 38 of the CRC, calling on states to accord children special protection during war and demanding that they "refrain from recruiting any person who has not attained the age of fifteen years into their armed forces." While the 1989 Convention on the Rights of the Child defines childhood as below the age of eighteen, fifteen is currently recognized as the minimum age for voluntary or compulsory recruitment into the armed forces. However, despite the opposition of the United States, momentum is now building for an optional protocol to the convention that would bring the minimum age to eighteen.

Despite these articles, wars continue to kill children in greater numbers than a century ago. Between 1990 and 2000 alone, an estimated two million children were killed in armed conflicts.[117] In the continuing war in the Sudan, as during the wars in Guatemala and Ethiopia, children are grabbed from cars, buses, or off the street, often on their way to their schools, homes, or churches, and forced to fight. A UNICEF series of twenty-four case studies of child soldiers, covering conflicts over the past thirty years, makes it clear that tens of thousands of children—many under the age of ten—have been recruited into armies around the world. In Liberia, children as young as seven have been found in combat, while in Cambodia, a survey of wounded soldiers found that 20 percent of them were between the ages of ten and fourteen when recruited. In Sri Lanka, of 180 Tamil Tiger guerrillas killed in one government attack, more than half were still in their teens, and 128 were girls.[118]

"CHILD SOLDIER VICTIM FROM HONDURAS," UNICEF REPORT

A case-study from Honduras illustrates one child's experience of joining armed groups:

At the age of 13, I joined the student movement. I had a dream to contribute to make things change, so that children would not be hungry . . . later I joined the armed struggle. I had all the inexperience and fears of a little girl. I found out that girls were obliged to have sexual relations "to alleviate the sadness of the combatants." And who alleviated our sadness after going with someone we hardly knew? At my young age I experienced abortion. . . . In spite of my commitment, they abused me, they trampled my human dignity. And above all, they did not understand that I was a child and that I had rights.

From Graça Machel, "Impact of Armed Conflict on Children."

In their efforts to escape from war, children have endured unthinkable horrors. In search of a safe haven from the ongoing civil war in the Sudan, thousands of unaccompanied Sudanese boys as young as seven and eight journeyed on foot in a desperate effort to reach the Kenyan border. En route, they became the prey of soldiers, militiamen, and wild animals, so that in the end, only a few reached their destination safely. A 1995 UNICEF study reported that in Angola, 20 percent of the country's children had been separated from their parents and relatives, and that during the devastating Cambodian war (1970–1975) and its genocidal aftermath (1975–1978), half the Cambodian population under the age of fifteen was left without adult care.[119] Article 22 of the 1989 CRC addresses this issue, enabling a child to receive either refugee assistance and protection or asylum status, whether or not accompanied by an adult.

International law may have adjusted to the specific needs of children in our era, yet they remain vulnerable. Those who are spared from war or the sex trade often lack even minimal healthcare, parenting, welfare, and education, all rights that are well-established in the industrialized countries and guaranteed under the convention. Consider the gap in infant mortality: 100 deaths per 1,000 births in the least developed countries versus 6 deaths per 1,000 births in the most developed states.[120] The gap in itself is staggering, pointing to the various ills that accompany poverty, which in turn affect the rights of the most vulnerable people in societies. While legal recognition of children's rights should be considered a first step, it cannot be a substitute for real international efforts to diminish the growing inequality between rich and poor countries.

For those children who have lost their innocence because of famine, sexual exploitation, war, or other forms of abuse, trying them as adults if they commit criminal offenses only perpetuates the cycle of abuse and violence, whether in Cambodia or in the United States. A critical plank of the children's rights movement is that regardless of the cruelty they may have been taught to inflict, children should not be tried as adults before the age of eighteen, as article 14 of the International Covenant on Civil and Political Rights stipulates. Instead, they should be rehabilitated, educated, and ultimately pardoned so that they can contribute to the development of their societies.[121] The strength of a civilization is not measured by the number of its prisons, or by the number of its forgotten children perishing in jails or electric chairs, but by its ability to break the cycle of violence generated by utter despair.

As has become increasingly clear in recent years, the globalization of the economy has produced various backlashes. When challenged, the "invisible hand" can be easily transformed into a controlling "iron fist" to restore social order. When necessary, delinquent children and other deviants can be threatened with exile from society. When opportune, a woman may be forced into a more subservient role within the family and society and reminded that her apparent victories in gaining control over her own body and reproduction may be ephemeral. In this context, the rights of the unborn can be elevated to the level of the rights of women in international human rights legal documents, such as the Convention on the Rights of the Child. When the efficient functioning of society is challenged, liberal prescriptions for globalization may intrude into what liberals pride themselves on cherishing the most: the realm of privacy. At that point, feminists, homosexuals, and lesbians can find themselves cast as the villains responsible for various forms of social instability.

The specter of the Stonewall riots in 1969 and the spread of homosexual and lesbian movements thereafter have haunted social conservatives, stimulating their eagerness to purge society of sexual deviance. The emergence of a Christian fundamentalist right wing in English-speaking countries was strengthened by the fiscal and social conservatism of Thatcher and Reagan and supported by a significant section of the corporate and business elite, who sought capitalist development unhampered by the welfare state, civil rights, and international human rights legislation. Gaining terrain in the last two decades of the twentieth century, in part by exploiting the fear of AIDS, religious fundamentalist groups have worked diligently to undo legislation supportive of women's and gay rights. It is in this context that in 1981 a Christian Voice fundraising letter urged its members not to "let militant gays, ultra liberals, atheists, and porno pushers, pressure Congress into passing Satan's agenda instead of God's." In 1988, the British House of Commons went as far as passing Clause 28, which forbade the teaching of tolerance toward homosexuals.[122]

Police raids against gays in Canada, Australia, and elsewhere reflected an emerging homophobic climate, which among other horrors inspired thugs to beat the young American university student Matthew Shepard (1977–1998) and leave him tied to a fence for eighteen hours to die in the cold. The hostile climate confronting gays and lesbians is far worse in many other countries. Over eighty countries in the world continue to criminalize sexual activity between consenting adults of the same sex. In other places, national or local legislation discriminates against lesbian, gay, bisexual, and transgender persons, imposing different standards for the legal age of consent and allowing indictments against them under various charges such as "scandalous conduct," "public indecency," loitering, and related charges.[123]

The degree of criminalization of sexual activity between consenting adults varies from country to country. The United Kingdom still bans lesbians and gays from military service; in 2001 the Zimbabwe Supreme Court upheld former president Canaan Banana's 1998 conviction for sodomy and indecent assault; in Egypt twenty-three men were recently sentenced for up to five years in jail for homosexual activities; and in Iran and Saudi Arabia captured gays are either severely lashed or publicly executed by hanging, stoning, or being thrown from a high place.[124]

Clearly, gays and lesbians do not suffer from the same level of persecution in Western industrialized countries as in the developing world. In 2001, the European parliament urged the European Union legislative body "to guarantee one-parent families, unmarried couples, and same-sex couples rights equal to those enjoyed by traditional couples and families, particularly as regards tax law, pecuniary rights and social rights." Among the most progressive nations, the Netherlands stands first for passing legislation permitting marriage between same-sex couples and granting adoption rights and access to the courts in cases of divorce. Next are countries such as Denmark, Greenland, Iceland, Norway, Sweden, France, Brazil, and Hungary, which have provisions for granting same-sex partners all the benefits of civil marriage with the exception of adoption.

Lesbians and gay men still lack the right to adopt children or acquire custody rights—rights that heterosexual individuals are eligible for under many international documents, such as article 24.1 of the Covenant on Civil and Political Rights, article 10 (3) of the Covenant on Economic, Social and Cultural Rights, and article 21 of the Convention on the Rights of the Child. If a lesbian can now enjoy parenting, thanks in part to artificial insemination technology, or co-parenting a child with a homosexual biological father, gays and lesbians lack the same access as heterosexuals to an impartial legal system for coping with disputes or divorce.

Another problem, accentuated by globalization, remains the absence of rights for gays and lesbians to immigrate in order to join their partners or to claim refugee status. There are currently fourteen countries that, while not allowing same-sex marriage, permit the sponsoring of a same-sex partner for immigration: Australia, Belgium, Canada, Denmark,

Finland, France, Iceland, Israel, the Netherlands, New Zealand, Norway, South Africa, Sweden, and the United Kingdom. Claiming refugee status for fear of persecution due to their same-sex preference presents additional obstacles for gays and lesbians. By recognizing under the "social group" criteria of the Convention Relating to the Status of Refugees the rights of individuals to apply for refugee status if they fear persecution on such grounds "as gender, linguistic background and sexual orientation,"[125] Canada leads other countries in its interpretation of refugee status for lesbians, gays, and heterosexual women. Its policies set an example for others to follow in moving beyond condemnations of same-sex preference as either a mental illness or a moral perversion.

World opinion has predictably shown more sympathy toward the physically impaired, the disabled, and the handicapped than toward gays and lesbians.[126] The rights of the disabled were recognized as early as 1948, in article 25 of the Universal Declaration of Human Rights, which states that each person has "the right to security in the event of unemployment, sickness, disability, widowhood, old age or other lack of livelihood in circumstances beyond his control." Further general condemnations of discrimination against the disabled were contained in various human rights instruments, such as the International Covenant on Civil and Political Rights and the International Covenant on Economic, Social and Cultural Rights. Other more specific but non-binding instruments relating to disability rights were subsequently adopted, such as the Declaration on the Rights of Disabled Persons (1975), the World Programme of Action concerning Disabled Persons (1982), the Declaration on the Rights of Mentally Retarded Persons (1971), and the Standard Rules on the Equalization of Opportunities for People with Disabilities (1993).

International awareness over disability problems was long overdue. The ranks of the disabled are swelling, now numbering over 500 million people, or about 10 percent of the world population. Approximately two-thirds live in developing countries, and in some developing countries nearly 20 percent of the general population is in some way disabled. When one considers the impact on their families, 50 percent of those populations is affected. Inadequate employment conditions, particularly for women, and poor medical care are among the most important problems confronting the disabled. As a cause of disabilities, the greatest single contributor is war.[127]

That "states should recognize the principles that persons with disabilities must be empowered to exercise their human rights, particularly in the field of employment" (ECOSOC [UN Economic and Social Council] Standard Rules 7) is guaranteed in many human rights documents.[128] Yet, maintains Ali Tari, special advisor to the ILO director general, the "new economic reality—growing global competition, shrinking profit margins, a declining resource base—is forcing firms all over the world to seek ways of decreasing personnel costs." Hence, "Staying in work has become more difficult for workers with disabilities in general, due to the deregulation of the labor market in many countries, and as a result of pressures on enterprises to remain competitive in an increasingly global market."[129] Women bear the greater burden of the disabled population, suffering a double discrimination. Not only do they have to deal with their own disabilities in societies that already stigmatize the work of nondisabled women, but they are also primary caretakers for disabled men, children, and older people.

Rampant wars have obviously been harsher on the disabled population, preventing people from resuming normal lives after peace and leaving them with less of a human rights recourse than other victims of war. In war-torn societies, unable to provide even minimal health and social services, they became the most wretched of the wretched of the earth.

UNITED NATIONS DECLARATION ON THE RIGHTS OF DISABLED PERSONS, 1975

3. Disabled persons have the inherent right to respect for their human dignity. Disabled persons, whatever their origin, nature and seriousness of their handicaps and disabilities, have the same fundamental rights as their fellow citizens of the same age, which implies first and foremost the right to enjoy a decent life, as normal and full as possible.

4. Disabled persons have the same civil and political rights as other human beings; paragraph 7 of the Declaration on the Rights of Mentally Retarded Persons applies to any possible limitation or suppression of those rights for mentally disabled persons.

5. Disabled persons are entitled to the measures designed to enable them to become as self-reliant as possible. . . .

10. Disabled persons shall be protected against all exploitation, all regulations and all treatment of a discriminatory, abusive or degrading nature.

11. Disabled persons shall be able to avail themselves of qualified legal aid when such aid proves indispensable for the protection of their persons and property. If judicial proceedings are instituted against them, the legal procedure applied shall take their physical and mental condition into account.

12. Organizations of disabled persons may be usefully consulted in all matters regarding the rights of disabled persons.

There are 300,000 disabled landmine survivors worldwide, a scale of suffering that finally galvanized UN passage of the Mine Ban Treaty (or the Convention on the Prohibition of the Use, Stockpiling, Production and Transfer of Anti-Personnel Mines and on Their Destruction) in March 1999, which aims not only to prevent new victims, but also to make the rights of landmine survivors part of international treaty law. Thanks to the global grassroots campaign led by Nobel Prize–winning activist Jody Williams, the treaty commits state parties to "do their utmost in providing assistance for the care and rehabilitation, including the social and economic reintegration, of mine victims." It is important, however, to note that the United States has joined Russia, China, Iran, Iraq, Libya, North Korea, Burma, Syria, and Cuba in refusing to sign the Mine Ban Treaty; the United States remains the only one of the fourteen NATO countries that has not signed the treaty. The United States possesses the third largest stockpile of antipersonnel mines in the world, totaling more than 11 million.[130]

Since World War II most of the conflicts in the world have been internal conflicts. A weapon of choice in those wars has all too often been landmines—to such a degree that today there are tens of millions of landmines contaminating approximately seventy countries around the world. The overwhelming majority of those countries are in the developing world, and they are primarily countries that do not have the resources to clear minefields or to care for the tens of thousands of landmine victims. The result is that the international community is now faced with a global humanitarian crisis.

At the dawn of the twenty-first century, the disabled, women, gays, and advocates for children have called for more attention to their groups'

JODY WILLIAMS, NOBEL PEACE PRIZE LECTURE ON LANDMINES, 1997

Landmines distinguish themselves because once they have been sown, once the soldier walks away from the weapon, the landmine cannot tell the difference between a soldier or a civilian—a woman, a child, a grandmother going out to collect firewood to make the family meal. The crux of the problem is that while the use of the weapon might be militarily justifiable during the day of the battle, or even the two weeks of the battle, or maybe even the two months of the battle, once peace is declared the landmine does not recognize that peace. The landmine is eternally prepared to take victims. In common parlance, it is the perfect soldier, the "eternal sentry." The war ends, the landmine goes on killing.

---

rights. They are joined in that clamoring for rights by various ethnic groups that invoke claims of repression to justify demands either for territorial secession or for more autonomy to exercise their cultural rights. While simmering ethnic tensions had been subsumed under the ideological banners of the superpowers' cold war rivalry, the end of that conflict unleashed a new explosion of ethnic conflicts in the former Soviet Union, Yugoslavia, Somalia, Rwanda, Afghanistan, and elsewhere. The cold war ideological battles between two opposing concepts of human rights were, in a sense, bypassed, as new conflicts were now traced to a collision of cultural values.

Whether or not globalization has led to clashes between civilizations, as Samuel Huntington forecast, or within them, it certainly has brought to the fore new international concerns over the rights of minorities. After the dismantling of the Soviet Union, twenty-five million ethnic Russians, reduced to minority status within former Soviet republics, became more vulnerable to human rights abuses. The treatment of its Albanian minority was far worse in Yugoslavia following its dissolution. Yet despite widespread persecution of minorities, neither the charter of the United Nations nor the Universal Declaration of Human Rights obliged the state to protect minorities.[131] While article 27 of the Covenant on Civil and Political Rights and the Helsinki Accords provided some support for minority rights, during the cold war states were reluctant to provide an expansive conception of minority rights, fearing the intensification of internal challenges to their sovereign control.

The post–cold war approach to minority rights has found expression in diverse documents such as the one adopted by the European Community as a result of the 1998 Badinter Commission Report and the 1992 UN Declaration on the Rights of Persons Belonging to National or Ethnic, Religious and Linguistic Minorities. Article 4 of that declaration stipulates that "[states] shall take measures to create favorable conditions to enable persons belonging to minorities to express their characteristics and to develop their culture, language, religion, traditions and customs, except where specific practices are in violation of national law and contrary to international standards." These international concessions, however, underlined a continuous historical tension between the states' right to sovereignty and the protection of minority rights.

That tension was experienced by many hundreds of ethnic groups throughout the twentieth century. More recently, however, as globalization has further broadened and deepened, threatening the cultures of indigenous peoples from Amazonia to the Arctic, it has also prompted indigenous quests, such as that led by the Guatemalan indigenous rights advocate Rigoberta Menchú Tum, for the preservation of cultural autonomy and lands. In the face of adversarial commercial interests, indigenous people have long sought to flourish as distinct communities, "determined to preserve, develop and transmit to future generations their ancestral territories, and their ethnic identity, as the basis of their continued existence as people in accordance with their own cultural patterns, social institutions and legal systems."[132] Today, international laws include a number of rulings benefiting indigenous peoples, granting them some control over their lands and some level of self-government, or effecting an imperfect compromise between state sovereignty and the protection of minorities, such as in the 1994 Resolution on Action Required Internationally to Provide Effective Protection for Indigenous Peoples and the 1997 American Declaration on the Rights of Indigenous People.[133]

With ever growing flows of migrants carrying different cultural values further and faster, along with the worldwide reconfiguration of economic production, globalization, for all the dangers it has posed, has simultaneously opened new spaces for the progress of human rights. Changes in economic production have provided new opportunities for middle-class women in the West, long trapped in their households, as well as for peasant women in the developing world, historically ensnared in rural misery. As women entered the workforce en masse, gay men and lesbians felt freer to redefine their sexual preference in societies paving the way for new gender and sexual definition. While women were fighting for liberation, their activism also advanced the rights and protection of children, who increasingly became the focus of international treaties. The formation of global human rights networks, abetted by the revolution in communications, has brought attention to the victims of wars, to the disabled, and to the plight of indigenous peoples. If the incorporation of human rights in numerous international treaties reflected growing awareness of social misery throughout the world, enforcing human rights still remains a problem and a pressing challenge of the new millennium. Finding the best arena in which to implement human rights is a formidable challenge that requires us to draw on the lessons of history, a task to which we now turn.

RIGOBERTA MENCHÚ TUM, ON INDIGENOUS RIGHTS, NOBEL PEACE PRIZE LECTURE, 1992

To us Mother Earth is not only a source of economic riches that give us the maize, which is our life, but she also provides so many other things that the privileged ones strive for. The Earth is the root and the source of our culture. She keeps our memories, she receives our ancestors and she, therefore, demands that we honor her and return to her, with tenderness and respect, the goods that she gives us. . . .

From these basic features derive behavior, rights and obligations in the American Continent, for the indigenous people as well as for the non-indigenous, whether they be racially mixed, blacks, whites or Asian. . . . The indigenous peoples never had, and still do not have, the place that they should have occupied in the progress of and benefits of science and technology, although they represented an important basis for this development.

If the indigenous civilization and European civilizations could have made exchanges in a peaceful and harmonious manner, without destruction, exploitation, discrimination and poverty, they could, no doubt, have achieved greater and more valuable conquests for Humanity.

INTER-AMERICAN COMMISSION ON HUMAN RIGHTS, AMERICAN DECLARATION ON THE RIGHTS OF INDIGENOUS PEOPLES, 1997

Section One: Indigenous Peoples

ARTICLE I: SCOPE AND DEFINITIONS

1. This Declaration applies to indigenous peoples as well as peoples whose social, cultural, and economic conditions distinguish them from other sections of the national community, and whose status is regulated wholly or partially by their own customs or traditions or by special laws or regulations. . . .

Section Two: Human Rights

ARTICLE II: FULL OBSERVANCE OF HUMAN RIGHTS

1. Indigenous peoples have the right to the full and effective enjoyment of the human rights and fundamental freedoms recognized in the Charter of the OAS, the American Declaration of the Rights and Duties of Man, the American Convention on Human Rights, and other international human rights law; and nothing in this Declaration shall be construed as in any way limiting or denying those rights or authorizing any action not in accordance with the instruments of international law including human rights law. . . .

ARTICLE V: NO FORCED ASSIMILATION

1. Indigenous peoples have the right to freely preserve, express and develop their cultural identity in all its aspects, free of any attempt at assimilation. . . .

Section Three: Cultural Development

ARTICLE VII: RIGHT TO CULTURAL INTEGRITY

2. Indigenous peoples are entitled to restitution in respect of the property of which they have been dispossessed, and where that is not possible, compensation on a basis not less favorable than the standard of international law. . . .

ARTICLE XIII: RIGHT TO ENVIRONMENTAL PROTECTION

1. Indigenous peoples have the right to a safe and healthy environment, which is an essential condition for the enjoyment of the right to life and collective well-being. . . .

Section Four: Organizational and Political Rights

ARTICLE XV: RIGHT TO SELF-GOVERNMENT

1. Indigenous peoples have the right to freely determine their political status and freely pursue their economic, social, spiritual and cultural development, and accordingly, they have the right to autonomy or self-government with regard to *inter alia* culture, religion, education, information, media, health, housing, employment, social welfare, economic activities, land and resource management, the environment and entry of nonmembers; and to determine ways and means of financing these autonomous functions. . . .

ARTICLE XVI: INDIGENOUS LAW

1. Indigenous law shall be recognized as a part of the states' legal system and of the framework in which the social and economic development of the states takes place. . . .

Section Five: Social, Economic and Property Rights

ARTICLE XIX: WORKERS RIGHTS

1. Indigenous peoples shall have the right to full employment of the rights and guarantees recognized under international labor law and domestic labor law; they shall also have the right to special measures to correct, redress and prevent the discrimination to which they have historically been subject. . . .

ARTICLE XXI: RIGHT TO DEVELOPMENT

1. The states recognize the right of indigenous peoples to decide democratically what values, objectives, priorities and strategies will govern and steer their development course, even where they are different from those adopted by the national government or by other segments of society. Indigenous peoples shall be entitled to obtain on a non-discriminatory basis appropriate means for their own development according to their preferences and values, and to contribute by their own means, as distinct societies, to national development and international cooperation.

Chapter Six

Promoting Human Rights in the Twenty-first Century

THE CHANGING ARENA OF STRUGGLE

Pakistani women rally
against religious
extremism, Karachi,
January 13, 2001.
AP photo/Zia Mazhar.

ARE WE MOVING TOWARD A MORE HARMONIOUS WORLD under the arches of McDonald's and before the screen of Microsoft? Or is the wave of solidarity expressed in the techno-plaza a mere illusionary space for the *vox populi* in matters of human rights? Despite the impact of globalization on human rights struggles, the popular voice seems less audible. Now digitized, this voice may be more easily subjugated to corporate interests and manipulations. New consumer needs are generated by the Gateses and Murdochs of a New World, in which control and dissemination of relevant information may be falling into the hands of the few.

In our new era, the state seems less able to ensure a fair diffusion of information and to secure the social environment necessary for real democratic debate. Forced out of the *piazza popolare* by corporate behemoths, progressives are either calling for the rebirth of local politics and communitarian solidarity or for global action—virtual or institutional. Whether progressives' activities are now local or global, civil society is gradually left at the mercy of tycoons. With the weakening of democratic forces in civil society as a buffer to state authority as those forces are more and more paralyzed by market imperatives and post–September 11 security concerns, the stage is set for authoritarian trends.

Historically, technology, economic development, and the state contributed first to the development *and only later* to the vanishing of social spaces of communication that are essential for human rights struggle. For instance, the railroad and the industrial revolution not only produced new urban sites of human interaction, but also created spaces for and spawned forms of resistance (trade unions, labor movements, etc.) often directed against the ramifications of these new economic developments. Today, the information age, globalization, and flexible production have fragmented and diluted that capacity for resistance. At the same time, these global forces are also carving out new social arenas propitious for the development of human rights. My assessment of these new opportunities draws on past historical lessons from the medieval period, the eighteenth-century democratic revolutions, the industrial revolution, the anti-colonial struggle, and globalization and its human rights critics.

Contemporary discussions about the best agency for the promotion of human rights (i.e., the feminist movement, the ecological movement, NGOs, the UN, the state, etc.) generally disregard how structural and institutional dynamics form a totality that has historically favored or restricted opportunities to advance human rights. Human rights scholars and activists tend to focus on civil society as the best arena for human rights struggle against the state, overlooking how different state apparatuses mold and shape their power in relationship to civil society.[1] Few have considered what impacts the manifold expressions of this dynamic have on the private realm (e.g., the individual right to privacy, gender relations, child rearing, our capacity for critical thinking, etc.). The following seeks to address these lacunae.

Accordingly, this chapter utilizes three categories: the state, civil society or the public sphere, and the private realm. Drawing on Antonio Gramsci's dialectic writing, *the state* as referred to here is an organism "reinforcing the relative power of the bureaucracy (civil and military), of high finance, and generally of all bodies relatively independent of the fluctuation of public opinion proper." With Gramsci, *civil society* is understood as the realm both of commodity exchange and social relations between dominant and subaltern groups, a social arena molded by the state to fit existing economic structures.[2] Following Jürgen Habermas, *the private sphere* indicates here either the realm of personal and gender relationships, or the household, a realm which becomes a separate entity with the emergence of the bourgeois public sphere.[3]

Emphasizing with Pierre Bourdieu that broad spatial and temporal experiences are the primary vehicles for the coding and reproduction of social relations,[4] one can evaluate, moving back through time, which types of institutional and spatial dynamics are most propitious for the advancement of human rights. For instance, the relative weakness of an as yet undeveloped civil society to resist the authoritarian, decentralized medieval feudal commonwealth allowed the state and the church to exercise control over social and private space in ways that are too often reminiscent of our times. Civil society today is more developed and more global in scope. Yet it has, at the same time, become more vulnerable as deterritorialized centers of economic power, along with the state, are increasingly able to contain those who dissent against the status quo in the public and the private sphere. The era in which human rights made more decisive progress, however, was one in which the state was relatively weakened by the burgeoning of popular participation in civil society, and in which the private realm escaped its control. This trend started during the eighteenth century's democratic revolutions and continued as the industrial revolution progressed throughout the nineteenth century. This concluding chapter asks, how can we counter the modern descent into a new medievalism concerning human rights and revive the democratic impulses of the eighteenth and nineteenth centuries? It addresses this question while examining some of the periods in the history of human rights already reviewed in this book, albeit through a different prism: the changing arenas of human rights struggle.

MEDIEVALISM AND THE ABSENCE OF CIVIL SOCIETY

The spheres of human rights debate and interaction tend to correspond to the prevailing locus of economic and public activity. In the medieval age, the countryside was the realm of such popular activities. With the exception of small numbers of merchants residing in medieval towns, the majority of the population worked the land and lived in rural settlements, with their churches, mills, and barns. The medieval landscape consisted, as Karl Marx explained, "on the one hand of landed property with serf-labor chained to it, and on the other of individual labor with small capital commanding the labor of journeymen."[5]

The close-knit character of most medieval communities stemmed from the relative immobility of the population and the nature of the feudal economy. While the church and warfare were international concerns in which a man might serve from one end of Europe to another, and though merchants traveled with their wares across a multitude of frontiers, the bulk of the agricultural population rarely journeyed more than a few miles from a given village, and many townspeople were equally confined. News traveled slowly and inaccurately, borne by pilgrims, peddlers, bailiffs, and beggars. Marriage outside the village was unusual, and local dialects contrasted sharply. With few technological resources and poor communications, all medieval communities were largely conditioned by their immediate physical environment.[6] Floods, pestilence, famines, and warfare between noblemen were constant hazards. The peasant was subjected by his professional activity to the dominion of meteorological time, to the cycle of seasons and the unpredictability of storms and other natural cataclysms. Against uncertainty and fear, one could find some consolation in time experienced collectively, with an order imposed by the cycle of seasons.

By the end of the fifteenth century, a great economic readjustment was taking place in Europe as ocean routes opened and commercial ventures expanded. The medieval economy began to give way to widening trade and to the development of new spaces for human interaction and activities. If populations had previously concentrated in settlements for political, ecclesiastic, and defensive reasons, it was now commercial activity that increasingly brought people together. These new opportunities led to the emergence of a merchant class residing in towns and flourishing city-states such as Venice, Florence, Hamburg, and Bruges: "For the merchants, the [commercial] environment superimposed a new and measurable time, in other words, an oriented and predictable time, on that of the natural environment."[7]

Along with bankers, merchants stood near the top of the non-noble population. In towns, journeymen lost their civic voice in public affairs and were subordinated to upper-bourgeois patricians who were interested in new and more adventurous commercial transactions. The interest of the master of the crafts guild was often opposed to those of the greater merchants, thereby producing a struggle for control over town governments. The concentration of the population in towns created the space for timely communication and conflict between associations, between the *popolo grasso* (big merchants) and the *popolo minuto* (lesser craftsmen and laborers). These conflicts were common in relatively autonomous city-states such as those in Italy. These new relations based on commercial interests pointed toward the birth of an active yet relatively small civil society.

One should not forget, however, that the bulk of taxation in feudal society was still generally extracted from the work of the peasantry, which constituted the majority of the population. In exchange for protection, feudal serfs had to pay heavy taxes to support wars and had to work the land for their masters. They had no public rights in relationship to their lords, who ranked as full masters of their dominions. Society was conceived as a hierarchy of lordships with the sovereign at its head and serfs at the bottom. The seeds from which all medieval institutions of central administration were to grow consisted of the immediate personal household of the king; its members were the only permanent staff he had, and their intimate personal association with their lord was the sole basis on which they could claim to represent his views and bear his authority. The kings instituted royal courts, under royal justice, to decide property disputes and to repress crimes. The king was supposed to act in council or in "court" with his vassals. Royal departments included the judiciary, exchequer, and military command. These departments, from which emerged the institution of parliament, represented vehicles for publicizing and strengthening royal authority. None of these assemblies, or parliaments, represented as yet the nation or the people, but instead represented the estates of the realm.[8] In such an authoritarian feudal state, no room was left for the advancement of political and economic rights.

The clergy helped in this respect: it sanctified the divine rule of the king and justified royal measures to the rest of the population. With the exception of urban independence on the Lombard or the Hanseatic model, most towns in France and Spain, and in parts of Germany and England, remained under the authority of royal government and the church. Between the monarchical state and the peasant society, no significant social space was carved out outside of the tutelage of the church. The church provided an important forum for convening individuals from disparate areas of the countryside. It provided a sense of community in which peasants could share their weekly experience and find comfort in the promise of heavenly reward for their present misery.

The church should not be seen as a free agent in feudal society, but as an intrinsic part of the apparatus of power itself. By pledging universal happiness in the kingdom of God in compensation for people's obedience and earthly poverty, the church shielded the feudal system from potential usurpers of power. It provided people with a sense of direction, escorting them from birth to death. It regulated commercial activities and condemned them, whenever they represented a threat to authority, as the devilish work of speculators and usurers. Religion permeated every pore of medieval life. The mutual duties of lord and vassal were confirmed by religious oaths, and bishops and abbots, as holders of land, became feudal personages themselves. The king was crowned by the chief churchman of his kingdom and adjured to rule with justice and piety. In towns, each guild served as a lay religious brotherhood and had a patron saint. Painting, art, and sculpture glorified religious imagery and decorated Gothic cathedrals.

In rural areas, despite economic change, no significant public space permitted democratic communication between the peasantry and feudal authorities. The notion of the public sphere in the medieval context referred mainly to a geographic location, compared to the modern association of a public sphere with active public participation. Public gatherings were often staged in order to display the feudal hierarchy: "The publicity of courtly-knightly representation which, appropriately enough, was fully displayed on feast days, the 'high holidays,' rather than on court days, was completely unlike a sphere of political communication. Rather, as the aura of feudal authority, it indicated social status."[9] Churches, with their rituals, liturgy, and mass processions, represented another space in which the crown could exhibit order, stability, and power.

During the Renaissance, however, places such as Milan, Florence, Venice, and Genoa emerged as independent city-states. With no kings to impose laws and largely immune to the influence of popes, a secular and republican spirit prevailed, alongside mercantilism, in the public sphere of these states: "Space was no longer indeterminate, unknowable or divine; it was a zone occupied by physical human beings, or one in which human beings might at least imagine themselves moving about."[10] The artistic imaginations of da Vinci and Michelangelo could flourish in this humanized space, which was now also creating room for the revival of Greek and Roman teachings about rights.

Where the influence of the Renaissance had been more limited, the churches' unique role as a space where individuals gathered on a regular basis gave it the potential to give vent to democratic impulses. Throughout Europe, Luther and other advocates of the Protestant Reformation called for more religious tolerance, viewing the Bible as the primary authority on issues of faith, insisting on a return to simple liturgies, asserting individual responsibility in matters of salvation and in seeking happiness on earth, the "real" realm of God's creation, and demanding separation of church and state.

These calls for more tolerance found wide support among the emerging middle class and illuminati. Enlightened priests such as Bartolomé de las Casas deplored the Spanish crown's use of Catholicism to exploit and persecute the Indian population. Descartes's skepticism inspired the Dutch legal scholar Hugo Grotius's call for greater religious freedom.[11] Thomas Hobbes's invocation of the use of scientific, rather than divine, criteria to evaluate political arrangements inspired the assault on revealed knowledge. One important consequence of this growing insistence on individual freedom was the Habeas Corpus Act of 1679, which protected individual liberty by proscribing illegal imprisonment by the state.

Calls for religious tolerance and for a new space for economic and social progress spread throughout Europe, sparking lengthy religious warfare pitting the Catholic League against the defenders of Protestantism. Internal religious war erupted for thirty years in Germany and spread to Holland, Spain, and Scotland. Finally, the 1648 Peace of Westphalia ended the wars of religion in central Europe and divided Europe in the following ways: Catholics and Protestants reached a balance of power in Germany, England became Anglican, the Low Countries embraced Calvinism, and France and Italy remained devoted to the papacy.[12]

Along with debates in church gatherings and meetings of notables in towns, the spread of the printing press helped disseminate political and religious ideas to a small yet significantly vocal stratum of the population: scientists. It also enabled collaboration at a distance, giving enormous impetus to the formation and effectiveness of the scientific community. In the search for academic freedom, intellectuals and scientists no longer needed to be confined to universities or other institutions strictly guided by religious dogma. The proliferation of scientific discoveries, combined with mercantile pursuits in the seventeenth century, marked the growing confidence of individuals interacting outside the space controlled by religious orthodoxy.

Yet the development of an independent democratic space, outside the direct control of the state and the church and separated from the private realm, remained embryonic. This was partly because, despite the progress of commerce, the notions of public (work on the land) and private (the household) were still closely intertwined in late medieval societies. Individuals were united by family bonds and by land.

> If we think of the land as the public sphere, then the house and the authority exercised by its masters must simply be considered a public authority of the second order: it is certainly private in relation to that of the land to which it is subordinated, but surely in a sense very different from how the term is understood in modern private law. Thus it seems quite intelligible . . . that "private" and "public" powers are so fused together into an indivisible unity that both are emanations from a single unified authority, that they are inseparable from the land and can be treated like legitimate private rights.[13]

If family life was organically shaped by the common economic activity of farming, a division of labor between women and men existed in the peasant family. Plowing and mowing, for example, were predominantly male tasks. Women's work in the fields included planting, weeding, and shearing sheep. Closer to home they also took care of the poultry, the dairy, and the garden.[14] They remained the main caretakers of children, while men's work was concentrated in the field. Such differences sharpened as the realm of economic activities gradually moved, during the nineteenth century, from the countryside to towns, thereby creating an even clearer separation between a female domestic sphere and a male public sphere.

Meanwhile, women's subordination to men was regarded as the

penalty for Eve's sin. Protestantism did not change this perception. Calvinist theologians composed treatises to demonstrate the need for patriarchal discipline. Condemning women as bad mothers and attempting to counter their "pernicious effects," Samuel Hochholtzer stated:

> How they [women] love to accept strange, false beliefs, and go about with benedictions and witches' handwork. When they are not firm in faith and the Devil comes to tempt them . . . they follow him and go about with supernatural fantasies. Daily experience also teaches us that many of them hide in the serious error that they could cure their children and others with blessings and devilish things, such as the many stories about herbs, which they first empowered with supernatural blessings.[15]

The perception of women's "natural weakness" justified prejudice and the medieval belief in witchcraft. Far more women than men died accused as witches in Germany, and the pressure to put witches on trial came not only from higher authority but also from communal searches for scapegoats for famines, epidemics, and harm done to animals. Women suffered ill treatment regardless of their rank. Even noble ladies "married and unmarried, . . . the bright jewels of festivals and tourneys, were wholly subject to the domestic power of father and husband, were not infrequently ill-treated and were jealously watched as though they were ladies of the harem."[16] As Max Horkheimer astutely remarked, "The familial role of the woman strengthens the authority of the status quo in two ways. Being dependent on her husband's position and earnings, she is also circumscribed by the fact that the head of the family adapts himself to the situations he meets and under no circumstances rebels against the powers that be but does his utmost to better his position."[17] In the context of the Reformation, the feudal and religious hierarchy continued to be replicated at every level: higher authorities reduced prospects for rebellions by granting men absolute patriarchal authority over their wives or by unleashing their frustrations onto other women.

In sum, commercial transactions during the medieval age might have prompted the development of new spaces for human rights interaction, yet disequilibria between a strong feudal power and a still embryonic civil society continued to constrain the development of human rights opportunities. As long as the public realm was dormant, closely linked to the private realm, and subservient to religious and feudal authority, the state, however backward, was still uncontested. State control was further eased by the imposition of patriarchal authority onto a shapeless public and private society. Commerce and the burgeoning of city-states and towns with relatively less state control than was present in the countryside, however, generated new space for economic activity, which often pitted the interests of journeymen against those of big merchants. If the agrarian economy was not conducive to mass gatherings and active public participation, the church, whose function was to ensure the people's allegiance to the crown, was.

Despite its efforts to preserve the status quo, the church provided both a new space for resistance and the language to confront power on different religious and social terms. Because the liturgies and stratification of the church replicated the political and social hierarchy inherent in feudalism, Protestantism struggled against papal hierarchy, entrusted individuals with the ability to interpret the Holy Scriptures, and, along with the new merchant class, called for a separation of church and state. Despite a still small commercial economy, which coexisted with the agrarian economy, the advent of the Reformation added strength and legitimacy to the merchant class. Freed from the moral jurisdiction of the church in matters of commerce and speculation, the merchant economy was able to expand. The medieval agrarian and social landscapes were now dotted with urban niches in which rapid communication between individuals would prove decisive for the development of commerce and human rights struggles predicated on individual rights in the seventeenth and eighteenth centuries.

THE EMERGENCE OF CIVIL SOCIETY
DURING THE ENLIGHTENMENT

The further development of commerce, now undertaken by different countries, encouraged the growth of towns, intensified social divisions, and led to the subsequent democratic revolutions of the eighteenth century. The emerging global economy, which had initially profited the Portuguese and the Spanish in the sixteenth century, was now moving to serve the interests of the British, the French, and the Dutch. The new wealth of these emerging powers was produced by increased scientific knowledge, a detachment from blind subservience to religious dogma, a newly asserted independence from the feudal and rural economy, and slavery. In Europe, and more particularly in northern Europe, the growth of towns benefited from new mercantile initiatives. Transformed by overseas ventures, a new commercial class of city dwellers began to challenge the heretofore uncontested supremacy of the landowning aristocracy.

Despite the growing impact of urban life, most people in the eighteenth century did not live in towns. Cities remained small relative to those of the nineteenth century: "The largest cities of Europe did not exceed 600,000 or 700,000 people and the next largest cities did not much exceed 200,000 people."[18] Though agriculture was still the main form of production, the emerging wealthy mercantile class (drawn from both the nobility and the merchant class) had begun to develop free-trading internal markets in which towns served as hubs for regional trade, promoting a shift in power from the rural sector toward the towns. The creation of commercial towns, homogenized and structured in order to secure commodity exchanges beyond feudal tariff barriers, became essential for the advance of human rights. Such spaces offered the possibility for individuals to gather and confront the absolutism of the state. Clear scientific mapping of new geographical spaces contributed to the further expansion of commerce and provided a new territorial base for popular rebellions.

Mercantilism coincided with the European age of royal grandeur and absolutism. Palaces were built in the principal capitals, such as Paris, St. Petersburg, London, and Vienna, displaying the splendor of the new era.[19] The state was becoming increasingly centralized under the absolute authority of the king. In the early days of state making, medieval kings had to depend for aid on the nobility and the clergy, neither of which was single-mindedly devoted to serving royal interests. With the growth of the state, the need to secure consent for important action and, concurrently, the need to get help with administrative work resulted in a blanketing of Europe with political assemblies at all levels. The challenge to royal ambitions represented by these assemblies motivated princes to seek to reduce or destroy them. The restoration of the English monarch Charles II after the crushing of the "Long Parliament," and Louis XIV's (1638–1715) dissolution of the Estates General, announcing that he would govern by himself, evidenced these efforts. Louis XIV's motto, "L'état, c'est moi!" (the state is me), celebrated royal absolutism and inspired monarchs throughout Europe to follow in his footsteps. The armed forces and formerly private enterprises were now also centralized with a more complex administration under the authority of the king. Inspired by the political theorist Bishop Bossuet (1627–1704), the Sun King espoused the idea that law and force within any country should be monopolized by absolute yet lawful kings as the sole representatives of God on earth. The grandeur of France's royal absolutism as manifested in painting, architecture, and engineering was emulated in Denmark-Norway, Poland, England, and elsewhere throughout Europe.

If the economic interests of the bourgeois and the monarchy went hand in hand during the early phase of mercantilism and absolutism, they began to enter into conflict during the eighteenth century. International trade still suffered under the rudimentary financial institutions of feudal society, which restrained the growth of merchants' wealth and influence. Excluded from political and religious affairs, the bourgeoisie channeled its frustrations into a developing public space that coincided with the expansion of towns as the new heart of economic power. A bourgeois civil society, with its new institutions, grew between the state and the private sphere, forming a buffer zone that began to check royal authority. The 1688 English Glorious Revolution, which reestablished the authority of the parliament, illustrates this shift.

By the late eighteenth century, the political debates within European civil society had had a profound influence on the ideas of the American Revolution. Thomas Jefferson's American Declaration of Independence was inspired by natural rights theorists such as Jean Jacques Rousseau. Europeans had developed a broader worldview, thanks to their overseas discoveries and trade with America, Africa, and Asia. There was much speculation on the diversity of human races and cultures, and a growing belief that individuals across the world should enjoy similar rights. Traveling between the United States and France, Thomas Paine praised, in the spirit of his age, the virtue of civil society. "[Civil] society," he wrote, "is produced by our wants, and governments by our wickedness; the former promotes our happiness positively by uniting our affections, the latter negatively by restraining our vices. The one encourages intercourse, the other creates distinction. The first is a patron, the latter a punisher."[20] Civil society was legitimized as the realm of natural rights; the state was justified only insofar as it enforced these universal rights. Among the most important rights discussed were the rights to private property and to political freedom.

The growing literacy of the bourgeoisie, amidst the still generally illiterate and impoverished masses, increased the active leadership of this new emerging class in civil society. Previously focusing on royal court affairs, news now broadened to address the needs of commerce.[21] With the growing tension between towns and courts, gazettes were also reporting philosophical and political views discussed in universities and salons. Finally, gathering places such as theaters and concert halls, long used for the display of court power, were now opening to a wider public.

Activities within civil society and the public space reached a new height with the advent of the American and the French revolutions. Though

Rousseau, Voltaire, and Diderot had all demanded freedom of the press since the 1750s, that right was first enjoyed in America. With the *Boston Gazette and Country Journal,* John Adams was perhaps the first to realize the revolutionary possibilities of the press as a tool for changing the organization of power.[22] In pre-revolutionary North America, it fanned the flames of political associations such as the Sons of Liberty and the Committees of Correspondence.[23]

By the time of the American Revolution, demands for a free press and free association were sweeping across Europe and were soon adopted by revolutionary France, where the 1789 Declaration of the Rights of Man and of the Citizen inaugurated the "free communication of ideas and opinions as one of the most precious rights of men."[24] Jacques-Pierre Brissot's (1754–1793) *Patriote français* (1789) was among the first of an extraordinary wave of newspapers that circulated in France. Some royalist papers, like Antoine Rivarol's (1753–1801) *Actes des apôtres* and the Abbé Royou's (1741–1792) *Ami du roi* (1790), were printed, but conservative publications were no match for their revolutionary competitors. Mirabeau (1749–1791) initiated the *États généraux* (1789) after the fall of the Bastille, Louis Prudhomme started the important *Révolutions de France* (1789), and Jean-Paul Marat (1743–1793) launched the *Ami du peuple* (1789).[25] The rest of France used these major papers as a model, and newspapers multiplied throughout the revolutionary period.

Along with other new rights, the French revolution encouraged free political association. The spread of numerous clubs and political associations throughout France, such as the Friends of Liberty and Equality and the Jacobin clubs, also animated public debate and the life of the public sphere, until the Chapelier Law of 1791 restricted political associations in France. The spread of public associations in France encouraged similar enterprises throughout Europe. Despite the still faint development of the bourgeoisie in the German, Italian, and Swiss states, societies and reading circles everywhere found new impetus. In Germany, for instance, one could count 270 bourgeois reading societies.[26]

The burgeoning of the public sphere in cities coincided with the development of the bourgeois family. Friedrich Hegel referred later to the emergence of such a family as the romantic realm, in opposition to the impersonal character of civil society. That development called for a sharper division of labor between men and women, one in which marital love and child care were identified as the realm of women and business and civic loyalty as the sphere of men.[27] Monogamy as conceived by the bourgeois family suggested female isolation from a patriarchal public sphere and women's economic dependence on male activities.[28] During the politically animated period of the eighteenth century, excluded from discussions in the coffeehouses (an institution in the public sphere), urban educated middle-class women like Madame de Staël (1766–1817) would host philosophical salons in their homes and lend their voices in support of the largely illiterate population of women in the countryside.[29]

With the progress of the French Revolution, journals and pamphlets were read aloud and debated in public spaces where common women congregated, and women picked up some of the language and content of the revolutionary debate. Oral communication within cities was essential for the new activism of women from poor and working-class backgrounds. In Paris, women once confined to home and church now encountered each other daily in the streets, the market, the gaming halls of the Palais royale, and later in the workshops, breadlines, section assemblies, popular assemblies, galleries of clubs, and so on.[30] In late summer 1789, when a shortage of grain raised bread prices to new levels, women rallied in opposition. Tensions reached a zenith in early October when women marched to demand bread from the king and the National Assembly. In this context, Olympe de Gouge, following Etta Palm d'Aelders and others, called for legal reforms on behalf of women. Her 1791 Declaration of the Rights of Women, addressed to Queen Marie-Antoinette, remains a key historical document heralding the revolutionary fight for the promotion of the rights of women. The Thermidorian reaction, however, ended women's political activities and revoked for a long period the gains promised by the French Revolution.

In short, during the Enlightenment, the development of commerce redefined the temporal experience of economic, political, and social activities, producing new social spaces that stimulated individuals' capacity to resist monarchical power. The convergence of an invigorated bourgeois patriarchal civil society and an emerging feminine private realm created critical opportunities for the spread of human rights militancy, culminating in the eighteenth-century democratic revolutions. While the private sphere had become the intimate realm that, through a sharper division of labor between the sexes, supported the development of a patriarchal bourgeois society, growing towns were the geographical unit in which civil society—and the liberal notion of individual private property—predominated, even as the state became the relevant space toward which the mercantile economy gravitated.

As the emerging liberal civil society confronted the absolutist state, tensions were inevitable. In the late seventeenth century, the English Bill of Rights, issued following the English Glorious Revolution, concluded with the reinstitution of the parliament and limitations on the executive power of the newly installed King William of Orange, demonstrating the capacity of the affluent bourgeoisie to extract concessions from the British monarchy. The success of the American Revolution dramatized the potential of bourgeois civil society predicated upon property rights to confront and defeat a monarchical state. The French Revolution, the result of a political and economic crisis between the Third Estate and the nobility, ultimately consolidated the gains of a politically ambitious bourgeoisie. With these revolutions, popular participation in civil society had finally reached a boiling point.

THE EXPANSION OF CIVIL SOCIETY IN THE INDUSTRIAL AGE

Social conflicts did not halt after the French Revolution. A new wave of commercial and technological development, led by Great Britain, was transforming the European social landscape, changing the balance between the state, civil society, and the private realm and providing new venues for human rights struggles. While France after the French Revolution was still divided between royalist and republican factions, Britain, France's old rival, was ruling an overseas empire and expanding its markets abroad. Britain's economic precocity relative to France and other nations was due to a host of factors: its early initiation of agrarian enclosure policies, an empire that provided access to vast supplies of raw materials, a superior commercial fleet that gave the country easy contact with suppliers and overseas markets, naval power to protect its commerce, abundant coal and iron resources, a free internal trade policy, and a capacity for technological innovation, most notably represented by the steam engine. These advantages propelled England's transition from an agricultural economy, making it the leader of the industrial revolution.

Though other European nations followed, England showed the way. The process of its industrialization, including the development of rapid transportation, thanks to the railroad, revolutionized people's spatial lifestyle and temporal experience. From 1750 to 1850, the combined population of England and Ireland tripled, rising from about ten million in 1750 to about thirty million in 1850.[31] Expanding coal and iron production drew a migration of people from the south, contributing to the growth of cities like Manchester and Liverpool, which rose out of nothing in the north of England.[32] Outside of England, industrialization and urbanization began in the mid–nineteenth century in Belgium and north-eastern France and spread to Germany, the Netherlands, southern Scandinavia, and other areas in conjunction with the construction of railways.

While various forms of social turmoil accompanying the process of industrialization weakened the feudal state, feudalism and absolute monarchy retained a strong hold over Europe at the beginning of the nineteenth century. Royalists continued to strive for control and to repress liberal ideas after the Thermidor reaction in France and throughout many countries in which the ideas of the French Revolution had taken hold. Following the defeat of Napoleon Bonaparte, the Congress of Vienna in 1815 represented a determined European effort to restore old dynastic powers and erect a barrier along France's eastern frontier. The Bourbon line was restored with the French king Louis XVIII, the Prussian king Frederick William III ruled over the large German confederation of states, the Dutch republic was revived as the kingdom of the Netherlands, and the Italian kingdom of Sardinia was restored and strengthened by the addition of the defunct republic of Genoa. In the rest of Italy, the restoration of the pope in the Papal States was recognized, and the Austrian Empire annexed the Lombardo-Venetian kingdom in northern Italy.[33]

Despite the reestablishment of old monarchies, the incremental transition from an agricultural to an industrial economy had continuously fed the creation or improvement of public spaces, facilitating social interaction and stimulating prospects for resistance against feudal and royalist obstacles. In the United Kingdom, the establishment of parliamentary power, as a result of the Glorious Revolution, along with the free traffic of commodities, had already contributed to the substantial growth of English bourgeois civil society. In *The Wealth of Nations,* published in 1776, Adam Smith had praised the virtues of a laissez-faire economy. The benefits of the "invisible hand," whose capacity to produce wealth required the absence of governmental interference, were later acclaimed by Thomas Malthus (1766–1834) and David Ricardo (1772–1823). Throughout Europe, the passage of laws securing private affairs from intrusion by the state demonstrated growing individual autonomy from state control.

Hegel, among other important philosophers, was inspired by this trend. He celebrated civil society, the realm of private interests, as the arena of freedom and individual will actualized in a new forum. Both Hegel and John Stuart Mill predicted that the middle class would become the liberal bastion of social stability. For Hegel, the state, as represented in the person of a constitutional monarch, legitimized the gains individuals acquired in civil society and transcended their particularism. His endorsement of a strong monarch reflected German and Italian liberals' yearning for the consolidation of national power as a prerequisite for initiating the process of industrialization already undertaken by England and France.

In countries such as Germany and Italy, where the bourgeoisie was still in its embryonic stage and civil society almost nonexistent, liberals endorsed the development of a strong national state. Referring to the Italian Risorgimento (unification), Antonio Gramsci suggested that when civil society is not yet developed and remains "gelatinous," when no group is clearly dominant, the functions of the state and civil society are initially fused together. In other words, the state develops as a coercive apparatus "which legally enforces discipline on those groups who do not 'consent' either actively or passively."[34] In the Italian context, forces in the north were eager to proceed with industrialization, while the south was still characterized by agricultural backwardness. To modernize, national unification between the north and the south was imperative. The liberal thinker Giuseppe Mazzini's nationalist appeal to the Italians was clear: "Your Country is one and indivisible . . . [it] is the token of the mission which God has given you to fulfill in Humanity."[35] In Germany, Max Weber and others endorsed the same nationalist perspective as Italian liberals.[36]

In England and France, where industrialization was more advanced and feudal power diminished, civil society became a battlefield between various social groups. If freedom from feudal domination and the state meant freedom to trade, it also meant, for the bourgeoisie, freedom from labor laws. In these countries, however, laissez-faire industrialization had already revealed the dark face of urbanization and the harsh living conditions of the emerging working class. The migration of workers from the rural sectors to urban sites created factory towns where life was physically and psychologically deadening. Observing the miserable conditions of workers in Manchester, Engels reported that "if anyone wishes to see in how little space a human being can move, how little air—and such air!—he can breathe, how little of civilization he may share and yet live, it is only necessary to travel hither."[37] Gathered in cities, talking and mingling in denser social spaces than those of the medieval countryside, workers could share their daily experience in coal mining and textile mills, and in doing so, develop a sense of solidarity and class awareness. Modern industry and faster communication created by social density, rail transport, and advances in printing and papermaking combined to facilitate unity among workers and the establishment of trade unions. "It was just this contact," Marx observed, "that was needed to centralize the numerous local struggles, all of the same character, into one national struggle between classes. But every class struggle is a political struggle. And that union, to attain which the burghers of the Middle Ages, with their miserable highways, required centuries, the modern proletarians, thanks to railways, achieved in a few years."[38]

Easier and faster communication between workers was conducive to the formation of trade unions and labor movements and to the spread of socialist ideas after 1830. In England, those socialist ideas fused with the movement for further parliamentary reforms. Through mass agitation, the Chartist movement focused on winning working-class representation in parliament, universal suffrage for all adult males, and the reduction of working hours. In France, socialism was mixed with revolutionary republicanism. Cheap reprints of Robespierre's writings circulated in working-class areas of 1830s Paris. Abhorring the flagrant greed of the rising industrialist class, Pierre-Joseph Proudhon professed that "property is theft" and envisioned a new space for worker collaboration by preaching mutualism (or worker cooperative associations). Louis Blanc similarly recommended the formation of "National Workshops."

In 1848, facing King Louis-Philippe's intransigent opposition to any type of reforms—whether liberal or radical—the National Workshops mobilized in Paris the most distressed elements of the working class.[39] Tens of thousands were brought together to talk, read journals, listen to speeches, and organize common action against the king.[40] At the early stage of industrialization, such common action was not without obstacles. Workers did not fight the bourgeoisie but the enemy of the bourgeoisie, the remnant of absolute monarchy, as evidenced by the struggle between royalists and republican forces (which united both socialists and liberals) in France under Louis-Philippe. With the progress of industrialization and the eradication of absolutism, the tension between the bourgeois and workers, in a Dickensian "tale of two cities," intensified.

As long as the state apparatus remained a hindrance to further reforms and common action, new strategies had to be devised. The ill effects of industrialization were apparent across borders, and socialists envisioned a wider political space to counter such consequences. Karl Marx inaugurated in 1864 the First International, the first working-class organization to gather socialists from all over the world. The aim of the organization was to promote a broader alliance between socialist movements. "Workers of the world, unite!" was not just a rhetorical motto for rallying the working-class movement, but signified the vast space across which labor would have to confront an increasingly global web of unregulated private enterprise.[41]

Marking the global scale of their resistance effort, the socialists forged a comprehensive political agenda, advocating universal suffrage, the abolition of the right to property, the right to education, a heavily progressive income tax, the abolition of the right to inheritance, the reduction of working hours, the amelioration of health and safety conditions in the workplace, the restriction of child labor, the emancipation of women, and the abolition of slavery. This agenda proved appealing, and despite initial attempts to suppress the development of socialist movements, as occurred in Otto von Bismarck's Germany, the ranks of the socialists swelled throughout the industrialized regions of Europe. In the less industrialized parts of Europe, particularly in Italy and Spain, anarchist rather than socialist tendencies were the dominant anti-capitalist forces.

The growing militancy of social groups in industrialized civil societies benefited from the private-public divide imposed by the changing space of the market economy. Regardless of class, women were reduced, in Engels's view, to a "proletarian," that is, economically dependent, position, compared to their "bourgeois" husbands.[42] To be more precise, women's work in the private realm was not remunerated. Women from the middle class were clearly secluded within the private sphere, where their primary tasks were to secure the domestic comforts of the husband and to supervise the education of the children. "An ideal middle-class residence," observed British historian Carol Dyhouse, "had to be large enough to give physical and spatial expression to distances between social groups based upon sex, class and age, and to social hierarchy."[43] Less remunerated than men in their respective class, working-class women, on the other hand, were involved in a less demarcated private and public sector, both in child care and factory work. As industrialization progressed, working-class family lifestyles, and particularly women's, were grafted onto the activities of the factories. Children were sent off to work at a tender age, and employers often paid parents directly for their children's labor. In the cities, working-class children lived at home or in boarding houses and labored in the factories.[44]

Though initially confined within the private sphere, in contrast to working-class women, educated middle-class women gradually lent their voices to improving women's condition and to assuming leadership of suffragist movements. The education young middle-class women received was targeted toward child rearing tasks and provision of adequate companionship for cultivated husbands. With the 1792 publication of *A Vindication of the Rights of Women,* Mary Wollstonecraft had argued that the best way to ensure women's education was to educate those who were to become the mothers and teachers of future generations. With the development of capitalism and the widening education of middle-class women, the cult of feminine domesticity was transformed into the craft of professional homemaking management as home caretaking activities evolved into nursing, teaching, and charity tasks in the public sector. Consistent with their traditionally subordinate role as caretakers in the private sphere, these middle-class women encountered in the public sphere various obstacles rooted in their lack of private and political rights. For instance, though they were pulled into the public space as new consumers, they were not allowed to sign checks, to disburse funds, to speak in public, or to vote.[45] With the support of radical feminists, the agenda of the suffragists in the United States and in the more advanced industrialized countries like England and France began to emphasize voting rights and the right to acquire private property. Despite August Bebel's warning of possible class antagonism within the suffragist movement, that movement helped add critical momentum to the drive for human rights in the late nineteenth century.[46]

In sum, industrialization, steam-powered ships, the railroad, and the growth of urban sites all produced new spatial opportunities for timely communication and the progress of human rights, first uniting workers and the bourgeoisie against royalists and the vestiges of feudalism, later uniting workers against the bourgeoisie in their fight against capitalist greed and the ill effects of industrialization, and finally bringing together women as they entered the workforce and the public realm and fought to promote their rights. The very technologies that helped create manufacturing centers and expedite the circulation of commodities and capital also augmented the pace and scope of human rights struggle. The British ten-hour workday limitation bill was in this respect critical, for it offered collective time for planning and conducting working-class struggles. As the new form of oppression associated with early capitalism spread, enlarging the economic inequality between nations and individuals, workers' calls for emancipation began to be formulated in terms of global economic equality.

What in particular advanced the human rights struggle in the nineteenth century was a unique structural dynamic between various social agencies and institutions that characterized the weakening of the feudal state in the face of industrialization and allowed various groups (bour-geoisie, workers, and suffragists) to fight more actively in civil society for more control over the state. Ironically, despite the entrance of women (in particular working-class women) into the workforce and the public realm, human rights militancy in civil society took advantage of the establishment of a feminine private realm shaped by the new market economy, a realm that was supportive yet separated and uncompensated. Where industrialization lagged behind and civil society was still undeveloped (or less active), as in Germany and Italy, nationalist ideas were promulgated in order to galvanize state modernization. The expression of nationalism as part of the human rights agenda would become more evident in the twentieth century, in countries that sought national independence either from crumbling empires, like the Ottoman and Austrian Empires, or from European colonizers.

THE ANTI-COLONIAL STRUGGLE

Given the legacy of the industrial revolution, it is not difficult to understand why many would anticipate the twentieth century as the age that would bring civilization to new levels of comfort. Auguste Comte (1798–1857) had already announced the inexorable progress of positive science and the impending improvement of social conditions for everyone. Even colonialism was justified, as the effort of civilized nations to elevate "barbarous" countries to a better economic and social condition. Commenting on the British colonies, John Stuart Mill had argued in the nineteenth century that "[this] mode of government is the one in which the existing state of civilization of the subject people, most facilitates their transition to a higher stage of improvement."[47] The economic and technological superiority of Western Europeans, envied by most, was widely equated with the development of democratic institutions. Western democracies and the pace of social and economic progress were not easy to replicate, however, in colonized countries suffering from backward industries and inactive civil societies.

By spreading its metallic tentacles throughout the rest of the world, the railroad opened new venues of economic opportunity for the French and the British, who had split between themselves most of the African continent. Railroad transport helped carry raw materials and goods from the interior of the colonies to the world market. It also facilitated French control of Indochina, British colonization of India, and the Dutch occupation of most of Indonesia. By the beginning of the twentieth century, the race for raw materials had increased tensions between European powers, tensions that culminated in the dramatic events of World War I.

Despite its devastating effects on Europeans, World War I kindled new forms of international communication. The use of aircraft for surveillance and aerial bombardment helped intensify the postwar interest in commercial aviation. The search for reliable communication between ground and air stimulated improvement in radio technology. Airmail service was established between London and Paris, and soon afterward between New York and San Francisco. In 1929, commercial flights began between London and India, a trans-Pacific route between the United States and the Philippines was inaugurated in 1935, and a trans-Atlantic route started in 1939.[48] On the ground, the automobile also advanced globalization in various ways. Trucks and cars moved goods faster and further, bringing goods to urban, suburban, and rural markets distant from other forms of transportation. The mass production of cars, coinciding with the construction of new roads and networks of highways, increased traffic between major cities and towns and provided a new impetus for the growth of metropolitan areas. Initially, the same development of communication technology that enabled Europeans to create the social terrain necessary to promote human rights domestically also helped European states consolidate their colonial power. Strategic opportunities for human rights advances in the colonies would remain stagnant until World War II, due to the coercive effectiveness of the colonial state apparatus.

State rule in the colonies differed substantially from state rule in the mother countries. Parliamentary democracies in the mother countries could afford to make concessions to the subordinated classes in civil society, in exchange for their acceptance of the prevailing capitalist form of production, along with bourgeois leadership. In that context, Gramsci argued, the dominant class did not need to participate actively in state affairs as long as the political elite recognized the hegemonic structure of civil society. State rule in the colonies, however, was different. Though the colonies may have adopted some economic and cultural aspects of the hegemonic core, they were less able to adopt its political models. There, Europeans used the coercive apparatus of government to suppress dissent, while using control over education and the press to help legitimize colonial rule. The level of repression varied from country to country depending on the relative level of popular legitimacy and consent acquired by the colonizers. For example, compared to the French, Portuguese, and Dutch colonies, the colonized people of the British Commonwealth enjoyed relatively less political oppression in return for their subscription to British economic order and the British crown.[49]

The state's ability to control people in colonized society was also due to the peasant character of the still unformed civil society, which bore many similarities to European late feudal and early industrial periods. Gramsci noted the elementary shape of civil society in eastern feudal Europe in comparison to western Europe. "In Russia," he wrote, "the State was everything, civil society was primordial and gelatinous; in the West, there was a proper relation between State and civil society, and when the State trembled a sturdy structure of civil society was at once revealed."[50] Further, colonizing states often used preferential treatment to pit one group or one tribe against another, enabling the colonizers to divide and conquer. For instance, Belgium kept control of Rwanda by privileging Tutsis over Hutus, and the British conveniently maintained tensions between Muslims, Sikhs, and Hindus in India, as well as strife between the Malays and the Chinese in the Malayan territories. European "divide and rule" and co-optation methods retarded and blocked national awareness and unity that might have threatened their colonial rule.

Just as the weakening of the feudal state engendered active human rights militancy in the civil space of nineteenth-century Europe, the dramatic weakening of European governmental control over the colonies after World War II prompted human rights activities in the colonized territories. For various reasons, effective resistance against European colonization first emerged in the Asian colonies. Independence movements in Asia had been brewing since the beginning of the twentieth century, and by the end of World War II they had become explosive. Asian people's self-confidence can be traced in part to Japan's pledge at the outset of the war to free Asia from the chains of Western imperialism. Though the Japanese simply replaced the previous colonial regimes with their own, they also accelerated nationalist aspirations throughout the region. The initial Japanese victory over European forces signaled to Indonesians, Vietnamese, Burmese, and others that the Europeans were not as invincible as they had previously imagined. National awareness occurred later in Africa, which was less industrialized and more deeply divided by ethnic tensions. While Europeans tried to suppress any form of rebellion, colonial rule was nonetheless responsible for developing an African civil society, however embryonic its early shape.[51] The search for cheap labor had engendered a working class, just as the need for local management had created educational and economic opportunities for an indigenous elite. The most privileged benefited from overseas Western education and learned the principles of democracy and human rights. Ironically, colonizers were planting the seeds of their own destruction.

With the growth of political awareness, struggle toward independence became imminent. Human rights struggle took different forms in the West and the colonized countries. One can identify two forms of political struggle, drawn from Gramsci's analogy of military strategy: the war of position and the war of movement. Each is linked to different stages of development in civil society. In the West, where one group or class is hegemonic in civil society, the war of position, or of political struggle, is waged by another group or class seeking to gain political and tactical leverage. In the colonies, where no group or class is sufficiently anchored in an as yet unformed civil society, a war of movement, or a political struggle by one group or class aimed at taking over the state apparatus, is a possible option—such was the strategy adopted by the Bolshevik vanguard party. Political control of the state and eviction of the foreign presence were primary items on the agenda of the leaders of national liberation movements, and henceforth the war of movement was a preferred alternative in places such as Mozambique, Vietnam, and Angola. Yet an attack on the state in a war of movement could not pave the way for a transition to economic and structural arrangements distinctive from those shaped by the European colonizers.[52] It is therefore not surprising that the unequal social distribution that existed during the period of colonialism was perpetuated under the rule of the indigenous local bourgeois after independence.

Indeed, the indigenous local elite reinstated bourgeois dominance of civil society and trade links with former colonizers. Wages were kept low, ethnic divisions and social inequality maintained, and authoritarianism restored in an effort to forge ahead with modernization, attract foreign investment, and achieve better social control. This happened in Mobutu Sese Seko's Zaire (1960–1997), Johnson Aguiyi-Ironsi's Nigeria (1966), Isakander Mirza's Pakistan (1956–1958), and Ferdinand Marcos's Philippines (1965–1983). In a divided and non-hegemonic civil society, the political elite encouraged nationalist allegiance in order to supersede inequality and division. Frantz Fanon observed how in this phase the local indigenous bourgeois ended up emulating the models of repression of the colonial period while internalizing the values of the Western bourgeoisie: "The casinos of Havana and of Mexico, the beaches of Rio, the little Brazilian and Mexican girls, the half-breed thirteen-year-olds, the ports of Acapulco and Copacabana—all these are the stigma of this depravation of the national middle class."[53] Formal nationalism and a single coercive party system were reestablished in a "non-homogenous" civil society to divert popular discontent arising out of economic hardship or to hide social division.

Nationalism also helped obscure and maintain post-colonial divisions that existed between indigenous men and women and between white and autochthonous women. Such splits in both the domestic and public sphere replicated the colonial hierarchy of power. By entrusting indigenous men with patriarchal authority, the colonial administration could suppress eventual male rebellions. By elevating the status of European women in comparison to indigenous women, the colonial state was able to further social control, breaking the early-nineteenth-century feminist spirit of solidarity that existed between suffragist and abolitionist in the mother countries, on the one hand, and anti-slavery and anti-colonialism forces, on the other hand. "The English woman abroad," American sociologist Vron Ware has remarked, "could be at once a many-faceted figure: from an intrepid adventuress defying racial and sexual boundaries to heroic mother responsible for the preservation of the white race; from the devoted missionary overseeing black souls to the guardian of white morals; from determined pioneer and companion to the white man to a vulnerable defenceless piece of his property—'the greatest gift God gave to man.'"[54]

If feminism needed to prevail over class differences, as the British feminist Josephine Butler argued in the early twentieth century, colonial life only appeared to widen the gap between women of different cultural extractions and economic status.[55] Class differences were often evidenced in legislation, such as the strict regulation of prostitution and interracial marriage, as well as in different moral and social norms for indigenous and European women.[56] Yet even long after independence, the continuing subordination of women to male authority under the aegis of religious authorities in many African and Muslim societies illustrates the extreme forms indigenous authoritarianism has taken in ethnically and economically divided societies. This underlines the absence of an active civil society and reveals the need for the state to control the private realm and to repress possible rebellions.

In summary, the global economy may have expanded its space of production and economic opportunity, and may even have generated a universal social space of resistance in the colonies after World War II. Human rights opportunities in the colonies, however, were different than in Europe due to a host of structural factors, including lack of industrial development and a shapeless (and non-hegemonic) pre-independence civil society. Despite the weakening of European power in the colonies, the human rights agenda was expressed in nationalist terms, through the taking over of the state and the eviction of foreigners. The absence of civil society also hampered human rights advances after national independence, accounting for post-colonial states' inability to move beyond the repressive nature of the state.

Divide-and-control methods learned from the European colonizers helped indigenous elites maintain tensions between groups, classes, and sexes in the newly independent states. Even as a revolution in transportation and communication extended the sense of global reach, colonial competition between major industrialized countries generated parochial and nationalist sentiments in both the mother countries and their dominions. One has to bear in mind that nationalism, often translated as a human rights aspiration, can be used as a force for domination just as easily as it can be used against oppression. Whereas during the first half of the twentieth century, nationalism in industrialized countries aimed to expand economic opportunity and superiority in a yet non-hegemonic global civil and economic space, the flames of nationalist sentiment in the colonies were fanned to reject the colonizers and to secure state control and the entrenchment in power of one group or class in a still shapeless sphere of civil society.

THE GLOBALIZATION OF CIVIL SOCIETY?
OR AN ASSAULT ON THE PRIVATE REALM?

In relatively more hegemonic and vibrant civil societies, such as in the West, popular participation in the public sphere has also been curtailed. While information technology has facilitated the development of a worldwide civil society, globalization has shown a propensity to absorb and divide dissenting voices. One may even wonder whether globalization has had an adverse effect on traditional channels for promoting human rights (i.e., the state and various domestic and international associations within civil society), and whether new human rights strategies must now be devised. As a new cartography of power reshapes the international order after September 11, one should consider, now more than before, whether the state today is still able to ensure fair access to information and to secure the social environment necessary for real democratic debate and human rights. Has civil society, both locally and globally, become an arena dominated by either consumerism or security interests? With the weakening of democratic forces as a buffer zone between the state and the private realm, how can one protect private individuals from deepening incursions by the state and the market?

Globalization and the State

World War II prompted a regrowth of state interventionism (which had already been stimulated by the Great Depression of the 1930s), first to sustain wartime mobilization and then to stimulate postwar recovery. As the price for preserving the stability of capitalist production, the state recognized the rights of trade unions and granted extensive social benefits to the workforce. The welfare state served as a regulator in the economic sphere, stimulating demand during downturns through public expenditure and absorbing surplus labor by increasing public employment. In addition, under the hegemony of the United States, the dollar became the standard international currency. Core countries controlled the sources and prices of raw materials, mostly produced by the still largely colonized world; this control persisted during the emergence of newly independent states.

With the oil crisis of the 1970s disrupting the flow of global capital and fueling a cycle of inflation, austerity policies, and recession, the capacity of states to serve as brokers between capital and labor came under increasing pressure. As labor power diminished, Keynesian economic policies were challenged. The new economic model that emerged in the late 1970s emphasized higher productivity from technological innovations, while reducing the state's capacity to protect working conditions. State intervention was now increasingly designed to support the interests of private capital. The economic policies of Thatcher and Reagan served as the leading models.

Compared to the West, the developing world faced far more severe economic hardship and corresponding political repression. Developing countries, initially immersed in anti-colonial struggle, continued to lag far behind the Western world. For newly independent and other developing states, modernization was accompanied by severe human rights abuses. Unsurprisingly, the oil crisis struck most deeply at countries struggling to compete as new state actors in the international economy. Elites in those developing states, which had borrowed heavily to sustain modernization projects, were now driven to impose austerity measures that required tightened social control, such as occurred in Argentina and Brazil. In Latin American and Africa, these tighter controls reflected the weakened capacities of states to secure either a decent living standard for their citizens or their basic political rights.

In the Soviet Union and other communist countries, state-controlled economies struggled to implement a modern industrial system that would rival Western economic successes under the banner of socialism. Though successful in the wartime economy of the 1940s, communist centralized planning failed during peacetime. Rapid economic decline finally prompted Soviet leader Mikhail Gorbachev's *perestroika* policy, a belated and incomplete effort to introduce features of a market economy— a process that was radically accelerated by the subsequent collapse of the communist regime. Indeed, with the disappearance of the Soviet empire, and with the embrace of capitalism by China, virtually the entire world came under the rubric of a single increasingly integrated market system.

Under the pressure of globalization, the capacity of states is now under greater assault. Many argue that a global grid, connecting sources of economic power and information, now rivals the traditional state apparatus, blurring the old binary distinction between north and south and creating a new medieval landscape of power centers.[57] While written from differing ideological perspectives, the post–cold war academic literature announcing the demise of the state has generally questioned the state's ability to curtail market forces and to ensure social benefits and human rights. Global economic integration, goes the argument, is eroding hard-won rights—especially workers' rights—in the developed West, while precluding the achievement of those rights in the developing world.[58]

While the state is indeed changing as it apparently blends into a new kaleidoscopic world, it is hardly disappearing. Far from it, as the progress of globalization requires a strong state either to guarantee sufficient education and living standards to enable citizens to maintain purchasing power, or to maintain authoritarian governmental structures that ensure cheap labor and suppress opposition.[59] To be more precise, it is not the state that is weakened, despite widespread belief to the contrary, but its capacity to sustain the redistributive policies associated with the welfare state. More than that, if the old imperialist divide between southern and northern states has been challenged by the emergence of East Asian states and other new economic loci of power, northern or Western states remain far more influential. It is Western authority that prevails in international organizations (the UN, the WTO, the IMF, etc.), and it is the West that has the ability to dispatch military forces to retaliate against challengers or to secure its interests in the new global order.

No sooner had the cold war ended than that order was tested by the

Iraqi invasion of Kuwait. Whatever the virtues of the U.S.-led coalition's proclaimed commitment to the sovereignty of threatened states, the propelling force behind the Desert Storm campaign was surely to ensure Western access to the world's oil supply.[60] Yet such blatant economically and geopolitically driven interventions cannot command the world respect needed to sustain American (or Western) hegemony. That instrumental goal was better served by the 1999 Kosovo intervention, which helped secure regional stability for Europe's troubled backyard, as even critics of NATO's bombardment conceded.[61] Moreover, the bombing arguably prevented even greater massacres and human rights abuses, as evidenced by the record of Slobodan Milosevic's (1941–) Serbian forces when left free to conduct a war in Bosnia.

If hegemony, as Gramsci understood it, requires a moral justification of power, the Western powers have met that standard only intermittently, notably failing to intervene even in cases of genocide. It is certainly true that the British intervention in Sierra Leone in 1999 put a halt to massive bloodshed, just as an Australian-led force halted the slaughter in East Timor that same year. Yet no one, despite faint gestures of interest, intervened to interrupt the 1994 genocide in Rwanda, in which hundreds of thousands of women, children, and men met terrible deaths.[62] For too many years, the West remained motionless in the face of monstrous oppression, particularly against women, under the Taliban regime, until the appalling wakeup call of September 11, 2001. Morality and interest need to be continuously wed to ensure the perpetuation of hegemonic dominance. Even if some response toward a regime as repressive as the Taliban was long overdue, it surely would not have occurred had not the security of the world's most powerful state been put directly in jeopardy.

This and other military actions, years after the end of the cold war, remind us that the state is not about to fade away, and that it might even promote humanitarian causes within the framework of new just-war theories. If anything, effective use of force ultimately strengthens the very juridical and moral apparatus of a globalized world in the service of its most privileged custodians, who without hesitation warn belligerent defiers of core centers of globalization of the terrible price of rebellion and disruption. In this sense, globalization appears "in the form of a very high tech machine: it is virtual, built to control the marginal event, and organized to dominate and when necessary intervene [with the assistance of states], in the event of the breakdown of the system."[63]

Clearly, attacks against nerve centers of economic and military power, exemplified by the World Trade Center and the Pentagon and subsequent retaliation by powerful state actors against terrorists, hinder investment and lower consumer confidence. Yet force, used as a last resort, can also be a remedy of choice for strengthening faith in a speedy return to business as usual and enhancing the communal spirit. In the fight against terrorism, the world fearfully coalesces behind the power of "civilization," which, in a not too distant past, was guilty of the greatest indifference to human suffering. Of course, skepticism toward the current embrace of idealistic rationales (e.g., women's rights, democracy, and development) for the war on terror should not suggest that patterns of past wrongdoing should not be redressed, and that interventions—diplomatic, economic or military—should not be invoked to halt genocide or stop severe human rights violations.

Defenders of humanitarian interventions (who understand that human rights rhetoric may mask instrumental interests) should remain cautious, however, in defending the use of all possible means in the pursuit of human rights ends. Thus, human rights advocates had good cause for concern that an intervention aimed at toppling Iraqi dictator Saddam Hussein, who undertook a genocidal assault on his own Kurdish population in 1988, might have intensified a broader conflict in the Middle East, or more generally led to consequences that would mock the long-term goal of peace and human rights. In some cases the costs are obviously prohibitive, making rescue of the oppressed unimaginable. Could anyone envision a military intervention to liberate the Chechens from abusive Russians or the Tibetans from suppression by China?

While global economic integration ostensibly weakens the state, the primary economic beneficiaries of globalization need a strong state to protect property rights and to crush popular or ethnic challenges. Yet the fact that the state is porous to global market pressures should not imply that human rights activists should abandon *in toto* the capacity of the state to legislate and enforce democracy and human rights. To do so would be to accept as inevitable a reshaping of state power in which the strengthening of the coercive machinery used to crush domestic or foreign opponents proceeds in tandem with a weakening of welfare, workers' rights, and democratic governance—a world designed to offer carte blanche to corporate and geopolitical interests.

Globalization and Civil Society

If global economic integration and post-Fordist production have weakened the welfare capacity of the state, they have also restructured civil society worldwide by strengthening corporate interests and adjusting the role of the state to conform to new economic rules. One can hope, drawing from the lessons of the nineteenth century, that the weakening of the state will be conducive to the expansion of a vibrant civil society. As new forms of production and global economic integration have undermined the state's ability to enforce workers' rights and social justice, is civil society (understood as being both local and international) emerging as a better forum for the advancement of human rights? One can identify two trends with respect to human rights in civil society: a negative trajectory, if we consider the ascension of nationalist forces and the weakening of democratic ones in the domestic realm, particularly after September 11; and a more positive path, should we consider the proliferation of international human rights institutions and the growth of the anti-globalization movement in the realm of civil society.

In the West, the decline of organized labor, whose unified agenda has been supplanted by the diverging interests of groups promoting feminist, environmental, racial, ethnic, and gay issues, reflects such a negative trend. Given their inability to reach a meaningful alliance—essential for channeling demands and for collective bargaining—the influence of progressive forces has also been substantially curtailed in the West since the 1970s. Paralleling the trend in the United States, trade unions have also been severely weakened in Europe, as evidenced by the 1991 Maastricht agreement.

The frustration of nationally based labor unions in the West has been echoed by the embattled efforts to develop peasant solidarity in developing areas such as India, Bangladesh, and Sri Lanka, coupled with a failure thus far to broaden what remain disconnected local struggles from Beijing to Chiapas, Jakarta, Seoul, and elsewhere. The paradox, observe Michael Hardt and Antonio Negri, is that "in our age of communicability, *struggles have become all but incommunicable,*" and the very notion of international struggle based on the communication of common desires seems to have vanished.[64] In the cracks of this fractured social terrain, the seeds of nationalism have sprouted and sunk new roots.

Despite democratic pockets of resistance, whether in the form of the Western social movement activism of the 1960s and 1970s or in forms of local contestation, nationalist movements from Le Pen's party in France to the Hamas movement in the West Bank have been the predominant forms of resistance everywhere against the permeation of globalized capital and Western cultural influence. Nevertheless, if nationalists despise globalization in principle, they have not hesitated to utilize the technologies unleashed by globalization to acquire weapons and to dissem- inate their message. Indeed, Iranian clergy, Hutus, and Serbs, among oth- ers, have relied heavily on the mass media to fuel nationalist, religious, or ethnic fervor, while in the United States, fundamentalist Christian groups and neo-Nazis have utilized sophisticated websites and Internet campaigns to recruit new members, coordinate activities, and dissemi- nate their agendas.[65]

Ironically, many groups, from the extreme right to the left, among them nationalists, religious fundamentalists, and peasant movements world- wide, share a common spatial and communal orientation in their reac- tion against the acceleration of time and the obtrusion of globalized cap- ital upon every localized identity. Rejecting a civil society shaped by the rule of *homo economicus,* many have sought to invest their strength in local politics. In the post-communist world and in developing countries as well, abhorrence of the state and a focus on civil society have been the prevailing impulses for many dissenters and activists. What was not anticipated by grassroots activists in these societies, however, was the ability of stronger corporate forces to take substantial control over civil society and to trample resistance—especially progressive resistance— without any fear of corrective state regulation.

In the Western world, a similar trend has been noticeable. From the religious right, typified by the American evangelist Jerry Falwell, which emphasizes communal love centered around the institution of the church, to Canadian and American liberals like Charles Taylor and Alvin Toffler, who ask for non-interference in community or local politics centered around civic organizations or "virtual" communities, to ecologists cele- brating local as well as global militancy, the state and the global economy are similarly regarded as unwelcome intrusions into civil society.[66] Yet it is doubtful that such personal or local politics within civil society will be any more impervious to the market-driven forces of the information age than the state has been.[67] If anything, local spaces of contestation, whether on the right or the left, can be easily commodified, co-opted, and, when necessary, violently neutralized by globalizing forces.

The game is not entirely one-sided, however. One can witness, indeed, a more positive trend for human rights opportunities on the international front of civil society. In 1956, for instance, there were 973 transnational nongovernmental organizations, whereas in 1996 there were over 5,000.[68] One may now count over 200 NGOs associated with human rights issues in the United States, a comparable number in the United Kingdom, and a growing number of similar organizations in the developing world.[69] Lester Salamon, director of Johns Hopkins's Institute for Policy Studies, notes the general difficulty in compiling systematic data, given the "varying terminology and widely divergent functions" of the nonprofit civil sector.[70] Nevertheless, the rapid global expansion of the organized human rights movement since the 1970s is beyond dispute, and one should consider how the emergence of such global issues as development and environmental protection are associated with the rapid proliferation of supranational organizations aspiring to fulfill functions traditionally assumed by the welfare state.[71]

Paralleling this expansion, one can also observe the proliferation of human rights legal documents ratified by a growing number of international governmental organizations (IGOs). There were only 37 IGOs in 1909; today one can count nearly 241 IGOs, 2,072 multilateral treaties and intergovernmental agreements, and a significant increase in the level of diplomatic interaction.[72] Along with increasing trade, foreign investment, cultural exchanges, and tourism, there has been an unprecedented spread of global human rights mechanisms—for example, in the form of organizations like the European Commission on Human Rights, the Inter-American Committee on Human Rights, and many others—a trend propitious for the passage of international human rights legislation and for the development of what some have called a human rights regime.[73]

There have indeed been indications of strengthened international law pertaining to perpetrators of war crimes and crimes against humanity, exemplified by the indictment of former Chilean ruler Augusto Pinochet (1915–) and former Serbian president Slobodan Milosevic. Also noteworthy has been the development, in South Africa, of an alternative to such prosecutions, as the Truth and Reconciliation Commission offered freedom to those guilty of murderous abuses during apartheid in exchange for a full confession of their crimes. That innovation has proven a creative approach that publicly documents human rights violations, airs the grievances of survivors, and engenders a healing process that exchanges vengeance for reconciliation and the promise of a better future. While power politics continues to prevail, as illustrated by the unwillingness of the United States to recognize the International Criminal Court, the near unanimous rejection of the U.S. view by the international community reflects apparent progress in the construction of a global human rights regime.

These and other human rights initiatives have benefited from growing visibility as information technology has enhanced the expansion, influence, and networking capacity of human rights–oriented NGOs and IGOs. From the growing prominence of groups like Amnesty International, Human Rights Watch, and Médecins sans frontières, to the post–cold war appeal of arguments for humanitarian intervention, human rights discourse is now playing an important role in world politics. Human rights websites have become a major tool for the dissemination of information about human rights violations, for rallying popular outrage, and for pressuring governments to redress human rights transgressions. Repressive states can no longer easily insulate their populations from the diffusion of information as radio broadcasts of unauthorized views (such as by the Voice of America and BBC World Service) have been supplemented by the interactive capabilities represented by websites and e-mail.

Proposals to counter encroachments on human rights by the market and the state, either by strengthening global democratic institutions or by developing a global virtual space for human rights action, have become subjects of great academic interest. Robert Keohane, Joseph Nye, and John Ruggie, among others, have identified the importance of new regimes as ways to sanction abusive governments.[74] Robert Johansen and David Held have proposed ways to restructure international institutions, such as the UN and its Security Council, to make them more democratically representative.[75] Others, like Jessica Matthew Tuchman, Ian MacLean, Margaret E. Keck, and Katheryn Sikkink, have shown the importance of NGOs and the use of information technology to pressure repressive governments to adopt human rights measures, citing the Chiapas rebellion and other cases where challenges to ruling elites tempt repressive governmental responses.[76]

Without questioning the important contributions of transnational institutionalism and the diffusion of information, it remains unclear why, in a non-regulated global environment, corporate interests would not once again be better equipped (given their enormous financial resources) to control global institutions as well as the virtual civil society (through ownership of the telecommunications industry, advertisements, control of web portals, etc.), while seeking legitimacy by maintaining a largely cosmetic universalist rhetoric of rights. As Habermas reminds us, "[T]he most fortunate nations had learned in the eighteenth century how sheer power can domesticate legitimate law."[77]

Is the human rights regime, after all, mere window dressing, serving mainly to conceal the interests and clout of the powerful? Positive international human rights laws, while important, are far from sufficient:

one needs to offer new channels through which repressed inhabitants of countries with weak or nonexistent liberal institutions can express their demands for democratic accountability. Already, there are signs—if only tentative and intermittent ones—that the mass protests at recent meetings of the IMF and G8 or the establishment of a World Social Forum (2001) are having an impact, as the policy of imposing austerity measures on debtor nations yields to greater recognition of the need to address the problems of the world's poor.[78] If shifting our focus toward popular democratic and collective action is critical, we should not forget that local and transnational human rights efforts remain fragmented both on theoretical and strategic grounds.

Theoretically, while the anti-neo-liberal globalization movement provides new hopes and opportunities for the development of a more vibrant global civil society and integrated human rights dialogue, it still lacks a common progressive political, economic, and social agenda, an important denominator needed to unite more effectively a variety of human rights interests. Strategically, and particularly in light of September 11, a more comprehensive universalist agenda should engage the reality of the new security order and seize opportunities wherever they present themselves.[79] Hence, it would seem natural for human rights activists to explore more systematically ways to coordinate local and global human action, thereby avoiding needless duplication and redirecting resources where most needed.

In short, a human rights agenda built on greater political, social, and economic cohesiveness and deployed to coordinate local and global human rights action might advance the ongoing struggle to strengthen the capacity of the state to resist corporate demands for deregulatory policies. Whether human rights efforts are invested locally or transnationally, they are often conducted outside and against the state, a forum that remains, despite many skeptics of the legitimacy of the Westphalian system, a critical vehicle for the promotion of human rights. In the absence of a buffer zone able to maintain and regulate the state and the global economy, the private realm (including the family as well as the realm of privacy) faces greater challenges.

Globalization and the Private Realm

Since World War II, the realm of the family has been substantially transformed in relationship to the economy and the state. Shortly after World War II, France, Yugoslavia, and China were added to the group of nations (which already included the United States and Great Britain) that had granted women voting rights. In the Western world, the 1960s and 1970s saw the flourishing of women's movements that, along with the development of the counterculture, the New Left, the new social movements, and gay organizations, joined the struggle against individualism, conservative family values, and the war in Vietnam. The feminist movement in particular changed the social landscape. With the development of affirmative action, abortion rights, and other forms of legal protection, women have grown more disposed to assert their independence, to divorce when they wish, and to enter in growing numbers, a predominantly male public space.

As inflation and recession in the 1970s made it hard to support even intact families on a single income, a great number of women, including those with young children, entered the workforce. The market, unsurprisingly, did not reject this influx of a new surplus labor pool willing to work for lower wages—especially given the resultant downward pressure on men's salaries. As the number of divorces started rivaling the number of marriages, and harsher competition between men and women in the workplace triggered a new "battle of the sexes," affirmative action was challenged in a process that Susan Faludi has aptly described as the "backlash" against feminism.[80] The attack on welfare during the Thatcher and Reagan era ultimately undercut women's living conditions, particularly those of single mothers, increasing numbers of whom fell below the poverty line.[81] Not only did the disintegration of the family parallel the fragmentation of democratic forces in civil society, it also destroyed the equilibrium between a patriarchal civil society and a feminine domestic household. With the gradual disappearance of a rigid gender division of labor, and without the sanctuary of a secure private household under the care of women, the struggle for survival in the public sphere became harsher.

It is in this context that one can explain the success of politicians in their crusade for anachronistic notions of "family values," the attack on affirmative action (which in the United States has also affected the black population) as well as on women's reproductive freedom, and the widespread disdain for feminism at every level of society. From the bombing of abortion clinics to the Southern Baptist Church's insistence on a wife's subordination to her husband, the backlash against American feminism is in full swing. In less stable and more violence-prone regions of the world, women were prone to losing even minimal protections—as witnessed by the abolition of women's education by the Taliban in Afghanistan, the killing of secular women by Islamist insurgents in Algeria, the "rape camps" run by the Serbian paramilitary units in the former Yugoslavia, and the spread of Islamic "laws" (from Saudi Arabia to Iran to Nigeria) under which women convicted of adultery in all-male courts may be stoned to death.

Social stability is challenged when both the family and civil society are in disarray. In the absence of democratic forces in the public space, should we be surprised that patriarchal control over women in Middle Eastern societies, a replica of authoritarian power on the domestic level, appeases and empowers Muslim men while diverting them from unleashing their frustration against the repressive state? Should we be surprised that in the absence of a vibrant civil society in the West, political interest, as in the United States, often takes the form of a fascination with sexual politics, as illustrated by the preoccupation with President Bill Clinton's liaisons with Gennifer Flowers, Monica Lewinsky, and, purportedly, others, with Princess Diana's romantic life, with O. J. Simpson's battered and murdered wife, or with endless revelations of the private lives of Kennedys, living or dead? Should we be surprised when the media mirror household concerns in the political realm, or when affairs of state are reduced to the politics of domesticity?

Did we too hastily desert the public space for the magical realism of tabloid politics? The vanishing of a physical democratic public space at the local level is already well advanced once public discourse has been supplanted by media talking heads, when participatory democracy has been superseded by opinion polls, when teenagers meet in the malls but are rarely seen at political rallies or as volunteers for political organizations, and when Monica Lewinsky becomes more politically important than the plight of Afghan, Nigerian, or Saudi women.[82]

While connecting us faster, information technology is now more than ever invading our realm of privacy, whether one is a celebrity or an ordinary citizen. Concerns over the protection of private information, fears of outsiders' reading of e-mails, employers' identification of prospective employees' choices of websites, and issues of intellectual property on the web: all underline the fragility of individual rights.[83] In the wake of terrorist attacks, we recognize that we have become even more vulnerable as we became more globally linked. Border and airport controls have been tightened, measures protecting privacy have been removed, and identification requirements and background checks proliferate, paving the way to an ever more pervasive surveillance society.

If greater state control provides more security, it ultimately undermines civil liberties and the fundamental right to privacy. Sophisticated face-recognition technology and cameras deployed throughout England as part of a broad national surveillance plan provide a glimpse of what may be in store for America. If designed initially to combat terrorism, British video surveillance is now mainly used to follow car thieves and traffic offenders, confess officials in the monitoring room for the City of London. It is also used to keep punks out of shopping malls, and "rather than thwarting serious crime, the [dummy as well as real] cameras are being used to enforce social conformity."[84]

The British utilitarian philosopher Jeremy Bentham (1748–1832) understood the appeal of constant surveillance more than two centuries ago, when he described the social benefits of building an inspection tower that gazes over the inner walls of a prison, whose inmates must henceforth live in constant fear of being watched. That uncertainty, he believed, would deter inhabitants of this "model" prison, which he called the Panopticon (Greek for "all seeing place"), from engaging in anti-social behavior:

> The more constantly the persons to be inspected are under the eyes of the persons who should be inspecting, the more perfectly will the purpose of the establishment have been attained. Ideal perfection, if that were the object, would require each person should actually be in that predicament, during every instant of time. This being impossible the next thing to be wished for is, that, at every instant, seeing reason to believe as much, not being able to satisfy himself to the contrary, he should *conceive* himself to be so.[85]

Technology, as Michel Foucault has observed, has finally approached realization of Bentham's vision of modern surveillance, facilitating, as each individual internalizes the sense that all behavior is being monitored, the implementation of ever more efficient and less visible forms of state control.[86] In contrast to the often brutal and public forms of punishment of the past, modernity and globalization, claims Foucault, have introduced cleaner and more rational forms of social control and punishment.

The expansion of counterterrorist activities, then, did not instigate but rather accelerated the rise of a more bureaucratized, cyber-controlled society.[87] Max Weber predicted this trend almost a century ago, observing the depersonalization of civil society at a far earlier stage of bureaucratization. More recently, L. Ron Hubbard, the founder of Scientology, tapped that source of individual anxiety in the West when he proposed elevating science to a religious faith, while in some less developed regions of the world, mullahs find new responsiveness to a more traditional vehicle for depersonalization. One can argue that we have moved back toward a new form of medieval and religious social landscape in which the focus on the local and the fragility of the private realm underline the absence of sufficient democratic participation in civil society against the state.

Protecting the space for critical thinking and privacy, as well as reallocating individual roles within the family in the direction of greater fairness, are important preconditions for revitalizing democratic participation in an increasingly consumer-oriented society. In general, new participatory arenas must be sought to enable citizens to resist the increasingly unregulated intrusion of the state and commercial interests into various arenas of social and personal activity. In turn, a stronger domestic and international participatory civil society can also provide the state with the legitimacy to resist such intrusions by self-interested economic forces, and to act as a more impartial arbitrator between powerful entities and ordinary citizens.

Post-Fordism after World War II has created new informational sites of economic activity and at the same time decentralized the arenas of social and economic interaction. Yet global deregulatory economic policies, hastened by the economic crisis of the 1970s, have drastically weakened the state's capacity to mediate between capital, on the one hand, and workers and the poor, on the other hand. These changes have allowed the global economy to penetrate more deeply into civil society and the private realm, a trend made manifest by Western politicians' preoccupation with "smaller" governments and private morality.

Disenchanted with the impersonal greed and cynicism of civil society and the crisis of the nuclear family, many disconnected individuals are searching for havens in communities or under the auspices of churches, mosques, and temples. Despite important efforts to advance global communication, particularist, nationalist, and fundamentalist forces are on the rise everywhere, in both virtual and non-virtual spaces. In the absence of physical spaces for participatory democracy and of discourse premised on the promotion of social and economic fairness, the state and the market are able to extend their control over the private realm, well beyond computer and television screens and well beyond the consciousness of the citizen-spectator of the new Orwellian world, a one-dimensional world of consumerism that reduces citizens to a life of conformism and uncritical thinking. Herbert Marcuse, later echoed by Vaclav Havel, Benjamin Barber, and others, offered this characterization of modern society as far back as the 1960s.

How can we counter such a return to medieval levels of authoritarian intrusiveness in the private sphere while reviving the internationalist human rights drive of eighteenth- and nineteenth-century civil society? What venues of human rights hold promise, given the shrinking social spaces, that gather individuals in one setting in a way that enables them to recognize and pursue their collective and global concerns? The struggles for spatial interaction in the face of an atomized or repressed civil society have never been more important. Though communitarians and nationalists are showing us one path, their narrow spatial and anti-economic foci feed the interests of a dominant economic elite whose stability and control depend on the structural division of diverse social spaces.

If, by contrast, the increase in human rights activism and the subsequent adoption of hundreds of human rights treaties offer new hope, enduring change will require the coordination of human rights campaigns with democratic agencies at the level of national and local governance. The struggle for human rights needs to continue both within and beyond the legal debates and the corridors of international organizations. It needs to counter the bureaucratization of the institutionalized human rights regime with mobilization efforts in the streets of locales from Gaza to Guatemala, from Genoa to Kabul. Developing solidarity among different agencies of change at the local and global levels of civil society in turn requires greater efforts to develop an economic and social agenda that unites different human rights efforts.

A more vibrant civil society could thwart undemocratic policies associated with the unfettered march of neo-liberal globalization, protect the realm of privacy against unwelcome state intrusion, and stimulate critical thinking. One should not forget that the popular forces galvanized in 1789 and 1848 benefited, even if temporarily, from the creation of a nurturing and unremunerated private realm. The feminist movement since the 1970s in the West, however, has critically challenged that bastion of female subjugation, offering a destabilizing alternative to authoritarian and predominantly patriarchal societies. Today, protecting the realm of privacy and individual rights (as opposed to the hierarchy of the household) could provide the necessary energy to arouse more egalitarian democratic forces against repressive states, demanding girls- and women-related rights inside and outside the family and broadening political and social welfare for all citizens, just as such efforts stimulated democratic impulses in Western civil societies.

One cannot entrust the task of building such a civil society to the whims of history. That mission belongs to the active involvement of a global and local human rights civil society, which in our current political environment must counter narrowly conceived national and economic interests. There is a pressing need to coordinate global and local action while protecting the private realm. The task of the human rights community continues to span different spatial levels. That community now confronts the need to rescue and strengthen the progressive aspirations once embodied by the state, to enhance democratic control in civil society both domestically and internationally, to defend privacy and women's rights, and to strengthen existing human rights supranational institutions (however limited their current power).

Walter Benjamin's *Angel of History* shows us, through the drama and struggles of the past, the steps leading toward a new paradise. Events are now as before irresistibly propelling our angel of progress into the future, in which dreams of justice are rekindled. Yet each designer of utopia has been marked by previous catastrophes and failures. If it is with trepidation born of past tragedy that we carry the lantern of hope through the uncertain dawn of this new millennium, it is with the confidence gained from past progress that we aspire to a greater measure of justice for all.

Appendix

A Chronology of Events and Writings Related to Human Rights

TABLE A.1
THE ENLIGHTENMENT

British Context	Other European Context	Human Rights Speeches, Writings, and Documents
		1545 Bartolomé de las Casas, *In Defense of the Indians*
	1600–1700 English, Dutch in America; Dutch in Indonesia and South Africa	
	1618–1648 Thirty Years' War	
1625–1649 Charles I		1625 Hugo Grotius, *Law of War and Peace*
	1635 France enters Thirty Years' War	
1637 Ship Money Case		
1640–1660 Long Parliament		
1642–1648 Puritan Revolution		
		1643 John Milton, *Areopagetica*
1646 Putney debate		
	1648 Treaty of Westphalia	
1649 execution of Charles I		
1649–1653 commonwealth		
1649–1658 rule of Cromwell		
		1652 Thomas Hobbes, *Leviathan*
1653–1669 protectorate		
1660 restoration		

continued on next page

continued

British Context	Other European Context	Human Rights Speeches, Writings, and Documents
1660–1685 Charles II		
1670 rise of Whigs and Tories		
1673 Test Act		
		1679 Habeas Corpus Act
1685–1688 James I		
1688 Glorious Revolution		
1688–1702 William and Mary		
		1689 Tolerant Act; English Bill of Rights
		1690 John Locke, *Second Treatise* and *Letter concerning Toleration*

American Context	European Context	Human Rights Speeches, Writings, and Documents
	1695 revocation of prepublication censorship	
		1748 Baron de Montesquieu, *Spirit of Laws*
1750s spread of Calvinism		
1754–1763 French-Indian War		
1756–1763 Seven Years' War	1756–1763 Seven Years' War	1756 Cesare Beccaria, *Treatise on Crimes and Punishments*
		1761 Jean-Jacques Rousseau, *Social Contract*
1765 British Stamp Act		
1769 Watt's steam engine; Arkwright's water frame		
1775–1778 American War of Independence		1775 Thomas Paine, "African Slavery in America"
		1776 U.S. Declaration of Independence; Adam Smith, *Wealth of Nations;* Abigail Adams, "Remember the Ladies"
1786–1787 Shay's Rebellion		

American Context	European Context	Human Rights Speeches, Writings, and Documents
	1790–1791 slave rebellion (Haiti, St. Domingue, Guadeloupe, Martinique)	
		1791 U.S. Bill of Rights
		1792 Mary Wollstonecraft, *A Vindication of the Rights of Woman*
1793–1814 war with France		
1798 Sedition Act	1798 Rebellion of Ireland	
	1807 Britain outlaws slave trade	

French Context	Other European Context	Human Rights Speeches, Writings, and Documents
1789 French Revolution begins		1789 French Declaration of the Rights of Man and of the Citizen
1790–1791 slave rebellion (Haiti, St. Domingue, Guadeloupe, Martinique)		1790 Olympe de Gouge, Declaration of the Rights of Woman
1791 constitutional monarchy; National Assembly decrees emancipation of Jews		
1792 republic declared	1792–1797 War of the First Coalition	
1793 execution of Louis XVI		1793 French Constitution; Maximilien de Robespierre, "On Property"
1794 fall of Robespierre; Thermidor reaction; France abolishes slavery		
1795–1799 Directory		1795 Immanuel Kant, *Perpetual Peace*
1797 rise of Napoleon Bonaparte		1797 Kant, "Metaphysics of Morals"
1799–1804 consulate	1799–1802 War of the Second Coalition	

continued on next page

continued

American Context	European Context	Human Rights Speeches, Writings, and Documents
1802 Napoleon restores colonial slavery		
1804–1814 First Grand Empire	1806–1812 Napoleon's continental system	
	1805 War of the Third Coalition	
	1815 Battle of Waterloo; Congress of Vienna	

TABLE A.2
THE INDUSTRIAL AGE

Social and Political Context after 1800	Human Rights Speeches, Writings, and Documents
1802 Napoleon restores slavery in French colonies	1802 Factory Health and Morals Act
1807 Britain abolishes slave trade	
1810 Venezuela abolishes slavery	
1810–1824 civil wars and revolutions in Spanish colonial possessions	
1812 Argentina abolishes slavery	
	1815 Eight Power Declaration
	1817 Robert Owen, *New View of Society*
	1820 Missouri Compromise
	1821 G. W. F. Hegel, *Philosophy of Rights*
1823 Chile abolishes slavery	
1829 Mexico abolishes slavery	
1830 Revolution; election of Louis-Philippe in France; Greek independence; Belgian independence	
	1832 First Reform Bill
1833 British Abolition Act	1833 Factory Act
1834 Britain frees Caribbean slaves	1834 Poor Law
	1835 Municipal Corporations Act
	1837 Chartist petition
1838–1848 Chartism	1838 People's Charter

Social and Political Context after 1815	Human Rights Speeches, Writings, and Documents
1840 World Anti-Slavery Conference	1840 Louis Blanc, *L'organisation du travail;* Pierre-Joseph Proudhon, *What Is Property?*
1846 repeal of Corn Law	1847 Ten Hours Act
1848 Revolutions; Bloody June Days in Paris; Seneca Falls Convention	1848 Karl Marx and Friedrich Engels, "Manifesto of the Communist Party"; Susan B. Anthony and Elizabeth Cady Stanton, "Declaration of Sentiments" at Seneca Falls Convention
	1851 Sojourner Truth, "Ain't I a Woman?"
1852 Second Empire	1852 Harriet Beecher Stowe, *Uncle Tom's Cabin*
1854 Peru abolishes slavery	
1859 Battle of Solferino	
1860 Abraham Lincoln elected U.S. president	
1861 Alexander II (Russia) abolishes serfdom; 1861–1865 American Civil War	
	1862 Henri Dunant, *Memory of Solferino*
	1863 Lieber Code
1864 International Workingmen's Association founded; International Red Cross founded	1864 Geneva Convention; Marx, inaugural address at First International
	1865 Marx, "Letter to Abraham Lincoln"
	1866 Marx, "Instruction to the Delegates to the Geneva Congress"
	1867 Second Reform Act (extension of suffrage)
1871 Paris Commune	
1872 Hague Conference	
1880–1886 Cuba abolishes slavery	
1883–1886 Brazil abolishes slavery	1883 New Corruption Practices Act; August Bebel, *Women and Socialism*
	1884 General Act of the Berlin Conference; Engels, *On the Origin of the Family, Private Property, and the State*
1885 Belgian Labor Party founded	
1888 Austrian Social Democratic Party founded	

continued on next page

continued

Social and Political Context after 1815	Human Rights Speeches, Writings, and Documents
1889 Swedish Socialist Movement founded; Women's Franchise League founded; Second International	
1890 International Labor Conference in Berlin	
1893 New Zealand grants universal suffrage	
1894 Dreyfus Affair	
1897 National Union of Women's Suffrage Societies founded	
	1898 Emile Zola, "J'accuse"
1900 Paris Congress	
1902 Australia grants universal suffrage	
1906 Finland grants universal suffrage	
1910 China abolishes slavery	
1913 Norway grants universal suffrage	
1920 United States grants universal suffrage	
	1921 Marcel Proust, *Sodom and Gomorrah*
	1926 League of Nations, Convention to Suppress the Slave Trade and Slavery

TABLE A.3
THE WORLD WARS

Important World Events	Human Rights Speeches, Writings, and Documents
Before World War I	
1867 Italian unification	
1868–1912 Japanese unification	
1871 German unification	
1899 The Hague Peace Conference	
	1902 V. I. Lenin, "What Is to Be Done?"
	1904 Amsterdam Congress Resolution against Colonialism
1905 Polish League; Russian Revolution; Japan defeats Russia; "Bloody Sunday" in Russia	

Before World War I	
	1907 Stuttgart Resolution on Militarism and International Conflicts; Otto Bauer, *Question of Nationalities and Social Democracy*
	1909 Rosa Luxemburg, *The National Question and Autonomy;* Mahatma Gandhi, "Passive Resistance"
1910 Japanese annexation of Korea	
1911 Crisis of Agadir	

World War I	
1914 World War I begins	1914 Lenin, "The Right of Nations to Self-Determination"
1914–1918 Spartacus League	
1915–1916 deportation and massacre of Armenians	1915 Leonard Woolf, *International Government*
1917 Bolshevik Revolution	
1918 Peace Treaty of Brest Litovsk; World War I ends	1918 Declaration of the Rights of the Toiling and Exploited Peoples; Woodrow Wilson, "Fourteen Points" speech; Lenin, *The Emancipation of Women*

Interwar Period	
1919 Paris Conference; League of Nations founded; International Labor Organization founded; permanent Court of Justice founded at the Hague	1919 International Labor Organization Charter; Covenant of the League of Nations; Polish Minority Treaty; Karl Kautsky, *Terrorism and Communism*
1920 Geneva Congress	1920 Lenin, *On the National Liberation Movement*
	1921 International Convention for the Suppression of the Traffic in Women and Children
1922–1943 fascist Italy under Benito Mussolini	
	1924 Declaration of the Rights of Children; Gandhi, "Appeal to the Nation"
	1926 Slavery Convention
1929–1941 Great Depression	
1933–1945 Nazi Germany under Adolf Hitler	
	1936 Soviet Constitution

continued on next page

continued

Interwar Period

1937 "Rape of Nanking," China,
by Japanese forces

World War II

1939 World War II begins	1939 Albert Camus, indictment of Algerian conflict
1941 Atlantic Charter	1941 Franklin Roosevelt, "Four Freedoms" speech
1944 Dumbarton Oaks Conference	
1945 World War II ends	

Aftermath of World War II

1945 United Nations (UN) founded; International Court of Justice founded; Bretton Woods; Marshall Plan; Yalta Conference; San Francisco Conference	1945 UN Charter; Ho Chi Minh, Vietnamese Declaration of Independence; Martin Niemöller, "They Came"
1945–1946 Nuremberg trials	
	1948 UN Universal Declaration of Human Rights

Age of Decolonization and Cold War

1947 Indian independence; creation of Pakistan; Sri Lankan independence	
1948 creation of Israel; Burmese independence	
1949 Communist Revolution in China; NATO founded	1949 Simone de Beauvoir, *Second Sex*
1950 Schuman plan for Franco-German coal and steel production	1950 European Convention for the Protection of Human Rights and Fundamental Freedoms
	1951 UN Convention on the Prevention and Punishment of the Crime of Genocide; Convention Related to the Status of Refugees; Hannah Arendt, "On the Rights of Stateless People"
	1953 Convention on the Political Rights of Women
1954 division of Vietnam at 17th parallel; Battle of Dien Bien Phu	
1954–1975 Vietnam War	
1955 Warsaw Pact	

TABLE A.4
GLOBALIZATION

1956–1989 Events	Human Rights Speeches, Writings, and Documents
1956 Hungarian uprising	
1958 General Agreement on Tariffs and Trade	
	1959 Declaration of the Rights of the Child
	1960 Kwame Nkrumah, UN speech on African self-determination
	1961 Léopold Senghor, *On African Nationalism*
1962 Algerian independence	
1963 John F. Kennedy assassinated	1963 Betty Friedan, *Feminine Mystique;* Martin Luther King, Jr., "I Have a Dream" speech; Frantz Fanon, *Wretched of the Earth*
	1964–1965 Che Guevara, speeches before the UN General Assembly and the Afro-Asian Solidarity Conference
	1966 UN International Covenant on Civil and Political Rights; UN International Covenant on Economic, Social and Cultural Rights; Convention on the Elimination of All Forms of Racial Discrimination
	1967 Convention on the Elimination of Discrimination against Women
1968 student uprisings in Europe and the United States; Prague Spring; Martin Luther King, Jr., assassinated; Robert Kennedy assassinated	1968 Protocol Relating to the Status of Refugees
1969 Stonewall Riots	1969 Kate Millett, *Sexual Politics;* Convention Governing the Specific Aspects of Refugee Problems in Africa
1970–1975 Cambodian War	
	1971 UN Declaration on the Rights of Mentally Retarded Persons
1972 U.S. President Richard Nixon visits China	1972 London Dumping Convention; Heinz Heger, *The Men with the Pink Triangle*
1973 oil crisis	
1974 Nixon resigns	

continued on next page

continued

1956–1989 Events	Human Rights Speeches, Writings, and Documents
	1975 Declaration on the Rights of Disabled Persons; Helsinki Accords
	1978 Vaclav Havel, *Power of the Powerless;* MARPOL Convention; UNESCO Convention on Race and Racial Prejudice
1979 Margaret Thatcher elected prime minister of United Kingdom	1979 UN Convention on the Elimination of All Forms of Discrimination against Women
1980 Ronald Reagan elected U.S. president	
1981 Soviets crack down on Solidarity movement in Poland	
	1982 World Programme of Action concerning Disabled Persons; UN Law of the Sea
1985 Vienna Protocol; Mikhail Gorbachev becomes general secretary of the Communist Party of the USSR	
1986 Chernobyl nuclear disaster; Mikhail Gorbachev unveils economic reforms *(perestroika)*	1986 African Charter on Human and Peoples' Rights
1987 Montreal Protocol	
1989 Berlin Wall falls; Eastern European "Velvet Revolutions"; Tiananmen Square uprising, Beijing	

The Aftermath of 1989	Human Rights Speeches, Writings, and Documents
	1989 Indigenous and Tribal Peoples Convention; Basel Convention; Convention on the Rights of the Child
	1990 UN Convention on the Protection of the Rights of All Migrant Workers and Their Families
1991 Persian Gulf War; Slovenia, Croatia, Bosnia-Herzegovina, and Macedonia declare independence from Yugoslavia; Maastricht Treaty	1991 UN High Commissioner for Refugees guidelines established

The Aftermath of 1989	Human Rights Speeches, Writings, and Documents
1992 NAFTA; Zapatista rebellion; ASEAN Free Trade Area established	1992 UN Declaration on the Rights of Persons Belonging to National or Ethnic, Religious and Linguistic Minorities; Rio Declaration on Environment and Development; Rigoberta Menchú Tum, Nobel Prize lecture on indigenous rights
1992–1993 humanitarian intervention in Somalia	
1993 international criminal tribunal for the former Yugoslavia	
1994 genocide in Rwanda; creation of international criminal tribunal for Rwanda	Resolution on Action Required Internationally to Provide Effective Protection for Indigenous Peoples; Standard Rules on the Equalization of Opportunities for Persons
1995 International Women's Conference, Beijing	1995 Beijing Declaration; Subcomandante Marcos, "A Letter Addressed to the People of the United States"
1997 Hong Kong returned to China; Kyoto Treaty	1997 American Declaration on the Rights of Indigenous People; Jody Williams, Nobel Prize lecture on landmines
1999 WTO protests, Seattle; Chechen war begins	1999 Mine Ban Treaty; José Bové, "McDonald's as a Symbol" interview; Amartya Sen, *Development as Freedom*
2000 IMF protests, Buenos Aires; World Bank and IMF protests, Prague; UN declares December 4 International Migrants' Day	2000 Charter of Fundamental Rights; Bové, "Seattle-on-Tarn" interview
2001 Single Europe Act; terrorist attacks on United States; United States passes Patriot Act; G8 protests, Genoa	
2002 World Economic Forum protests, Washington, D.C.	

Notes

INTRODUCTION

1. For an insightful criticism of a realist approach to history, see Edward Hallett Carr, *The Twenty Years' Crisis*, 91–93. See also Michel Foucault, "Truth and Power," in *Power/Knowledge*, and Costas Douzinas, *The End of Human Rights*.

2. Walter Benjamin, "The Theses on the Philosophy of History," in *Illuminations*, 257–258.

3. While voting rights are often seen in human rights discourses as being linked to the first generation of liberal rights, I show in this book that they should belong to the second generation of socialist rights.

4. Karl Marx, "British Political Parties," in *Selected Writings*, 332.

5. Samuel Huntington, "The Clash of Civilizations?"

6. See Bikhu Parekh, "Non-Ethno-Centric Universalism," in Tim Dunne and Nicholas Wheeler, *Human Rights in Global Politics*, 128–159.

7. See Jack Donnelly, *Universal Human Rights in Theory and Practice*; Alison Dundes Renteln, "Relativism and the Search for Human Rights," 56–72; R. Panikar, "Is the Notion of Human Rights a Western Concept?" 75–102; Rhoda Howard, *Human Rights and the Search for Community*; William Felice, *Taking Rights Seriously*.

8. See references in Micheline Ishay and Omar Dahbour, *The Nationalism Reader*.

9. This point is further discussed in my *Internationalism and Its Betrayal*.

CHAPTER I

1. Herodotus, *The Histories*, 219–220.

2. For a fascinating profile of the drafters of the human rights commission, see Mary Ann Glendon, *A World Made New*, xx. Also see chapter 4 of this book.

3. Jacques Maritain, *Human Rights*, 10; see also Maritain, *The Rights of Man and Natural Law*.

4. See Maritain, *Human Rights*, 260.

5. René Cassin, "Religions et droits de l'homme," in *Amicorum discipulorumque liber*, vol. 4, 98 (my translation).

6. Cited in Dayan Berkovitz, "A Halachic Viewpoint." This chapter does not support the idea that modern notions of human rights are equivalent to ancient religious conceptions of the common good, but one can easily find the spirit of some religious injunctions in modern definitions of rights.

7. With the exception of a list of moral precepts that were learned by boys

of the Egyptian ruling class ca. 3000 B.C.E., as well as some scattered Sumerian and old Acadian laws. G. R. Driver and John C. Miles, *The Babylonian Laws,* vol. 1, 54.

8. Milton R. Konvitz, "Many Are Chosen and Many Are Called," in *Judaism and Human Rights,* 79; see also Abraham Kaplan, "Human Rights and Human Relations in Judaism," in Alan S. Rosenbaum, *The Philosophy of Human Rights,* 66–67.

9. Cassin, "Religions et droits de l'homme," in *Amicorum discipulorumque liber.*

10. S. V. Puntambekar, *Human Rights,* in Maritain, *Human Rights,* 197.

11. See R. C. Pandeya, "Human Rights: An Indian Perspective," in *Philosophical Foundations of Human Rights,* 267.

12. John Strong, *The Experience of Buddhism,* 191–193.

13. Chung-Shu Lo, "Human Rights in the Chinese Tradition," in Maritain, *Human Rights,* 186–187.

14. Confucius, *Analects,* bk. 18, 6, 150.

15. Irene Bloom, "Fundamental Institutions and Consensus Statement: Mencian Confucianism and Human Rights," in William Theodore de Bary and Tu Weiming, *Confucianism and Human Rights,* 96.

16. Confucius, *Analects,* bk. 16, 9, 140.

17. Ibid., bk. 15, 31–32; see also Tu Wei-ming, "Confucianism," in Arvind Sharma, *Our Religions,* 186; and Leonard Shihlien Hsü, *The Political Philosophy of Confucianism,* 156.

18. Tu Wei-ming, "Confucianism," in Sharma, *Our Religions,* 144.

19. Confucius, *Analects,* bk. 13, 13, 120.

20. Ibid., bk. 12, 5, 113.

21. Richard McKeon, *The Philosophic Bases and the Material Circumstances of the Rights of Man,* in Maritain, *Human Rights,* 36.

22. Jean Graven, quoted in René Cassin, *Amicorum disciplinorumque liber,* vol. 2, 10 (my translation).

23. Plato, *The Republic,* bk. 4, 1, or in Micheline Ishay, *The Human Rights Reader,* 12–13.

24. Epictetus, *The Discourses,* in *"The Discourses" and "Enchiridon,"* bk. 4, chap. 7, 29–34.

25. Marcus Tullius Cicero, *The Laws,* in *"De Republica" and "De Legibus,"* bk. 1, or in Ishay, *The Human Rights Reader,* 23.

26. Cicero, *On the Commonwealth,* bk. 3, 22, 215.

27. Cicero, *The Laws,* in *"De Republica" and "De Legibus,"* bk. 1, or in Ishay, *The Human Rights Reader,* 26, 29.

28. Teilhard de Chardin, "Some Reflections on the Rights of Man," in Maritain, *Human Rights,* 105.

29. Sergius Hessen, "The Rights of Man in Liberalism, Socialism and Communism," in Maritain, *Human Rights,* 117.

30. The tension around the idea of the Jews as the chosen people is discussed later in this chapter.

31. Humayun Kabir, "Human Rights: The Islamic Tradition and the Problems of the World Today," in Maritain, *Human Rights,* 191.

32. All excerpts from the Quran are drawn from Abdullah Yusuf Ali, *The Meaning of the Holy Qur'an.*

33. Driver and Miles, *The Babylonian Laws,* vol. 1, 54, 78.

34. Ibid., vol. 1, 65.

35. Norman Bentwich, *The Religious Foundations of Internationalism,* 61–62; Konvitz, *Judaism and Human Rights,* 95–97.

36. *The Arthashastra,* 4.9.17, 18.

37. Bentwich, *The Religious Foundations of Internationalism,* 182–185.

38. *The Arthashastra,* 4.11.1–2, 5, 7, 13, 15, 16–20, 22; 4.11.11, 12.

39. Ibid., 4.10.1–2, 8, 11, 13, 16.

40. Ibid., 4.8.14, 17–20; 4.8.15–16, 21–24.

41. Frederick Franck, "The Awakening of Self in Buddhism," in *The Buddha Eye,* 22–33; or see Taitetsu Unno, "Personal Rights and Contemporary Buddhism," in Leroy Rouner, *Human Rights and the World's Religions,* 131.

42. For a clear account of different schools of Buddhism (Theravada, Mahayana, Tantra, and Zen), see Masao Abe, "Buddhism," in Sharma, *Our Religions,* 85–101.

43. See Masao Abe, "Religious Tolerance and Human Rights: A Buddhist Perspective," in Leonard Swidler, *Religious Liberty and Human Rights,* 210.

44. Kenneth Inada, "The Buddhist Perspective on Human Rights," in Arlene Swidler, *Human Rights in Religious Traditions,* 73; for a detailed explanation of these precepts, see also Peter Harvey, *An Introduction to Buddhism,* 202–205.

45. From the *Mahavastu,* in Strong, *The Experience of Buddhism,* 33.

46. Cited and discussed in Bentwich, *The Religious Foundations of Internationalism,* 188.

47. Ibid., 196.

48. Confucius, *Analects,* bk. 20, 2, 159–160.

49. Bentwich, *The Religious Foundations of Internationalism,* 196.

50. See Lin Yutang, *The Wisdom of Confucius,* 164.

51. Confucius, *Analects,* bk. 15, 39, 137.

52. Ibid., bk. 17, 8, 144–145.

53. See D. C. Lau's interpretation in Confucius, *Analects,* Introduction, 36–37, versus Hsü's in *The Political Philosophy of Confucianism,* 156.

54. Plato, *The Statesman,* 293c, 131.

55. Aristotle, *The Politics,* bk. 3, chap. 13, 313.

56. Ibid.

57. Cited in Majid Khadduri, *The Islamic Conception of Justice,* 1.

58. David Little, John Kelsay, and Abdulaziz A. Sachedina, *Human Rights and the Conflict of Culture,* 64.

59. Surah 2:256, 257; see also surah 5:44–48. For a universalist interpretation of these verses, see Little, Kelsay, and Sachedina, *Human Rights and the Conflict of Culture,* 68; Riffat Hassan, "On Human Rights and the Qur'anic Perspective," in Arlene Swidler, *Human Rights in Religious Traditions,* 61; and Mohammmed Allal Sinaceur, "Islamic Tradition and Human Rights," in *Philosophical Foundations of Human Rights,* 215–217.

60. Bentwich, *The Religious Foundations of Internationalism,* 167.

61. Ann Elizabeth Mayer, *Islam and Human Rights,* 98–99, 164.

62. See Riffat Hassan, "On Human Rights and the Qur'anic Perspective," in Swidler, *Human Rights in Religious Traditions,* 61.

63. Driver and Miles, *The Babylonian Laws,* vol. 1, 417.

64. Ibid., vol. 1, 112.

65. Ibid., vol. 2, sec. 9–13, 17–19.

66. Ibid., vol. 1, sec. 264, 456.

67. It is important to remind the reader that the notion of economic entitlement does not correspond exactly to the notions of property rights and other social rights, such as the nineteenth-century right to work, that were more clearly defined with the development of capitalism.

68. On a similar topic, see Eric G. Freudenstein, "Ecology and the Jewish Tradition," 265–274.

69. *The Arthashastra,* 96, 320–322.

70. Upanisads 1.3.22, cited in S. Cromwell Crawford, *The Evolution of Hindu Ideals,* 50; see also Brahadaranyaka Upanisad 1.3.22 and Chandogya Upanisad 5.3.1–5.10.9, in Patrick Olivelle, *Upanisads,* 12.

71. Ramachandra Guha, "Radical Environmentalism and Wilderness Preservation," 71–83; and article 12 of the United Nations International Covenant on Economic, Social and Cultural Rights (1966) in Ishay, *The Human Rights Reader,* 437.

72. *The Arthashastra,* 3.9.19–20; 3.16.25–28.

73. Klaus K. Klostermaier, *A Survey of Hinduism,* 322–323.

74. Ibid., 168.

75. *The Arthashastra,* 3.14.2, 5–9, 11.

76. See, for example, the Khuddaka-patha and Digha Nikaya; relevant sections in Strong, *The Experience of Buddhism,* 112–114.

77. Robert Thurman, "Social and Cultural Rights in Buddhism," in Rouner, *Human Rights and the World's Religions,* 157–158; see also Thurman, "Guidelines for Buddhist Social Activism Based on Nagarjuna's Jewel Garland of Royal Counsels," 37–38.

78. Masao Abe, "Buddhism," in Sharma, *Our Religions,* 83.

79. De Bary, "Neo-Confucianism and Human Rights," 192.

80. Confucius, *Analects,* bk. 16, 1, 138–139.

81. Ibid., bk. 20, 2, 159; bk. 6, 4, 81.

82. Plato, *The Republic,* bk. 5, pt. 464, 222.

83. Aristotle, *The Politics,* bk. 2, chap. 5, 1263b15, 116.

84. Ibid., bk. 2, chap. 5, 1263a8–1263a40, 114–115.

85. Ibid., bk. 3, chap. 2, 1275b22–1276a6, 171–172.

86. Ibid., bk. 7, chap. 9, 1329a17, 416.

87. See "The Sermon of the Mountains," Matthew 5:21, Matthew 15:19–20, Mark 7:20–23, Ephesians 4:22–28 NEB.

88. Regarding the protection of children, see surahs 2:233, 4:2–33, 6:152, and 17:31.

89. For relevant excerpts from the Quran, see also Ishay, *The Human Rights Reader,* 41–57.

90. *The Laws of Manu,* 10.63.

91. *The Arthashastra,* 7.5.19–26, 27–37.

92. Cited in Harvey, *An Introduction to Buddhism,* 202.

93. Thurman, in Rouner, *Human Rights and the World's Religions,* 158.

94. Confucius, *Analects,* bk. 16, 8, 203.

95. *Mencius,* bk. 7, pt. B2–4, 195.

96. De Bary, introduction to de Bary and Tu Weiming, *Confucianism and Human Rights,* 8.

97. Plato, *The Republic,* bk. 5, pt. 470–471, 229–230.

98. Ibid., bk. 5, pt. 469–470, 228–229.

99. Graven, in Cassin, *Amicorum disciplinorumque liber,* 12.

100. Cicero, *De Republica,* XXIII, 213.

101. Bentwich, *The Religious Foundations of Internationalism,* 84.

102. Saint Augustine, *The City of God,* or in Ishay, *The Human Rights Reader,* 37–41.

103. Thomas Aquinas, *Summa theologica,* or in Ishay, *The Human Rights Reader,* 58–65.

104. See also Khadduri, *The Islamic Conception of Justice,* 85; and Little, Kelsay, and Sachedina, *Human Rights and the Conflict of Culture,* 85.

105. Cited in Abul A'la Mawdudi, *Human Rights in Islam,* 36–38.

106. Cited in Bentwich, *The Religious Foundations of Internationalism,* 163–164.

107. Driver and Miles, *The Babylonian Laws,* vol. 2, par. 154–155, 61.

108. Ibid., vol. 2, par. 154, 61.

109. Ibid., vol. 2, par. 131–132, 53.

110. Ibid., vol. 2, par. 153, 59.

111. Ibid., vol. 1, 313, note 3.

112. Ibid., vol. 1, 222–223.

113. Ibid., vol. 2, par. 117, 48–49.

114. One should bear in mind that the Hebrew word *eved* simply means "worker," and that there was little difference between the hired worker and the Hebrew slave.

115. One should bear in mind that the Hebrew word *kaniti* in the Bible can also mean "I acquired."

116. See also Lewis Jon Eron, "Homosexuality and Judaism," in Arlene Swidler, *Homosexuality and World Religions,* 116.

117. Ibid., 120.

118. *The Laws of Manu,* 3.15, 3.18, 9.156–157, 10.64–66.

119. Ibid., 8.41.

120. Ibid., 8.124.

121. *The Arthashastra,* 4.8.28, 29.

122. Ibid., 3.3.8; 3.4.1.

123. *The Laws of Manu,* 8.299.

124. Ibid., 5.148–149.

125. *The Arthashastra,* 3.16.32.

126. Ibid., 3.3.20–24.

127. Arvind Sharma, "Homosexuality and Hinduism," in Swidler, *Homosexuality and World Religions,* 54–55, 70.

128. R. K. Mookerjee's view, cited in *The Arthashastra,* 446.

129. Ibid., 447.

130. *The Arthashastra* 3.13.21–22, 25.

131. Edwin Burtt, *The Teachings of the Compassionate Buddha*, 71–73.

132. "The Acceptance of Women into the Order," in ibid., 52–56.

133. "The Twelve Vows of Healing Buddha," in Strong, *The Experience of Buddhism*, 192.

134. "Karma and the Six Realms of Rebirth," in Strong, *The Experience of Buddhism*, 31.

135. José Ignacio Cabezón, "Homosexuality and Buddhism," 91.

136. Han Fei Tzu, note 81, cited in Tu Wei-ming, "Confucianism," in Sharma, *Our Religions*, 193.

137. Confucius, *Analects*, bk. 20, 2, 160.

138. Hsü, *The Political Philosophy of Confucianism*, 172–173.

139. Ibid., 188.

140. Confucius, *Analects*, bk. 17, 25, 148.

141. Hsü, *The Political Philosophy of Confucianism*, 188; Bryan W. Van Norden, "Introduction," and Lisa A. Raphals, "A Woman Who Understood the Rites," in Van Norden, *Confucius and the Analects*, 10, 275, 295.

142. Sandra Wawrytko, "Homosexuality and Chinese and Japanese Religions," in Swidler, *Homosexuality and World Religions*, 204–205.

143. Plato, *The Republic*, bk. 5, 455.

144. Plato, *Symposium*, 181b, 191-92; *The Laws*, bk. 1, 631, 636; bk. 8, 836–837, 838–839, 841; *The Republic*, bk. 3, pt. 403, 144.

145. Aristotle, *The Politics*, bk. 1, chap. 4, 64–65.

146. Ibid., bk. 1, chap. 5, 68.

147. Aristotle, *The Nicomachean Ethics*, bk. 7, sec. 5, 189, 190.

148. Ibid., 8.4.1157a, 221.

149. See also 1 Timothy 1:10, and for a brief reference to lesbianism, see Romans 1:26–27 NB.

150. For a discussion of the distinction between female and male homosexuality, see Denise Carmody and John Carmody, "Homosexuality and Roman Catholicism," in Swidler, *Homosexuality and World Religions*, 135–142.

151. See Seyed Hosseyin Nasr, "Islam," in Sharma, *Our Religions*, 460–461.

152. See Mayer, *Islam and Human Rights*, 110–112.

153. For a discussion of the difference between religious prohibition and cultural acceptance of homosexuality in Islamic countries, see Khalid Duran, "Homosexuality and Islam," in Swidler, *Homosexuality and World Religions*, 181–197.

154. These linkages are further developed in chapter 2.

155. See Jack Donnelly, "Human Rights and Cultural Values: Caste in India," in *Universal Human Rights in Theory and Practice*, 126–137.

156. Anguttara-nikaya, viii, ii.ix, cited in Masao Abe, "Buddhism," in Sharma, *Our Religions*, 72.

157. The Gush Emunim (Bloc of Faith) refers to a Jewish religious and nationalist movement of West Bank settlers; Hamas is a fundamentalist Muslim group predominant in the West Bank and the Gaza territories; BJP (the Bharatiya

Janata Party) refers to a Hindu nationalist party; and Komeito (the Clean Life Party) is a Japanese conservative Buddhist party.

CHAPTER 2

1. G. W. F. Hegel, *The Philosophy of Right,* par. 39, 218.

2. J. M. Roberts, *The History of the World,* 441.

3. Ibid.

4. Ibid., 434.

5. Samir Amin, "The Ancient World-Systems versus the Modern Capitalist World System," 357. Amin defines the categorization of this vast region, whose centers of power shifted over time.

6. Roberts, *The History of the World,* 330.

7. Ibid., 187.

8. Ibid., 331.

9. Stephen K. Sanderson, *Civilizations and World Systems;* Joseph Needham, *Science and Civilization;* Amin, "The Ancient World-Systems versus the Modern Capitalist World System"; and Amin, *Eurocentrism.*

10. E. L. Jones, *The European Miracle,* 200.

11. Ibid., 194.

12. Roberts, *The History of the World,* 420.

13. Ibid., 203.

14. Jared Diamond, *Guns, Germs, and Steel,* 412–413.

15. Maxime Rodinson, *Islam and Capitalism.*

16. Jones, *The European Miracle,* 177.

17. Ibid.

18. Ibid., 187.

19. Parts of the following section are drawn from Ishay, *Internationalism and Its Betrayal,* 5–10.

20. For a discussion of the conditions of the development of mercantilism, see Eli F. Hecksher, *Mercantilism,* vol. 1, chap. 7, 326–456; and also Laurence B. Packard, *The Commercial Revolution,* 7–20.

21. See Karl Marx and Friedrich Engels, *The German Ideology,* 63.

22. Robert Palmer and Joel Colton, *History of the Modern World,* 102–103.

23. Numerous explanations of these revolutions are possible. Class-based analyses have been recently challenged by a variety of alternative historical explanations. Egret and Eisenstein contest the class demarcation of the revolutionary movement; Furet emphasizes the struggle of the political elites; Skocpol focuses on the structural weakness of the state; and Goldstone concentrates on population growth. What is important, however, for the purposes of this book is to identify a trend: the expansion of capitalism and its relationship to the evolving worldview of a class in formation. For more detailed accounts and interpretations of these revolutions, see Albert Mathiez, *The French Revolution;* Albert Soboul, *Histoire de la révolution française;* Georges Lefebvre, *La révolution française;* Simon Schama, *Citizens;* Jean Egret, *The French Pre-Revolution;* Elizabeth Eisenstein, "Who Intervened in 1788?"; François Furet, *Penser la révolu-*

tion française; Theda Skocpol, *States and Social Revolutions;* Jack Goldstone, *Revolution and Rebellion in the Early Modern World;* and Herbert G. Gutman, *Who Built America?*

24. Bartolomé de las Casas, *In Defense of the Indians.*

25. Martin Luther, "The Liberty of the Christian Man," in G. R. Elton, *Renaissance and Reformation, 1300–1648,* 148.

26. Hugo Grotius, *The Rights of War and Peace,* bk. 2, chap. 22, sec. 14, 271.

27. C. W. Firth, ed., *The Clarke Papers,* vol. 3, 351.

28. The Treaty of Westphalia, in Elton, *Renaissance and Reformation,* 241.

29. John Locke, *A Letter concerning Toleration,* 44.

30. Ibid.

31. John Milton, *Areopagetica: A Speech for the Liberty of Unlicensed Printing, to the Parliament of England,* in *Selected Essays of John Milton,* 42.

32. Ibid., 128.

33. William H. Marnell, *The First Amendment,* 57.

34. Ibid., 60.

35. Ibid., 93.

36. Ibid., 144.

37. Thomas Paine, *Common Sense,* 34, 52.

38. Thomas Jefferson, "Address to a Committee of the Danbury Baptist Association, in the State of Connecticut, Washington, January 1, 1802," in *The Life and Selected Writings of Thomas Jefferson,* 332.

39. "An Act for Establishing Religious Freedom (1779)," passed in the Assembly of Virginia in the beginning of the year 1786, in Jefferson, *The Life and Selected Writings of Thomas Jefferson,* 311–313.

40. Marnell, *The First Amendment,* 144.

41. "The Sedition Act" (July 14, 1798), in *The People Shall Judge,* 435.

42. Jefferson, "First Inaugural Address, 1801," in *The People Shall Judge,* 427.

43. See Baron de Montesquieu, *Lettres persanes,* letters 83 and 85; Voltaire, "Toleration," in *Philosophical Dictionary,* 360–361, and *Oeuvres complètes;* Jean-Jacques Rousseau, "Profession du Vicaire Savoyard," in *Oeuvres complètes;* Denis Diderot, *Oeuvres complètes.*

44. Deism is a belief advocating a natural religion emphasizing human over revealed morality.

45. Voltaire, "Toleration," in *Philosophical Dictionary,* 360–361.

46. Article 11 of the French Declaration of the Rights of Man and of the Citizen, in Ishay, *The Human Rights Reader,* 139.

47. See also Ishay, *Internationalism and Its Betrayal,* 53–55.

48. Thomas Hobbes, "The Leviathan," in Ishay, *The Human Rights Reader,* 84.

49. Ibid., 85.

50. Ibid., 88.

51. The Habeas Corpus was directly inspired by clause 39 of the Magna Carta, which states, "No freeman shall be arrested, or detained in prison, or outlawed, or banished, or in any way molested; and we will not set forth against

him nor send against him, unless by the lawful judgment of his peers and by the law of the land." In George B. Adams, *The Origin of the English Constitution,* chap. 5.

52. English Bill of Rights, in Ishay, *The Human Rights Reader,* 93.

53. Brian Innes, *The History of Torture,* 86–96; see also John H. Langbein, *Torture and the Law of Proof.*

54. Innes, *The History of Torture,* 147–155.

55. Hobbes, "The Leviathan," in Ishay, *The Human Rights Reader,* 88.

56. Cesare Beccaria, *Treatise on Crimes and Punishments,* chap. 2, in Ishay, *The Human Rights Reader,* 120–122.

57. George R. Havens, *Selections from Voltaire,* 384 (my translation); see also "Torture" in Voltaire, "The Philosophical Dictionary," in *The Works of Voltaire,* 119.

58. See article 5 of the UN Universal Declaration, article 7 of the Covenant on Civil and Political Rights, article 3 of the European Convention, article 5.2 of the American Convention, and article 5 of the African Charter; see also Nigel S. Rodley, *The Treatment of Prisoners under International Law.*

59. Rousseau, *"The Social Contract" and "Discourses,"* 105.

60. More precisely, see articles 3, 5, and 8 of the UN Universal Declaration; articles 2 and 3 of the European Convention; and articles 6 and 7 of the Covenant on Civil and Political Rights (in the documents section in Ishay, *The Human Rights Reader*).

61. Michel Foucault, *Discipline and Punish,* 38.

62. Norberto Bobbio, *The Age of Rights,* 128.

63. See John Simmons, *The Lockean Theory of Rights,* 148–149.

64. Locke, *The Second Treatise,* in Ishay, *The Human Rights Reader,* 96.

65. Rousseau, "The Right of Life and Death," in *"The Social Contract" and "Discourses,"* 209.

66. Immanuel Kant, "The Metaphysics of Morals," in *Kant's Political Writings,* 156.

67. Ibid., 157.

68. Ibid.

69. Foucault, *Discipline and Punish,* 48–49.

70. Beccaria, *Treatise on Crimes and Punishments,* chap. 2, in Ishay, *The Human Rights Reader,* 124.

71. Ibid., 126.

72. Ibid., 123.

73. Quoted in James J. Megivern, *The Death Penalty,* 302–303.

74. Voltaire, "Commentaires sur le livre des délits et des peines," in *Oeuvres de Voltaire,* 58. Voltaire's work referred to Beccaria's. Although the German philosopher Hegel repudiated Beccaria's abolitionist view, he nonetheless recognized in his *Philosophy of Right* that "Beccaria's effort to abolish the death penalty had some advantageous effects; even if neither Joseph II nor the French have ever managed its total abolition, there has been more awareness of which crimes are punishable and which are not" (par. 100).

75. Maximilien de Robespierre, "On the Abolition of the Death Penalty" (Constituent Assembly, May 30, 1791), in *Robespierre,* 24.

76. Robespierre, "On the Action to be Taken against Louis XVI" (December 3, 1792), in *Robespierre*, 31.

77. See also Bobbio, *The Age of Rights*, 143–162.

78. See C. B. Macpherson, *The Political Theory of Possessive Individualism*, 138.

79. Henry Ireton, "Extract from the Debates at Putney" (October 29, 1647), in Andrew Sharp, *The English Levellers*, 108–109.

80. Sharp, *The English Levellers*, 110.

81. Richard Overton, "An Arrow against All Tyrants," in ibid., 55.

82. See Macpherson, *The Political Theory of Possessive Individualism*, 148.

83. See Christopher Hill, *The World Turned Upside Down*, 15.

84. Locke, "On Property," *The Second Treatise*, in Ishay, *The Human Rights Reader*, 97.

85. C. Edward Merriam, *American Political Theories*, 75.

86. Ibid., 84.

87. Ibid., and see A. J. Beitzinger, *A History of American Political Thought*, 183.

88. Beitzinger, *A History of American Political Thought*, 280.

89. Ibid., 295.

90. R. R. Palmer, *The Age of the Democratic Revolution*, vol. 1, 225.

91. Merriam, *American Political Theories*, 85.

92. Ibid.

93. "The 1789 Declaration of the Rights of Man and of the Citizen," in Ishay, *The Human Rights Reader*, 139.

94. Abbé de Sieyès, Preliminary to the French Constitution, August 1789, in Lynn Hunt, *The French Revolution and Human Rights*, 81.

95. Robespierre, "On the Right to Vote," delivered variously in the Constituent Assembly 1789–1791 and the National Convention (September 1792–July 1794), in *Robespierre*, 21–22.

96. Robespierre, "On Property" (April 24, 1793), in *Robespierre*, 51–57.

97. See Bartolo da Sassoferato, *La Tiberiade*; Cecil Nathan Sidney Woolf, *Bartolo de Sassoferato*; Joseph Canning, *The Political Thought of Baldus de Ubaldi*; and Francisco de Vitorio, *Relaciones sobre los indios y el derecho de guerra* and *Political Writings*.

98. Samuel Pufendorf, *On the Law of Nature and of Nations in Eight Books*, in *The Political Writings of Samuel Pufendorf*, 258; Richard Zouche, *Juris et judicii fecialis*, vol. 2; Emmerich de Vattel, *Le droit des gens ou principe de la loi naturelle*, vol. 2.

99. John Kelsay and James Turner Johnson, *Just War and Jihad*; Terry Nardin, *The Ethics of War and Peace*.

100. Grotius, *The Rights of War and Peace*, bk. 2, chap. 1, sec. 1–4, 73–84, and bk. 2, chap. 20, sec. 1–3, 220–255; see also Peter R. Remec, *The Position of the Individual in International Law according to Grotius and Vattel*, 88–89.

101. Grotius, *The Rights of War and Peace*, bk. 2, chap. 22, sec. 12, 398.

102. Samuel Pufendorf, *On the Law of Nature and of Nations in Eight Books*, in *The Political Writings of Samuel Pufendorf*, 258; and Vattel, *Le droit des gens ou principe de la loi naturelle*, vol. 2, chap. 3, par. 42–50.

103. Pufendorf, *On the Law of Nature and of Nations in Eight Books*, in *The Political Writings of Samuel Pufendorf*, 259.

104. Grotius, *The Rights of War and Peace*, bk. 1, chap. 1, sec. 14, 25.

105. Ibid., bk. 1, chap. 3, sec. 7, 62.

106. Adam Smith, *The Wealth of Nations*, bk. 1, 477; and Smith, *The Theory of Moral Sentiments*, 304.

107. See Smith, *The Wealth of Nations*, bk. 1 and 2.

108. Ibid., bk. 5, 236.

109. See ibid., bk. 4.

110. Paine, "The Rights of Man," in *The Essential Thomas Paine*, 267.

111. Kant, "Idea of a Universal History," in *Kant's Political Writings*, 50.

112. By focusing on commerce, Adam Smith later reversed what the Physiocrats thought was profitable.

113. Rousseau, *Considération sur le gouvernement de Pologne et sur sa réformation projetée*, in *The Political Writings of Jean-Jacques Rousseau*, vol. 2, 477.

114. Abbé Charles de Saint-Pierre, *Abridgement of the Project for Perpetual Peace*, in Ishay, *The Human Rights Reader*, 104–110.

115. Rousseau, *Judgement on Perpetual Peace*, in Ishay, *The Human Rights Reader*, 110–114.

116. Quoted in Ishay, *Internationalism and Its Betrayal*, 59.

117. Kant, "The Metaphysics of Morals," in *Kant's Political Writings*, 174, or in Ishay, *The Human Rights Reader*, 172.

118. J. W. Thornton, *The Pulpit of the American Revolution*, 250.

119. The United States Declaration of Independence, in Ishay, *The Human Rights Reader*, 127.

120. Paine, "Address to the People of France," in *Complete Writings of Paine*, 540.

121. Robespierre, National Convention, February 15, 1794, in *Oeuvres*, vol. 3, 538–539 (my translation).

122. Robespierre, National Convention, December 25, 1793, in ibid. (my translation).

123. Kant, "The Contest of the Faculties," in *Kant's Political Writings*, 182.

124. Kant, *On the Old Saw: That May Be Right in Theory but It Won't Work in Practice*, 67.

125. Refers to Kant, *Perpetual Peace*, in *Kant's Political Writings*, 94–96.

126. Gerrard Winstanley, "A New Yeers Gift (1650)," in David Wooton, *"Divine Right and Democracy,"* 322; see also Winstanley, *Selections from His Works*.

127. Jefferson, "Letter to Madison," Fontainebleau (October 28, 1785), in *The Life and Selected Writings of Thomas Jefferson*, 389.

128. See Monroe Stearns, *Shay's Rebellion*.

129. Friedrich Engels, "The Book of Revelation," in Marx and Engels, *Collected Works*, vol. 26, 112–117. (Originally published in *Progress* 2, no. 2 [August 1883]: 113.)

130. Hill, *The World Turned Upside Down*, 306.

131. Ibid., 314.

132. Ibid., 308.

133. Carole Pateman, *The Sexual Contract,* 53.

134. Mary Astell, "Some Reflections upon Marriage," in Isaac Kramnick, *The Enlightenment Reader,* 563.

135. Paine, "An Occasional Letter to the Female Sex," 362.

136. Abigail Adams to John Adams (March 31, 1776), and John Adams to Abigail Adams (April 14, 1776), in Lyman Tower Sargent, *Political Thought in the United States,* 66–67.

137. Olympe de Gouge, The Declaration of the Rights of Woman (1790), in Ishay, *The Human Rights Reader,* 140–147; see also Marquis de Condorcet, "On the Admission of Women to the Rights of Citizenship" (July 1790), and Etta Palm d'Aelders, "Discourse on the Injustice of the Laws in Favor of Men, at the Expense of Women" (December 30, 1790), in Hunt, *The French Revolution and Human Rights,* 119–123.

138. Mary Wollstonecraft, *A Vindication of the Rights of Woman.*

139. Louis-Marie Prudhomme, "On the Influence of the Revolution on Women" (February 12, 1791), in Hunt, *The French Revolution and Human Rights,* 131.

140. Philippe Fabre d'Eglantine (National Convention, October 19, 1793), Jean Baptiste Amar (Committee of Public Safety, October 30, 1793), Pierre Chaumette (*Moniteur Universel,* November 19, 1793), in Hunt, *The French Revolution and Human Rights,* 135–139.

141. Soon after, Holland granted emancipation to its Jewish population. See Pierre Birnbaum and Ira Katznelson, *Paths of Emancipation,* 24.

142. Vern L. Bullough, *Homosexuality,* 45, and generally chap. 3.

143. Lefebvre, *The French Revolution,* vol. 1, 151.

144. "Motion Made by Vincent Ogé the Younger to the Assembly of Colonists, 1789," in Hunt, *The French Revolution and Human Rights,* 103–104.

145. "Speech of Barnave," March 8, 1790, in Hunt, *The French Revolution and Human Rights,* 109.

146. On April 6, 1793, a Committee of Public Security was created as a political police designed to protect the revolutionary republic from its internal and external enemies.

147. Paine, "African Slavery in America" (1775), in Ishay, *The Human Rights Reader,* 130–133.

148. See Jefferson, *Notes on Virginia* (1784), in *The Life and Selected Writings of Thomas Jefferson,* 210–213, 255; see also Eugene D. Genovese, *The Political Economy of Slavery.*

149. Robert Ferguson, "The American Enlightenment," in Sacvan Bercovitch and Cyrus R.K. Patell, *The Cambridge History of American Literature,* 496.

150. Prince de Broglie, "The Jewish Question," December 24, 1789, in Hunt, *The French Revolution and Human Rights,* 92.

151. La Fare, Bishop of Nancy, "Opinion on the Admissibility of Jews to Full Civil and Political Rights," spring 1790, in Hunt, *The French Revolution and Human Rights,* 97–98.

152. Admission of Jews to Rights of Citizenship, September 27, 1791, in Hunt, *The French Revolution and Human Rights,* 99.

153. Jacob Katz, *Out of the Ghetto*, 2; Birnbaum and Katznelson, *Paths of Emancipation*, 128; Pierre Pluchon, *Nègres et juifs au XVIIIe siècle*.

154. Some passages of the following section are drawn from Ishay, *Internationalism and Its Betrayal*, 78–82.

155. *The New Cambridge Modern History*, vol. 8, 711; or Palmer, *The World of the French Revolution*,

156. See A. J. Grant and Harold Temperley, *Europe in the Nineteenth and Twentieth Centuries*, 197.

CHAPTER 3

1. On this question, see Stephen Lukes, *Marxism and Morality*, 61–70, or his "Can a Marxist Believe in Human Rights?" in *Moral Conflict and Politics,*173–188; and Michel Foucault, "Two Lectures," 79–108, and "Truth and Power," 109–133, in *Power/Knowledge*. See also Claude Lefort, *L'invention démocratique*, 46.

2. Joel Colton and Robert Palmer, *History of the Modern World*, 464.

3. From about 1760 on, enclosure meant the transformation of formerly common or open fields into private property. Because of their control over parliament, landlords succeeded in accelerating the conversion of land. The result was a patchwork of individual ownership in which landlords employed wage workers. This enabled independent farmers, freed from old custom-based restrictions, to improve commercially cultivated lands.

4. See H. de B. Gibbens, *Industry in England*, 343–347.

5. See Eric Hobsbawm, *The Age of Revolutions*. For an interesting discussion of the impact of 1848, see Stephen Bronner, *Socialism Unbound*, 12–15.

6. William L. Langer, *Political and Social Upheaval*.

7. Norman Davies, *Europe*, 802.

8. Jay Kinsbruner, *Independence in Spanish America*; see also Michael Costeloe, *Response to Revolution*.

9. Davies, *Europe*, 803–804.

10. Colton and Palmer, *History of the Modern World*, 499.

11. The People's Charter was a bill drafted by the London radical William Lovett in May 1837. See Mark Hovell, *The Chartist Movement*.

12. For an interesting discussion of Chartism, see Gareth Stedman Jones, "Rethinking Chartism," in *Languages of Class*.

13. Georges Duveau, *The Making of a Revolution*, 33–44.

14. Colton and Palmer, *History of the Modern World*, 515.

15. Hobsbawm, *The Age of Revolutions*, 140.

16. Alice Bullard, "Paris 1871 / New Caledonia 1878: Human Rights and the Managerial State," in Lynn Hunt, Jeffrey Wasserstrom, and Marilyn B. Young, *Human Rights and Revolutions*, 79.

17. Henry David Thoreau, *On the Duty of Civil Disobedience*.

18. James M. McPherson, *Drawn with the Sword*; Brian Holden Reid, *The American Civil War and the Wars of the Industrial Revolution*; Marshall DeRosa, *The Politics of Dissolution*.

19. Alan Trachtenberg, *The Incorporation of America,* 75–76.

20. See Edmund Burke, *Reflections on the Revolutions in France,* 123; and Joseph de Maistre, *Etudes sur la souveraineté,* in *Oeuvres complètes,* vol. 1, chap. 10, 377.

21. See Davies, *Europe,* 795; Friedrich Schleiermacher, *Über die Religion reden;* Félicité Robert de Lamennais, *Paroles d'un croyant;* Johann J. Ignaz von Döllinger, *Der Papst und das Konzil;* and Søren Kierkegaard, *Fear and Trembling* and *The Concept of Dread.*

22. Johann Gottlieb Fichte, *Address to the German Nation;* and see G. W. F. Hegel, *The Philosophy of Right,* sec. 358, 222. See also Hegel, *Reason in History.*

23. Micheline Ishay, *Internationalism and Its Betrayal,* 80–82.

24. Claude Henri Saint-Simon, "The New Christianity," 116; Charles Fourier, *Théorie de l'universelle* (1838), in *Selections from the Works of Fourier,* 157.

25. Robert Owen, "Address to the Inhabitants of Lanark" (1816), in Albert Fried and Ronald Sanders, *Socialist Thought.*

26. Karl Marx, *The Eighteenth Brumaire of Louis Bonaparte,* 26.

27. Karl Marx and Friedrich Engels, *The German Ideology, Including the Theses of Feuerbach and the Introduction to the Critique of Political Economy,* 35.

28. Donald Kitchin, John Lewis, and Karl Polanyi, *Christianity and the Social Revolution;* Philip N. Backstrom, *Christian Socialism and Cooperation in Victorian England;* Peter d'Alroy Jones, *The Christian Socialist Revival;* James Dombrowski, *The Early Days of Christian Socialism in America.*

29. Marx, "On the Jewish Question," in *Selected Writings,* 39, or in Ishay, *The Human Rights Reader,* 189.

30. Marx, "On the Jewish Question," in *Selected Writings,* 41, or in Ishay, *The Human Rights Reader,* 192.

31. Marx, "On the Jewish Question," in *Selected Writings,* 43–45, or in Ishay, *The Human Rights Reader,* 197.

32. Hegel, *The Philosophy of Right,* addition to sec. 297, 291. Hegel also wrote: "Civil servants and the members of the executive constitute the greater part of the middle class, the class in which the consciousness of right and the developed intelligence of the mass of people is to be found" (sec. 297, 193).

33. Marx and Engels, *The German Ideology, Including the Theses of Feuerbach and the Introduction to the Critique of Political Economy,* 37.

34. Engels, "Herr Eugen Dühring's Revolution in Science," in Engels and Marx, *Basic Writings on Politics and Philosophy,* 270; or see Engels, *The Anti-Dühring,* in Ishay, *The Human Rights Reader,* 212.

35. Karl Vorländer, *Kant und Marx;* excerpt translated in Otto Bauer, "Marxismus und Ethik," in Tom Bottomore and Patrick Goode, *Austro-Marxism,* 78–84. See also Karl Kautsky, *Ethik und materialistische Geschichstauffassung,* 127–144; Max Horkheimer, *The Eclipse of Reason;* Alan Gilbert on moral objectivity in *Democratic Individuality;* and Shlomo Avineri, *The Social and Political Thought of Karl Marx.*

36. See Marx and Engels, "Alienation and Social Classes," excerpts from *The Holy Family,* in *The Marx-Engels Reader,* 105. More recently, the liberal philosopher John Rawls has entertained a similar position by calling on individuals, regardless of their class position, to envision social justice as if they were wearing

a "veil of ignorance" concealing their future status in society. See Rawls, *A Theory of Justice,* 118–123.

37. Engels, *The Anti-Dühring,* in Ishay, *The Human Rights Reader,* 213.

38. Gracchus Babeuf, *La doctrine des égaux.*

39. George Lichtheim, *The Origins of Socialism,* 17–18.

40. Charles Seymour and Donald Paige Frary, *How the World Votes,* 344.

41. Lichtheim, *The Origins of Socialism,* 29.

42. Moses Hess, "The Philosophy of the Act," 264; see also Lichtheim, *The Origins of Socialism,* 180.

43. Giuseppe Mazzini, *The Duties of Man,* in Micheline Ishay and Omar Dahbour, *The Nationalism Reader,* 89.

44. The famous phrase is from Charles Dickens, *A Tale of Two Cities,* 9; Dickens also evokes the horrors of British factory life during this period in his novel *Hard Times.*

45. In T. H. Marshall's words, "The Poor Law treated the claims of the poor not as an integral part of the rights of citizens, but as an alternative to them—as claims which could be met only if the claimants ceased to be citizens in any true sense of the word. For paupers forfeited in practice the civil right of personal liberty, by internment in the workhouse, and they forfeited by law any political rights they might possess." Marshall, *Class, Citizenship, and Social Development,* 88. See also Karl Polanyi, *The Great Transformation,* 77–102.

46. Polanyi, *The Great Transformation,* 80.

47. Chartist Petition agreed to at the Crown and Anchor Tavern Meeting in London, February 28, 1837; in Dorothy Thompson, *The Early Chartists,* 62.

48. Pierre-Joseph Proudhon, *What Is Property?* vol. 1, 48, or in Ishay, *The Human Rights Reader,* 179.

49. Marx, "On the Jewish Question," in *Selected Writings,* 54, or in Ishay, *The Human Rights Reader,* 196.

50. Seymour and Frary, *How the World Votes,* 351.

51. Ibid., 354–355.

52. Louis Blanc, *L'organisation du travail;* translated in Fried and Sanders, *Socialist Thought,* 235.

53. Blanc, *Organization of Work,* 46.

54. Fourier, "Attractive Labour," in *Selections from the Work of Fourier,* 163–170.

55. Marx, "The Class Struggles in France, 1848–1850," in *Karl Marx on Revolution,* 181; for an interesting discussion of Marx and Engels's position on universal suffrage and of Marx's politics in general, see Alan Gilbert, *Marx's Politics,* 335–338.

56. Marx, "Universal Suffrage," in *Selected Writings,* or in Ishay, *The Human Rights Reader,* 201.

57. Seymour and Frary, *How the World Votes,* 133.

58. John Stuart Mill, *Considerations on Representative Government,* in *"On Liberty" and Other Essays,* 330.

59. Seymour and Frary, *How the World Votes,* 141–144; see also George Kent, *Memoirs and Letters of Chancellor Kent.*

60. Marshall, *Class, Citizenship, and Social Development,* 85–86.

61. George Henry Evans, "The Working Men's Declaration of Independence," December 1829, in Philip S. Foner, *We, the Other People,* 48.

62. Seymour and Frary, *How the World Votes,* 234–235.

63. William Wells Brown, *The Negro in the American Rebellion,* 360.

64. Quoted in Stetson Kennedy, *Jim Crow Guide to the U.S.A.,* 150; see also Donald G. Nieman, *Promises to Keep.*

65. Adam Przeworski and John Sprague, *Paper Stones,* 36.

66. Ibid., 50.

67. See Marx, *Capital,* vol. 1, 523–526, 613–614, 628–629; Marx and Engels, *The German Ideology,* vol. 1, pt. 1; Marx, *Critique of the Gotha Programme,* sec. 3, 22, or in Ishay, *The Human Rights Reader,* 210–211; Engels, *Principles of Communism,* in Marx and Engels, *Collected Works,* vol. 6, 351.

68. Marx, "Instruction to the Delegates to the Geneva Congress," in *The First International and After,* 88–89.

69. Marshall, *Class, Citizenship, and Social Development,* 89.

70. Marx, "Instruction to the Delegates to the Geneva Congress," in *The First International and After,* 89.

71. Quoted in Marshall, *Class, Citizenship, and Social Development,* 89.

72. Immanuel Kant, "Idea for a Universal History," in *Kant's Political Writings,* 50.

73. Thomas Paine, in *The Essential Thomas Paine,* 267.

74. Proudhon, *What Is Property?* vol. 2, 272, or in Ishay, *The Human Rights Reader,* 183.

75. Mikhail Bakunin, speech to the International Workingmen's Association at the Basel Congress of 1869, in *From out of the Dustbin,* 140.

76. See Bakunin, "Organization and General Strike," in *From out of the Dustbin,* 149–150.

77. Marx, "Class Struggle in France," in Marx and Engels, *Collected Works,* vol. 10, 80–81; and Antonio Gramsci, *Selections from the Prison Notebooks of Antonio Gramsci,* 219–223.

78. Engels, *The Origin of the Family, Private Property, and the State,* 157.

79. Marx and Engels, "Manifesto of the Communist Party," in *Collected Works,* vol. 6, 493, or in Ishay, *The Human Rights Reader,* 325.

80. Marx, "The Class Struggles in France 1848–1850," in Marx and Engels, *Collected Works,* vol. 10, 203, or in Ishay, *The Human Rights Reader,* 326.

81. Marx, "Speech at the Hague Congress" (September 8, 1872), in Marx and Engels, *Collected Works,* vol. 20, or in Ishay, *The Human Rights Reader,* 327.

82. Marx, *Civil War in France,* in Marx and Engels, *Collected Works,* vol. 22, 331, 333 (italics added); and Kautsky, *The Dictatorship of the Proletariat,* in *Selected Political Writings,* 115, or in Ishay, *The Human Rights Reader,* 336.

83. In German: "Der Staat ist es welcher die Funktion hat, diese Entwicklung der Freiheit, diese Entwicklung des Menschengeschlechtes zur Freiheit zu vollbringen." Ferdinand Lassalle, *Arbeiterprogramm,* 43.

84. Eduard Bernstein, *Evolutionary Socialism;* and Kautsky, "Dictatorship and Democracy" and "The Transition to Capitalism," in *Selected Political Writings.*

85. Sidney Webb, "English Progress toward Social Democracy," 3, 9. The Fabians founded a socialist society in London in 1883, its goal being the estab-

lishment of a democratic socialist state in Great Britain. Leaders included George Bernard Shaw, Sidney Webb, Annie Besant, Edward Pease, and Graham Wallas. Shaw and Webb, later joined by Webb's wife, Beatrice, were for many years the most influential leaders of the society.

86. Ibid., 3.

87. Jean Jaurès, *Idealism in History,* 410.

88. Marx and Engels, "Manifesto of the Communist Party," in *Collected Works,* vol. 6, 488.

89. For an interesting account of the Internationals, see Julius Braunthal, *The History of the International.*

90. See James Joll, "The Struggle with Anarchists" (chap. 2) and "Reformists and Revolutionaries" (chap. 3) in *The Second International, 1889–1914.*

91. Kautsky, quoted in Braunthal, *The History of the International,* vol. 1, 272–273.

92. Kant, *Perpetual Peace,* in *Kant's Political Writings,* 94, 95, 96.

93. Henri Dunant, *Un souvenir de Solferino,* published in English as *Memory of Solferino.*

94. See appendix D, "The International Peace Conference at the Hague," in George B. Davis, *The Elements of International Law.*

95. Paul Gordon Lauren, *The Evolution of International Human Rights,* 60–61.

96. Jean-Jacques Rousseau, *L'état de guerre,* in *The Political Writings of Jean-Jacques Rousseau,* 300; see also Robert Derathé, *Jean-Jacques Rousseau et la science politique de son temps,* 134; see also Rosa Luxemburg, "The Militia and Militarism," in *Selected Writings,* 76–92; and Karl Liebknecht, *Militarism and Anti-Militarism.*

97. Braunthal, *The History of the International,* vol. 1, 321.

98. Minutes of the General Council, June 19 and 26 and July 3, 10, and 17, 1866, noted in ibid., vol. 1, 321.

99. Ibid.

100. Ibid., vol. 1, 328.

101. Marx, "Letter to Abraham Lincoln, President of the United States of America" (1864), in Marx and Engels, *Collected Works,* vol. 20, 19–20.

102. George Bernard Shaw, *Fabianism and the Empire,* 22–38.

103. John Stuart Mill, *Considerations on Representative Government,* in *Three Essays,* 380–388, 401–404, 408–412, or in Ishay and Dahbour, *The Nationalism Reader,* 98–107; Braunthal, *The History of the International,* vol. 1, 308; Bernstein, *Die Voraussetzungen des Sozialismus* (1899), translated as *The Preconditions of Socialism.* See also Manfred Steger, *The Quest for Evolutionary Socialism;* for a critique of Bernstein's position, see Kautsky, *Socialism and Colonial Policy,* 12–17.

104. Braunthal, *The History of the International,* vol. 1, 308.

105. Amsterdam's Resolution, quoted in ibid., vol. 1, 319.

106. "The Stuttgart Resolution on Militarism and the International Conflicts," in Braunthal's appendix, *The History of the International,* vol. 1, 363.

107. Gérard M. Laurent, *Coup d'oeil sur la politique de Toussaint-Louverture.*

108. Arthur de Gobineau, *The Inequality of the Human Races,* 25.

109. G. W. F. Hegel, *Philosophy of Mind,* sec. 393, 42.

110. See Charles Darwin, *The Descent of Man,* chap. 7; Francis Galton, *Hereditary Genius.* For a very insightful discussion on racism and science see Stephen Gould, *The Mismeasure of Man.*

111. See also Thomas Clarkson, *The History of the Rise, Progress, and Accomplishment of the Abolition of the Slave Trade.*

112. Quoted in William Law Mathieson, *British Slavery and Its Abolition, 1823–1838,* 51.

113. Ibid., 55.

114. Gary Y. Okihiro, *In Resistance.*

115. William Lloyd Garrison, "Exciting the Minds of the People," in Louis Giller, *Abolition and Social Justice,* 106.

116. *The Complete Poetical Works of John Greenleaf Whittier;* James Russell Lowell, "The Bigelow Papers," in his *Complete Poetical Works;* and Lydia Maria Child, *Freedmen's Book;* and from the free-black community, Frederick Douglass, *Selected Speeches and Writings;* and William Wells Brown, *The Black Man.*

117. See James Long, *Russian Serf Emancipation;* for a discussion on the possible reasons for the abolition of serfdom, see Peter Kolchin, "After Serfdom: Russian Emancipation in Comparative Perspective," in Stanley L. Engerman, *Terms of Labor,* 88–89.

118. United Kingdom Foreign and Commonwealth Office, "Déclaration des huit cours relative à l'abolition universelle de la traîte des nègres," 971–972; see also Paul Gordon Lauren, *The Evolution of International Human Rights,* 40–41.

119. Lauren, *The Evolution of International Human Rights,* 41.

120. Later to become the Anti-Slavery International for the Protection of Human Rights, one of the first human rights NGOs.

121. The General Conference of Berlin, February 6, 1885, in Arthur B. Keith, *The Belgian Congo and the Berlin Act,* 305.

122. Adam Smith, *The Wealth of Nations,* 413.

123. Ibid.

124. For more details on the economic justification of the British and American anti-slavery movements, see Engerman, *Terms of Labor,* 59–86.

125. Marx, *Capital,* vol. 1, 1033.

126. Barbara Wolfe Jancar, *Women under Communism,* 74; Sheila Rowbotham, *Hidden from History.*

127. Clara Zetkin, "Nur mit der proletarischen Frau wird der Sozialismus siegen!" vol. 1, 3–11; translated by Hal Draper and Anne Lipow in Ralph Miliband and John Saville, *Socialist Register,* 193.

128. Priscilla Murolo, *The Common Ground of Womanhood,* 53.

129. Zetkin, "Proletarian Women and Socialist Revolution," in Miliband and Saville, *Socialist Register,* 194.

130. Ivy Pinchbeck, *Women Workers and the Industrial Revolution,* 240–281.

131. Zetkin, "Proletarian Women and Socialist Revolution," in Miliband and Saville, *Socialist Register,* 196; see also Lise Vogel, *Marxism and the Oppression of Women,* 110.

132. August Bebel, *Women and Socialism,* 4, or, as translated here, see Ishay,

The Human Rights Reader, 228; on women's emancipation see also Engels, *The Origin of the Family, Private Property, and the State,* 148, 158; for an account of the Marxist view of women, see Vogel, *Marxism and the Oppression of Women.*

133. Engels, *The Origin of the Family, Private Property, and the State,* 72, or in Ishay, *The Human Rights Reader,* 224.

134. Janet Saltzman Chafetz and Anthony Gary Dworkin, *Female Revolt,* 119–121.

135. Ibid., 114; see also Andrew Sinclair, *The Emancipation of the American Woman.*

136. See Ellen Carol Dubois, *Woman Suffrage and Women's Rights,* 266–267.

137. Ibid., 269.

138. Lettres de Colbert III: ii 395—Proclamations of 1669, quoted in Eli F. Hecksher, *Mercantilism,* vol. 2, 155–156.

139. The 1802 preamble ran as follows: "Whereas it hath of late become a practice in cotton and woollen mills, and in cotton and woollen factories, to employ a great number of male and female apprentices, and other persons, in the same building, in consequence of which certain regulations are now necessary to preserve the health and morals of such apprentices." Richard Whately Cooke-Taylor, *The Modern Factory System,* or see http://www.spartacus.schoolnet.co.uk/IR1802.htm.

140. Robert D. Owen, *An Outline of the System of Education at New Lanark;* see also Eileen Yeo, "Robert Owen's Reputation as an Educationist," 65–84.

141. Colton and Palmer, *History of the Modern World,* 503.

142. Walter I. Trattner, *Crusade for the Children,* 29, note 18.

143. Ibid., 30–33.

144. Industriels de la Champagne (1835), quoted in Edouard Ducpétiaux, *De la condition physique et morale des jeunes ouvriers,* vol. 1, 29, and cited in Lee Shai Weissbach, *Child Labor Reform in Nineteenth-Century France,* 11.

145. Weissbach, *Child Labor Reform in Nineteenth-Century France,* 66.

146. For an interesting discussion on this issue (and generally for a very good book on the history of homosexuality), see David F. Greenberg, *The Construction of Homosexuality,* 383–396.

147. Ibid., 347–396.

148. Ibid., 387–388.

149. Oscar Wilde, *The Soul of Man under Socialism;* Walt Whitman, the *Calamus* section of *Leaves of Grass* and *Democratic Vistas,* in *The Portable Walt Whitman;* Edward Carpenter, *The Intermediate Sex;* André Gide, *L'immoraliste* and *Corydon.*

150. Vern Bullough, *Homosexuality,* 37–38.

151. Jacob Katz, *Out of the Ghetto,* 195–197.

152. For a very interesting account of the forgery of these documents and the context in which they spread, see Stephen Bronner, *A Rumor about the Jews.*

153. Paul Johnson, *A History of the Jews,* 365.

154. Michael Stanislawski, "Russian Jewry and Jewish Emancipation," in Pierre Birnbaum and Ira Katznelson, *Paths of Emancipation,* 281. The fate of Jewish emancipation under the Bolshevik regime is a complicated issue that is beyond the scope of this book. See also Johnson, *A History of the Jews,* 359.

155. The Sephardim were Jews of Hispanic origin who, after the Spanish Inquisition in the fifteenth century, resided around the Mediterranean Sea, in southern Europe, North Africa, and the Arab world.

156. Dan V. Segre, "The Emancipation of Jews in Italy," in Birnbaum and Katznelson, *Paths of Emancipation*, 224–225.

157. Aron Rodrigue, "From Millet to Minority: Turkish Jewry," in Birnbaum and Katznelson, *Paths of Emancipation*, 239, 242.

158. Johnson, *A History of the Jews*, 380.

159. "J'accuse" was published in *Aurore*, January 13, 1898.

160. See Theodore Herzl, *A Jewish State*.

161. For a fascinating account of Zionism, see Shlomo Avineri, *The Making of Modern Zionism*, 10–11.

162. Luxemburg, "The Junius Pamphlet," in *Rosa Luxemburg Speaks*, 326–327.

CHAPTER 4

1. The concept of third-generation rights is often associated with group rights, which are perceived as distinct from individual rights (or first-generation rights). Ironically, group rights have been also defended by liberals like Mazzini and Wilson, and for different reasons by socialists like Lenin.

2. See both Max Weber, "Economic Policy and the National Interest in Germany," and Leopold Ranke, "The Great Powers," in Micheline Ishay and Omar Dahbour, *The Nationalism Reader*, 119–129, 156–159; see also Norman Davies, *Europe*, 824–826; W. G. Beasley, *The Rise of Modern Japan*, 84–96. For an explanation on the way the absence of a peasant revolution shaped modern Japan, see Barrington Moore, *Social Origins of Dictatorship*, 254–275.

3. Joel Colton and Robert Palmer, *History of the Modern World*, 599, 703; Sidney Giffard, *Japan among the Powers*, 24–44.

4. Parts of this section are drawn from Micheline Ishay and David Goldfischer, "Human Rights and Security," 129–139 (also in Ishay, *The Human Rights Reader*, 377–402).

5. Friedrich Nietzsche, *"The Birth of Tragedy" and "Genealogy of Morals,"* 298.

6. Theodore H. von Laue, "Soviet Diplomacy: G. V. Chicherin, People's Commissar for Foreign Affairs, 1918–1930," in Gordon Craig and Felix Gilbert, *The Diplomats*, vol. 1, 235; also quoted in Kenneth Waltz, *Theory of International Politics*, 128.

7. Woodrow Wilson, "An Address at Guildhall," December 28, 1918, in *The Papers of Woodrow Wilson*, vol. 53, 532.

8. Wilson, "Address to Senate, January 22, 1917," in *The Papers of Woodrow Wilson*, vol. 40, 536.

9. Franklin D. Roosevelt, "Address to Congress, March 1, 1945," in *The Public Papers and Addresses of Franklin D. Roosevelt*, vol. 13, 570.

10. In the French elections of October 1945, the Communists ranked first, receiving the highest percentage of the vote ever won by a single party in French history. In Italy, a coalition between the communist and socialist parties became

the dominant force in the Italian government. See Louis J. Halle, *The Cold War as History,* 87–88, 139–140.

11. Ibid., 73.

12. Quoted in William Roger Louis, *Imperialism at Bay,* 121. Cited in Kissinger, *Diplomacy,* 401.

13. In this regard, Fouad Ajami has written that "Zaïrean President Mobutu Sese Seko's cult of the bush and of the ancestors, Pakistani President Zia ul-Haq's Islam, Anwar Sadat's cult of ancient Egypt, Ayatollah Khomeini's Islamic Republic and countless others all have a common message: imported ideologies and standards have alienated societies from themselves. Somewhere in the past, there was a social order that worked, and it could conceivably be recovered." Ajami, "The Third World Challenge," 379. See also Kanan Makiya, *Cruelty and Silence,* 278–283.

14. Of course, both superpowers produced arguments that sought to reconcile support for regimes that trampled on the values each espoused with the long-term promotion of those very values. In the United States, the leading example was Jeane Kirkpatrick's "Dictatorships and Double Standards," which argued that there was no liberal middle ground between rightist dictatorships (which supported the United States) and leftist totalitarian regimes (which would promote Soviet geostrategic ambitions). Moreover, authoritarian regimes might, over a long period of domestic political development, yield to the gradual establishment of the preconditions for liberal democracy. The oppression of Soviet-backed regimes, by contrast, would last forever. The Soviets also found arguments to justify support for non-socialist dictatorships. Here, the debate centered on the historical stages of development toward socialism, in which Third World "bourgeois nationalism" could be regarded as a necessary step. See Jerry Hough, *The Struggle for the Third World,* 120–121, 142–183 (especially 149–156).

15. Thus, the United States could support showcases for liberal democracy in places like Costa Rica (which could also be used as a base for countering leftist movements elsewhere in Central America). Under the Carter administration, promotion of liberal rights sometimes challenged realpolitik concerns, as continuing support for "friendly" dictators was intermingled, at least sporadically, with calls to ease domestic repression (e.g., in Iran under the Shah, in Somoza's Nicaragua, and in Pinochet's Chile). For the Soviets, Cuba and Vietnam exemplified cases where serious efforts to build socialism domestically coincided with Soviet geostrategic ambitions. As with human rights during the Carter administration, Soviet leaders were also sometimes willing to risk foreign policy setbacks by supporting socialist challenges to Third World regimes they were courting diplomatically. Thus, Hough writes, "In areas such as the Middle East, continuing Soviet support for local communists and radical reforms seriously interfered with the promotion of governmental interests" (*The Struggle for the Third World,* 150).

16. Davies, *Europe,* 828.

17. Karl Marx and Friedrich Engels, "Manifesto of the Communist Party," in Marx and Engels, *The Marx-Engels Reader,* 488.

18. See Marx's discussion on Ireland, Marx to Engels, November 2, 1867, in Marx, *The First International and After,* 117–120, 158–171: "I used to regard

Ireland's separation from England as impossible, I now think it is inevitable, although federation may follow separation" (158). Marx's later position contrasted sharply with his view of British colonialism in India, which he believed beneficial for Indians insofar as it would destroy their feudal and absolutist vestiges and create a fertile soil for capitalist development and later working class solidarity. For Marx's views on India, see David Fernbach, ed, *Surveys from Exile*, 301–324.

19. Otto Bauer, quoted by Lenin in *"Critical Remarks on the National Question" and "The Right of Nations to Self-Determination,"* 116.

20. Bauer, *The Question of Nationalities and Social Democracy,* 117–118, or in Ishay and Dahbour, *The Nationalism Reader,* 184.

21. Ishay and Dahbour, *The Nationalism Reader,* 186. See also Bauer, *The Question of Nationalities and Social Democracy,* 157–258.

22. Michael Forman, *Nationalism and the International Labor Movement,* 107–108.

23. Bauer, *The Question of Nationalities and Social Democracy,* 410, or in Ishay and Dahbour, *The Nationalism Reader,* 189.

24. Rosa Luxemburg, *The National Question and Autonomy* (originally published in 1909), in Ishay, *The Human Rights Reader,* 292.

25. Ibid., 296.

26. Ibid., 291, 293.

27. Ibid., 292.

28. Ibid.

29. Lenin, *"Critical Remarks on the National Question" and "The Right of Nations to Self-Determination,"* 43, or in Ishay and Dahbour, *The Nationalism Reader,* 209.

30. Lenin, *"Critical Remarks on the National Question" and "The Right of Nations to Self-Determination,"* 66, or in Ishay and Dahbour, *The Nationalism Reader,* 212.

31. Lenin, *On the National Liberation Movement,* 56.

32. Michael Löwy, "Marxism and the National Question," 81–100.

33. Joseph Stalin, *Marxism and the National-Colonial Question,* 22, or in Ishay and Dahbour, *The Nationalism Reader,* 192.

34. Stalin, *Marxism and the National-Colonial Question,* 57, or in Ishay and Dahbour, *The Nationalism Reader,* 194, 195, 196.

35. Stalin, *Marxism and the National-Colonial Question,* 122–135.

36. Wilson, "The Fourteen Points Address" (1918), in Ishay, *The Human Rights Reader,* 303–304.

37. Jean Lacouture, *Ho Chi Minh,* 24–25.

38. The Covenant of the League of Nations (1919), in Ishay, *The Human Rights Reader,* 305.

39. The Polish Minority Treaty (1919), in Ishay, *The Human Rights Reader,* 309–310.

40. Benito Mussolini, *Fascism,* in Ishay and Dahbour, *The Nationalism Reader,* 226.

41. Cited in Patrick Thornberry, *International Law and the Rights of Minorities.* For a discussion of these problems, see also Henry Kissinger, *Diplomacy,* 239–241.

42. Mahatma Gandhi, "Appeal to the Nation" (July 17, 1924), in Ishay, *The Human Rights Reader*, 352.

43. Jawaharlal Nehru, *The Discovery of India*, 384–387, 391–395, and 543–546, or in Ishay and Dahbour, *The Nationalism Reader*, 253.

44. Ruth Leger Sivard, *World Military and Social Expenditures 1993*, cited in Yahya Sadowski, *The Myth of Global Chaos*, 137.

45. Ho Chi Minh, "Declaration of Independence of the Democratic Republic of Vietnam" (September 2, 1945), in his *On Revolution*, 143–144; Harry Piotrowski and Wayne C. McWilliams, *The World since 1945*, 112, 116.

46. There is a voluminous literature on this war. For a succinct account, see Stephen E. Ambrose and Douglas G. Brinkley, *Rise to Globalism*, 134–141, 190–206.

47. Herbert R. Lottman, *Albert Camus*, 214; see also Stephen Bronner, *Camus*.

48. Piotrowski and McWilliams, *The World since 1945*, 121–138.

49. Leopold Sédar Senghor, *On African Socialism*, 80.

50. Frantz Fanon, "The Wretched of the Earth," in Ishay, *The Human Rights Reader*, 316.

51. See Steve Roach, "The Question of Cultural Autonomy."

52. Richard Stites, "The Russian Empire and the Soviet Union, 1900–1945," in Michael Howard and William Roger Louis, *The Oxford History of the Twentieth Century*, 118.

53. Sheila Fitzpatrick, *The Russian Revolution*, 42–43.

54. See also comments on the 1918 document in E. H. Carr, *The Rights of Man*, in Jacques Maritain, *Human Rights*, 20.

55. Lenin, "What Is to Be Done?" in *The Lenin Anthology*, 50.

56. Lenin, "The State and Revolution," in *Lenin's Selected Works*, 325.

57. For a good comparative discussion of the French terror and the Bolshevik terror, see Arno J. Meyer, *The Furies*.

58. Karl Kautsky, *Selected Political Writings*, 141.

59. Luxemburg, "The Russian Revolution," in *Rosa Luxemburg Speaks*, 387, 389.

60. Kautsky, *Selected Political Writings*, 138.

61. Ibid., 147.

62. Leon Trotsky, "Their Morals and Ours," in Ishay, *The Human Rights Reader*, 338.

63. Ibid., 341.

64. Ibid., 342.

65. Luxemburg, "The Old Mole" (*Spartacus*, no. 5, May 1917), in *Selected Writings*, 233–234.

66. Lenin, "Report on War and Peace," in *The Lenin Anthology*, 545.

67. Luxemburg, "The Russian Tragedy" (*Spartacus*, no. 11, September 1918), in *Selected Writings*, 235–236.

68. Leonard S. Woolf and the Fabian Society, *International Government*.

69. Braunthal, *The History of the International*, vol. 2, 154.

70. American Association for the United Nations, Educational Committee, *A Brief History of the League*, 13–32.

71. The Covenant of the League of Nations, in Ishay, *The Human Rights Reader,* 304.

72. Quoted in Braunthal, *The History of the International,* vol. 2, 160.

73. For an important contribution on this connection, see Bruce D. Porter, *War and the Rise of the State,* 159.

74. Ibid., 165–166.

75. Ibid., 168.

76. Ibid., 181–182, 186.

77. Robert Schuman, quoted in Halle, *The Cold War as History,* 249. Schuman was French foreign minister when he made this proposal, which led to the creation of the European Coal and Steel Community.

78. Jean Monnet, *Memoirs,* 221.

79. Franklin Roosevelt, "The Four Freedoms" (1941), in Ishay, *The Human Rights Reader,* 403–406.

80. Franklin Roosevelt, "Address to Congress, March 1, 1945," in *The Public Papers and Addresses of Franklin D. Roosevelt,* vol. 13, 570.

81. See *The United Nations Conference on International Organization Journal,* San Francisco, April 25, 1945.

82. See Paul Gordon Lauren, *The Evolution of International Human Rights,* 188.

83. William Korey, *NGOs and the Universal Declaration of Human Rights,* 36, 38.

84. The Trusteeship Council, whose main function was to supervise non-strategic trust for the General Assembly and strategic trust for the Security Council, was endowed with only recommendation powers.

85. Roger W. Smith, Eric Markusen, and Robert Jay Lifton, *Professional Ethics and the Denial of the Armenian Genocide,* in Richard G. Hovannisian, *Remembrance and Denial,* 271–296; Hovannisian, *The Armenian Genocide.* See also G. S. Graber, *Caravans to Oblivion.*

86. Iris Chang, *The Rape of Nanking.*

87. Michael R. Marcus, *The Nuremberg War Crimes Trial.*

88. Korey, *NGOs and the Universal Declaration of Human Rights,* 205, 209.

89. Eleanor D. Roosevelt, "Statements by E. Roosevelt," *Department of State Bulletin,* December 19, 1948, 867.

90. Habib C. Malik, *The Challenge of Human Rights,* 117.

91. Eleanor Roosevelt, "The Promise of Human Rights," *Foreign Affairs,* April 1948, in *Courage in a Dangerous World,* 157.

92. For the UNESCO symposium, see Maritain, *Human Rights;* see also Mary Ann Glendon, *A World Made New,* chap. 5.

93. Maritain, *Human Rights,* 259, 260.

94. Human Rights Commission, First Session, Summary Records (E/CN.4/SR.8, 4), quoted in Glendon, *A World Made New,* 39.

95. Verbatim record, in Malik, *The Challenge of Human Rights,* 27.

96. Glendon, *A World Made New,* 116.

97. Ibid., 36.

98. Human Rights Commission, Third Session, Summary Records (E/CN.4/132), quoted in Glendon, *A World Made New,* 116.

99. Franklin Roosevelt, "The Four Freedoms," in Ishay, *The Human Rights Reader*, 403–406.

100. There is continuing debate over who was the main drafter of the Universal Declaration of Human Rights. Was it John Humphrey or René Cassin? This author was persuaded by the evidence provided by Marc Agi, who has argued that Cassin filled that role. See Marc Agi, *René Cassin*, 229–266.

101. As explained in the introduction and in chapter 3, articles related to political rights belong in the second generation of rights. For a useful account of the history of the declaration, see Johannes Morsink, *The Universal Declaration of Human Rights*.

102. The USSR also disliked three specific rights: freedom of movement and the right to asylum and to a nationality.

103. Eleanor Roosevelt, "Statement on Draft Covenant on Human Rights," in *Courage in a Dangerous World*, 168.

104. Ibid., 164.

105. For a well-documented book on NGOs and the early days of the UN, see Korey, *NGOs and the Universal Declaration of Human Rights*.

106. Jack C. Plano and Robert E. Riggs, *The United Nations*, 127.

107. The following section contains passages from Ishay and Goldfischer, "Human Rights and Security," in Ishay, *The Human Rights Reader*, 395–398.

108. A. G. Mileikovskii, *International Relations after the Second World War*, 259. Quoted by Adam Ulam, *Expansion and Coexistence*, 436.

109. State Department Policy Planning Staff Document PPS23, February 1948. Quoted by Noam Chomsky, "Intervention in Vietnam and Central America: Parallels and Differences" (1985), in James Peck, *The Chomsky Reader*, 318.

110. For a description of covert CIA involvement in Italy in 1947–1948, see Rhodri Jeffreys-Jones, *The CIA and American Democracy*, 50–52.

111. For a recent account of U.S. suppression of democracy in Japan, South Korea, and elsewhere, see Chalmers Johnson, *Blowback*.

112. Eric Hobsbawm, *The Age of Extremes*, 212.

113. Ibid., 215.

114. Lenin, *The Emancipation of Women*, 69; see also Peter H. Juviler, "Women and Sex in Soviet Law," 244–245; Lise Vogel, *Marxism and the Oppression of Women*, 122.

115. Kate Millett, *Sexual Politics*, 172.

116. Memorandum from the German Ministry of Labor to the German minister of foreign affairs on international labor legislation at the peace conference (December 28, 1918), in James Thompson Shotwell, *The Origins of the International Labor Organization*, vol. 1, 112–113.

117. Francis Graham Wilson, *Labor in the League System*, 172–174.

118. Paula Siber, "The Women's Issue and Its National Socialist Solution," reprinted in Walter Gehl, *Der Nationalsozialistischer Staat*, 127–130.

119. Amy Hackett, "The German Woman's Suffrage, 1890–1914: A Study of National Feminism," in Robert J. Bezucha, *Modern European Social History*, 371; see also George L. Mosse, *Nationalism and Sexuality*, 111.

120. Eleanor Roosevelt, "UN Deliberations on Draft Convention on the Po-

litical Rights of Women," *Department of State Bulletin,* December 31, 1951, in *Courage in a Dangerous World,* 180.

121. A. Goikhbarg, cited in Bernice Q. Madison, *Social Welfare in the Soviet Union,* 36; Judith Harwin, *Children of the Russian State,* 4–5; Ester Conus, *Protection of Motherhood and Childhood in the Soviet Union,* 39–40.

122. Harwin, *Children of the Russian State,* 13.

123. Eileen Heyes, *Children of the Swastika,* 57.

124. Herbert W. Schneider and Shepard B. Clough, *Making Fascists,* 84; Wilhelm Ronald, "España Nuestra."

125. Sharon Detrick, *A Commentary on the United Nations Convention on the Rights of the Child,* 15.

126. Neil Miller, *Out of the Past,* 112.

127. Dr. von Baktis, *Die Sexual Revolution in Russland,* 22; see also Barry Adam, *The Rise of a Gay and Lesbian Movement,* 50.

128. Robert Conquest, *The Great Terror;* Miller, *Out of the Past,* 205, 207.

129. Herbert Marcuse, *Soviet Marxism.*

130. Miller, *Out of the Past,* 265.

131. Per Kleis, "Homosexual Retrospect," cited in Adam, *The Rise of a Gay and Lesbian Movement,* 65.

132. Miller, *Out of the Past,* 292.

133. See Jeffrey Weeks, *Coming Out.*

134. See Dennis Altman, *Homosexual.*

135. See Houston Steward Chamberlain, *The Foundations of the Nineteenth Century;* see also Pierre Birnbaum and Ira Katznelson, *Paths of Emancipation,* 7.

136. Thomas D. Musgrave, *Self-Determination and National Minorities,* 42.

137. Paul Mendes-Flohr and Jehuda Reinharz, *The Jew in the Modern World,* 349.

138. Michael Stanislawski, "Russian Jewry and Jewish Emancipation," in Birnbaum and Katznelson, *Paths of Emancipation,* 283.

139. Ishay, *The Human Rights Reader,* 421.

140. Cited in Musgrave, *Self-Determination and National Minorities,* 131.

141. Ishay, *The Human Rights Reader,* 432, 453.

CHAPTER 5

1. Charles Krauthammer, "The Unipolar Moment." See also Samuel Huntington, "Why International Primacy Matters," 68–83; Joseph S. Nye, Jr., *Bound to Lead;* Joseph Joffee, "Entangled Forever"; Joshua Muravchick, "At Last, Pax Americana."

2. Francis Fukuyama, "The End of History?" 3–18.

3. Thomas Friedman and Ignacio Ramonet, "Dueling Globalizations." Others, including Peter Martin and Martin Wolf, have also celebrated the moral and economic benefits of globalization (Martin, "The Moral Case for Globalization," and Wolf, "Why This Hatred of the Market?").

4. Friedman and Ramonet, "Dueling Globalizations," 118, 125. Others, like Benjamin Barber, also see justice and democracy succumbing to the formation of an ever more arrogant consumer society (see Barber, *Jihad vs. McWorld*). What

characterizes the new globalized era, deplore Antonio Negri and Michael Hardt, is its capacity to cloak under the rhetoric of universality and human rights its ever more controlling policing apparatus, which is used to repress or co-opt protest movements. See Hardt and Negri, *Empire*.

5. Eric Hobsbawm, *The Age of Extremes*, 447.

6. Stephen Bronner, *Ideas in Action*, 226.

7. An exception occurred in the early 1980s, during the last round of the cold war, when there were widespread European protests against the planned U.S. deployment of intermediate-range nuclear forces coupled with a mass nuclear freeze movement in the United States.

8. George Black and Robin Munro, *Black Hands of Beijing*, 221.

9. Lee Fiagon, *China Rising*, 239–241.

10. Boris Kagarlitsky, "The Road to Consumption," 54.

11. Desmond Dinan, *Ever Closer Union*, 423–429; see also Anthony Forster, *Britain and the Maastricht Negotiations*, 128.

12. Harry Cleaver, "Zapatistas and the Electronic Fabric of the Struggle," in John Holloway and Eloína Peláez, *Zapatista*.

13. See Manfred Steger, *Globalism*, chap. 5.

14. Agence France-Presse, "Argentine Union Calls for Strike to Protest IMF Austerity Plan." Organizers estimated 80,000 protesters, whereas Reuters reported around 20,000 workers.

15. Luis Alfredo Martinez, "Honduras—Protest Unrest Increasing in Honduras, despite President's Popularity"; Global News Wire and Global Organizations, "Public Protests around the World."

16. Cited by John Kifner, "The World through the Serbian Mind's Eye"; also cited in Barber, *Jihad vs. McWorld*, 195.

17. Frank Lechner, "Global Fundamentalism," in William H. Swatos, *A Future for Religion?* 27–37; see also JoAnn Chirico and Roland Robertson, "Humanity, Globalization and Worldwide Religious Resurgence." Here, one should note that free-marketers have often argued that fundamentalism in Afghanistan and Sudan was rooted precisely in areas in which economic integration and secular cultural penetration have not made significant inroads.

18. Pat Regnier, "Changing Their Tune," 78.

19. Immanuel Wallerstein has suggested that globalization represents an intensification of the contradictions of capitalism (an extension of Lenin's imperialist thesis). By contrast, Alvin Toffler, among others, perceives a revolutionary break from old social and economic patterns as unique as those of the agricultural and industrial ages. The theoretical debate over globalization's place in the evolution of world capitalism, while important, is beyond the scope of this book. (Immanuel Wallerstein, "The Rise and Future Demise of the World Capitalist System"; Alvin Toffler, *The Third Wave*.)

20. David Held et al., *Global Transformations*, 201; see also John G. Ruggie, "International Regimes, Transactions and Change."

21. See Manuel Castells, *The Rise of Network Society*.

22. Robert P. Clark, *The Global Imperative*.

23. Karl Marx and Friedrich Engels, "Manifesto of the Communist Party," in Marx and Engels, *The Marx-Engels Reader*, 477.

24. Martin, "The Moral Case for Globalization."

25. Wolf, "Why This Hatred of the Market?"

26. Ted Fisherman, "The Joys of Global Investment," 35–42.

27. African News Service, "Foreign Direct Investment in Africa Shrinks; Making First Decline since Mid-1990s"; World Bank, *World Development Report 2000–2001*, 22.

28. United Nations, Economic Commission for Latin America and the Caribbean, Social Panorama Publication 2001–2002, chap. 1.

29. Held et al., *Global Transformations*, 245–262.

30. Bernard Cassen, "Pour sauver la société."

31. Kenneth E. Boulding, *Principles of Economic Policy*, 94; Harry Johnson, *Money, Trade, and Economic Growth*, 153; Walt W. Rostow, *The Stages of Economic Growth*; Immanuel Wallerstein, *The Modern World System*. For a discussion on development and human rights trade-offs, see Jack Donnelly, *Universal Human Rights in Theory and Practice*, 161–202.

32. Amartya Sen, *Development as Freedom*, 35–37.

33. John Cassidy, "Helping Hands."

34. Eduardo Aninat, "Surmounting the Challenges of Globalization," 5.

35. Matthew J. Slaughter and Philip Swagel, "Does Globalization Lower Wages and Export Jobs?" 178.

36. Juliet Lodge, *The European Challenge of the Future*, 157; Dinan, *Ever Closer Union*, 427.

37. Slaughter and Swagel, "Does Globalization Lower Wages and Export Jobs?" For a discussion on the gap between high-skilled and low-skilled workers, see Adrian Wood, *North-South Trade, Employment and Inequality*, 14–15, and "Trade Hurts Unskilled Workers," 57–80; Timothy Taylor, "The Truth about Globalization," 31–32.

38. Quoted in Michael Dreyling, *Solidarity and Contention*, 146.

39. Quoted in Stephen J. Kobrin, "The MAI and the Clash of Civilizations," 97–98, 102.

40. Robert Cox, "Civil Society at the Turn of the Millennium," 3–28; Jay Manzur, "Labor's New Internationalism," 79–93; Kathleen Newland, "Workers of the World, Now What?" 53–65.

41. Amnesty International, "AI on Human Rights and Labor Rights" (1998), in Frank J. Lechner and John Boli, *The Globalization Reader*, 187.

42. Held et al., *Global Transformations*, 391.

43. Ibid., 399–400.

44. Friedrich Engels, "Dialectics of Nature," in Friedrich Engels and Karl Marx, *Marx and Engels on Ecology*, 179–180.

45. John Micklethwait and Adrian Woldridge, "Why the Globalization Backlash Is Stupid," 17–18.

46. Held et al., *Global Transformations*, 397.

47. See Dave Foreman, "A Modest Proposal for a Wilderness System"; for a critique of deep ecology, see Ramachandra Guha, "Radical Environmentalism and Wilderness Preservation," 71–83.

48. Vandana Shiva, *Staying Alive*, 5.

49. Mary Daly, *Gyn/Ecology*; and Susan Griffin, *Woman and Nature*.

50. See Val Plumwood, "Ecosocial Feminism as a General Theory of Oppression," in Ronnie Harding, *From Ecology V Proceedings*, 63–72; Ynestra King, "Feminism and the Revolt of Nature," 12–16; James O'Connor, "Socialism and Ecology," 1.

51. Herbert Marcuse, "Ecology and Revolution," 11.

52. Steve Charnovitz and Michael M. Weinstein, "The Greening of the WTO," 147–157.

53. Alan Binder, "Cleaning Up the Environment: Sometimes Cheaper Is Better," in *Hard Heads and Soft Hearts*, 138–159.

54. Held et al., *Global Transformations*, 389.

55. Cited and discussed in Maryellen Fullerton, "The International and National Protection of Refugees," in Hurst Hannum, *Guide to International Human Rights Practice*, 213.

56. Held et al., *Global Transformations*, 312; Jorge Bustamente, "Measuring the Flows of Undocumented Immigrants," in Jorge A. Bustamante and Wayne A. Cornelius, *Mexican Migration to the United States*.

57. Clifford Geertz, "The Integrative Revolution: Primordial Sentiments and Civil Politics in the New States," in *Old Societies and New States*, 107–113.

58. Rogers Brubaker, "Immigration, Citizenship, and the Nation-State in France and Germany," in Gershon Shafir, *The Citizenship Debates*, 150.

59. Barber, *Strong Democracy*, 232; see also John Rawls, "The Domain of Political and Overlapping Consensus," 241.

60. Brubaker, "Immigration, Citizenship, and the Nation-State in France and Germany," in Shafir, *The Citizenship Debates*, 136.

61. Will Kymlicka, "Multicultural Citizenship," in Shafir, *The Citizenship Debates*, 171.

62. "What are the possible sources of unity in a multinational state which affirms, rather than denies, its national differences? I do not have a clear answer to this question," writes Kymlicka. Ibid., 179.

63. Julia Malone, "Lagging Latino Appeal Looms over Bush Trip."

64. Ellen Hale, "How Denmark and Other European Nations are Tackling Immigration Issues in the Wake of the September 11 Attacks and the War on Terrorism."

65. Jürgen Habermas, "Citizenship and National Identity: Some Reflections on the Future of Europe," in Micheline Ishay and Omar Dahbour, *The Nationalism Reader*, 342.

66. Hobsbawm, "The Universalism of the Left," in Micheline Ishay, *The Human Rights Reader*, 277–280.

67. Bob Sutcliffe, "Freedom to Move in the Age of Globalization," in Dean Baker, Gerald Epstein, and Robert Polin, *Globalization and Progressive Economic Policy*, 325–336.

68. Hardt and Negri, *Empire*, 400.

69. James H. Mittelman, *Globalization Syndrome*, 73.

70. International Labor Organization, *Provisions of the ILO Conventions and Recommendations concerning Migrant Workers*.

71. Yasemin Nuhoğly Soysal, "Toward a Postnational Model of Membership," in Shafir, *The Citizenship Debates*, 197–198.

72. Saskia Sassen, "The De Facto Transnationalizing of Immigrant Policy," in *Globalization and Its Discontents,* 5–30.

73. Barber, *Jihad vs. McWorld,* 24–25.

74. Barber, "Democracy at Risk," 30.

75. For a cultural and sociological interpretation of *Dallas,* see John Tomlinson, *Cultural Imperialism,* 45–50.

76. See Lechner, "Global Fundamentalism," in Swatos, *A Future for Religion?* 27–32.

77. Alison Dundes Renteln, "Relativism and the Search for Human Rights," 68.

78. Jane Flax, "Postmodernism and Gender Relations in Feminist Theory," 621–643.

79. Richard Rorty, "Human Rights, Rationality, and Sentimentality," in Ishay, *The Human Rights Reader,* 263; see also Rorty, "Feminism, Ideology, and Deconstruction," 96–103.

80. Rawls, *The Law of Peoples;* Hobsbawm, "The Universalism of the Left," in Ishay, *The Human Rights Reader,* 277–280. See also Alan Gilbert, *Democratic Individuality.*

81. Bikhu Parekh, "Non-Ethno-Centric Universalism," in Tim Dunne and Nicholas J. Wheeler, *Human Rights in Global Politics,* 128–159.

82. Abdullai Ahmed An-Na'im, *Human Rights in Cross-Cultural Perspectives,* 427–435; Jack Donnelly, "The Social Construction of International Human Rights," in Dunne and Wheeler, *Human Rights in Global Politics,* 71–102; Habermas, *The Theory of Communicative Action;* Hans Küng, *A Global Ethics for Politics and Economics;* Will Kymlicka, *Multicultural Citizenship.*

83. This 1989 convention was a revision of the 1957 ILO document on the same topic. International Labor Organization, *Convention (No. 169) concerning Indigenous and Tribal Peoples in Independent Countries,* report 4, no. 1.

84. Sebastian M. Poulter, *English Law and Ethnic Minority Customs;* Soysal, "Toward a Postnational Model of Membership," in Shafir, *The Citizenship Debates,* 198.

85. Quoted in Kevin Galvin, "Rights and Wrongs." See also Ann McFeatters, "Bush Signs Anti-Terror Bill"; Edward Helmore, "The U.S. Refuses to Either Charge or Free Those Suspected of Terrorism"; Bob Egelko, "FBI Checking Out Americans' Reading Habits"; Frank Gardner, "Muslims Condemn U.S. Terror 'Profiling.'"

86. Quoted in Lee Dembart, "Privacy Undone," 11.

87. Agence France-Presse, "Amnesty Fears Terrorist Crackdown Could Mean Repression in China."

88. "EU/Chechnya: MEPS Say Russia Uses Terrorism as Excuse for Human Rights Abuses."

89. See Bruce Porter, *War and the Rise of the State.*

90. See also Paul L. Murphy, *World War I and the Origin of Civil Liberties in the United States.*

91. Kevin Phillips, *Wealth and Democracy.*

92. See, for example, Fareed Zakaria, "The End of the End of History."

93. Condoleezza Rice, "America Has the Muscle, but It Has Benevolent Values."

94. Noam Chomsky, *The New Militarism;* Hardt and Negri, *Empire.*

95. Michael Ignatieff, "The Burden."

96. Wendy Patten, "United States."

97. Michael Walzer, *Just and Unjust War.*

98. Meeting since 1975, the Group of Seven, or G7, comprised the major market-oriented democracies: the United States, Canada, France, Germany, Italy, Great Britain, and Japan. The group became the G8 after the post–cold war addition of Russia. G8 Miyazaki Initiatives on Conflict Prevention, http://www.mofa .go.jp/policy/economy/summit/2000/documents/initiative.html.

99. Marx, *Capital,* vol. 1, pt. 1 and 8.

100. On this subject, see Leo Panitch, "Globalization and the State."

101. International Confederation of Free Trade Unions, "The Global Market: Trade Unionism's Greatest Challenge," introduction.

102. Kevin Bales, *Disposable People,* 9.

103. Jean-Jacques Rousseau, *Fragments,* in *The Political Writings of Jean-Jacques Rousseau,* vol. 1, 310.

104. Bales, *Disposable People,* chap. 3.

105. These statistics are based on a 1999 comparison of a few random countries in the highest and lowest development categories. UN Human Development Report (2001), www.undp.org/hdr2001.

106. United Nations Expert Group Meeting on International Migration Policies and the Status of Female Migrants, *International Migration Policies and the Status of Female Migrants,* 2–3, 6.

107. Manolo I. Abella, "Sex Selectivity of Migration Regulations Governing International Migration in Southern and South-Eastern Asia," and Sharon Stanton Russell, "Policy Dimensions of Female Migration to the Arab Countries of Western Asia," in United Nations Expert Group Meeting on International Migration Policies and the Status of Female Migrants, *International Migration Policies and the Status of Female Migrants,* 242–243, 253–266.

108. Pamela Goldberg, "Where in the World Is There Safety for Me? Women Fleeing Gender-Bias Persecution," in Julie Peters and Andrea Wolper, *Women's Rights, Human Rights,* 350.

109. Sima Wali, "Human Rights for Refugee and Displaced Women," in Peters and Wolper, *Women's Rights, Human Rights,* 337; see also http://www .amnestyusa.org/women.

110. See the Lieber Code, General Orders No. 20, 1863; the Hague Conventions of 1899 and 1907; the Tokyo Charter of the International Military Tribunal for the Far East of 1946; Control Council Law No. 10; and Draft Codes of Offense against Peace and Security of Mankind, all in Yougindra Khushalani, *Dignity and Honour of Women as Basic and Fundamental Human Rights,* 5, 9, 21, 23, 31.

111. David J. Scheffer, Ambassador-at-Large for War Crimes Issues, remarks at Fordham University, New York, October 29, 1999, at http://www.converge.org .nz/pma/arape.htm.

112. Sharon Detrick, *A Commentary on the United Nations Convention on the Rights of the Child,* 558.

113. Abdelwahab Bouhdiba, *Exploitation of Child Labour,* 2, 3, 11, 20.

114. Detrick, *A Commentary on the United Nations Convention on the Rights of the Child,* 588.

115. Kenneth J. Herman, Jr., and Michael Jupp, "International Sex Trade," in Daniel S. Campagna and Donald L. Poffenberger, *The Sexual Trafficking in Children,* 147.

116. For figures for Thailand and Brazil, see UNICEF, "The Progress of Nations 1994." For India, see Bureau of Democracy, Human Rights and Labor, U.S. State Department, "Country Reports on Human Rights Practices," March 31, 2003, at http://www.state.gov/g/drl/rls/hrrpt/2002.

117. UNICEF, *State of the World's Children 2002,* 42.

118. UNICEF, "Children at Both Ends of the Gun," and Graça Machel, "Impact of Armed Conflict on Children." See also Ilene Cohn and Guy S. Goddwin-Gill, *Child Soldiers.*

119. UNICEF Report from 1995, cited in Machel, "Impact of Armed Conflict on Children."

120. These statistics are based on a 1999 comparison of a few random countries in the highest and lowest development categories. UN Human Development Report (2001), www.undp.org/hdr2001.

121. Detrick, *A Commentary on the United Nations Convention on the Rights of the Child,* 680.

122. Cited in Barry Adam, *The Rise of a Gay and Lesbian Movement,* 121, 125.

123. Human Rights Watch, "Lesbian and Gay Rights," in "World Report 2001."

124. Ibid.

125. Rob Hughes, "Refugee Claims Based on Sexual Orientation."

126. The UN divides reductions of human capacity into three categories: Impairment refers to "any loss or abnormality of psychological, physiological, or anatomical structure or function"; disability means a "restriction or lack of ability to perform an activity in the manner or within the range considered normal for a human being"; a handicap is "a disadvantage for a given individual, resulting from an impairment or disability, that limits or prevents the fulfillment of a role that is normal (depending on age, sex and social and cultural factors) for that individual." World Programme of Action concerning Disabled Persons, adopted by the UN General Assembly on December 3, 1982; http://www.un.org/esa/socdev/enable/diswpa00.htm.

127. United Nations, Second Meeting of the Ad Hoc Committee on an International Convention, *The United Nations and Disabled Persons,* chap. 1.

128. Standard Rules on the Equalization of Opportunities for Persons with Disabilities, http://www.un.org/esa/socdev/enable/dissre00.htm. See also ILO Convention 142, focusing on training and human resource development; the ILO's Vocational Rehabilitation and Employment Convention (159); and ILO Recommendation 168, ILOLEX Database of International Labor Standards, http://www.ilolex.ilo.ch:1567/english/index.htm.

129. Cited in International Confederation of Free Trade Unions, "A Lame Excuse," 3.

130. Human Rights Watch, "The United States and Antipersonnel Mines—2001."

131. Patrick Thornberry, *International Law and the Rights of Minorities*, 241; Thomas D. Musgrave, *Self-Determination and National Minorities*, 141–142.

132. United Nations Subcommission on the Prevention of Discrimination and Protection of Minorities, "Study of the Problem of Discrimination against Indigenous Populations," UN Doc. ECN.4/Sub.2/1986/7/Add. 4, par. 379 (1986).

133. S. James Anaya, *Indigenous Peoples in International Law*, 183–184.

CHAPTER 6

1. Benjamin Barber, "An American Civic Forum," 269–283; Michael Walzer, "Rescuing Civil Society," 62–67. There are of course exceptions, among them John Ehrenberg, *Civil Society;* John Keane, *Civil Society,* 15–18; Andrew Arato and Jean Cohen, "Social Movements, Civil Society and the Problem of Sovereignty," 266–283; Robert Cox, "Civil Society at the Turn of the Millennium," 3–28.

2. Antonio Gramsci, *Selections from the Prison Notebooks of Antonio Gramsci,* 210. The reader should bear in mind that the relationship I depict between the economy and human rights should be understood not as one of cause and effect, but dialectically, for human rights activities have also helped shape the social and economic activities of each of the aforementioned periods.

3. Jürgen Habermas, *The Structural Transformation of the Public Sphere,* chap. 1.

4. David Harvey, *The Condition of Postmodernity,* 242.

5. Karl Marx and Friedrich Engels, *The German Ideology,* 12.

6. See Marc Bloch, *Feudal Society,* vol. 1, pt. 2, chap. 5.

7. Jacques Le Goff, *Time, Work and Culture in the Middle Ages,* 35.

8. See Bloch, *Feudal Society,* vol. 2, pt. 7.

9. Habermas, *The Structural Transformation of the Public Sphere,* 8.

10. Joel Colton and Robert Palmer, *History of the Modern World,* 54.

11. Hugo Grotius, *The Law of War and Peace,* "Prolegomena," 12, 141.

12. Roy Porter, Bob Scribner, and Mikuláš Teich, *The Reformation in National Context;* Peter Blickle, "Social Protest and Reformation Theology."

13. Otto Brunner, *Land und Herrschaft,* cited in Habermas, *The Structural Transformation of the Public Sphere,* 5–6.

14. Chris Middleton, "The Familiar Fate of the *Famulae:* Gender Divisions in the History of Wage Labour," in E. E. Pahl, *On Work,* 28.

15. Quoted in R. Po-Chia Hsia, *Social Discipline in the Reformation,* 147–148; see also Steven Ozment, *When Fathers Ruled.*

16. J. Bühler, *Die Kultur des Mittelalters,* 305–306, cited in Max Horkheimer, *Critical Theory,* 119.

17. Horkheimer, *Critical Theory,* 120.

18. Colton and Palmer, *History of the Modern World,* 26.

19. See Eli Ecksher, *Mercantilism;* Michael Mann, "Approaching a Histori-

cal Explanation," in Jean Baechler, John A. Hall, and Michael Mann, *Europe and the Rise of Capitalism.*

20. Thomas Paine, *Common Sense,* in *The Essential Thomas Paine,* 24.

21. Habermas, *The Structural Transformation of the Public Sphere,* 21.

22. Anthony Smith, *The Newspaper,* 74–76.

23. A. J. Langguth, *Patriots,* 51, 200–201.

24. Declaration of the Rights of Man and of the Citizen, in Micheline Ishay, *The Human Rights Reader,* 139.

25. Jeremy D. Popkin, *Revolutionary News;* Hugh Gough, *The Newspaper Press in the French Revolution.*

26. I. Jentsch, "Zur Geschichte des Zeitungswesens in Deutschland," and N. Braubach, "Ein publizistischer Plan der Bonner Lesegesellschaft," cited in Habermas, *The Structural Transformation of the Public Sphere,* 72.

27. G. W. F. Hegel, *The Philosophy of Right,* 114.

28. Engels, *The Origins of the Family, Private Property, and the State,* in Ishay, *The Human Rights Reader,* 219–226.

29. See Habermas, *The Structural Transformation of the Public Sphere,* 33.

30. Darline Gay Levy, Harriet Branson Applewhite, and Mary Durham Johnson, *Women in Revolutionary Paris,* 10.

31. Colton and Palmer, *History of the Modern World,* 468.

32. See Eric Hobsbawm, *Industry and Empire.*

33. Colton and Palmer, *History of the Modern World,* 458–459; see also Norman Davies, *Europe,* 805.

34. Gramsci, *Selections from the Prison Notebooks of Antonio Gramsci,* 12; see also 44–122.

35. Giuseppe Mazzini, "The Duties of Man," in Micheline Ishay and Omar Dahbour, *The Nationalism Reader,* 94.

36. Max Weber, "Economic Policy and the National Interest in Germany," in Ishay and Dahbour, *The Nationalism Reader,* 119–124.

37. Engels, "Working-Class Manchester," in Karl Marx and Friedrich Engels, *The Marx-Engels Reader,* 584.

38. Marx and Engels, "Manifesto of the Communist Party," in Marx and Engels, *The Marx-Engels Reader,* 481.

39. Charles Breunig, *The Age of Revolution and Reaction,* 254–260.

40. Colton and Palmer, *History of the Modern World,* 514.

41. Harvey, "The Geography of the Manifesto," in *Spaces of Hope,* chap. 2.

42. See Engels, *The Origins of the Family, Private Property, and the State,* in Ishay, *The Human Rights Reader,* 219–226.

43. Carol Dyhouse, "Mothers and Daughters in the Middle-Class Home c. 1870–1914," in Jane Lewis, *Women's Experience of Home and Family,* 29.

44. See Julie Matthaei, *An Economic History of Women in America,* 144.

45. Ibid., 182.

46. August Bebel, "Women and Socialism," in Ishay, *The Human Rights Reader,* 228.

47. John Stuart Mill, "Considerations on Representative Government," in Ishay and Dahbour, *The Nationalism Reader,* 105.

48. Robert P. Clark, *The Global Imperative,* 114.

49. See Colston Papers and Symposium of the Research Society and the University of Bristol, in *Principles and Methods of Colonial Administration*.

50. Gramsci, *Selections from the Prison Notebooks of Antonio Gramsci*, 239.

51. This should not suggest that there were no sites whatsoever of social protest. See for example Allen Isaacman, "Peasants and Rural Social Protest in Africa."

52. Even the Bolsheviks' apparent success in transforming the state encountered similar economic and structural obstacles after the revolution.

53. Frantz Fanon, *The Wretched of the Earth*, 154.

54. Vron Ware, *Beyond the Pale*, 120.

55. See Antoinette Burton, *Burdens of History*, particularly chap. 5, on Josephine Butler and the Indian Company (127–169).

56. See M. Jaqui Alexander, "Redrafting Morality: The Postcolonial State and the Sexual Offence Bill of Trinidad and Tobago," in Chandra Talpade Mohanty, Ann Russo, and Lourdes Torres, *Third World Women and the Politics of Feminism*, 133–152.

57. On the demise of the state, see Ken'ichi Ohmae, *The End of the Nation-State;* Walter B. Wriston, *The Twilight of Sovereignty;* J. M. Guehenno, *The End of the Nation-State;* Susan Strange, *The Retreat of the State;* Michael Hardt and Antonio Negri, *Empire*.

58. Charles Tilly, "Globalization Threatens Labor's Rights."

59. For an insightful discussion on the importance of the state in the global economy, see Leo Panitch, "Globalization and the State," 60–93.

60. For an interesting account on intervention, see William I. Robinson, *Promoting Polyarchy*.

61. Noam Chomsky, *The New Militarism*.

62. On the issue of indifference, see Samantha Power, *A Problem from Hell;* Richard Falk, *Human Rights Horizons,* chap. 9.

63. Hardt and Negri, *Empire,* 39.

64. Ibid., 54.

65. See Chip Berlet, "Who Is Mediating the Storm? Right-Wing Alternative Information Networks," in Linda Kuntz and Julia Lesage, *Media, Culture and the Religious Right,* 249–274.

66. Charles Taylor, *Multiculturalism;* Alvin Toffler, *The Third Wave*.

67. See Barber, *Jihad vs. McWorld*.

68. Thomas Friedman, *The Lexus and the Olive Tree*.

69. David Held et al., *Global Transformations,* 67.

70. Lester Salamon, "The Rise of the Nonprofit Sector," 110.

71. Ibid.

72. Union of International Associations, *Yearbook of International Organizations,* vol. 1B, 2406.

73. Held et al., *Global Transformations,* 52–57, 67; see also Jack Donnelly, "The Social Construction of International Human Rights," in Tim Dunne and Nicholas J. Wheeler, *Human Rights in Global Politics,* 71–102; James Crawford, *Democracy in International Law*.

74. Joseph Nye, "America's Information Edge," 20–36; Robert Keohane, *After Hegemony;* John Gerard Ruggie, "What Makes the World Hang Together?" 855–885.

75. Robert Johansen, "Building World Security," in Michael T. Klare and Daniel C. Thomas, *World Security Challenges for a New Century,* 394–395; Held, *Cosmopolitan Democracy.*

76. See Jessica T. Matthews, "Power Shift," 50–66; Ian MacLean, *Democracy and the New Technology;* Margaret E. Keck and Kathryn Sikkink, *Activists beyond Borders.*

77. Habermas, *The Postnational Constellation,* 120.

78. In recent G8 meetings, the United States, Britain, France, Germany, Japan, Canada, and Italy have been joined by Russia.

79. For additional discussion of this issue, see Ishay, "Globalism and the New Realism of Human Rights."

80. Susan Faludi, *Backlash.*

81. Gwendolyn Mink, *Welfare's End,* 42–43, 129; Irvin Garfinkel and Sara S. McLanahan, *Single Mothers and Their Children,* 139, 141, 162; Dorothy K. Seavey, *Back to Basics,* 58–59.

82. Serge Halimi, "Face au journalisme de marché."

83. Stephen Doheny-Farnia, *The Wired Neighborhood,* 188; see also Laura Gurak, *Persuasion and Privacy in Cyberspace.*

84. Jeffrey Rosen, "A Watchful State," 42.

85. Jeremy Bentham, *The Panopticon Writings,* 34.

86. Michel Foucault, *Discipline and Punish,* 201.

87. David Lyons, *The Electronic Eye,* chap. 2.

References

Abella, Manolo I. "Sex Selectivity of Migration Regulations Governing International Migration in Southern and South-Eastern Asia." In United Nations Expert Group Meeting on International Migration Policies and the Status of Female Migrants, *International Migration Policies and the Status of Female Migrants*. New York: United Nations, 1995.

Adam, Barry. *The Rise of a Gay and Lesbian Movement*. New York: Twayne, 1995.

Adams, George B. *The Origin of the English Constitution*. New Haven: Yale University Press, 1912.

African News Service. "Foreign Direct Investment in Africa Shrinks; Making First Decline since Mid-1990s." September 18, 2001. http://ro.unctad.org/en/press/pro124en.htm [April 2002].

Agence France-Presse. "Amnesty Fears Terrorist Crackdown Could Mean Repression in China." October 12, 2001. http://www.islam-online.net/English/News/2000-10/13/article7/shtml [December 2001].

———. "Argentine Unions Call for Strike to Protest IMF Austerity Plan." May 31, 2000. http://venus.uwindsor.ca/flipside/vol3/juno0/oojno6a.htm.

Agi, Marc. *René Cassin, 1887–1976: Prix Nobel de la paix, père de la Déclaration universelle des droits de l'homme*. Paris: Perrin, 1998.

Ajami, Fouad. "The Third World Challenge: The Fate of Nonalignment." *Foreign Affairs* 59, no. 2 (Winter 1980–1981).

Ali, Abdullah Yusuf, ed. and trans. *The Meaning of the Holy Qur'an*. Beltsville, Md.: Amana Publications, 1989.

Altman, Dennis. *Homosexual: Oppression and Liberation*. New York: Outerbridge & Dienstfrey, 1971.

Ambedkar, B. R. *Annihilation of Caste: With a Reply to Mahatma Gandhi*. Bombay: Bharat Bhushan Press, 1945.

Ambrose, Stephen E., and Douglas G. Brinkley. *Rise to Globalism: American Foreign Policy since 1938*. 8th rev. ed. New York: Penguin, 1997.

American Association for the United Nations, Educational Committee. *A Brief History of the League*. New York: Educational Committee, League of Nations Association, 1934.

Amin, Samir. "The Ancient World-Systems versus the Modern Capitalist World System." *Review* 3 (Summer 1991).

———. *Eurocentrism*. New York: Monthly Review Press, 1989.

Anaya, S. James. *Indigenous Peoples in International Law*. Oxford: Oxford University Press, 2000.

Aninat, Eduardo. "Surmounting the Challenges of Globalization." *Finance and Development* 39, no. 1 (March 2002).

An-Na'im, Abdullai Ahmed, ed. *Human Rights in Cross-Cultural Perspectives: A Quest for Consensus*. Philadelphia: University of Pennsylvania Press, 1992.

Arato, Andrew, and Jean Cohen. "Social Movements, Civil Society and the Problem of Sovereignty." *Praxis International* 4, no. 3 (1984).

Arendt, Hannah. *The Origins of Totalitarianism*. New York: Harcourt, 1951.

Aristotle. *The Nicomachean Ethics*. Trans. Martin Ostwald. New York: Bobbs-Merrill, 1962.

———. *The Politics*. Trans. T. S. Sinclair. London: Penguin, 1962.

The Arthashastra. Ed. and trans. L. N. Rangarajan. London: Penguin, 1992.

Augustine, Saint. *The City of God*. New York: Modern Library, 1994.

Avineri, Shlomo. *The Making of Modern Zionism*. New York: Basic Books, 1981.

———. *The Social and Political Thought of Karl Marx*. Cambridge: Cambridge University Press, 1968.

Babeuf, Gracchus. *La doctrine des égaux: Extraits des oeuvres complètes*. Paris: E. Cornély, 1906.

Backstrom, Philip N. *Christian Socialism and Cooperation in Victorian England*. London: Croom Helm, 1974.

Baechler, Jean, John A. Hall, and Michael Mann, eds. *Europe and the Rise of Capitalism*. Oxford: Basil Blackwell, 1988.

Baker, Dean, Gerald Epstein, and Robert Polin, eds. *Globalization and Progressive Economic Policy*. Edinburgh: Cambridge University Press, 1998.

Baktis, Dr. von. *Die sexual Revolution in Russland*. Berlin: Verlag der Syndikalist, 1925.

Bakunin, Mikhail. *From out of the Dustbin: Bakunin's Basic Writings, 1869–1871*. Ed. and trans. Robert M. Cutler. Ann Arbor: Ardis Publishers, 1985.

Bales, Kevin. *Disposable People: New Slavery in the Global Economy*. Berkeley: University of California Press, 1999.

Barber, Benjamin. "An American Civic Forum: Civil Society between Market Individuals and the Political Community." *Social Philosophy and Policy Foundation* 13, no. 1 (1996).

———. "Democracy at Risk: American Culture in a Global Culture." *World Policy Journal* 15, no. 2 (Summer 1998).

———. *Jihad vs. McWorld*. New York: Random House, 1995.

———. *Strong Democracy*. Berkeley: University of California Press, 1984.

Bauer, Otto. "Marxismus und Ethik." *Neue Zeit* 24, no. 2 (1906): 82.

———. *The Question of Nationalities and Social Democracy*. Minneapolis: University of Minnesota Press, 2000.

Beasley, W. G. *The Rise of Modern Japan: Political, Economic and Social Change since 1850*. New York: St. Martin's Press, 1995.

Beauvoir, Simone de. *The Second Sex*. New York: Vintage Books, 1989.

Bebel, August. *Women and Socialism*. New York: Source Book Press, 1904.

Beitzinger, A. J. *A History of American Political Thought*. New York: Dodd, Mead, 1972.

Benjamin, Walter. *Illuminations*. Ed. Hannah Arendt, trans. Harry Zohn. New York: Harcourt Brace Jovanovich, 1968.

Bentham, Jeremy. *The Panopticon Writings*. Ed. and intro. Miran Bozovic. London: Verso, 1995.

Bentwich, Norman. *The Religious Foundations of Internationalism: A Study of International Relations through the Ages*. New York: Bloch Publishing, 1959.

Bercovitch, Sacvan, and Cyrus R. K. Patell, eds. *The Cambridge History of American Literature*. New York: Cambridge University Press, 1994.

Berkovitz, Dayan. "A Halachic Viewpoint." http://www.icjw.org/halachic.htm [May 2002].

Bernstein, Eduard. *Evolutionary Socialism*. Trans. Edith C. Harvey. New York: Schocken Books, 1961.

————. *The Preconditions of Socialism*. Ed. and trans. Henry Tudor. Cambridge: Cambridge University Press, 1993.

Bezucha, Robert J., ed. *Modern European Social History*. Lexington, Mass.: D. C. Heath, 1972.

Binder, Alan. *Hard Heads and Soft Hearts: Tough-Minded Economics for a Just Society*. Reading, Mass.: Addison-Wesley, 1987.

bin Laden, Osama. "Fatwah." *Al-Quds al-'Arabi*. February 23, 1998. http://www.ict.org.il/articles/fatwah.htm.

Birnbaum, Pierre, and Ira Katznelson, eds. *Paths of Emancipation: Jews, States, and Citizenship*. Princeton, N.J.: Princeton University Press, 1995.

Black, George, and Robin Munro. *Black Hands of Beijing*. New York: John Wiley, 1993.

Blanc, Louis. *L'organisation du travail*. Paris: Société de l'industrie fraternelle, 1848. Trans. Marie Paula Dickore as *Organization of Work*. Cincinnati: University of Cincinnati Press, 1911.

Blickle, Peter. "Social Protest and Reformation Theology." In Kaspar von Greyerz, ed., *Religion, Politics, and Social Protest: Three Studies on Early Modern Germany*. London: George Allen & Unwin, 1984.

Bloch, Marc. *Feudal Society*. 2 vols. Trans. L. A. Manyon. Chicago: University of Chicago Press, 1961.

Bobbio, Norberto. *The Age of Rights*. Oxford: Polity Press, 1996.

Bottomore, Tom, and Patrick Goode, eds. *Austro-Marxism*. Oxford: Clarendon Press, 1978.

Bouhdiba, Abdelwahab. *Exploitation of Child Labour*. New York: United Nations, 1982.

Boulding, Kenneth E. *Principles of Economic Policy*. Englewood Cliffs, N.J.: Prentice-Hall, 1958.

Bové, José, and François Dufour. *The World Is Not for Sale: Farmers against Junk Food*. Trans. Anna de Casparis. New York: Verso, 2001.

Braubach, N. "Ein publizistischer Plan der Bonner Lesegesellschaft." In A. J. M. Herrmann, ed., *Aus Geschichte und Politik: Festschrift zum 70. Geburtstag von Ludwig Bergsträsser*. Düsseldorf: Droste-Verlag, 1954.

Braunthal, Julius. *The History of the International*. 3 vols. Trans. Henry Collins and Kenneth Mitchell. New York: Praeger, 1967–1980.

Breunig, Charles. *The Age of Revolution and Reaction, 1789–1850*. New York: W. W. Norton, 1977.

Bronner, Stephen. *Camus: Portrait of a Moralist*. Minneapolis: University of Minnesota Press, 1999.

———. *Ideas in Action*. Oxford: Rowman & Littlefield, 1999.

———. *A Rumor about the Jews: Reflections on Antisemitism and the Protocols of the Learned Elders of Zion*. New York: St. Martin's Press, 2000.

———. *Socialism Unbound*. 2nd ed. Boulder: Westview, 2001.

Brown, William Wells. *The Black Man: His Antecedents, His Genius, and His Achievements*. New York: Thomas Hamilton, 1863; repr. New York: Johnson Reprint, 1968.

———. *The Negro in the American Rebellion: His Heroism and His Fidelity*. Boston: Lee & Shepard, 1867; repr. New York: Kraus Reprint, 1969.

Bühler, J. *Die Kultur des Mittelalters*. Leipzig: A. Kröner, 1930.

Bullough, Vern L. *Homosexuality: A History*. New York: New American Library, 1979.

Burke, Edmund. *Reflections on the Revolutions in France*. Ed. and intro. J. G. A. Pocock. Indianapolis: Hackett Publishing, 1978.

Burton, Antoinette. *Burdens of History*. Chapel Hill: University of North Carolina Press, 1994.

Burtt, Edwin, ed. *The Teachings of the Compassionate Buddha*. New York: New American Library, 1955.

Bustamente, Jorge A., and Wayne A. Cornelius, eds. *Mexican Migration to the United States: Origins, Consequences and Policy Options*. La Jolla: Center for U.S.-Mexican Studies, University of California, 1989 and 1994.

Cabezón, José Ignacio. "Homosexuality and Buddhism." In Arlene Swidler, ed., *Homosexuality and World Religions*. Valley Forge, Pa.: Trinity Press International, 1993.

Campagna, Daniel S., and Donald L. Poffenberger, eds. *Sexual Trafficking in Children: An Investigation of the Child Sex Trade*. Dover, Mass.: Auburn House, 1988.

Canning, Joseph. *The Political Thought of Baldus de Ubaldi*. Cambridge: Cambridge University Press, 1987.

Carpenter, Edward. *The Intermediate Sex*. London: George Allen & Unwin, 1941.

Carr, Edward Hallett. *The Twenty Years' Crisis, 1919–1939*. London: Macmillan, 1961.

Cassen, Bernard. "Pour sauver la société." *Le monde diplomatique*, May 1997.

Cassidy, John. "Helping Hands: How Foreign Aid Could Benefit Everybody." *New Yorker*, March 18, 2002.

Cassin, René. *Amicorum discipulorumque liber: Méthodologie des droits de l'homme*. 4 vols. Paris: Editions A. Pedone, 1972.

Castells, Manuel. *The Rise of Network Society*. London: Blackwell Publishers, 1996.

Chafetz, Janet Saltzman, and Anthony Gary Dworkin. *Female Revolt: Women's Movements in World and Historical Perspective*. Totowa, N.J.: Rowman & Allanheld, 1986.

Chamberlain, Houston Steward. *The Foundations of the Nineteenth Century*. New York: J. Lane, 1911.

Chang, Iris. *The Rape of Nanking: The Forgotten Holocaust of World War II*. New York: Basic Books, 1997.

Charnovitz, Steve, and Michael M. Weinstein. "The Greening of the WTO." *Foreign Affairs* 80, no. 6 (November-December 2001).

Child, Lydia Maria. *Freedmen's Book*. Boston: Ticknor and Fields, 1865.

Chirico, JoAnn, and Roland Robertson. "Humanity, Globalization and Worldwide Religious Resurgence." *Sociological Analysis* 46, no. 3 (Fall 1985).

Chomsky, Noam. *The New Militarism: Lessons from Kosovo*. Monroe, Maine: Common Courage Press, 1999.

Cicero, Marcus Tullius. *On the Commonwealth*. Trans. George Sabine and Stanley Smith. Indianapolis: Bobbs-Merrill, 1950.

———. *De Republica*. Trans. Clinton Walker Keyes. Cambridge, Mass.: Harvard University Press, 1966.

———. *"De Republica" and "De Legibus."* Trans. Clinton W. Keyes. Cambridge, Mass.: Harvard University Press, 1961.

Clark, Robert P. *The Global Imperative: An Interpretive History of the Spread of Humankind*. Boulder: Westview, 1997.

Clarkson, Thomas. *The History of the Rise, Progress, and Accomplishment of the Abolition of the Slave Trade*. 2 vols. London: Frank Cass, 1968.

Clough, Shepard B., and Herbert W. Schneider. *Making Fascists*. Chicago: University of Chicago Press, 1929.

Cohn, Ilene, and Guy S. Goddwin-Gill. *Child Soldiers: The Role of Children in Armed Conflict*. Oxford: Clarendon Press, 1984.

Colton, Joel, and Robert Palmer. *History of the Modern World*. 4th ed. New York: Knopf, 1911.

Confucius. *The Analects*. Ed. and trans. Arthur Waley. London: George Allen & Unwin Ltd., 1956.

Conquest, Robert. *The Great Terror: A Reassessment*. New York: Oxford University Press, 1990.

Conus, Ester. *Protection of Motherhood and Childhood in the Soviet Union*. Trans. Vera Fediavsky. Moscow: State Medical Editorship, 1933.

Cooke-Taylor, Richard Whately. *The Modern Factory System*. London: K. Paul, Trench, Trübner, 1891.

Costeloe, Michael. *Response to Revolution: Imperial Spain and the Spanish American Revolutions, 1810–1840*. London: Cambridge University Press, 1986.

Cox, Robert. "Civil Society at the Turn of the Millennium: Prospects for an Alternative World Order." *Review of International Studies* 25, no. 1 (January 1999).

Craig, Gordon, and Felix Gilbert. *The Diplomats, 1919–1939*. 2 vols. New York: Atheneum, 1963.

Crawford, James. *Democracy in International Law: Inaugural Lecture*. Cambridge: Cambridge University Press, 1994.

Crawford, S. Cromwell. *The Evolution of Hindu Ideals*. Honolulu: University Press of Hawaii, 1982.

Dalai Lama. "Human Rights and Universal Responsibilities." In *The Dalai Lama: A Policy of Kindness*. Ed. Sidney Piburn. Ithaca, N.Y.: Snow Lion Publications, 1990.

Daly, Mary. *Gyn/Ecology: The Meta-Ethics of Radical Feminism*. Boston: Beacon Press, 1978.

Darwin, Charles. *The Descent of Man*. New York: New York University Press, 1989.

Davies, Norman. *Europe: A History*. New York: Oxford University Press, 1996.

Davis, George B. *The Elements of International Law*. New York: Harper & Brothers, 1916.

De Bary, William Theodore. "Neo-Confucianism and Human Rights." In Leroy Rouner, ed., *Human Rights and the World's Religions*. Notre Dame, Ind.: University of Notre Dame Press, 1988.

De Bary, William Theodore, and Tu Weiming, eds. *Confucianism and Human Rights*. New York: Columbia University Press, 1998.

Dembart, Lee. "Privacy Undone: The EU's Internet Plan Takes Liberties with Personal Rights." *International Herald Tribune*, June 10, 2002, p. 11.

Derathé, Robert. *Jean-Jacques Rousseau et la science politique de son temps*. Geneva: Slatkine Reprints, 1979.

DeRosa, Marshall, ed. *The Politics of Dissolution: The Quest for a National Identity and the American Civil War*. London: Transaction Publishers, 1998.

Detrick, Sharon. *A Commentary on the United Nations Convention on the Rights of the Child*. The Hague: Martinus Nijhoff, 1999.

Diamond, Jared. *Guns, Germs, and Steel*. New York: W. W. Norton, 1997.

Dickens, Charles. *Hard Times*. London: New English Library, 1961.

———. *A Tale of Two Cities*. New York: Signet Classics, 1960.

Diderot, Denis. *Oeuvres complètes*. Ed. Herbert Dieckman, Jean Fabre, Jacques Proust, and Jean Varlant. Paris: Hermann, 1975.

Dinan, Desmond. *Ever Closer Union: An Introduction to European Union*. Boulder: Lynne Rienner, 1999.

Doheny-Farnia, Stephen. *The Wired Neighborhood*. New Haven: Yale University Press, 1996.

Döllinger, Johann J. Ignaz von. *Der Papst und das Konzil*. Frankfurt: Minerva, 1968.

Dombrowski, James. *The Early Days of Christian Socialism in America*. New York: Columbia University Press, 1936.

Donnelly, Jack. *Universal Human Rights in Theory and Practice*. Ithaca, N.Y.: Cornell University Press, 1989.

Douglass, Frederick. *Selected Speeches and Writings*. Ed. Philip S. Foner. Chicago: University of Chicago Press, 1999.

Douzinas, Costas. *The End of Human Rights*. Oxford: Hart Publishing, 2000.

Dreyling, Michael. *Solidarity and Contention*. New York: Garland Publishing, 2001.

Driver, G. R., and John C. Miles, eds. *The Babylonian Laws*. 2 vols. Oxford: Clarendon Press, 1956.

Dubois, Ellen Carol. *Woman Suffrage and Women's Rights*. New York: New York University Press, 1998.

Ducpétiaux, Edouard. *De la condition physique et morale des jeunes ouvriers*. 2 vols. Brussels: n.p., 1843.

Dunant, Henri. *Un souvenir de Solferino.* 1862; repr. Lausanne: L'age d'homme, 1986. Trans. as *Memory of Solferino.* Washington, D.C.: American National Red Cross, 1939.

Dunne, Tim, and Nicholas J. Wheeler, eds. *Human Rights in Global Politics.* Cambridge: Cambridge University Press, 1999.

Duveau, Georges. *The Making of a Revolution.* New York: Pantheon Books, 1967.

Ecksher, Eli. *Mercantilism.* London: George Allen & Unwin, 1935.

Egelko, Bob. "FBI Checking Out Americans' Reading Habits." *San Francisco Chronicle,* June 23, 2002, A5.

Egret, Jean. *The French Pre-Revolution.* Chicago: University of Chicago Press, 1977.

Ehrenberg, John. *Civil Society: The Critical History of an Idea.* New York: New York University Press, 1999.

Eisenstein, Elizabeth. "Who Intervened in 1788? A Commentary on the Coming of the French Revolution." *American Historical Review* 71 (October 1965): 77–103.

Elton, G. R., ed. *Renaissance and Reformation, 1300–1648.* New York: Macmillan, 1963.

Engels, Friedrich. *The Origin of the Family, Private Property, and the State.* New York: International Publishers, 1942.

Engels, Friedrich, and Karl Marx. *Basic Writings on Politics and Philosophy.* Ed. Lewis S. Feuer. Garden City, N.Y.: Doubleday, 1959.

———. *The German Ideology.* New York: International Publishers, 1960.

———. *Marx and Engels on Ecology.* Ed. Howard Parsons. Westport, Conn.: Greenwood Press, 1977.

———. *The Marx-Engels Reader.* Ed. Robert C. Tucker. New York: W. W. Norton, 1972.

Engerman, Stanley L., ed. *Terms of Labor: Slavery, Serfdom and Free Labor.* Stanford, Calif.: Stanford University Press, 1999.

Epictetus. *"The Discourses" and "Enchiridon."* New York: Walter J. Black, 1944.

"EU/Chechnya: MEPS Say Russia Uses Terrorism as Excuse for Human Rights Abuses." *European Report,* April 12, 2002.

Falk, Richard. *Human Rights Horizons: The Pursuit of Justice in a Globalizing World.* London: Routledge, 2000.

Faludi, Susan. *Backlash: The Undeclared War against Feminism.* New York: Crown, 1991.

Fanon, Frantz. *The Wretched of the Earth.* New York: Grove Press, 1968.

Farer, Tom J. *Beyond Sovereignty: Collectively Defending Democracy in the Western Hemisphere.* Baltimore: Johns Hopkins University Press, 1995.

———. *The Grand Strategy of the United States in Latin America.* New Brunswick, N.J.: Transaction Books, 1988.

———. *Transnational Crime in the Americas.* New York: Routledge, 1999.

Felice, William. *Taking Rights Seriously: The Importance of Collective Human Rights.* Albany: SUNY Press, 1996.

Fernbach, David, ed. *Surveys from Exile.* New York: Vintage Books, 1974.

Fiagon, Lee. *China Rising*. Chicago: Ivan R. Dee, 1990.

Fichte, Johann Gottlieb. *Address to the German Nation*. Ed. and intro. G. Armstrong Kelly. New York: Harper Torchbooks, 1968.

Firth, C. H., ed. *The Clarke Papers*. Vol. 3. London: Camden Society Publications, 1891–1901.

Fisherman, Ted. "The Joys of Global Investment." *Harper's*, February 1997.

Fitzpatrick, Sheila. *The Russian Revolution*. Oxford: Oxford University Press, 1982.

Flax, Jane. "Postmodernism and Gender Relations in Feminist Theory." *Signs* 12, no. 4 (1987).

Foner, Philip S., ed. *We, the Other People*. Urbana: University of Illinois Press, 1976.

Foreman, Dave. "A Modest Proposal for a Wilderness System." *Whole Earth Review*, no. 53 (Winter 1986–1987).

Forman, Michael. *Nationalism and the International Labor Movement: The Idea of the Nation in Socialist and Anarchist Theory*. Philadelphia: University of Pennsylvania Press, 1998.

Forster, Anthony. *Britain and the Maastricht Negotiations*. London: Macmillan, 1999.

Foucault, Michel. *Discipline and Punish: The Birth of the Prison*. Trans. Alan Sheridan. New York: Pantheon Books, 1977.

———. *Power/Knowledge*. Ed. and trans. Colin Gordon. New York: Pantheon Books, 1980.

Fourier, Charles. *Selections from the Work of Fourier*. Ed. Charles Gide, trans. Julia Franklin. London: Swan Sonnenschein, 1901.

Franck, Frederick, ed. *The Buddha Eye*. New York: Crossroad, 1982.

Freudenstein, Eric G. "Ecology and the Jewish Tradition." In Milton R. Konvitz, ed., *Judaism and Human Rights*. New York: W. W. Norton, 1972.

Fried, Albert, and Ronald Sanders, eds. *Socialist Thought*. New York: Columbia University Press, 1993.

Friedman, Thomas. *The Lexus and the Olive Tree*. New York: Farrar, Straus and Giroux, 1999.

Friedman, Thomas, and Ignacio Ramonet. "Dueling Globalizations." *Foreign Policy* (Fall 1999).

Fukuyama, Francis. "The End of History?" *National Interest* 16 (Summer 1989).

Furet, François. *Penser la révolution française*. Paris: Gallimard, 1978.

Galton, Francis. *Hereditary Genius: An Inquiry into Its Laws and Consequences*. New York: New York University Press, 1989.

Galvin, Kevin. "Rights and Wrongs: Why New Law-Enforcement Powers Worry Civil Libertarians." *Seattle Times*, December 7, 2001, A3.

Gandhi, Mahatma. "Appeal to the Nation." In *The Writings of M. K. Gandhi*. Ed. Raghavan Iyer. Ahmedabad: Navajivan Trust, 1990.

———. "Passive Resistance." In *The Selected Works of Mahatma Gandhi*. Vol. 4. Ahmedabad: Navajivan Press, 1968.

Gardner, Frank. "Muslims Condemn U.S. Terror 'Profiling.'" BBC News, June 26, 2002. http://news.bbc.co.uk/2/hi/americas/2068038.stm.

Garfinkel, Irvin, and Sara S. McLanahan. *Single Mothers and Their Children.* Washington, D.C.: Urban Institute Press, 1986.

Geertz, Clifford, ed. *Old Societies and New States: The Quest for Modernity in Asia and Africa.* New York: Free Press, 1963.

Gehl, Walter, ed. *Der nationalsozialistischer Staat.* Breslau: Ferdinand Hirt, 1933.

Genovese, Eugene D. *The Political Economy of Slavery.* New York: Vintage Books, 1967.

Gibbins, H. de B. *Industry in England: Historical Outlines.* New York: Charles Scribner's Sons, 1897.

Gide, André. *Corydon.* Paris: Gallimard, 1925.

———. *L'immoraliste.* Paris: Mercure de France, 1917.

Giffard, Sidney. *Japan among the Powers, 1890–1990.* New Haven: Yale University Press, 1994.

Gilbert, Alan. *Democratic Individuality.* Cambridge: Cambridge University Press, 1990.

———. *Marx's Politics.* New Brunswick, N.J.: Rutgers University Press, 1981.

Giller, Louis, ed. *Abolition and Social Justice.* New York: Harper & Row, 1972.

Glendon, Mary Ann. *A World Made New: Eleanor Roosevelt and the Universal Declaration of Human Rights.* New York: Random House, 2001.

Global News Wire and Global Organizations. "Public Protests around the World." January 10, 2003. http://www.globalissues.org/TradeRelated/FreeTrade/Protests.asp.

Gobineau, Arthur de. *The Inequality of the Human Races.* Trans. A. Collins. London: William Heinemann, 1915.

Goldfischer, David, and Micheline Ishay. "Human Rights and Security: A False Dichotomy." *New Political Science* 35 (Spring 1996).

Goldstone, Jack. *Revolution and Rebellion in the Early Modern World.* Berkeley: University of California Press, 1991.

Gough, Hugh. *The Newspaper Press in the French Revolution.* Chicago: Dorsey Press, 1998.

Gould, Stephen. *The Mismeasure of Man.* New York: W. W. Norton, 1981.

Graber, G. S. *Caravans to Oblivion: The Armenian Genocide, 1915.* New York: John Wiley, 1996.

Gramsci, Antonio. *Selections from the Prison Notebooks of Antonio Gramsci.* Ed. and trans. Quintin Hoare and Geoffrey Nowell Smith. New York: International Publishers, 1980.

Grant, A. J., and Harold Temperley. *Europe in the Nineteenth and Twentieth Centuries, 1789–1950.* London: Longmans, 1953.

Greenberg, David F. *The Construction of Homosexuality.* Chicago: University of Chicago Press, 1988.

Griffin, Susan. *Woman and Nature: The Roaring inside Her.* New York: Harper & Row, 1979.

Grotius, Hugo. *The Law of War and Peace.* Trans. F. W. Keisley, intro. J. B. Scott. New York: Bobbs-Merrill, 1925.

———. *The Rights of War and Peace.* Ed. and trans. A. C. Campbell. New York: M. W. Dunne, 1901.

Guehenno, J. M. *The End of the Nation-State*. Minneapolis: University of Minnesota Press, 1995.

Guevara, Ernesto. *Che: Selected Works of Ernesto Guevara*. Ed. Rolando F. Bonachea and Nelson P. Valdes. Cambridge, Mass.: MIT Press, 1969.

Guha, Ramachandra. "Radical Environmentalism and Wilderness Preservation: A Third World Critique." *Environmental Ethics* 2 (Spring 1989).

Gurak, Laura. *Persuasion and Privacy in Cyberspace*. New Haven: Yale University Press, 1997.

Gutiérrez, Gustavo. *The Density of the Present: Selected Writings by Gustavo Gutiérrez*. Maryknoll, N.Y.: Orbis, 1992.

Gutman, Herbert G., ed. *Who Built America?* New York: Pantheon Books, 1989.

Habermas, Jürgen. *The Postnational Constellation: Political Essays*. Trans., ed., and intro. Max Pensky. Cambridge, Mass.: MIT Press, 2001.

———. *The Structural Transformation of the Public Sphere*. Trans. Thomas Burger. Cambridge, Mass.: MIT Press, 1991.

———. *The Theory of Communicative Action*. Trans. Thomas McCarthy. Boston: Beacon Press, 1984.

Hale, Ellen. "How Denmark and Other European Nations Are Tackling Immigration Issues in the Wake of the September 11 Attacks and the War on Terrorism." *USA Today*, March 20, 2002.

Halimi, Serge. "Face au journalisme de marché: Encourager la dissidence." *Le monde diplomatique*, May 1997.

Halle, Louis J. *The Cold War as History*. New York: Harper Perennial, 1991.

Hannum, Hurst, ed. *Guide to International Human Rights Practice*. Philadelphia: University of Pennsylvania Press, 1992.

Harding, Ronnie, ed. *From Ecology V Proceedings*. Kensington: Center for Liberal and General Studies, University of New South Wales, 1992.

Hardt, Michael, and Antonio Negri. *Empire*. Cambridge, Mass.: Harvard University Press, 2000.

Harvey, David. *The Condition of Postmodernity*. London: Blackwell, 1990.

———. *Spaces of Hope*. Berkeley: University of California Press, 2000.

Harvey, Peter. *An Introduction to Buddhism: Teachings, History and Practices*. Cambridge: Cambridge University Press, 1990.

Harwin, Judith. *Children of the Russian State, 1917–1995*. Aldershot, England: Avebury, 1996.

Havel, Vaclav, et al. *The Power of the Powerless: Citizens against the State in Central-Eastern Europe*. Ed. John Keane. Armonk, N.Y.: M. E. Sharpe, 1985.

Havens, George R. *Selections from Voltaire*. New York: D. Appleton-Century, 1930.

Hecksher, Eli F. *Mercantilism*. 2 vols. Trans. Mendel Shapiro. London: George Allen & Unwin, 1935.

Hegel, G. W. F. *Philosophy of Mind*. Trans. William Wallace and A. V. Miller. Oxford: Oxford University Press, 1971.

———. *The Philosophy of Right*. Ed. T. M. Knox. London: Oxford University Press, 1952.

———. *Reason in History: A General Introduction to the Philosophy of History*. Trans. and intro. Robert S. Hartman. New York: Macmillan, 1953.

Heger, Heinz. *The Men with the Pink Triangle.* Trans. David Fernbach. Cucugnan, France: Heretic Books, 1972.

Held, David. *Cosmopolitan Democracy: An Agenda for Building a New World Order.* Cambridge, Mass.: Polity Press, 1995.

Held, David, Anthony McGrew, David Goldblatt, and Jonathan Perraton. *Global Transformations.* Stanford, Calif.: Stanford University Press, 1999.

Helmore, Edward. "The U.S. Refuses to Either Charge or Free Those Suspected of Terrorism." *Guardian,* May 7, 2002.

Herodotus. *The Histories.* Trans. Audrey de Sélincourt, rev. and intro. A. R. Burn. Middlesex: Penguin, 1974.

Herzl, Theodore. *A Jewish State.* Trans. S. D. Avigdor. New York: Maccabbean Publishing, 1904.

Hess, Moses. "The Philosophy of the Act." In Albert Fried and Ronald Sanders, eds., *Socialist Thought.* New York: Columbia University Press, 1993.

Heyes, Eileen. *Children of the Swastika: The Hitler Youth.* Brookfield, Conn.: Millbrook Press, 1993.

Hill, Christopher. *The World Turned Upside Down.* London: Temple Smith, 1972.

Hobsbawm, Eric. *The Age of Extremes.* New York: Vintage Books, 1994.

———. *The Age of Revolutions, 1789–1848.* London: New American Library, 1962.

———. *Industry and Empire.* New York: Pantheon Books, 1968.

Ho Chi Minh. *On Revolution: Selected Writings, 1920–1966.* Ed. Bernard B. Fall. New York: Praeger, 1967.

Holloway, John, and Eloína Peláez, eds. *Zapatista.* London: Pluto Press, 1998.

Horkheimer, Max. *Critical Theory: Selected Essays.* New York: Continuum, 1982.

———. *The Eclipse of Reason.* New York: Continuum, 1987.

Hough, Jerry. *The Struggle for the Third World: Soviet Debates and American Options.* Washington, D.C.: Brookings Institution, 1986.

Hovannisian, Richard G. *The Armenian Genocide.* New York: St. Martin's Press, 1992.

———, ed. *Remembrance and Denial.* Detroit: Wayne State University Press, 1998.

Hovell, Mark. *The Chartist Movement.* New York: August M. Kelley, 1967.

Howard, Michael, and William Roger Louis, eds. *The Oxford History of the Twentieth Century.* Oxford: Oxford University Press, 1998.

Howard, Rhoda. *Human Rights and the Search for Community.* Boulder: Westview, 1995.

Hsia, R. Po-Chia. *Social Discipline in the Reformation: Central Europe, 1550–1750.* London: Routledge, 1989.

Hsü, Leonard Shihlien. *The Political Philosophy of Confucianism: An Interpretation of the Social and Political Ideas of Confucius, His Forerunners, and His Early Disciples.* New York: Dutton, 1932.

Hughes, Rob. "Refugee Claims Based on Sexual Orientation." OUT/LAW Online. June 3, 2002. http://www.smith-hughes.com/papers/refugees.htm.

Human Rights Watch. "The United States and Antipersonnel Mines—2001." http://www.hrw.org/press/2001/03/lmfacts.htm [November 2001].

————. "World Report 2001." http://www.hrw.org/wr2k1/.

Hunt, Lynn, ed. and trans. *The French Revolution and Human Rights: A Brief Documentary History*. New York: St. Martin's Press, 1996.

Hunt, Lynn, Jeffrey Wasserstrom, and Marilyn B. Young, eds. *Human Rights and Revolutions*. Oxford: Rowman & Littlefield, 2000.

Huntington, Samuel. "The Clash of Civilizations?" *Foreign Affairs* 72, no. 3 (Summer 1993).

————. "Why International Primacy Matters." *International Security* 17, no. 4 (Spring 1993).

Ignatieff, Michael. "The Burden." *New York Times Magazine*, January 5, 2003.

————. *Human Rights as Politics and Idolatry*. Ed. and intro. Amy Gutman. Princeton, N.J.: Princeton University Press, 2001.

Innes, Brian. *The History of Torture*. New York: St. Martin's Press, 1998.

International Confederation of Free Trade Unions. "The Global Market: Trade Unionism's Greatest Challenge." *Report for the Sixteenth World Congress of the ICFTU*. June 27, 1996. http://www.icftu.org.

————. "A Lame Excuse: A Fight for the Rights of Workers with Disabilities." *Report of the International Confederation of Free Trade Unions*. April 6, 2000. http://www.icftu.org.

International Labor Organization. *Convention (No. 169) concerning Indigenous and Tribal Peoples in Independent Countries*. Geneva: International Labor Organization, 1989.

————. *Provisions of the ILO Conventions and Recommendations concerning Migrant Workers*. Geneva: ILO Publications, n.d.

Isaacman, Allen. "Peasants and Rural Social Protest in Africa." *African Studies Review* 33, no. 2 (September 1990).

Ishay, Micheline. "Globalization and the New Realism of Human Rights." In Manfred Steger, ed., *Rethinking Globalism*. Lanham, Md.: Rowman & Littlefield, forthcoming.

————. *Internationalism and Its Betrayal*. Minneapolis: University of Minnesota Press, 1995.

————, ed. *The Human Rights Reader: Major Political Writings, Essays, Speeches, and Documents from the Bible to the Present*. New York: Routledge, 1997.

Ishay, Micheline, and Omar Dahbour, eds. *The Nationalism Reader*. Atlantic Highlands, N.J.: Humanities Press, 1995; repr. New York: Prometheus, 1999.

Jancar, Barbara Wolfe. *Women under Communism*. Baltimore: Johns Hopkins University Press, 1978.

Jaurès, Jean. *Idealism in History*. In Albert Fried and Ronald Sanders, eds., *Socialist Thought*. New York: Columbia University Press, 1993.

Jefferson, Thomas. *The Life and Selected Writings of Thomas Jefferson*. Ed. Adrienne Koch and William Peden. New York: Modern Library, 1944.

Jeffreys-Jones, Rhodri. *The CIA and American Democracy*. New Haven: Yale University Press, 1989.

Jentsch, I. "Zur Geschichte des Zeitungswesens in Deutschland." Ph.D. diss., University of Leipzig, 1937.

Jerusalem Bible. Jerusalem: Koren Publishers, 1977.

Joffee, Joseph. "Entangled Forever." *National Interest* 21 (Fall 1990).

Johnson, Chalmers. *Blowback*. New York: Henry Holt, 2000.

Johnson, Harry. *Money, Trade, and Economic Growth*. Cambridge, Mass.: Harvard University Press, 1962.

Johnson, James Turner, and John Kelsay, eds. *Just War and Jihad*. New York: Greenwood Press, 1991.

Johnson, Paul. *A History of the Jews*. New York: Harper & Row, 1987.

Joll, James. *The Second International, 1889–1914*. New York: Harper & Row, 1966.

Jones, E. L. *The European Miracle*. Cambridge: Cambridge University Press, 1981.

Jones, Gareth Stedman. *Languages of Class: Studies in English Working-Class History, 1832–1982*. Cambridge: Cambridge University Press, 1983.

Jones, Peter d'Alroy. *The Christian Socialist Revival, 1877–1914*. Princeton, N.J.: Princeton University Press, 1968.

Juviler, Peter H. "Women and Sex in Soviet Law." In Dorothy Atkinson, Alexander Dallin, and Gail Warshofsky Lapidus, eds. *Women in Russia*. Stanford, Calif.: Stanford Unviersity Press, 1977.

Kagarlitsky, Boris. "The Road to Consumption." In George Katsiaficas, ed., *After the Fall: 1989 and the Future of Freedom*. New York: Routledge, 2001.

Kant, Immanuel. *Kant's Political Writings*. Ed. Hans Reiss. Cambridge: Cambridge University Press, 1970.

———. *On the Old Saw: That May Be Right in Theory but It Won't Work in Practice*. Trans. E. B. Ashton. Philadelphia: University of Pennsylvania Press, 1974.

Katz, Jacob. *Out of the Ghetto: The Social Background of Jewish Emancipation, 1770–1870*. Cambridge, Mass.: Harvard University Press, 1973.

Kautsky, Karl. *Ethik und materialistische Geschichtsauffassung*. Stuttgart: n.p., 1906.

———. *Karl Kautsky: Selected Political Writings*. Ed. and trans. Patrick Goode. New York: St. Martin's Press, 1983.

———. *Socialism and Colonial Policy: An Analysis*. Belfast: Athol Books, 1975.

Keane, John. *Civil Society: Old Images, New Visions*. Stanford, Calif.: Stanford University Press, 1998.

Keck, Margaret E., and Kathryn Sikkink. *Activists beyond Borders*. Ithaca, N.Y.: Cornell University Press, 1998.

Keith, Arthur B. *The Belgian Congo and the Berlin Act*. Oxford: Clarendon Press, 1919.

Kennedy, Stetson. *Jim Crow Guide to the U.S.A.* London: Lawrence & Wishhart, 1959.

Kent, George. *Memoirs and Letters of Chancellor Kent*. Ed. William Kent. Boston: Little, Brown, 1898.

Keohane, Robert. *After Hegemony: Cooperation and Discord in the World Political Economy*. Princeton, N.J.: Princeton University Press, 1984.

Khadduri, Majid. *The Islamic Conception of Justice*. Baltimore: Johns Hopkins University Press, 1984.

Khushalani, Yougindra. *Dignity and Honour of Women as Basic and Fundamental Human Rights*. The Hague: Martinus Nijhoff, 1982.

Kierkegaard, Søren. *The Concept of Dread*. Ed. and trans. Walter Lowrie. Princeton, N.J.: Princeton University Press, 1957.

———. *Fear and Trembling*. Ed. and trans. Walter Lowrie. Princeton, N.J.: Princeton University Press, 1941.

Kifner, John. "The World through the Serbian Mind's Eye." "The Week in Review," *New York Times,* April 10, 1994, section 4, p. 1.

King, Martin Luther, Jr. *A Testament of Hope*. Ed. James M. Washington. San Francisco: Harper & Row, 1986.

King, Ynestra. "Feminism and the Revolt of Nature." *Heresies,* no. 13 (1981).

Kinsbruner, Jay. *Independence in Spanish America*. Albuquerque: University of New Mexico Press, 1994.

Kirkpatrick, Jeane. "Dictatorships and Double Standards." *Commentary* 8, no. 5 (November 1979).

Kissinger, Henry. *Diplomacy*. New York: Simon & Schuster, 1994.

Kitchin, Donald, John Lewis, and Karl Polanyi, eds. *Christianity and the Social Revolution*. New York: C. Scribner's, 1936.

Klare, Michael T., and Daniel C. Thomas. *World Security Challenges for a New Century*. New York: St. Martin's Press, 1994.

Klostermaier, Klaus K. *A Survey of Hinduism*. Albany: SUNY Press, 1989.

Kobrin, Stephen J. "The MAI and the Clash of Civilizations." *Foreign Policy* (Fall 1998).

Konvitz, Milton, ed. *Judaism and Human Rights*. New York: W. W. Norton, 1972.

Korey, William. *NGOs and the Universal Declaration of Human Rights*. New York: Palgrave, 2001.

Kramnick, Isaac, ed. *The Enlightenment Reader*. Baltimore: Penguin, 1995.

Krauthammer, Charles. "The Unipolar Moment." *Foreign Affairs* 70, no. 1 (1990–1991).

Küng, Hans. *A Global Ethics for Politics and Economics*. Oxford: Oxford University Press, 1998.

Kuntz, Linda, and Julia Lesage. *Media, Culture and the Religious Right*. Minneapolis: University of Minnesota Press, 1998.

Kymlicka, Will. *Multicultural Citizenship: A Liberal Theory of Minority Rights*. Oxford: Clarendon Press, 1995.

Lacouture, Jean. *Ho Chi Minh: A Political Biography*. New York: Random House, 1968.

Lamennais, Félicité Robert de. *Paroles d'un croyant*. Paris: P. d'Aubrée et Cailleux, 1836–1837.

Langbein, John H. *Torture and the Law of Proof*. Chicago: University of Chicago Press, 1976.

Langer, William L. *Political and Social Upheaval, 1832–1852*. New York: Harper & Row, 1969.

Langguth, A. J. *Patriots: The Men Who Started the American Revolution*. New York: Simon & Schuster, 1988.

Las Casas, Bartolomé de. *In Defense of the Indians*. Trans. Stefford Poole. De Kalb: Northern Illinois University Press, 1970.

Lassalle, Ferdinand. *Arbeiterprogramm*. Stuttgart: Reclam Dietzing, 1973.

Lauren, Paul Gordon. *The Evolution of International Human Rights: Visions Seen*. Philadelphia: University of Pennsylvania Press, 1998.

Laurent, Gérard M. *Coup d'oeil sur la politique de Toussaint-Louverture*. Port-au-Prince, Haiti: H. Deschamps, 1949.

Laws of Manu. Trans. Wendy Doniger and Brian K. Smith. London: Penguin, 1991.

Lechner, Frank J., and John Boli, eds. *The Globalization Reader*. Malden, Mass.: Blackwell Publishers, 2000.

Lefebvre, Georges. *La révolution française*. Paris: Presses Universitaires de France, 1968.

Lefebvre, Georges. *The French Revolution: From Its Origins to 1793*. Vol. 1. New York: Columbia University Press, 1962.

Lefort, Claude. *L'invention démocratique: Les limites de la domination totalitaire*. Paris: Fayard, 1981.

Le Goff, Jacques. *Time, Work and Culture in the Middle Ages*. Trans. Arthur Goldhammer. Chicago: University of Chicago Press, 1980.

Lenin, V. I. *Collected Works*. 45 vols. Moscow: Progress Publishers, 1960–1970.

———. *"Critical Remarks on the National Question" and "The Right of Nations to Self-Determination."* Moscow: Progress Publishers, 1974.

———. *The Emancipation of Women*. New York: International Publishers, 1966.

———. *The Lenin Anthology*. Ed. Robert C. Tucker. New York: Norton, 1975.

———. *Lenin's Selected Works*. Moscow: Progress Publishers, 1977.

———. *On the National Liberation Movement*. San Francisco: Proletarian Publishers, 1975.

———. *Women and Society*. New York: International Publishers, 1938.

Levy, Darline Gay, Harriet Branson Applewhite, and Mary Durham Johnson. *Women in Revolutionary Paris*. Urbana: University of Illinois Press, 1979.

Lewis, Jane, ed. *Women's Experience of Home and Family, 1850–1940*. Oxford: Basil Blackwell, 1986.

Lichtheim, George. *The Origins of Socialism*. New York: Praeger, 1969.

Liebknecht, Karl. *Militarism and Anti-Militarism*. New York: Howard Fertig, 1969.

Lin Yutang, ed. and trans. *The Wisdom of Confucius*. New York: Modern Library, Random House, 1938.

Little, David, and Sumner B. Twiss. *Comparative Religious Ethics*. New York: Harper & Row, 1973.

Little, David, John Kelsay, and Abdulaziz A. Sachedina. *Human Rights and the Conflict of Culture: Western and Islamic Perspectives on Religious Liberty*. Columbia: University of South Carolina Press, 1988.

Locke, John. *A Letter concerning Toleration*. Ed. John Horton and Susan Mendus. London: Routledge, 1991.

Lodge, Juliet. *The European Challenge of the Future*. New York: St. Martin's Press, 1993.

Long, James. *Russian Serf Emancipation: Four Letters on Origin, Evils and Abolition; Addressed to the Committee of the British and Foreign Anti-Slavery Society*. 27 New Broad Street, London: n.p., 1884.

Lottman, Herbert R. *Albert Camus*. Paris: Seuil, 1978.

Louis, William Roger. *Imperialism at Bay: The United States and the Decolonization of the British Empire, 1941–1945*. New York: Oxford University Press, 1978.

Lowell, James Russell. *Complete Poetical Works*. Boston: Houghton-Mifflin, 1897.

Löwy, Michael. "Marxists and the National Question." *New Left Review,* no. 96 (March-April 1976).

Lukes, Stephen. *Marxism and Morality*. Oxford: Clarendon Press, 1985.

———. *Moral Conflict and Politics*. Oxford: Clarendon Press, 1991.

Luxemburg, Rosa. *Rosa Luxemburg: Selected Writings*. Ed. and intro. Robert Looker. London: Jonathan Cape, 1972.

———. *Rosa Luxemburg Speaks*. Ed. Mary-Alice Waters. London: Pathfinder Press, 1970.

Lyons, David. *The Electronic Eye: The Rise of Surveillance Society*. Minneapolis: University of Minnesota Press, 1994.

Machel, Graça. "Impact of Armed Conflict on Children." August 26, 1996. http://www.unicef.org/graca/a51–306_en.pdf.

Machiavelli, Niccolò. *Il principe*. Intro. Luigi Rosso. Florence: Sansoni, 1958.

MacKinnon, Catherine A. "Crimes of War, Crimes of Peace." In Stephen Shute and Susan Hurley, eds., *On Human Rights*. New York: Basic Books, 1993.

MacLean, Iain. *Democracy and the New Technology*. Cambridge: Polity Press, 1989.

Macpherson, C. B. *The Political Theory of Possessive Individualism: From Hobbes to Locke*. Oxford: Oxford University Press, 1962.

Madison, Bernice Q. *Social Welfare in the Soviet Union*. Stanford, Calif.: Stanford University Press, 1968.

Mahmassani, Sobhi. "The Principle of International Law in Light of Islamic Doctrine." In Hague Academy for International Law, *Recueil des cours*. The Hague: Hague Academy for International Law, 1966.

Maistre, Joseph de. *Oeuvres complètes*. 2 vols. Geneva: Slatkine Reprints, 1979.

Makiya, Kanan. *Cruelty and Silence: War, Tyranny, Uprising and the Arab World*. New York: W. W. Norton, 1993.

Malik, Habib C., ed. *The Challenge of Human Rights: Charles Malik and the Universal Declaration*. Oxford: Center for Lebanese Studies, 2000.

Malone, Julia. "Lagging Latino Appeal Looms over Bush Trip." *Atlanta Journal and Constitution,* March 29, 2002.

Manzur, Jay. "Labor's New Internationalism." *Foreign Affairs* 79, no. 1 (January-Febuary 2000).

Marcos, Subcomandante. *Our Word Is Our Weapon: Selected Writings*. Ed. Juana Ponce de León. New York: Seven Stories Press, 2001.

Marcus, Michael R. *The Nuremberg War Crimes Trial, 1945–46*. New York: St. Martin's Press, 1997.

Marcuse, Herbert. "Ecology and Revolution." *Liberation* 17, no. 6 (September 1972): 10–12.

———. *Soviet Marxism*. New York: Vintage Books, 1961.

Maritain, Jacques, ed. *Human Rights: Comments and Interpretations*. New York: Columbia University Press, 1949.

———. *The Rights of Man and Natural Law.* New York: Charles Scribner's Sons, 1951.

Marnell, William H. *The First Amendment.* New York: Doubleday, 1964.

Marshall, T. H. *Class, Citizenship, and Social Development.* New York: Anchor Books, 1965.

Martin, Peter. "The Moral Case for Globalization." *Financial Times,* May 1997.

Martinez, Luis Alfredo. "Honduras—Protest Unrest Increasing in Honduras, despite President's Popularity." *Financial Times,* July 2000.

Marx, Karl. *Capital.* London: Penguin, 1976.

———. *Critique of the Gotha Programme.* New York: International Publishers, 1938.

———. *The Eighteenth Brumaire of Louis Bonaparte.* New York: International Publishers, 1964.

———. *The First International and After.* Vol. 3 of *Political Writings.* London: Penguin, 1992.

———. *Karl Marx on Revolution.* Ed. Saul K. Padover. New York: McGraw-Hill, 1971.

———. *Karl Marx: Selected Writings.* Ed. David McLelland. London: Oxford University Press, 1977.

Marx, Karl, and Friedrich Engels. *Collected Works.* 49 vols. New York: International Publishers, 1975–2001.

———. *The German Ideology.* New York: International Publishers, 1939.

———. *The German Ideology, Including the Theses of Feuerbach and the Introduction to the Critique of Political Economy.* New York: Prometheus, 1998.

———. *The Marx-Engels Reader.* 2nd ed. Ed. Robert C. Tucker. New York: W. W. Norton, 1978.

Mathieson, William Law. *British Slavery and Its Abolition, 1823–1838.* London: Longmans, 1926.

Mathiez, Albert. *The French Revolution.* New York: Gallimard, 1962.

Matthaei, Julie. *An Economic History of Women in America.* New York: Schocken Books, 1982.

Matthews, Jessica T. "Power Shift." *Foreign Affairs* 76, no. 1 (January-February 1997).

Mawdudi, Abul A'la. *Human Rights in Islam.* Leicester: Islamic Foundation, 1976–1980.

Mayer, Ann Elizabeth. *Islam and Human Rights.* Boulder: Westview, 1991.

McFeatters, Ann. "Bush Signs Anti-Terror Bill." *Pittsburgh Post-Gazette,* October 27, 2001, A6.

McPherson, James M. *Drawn with the Sword: Reflections on the American Civil War.* New York: Oxford University Press, 1996.

Megivern, James J. *The Death Penalty.* New York: Paulist Press, 1997.

Mencius. Trans. and intro. D. C. Lau. London: Penguin, 1970.

Mendes-Flohr, Paul, and Jehuda Reinharz, eds. *The Jew in the Modern World.* New York: Oxford University Press, 1980.

Merriam, C. Edward. *American Political Theories.* New York: Macmillan, 1903.

Meyer, Arno J. *The Furies.* Princeton, N.J.: Princeton University Press, 2000.

Micklethwait, John, and Adrian Woldridge. "Why the Globalization Backlash Is Stupid." *Foreign Policy* (September-October 2001).

Mileikovskii, A. G., ed. *International Relations after the Second World War.* Moscow: n.p., 1962.

Miliband, Ralph, and John Saville, eds. *Socialist Register.* London: Merlin Press, 1976.

Mill, John Stuart. *"On Liberty" and Other Essays.* Ed. John Gray. Oxford: Oxford University Press, 1991.

———. *Three Essays.* New York: Oxford University Press, 1975.

Miller, Neil. *Out of the Past: Gay and Lesbian History from 1869 to the Present.* New York: Vintage Books, 1995.

Millett, Kate. *Sexual Politics.* New York: Avon, 1969.

Milton, John. *Selected Essays of John Milton.* Ed. Laura E. Lockwood. Cambridge, Mass.: Houghton Mifflin, n.d.

Mink, Gwendolyn. *Welfare's End.* Ithaca, N.Y.: Cornell University Press, 1998.

Mittelman, James H. *Globalization Syndrome: Transformation and Resistance.* Princeton, N.J.: Princeton University Press, 2000.

Mohanty, Chandra Talpade, Ann Russo, and Lourdes Torres, eds. *Third World Women and the Politics of Feminism.* Indianapolis: Indiana University Press, 1991.

Monnet, Jean. *Memoirs.* New York: Doubleday, 1978.

Montesquieu, Baron de. *Lettres persanes.* Ed. Antoine Adam. Geneva: Droz, 1954.

Moore, Barrington. *Social Origins of Dictatorship.* Boston: Beacon Press, 1966.

Morsink, Johannes. *The Universal Declaration of Human Rights.* Philadelphia: University of Pennsylvania Press, 1999.

Mosse, George L. *Nationalism and Sexuality: Middle-Class Morality and Sexual Norms in Modern Europe.* Madison: University of Wisconsin Press, 1985.

Muravchick, Joshua. "At Last, Pax Americana." *New York Times,* January 24, 1991, A19.

Murolo, Priscilla. *The Common Ground of Womanhood: Class, Gender, and Working Girls' Clubs, 1884–1928.* Urbana: University of Illinois Press, 1997.

Murphy, Paul L. *World War I and the Origin of Civil Liberties in the United States.* New York: W. W. Norton, 1979.

Musgrave, Thomas D. *Self-Determination and National Minorities.* Oxford: Clarendon Press, 1997.

Nardin, Terry, ed. *The Ethics of War and Peace: Religious and Secular Perspectives.* Princeton, N.J.: Princeton University Press, 1996.

Needham, Joseph. *Science and Civilization.* Cambridge: Cambridge University Press, 1954.

Nehru, Jawaharlal. *The Discovery of India.* New York: Oxford University Press, 1990.

New Cambridge Modern History. Vol. 8. Cambridge: Cambridge University Press, 1965.

New English Bible: The New Testament. New York: Oxford University Press, 1970.

Newland, Kathleen. "Workers of the World, Now What?" *Foreign Policy* (Spring 1999).

Nieman, Donald G. *Promises to Keep: African Americans and the Constitutional Order, 1776 to the Present.* Oxford: Oxford University Press, 1991.

Nietzsche, Friedrich. *"The Birth of Tragedy" and "Genealogy of Morals."* Trans. Francis Golffing. New York: Doubleday, 1956.

Nkrumah, Kwame. *I Speak of Freedom: A Statement of African Ideology.* New York: Praeger, 1961.

Nye, Joseph S., Jr. "America's Information Edge." *Foreign Affairs* 75, no. 2 (March 1996).

———. *Bound to Lead: The Changing Nature of American Power.* New York: Basic Books, 1990.

O'Connor, James. "Socialism and Ecology." In *Capitalism, Nature, Socialism* 2, no. 3 (October 1991).

Ohmae, Ken'ichi. *The End of the Nation-State.* New York: New York University Press, 1995.

Okihiro, Gary Y., ed. *In Resistance: Studies in African, Caribbean, and Afro-American History.* Amherst: University of Massachusetts Press, 1986.

Olivelle, Patrick, trans. *Upanisads.* Oxford: Oxford University Press, 1996.

Owen, Robert D. *A New View of Society: A Facsimile Reproduction of the Third Edition Printed in London in 1817.* Glencoe, Ill.: Free Press, 197?.

———. *An Outline of the System of Education at New Lanark.* Glasgow: Glasgow University Press, 1824.

Ozment, Steven. *When Fathers Ruled: Family Life in Reformation Europe.* Cambridge, Mass.: Harvard University Press, 1983.

Packard, Laurence B. *The Commercial Revolution.* New York: Henry Holt, 1927.

Pahl, E. E., ed. *On Work.* Oxford: Basil Blackwell, 1988.

Paine, Thomas. *Common Sense.* New York: Liberal Arts Press, 1953.

———. *Complete Writings of Paine.* Ed. Philip Foner. New York: Citadel, 1969.

———. *The Essential Thomas Paine.* Ed. Sidney Hook. New York: Mentor Books, 1969.

———. "An Occasional Letter to the Female Sex." *Pennsylvania Magazine,* August 1775.

Palmer, R. R. *The Age of the Democratic Revolution, 1760–1800.* 2 vols. Princeton, N.J.: Princeton University Press, 1969.

———. *The World of the French Revolution.* New York: Harper & Row, 1967.

Panikar, R. "Is the Notion of Human Rights a Western Concept?" *Diogenes* 120 (Winter 1982).

Panitch, Leo. "Globalization and the State." *Socialist Register,* 1994.

Pateman, Carole. *The Sexual Contract.* Stanford, Calif.: Stanford University Press, 1988.

Patten, Wendy. "United States: Include Key Rights Protections in Homeland Security Bill." A Human Rights Watch Letter to the U.S. Senate. September 26, 2002. http://www.hrw.org/press/2002/09/us-hr0926.htm.

Peck, James, ed. *The Chomsky Reader.* New York: Pantheon Books, 1987.

The People Shall Judge: Readings in the Formation of American Policy. Ed. the

Staff, Social Sciences 1, the College of the University of Chicago. Chicago: University of Chicago Press, 1949.

Peters, Julie, and Andrea Wolper, eds. *Women's Rights, Human Rights: International Feminist Perspectives.* New York: Routledge, 1995.

Phillips, Kevin. *Wealth and Democracy: The Politics of the American Rich.* New York: Broadway Books, 2002.

Philosophical Foundations of Human Rights. Intro. Paul Ricoeur. Paris: UNESCO, 1986.

Pinchbeck, Ivy. *Women Workers and the Industrial Revolution, 1750–1850.* London: Frank Cass, 1968.

Piotrowski, Harry, and Wayne C. McWilliams. *The World since 1945.* Boulder: Lynne Rienner, 1993.

Plano, Jack C., and Robert E. Riggs. *The United Nations: International Organization and World Politics.* Chicago: Dorsey Press, 1988.

Plato. *The Laws.* Ed. Trevor J. Saunders. Harmondsworth: Penguin, 1970.

———. *The Republic.* Trans. H. D. P. Lee. London: Penguin, 1955.

———. *The Statesman.* Trans. Harold Fowler. Cambridge, Mass.: Harvard University Press, 1962.

———. *Symposium.* Ed. W. Hamilton. Baltimore: Penguin, 1951.

Pluchon, Pierre. *Nègres et juifs au XVIIIe siècle: Le racisme au siècle des lumières.* Paris: Editions Tallandier, 1984.

Polanyi, Karl. *The Great Transformation.* New York: Farrar & Rinehart, 1944.

Polis, Adamantha, and Peter Schwab, eds. *Human Rights: Cultural and Ideological Perspectives.* New York: Praeger, 1980.

Popkin, Jeremy D. *Revolutionary News: The Press in France, 1789–1799.* Durham: Duke University Press, 1990.

Porter, Bruce D. *War and the Rise of the State: The Military Foundations of Modern Politics.* New York: Free Press, 1994.

Porter, Roy, Bob Scribner, and Mikuláš Teich. *The Reformation in National Context.* Cambridge: Cambridge University Press, 1999.

Poulter, Sebastian M. *English Law and Ethnic Minority Customs.* London: Butterworth, 1986.

Power, Samantha. *A Problem from Hell: America and the Age of Genocide.* New York: Basic Books, 2002.

Principles and Methods of Colonial Administration. Ed. C. M. MacInnes. London: Butterworths Scientific Publications, 1950.

Proudhon, Pierre-Joseph. *What Is Property? Or an Inquiry into the Principle of Right and of Government.* 2 vols. Ed. and trans. Benjamin R. Tucker. London: New Temple Press, 1902.

Proust, Marcel. *Sodom and Gomorrah.* Trans. C. K. Scott Moncrieff and Terence Kilmartin. New York: Modern Library, 1934.

Przeworski, Adam, and John Sprague. *Paper Stones: A History of Electoral Socialism.* Chicago: University of Chicago Press, 1986.

Pufendorf, Samuel. *The Political Writings of Samuel Pufendorf.* Ed. Craig L. Carr, trans. Michael J. Seidler. New York: Oxford University Press, 1994.

Rawls, John. "The Domain of Political and Overlapping Consensus." *New York University Law Review* 64, no. 2 (1989).

———. *The Law of Peoples*. Cambridge, Mass.: Harvard University Press, 1999.

———. *A Theory of Justice*. Rev. ed. Cambridge, Mass.: Harvard University Press, 1999.

Regnier, Pat. "Changing Their Tune." *Time International*, December 3, 2001.

Reid, Brian Holden. *The American Civil War and the Wars of the Industrial Revolution*. London: Cassell, 1999.

Remec, Peter R. *The Position of the Individual in International Law according to Grotius and Vattel*. The Hague: Martinus Nijhoff, 1960.

Renteln, Alison Dundes. "Relativism and the Search for Human Rights." *American Anthropologist* 90, no. 1 (1988).

Rice, Condoleezza. "America Has the Muscle, but It Has Benevolent Values." *Daily Telegraph*, London, October 17, 2002, p. 26.

Roach, Steve. "The Question of Cultural Autonomy: Reassessing the Merits of Cultural Autonomy during the Post–Cold War." Ph.D. diss., University of Denver, January 2002.

Roberts, J. M. *The History of the World*. Middlesex: Penguin, 1976.

Robespierre, Maximilien de. *Oeuvres*. 3 vols. Ed. Lapponneraye. New York: Burt Franklin, 1970.

———. *Robespierre*. Ed. George Rudé. Englewood Cliffs, N.J.: Prentice-Hall, 1967.

Robinson, William I. *Promoting Polyarchy: Globalization, U.S. Intervention and Hegemony*. Cambridge: Cambridge University Press, 1996.

Rodinson, Maxime. *Islam and Capitalism*. Austin: University of Texas Press, 1978.

Rodley, Nigel S. *The Treatment of Prisoners under International Law*. 2nd ed. Oxford: Clarendon Press, 1999.

Ronald, Wilhelm. "España Nuestra: The Molding of Primary School Children for a Fascist Spain." *Journal of Curriculum and Supervision* 13, no. 3 (Spring 1998).

Roosevelt, Eleanor D. *Courage in a Dangerous World: The Political Writings of Eleanor Roosevelt*. Ed. Allida M. Black. New York: Columbia University Press, 1999.

———. "Statements by E. Roosevelt." In *Department of State Bulletin*. December 19, 1947. Washington, D.C.: U.S. Department of State.

Roosevelt, Franklin D. *The Public Papers and Addresses of Franklin D. Roosevelt*. Vol. 13. Ed. Samuel I. Roseman. New York: Harper & Brothers, 1950.

Rorty, Richard. "Feminism, Ideology, and Deconstruction: A Pragmatist View." *Hypatia* 8, no. 2 (special issue: "Feminism and Pragmatism") (Spring 1993).

Rosen, Jeffrey. "A Watchful State." *New York Times Magazine*, October 7, 2001, p. 42.

Rosenbaum, Alan S., ed. *The Philosophy of Human Rights: International Perspectives*. Westport, Conn.: Greenwood Press, 1980.

Rostow, Walt W. *The Stages of Economic Growth: A Non-Communist Manifesto*. Cambridge: Oxford University Press, 1960.

Rouner, Leroy, ed. *Human Rights and the World's Religions*. Notre Dame, Ind.: University of Notre Dame Press, 1988.

Rousseau, Jean-Jacques. "Judgement on Saint-Pierre Project for Perpetual Peace."

In M. G. Forsyth, H. M. A. Keens-Soper, and P. Savigaaer, eds., *The Theory of International Relations*. Englewood Cliffs, N.J.: Prentice-Hall, 1970.

———. *Oeuvres complètes*. Ed. Bernard Gagnebin and Marcel Raymond. Paris: Gallimard, 1964.

———. *The Political Writings of Jean-Jacques Rousseau*. 2 vols. Ed. C. E. Vaughn. Oxford: Basil Blackwell, 1962.

———. *"The Social Contract" and "Discourses."* Trans. and rev. G. D. H. Cole. London: J. M. Dent and Sons, 1973.

Rowbotham, Sheila. *Hidden from History: Rediscovering Women in History from the Seventeenth Century to the Present*. London: Pantheon Books, 1973.

Ruggie, John G. "International Regimes, Transactions and Change: Embedded Liberalism in the Postwar Economic Order." *International Organization* 36, no. 2 (Spring 1982).

———. "What Makes the World Hang Together? Neo-Utilitarianism and the Social Constructivist Challenge." *International Organization* 52, no. 4 (Autumn 1998).

Sadowski, Yahya, ed. *The Myth of Global Chaos*. Washington, D.C.: Brookings Institution, 1998.

Saint-Simon, Claude Henri. "The New Christianity." In *Selected Writings*. Ed. and trans. F. M. H. Markham. New York: Macmillan Company, 1952.

Salamon, Lester. "The Rise of the Nonprofit Sector." *Foreign Affairs* 73, no. 4 (July-August 1994).

Sanderson, Stephen K., ed. *Civilizations and World Systems*. Walnut Creek, Calif.: AltaMira Press, 1995.

Sargent, Lyman Tower, ed. *Political Thought in the United States: A Documentary History*. New York: New York University Press, 1997.

Sassen, Saskia. *Globalization and Its Discontents*. New York: New Press, 1998.

Sassoferato, Bartolo. *La tiberiade*. Rome: G. Gigliotto, 1587.

Schama, Simon. *Citizens: A Chronicle of the French Revolution*. New York: Knopf, 1989.

Schleiermacher, Friedrich. *Über die Religion reden*. Berlin: Realschulbuchhandlung, 1806.

Seavey, Dorothy K. *Back to Basics: Women's Poverty and Welfare Reform*. Wesley, Mass.: Center for Research on Women, 1996.

Sen, Amartya. *Development as Freedom*. New York: Anchor Books, 1999.

Senghor, Leopold Sédar. *On African Socialism*. Trans. M. Cook. New York: Praeger, 1964.

Seymour, Charles, and Donald Paige Frary. *How the World Votes: The Story of Democratic Development in Elections*. Springfield, Mass.: C. A. Nichols, 1918.

Shafir, Gershon, ed. *The Citizenship Debates*. Minneapolis: University of Minnesota Press, 1998.

Sharma, Arvind, ed. *Our Religions*. New York: HarperCollins, 1999.

Sharp, Andrew, ed. *The English Levellers*. Cambridge: Cambridge University Press, 1998.

Shaw, George Bernard. *Fabianism and the Empire*. London: Fabian Society, 1900.

Shiva, Vandana. *Staying Alive: Women, Ecology, and Development.* London: Zed Books, 1988.

Shotwell, James Thompson, ed. *The Origins of the International Labor Organization.* 2 vols. New York: Columbia University Press, 1934.

Simmons, John. *The Lockean Theory of Rights.* Princeton, N.J.: Princeton University Press, 1992.

Sinclair, Andrew. *The Emancipation of the American Woman.* New York: Harper & Row, 1965.

Sivard, Ruth Leger. *World Military and Social Expenditures 1993.* Washington, D.C.: World Priorities, 1993.

Skocpol, Theda. *States and Social Revolutions: A Comparative Analysis of France, Russia and China.* Cambridge: Cambridge University Press, 1979.

Slaughter, Matthew J., and Philip Swagel. "Does Globalization Lower Wages and Export Jobs?" *International Monetary Fund,* 1997.

Smith, Adam. *The Theory of Moral Sentiments.* Indianapolis: Liberty Classics, 1969.

———. *The Wealth of Nations.* Intro. Edwin Cannan. Chicago: University of Chicago Press, 1976.

Smith, Anthony. *The Newspaper: An International History.* London: Thames and Hudson, 1979.

Soboul, Albert. *Histoire de la révolution française.* Paris: Gallimard, 1962.

Stalin, Joseph. *Marxism and the National-Colonial Question.* San Francisco: Proletarian Publishers, 1975.

Stearns, Monroe. *Shay's Rebellion: Americans Take Up Arms against Unjust Laws, 1786–7.* New York: Franklin Watts, 1968.

Steger, Manfred. *Globalism: The New Market Ideology.* Boulder: Rowman & Littlefield, 2002.

———. *The Quest for Evolutionary Socialism: Eduard Bernstein and Social Democracy.* Cambridge: Cambridge University Press, 1997.

Strange, Susan. *The Retreat of the State: The Diffusion of Power in the World Economy.* Cambridge: Cambridge University Press, 1996.

Strong, John. *The Experience of Buddhism: Sources and Interpretations.* Belmont, Calif.: Wadsworth Publishing Company, 1995.

Swatos, William H., ed. *A Future for Religion?* Newbury Park, Calif.: Sage Publications, 1989.

Swidler, Arlene, ed. *Homosexuality and World Religions.* Valley Forge, Pa.: Trinity Press International, 1993.

———. *Human Rights in Religious Traditions.* New York: Pilgrim Press, 1982.

Swidler, Leonard, ed. *Religious Liberty and Human Rights.* New York: Hippocrene Books, 1986.

Taylor, Charles. *Multiculturalism.* Ed. and intro. Amy Gutman. Princeton, N.J.: Princeton University Press.

Taylor, Timothy. "The Truth about Globalization." *Public Interest* (Spring 2002).

Thomas Aquinas. *Summa theologica.* Ed. Fathers of the English Dominican Province. Hampshire: Eyre & Spottiswoode, 1947.

Thompson, Dorothy. *The Early Chartists*. Columbia: University of South Carolina Press, 1971.

Thoreau, Henry David. *On the Duty of Civil Disobedience*. London: A. C. Fifield,
1905.

Thornberry, Patrick. *International Law and the Rights of Minorities*. Oxford:
Clarendon Press, 1991.

Thornton, J. W. *The Pulpit of the American Revolution*. Boston: n.p., 1860.

Thurman, Robert. "Guidelines for Buddhist Social Activism Based on Nagarjuna's
Jewel Garland of Royal Counsels." *Eastern Buddhist* 9 (1983).

Tilly, Charles. "Globalization Threatens Labor's Rights." *International Labor
and Working Class History*, no. 47 (Spring 1995).

Toffler, Alvin. *The Third Wave*. London: Bookmarks, 1994.

Tomlinson, John. *Cultural Imperialism: A Critical Introduction*. London: Pinter
Publishers, 1991.

Trachtenberg, Alan. *The Incorporation of America*. New York: Hill and Wang,
1982.

Trattner, Walter I. *Crusade for the Children*. Chicago: Quadrangle Books, 1970.

Ulam, Adam. *Expansion and Coexistence: Soviet Foreign Policy, 1917–73*. New
York: Praeger, 1974.

UNESCO. "The Race Question." *UNESCO and Its Programme*, vol. 3. Paris:
UNESCO, 1950.

UNICEF. "Children at Both Ends of the Gun." http://www.unicef.org/graca/kid-
soldi.htm.

———. *State of the World's Children 2002*. New York: UNICEF House, 2002.

Union of International Associations. *Yearbook of International Organizations*.
Vol. 1B. Munich: K. G. Saur Verlag, 2000.

United Kingdom Foreign and Commonwealth Office. "Déclaration des huit cours
relative à l'abolition universelle de la traîte des nègres." In *British and State
Papers, 1815–1816*. Kew: Public Records Office, National Archives, 1815.

United Nations, Economic Commission for Latin America and the Caribbean.
Social Panorama Publication 2001–2002. Santiago, Chile: ECLAC, 2002.

United Nations, Second Meeting of the Ad Hoc Committee on an International
Convention. *The United Nations and Disabled Persons: The First Fifty Years*.
New York: United Nations, 2003.

United Nations Expert Group Meeting on International Migration Policies and
the Status of Female Migrants. *International Migration Policies and the Status of Female Migrants*. New York: United Nations, 1995.

Van Norden, Bryan W. *Confucius and the Analects*. Oxford: Oxford University
Press, 2002.

Vattel, Emmerich de. *Le droit des gens ou principe de la loi naturelle*. Vol. 2.
Washington, D.C.: Carnegie Institution of Washington, 1916.

Vitorio, Francisco de. *Political Writings*. Ed. Anthony Pagden and Jeremy
Lawrence. New York: Cambridge University Press, 1991.

———. *Relaciones sobre los indios y el derecho de guerra*. Buenos Aires: Espasa-
Valpe Argentina, 1946.

Vogel, Lise. *Marxism and the Oppression of Women*. New Brunswick, N.J.: Rutgers University Press, 1983.

Voltaire. *Oeuvres complètes.* Paris: Furne, 1835–1838.
———. *Oeuvres de Voltaire.* Paris: P. Pourrat Frères, 1839.
———. *Philosophical Dictionary.* Boston: J. P. Mendum, 1881.
———. *The Works of Voltaire.* Paris: E. R. Dumont, 1901.
Vorländer, Karl. *Kant und Marx: Ein Beitrag zur Theorie des Sozialismus.* Tübingen: Verlag von J. C. B. Mohr, 1926.
Wallerstein, Immanuel. *The Modern World System.* New York: Academic Press, 1974.
———. "The Rise and Future Demise of the World Capitalist System: Concepts for Comparative Analysis." *Comparative Studies in Society and History* 16 (1974).
Waltz, Kenneth. *Theory of International Politics.* Reading, Mass.: Addison-Wesley, 1979.
Walzer, Michael. *Just and Unjust War.* New York: Basic Books, 1977.
———. "Rescuing Civil Society." *Dissent* 46, no. 1 (Winter 1999).
Ware, Vron. *Beyond the Pale: White Women, Racism and History.* London: Verso, 1992.
Webb, Sidney. "English Progress toward Social Democracy." In *Fabian Tracts.* London: Fabian Society, 1892; repr. Fabian Society, 1906.
Weeks, Jeffrey. *Coming Out.* London: Quartet, 1977.
Weissbach, Lee Shai. *Child Labor Reform in Nineteenth-Century France.* Baton Rouge: Lousiana State University Press, 1989.
Whitman, Walt. *The Portable Walt Whitman.* Ed. Mark Van Doren. Harmondsworth: Penguin, 1945.
Whittier, John Greenleaf. *The Complete Poetical Works of John Greenleaf Whittier.* Boston: Houghton Mifflin, 1894.
Wilde, Oscar. *The Soul of Man under Socialism.* New York: M. N. Maisel, 1911.
Wilson, Francis Graham. *Labor in the League System.* Stanford, Calif.: Stanford University Press, 1934.
Wilson, Woodrow. *The Papers of Woodrow Wilson.* 69 vols. Ed. Arthur S. Link. Princeton, N.J.: Princeton University Press, 1966.
Winstanley, Gerrard. *Selections from His Works.* Ed. Leonard Hamilton. London: Cresset Press, 1944.
Wolf, Martin. "Why This Hatred of the Market?" "Global Opportunities," *Financial Times,* May 6, 1997.
Wollstonecraft, Mary. *A Vindication of the Rights of Woman.* 2nd ed. Ed. Carole H. Poston. London: Norton, 1988.
Wood, Adrian. *North-South Trade, Employment, and Inequality: Changing Fortunes in a Skill-Driven World.* Oxford: Oxford University Press, 1994.
———. "Trade Hurts Unskilled Workers." *Journal of Economic Perspectives* 9, no. 3 (Summer 1995).
Woolf, Cecil Nathan Sidney. *Bartolo de Sassoferato: His Position in the History of Medieval Thought.* Cambridge: Cambridge University Press, 1913.
Woolf, Leonard S., and the Fabian Society. *International Government: Two Reports.* New York: Brentano, 1916.
Wooton, David, ed. *"Divine Right and Democracy": An Anthology of Political Writing in Stuart England.* London: Penguin, 1986.

World Bank. *World Development Report 2000–2001: Attacking Poverty.* New York: Oxford University Press, 2001.

Wriston, Walter B. *The Twilight of Sovereignty.* New York: Charles Scribners Sons, 1992.

Yeo, Eileen. "Robert Owen's Reputation as an Educationist." In Sidney Pollard and John Salt, eds., *Robert Owen, Prophet of the Poor: Essays in Honour of the Two-Hundredth Anniversary of His Birth.* Lewisburg, Pa.: Bucknell University Press, 1971.

Zakaria, Fareed. "The End of the End of History." *Newsweek.* September 24, 2001. http://www.msnbc.com/news/629514.asp.

Zetkin, Clara. "Nur mit der proletarischen Frau wird der Sozialismus siegen!" In *Ausgewählte Reden und Schriften.* 3 vols. Berlin: Dietz Verlag, 1957.

Zola, Emile. "J'accuse." *Aurore,* January 13, 1898.

Zouche, Richard. *Juris et judicii fecialis.* 2 vols. Ed. Thomas E. Holland, trans. J. L. Briefly. Washington, D.C.: Carnegie Institution of Washington, 1911.

Index

Italicized page numbers refer to boxed inserts.

Text:	10/13 Sabon
Display:	Sabon
Indexer:	Sharon H. Sweeney
Compositor:	Integrated Composition Systems
Printer:	Maple-Vail Manufacturing Group